ALBERT R. KITZHABER

Professor of English, University of Oregon

ADVISORY EDITOR TO DODD, MEAD & COMPANY

THE DIMENSIONS OF POETRY

A Critical Anthology

Do not go gentle into that good night,
~~Old age~~ should be a tempest near the grave;
Rage, rage against the dying of the light.'
Old
~~Good~~ men at clo~~s~~e of day know dark is right,   frail
But, if their ~~grey~~ hearts move them to be brave,
Do not go gentle into that good night.

~~They~~
Very near death they see that ~~th~~ life cd have /
been wonderful, & they rage against the
dying of the light.
                                        but they had
                                        worked against it,
There cd have been light all their days
even at the darkest times, and so they
cannot die gently.

They understand, now they are dying, that
impossible love cared have been their sun)
but that they helped to kill it, & so they
rage against its dying.

Now you, my father, dying, have taught me this.

                    ⚌   539

How might the

    The darkest

Good men
Good men in the dark sea learn

One of the earliest manuscript versions of Dylan Thomas's "Do
Not Go Gentle into That Good Night." See the poem (p. 705)
and the discussion of its revisions (p. 716). (*Reproduced by permission of the Harvard College Library and New Directions.*)

THE DIMENSIONS

OF POETRY

A Critical Anthology

JAMES E. MILLER, JR.

and BERNICE SLOTE

The University of Nebraska

DODD, MEAD & COMPANY

NEW YORK · TORONTO

1962

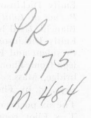

POETRY ACKNOWLEDGMENTS

"Risselty Rosselty" (anonymous) is reprinted from *Kansas Folklore,* S. J. Sackett and William E. Koch, eds., Lincoln: University of Nebraska Press, 1961. Used by permission of the University of Nebraska Press.

A. J. Arberry's translation of a rubáiyát of Omar Khayyám is used with the permission of Professor Arberry.

W. H. Auden's "As I Walked Out One Evening" and "Musée des Beaux Arts" are reprinted from *The Collected Poetry of W. H. Auden,* copyright 1940 by W. H. Auden and used by permission of Random House, Inc. The paragraph on Tennyson by W. H. Auden is from the introduction by W. H. Auden (copyright 1944 by W. H. Auden) to *A Selection from the Poems of Alfred Lord Tennyson.* Reprinted by permission of Doubleday & Company, Inc.

Hart Crane's "To Brooklyn Bridge" is reprinted from *The Collected Poems of Hart Crane.* By permission of Liveright, Publishers, N. Y. Copyright © R 1961, by Liveright Publishing Corp.

E. E. Cummings' "anyone lived in a pretty how town" is reprinted from *Poems 1923–1954* by E. E. Cummings, copyright, 1940, by E. E. Cummings and used by permission of Harcourt, Brace & World, Inc.

Emily Dickinson's "My Life had stood" is reprinted from *The Complete Poems of Emily Dickinson,* copyright 1929, © 1957, by Martha Dickinson Bianchi. Used by permission of Little, Brown & Co. The rest of the poems of Emily Dickinson included in this book are reprinted by permission of The President and Fellows of Harvard College and the Trustees of Amherst College from Thomas H. Johnson, Editor, *The Poems of Emily Dickinson.* Cambridge, Mass.: The Belknap Press of Harvard University Press, Copyright, 1951, 55, by The President and Fellows of Harvard College.

The six poems of T. S. Eliot are reprinted from *Collected Poems 1909–1935* by T. S. Eliot, copyright, 1936, by Harcourt, Brace & World, Inc. and used with their permission.

The twenty poems of Robert Frost are reprinted from *Complete Poems of Robert Frost.* Copyright 1916, 1921, 1923, 1928, 1930, 1935, 1939, 1947 by Holt, Rinehart and Winston, Inc. Copyright renewed 1944, 1951, © 1956 by Robert Frost. Copyright 1936, 1942 by Robert Frost. Used by permission of Holt, Rinehart and Winston, Inc.

Thomas Hardy's "The Darkling Thrush" and "In Church" are reprinted from *Collected Poems* by Thomas Hardy, copyright 1925 by The Macmillan Company and used with their permission.

iv

PREFACE

THIS BOOK has been made for the use and pleasure of those who are beginning the study of poetry, or who wish to have materials for continued reading. It begins with the close study of the individual poem and what it is (the vertical view), and expands to combine such reading with a knowledge of the poem's relationship to other poems (the horizontal view). We have tried to present a large selection of material in a usable, adaptable form, including study questions and illustrative essays, and emphasizing throughout that no one narrow critical formula will serve for the study of poems. For a poem is best understood and experienced when it is read many times and viewed as a living thing with many dimensions.

In the four chapters of Part I (The Vertical View), we have discussed in logical order the problems that a reader may encounter: learning what a poem is and what reading a poem means, how poems fit into types and traditions, how the reader can make interpretations and judgments, and what approaches he can use in studying a poem. Here we have given many individual poems for illustrations, with some suggested critical questions.

The larger section of the book, Part II (The Horizontal View), presents eighteen major poets in general chronological order (Hopkins has been shifted to join his fellow Victorian poets). Each poet is represented in depth with a substantial group of poems, a biography, and a list of suggested readings. Here the reader is left free to transfer to these poems the study techniques discussed in Part I. A particular feature of this section and the book is the series of essays and notes, one or more related to each major poet, in which are illustrated a variety of critical approaches to the understanding of poems.

In preparing *The Dimensions of Poetry,* we have observed the following principles as to

SELECTION: Poets. The eighteen poets in Part II were chosen not only because of their individual importance but in order to show the pattern of historical development in English and American literature. For example, Dryden is included to give a full picture of the seventeenth and eighteenth centuries. Shelley is omitted to avoid overbalancing the Romantic period and the nineteenth century.

Poems. The poems in Part I are in general selected from writers not included in Part II. See the Chronological Guide (pp. xxiii–xxv) for a complete listing of poets represented in the book. This Guide may also be used for an expanded chronological study of the poetry. We have included both the favorite, well-known poems from each major writer and some fresh material for each. With only a few exceptions, we have used complete poems. Because of space, some long works have had, of course, to be omitted. Nevertheless, poems like *The Rape of the Lock, The Rime of the Ancient Mariner,* and "The Eve of St. Agnes" are here; and *Paradise Lost* is represented by a series of excerpts linked by brief summaries of the action of the poem. These passages from Milton are chosen to show something of the brilliant variety of his poetry, even within one poem.

Essays. The critical essays in Part II were selected as good examples of various kinds of criticism. They vary in style, point of view, and complexity (just as poems do), but in each one a valid and carefully considered approach to a poem or to an author's work is illustrated.

TEXTS: In order to eliminate as far as possible the initial language barrier of the earlier poets, we have modernized and Americanized the spelling and some punctuation of the poems from Shakespeare, Donne, Milton, Dryden, and Pope (except in quotations used in the critical essays), basing our versions on the most authentic early texts. From Blake on, the texts of the poems have been kept as nearly as possible in the style intended by the poet. In modernizing the texts of the earlier poets, we have made one careful distinction. An apostrophe used to show that the word is to be pronounced with an omitted syllable (*ev'ry, heav'nly*) has been retained when that reading is necessary to keep the original metrical plan of the line. This distinction is very important in writers like Pope, who tried to keep a consistent ten-syllable line in the heroic couplet. Adding the extra syllable would distort the intended rhythm of the writer, and sometimes our view of his poetic skill. Punctuation, too, has been carefully adjusted to the apparent rhythmic intention of the writer, not to prose logic, although some marks have been added when necessary to clarify the grammar. After becoming familiar with the poems now modernized, the reader should also consult the original texts.

ARRANGEMENT: In the major sections of Part II (and in some of the smaller collections in Part I) the poems are arranged in a general chronological order. Selections from modern poets are given in the order in which they appear in the collected works.

OTHER READING: Notes prefacing each major poet in Part II give suggested introductory readings, chosen from older works of proved value and from the most recent critical studies. These readings are only places to begin. The essays included in Part II as examples of criticism are also beginnings.

The reader can find explications and essays on many other subjects and from other points of view by checking some of the standard bibliographies. See the magazine, *The Explicator*; *Poetry Explication,* ed. Arms and Kuntz; *Articles on American Literature,* ed. Leary; *Cambridge Bibliography of English Literature*; *English Literature, 1660–1800: A Bibliography of Modern Studies,* ed. Landa; and the bibliographies that appear regularly in *PMLA* and *Philological Quarterly.*

For most poets, the reader will find a Cambridge or Oxford edition of the complete works that will be standard and useful. Other important editions have been listed in the notes on suggested reading. And we repeat that this book is intended to be an *introduction* to poetry. For the greatest enjoyment, the reader will want to hold in his hands the volumes that are the whole works of a poet, and read and discover there some things that only he could find for himself.

JAMES E. MILLER, JR.
BERNICE SLOTE

Lincoln, Nebraska
February 1962

CONTENTS

CHAPTER 3. POETRY AND JUDGMENT   97

Poems

WILLIAM BUTLER YEATS (*1865–1939*) *622*

CHRONOLOGICAL GUIDE

PART I
THE
VERTICAL VIEW

Part 1

The
Vertical View

CHAPTER 1

INSIDE THE POEM

THE NATURE OF A POEM

POETRY is simply a deep kind of pleasure—like roses, or music, or love. It may, in fact, contain in itself all three of these familiar delights:

> O my luve is like a red, red rose,
>   That's newly sprung in June.
> O my luve is like the melodie
>   That's sweetly played in tune.

The pleasure from these lines by Robert Burns comes partly from their own lilt and rhythm, their *tune*. It comes also from the exactness, the *intensity*, of what is named: the double redness of the opening summer rose, the finished harmony of music. But it comes most richly from the fusion of all the elements that are brought into a pattern of relationships—love (and the implied lovers), the rose, and the song. An *order* is made of miscellaneous experiences, and separate things are made one whole.

The rest of the poem shows some variations. While the pattern of the first stanza has mainly physical and emotional responses, the second stanza introduces some mental gymnastics of definition, measurement, conviction, and argument:

> As fair art thou, my bonie lass,
>   So deep in luve am I;
> And I will luve thee still, my dear,
>   Till a' the seas gang dry.

The lover is a poetic engineer, measuring the depth and the length of love by beauty and all time. He convincingly promises the impossible. Some of the pleasures in poetry come from the

3

agile mind that must turn about in such a little drama of words.
The closing stanzas of the poem remind us that when we mention the "pleasure" of poetry, or roses, or love, we do not mean
that they are without tragedy. Roses die, and lovers part. So the
physical images of the last stanzas become harsh, fearful, dry, and
violent, a matter of desperate promises at a parting that may be,
for all any one knows, a final one. "And I will luve thee still," he
says,

> Till a' the seas gang dry, my dear,
>   And the rocks melt wi' the sun!
> And I will luve thee still, my dear,
>   While the sands o' life shall run.
>
> And fare thee weel, my only luve,
>   And fare thee weel a while!
> And I will come again, my luve,
>   Tho' it were ten thousand mile!

Our response to this poem is certainly a mixture of joy and sorrow, just as the poem itself has many sides. We can think of the
sound it makes, and the beat of the lines; of the persons and the
story it implies; of the shape and reality of physical things; of the
way we feel when we imagine that the lines apply to something
in our own experience. We might even consider how the old Scottish song of the eighteenth century involves a universal experience
and set it beside these stanzas from a twentieth-century ballad,
W. H. Auden's "As I Walked Out One Evening" (p. 47). Here
the lover says that "Love has no ending," and so

> "I'll love you, dear, I'll love you
>   Till China and Africa meet,
> And the river jumps over the mountain
>   And the salmon sing in the street.
>
> I'll love you till the ocean
>   Is folded and hung up to dry,
> And the seven stars go squawking
>   Like geese about the sky.
>
> The years shall run like rabbits,
>   For in my arms I hold
> The Flower of the Ages,
>   And the first love of the world."

He is making the same old beautiful promises, and perhaps his "Flower of the Ages" is the same rose that Burns saw in his "luve." In one sense, the "red, red rose" never dies. Perhaps this is what poetry is all about.[1]

There are two main ways of looking at a poem—as a physical object and as a process. Of the two, the process, or the experience created in himself by the reader, is more important. Whitman said (in "A Song for Occupations") that "all architecture is what you do to it when you look upon it." The physical object which is the poem has the architecture of lines and shape, scenes and stories, but the poem is also the experience—what the reader *does*, and what happens to him when all the elements of the poem come alive in him.

As a physical object, the poem has two fundamental characteristics that distinguish it from prose. It is, first of all, a *concentration*. Think of a poem as a compact, condensed structure of language, in itself smaller, more formal, more patterned and complicated than prose. From it, multiple explosions of the senses, emotions, and understanding may take place. It operates by indirection, suggestion, and fused meanings. Secondly, it has a deliberate pattern of sound and rhythm—not words set to music but words *in* music. Here the difference from prose is that a poem will have not only a more recognizable but a *continuous* and total rhythmic pattern.

As a process, the poem is the experience which the reader creates in himself. He sees, hears, feels, and knows. Like all experiences, the poem is a way of living—even of becoming more completely alive—for such a physical and imaginative act can extend a person's world and sharpen his vision. The process is both exciting and demanding: The reader can set off an explosion from the chemicals the poet provides, making a carnival of stars out of a few plain words. But he must also approach the creation of a poem, through his own craft of imaginative reading, with the same close awareness, attention, and practiced skill that a pianist gives to music, or a skier to motion in sky and snow.

To become more skilled as readers who create a poem, we can learn to attend to different elements, looking at them separately at first and later putting them together in full understanding.

[1] Exercises based on the poems in this chapter appear on pages 31–35.

First, we need to take a vertical view. We can go inside the physical world of the poem to see what is there.

THE PHYSICAL WORLD OF THE POEM

Images and Metaphor: Singleness and Doubleness

To see the landscape in a poem clearly, one must first of all hold to the virtue of simple accuracy. Accuracy applies to the meanings of words and the direction of grammar. A reader may have to look up a word, or straighten out a subject or a modifier. Accuracy also applies to the notion of persons and their situation. What characters are here? Who is speaking—a character, or the poet? And is it the poet in his own personality, or what Emily Dickinson called a "supposed person"? Poets are great actors, and you may find that a young woman writer is pretending for the moment to be an old man. (Note, for instance, that the "I" of Emily Dickinson's "Because I Could Not Stop for Death" is not the poet but a person dead for centuries.) At least, one should keep the poet clear of his characters. A good many hasty readers of Robert Frost's "Mending Wall" wisely nod and affirm that *Frost* says, "Good fences make good neighbors," when it is actually the habit-blind farmer who says it, and the intent of the whole poem is to show up his wrongheadedness.

First of all, then, we need a clear sense of the facts, of people, places, and events. We need to put them on the stage of our mind and let the play go on. Sometimes we will simply hear a voice talking, making direct statements of ideas, nothing fancy:

TO SABIDIUS [1]

I love thee not, Sabidius,
     I can not tell thee why;
I can say nought but this alone,—
     I do not love thee, I.

But direct statements rarely occur alone. They are almost always a part of a story, or a comment on a physical scene or object. They need their own context of person, place, and thing. With that physical world the reader must come to terms.

[1] One of many English versions of an epigram by the Latin poet Martial. "To Sabidius" appeared in Timothe Kendall's *Flowers of Epigrams*, 1577.

Going into the poem, the reader generally finds himself in a physical world. Though he may be breathing through his imagination rather than his lungs, the facts of his life are exactly the same. He must make contact with the realities of the senses, noticing colors and shapes, sounds and smells, touch and feeling. In the poem, objects are named, and the reader responds by seeing, hearing, feeling all of their qualities. He can have an experience on one level simply by letting his imagination re-create these images of the senses in his mind (red wagon, creaking wheels, fried onions, snow). Such *naming* of sensory details in a poem is called its *imagery*. An image can be caught in the mind as single, sharp, intense, and clear. That is the first step in having an experience to notice and attend to what is there. Such awareness is the reader's first tool. If it is the only pleasure he finds in poetry, it may still be enough. To give attention to a blade of grass or the color of a pomegranate or an old man's cough or the smell of gasoline is to be more completely alive. It is, then, the *imagery* of the poem in all its concrete sensory detail that makes up the first level of meaning, or significance, in a poem—the *singleness* with which a reader must first of all engage.

But in the physical world of the poem, images rarely come by themselves and for themselves. For poetry is a complex order of experience, and order implies relationship, connection, *doubleness*. One of the most characteristic acts of poetry is to take two or more separate, apparently unrelated things (images, objects, persons, qualities) and put them together. They turn out, in the context of the poem, to be related after all (in at least one respect), and to reveal something new and unexpected and convincing about the nature of things. In a real sense, the lion lies down with the lamb. A poem usually implies that the world is not composed of isolated facts; life is whole, and all things go together in some kind of order.

The easiest kind of combination to recognize in poetry is the form of expression called *simile,* or a plainly stated comparison. One thing is like another thing. My love is like a rose. My love is like a melody. Henry King illustrates more completely how the whole meaning can lie simply in the finding of such relationship.

SIC VITA

Like to the falling of a star,
Or as the flights of eagles are,
Or like the fresh spring's gaudy hue,
Or silver drops of morning dew,
Or like a wind that chafes the flood,   5
Or bubbles which on water stood:
Even such is man, whose borrowed light
Is straight called in, and paid to night:
   The wind blows out, the bubble dies,
   The spring entombed in autumn lies;   10
   The dew dries up, the star is shot,
   The flight is past, and man forgot.

HENRY KING, Bishop of Chichester (*1592–1669*)

The transience and brevity of life are made emotionally real by the accumulation of the images, the repeated comparisons. The theme is universal. The poet simply searches for a way to make the point fully realized and deeply felt.

Comparisons that are clearly stated as comparisons cause little trouble for the reader of poetry. The facts are as they are represented: My love is like a rose. Life is like a wind. But suppose the two objects of the comparison are actually fused together in a kind of imaginative shorthand: My love *is* a rose. Now here is a critical step in the reading of a poem, for this kind of language is not the exception but the habit in poetry. It is, in general, an *unliteral* language; that is, the statements do not mean what they say in objective fact. A literal comparison would say, "The man is *like* a lion," meaning that he has the lion's qualities of courage or fierceness or strength. The unliteral, or fused, form would say, "He *is* a lion," or "He is lion-hearted." Such an identification is direct, but comparatively simple. We might try fusing several things: The preacher became a lion roaring hot thunder. Now this statement is unliteral, but its exact meaning could not be duplicated in any other way—by listing *man, lion, heat,* and *thunder,* for instance—any more than a person ordering ice cream would expect to have set before him a bottle of milk, a bowl of sugar, and a couple of eggs. The unliteral phrase of poetry is more

than its parts. It has its own separate existence. Such language is condensed, compact, and forceful, with more suggestions, ideas, and imaginative possibilities than literal expression, which stays purely with objective fact. In one sense, poetry is like slang, which is almost totally an unliteral language. Like slang, poetry plays with words and creates new forms of language. The difference is that poetry's intention is serious, its form involved, and its life much longer.

The doubleness of unliteral language in poetry can be described in two ways. The most common form of *comparison* is the direct statement of assumed likenesses, or *metaphor,* which means a "carrying over": He is a lion; the bubble of reputation; his mind's geography. The principle of metaphor is so universally present in all of the language of poetry that the term is sometimes used to mean any comparison (including the more literal *simile*) or any unliteral statement that in some way derives from a comparison. If any one speaks of the "metaphorical" language of poetry, he means this general habit of combining different elements to show an order or a relationship.

Deriving from metaphor is a special category in which *representation* rather than comparison proper is the chief aim of the statement. One thing stands for another, or two things may be interchanged. The kinds of representation most often found in poetry are *symbol, personification,* and *allegory.*

A *symbol* is a physical thing which represents or stands for something else. In a symbol, one may equal one, but more often, the symbol is a focal point for a number of ideas, feelings, qualities, significances: A ring is a symbol or sign of marriage. Its circle stands for eternity and perfection, love and promise. The human world is full of such accepted or traditional symbols. A red rose stands for love, passion, and beauty; a willow tree for sorrow; a snake for evil; a dove for peace; gold for richness and value; the desert for sterility and death. These are traditional symbolic meanings, or representations. They usually appear in poetry as a part of a larger fabric of metaphorical language. But note how in some poems a symbol can be created with its own context. In Wordsworth's "Michael," the old shepherd becomes a symbol for the endurance of love; in D. H. Lawrence's "Snake" (p. 51) the traditional symbolic quality of the snake fades away, and it becomes a symbol of the innocence of the natural world misused by

man, a lost chance for man to become kinglike. At the end of
Browning's "My Last Duchess," the Duke turns to one more art
object:

>Notice Neptune, though,
>Taming a sea-horse, thought a rarity,
>Which Claus of Innsbruck cast in bronze for me!

In the context of the poem, both the act and the bronze piece take
on symbolic force, for the Duke in fact has been talking about
ownership, the taming of his wife.

Personification endows a quality or an idea with the characteristics of a person: Autumn wears a dress of crimson. Justice weeps
in the Capitol. An abstraction is thus made concrete, or exact and
physical. Personification may also identify a person with a single
abstraction or quality. One might say, "Abraham Lincoln was
democracy itself," or "In the play, the uncle was living confusion." For good examples of personification, see Gray's "Elegy"
(p. 72) and the second stanza of Keats's "To Autumn."

Allegory, usually found in longer poems, is customarily a narrative in which the pattern of what is named and what is represented holds throughout the extended piece. Point by point the
equivalents are worked out and developed. Often the characters
are personifications—qualities in the form of persons. Sometimes
the named figure represents an actual person. In longer pieces,
particularly satire, this kind of allegory is something to work out.
As in Dryden's "Mac Flecknoe," the game is to identify who and
what are meant. In shorter poems, allegory is a kind of continued
metaphor in which all the elements connect and relate to each
other. The following medieval poem, like many others of its time,
is an allegory in which the apparent secular terms represent in
various details the story of the death of Christ.

LULLY, LULLEY

>*Lully, lulley! lully, lulley!*
>*The faucon* [1] *hath borne my make* [2] *away!*

>He bare him up, he bare him down,
>He bare him into an orchard brown.

---

[1] *faucon* falcon   [2] *make* mate

In that orchard there was an halle,   5
That was hangèd with purple and pall.

And in that hall there was a bed,
It was hangèd with gold so red.

And in that bed there li'th a knight,
His woundes bleeding day and night.   10

At that bed's foot there li'th a hound,
Licking the blood as it runs down.

By that bed-side kneeleth a may,[3]
And she weepeth both night and day.

And at that bed's head standeth a stone,   15
Corpus Christi written thereon.

Lully, lulley! lully, lulley!
The faucon hath borne my make away.

ANONYMOUS

For other short poems in which a consistent allegory is worked out, see Spenser's "Like as a Ship" (p. 65) and Wyatt's "My Galley" (p. 64).

We might sum up the characteristics of the language of poetry by which one dimension of its physical world is created. The *singleness* in poetry is the exact, concrete, physical details of its imagery. Flicked into life by the imagination, these images give *intensity* to the experience. The *doubleness* in poetry (both comparison and representation) is the combination of two or more different elements to reveal a significant likeness. The unlikeness of the elements gives the tension of conflict to the action of the poem. The likeness establishes *order*. The doubleness in a poem is both a condensation and an explosion. A great deal is packed into a small space. It can also be the significance of a poem: to take two parts of the world and by putting them together in a meaningful relationship to perform the ritual of belief—that there is order, shape, unity, and sense in the cosmos.

[3] *may* maid

Voice and Movement

Another dimension of the poem is its physical voice and movement. Sound and rhythm are not subordinated or decorative devices added to the poem; they are part of its living body. The organic pulse and the harmony of sound of a poem can be both engaging and revealing, whether heard in the reader's voice or in his imagination.

Rhythm, like tides or breathing, is a regular rise and fall, in this case, of sound; in a drum pattern, it is the symmetrical beat that is felt through all variations. The beat in poetry depends mainly on the arrangement of accented syllables, although so much of the rhythm is determined by pauses, punctuation, the quality and extent of the sound, and the arrangement of words in lines, that no easy formula will help the reader classify or define the means by which any certain rhythm is produced. The system by which we may analyze the formal pattern of a line is called metrics. More detailed definitions of the types of metrical arrangements may be found in the Glossary, but here we are initially concerned with only the general principles of rhythm. Although they often overlap, we can distinguish two major kinds of rhythm in poetry: (1) *Common,* or *running,* rhythm assumes that comparable lines have an even number of syllables, arranged in a regular pattern of one stressed syllable alternating with one or two unstressed syllables. (2) *Speech* rhythm disregards any count of syllables, but rests upon an over-all symmetrical recurrence of heavy stresses, given to words or syllables according to natural speech or the sense of the line.

Common rhythm, based upon classical forms, establishes an ideal pattern to serve as a kind of undercurrent or norm—perhaps a line of ten syllables with alternating accents:

$$\smile / \smile / \smile / \smile /$$

or perhaps a line with twelve syllables in even groups of three:

$$\smile \smile / \smile \smile / \smile \smile / \smile \smile /$$

The ideal of common rhythm is like a design or blueprint made for a formal garden—everything is diagrammed and balanced. In reality, however, some flowers in the garden grow higher than others, and not every tree is exactly the same shape. Nevertheless the formal pattern is there; variations are within the measured whole. For example, Gray's "Elegy" (p. 72) begins with a regular metrical pattern of ten syllables and five stresses, or beats, to the line:

> ◡ / ◡ / ◡ / ◡ / ◡ /
> The curfew tolls the knell of parting day.

Since the pattern has been established, the second line can be read in an alternating sing-song:

> ◡ / ◡ / ◡ / ◡ / ◡ /
> The lowing herd wind slowly o'er the lea.

In actual reading, however, *wind* is given more emphasis and *o'er* less emphasis. The stanza then returns to the even measure:

> ◡ / ◡ / ◡ / ◡ / ◡ /
> The ploughman homeward plods his weary way. . . .

Later lines show other variations—an occasional extra syllable, an accent that is noticeably lighter than others (the *and* in the fourth line, for example), or a reversal of pattern:

> / ◡ ◡ /
> Rich with the spoils . . . (l. 50)

The second major type of rhythm is that which emphasizes the pulse of heavily stressed natural speech. Each stress gathers around it a cluster of unaccented syllables or slighter accents. Speech rhythm may occur in the long lines of Whitman:

> ◡ ◡ / ◡ ◡ ◡ /
> To the tally of my soul
> / ◡ / ◡ / / / ◡ / ◡ /
> Loud and strong kept up [*or* kept up] the gray brown [*or* gray
> / /
> brown] bird
> ◡ / ◡ / ◡ ◡ / / ◡ / ◡ ◡ /
> With pure deliberate notes spreading filling the night.

("When Lilacs Last in the Dooryard Bloom'd," ll. 163–165)

Here, there is no attempt to keep an even number of accents or syllables in each line. The pulse or rhythm is an over-all, sweeping

flow that rises and falls in a space larger than the line. A more
regular pattern of this kind can be followed in Hopkins, who
often has the same number of beats in comparable lines but
does not keep an even arrangement of the unaccented syllables.
(His own explanation of his prosody, which he calls "sprung
rhythm," should also be examined. He sounds more complicated,
but it all comes down to the same thing.) Hopkins indicated his
stresses in the first line of "God's Grandeur" to be

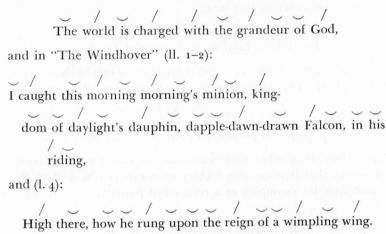

The world is charged with the grandeur of God,

and in "The Windhover" (ll. 1–2):

I caught this morning morning's minion, king-

dom of daylight's dauphin, dapple-dawn-drawn Falcon, in his

riding,

and (l. 4):

High there, how he rung upon the reign of a wimpling wing.

Common rhythm may seem the more artful, speech rhythm the
more natural; but usually neither is found in a pure form. Stresses
and pauses placed according to the sense of the words or the
speech flow may be used to different degrees in combination with
common rhythm. It is interesting to note that the worst poets
hold to jingly regularity, but that the poets most admired for
their verbal magic—Shakespeare, Milton, Keats—have used common rhythm as a substructure, but have built on and through it
music of remarkably intricate variations. And the poets most
successful in speech or stress rhythms have also exercised an artful
control of their own irregularities. In general, the *over-all* rhythm
or pulsing flow of the poem is what matters, and what the reader
giving a poem voice should aim to discover and feel.

The harmony of a poem is composed of various repetitions and
correspondences of sound, all blending in the imagination like a
chord of music that resolves itself. The most chordlike of all the
repetitions of sound in a poem is *rhyme,* which may be exact

(*moon / June*) or a bit slanting (*moon / moan — moon / sun*).
Rhyme can occur at the ends of lines, at any regular interval, or
even in the middle or beginning of the lines. Other repetitions
are important: *alliteration*—the same initial consonant (*sea /
sound*); *assonance*—the same vowel (m*oo*n / t*oo*l); or *consonance*—the same consonant in any location (roun*d* / *d*ecay).
Note how all of these repetitions make a close harmony in the last
lines of Shelley's "Ozymandias" (p. 142):

> Nothing beside remains. Round the decay
> Of that colossal wreck, boundless and bare
> The lone and level sands stretch far away.

Repetitions of words and phrases give both rhythm and harmony. See, for example, how the Whitman poems have a chording
of identical words and phrases at the beginnings of lines. All such
repetitions—and especially rhyme—emphasize the sense of a regular beat, or rhythm, in a poem.

Another use of sound is the word which resembles or suggests
whatever is named; in longer passages, the language would suggest the tone of the experience. A simple form of this device, or
onomatopoeia, is a word like *crash* or *tinkle.* In a large sense,
onomatopoeia functions when a passage about quiet things
sounds smooth and peaceful, a passage about wilder movement
has excitement. One can go too far with such correspondences, so
it is best to recognize only the most obvious uses of general
onomatopoeia in which the images and sound coincide. Compare, for example, two lines from Shelley's "Ode to the West
Wind" (p. 68) by reading them aloud. Of the storm he says,

> Black rain, and fire, and hail will burst: oh, hear!

A much closer harmony is used in the description of the dreaming Mediterranean:

> Lulled by the coil of his crystalline streams.

Or read the lines from Frost's "Birches" that describe the ice
breaking from the trees:

> Soon the sun's warmth makes them shed crystal shells
> Shattering and avalanching on the snow-crust—

or the water image in Yeats's "The Lake Isle of Innisfree":

I hear lake water lapping with low sounds by the shore.

Rhythms, too, can be suggestive, as in the galloping movement of Byron's "The Destruction of Sennacherib" (p. 49):

> The Assyrian came down like the wolf on the fold,
> And his cohorts were gleaming in purple and gold;

or the somnolence of Tennyson's "Lotos-Eaters":

> And in the stream the long-leaved flowers weep,
> And from the craggy ledge the poppy hangs in sleep.

The crisper tone of John Skelton makes a good contrast:

TO MISTRESS MARGARET HUSSEY

> Merry Margaret,
> As midsummer flower,
> Gentle as falcon
> Or hawk of the tower;
> With solace and gladness,   5
> Much mirth and no madness,
> All good, and no badness;
> So joyously,
> So maidenly,
> So womanly   10
> Her demeaning
> In every thing
> Far, far passing
> That I can endite,
> Or suffice to write   15
> Of merry Margaret,
> As midsummer flower,
> Gentle as falcon
> Or hawk of the tower;
> As patient and as still,   20
> And as full of good will,
> As fair Isaphill;
> Coriander,
> Sweet pomander,
> Good Cassander;   25
> Steadfast of thought,
> Well made, well wrought;
> Far may be sought

> Erst that ye can find
> So courteous, so kind   30
> As merry Margaret,
> This midsummer flower,
> Gentle as falcon,
> Or hawk of the tower.

JOHN SKELTON (c.1460–1529)

Quite aside from recognizable elements of sound and rhythm, the language of poetry has sometimes a memorable rightness in the way it fits together. We *like* the way the phrases fall. We say them over, like a kind of magic. We can recognize the language that works and the language that doesn't. Compare two versions of the same line, the famous opening line of Keats's *Endymion:* "A thing of beauty is a joy forever" was originally the flat statement "A thing of beauty is a constant joy." Whitman's phrase "Out of the cradle endlessly rocking" was first "Out of the rocked cradle." For magical lines we think of Shakespeare's "Bare ruined choirs where late the sweet birds sang" or "Ripeness is all." But each reader finds his own to remember.

Pattern

The reader who goes into the physical world of the poem will see that the singleness of concrete imagery, the doubleness of metaphor, the sound and motion of its language—all make a pattern. In one sense the pattern is external. The visual arrangement of the lines can make a difference: they may be either straggling or compact, in formal designs or in irregular positions that may tell a visual story or emphasize certain words and relationships. With internal logic, there may be arrangements of lines in some familiar patterns: the *couplet,* a pair of rhyming lines; the *stanza,* a regular grouping of lines, usually with a rhyme pattern. The *quatrain,* or four-line stanza, is one of the most common. Other larger arrangements of lines are *blank verse,* a series of unrhymed five-beat lines; and *free verse,* unrhymed irregular lines that have a strophic or rounded rising-falling paragraph rhythm instead of a formal metrical arrangement. Occasionally an entire poem, like a *sonnet,* will be formed in a specific pattern of lines and rhymes (see Chapter 2). These are outer patterns that can be grasped quickly by the reader. They are the formal signs of the ordered experience inside the poem.

Within the poem, the selection and the arrangement of the separate parts should make a significant order. Even in poems of nearly direct statement, the parts have importance *because* they are combined.

> A Book of Verses underneath the Bough,
> A Jug of Wine, a Loaf of Bread—and Thou
>   Beside me singing in the Wilderness—
> Oh, Wilderness were Paradise enow!

EDWARD FITZGERALD (1809–1883)

To have a book, a tree, bread, wine, two persons, and a wilderness equal to paradise is FitzGerald's particular magic with his translation of one of the four-line verses, or rubáiyát, by Omar Khayyám. To see how FitzGerald achieved the romantically vague tone he wanted, compare the original details in a literal translation of the same rubáiyát:

> If one may have a loaf of the flower of wheat, a two-maund (jar) of wine, a thigh of mutton, seated with a heart's darling in a ruined place—that is a pleasure that is not the attainment of any sultan.

translated by A. J. Arberry

Here the leg of mutton is enough to bludgeon some of the romance. What is chosen and what is left out—the combination—will make a difference in a poem.

The proper combination of details may give some words and images special significance. John Heywood's little dialogue (1562) is composed entirely of direct statements, but the last phrase gets its punning sharpness only from its context:

JACK AND HIS FATHER

> Jack (quoth his father) how shall I ease take?
> If I stand, my legs ache; and if I kneel
> My knees ache; if I go, then my feet ache;
> If I lie, my back ach'th; if I sit, I feel
> My hips ache; and lean I never so weel,   5
> My elbows ache. Sir (quoth Jack) pain to exile,
> Since all these ease not, best ye hang awhile.

JOHN HEYWOOD (c.1497–c.1580)

Images combined may also reshape each other. Read, for example, A. E. Housman's poem:

LOVELIEST OF TREES

Loveliest of trees, the cherry now
Is hung with bloom along the bough,
And stands about the woodland ride
Wearing white for Eastertide.

Now, of my threescore years and ten,   5
Twenty will not come again,
And take from seventy springs a score,
It only leaves me fifty more.

And since to look at things in bloom
Fifty springs are little room,   10
About the woodlands I will go
To see the cherry hung with snow.

A. E. HOUSMAN (*1859–1936*)

When Housman writes,

Loveliest of trees, the cherry now
Is hung with bloom along the bough,

bloom means blossoms, flowers. When later in the poem he writes of going "To see the cherry hung with snow," one knows that either bloom or snow must be unliteral; one is the fact and the other the likeness: blooming trees are white like snow, or the late snow on the trees is like blossoms. Most readers think the first meaning is the more natural; but it may even be possible to hold both interpretations in the mind at once and think of bloom and snow as the full range of the creative cycle of the year. One of the pleasures of poetry is that it enables you to lead a double life.

One of the clearest examples of pattern (or selection and combination) as meaning is in "Cargoes," by John Masefield. This is a naming poem, in which no comment is made other than to let the exact paralleling of imagery and form in each of the stanzas tell its own story of changing times and values:

CARGOES

Quinquireme of Nineveh from distant Ophir,
Rowing home to haven in sunny Palestine,
With a cargo of ivory,
And apes and peacocks,
Sandalwood, cedarwood, and sweet white wine.   5

Stately Spanish galleon coming from the Isthmus,
Dipping through the Tropics by the palm-green shores,
With a cargo of diamonds,
Emeralds, amethysts,
Topazes, and cinnamon, and gold moidores.   10

Dirty British coaster with a salt-caked smoke stack,
Butting through the Channel in the mad March days,
With a cargo of Tyne coal,
Road-rails, pig-lead,
Firewood, iron-ware, and cheap tin trays.   15

JOHN MASEFIELD (*1878–*   )

Ships, their regions, and their cargoes are named in order of history: the westward movement of civilization; the shift of sea and class power; the decline of rare romance and the rise of common good. The order of the parts in "Cargoes" makes the imagination move in certain directions: from past to present in time, from east to west in geography, from pleasure to practicality (or from beauty to ugliness, depending on one's point of view) in human values.

Such directed acts of the imagination make up an important internal order, or *psychological movement,* that should be considered in all poems. The particular kind of psychological movement gives shape to experience. Such a pattern of movement inside a poem can be quite individual, but for purposes of illustration we might note three of its most common forms. To coin some metaphors, we might call them the wheel, the chain, and the shuttle. The wheel and the chain are shapes that come primarily from the way in which the poem is developed and the order in which its parts are presented. The shuttle is one example of a form based on the direction taken by the events of the poem. All of them may overlap, and they are by no means the only shapes to find in poems. Using these as examples, however, the reader may go ahead to find his own variations.

The wheel is a round poem in which one central symbol or metaphor unifies all of the parts. We begin with one significant image (like the hub of a wheel) and let the details radiate out of it. A simple form of such a poem is the descriptive piece in which the focus is on an object or a single element; for example, "The Snow-Storm," by Ralph Waldo Emerson:

THE SNOW-STORM

Announced by all the trumpets of the sky,
Arrives the snow, and, driving o'er the fields,
Seems nowhere to alight: the whited air
Hides hills and woods, the river, and the heaven,
And veils the farm-house at the garden's end.
The sled and traveller stopped, the courier's feet
Delayed, all friends shut out, the housemates sit
Around the radiant fireplace, enclosed
In a tumultuous privacy of storm.

Come see the north wind's masonry.   10
Out of an unseen quarry evermore
Furnished with tile, the fierce artificer
Curves his white bastions with projected roof
Round every windward stake, or tree, or door.
Speeding, the myriad-handed, his wild work   15
So fanciful, so savage, nought cares he
For number or proportion. Mockingly,
On coop or kennel he hangs Parian wreaths;
A swan-like form invests the hidden thorn;
Fills up the farmer's lane from wall to wall,   20
Maugre the farmer's sighs; and at the gate
A tapering turret overtops the work.
And when his hours are numbered, and the world
Is all his own, retiring, as he were not,
Leaves, when the sun appears, astonished Art   25
To mimic in slow structures, stone by stone,
Built in an age, the mad wind's nightwork,
The frolic architecture of the snow.

RALPH WALDO EMERSON (*1803–1882*)

The center of the poem may be a metaphor. Sometimes the parallels that extend the metaphorical comparison are presented clearly for all to see, as in the comic exaggeration of Thomas Campion's poem on the Elizabethan admirer who had a vegetarian view of beauty:

THERE IS A GARDEN IN HER FACE

There is a garden in her face,
　Where roses and white lilies grow;
A heavenly paradise is that place,
　Wherein all pleasant fruits do flow:
There cherries grow, which none may buy　　　　5
Till "Cherry ripe" themselves do cry.

Those cherries fairly do enclose
　Of orient pearl a double row;
Which when her lovely laughter shows,
　They look like rosebuds filled with snow.　　10
Yet them nor peer nor prince can buy,
Till "Cherry ripe" themselves do cry.

Her eyes like angels watch them still;
　Her brows like bended bows do stand,
Threatening with piercing frowns to kill　　　　15
　All that attempt, with eye or hand,
Those sacred cherries to come nigh,
Till "Cherry ripe" themselves do cry.

A Book of Airs, 1601
THOMAS CAMPION (*1567–1620*)

Sometimes the central metaphor is more subtly involved in the structure of a poem and perhaps not immediately revealed. Note how in "The Sheaves," by E. A. Robinson, the one comparison of golden grain to golden hair determines all that is said:

THE SHEAVES

Where long the shadows of the wind had rolled,
Green wheat was yielding to the change assigned;
And as by some vast magic undivined
The world was turning slowly into gold.

Like nothing that was ever bought or sold   5
It waited there, the body and the mind;
And with a mighty meaning of a kind
That tells the more the more it is not told.

So in a land where all days are not fair,
Fair days went on till on another day   10
A thousand golden sheaves were lying there,
Shining and still, but not for long to stay—
As if a thousand girls with golden hair
Might rise from where they slept and go away.

EDWIN ARLINGTON ROBINSON (*1869–1935*)

The metaphor of sheaves—hair is more than visual likeness; it contains all the implications of growth, transient beauty, and the magic that informs all life.

For other poems with central metaphors and symbols, see Donne's "The Canonization," Milton's sonnet "On His Blindness," Blake's "The Tyger," Keats's "Ode on a Grecian Urn," Dickinson's "Hope Is the Thing with Feathers," and Eliot's "The Hollow Men." In their psychological movement, these poems turn on a central element, at the same time progressing in the development of a theme.

The chain poem is a series of images and events linked by repetition of lines, phrases, and refrains. Such a poem is ritualistic, emphasizing the importance of returning to the familiar forms and acts as signs of some greater unity. The ritual may be lighthearted, as in a good many children's poems that have refrains:

> To market, to market, to buy a fat pig,
> Home again, home again, jiggety jig.
> To market, to market, to buy a fat hog,
> Home again, home again, jiggety jog.

The chain of repetitions may also form a litany, as in Thomas Nashe's "Song" ("Adieu, farewell earth's bliss"), which is a series of variations on the theme of uncertain life:

SONG [1]

Adieu, farewell earth's bliss.
This world uncertain is;
Fond are life's lustful joys,
Death proves them all but toys.
None from his darts can fly;   5
I am sick, I must die.
        Lord, have mercy on us!

Rich men, trust not in wealth,
Gold cannot buy you health;
Physic himself must fade.   10
All things to end are made;
The plague full swift goes by.
I am sick, I must die.
        Lord, have mercy on us!

Beauty is but a flower,   15
Which wrinkles will devour;
Brightness falls from the air;
Queens have died young and fair;
Dust hath closed Helen's eye.
I am sick, I must die.   20
        Lord, have mercy on us!

Strength stoops unto the grave,
Worms feed on Hector brave;
Swords may not fight with fate;
Earth still holds ope her gate.   25
Come, come! the bells do cry.
I am sick, I must die.
        Lord, have mercy on us!

Wit with his wantonness
Tasteth death's bitterness;   30
Hell's executioner
Hath no ears for to hear
What vain art can reply.
I am sick, I must die.
        Lord, have mercy on us!   35

---

[1] From the play *A Pleasant Comedie, called Summers last will and Testament,*
acted in 1592, published in 1600. Summer's speech preceding the song: "Sing
me some doleful ditty to the Lute,/That may complaine my neere approaching death."

Haste therefore each degree
To welcome destiny;
Heaven is our heritage,
Earth but a player's stage.
Mount we unto the sky.   40
I am sick, I must die.
            Lord, have mercy on us!

THOMAS NASHE (*1567–1601*)

The haunting lines of the third stanza are the ones usually remembered. But beauty is only one of several uncertainties, and
the cry of the refrain becomes more poignant when it ends all
other human joys as well.

   The shuttle poem is one example of a form that depends on
the psychological movement, the general direction of a poem.
Does the poem, for example, go straight ahead, relying on logical
growth by addition, or does it reverse itself and eventually contradict what it began? All of the poems used so far in this section
have conclusions to which the first arrows point. We might look
at a few examples of some other kinds—of reversals, or shuttle
movements. In parts, any poem may use certain devices of opposition that form a shuttle: paradox, or apparent contradictions; irony of statement, in which the expressed meaning contradicts the implied meaning (to the one who has spilled his soup,
"Aren't you graceful?"); and irony of situation, in which experience contradicts itself and our usual expectations. Reversal occurs in the whole poem when the expected ending does not appear. The first statements are contradicted. For instance, note
that the chief pleasure in Housman's "When I Was One-and-
Twenty" is the way the whole thing flips over to the opposite
side:

WHEN I WAS ONE-AND-TWENTY

When I was one-and-twenty
   I heard a wise man say,
'Give crowns and pounds and guineas
   But not your heart away;
Give pearls away and rubies   5
   But keep your fancy free.'

But I was one-and-twenty,
  No use to talk to me.

When I was one-and-twenty
  I heard him say again,   10
'The heart out of the bosom
  Was never given in vain;
'Tis paid with sighs a-plenty
  And sold for endless rue.'
And I am two-and-twenty,   15
  And oh, 'tis true, 'tis true.

                                    A. E. HOUSMAN (*1859–1936*)

We get the same thing even more dramatically in Drayton's "Since There's No Help," in which the point is the same as in a modern song which urges the partner not only to call the whole thing off but also to call the calling-off off.

SINCE THERE'S NO HELP

1   Since there's no help, come let us kiss and part;
2   Nay, I have done, you get no more of me,
3   And I am glad, yea glad with all my heart
4   That thus so cleanly I myself can free;
5   Shake hands forever, cancel all our vows,   5
6   And when we meet at any time again,
7   Be it not seen in either of our brows
8   That we one jot of former love retain.
9   Now at the last gasp of Love's latest breath,
10 When, his pulse failing, Passion speechless lies,   10
11 When Faith is kneeling by his bed of death,
12 And Innocence is closing up his eyes,
13   Now if thou wouldst, when all have given him over,
14   From death to life thou mightst him yet recover.

                                    MICHAEL DRAYTON (*1563–1631*)

Many of Shakespeare's sonnets use this shuttle technique. Read also in Donne's ironic love poems, such as "Song: Go and Catch a Falling Star."

MEANING AND EXPERIENCE

The pleasure of a poem is in its physical world—its sharp, exact imagery; its revealing metaphors; its memorable rhythm; its shapely pattern. Beyond this, there are still other dimensions to recognize. Yes, you say, what of the *meaning*? Do we have to find the hidden meaning in a poem?

The truth is that there *is* no hidden meaning. There is, in poetry, only an involved meaning. It is involved because, like all experiences, it is made up of many simultaneous events and intricate relationships—the physical beat and melody of the lines, sensations imaged in the mind, the emotion and the understanding that come through a particular ordering of events. The poet is not playing tricks to hide his meaning. He is condensing to give force. And reading a poem is not the same as working a puzzle to find *one* answer. Involved in the poem are many things to realize and know, and these may change their shape somewhat with different readers and different times of reading. A poem has many dimensions. For this reason, a good poem can be read again and again, with more of the involved meaning discovered each time. Poems are like people: distrust those who have no mystery after the first meeting.

Poems in which the involved meaning is most highly developed are those which have many related metaphors and in which the significance goes far beyond a simple surface likeness. For example, in a poem about the atomic cloud, the lowest level of significance would be its visual appearance. The cloud looks like a cauliflower or a mushroom. Here the latter shape has more emotional suggestion. One might go deeper in significance and relate it to the genie rising out of Aladdin's lamp: a new world of magic and power is suggested. But a more unexpected, more involved and richer significance is in a comparison like that in "The Progress of Faust," by Karl Shapiro. The cloud is the reappearance of an undying Faust who has repeatedly sold his soul to some kind of devil.

THE PROGRESS OF FAUST

He was born in Deutschland, as you would suspect,
And graduated in magic from Cracow

In Fifteen Five. His portraits show a brow
Heightened by science. The eye is indirect,
As of bent light upon a crooked soul,   5
And that he bargained with the Prince of Shame
For pleasures intellectually foul
Is known by every court that lists his name.

His frequent disappearances are put down
To visits in the regions of the damned   10
And to the periodic deaths he shammed,
But, unregenerate and in Doctor's gown,
He would turn up to lecture at the fair
And do a minor miracle for a fee.
Many a life he whispered up the stair   15
To teach the black art of anatomy.

He was as deaf to angels as an oak
When, in the fall of Fifteen Ninety-four,
He went to London and crashed through the floor
In mock damnation of the playgoing folk.   20
Weekending with the scientific crowd,
He met Sir Francis Bacon and helped draft
"Colours of Good and Evil" and read aloud
An obscene sermon at which no one laughed.

He toured the Continent for a hundred years   25
And subsidized among the peasantry
The puppet play, his tragic history;
With a white glove he boxed the Devil's ears
And with a black his own. Tired of this,
He published penny poems about his sins,   30
In which he placed the heavy emphasis
On the white glove which, for a penny, wins.

Some time before the hemorrhage of the Kings
Of France, he turned respectable and taught;
Quite suddenly everything that he had thought   35
Seemed to grow scholars' beards and angels' wings.
It was the Overthrow. On Reason's throne
He sat with the fair Phrygian on his knees
And called all universities his own,
As plausible a figure as you please.   40

Then back to Germany as the sages' sage
To preach comparative science to the young
Who came from every land in a great throng

And knew they heard the master of the age.
When for a secret formula he paid   45
The Devil another fragment of his soul,
His scholars wept, and several even prayed
That Satan would restore him to them whole.

Backwardly tolerant, Faustus was expelled
From the Third Reich in Nineteen Thirty-nine.   50
His exit caused the breaching of the Rhine,
Except for which the frontier might have held.
Five years unknown to enemy and friend
He hid, appearing on the sixth to pose
In an American desert at war's end   55
Where, at his back, a dome of atoms rose.

KARL SHAPIRO (*1913*–   )

There is no one meaning to this poem. It joins several centuries
of man's unfinished business with himself.

We cannot isolate the "meaning" of a poem from the poem,
and neither the ideas nor the emotions involved are separate from
the total experience. The only way to find a meaning or have an
emotion is to go down *inside* the poem and let it have its way.
It is not the *being told* but the *finding out* that is important to
the reader. Meaning is acted out in the imagination. Afterwards
one will be able to say, this poem is *about* inconstancy of women,
or the fear of death, or the disillusionment of a soldier, or even
the fun of a catchy tune. We will recognize several *ways* of experience. Each poem is a view from somebody's little hill. By reading
poems, we can get around and see a great deal of territory.

There are obviously many differences in the kinds of experience poems provide. One further pleasure is to recognize the
variety. For example, look at two poems quite different in manner, tone, and effect, Ben Jonson's seventeenth-century poem "It
Is Not Growing Like a Tree" and D. H. Lawrence's twentieth-
century "Bavarian Gentians."

IT IS NOT GROWING LIKE A TREE [1]

It is not growing like a tree
In bulk, doth make man better be;

[1] From the ode "To . . . Sir Lucius Cary and Sir H. Morison"

Or standing long an oak, three hundred year,
To fall a log at last, dry, bald, and sear;
    A lily of a day   5
    Is fairer far in May,
Although it fall and die that night,
It was the plant and flower of light.
In small proportions we just beauties see;
And in short measures, life may perfect be.   10

BEN JONSON (*1572–1637*)

BAVARIAN GENTIANS

Not every man has gentians in his house
in Soft September, at slow, Sad Michaelmas.

Bavarian gentians, big and dark, only dark
darkening the day-time torch-like with the smoking blueness of
    Pluto's gloom,
ribbed and torch-like, with their blaze of darkness spread blue 5
down flattening into points, flattened under the sweep of white
    day
torch-flower of the blue-smoking darkness, Pluto's dark-blue daze,
black lamps from the halls of Dio, burning dark blue,
giving off darkness, blue darkness, as Demeter's pale lamps give
    off light,
lead me then, lead me the way.   10

Reach me a gentian, give me a torch!
let me guide myself with the blue, forked torch of this flower
down the darker and darker stairs, where blue is darkened on
    blueness
even where Persephone goes, just now, from the frosted September
to the sightless realm where darkness is awake upon the dark 15
and Persephone herself is but a voice
or a darkness invisible enfolded in the deeper dark
of the arms Plutonic, and pierced with the passion of dense
    gloom,
among the splendour of torches of darkness, shedding darkness on
    the lost bride and her groom.

D. H. LAWRENCE (*1885–1930*)

The Jonson poem has an even, balanced pattern. The metaphors and the comparisons they imply are familiar (tall as a tree, strong as an oak, the flower of a day). The poem is, however, more discourse than imagery, the voice of a speaker who is figuring things out, giving examples, concluding with an epigram that ties the rest together. The pleasure is in its neatness, its wholeness, the rightness of its observation, the exactness of its mark. The brevity of the poem and its symmetry in fact illustrate the point of the epigram. In it one does not move; he is still and reflects. The Lawrence poem, on the other hand, is a poem of rich physical imagery with the blue-black gentian as the symbolic flame to light the way to the underworld, Pluto's realm. The direction of the poem is to go down, down—down deep into the blueness, the darkness, of flower and the mystery of death. The tone is incantatory, repeating words and images to invoke the feeling of being absorbed into the darkness. The lines are not even, rhymed, and patterned, though they flow in the repetitions of free-verse rhythms. The central metaphor of blue-black flower as torch is not familiar but in context, and in its own way, it is exactly right for the experience of the poem. "Bavarian Gentians" is a poem of intense physical and emotional involvement. It is certain of only the reality of the descent into darkness and the final mystery. Jonson's poem, on the other hand, demonstrates what is certain and clearly understood. It has good sense, grace, and clarity; Lawrence's poem has richness, magic, and mystery.

Some of these distinctions may be helpful in remembering that the pleasures of poetry do not come with formulas. Taste may make one reader more at ease in Jonson's world, or another more alive in Lawrence's. But wherever he goes, the reader needs to *be* there himself. He must go through the actual experience, not simply hear it reported. In time, and with attention, he may even find that not one but many things will happen to him if he really is inside the poem.

EXERCISES

PAGE 4

1. In the poem "O My Luve Is Like a Red, Red Rose" what qualities are attributed to "my luve" by the comparisons with a rose and a

melody? Do the words "red, red," "newly sprung," and "sweetly played" add anything important to the comparison? Explain. What elements not in the rose and the melody are added in stanzas 3 and 4? 2. Read the poem aloud. What passages are the most melodious? What makes them so? Is there any reason for variation in the musical tone of the poem?

PAGE 6

1. Is "To Sabidius" a poem for any reason other than its rhyme? 2. What makes it somewhat more interesting than an ordinary direct statement? 3. Do you have any clue at all to the character or mood of the speaker?

PAGE 8

1. List the six particular images in *"Sic Vita"* that are presented in the comparisons of lines 1–6. In what ways do the images in each pair of rhyming lines (1 and 2, 3 and 4, 5 and 6) have a special relationship with each other? 2. Explain the phrases "borrowed light" and "paid to night." 3. Are there any qualities of man and life other than transience and brevity that are suggested in the six comparisons? For instance, why a falling *star* and not a falling *stone?*

PAGE 10

1. One might not recognize the allegorical significance of "Lully, Lulley" until the words "Corpus Christi" in the last line. Is it then possible to go back and identify some of the parallels with the story of Christ? What might the falcon represent? The orchard, the bed, the knight, the colors of purple and gold, the wounds, the maid, the stone? 2. The poem has sometimes been printed with the title, "The Knight of the Grail." Show that the details also fit such a story of medieval chivalry. Can both interpretations be held at the same time? Is there any advantage in doing so?

PAGE 16

1. Analyze the rhythmic pattern of "To Mistress Margaret Hussey." Is there a consistent arrangement of accented and unaccented syllables? Of rhyme? 2. Read the poem to yourself, stressing the accents and the swing of the lines. Explain how the sound of the poem supports what is said in it. *Check meanings and identify:* Isaphill (Hypsipyle), Coriander, pomander, Cassander (Cassandra).

PAGE 18

1. What details in the literal version of the "Rubáiyát" are omitted by FitzGerald? What details does he add? 2. Analyze the associations of

feeling and meaning in each of the two combinations. 3. What is the difference in the intention of the two versions (note the term "paradise" in one, "pleasure" in the other)? 4. Is there any logical reason (other than rhyme) for the order of details in FitzGerald's stanza?

PAGE 18

1. "Jack and His Father" is an example of light verse that is not altogether nonsense. What observation on human life and character can you detect? 2. Comment on the logical development of the statements (what prepares us to accept "hang" by the time we read the last line?). 3. Is the poem true literally or figuratively, or both?

PAGE 19

1. In the second stanza of "Loveliest of Trees" computation is important. Figure out carefully just how old the speaker is—it will make a great difference in the point of the poem. Explain fully. 2. Describe the difference in tone between stanzas 1 and 3 and stanza 2 and justify such an effect (or variation) in the poem. *Check meanings:* ride, score.

PAGE 20

1. Outline the poem "Cargoes" by giving the general time and place suggested in each stanza. Describe in detail what the cargoes tell of the culture and values in each civilization. Does the order of the poem suggest the progress or the fall of civilization? 2. What are some of the sensory suggestions in the terms "sandalwood," "diamonds," and "pig-lead"? 3. Why is cinnamon included in stanza 2? 4. How is the sound of stanza 3 different from that of stanza 1? What does its tone suggest? *Check meanings:* Quinquireme, moidores.

PAGE 21

1. Point out the various kinds of imagery used in "The Snow-Storm." Give examples of some of the most effective details and tell what each suggests in the description. 2. Explain: "tumultuous privacy of storm." In what way could this phrase be said to epitomize the poem? How do the details in the description support it? *Check meanings:* Parian, maugre.

PAGE 22

1. In "There Is a Garden" show how the term "heavenly paradise" unites all the metaphors, including the last stanza. Are these metaphors based on physical resemblances only, or are other qualities involved? 2. Most of these metaphors would be familiar to the reader of the sixteenth century, as they are now. What, if anything, saves the poem from being a cliché?

PAGE 22

1. In "The Sheaves" what is the significance of the words "assigned" and "undivined"? 2. Can you justify the plainness of lines 7 and 8? 3. How is repetition used in the poem? What is its effect?

PAGE 24

1. The first and last stanzas of "Song" are general statements. What is the central theme in each of the other four stanzas? 2. Point out the metaphors (the unliteral statements) in stanza 3 and discuss fully what they involve in suggestion and meaning. What is gained by the compact language? 3. Is there any difference in the significance of the refrain as it is used in the various stanzas? 4. Compare this poem with *"Sic Vita"* (p. 8). *Identify:* Helen.

PAGE 25

1. Can you justify the use of "give" in the first lines and of "paid" and "sold" in the last lines of "When I Was One-and-Twenty"? 2. Are the two statements of the wise man the same, or is there a development in the meaning? 3. To be honest, would you call the "truth" of this poem universal (for everyone) or personal (for the speaker of the poem)? *Check meanings:* crowns, pounds, guineas, rue.

PAGE 26

1. In "Since There's No Help" explain what persons are involved in what situation. 2. How do the last lines (especially "yet") change our understanding of the speaker's mood when he said earlier "no help" and "glad"? 3. Discuss the use of personification in this poem.

PAGE 27

1. Identify the historical events or characters represented in "The Progress of Faust." 2. Discuss as fully as you can the significance of joining Faust and the atom bomb, and the meaning involved in that imaginative view. 3. Look up the Faust legend and, if possible, compare its use here with that in Goethe's *Faust* and Marlowe's *Dr. Faustus.*

PAGE 29

1. Restate the poem "It Is Not Growing Like a Tree" in your own words without using any of the images or metaphors. Discuss some of the means by which Jonson has condensed this full idea into sharper, more compact language. 2. Analyze in detail the pattern of the poem (rhythm, rhyme, sound devices). 3. Define the meaning and use of "just beauties," "sear," "flower of light." 4. Is there any possible double meaning in "measures"? 5. Show how this poem develops imagery of space and time.

PAGE 30

1. What is the myth of Persephone and how does it function in "Bavarian Gentians"? 2. What is the scene at the beginning of the poem? At the end? Trace through the imagery the movement from one place to the other. 3. Comment on the effectiveness of color images in the poem. 4. Discuss the meaning and use of the gentian as a symbol.

CHAPTER 2
TYPES AND TRADITIONS

PART of knowing a poem is knowing its family, how it is linked to others of its kind. Poems are usually divided into two general types: *narrative,* those which emphasize a story or a sequence of events, and *lyric,* those which emphasize personal feeling or the songlike quality of the verse. In practice, a narrative poem will often contain lyrical passages. Coleridge's *The Rime of the Ancient Mariner* tells a story, but at certain moments both the music and the emotion of the verse are intensified. Likewise, a lyric poem almost always implies scene, characters, and events that precede and may follow the poem. The classification is mostly a matter of emphasis. To recognize some types of poems and some major traditions in English poetry will give additional pleasure to a reader. Four of the major types of narrative poems, each with its own conventions, are the *epic,* the *romance,* the *ballad,* and the *tale.* Four important types of lyrics are the *song,* the *sonnet,* the *ode,* and the *elegy.* We may define these forms and some familiar variations of them: the *dramatic* poem, the *didactic* poem of *discourse* or *satire,* poems in the *metaphysical* tradition, and poems in the *pastoral* tradition.

NARRATIVE POEMS

One question frequently tossed around by students of literature is, "Who will write the great American epic?" The one who does will no doubt be expected to follow the traditional idea of an epic—a long narrative poem in which heroic action of cosmic importance or national destiny is represented with dignity, grandeur, and poetic elevation. The great epics of other countries usually tell stories and depict heroes already important to a people. They involve both men and gods, combining legend, myth, and heroic adventure that may embody the ideals and beliefs of a tradition. The great Greek epics are Homer's *Iliad* and *Odyssey*. The Roman epic is Vergil's *Aeneid*. The most important epic in English is Milton's *Paradise Lost*. In these major poems, the epic follows the pattern set by Homer: conflict on a large scale between forces of good and evil, or (as in the *Odyssey*) a hero's search and wandering. In form, the classical epic is constructed in twelve or twenty-four books, the action beginning in the middle of the story with the preliminary events later recounted by one of the characters. Other conventions of the epic are the invocation to the gods or the muses, the catalogue of forces, the battles, the intervention of the gods, the concluding destiny of the hero. Pope's mock epic, *The Rape of the Lock,* is of additional interest when one can recognize in it these epic conventions on an ant-size scale.

Another traditional type of narrative poem is the *romance* or metrical romance. These exciting, often sophisticated, stories were first popular in the Middle Ages, when they were composed and sung or recited by skillful minstrels or gleemen who entertained at courts of kings and nobles. The romance told of the courageous deeds and courtly love of knights and ladies, the charmed circle of chivalry that held back a wilderness roamed by the enemy—beast, devil, and human foe. The form of the metrical romance was often elaborate, with musical, richly decorated verse that seemed to emphasize the civilized beauty it embodied. Stories of King Arthur and Charlemagne, in many variations, are perhaps the best examples of the romances that were especially popular in medieval France and Britain. One of the best modern examples of the romance, both in spirit and in form, is Keats's "The Eve of St. Agnes."

While the metrical romances entertained the court, the *ballads*, sung by anonymous individual leaders and occasionally larger groups, were part of the entertainment of the people. These story-poems, part of the oral folk-tradition of the Middle Ages, memorialized what was most important in experience. The subjects were usually tragic or awesome—death in love and war; spells, witches, and ghosts. The form and language were extremely simple and often repetitious (the better to be remembered). The story was stripped of all detail, and it was often presented as a dialogue, without comment or interpretation by the author. Commonly the lines were in rhyming pairs of seven or eight accents each; when written down, they were arranged in four-line stanzas, often followed by a refrain. The first important collection of the old English and Scottish ballads was the 1765 *Reliques of Ancient Poetry,* by Bishop Percy. Since then, the interest in preserving much of this kind of folk-art in both England and America has continued to grow. In the tradition of the ballad, the stories were fluid, one slipping into the other by character or phrase or act. Some very old popular ballads, like the cryptic "Lord Randal," will be found to exist in dozens of versions. A repertoire of representative ballads (many with their original music) would have to include the older "Sir Patrick Spens" or "Barbara Allen," western American ballads like "Sweet Betsy from Pike" and all the cowboy songs, and the literary imitations like Keats's "La Belle Dame sans Merci" or Coleridge's *The Rime of the Ancient Mariner.*

Ballads

SIR PATRICK SPENS

The king sits in Dunfermline town,
  Drinking the blude-red wine;
"O where will I get a gude skipper
  To sail this ship o' mine?"

O up and spake an eldern knight,   5
  Sat at the king's right knee:
"Sir Patrick Spens is the best sailor
  That ever sail'd the sea."

Our king has written a braid letter,
  And seal'd it with his hand,   10
And sent it to Sir Patrick Spens,
  Was walking on the strand.

"To Noroway, to Noroway,
  To Noroway o'er the faem;
The king's daughter o' Noroway,   15
  'Tis thou must bring her hame."

The first word that Sir Patrick read,
  A loud laugh laughèd he;

The next word that Sir Patrick read,
  The tear blinded his e'e.   20

"O who is this has done this deed
  And told the king o' me,
To send me out, at this time o' year,
  To sail upon the sea?

"Be it wind, be it weet, be it hail, be it sleet,   25
  Our ship must sail the faem;
The king's daughter o' Noroway,
  'Tis we must fetch her hame.

"Make haste, make haste, my merry men all;
  Our gude ship sails the morn."—   30
"Now ever alack, my master dear,
  I fear a deadly storm.

"I saw the new moone late yestreen,
  Wi' the auld moone in her arm;
And I fear, I fear, my master dear,   35
  That we will come to harm."

They hadna sail'd a league, a league,
  A league but barely three,
When the sky grew dark, and the wind blew loud,
  And angry grew the sea.   40

The anchors broke, the topmast split,
  It was sic a deadly storm:
And the waves came owre the broken ship
  Till a' her sides were torn.

O loath, loath, were our gude Scots lords   45
  To wet their cork-heel'd shoon;
But lang or a' the play was play'd
  Their hats they swam aboon.

O lang, lang may the ladies sit,
  Wi' their fans into their hand,   50
Before they see Sir Patrick Spens
  Come sailing to the strand.

And lang, lang may the maidens sit
  Wi' their gold kames in their hair.
A-waiting for their ain dear loves,   55
  For them they'll see nae mair.

Half-owre, half-owre to Aberdour,
   'Tis fifty fathoms deep;
And there lies gude Sir Patrick Spens,
   Wi' the Scots lords at his feet.   60

ANONYMOUS

1. The narrative in "Sir Patrick Spens" may be divided into four major scenes. Describe the events of each. 2. Are there any details that help to characterize persons, suggest motivation, describe visual scenes? 3. Why did Spens go on the voyage when he knew its danger? 4. Point out some lines or passages that illustrate the ballad qualities of restraint and suggestiveness rather than full, detailed explanation.

THE WIFE OF USHER'S WELL

There lived a wife at Usher's Well,
   And a wealthy wife was she;
She had three stout and stalwart sons,
   And sent them o'er the sea.

They hadna been a week from her,   5
   A week but barely ane,
Whan word came to the carlin wife
   That her three sons were gane.

They hadna been a week from her,
   A week but barely three,   10
Whan word came to the carlin wife
   That her sons she'd never see.

"I wish the wind may never cease,
   Nor fishes in the flood,
Till my three sons come hame to me,   15
   In earthly flesh and blood."

It fell about the Martinmass,
   When nights are lang and mirk,
The carlin wife's three sons came hame,
   And their hats were o' the birk.   20

It neither grew in syke nor ditch,
   Nor yet in ony sheugh;
But at the gates o' Paradise,
   That birk grew fair eneugh.

"Blow up the fire, my maidens,   25
    Bring water from the well!
For a' my house shall feast this night,
    Since my three sons are well."

And she has made to them a bed,
    She's made it large and wide,   30
And she's taen her mantle her about,
    Sat down at the bedside.

Up then crew the red red cock,
    And up and crew the gray;
The eldest to the youngest said,   35
    " 'Tis time we were away."

The cock he hadna craw'd but once,
    And clappd his wings at a',
When the youngest to the eldest said,
    "Brother, we must awa.   40

"The cock doth craw, the day doth daw,
    The channerin worm doth chide;
Gin we be·mist out o' our place,
    A sair pain we maun bide.

"Fare ye weel, my mother dear!   45
    Farewell to barn and byre!
And fare ye weel, the bonny lass
    That kindles my mother's fire!"

ANONYMOUS

1. What supernatural elements are in this poem? Is there an effect of horror? Explain. 2. If you were to take the mother as the central figure, what does the story consist of in terms of her actions and emotions? Does she believe the sons are "flesh and blood"?

THE CHERRY-TREE CAROL

Joseph was an old man,
    And an old man was he,
When he wedded Mary,
    In the land of Galilee.

Joseph and Mary walked   5
    Through an orchard good,

Where was cherries and berries,
      So red as any blood.

Joseph and Mary walked
      Through an orchard green,   10
Where was berries and cherries
      As thick as might be seen.

O then bespoke Mary,
      So meek and so mild:
"Pluck me one cherry, Joseph,   15
      For I am with child."

O then bespoke Joseph,
      With words most unkind:
"Let him pluck thee a cherry
      That brought thee with child."   20

O then bespoke the babe,
      Within his mother's womb:
"Bow down then the tallest tree,
      For my mother to have some."

Then bowed down the highest tree   25
      Unto his mother's hand;
Then she cried, "See, Joseph,
      I have cherries at command."

O then bespake Joseph:
      "I have done Mary wrong: 30
But cheer up, my dearest,
      And be not cast down."

Then Mary plucked a cherry,
      As red as the blood,
Then Mary went home   35
      With her heavy load.

Then Mary took her babe,
      And sat him on her knee;
"I pray thee now, dear child,
      Tell how this world shall be."   40

"O I shall be as dead, mother,
      As the stones in the wall;
O the stones in the street mother,
      Shall mourn for me all.

"Upon Easter-day, mother,   45
  My uprising shall be;
O the sun and the moon, mother,
  Shall both rise with me."

ANONYMOUS

1. This version of part of the Christian story is put into homely, familar terms. How is the sense of awe and mystery retained? 2. Comment on some of the symbolic meanings in the poem; for instance, the cherry "red as any blood," the stones, the sun and the moon. 3. Explain fully the significance of the last two lines.

LORD RANDAL

I

"O where hae ye been, Lord Randal, my son?
O where hae ye been, my handsome young man?"—
"I hae been to the wild wood; mother, make my bed soon,
For I'm weary wi' hunting, and fain wald lie down."

II

"Where gat ye your dinner, Lord Randal, my son?   5
Where gat ye your dinner, my handsome young man?"—
"I dined wi' my true-love; mother, make my bed soon,
For I'm weary wi' hunting, and fain wald lie down."

III

"What gat ye to your dinner, Lord Randal, my son?
What gat ye to your dinner, my handsome young man?"—   10
"I gat eels boil'd in broo'; mother, make my bed soon,
For I'm weary wi' hunting, and fain wald lie down."

IV

"What became of your bloodhounds, Lord Randal, my son?
What became of your bloodhounds, my handsome young man?"—
"O they swell'd and they died; mother, make my bed soon,   15
For I'm weary wi' hunting, and fain wald lie down."

V

"O I fear ye are poison'd, Lord Randal, my son!
O I fear ye are poison'd, my handsome young man!"—

"O yes! I am poison'd; mother, make my bed soon,
For I'm sick at the heart, and I fain wald lie down."   20

ANONYMOUS

1. As in all ballads, most of the detail in "Lord Randal" is omitted. We know that Lord Randal is dying, and we can guess why. But could there be some possible variations on the reason for (and cause of) his death? Give examples. 2. Point out some of the ballad devices in the poem.

BARBARA ALLEN

I

In Scarlet town, where I was born,
    There was a fair maid dwellin',
Made every youth cry *Well-a-way!*
    Her name was Barbara Allen.

II

All in the merry month of May,   5
    When green buds they were swellin',
Young Jemmy Grove on his death-bed lay,
    For love of Barbara Allen.

III

He sent his man in to her then,
    To the town where she was dwellin';   10
"O haste and come to my master dear,
    If your name be Barbara Allen."

IV

So slowly, slowly rase she up,
    And slowly she came nigh him,
And when she drew the curtain by—   15
    "Young man, I think you're dyin'."

V

"O it's I am sick and very very sick,
    And it's all for Barbara Allen."—
"O the better for me ye'se never be,
    Tho' your heart's blood were a-spillin'!   20

VI

"O dinna ye mind, young man," says she,
  "When the red wine ye were fillin',
That ye made the healths go round and round,
  And slighted Barbara Allen?"

VII

He turn'd his face unto the wall,   25
  And death was with him dealin':
"Adieu, adieu, my dear friends all,
  And be kind to Barbara Allen!"

VIII

As she was walking o'er the fields,
  She heard the dead-bell knellin';   30
And every jow the dead-bell gave
  Cried "Woe to Barabara Allen."

IX

"O mother, mother, make my bed,
  O make it saft and narrow:
My love has died for me to-day,   35
  I'll die for him to-morrow.

X

"Farewell," she said, "ye virgins all,
  And shun the fault I fell in:
Henceforth take warning by the fall
  Of cruel Barbara Allen."   40

ANONYMOUS

1. Analyze the sequence of reversals in the story of "Barbara Allen." Are they completely improbable, or can you justify them in any way?
2. Analyze the form of the poem: rhythm, stanza pattern, use of rhyme and other musical devices.

RISSELTY ROSSELTY

I married me a wife in the month of June,
With a wisselty wosselty wow, wow, wow,
Took her home by the light of the moon,

With a wisselty wosselty, ho John bobberty,
Nickerty, nockerty now, now, now.   5

She swept her floor but once a month,
With a wisselty wosselty wow, wow, wow.
And every stroke it brought a grunt,
With a wisselty wosselty, ho John bobberty,
Nickerty nockerty now, now, now.   10

She combed her hair but once a year,
With a wisselty wosselty wow, wow, wow,
And every stroke it brought a tear,
With a wisselty wosselty, ho John bobberty,
Nickerty nockerty now, now, now.   15

She churned her butter in dad's old boot,
With a wisselty wosselty wow, wow, wow,
Instead of a dash she wiggled her foot,
With a wisselty wosselty, ho John bobberty,
Nickerty nockerty now, now, now.   20

She peddled her butter all over town,
With a wisselty wosselty wow, wow, wow,
The print of her foot was on every pound,
With a wisselty wosselty, ho John bobberty,
Nickerty nockerty now, now, now.   25

She strained her cheese through dad's old sock,
With a wisselty wosselty wow, wow, wow,
The toe jam run down into the crock,
With a wisselty wosselty, ho John bobberty,
Nickerty nockerty now, now, now.   30

She went upstairs to make the bed,
With a wisselty wosselty wow, wow, wow,
She fell over the chair and bumped her head,
With a wisselty wosselty, ho John bobberty,
Nickerty nockerty, now, now, now.   35

She went outdoors to milk the cow,
With a wisselty wosselty wow, wow, wow,
She made a mistake and milked the sow,
With a wisselty wosselty, ho John bobberty,
Nickerty nockerty now, now, now.   40

ANONYMOUS

1. In what ways is this ballad (an American version) different from the five previous ballads in this section? For example, consider subject, story, tone, rhythm. 2. This version of the ballad does not have a real conclusion. Can you suggest one?

AS I WALKED OUT ONE EVENING

As I walked out one evening,
  Walking down Bristol Street,
The crowds upon the pavement
  Were fields of harvest wheat.

And down by the brimming river   5
  I heard a lover sing
Under an arch of the railway:
  "Love has no ending.

I'll love you, dear, I'll love you
  Till China and Africa meet,   10
And the river jumps over the mountain
  And the salmon sing in the street.

I'll love you till the ocean
  Is folded and hung up to dry,
And the seven stars go squawking   15
  Like geese about the sky.

The years shall run like rabbits,
  For in my arms I hold
The Flower of the Ages,
  And the first love of the world."   20

But all the clocks in the city
  Began to whirr and chime:
"O let not Time deceive you,
  You cannot conquer Time.

In the burrows of the Nightmare   25
  Where Justice naked is,
Time watches from the shadow
  And coughs when you would kiss.

In headaches and in worry
  Vaguely life leaks away,   30
And Time will have his fancy
  Tomorrow or today.

Into many a green valley
  Drifts the appalling snow;
Time breaks the threaded dances   35
  And the diver's brilliant bow.

O plunge your hands in water,
  Plunge them in up to the wrist;
Stare, stare in the basin
  And wonder what you've missed.   40

The glacier knocks in the cupboard,
  The desert sighs in the bed,
And the crack in the tea-cup opens
  A lane to the land of the dead.

Where the beggars raffle the banknotes   45
  And the Giant is enchanting to Jack,
And the Lily-white Boy is a Roarer,
  And Jill goes down on her back.

O look, look in the mirror,
  O look in your distress;   50
Life remains a blessing
  Although you cannot bless.

O stand, stand at the window
  As the tears scald and start;
You shall love your crooked neighbor   55
  With your crooked heart."

It was late, late in the evening,
  The lovers they were gone;
The clocks had ceased their chiming,
  And the deep river ran on.   60

                    W. H. AUDEN (*1907–*   )

1. Point out some of the ballad elements in this poem. 2. Some likeness
to Burns's "O My Luve Is Like a Red, Red Rose" has already been
suggested (p. 4). Discuss this relationship more fully. 3. What objects
and terms are used as symbols in Auden's poem? Discuss their meaning,
or what they represent.

Tales

A good many narrative poems do not fit into the tradition of
either the epic, the romance, or the ballad. They are *tales*—or

stories of people and events related in a variety of ways, from the medieval fable to the modern short story. One of the classic books of such narratives is Chaucer's *The Canterbury Tales,* in which stories and accounts of the people who tell them are interlaced (see the opening lines, p. 123). Frost's "The Witch of Coös" is a tale in dramatic form, much of the story implied. Gilbert's rollicking account of "The Ruler of the Queen's Navee" is a pointed story of a man's life.

Some tales are not quite so complete as a short story. Often a poem tells of one or more episodes in which either incident or character is emphasized. Some of these tales are semibiographies, like Wordsworth's "Michael." Others are restricted to some incident, as in Byron's "The Destruction of Sennacherib," Lawrence's "Snake," and Jeffers' "Hurt Hawks." Often these poems will suggest more than they tell, as in E. A. Robinson's "Richard Cory" (p. 85) or T. S. Eliot's "Journey of the Magi." In all cases, however, the tale finds its pattern and makes its point through a sequence of connected events.

THE DESTRUCTION OF SENNACHERIB

The Assyrian came down like the wolf on the fold,
And his cohorts were gleaming in purple and gold;
And the sheen of their spears was like stars on the sea,
When the blue wave rolls nightly on deep Galilee.

Like the leaves of the forest when Summer is green,   5
That host with their banners at sunset were seen:
Like the leaves of the forest when Autumn hath blown,
That host on the morrow laid withered and strown.

For the Angel of Death spread his wings on the blast,
And breathed in the face of the foe as he passed;   10
And the eyes of the sleepers waxed deadly and chill,
And their hearts but once heaved, and forever grew still!

And there lay the steed with his nostril all wide,
But through it there rolled not the breath of his pride:
And the foam of his gasping lay white on the turf,   15
And cold as the spray of the rock-beating surf.

And there lay the rider distorted and pale,
With the dew on his brow, and the rust on his mail;

And the tents were all silent, the banners alone,
The lances unlifted, the trumpet unblown.   20

And the widows of Ashur are loud in their wail,
And the idols are broke in the temple of Baal;
And the might of the Gentile, unsmote by the sword,
Hath melted like snow in the glance of the Lord!

GEORGE GORDON, LORD BYRON (*1788–1824*)

1. Tell the story of the destruction of Sennacherib as you learn it in
the poem. 2. Is there reason for some feeling of sympathy with both
the attacked and the attackers? Explain. 3. Analyze the rhythm, stanza
pattern, sound devices.

THE RULER OF THE QUEEN'S NAVEE [1]

When I was a lad I served a term
As office boy to an attorney's firm.
I cleaned the windows and I swept the floor,
And I polished up the handle of the big front door.
   I polished up that handle so carefullee   5
   That now I am the Ruler of the Queen's Navee!

As office boy I made such a mark
That they gave me the post of a junior clerk.
I served the writs with a smile so bland,
And I copied all the letters in a big round hand—   10
   I copied all the letters in a hand so free,
   That now I am the Ruler of the Queen's Navee!

In serving writs I made such a name
That an articled clerk I soon became;
I wore clean collars and a brand-new suit   15
For the pass-examination at the Institute.
   And that pass-examination did so well for me,
   That now I am the Ruler of the Queen's Navee!

Of legal knowledge I acquired such a grip
That they took me into the partnership.   20
And that junior partnership, I ween,
Was the only ship that I ever had seen.

[1] Sung by Sir Joseph Porter, First Lord of the Admiralty, in the Gilbert and
Sullivan *H. M. S. Pinafore*

But that kind of ship so suited me,
That now I am the Ruler of the Queen's Navee!

I grew so rich that I was sent   25
By a pocket borough into Parliament.
I always voted at my party's call,
And I never thought of thinking for myself at all.
   I thought so little, they rewarded me
   By making me the Ruler of the Queen's Navee!   30

Now, landsmen all, whoever you may be,
If you want to rise to the top of the tree,
If your soul isn't fettered to an office stool,
Be careful to be guided by this golden rule—
   Stick close to your desk and never go to sea,   35
   And you *all* may be Rulers of the Queen's Navee!

WILLIAM SCHWENCK GILBERT (*1836–1911*)

1. Is the sound and rhythm of this poem much different from that of "The Destruction of Sennacherib." One should be light and the other serious. Has the sound in each been adjusted to the subject? Discuss.
2. Why is this poem *not* a ballad?

SNAKE

A snake came to my water-trough
On a hot, hot day, and I in pyjamas for the heat,
To drink there.

In the deep, strange-scented shade of the great dark carob-tree
I came down the steps with my pitcher   5
And must wait, must stand and wait, for there he was at the
   trough before me.

He reached down from a fissure in the earth-wall in the gloom
And trailed his yellow-brown slackness soft-bellied down, over the
   edge of the stone trough
And rested his throat upon the stone bottom,
And where the water had dripped from the tap, in a small clear-
   ness,   10
He sipped with his straight mouth,
Softly drank through his straight gums, into his slack long body,
Silently.

Someone was before me at my water-trough,
And I, like a second comer, waiting.   15

He lifted his head from his drinking, as cattle do,
And looked at me vaguely, as drinking cattle do,
And flickered his two-forked tongue from his lips, and mused a
    moment,
And stooped and drank a little more,
Being earth-brown, earth-golden from the burning bowels of the
    earth   20
On the day of Sicilian July, with Etna smoking.

The voice of my education said to me
He must be killed,
For in Sicily the black, black snakes are innocent, the gold are
    venomous.

And voices in me said, If you were a man   25
You would take a stick and break him now, and finish him off.

But must I confess how I liked him,
How glad I was he had come like a guest in quiet, to drink at my
    water-trough
And depart peaceful, pacified, and thankless,
Into the burning bowels of this earth?   30

Was it cowardice, that I dared not kill him?
Was it perversity, that I longed to talk to him?
Was it humility, to feel so honoured?
I felt so honoured.

And yet those voices: 35
If you were not afraid, you would kill him!

And truly I was afraid, I was most afraid,
But even so, honoured still more
That he should seek my hospitality
From out the dark door of the secret earth.   40

He drank enough
And lifted his head, dreamily, as one who has drunken,
And flickered his tongue like a forked night on the air, so black,
Seeming to lick his lips,
And looked around like a god, unseeing, into the air,   45
And slowly turned his head,
And slowly, very slowly, as if thrice adream,

Proceeded to draw his slow length curving round
And climb again the broken bank of my wall-face.

And as he put his head into that dreadful hole,   5〔〕
And as he slowly drew up, snake-easing his shoulders, and entered
    farther,
A sort of horror, a sort of protest against his withdrawing into
    that horrid black hole,
Deliberately going into the blackness, and slowly drawing him-
    self after,
Overcame me now his back was turned.

I looked round, I put down my pitcher,   55
I picked up a clumsy log
And threw it at the water-trough with a clatter.

I think it did not hit him,
But suddenly that part of him that was left behind convulsed in
    undignified haste,
Writhed like lightning, and was gone   60
Into the black hole, the earth-lipped fissure in the wall-front,
At which, in the intense still noon, I stared with fascination.

And immediately I regretted it.
I thought how paltry, how vulgar, what a mean act!
I despised myself and the voices of my accursed human educa-
    tion.   65

And I thought of the albatross,
And I wished he would come back, my snake.

For he seemed to me again like a king,
Like a king in exile, uncrowned in the underworld,
Now due to be crowned again.   70

And so, I missed my chance with one of the lords
Of life.
And I have something to expiate;
A pettiness.

                          TAORMINA
              D. H. LAWRENCE (*1885–1930*)

1. Relate the events as they occur in this poem. 2. Why is so much time given to the description of the snake? What are some especially effective details in the description? 3. As in many short stories, the denouement is inside the central character. Explain.

HURT HAWKS

I

The broken pillar of the wing jags from the clotted shoulder,
The wing trails like a banner in defeat,
No more to use the sky forever but live with famine
And pain a few days: cat nor coyote
Will shorten the week of waiting for death, there is game without talons.   5
He stands under the oak-bush and waits
The lame feet of salvation; at night he remembers freedom
And flies in a dream, the dawns ruin it.
He is strong and pain is worse to the strong, incapacity is worse.
The curs of the day come and torment him   10
At distance, no one but death the redeemer will humble that head,
The intrepid readiness, the terrible eyes.
The wild God of the world is sometimes merciful to those
That ask mercy, not often to the arrogant.
You do not know him, you communal people, or you have forgotten him;   15
Intemperate and savage, the hawk remembers him;
Beautiful and wild, the hawks, and men that are dying, remember him.

II

I'd sooner, except the penalties, kill a man than a hawk; but the great redtail
Had nothing left but unable misery
From the bone too shattered for mending, the wing that trailed
under his talons when he moved.   20
We had fed him six weeks, I gave him freedom,
He wandered over the foreland hill and returned in the evening,
asking for death,
Not like a beggar, still eyed with the old
Implacable arrogance. I gave him the lead gift in the twilight.
What fell was relaxed,
Owl-downy, soft feminine feathers; but what   25
Soared: the fierce rush: the night-herons by the flooded river
cried fear at its rising
Before it was quite unsheathed from reality.

ROBINSON JEFFERS (*1887–1962*)

1. Give the plain narrative of "Hurt Hawks"—the series of events. 2. Who is the "him" of lines 15–17? 3. Comment on the use of "pillar," "jags," "lead gift." 4. Point out some devices of music and rhythm in the free verse (alliteration? repetition?). 5. Expand and explain the last two lines.

LYRIC POEMS

Songs

Because lyric poems were originally those meant to be sung to the accompaniment of a harp or lyre, we may take the *song* as the simplest form in this tradition. Words set to music have a lilt and rhythm that suggest a melody. The language is simple, emotional rather than intellectual. But the song is attractive for reading primarily because it creates its own music of rhythm and sound. Children chant loudly the verses of "Pease porridge hot/ pease porridge cold/ pease porridge in the pot/ nine days old." As they get older, they continue with lullabies, love laments, war cries, or hymns. The pleasure for all readers is in the melody, the sound of words, the refrains (jaunty or sad), the emotion. For the serious song goes beyond simple melody into the heart of human experience. It celebrates some moment of feeling, of sadness or joy, that is familiar enough for any reader to take as his own and sing silently for himself.

WESTERN WIND

Western wind, when will thou blow?
The small rain down can rain.—
Christ, if my love were in my arms
And I in my bed again!

ANONYMOUS

Describe what these brief lines suggest of season, weather, mood, situation.

THE BELLMAN'S SONG

Maids to bed and cover coal;
Let the mouse out of her hole;
Crickets in the chimney sing

Whilst the little bell doth ring:
If fast asleep, who can tell   5
When the clapper hits the bell?

ANONYMOUS (*c.1600–1620*)

Analyze the meter of these lines, noting any variations or irregularities.

THE SILVER SWAN

The silver swan, who living had no note,
When death approached, unlocked her silent throat;
Leaning her breast against the reedy shore,
Thus sung her first and last, and sung no more:
"Farewell, all joys; O death, come close mine eyes;   5
More geese than swans now live, more fools than wise."

ANONYMOUS (*c.1612*)

1. The swan traditionally sings only once—a beautiful song just before death. Comment on this swan's song. Does it have the expected beauty?
2. What exactly is meant by the last line?

MY TRUE LOVE HATH MY HEART

My true love hath my heart and I have his,
By just exchange one for another given;
I hold his dear, and mine he cannot miss,
There never was a better bargain driven.
    My true love hath my heart and I have his.   5

His heart in me keeps him and me in one,
My heart in him his thoughts and senses guides,
He loves my heart, for once it was his own,
I cherish his because in me it bides.
    My true love hath my heart and I have his.   10

SIR PHILIP SIDNEY (*1554–1586*)

1. Explain in detail (with special attention to pronouns) the meaning of lines 6–9. 2. This poem uses business terminology and legalistic argument. Give some examples. Do such devices harm or help a love poem?

SONG, TO CELIA

Drink to me only with thine eyes,
   And I will pledge with mine;
Or leave a kiss but in the cup,
   And I'll not look for wine.
The thirst that from the soul doth rise   5
   Doth ask a drink divine;
But might I of Jove's nectar sup,
   I would not change for thine.

I sent thee late a rosy wreath,
   Not so much honoring thee,   10
As giving it a hope that there
   It could not withered be.
But thou thereon didst only breathe,
   And sent'st it back to me,
Since when it grows and smells, I swear,   15
   Not of itself, but thee.

BEN JONSON (*1572–1637*)

1. This poem is so familiar as a song that many do not really notice what it says. Exactly what is the situation revealed in the poem? Has the lover been successful or not? 2. Show in what ways the lover makes the point that the lady is a really superior kind of goddess. 3. Compare the central metaphor of this poem with that in Shakespeare's "My Mistress' Eyes."

TO THE VIRGINS, TO MAKE MUCH OF TIME

Gather ye rose-buds while ye may,
   Old Time is still a-flying:
And this same flower that smiles today,
   Tomorrow will be dying.

The glorious lamp of heaven, the Sun,   5
   The higher he's a-getting,
The sooner will his race be run,
   And nearer he's to setting.

That age is best which is the first,
   When youth and blood are warmer;   10

> But being spent, the worse, and worst
>   Times still succeed the former.
>
> Then be not coy, but use your time,
>   And while ye may, go marry;
> For having lost but once your prime,   15
>   You may for ever tarry.

ROBERT HERRICK (*1591–1674*)

1. Are the metaphors in this poem apt in evoking a sense of urgency? What other purposes do they serve? 2. Is the tone of the poem comic? Entirely so?

WHY SO PALE AND WAN

> Why so pale and wan, fond lover?
>   Prithee, why so pale?
> Will, when looking well can't move her,
>   Looking ill prevail?
>   Prithee, why so pale?   5
>
> Why so dull and mute, young sinner?
>   Prithee, why so mute?
> Will, when speaking well can't win her,
>   Saying nothing do't?
>   Prithee, why so mute?   10
>
> Quit, quit, for shame, this will not move,
>   This cannot take her.
> If of herself she will not love,
>   Nothing can make her.
>   The devil take her!   15

SIR JOHN SUCKLING (*1609–1642*)

1. What is the pattern of the refrain? Does it have any variations? 2. Comment on resemblances in sound in stanzas 1 and 2. 3. Is this a poem about good sense or bad faith?

INTERROGATIVA CANTILENA

> If all the world were paper,
> And all the sea were ink;

If all the trees were bread and cheese,
How should we do for drink?

If all the world were sand-o,   5
Oh, then what should we lack-o?
If as they say, there were no clay,
How should we take tobacco?

If all our vessels ran-a,
If none but had a crack-a;   10
If Spanish apes eat all the grapes,
How should we do for sack-a?

If friars had no bald pates,
Nor nuns had no dark cloisters;
If all the seas were beans and peas,   15
How should we do for oysters?

If there had been no projects,
Nor none that did great wrongs;
If fiddlers shall turn players all,
How should we do for songs?   20

If all things were eternal,
And nothing their end bringing;
If this should be, then how should we
Here make an end of singing?

ANONYMOUS (from *Wit's Recreations*, 1641)

1. Analyze the pattern of sound and rhythm in this "Interrogative
Songlet." Notice the internal rhyme. 2. Discuss more completely the
meaning of stanza 5. 3. This poem is a combination of logical and
illogical elements. Point out some examples.

MINSTREL'S SONG FROM *AELLA*

O sing unto my roundelay,
    O drop the briny tear with me;
Dance no more at holiday;
    Like a running river be:
        My love is dead,   5
        Gone to his death-bed,
        All under the willow-tree.

Black his crine as the winter night,
    White his rode as the summer snow,

Red his face as the morning light;   10
  Cold he lies in the grave below.
    My love is dead,
    Gone to his death-bed,
    All under the willow-tree.

Sweet his tongue as the throstle's note,   15
  Quick in dance as thought can be,
Deft his tabor, cudgel stout;
  O he lies by the willow-tree.
    My love is dead,
    Gone to his death-bed,   20
    All under the willow-tree.

. . .

See! the white moon shines on high;
  Whiter is my true love's shroud:
Whiter than the morning sky,
  Whiter than the evening cloud.   25
    My love is dead,
    Gone to his death-bed,
    All under the willow-tree.

. . .

Come, with acorn-cup and thorn,
  Drain my heartès blood away;   30
Life and all its good I scorn,
  Dance by night, or feast by day.
    My love is dead,
    Gone to his death-bed,
    All under the willow-tree.   35

THOMAS CHATTERTON (*1752–1770*)

1. Part of the effectiveness of this poem is its medieval tone. Look up unfamiliar words, such as "roundelay," "crine," and "rode," and judge whether or not they have a special meaning in the poem. 2. Describe the stanza pattern. 3. This song is a kind of elegy. What details of imagery emphasize death and mourning?

WE'LL GO NO MORE A-ROVING

So we'll go no more a-roving
  So late into the night,

Though the heart be still as loving,
  And the moon be still as bright.

For the sword outwears its sheath,   5
  And the soul wears out the breast,
And the heart must pause to breathe,
  And Love itself have rest.

Though the night was made for loving,
  And the day returns too soon,   10
Yet we'll go no more a-roving
  By the light of the moon.

GEORGE GORDON, LORD BYRON (*1788–1824*)

1. Is the imagery of this poem specific or general? Give examples.
2. Explain the metaphor of stanza 2. 3. Note the number of stresses
in each line. Is the last line shorter than the others, or can you read it
to comply with the pattern?

WHEN WE TWO PARTED

When we two parted
  In silence and tears,
Half broken-hearted
  To sever for years,
Pale grew thy cheek and cold,   5
  Colder thy kiss;
Truly that hour foretold
  Sorrow to this.

The dew of the morning
  Sunk chill on my brow—   10
It felt like the warning
  Of what I feel now.
Thy vows are all broken,
  And light is thy fame;
I hear thy name spoken,   15
  And share in its shame.

They name thee before me,
  A knell to mine ear;
A shudder comes o'er me—
  Why wert thou so dear?   20
They know not I knew thee,
  Who knew thee too well:—

Long, long shall I rue thee,
    Too deeply to tell.

In secret we met—   25
    In silence I grieve
That thy heart could forget,
    Thy spirit deceive.
If I should meet thee
    After long years,   30
How should I greet thee?—
    With silence and tears.

GEORGE GORDON, LORD BYRON (1788–1824)

Are you most aware of music, mood, or logical development of idea
in this poem? Are all three present in some degree? Explain fully,
especially noting whether any one element reinforces the others.

A DIRGE

Rough wind, that moanest loud
    Grief too sad for song;
Wild wind, when sullen cloud
    Knells all the night long;
Sad storm, whose tears are vain,   5
Bare woods, whose branches strain,
Deep caves and dreary main,—
    Wail, for the world's wrong!

PERCY BYSSHE SHELLEY (1792–1822)

1. How does Shelley fit the words and the sound to the subject? 2. Point
out examples of alliteration, assonance, and other resemblances in
sound. 3. Is there any logical sequence in the imagery?

Sonnets

Sonnet means "little song," and in the early Italian twelfth-
century forms the term meant any short, musical poem. Although
now the sonnet has settled down to a regular structure of fourteen lines with one of several accepted rhyme patterns, as late as
the sixteenth century it had anywhere from twelve to thirty lines.
The fixing of the sonnet form has established one of the most
rigid and most satisfying traditions in English poetry, for the sonnet has become a kind of ritual that has been performed for cen-

turies by poets who have found it to be the perfect expression of a single feeling or idea. In a sense, every sonnet belongs to all the others that have gone before it and that helped to shape its form. Most sonnets treat the old subjects and attitudes of love, religious devotion, the transience of life, or the exaltation of beauty. Their appeal is in both the perfection of the form (the ordering of the experience) and the memorable rightness of the language.

The English sonnet has two principal forms. One follows the pattern developed by the Italian poet Petrarch, whose twelfth-century sonnets were the models for many of the later English poets. The Petrarchan sonnet of fourteen lines is divided into two sections: the first eight lines (the octave) present one idea or aspect of the subject; the last six lines (the sestet) give a conclusion, or an answer, or a variation. The octave has only two rhymes —*abbaabba*. The sestet has various arrangements of three additional rhymes—*cdcdee* or *cdecde*. For example, the octave of Sidney's sonnet "Leave Me, O Love" (p. 65) rejects earthly love; the sestet embraces heavenly love, and the concluding couplet summarizes the argument. The Shakespearean sonnet is constructed in three quatrains with alternating rhymes and a final couplet that summarizes and applies what has been said: *abab cdcd efef gg*. The best examples are, of course, in Shakespeare himself. Note the famous Sonnet 73, "That Time of Year," in which the three metaphors coincide with the three quatrains.

The Elizabethans were great sonneteers. In the following section, the individual sonnets by Wyatt, Spenser, and Sidney are taken from long "cycles," or groups of related sonnets, usually dedicated to some friend or ideal love. See also the sonnets of four major poets who excelled in that form: Shakespeare, Milton, Wordsworth, and Keats. Examples which could be called "master sonnets" by these poets are Shakespeare's "That Time of Year," Milton's "On His Blindness," Wordsworth's "The World Is Too Much With Us," and Keats's "On First Looking into Chapman's Homer."

I FIND NO PEACE

DESCRIPTION OF THE CONTRARIOUS PASSIONS IN A LOVER

I find no peace, and all my war is done;
I fear and hope; I burn, and freeze like ice;
I fly above the wind, yet can I not arise;

And nought I have, and all the world I season.
That looseth [1] nor locketh holdeth me in prison,   5
And holds me not, yet can I 'scape no wise;
Nor lets me live, nor die, at my devise,
And yet of death it giveth none occasion.
Without eye, I see; without tongue, I plain;
I desire to perish, and yet I ask health;   10
I love another, and thus I hate myself;
I feed me in sorrow, and laugh in all my pain.
Likewise displeaseth me both death and life;
And my delight is causer of this strife.

SIR THOMAS WYATT (*1503–1542*)

1. Explain the logic of four or five of the "contraries." 2. Is this sonnet in a consistent Petrarchan form? Consider both the rhyme pattern and the break between the octave and the sestet.

MY GALLEY

THE LOVER COMPARETH HIS STATE TO A SHIP IN PERILOUS STORM
TOSSED ON THE SEA

My galley chargèd with forgetfulness
Thorough sharp seas, in winter nights, doth pass
'Tween rock and rock; and eke mine enemy,[1] alas,
That is my lord, steereth with cruelness;
And every oar a thought in readiness,   5
As though that death were light in such a case.
An endless wind doth tear the sail apace,
Of forcèd sighs and trusty fearfulness;
A rain of tears, a cloud of dark disdain,
Have done the wearied cords great hinderance;   10
Wreathèd with error and eke with ignorance.
The stars be hid that led me to this pain;
Drowned is reason, that should me consort,
And I remain despairing of the port.

SIR THOMAS WYATT (*1503–1542*)

[1] *That looseth . . . wise* (ll. 5–6) These lines might be paraphrased as "What neither looses nor locks [love] holds me in prison; and although it does not really hold me, I cannot escape."

---

[1] *enemy* love

Both this sonnet and the following one by Spenser ("Like as a Ship") are based on a metaphor used by Petrarch in several of his sonnets. State as exactly as you can the central metaphor as Wyatt uses it. Show how the details in the extended metaphor (or allegory) fit into the whole.

LIKE AS A SHIP

Like as a ship, that through the ocean wide,
By conduct of some star doth make her way,
Whenas a storm hath dimmed her trusty guide,
Out of her course doth wander far astray;
So I, whose star, that wont with her bright ray,   5
Me to direct, with clouds is overcast,
Do wander now in darkness and dismay,
Through hidden perils round about me placed.
Yet hope I well, that when this storm is past
My Helice, the lodestar of my life,   10
Will shine again, and look on me at last,
With lovely light to clear my cloudy grief.
Till then I wander carefull comfortless,
In secret sorrow and sad pensiveness.

Amoretti, 34
EDMUND SPENSER (*1552–1599*)

Compare this sonnet with Wyatt's "My Galley," showing points of likeness and difference. For example, note whether the central metaphors have exactly the same comparisons, whether the imagery is more vivid in one than in the other, whether the moods of the speakers are the same. Are the last two lines part of the comparison? *Check meaning:* Helice.

LEAVE ME, O LOVE

Leave me, O love which reachest but to dust;
And thou, my mind, aspire to higher things;
Grow rich in that which never taketh rust,
Whatever fades but fading pleasure brings.
Draw in thy beams, and humble all thy might   5
To that sweet yoke where lasting freedoms be;
Which breaks the clouds and opens forth the light,
That doth both shine and give us sight to see.
O take fast hold; let that light be thy guide

In this small course which birth draws out to death,   10
And think how evil becometh him to slide,
Who seeketh heav'n, and comes of heav'nly breath.
  Then farewell, world; thy uttermost I see;
  Eternal Love, maintain thy life in me.

SIR PHILIP SIDNEY (1554–1586)

1. The conflict here is between two kinds of love. Explain what kind
is referred to in the first line; in the last line. 2. What other contrasts
and oppositions are involved in the poem? 3. Comment on the meaning
of "reachest," "lasting freedoms," "uttermost."

WITH HOW SAD STEPS, O MOON

With how sad steps, O Moon, thou climb'st the skies!
How silently, and with how wan a face!
What! may it be that even in heav'nly place
That busy archer his sharp arrows tries?
Sure, if that long-with-love-acquainted eyes   5
Can judge of love, thou feel'st a lover's case;
I read it in thy looks, thy languished grace
To me, that feel the like, thy state descries.
Then, ev'n of fellowship, O Moon, tell me,
Is constant love deemed there but want of wit?   10
Are beauties there as proud as here they be?
Do they above love to be loved, and yet
Those lovers scorn whom that love doth possess?
Do they call virtue there ungratefulness?

SIR PHILIP SIDNEY (1554–1586)

1. Is the appearance of the moon as described in lines 1–8 inherent in
the moon, or is it a reflection of the speaker's attitude? 2. What kind
of society do the last six lines suggest? 3. Explain line 10.

GO FROM ME

Go from me. Yet I feel that I shall stand
Henceforward in thy shadow. Nevermore
Alone upon the threshold of my door
Of individual life, I shall command
The uses of my soul, nor lift my hand   5

Serenely in the sunshine as before,
Without the sense of that which I forebore, . .
Thy touch upon the palm. The widest land
Doom takes to part us, leaves thy heart in mine
With pulses that beat double. What I do   10
And what I dream include thee, as the wine
Must taste of its own grapes. And when I sue
God for myself, He hears that name of thine,
And sees within my eyes, the tears of two.

Sonnets from the Portuguese, 6
ELIZABETH BARRETT BROWNING (*1806–1861*)

1. Compare the abrupt, rapid movement of the first line with the long, slow beginning of Sidney's sonnet "With How Sad Steps, O Moon," and justify each in the contexts of the poems. 2. Discuss the use of contrasts, or the union of opposing elements, in developing the theme of the poem.

HOW STRANGE THE SCULPTURES

How strange the sculptures that adorn these towers!
  This crowd of statues, in whose folded sleeves
  Birds build their nests; while canopied with leaves
  Parvis and portal bloom like trellised bowers,
And the vast minster seems a cross of flowers!   5
But fiends and dragons on the gargoyled eaves
  Watch the dead Christ between the living thieves,
  And, underneath, the traitor Judas lowers!
Ah! from what agonies of heart and brain,
  What exultations trampling on despair,   10
  What tenderness, what tears, what hate of wrong,
What passionate outcry of a soul in pain,
  Uprose this poem of the earth and air,
  This mediaeval miracle of song!

Divina Commedia, 2
HENRY WADSWORTH LONGFELLOW (*1807–1882*)

Longfellow's sonnet sequence *Divina Commedia* is an extended comparison of Dante's poem *Divina Commedia* (*The Divine Comedy*) and a medieval cathedral. 1. What is the view of the cathedral in this sonnet—exterior or interior? 2. What do the details of the poem suggest about the content of Dante's *Divina Commedia?* 3. Show how the last six lines can fit both sides of the metaphor—poem and cathedral. *Check meanings:* Parvis, minster, gargoyled.

Odes

Both songs and sonnets have been known to be funny. See, for example, Suckling's "Why So Pale and Wan" and Shakespeare's sonnet "My Mistress' Eyes." But the ode and the elegy are forms of the lyric that are consistently serious (except when they are used for parody and satire) and usually complex. Both are thoughtful; both have some object to consider. To make one distinction—an ode seems usually to be advancing *toward* its object; an elegy moves away.

An *ode* is a lyric of stately or exalted tone, usually a serious meditation on or praise of some subject or person (autumn, music, duty, the Duke of Wellington). In form, the ode may follow the pattern of the Greek poet Pindar, with elaborate stanzas that imitate the movements of the choral odes of the Greek dramas. As the chorus of the Greek play chanted the lines, it would circle first to one side (the strophe), then to the other (the antistrophe), and finally stand still (the epode). Such movements (as repeated several times in the dance) are paralleled in the English ode by stanza patterns and sometimes by reversals and conclusions in the subject matter. Sometimes the English ode will look like the regular variations of the Pindaric ode but will actually be an artfully designed, irregular symphonic piece, like Wordsworth's "Ode: Intimations of Immortality." Another type of ode (like those of Horace) may be written in uniform but intricately patterned stanzas. Perhaps the most noted examples of the ode in English poetry are the five by Keats (pp. 452–460). Although the English ode has often varied from the original Greek and Latin forms, it keeps the dignity and thoughtful depth of the traditional ode, as well as its complexity. Themes are interwoven and contrasted; the structure is artfully elaborate.

ODE TO THE WEST WIND

1

O wild West Wind, thou breath of Autumn's being,
Thou, from whose unseen presence the leaves dead
Are driven, like ghosts from an enchanter fleeing,

Yellow, and black, and pale, and hectic red,
Pestilence-stricken multitudes: O thou,   5
Who chariotest to their dark wintry bed

The wingèd seeds, where they lie cold and low,
Each like a corpse within its grave, until
Thine azure sister of the Spring shall blow

Her clarion o'er the dreaming earth, and fill   10
(Driving sweet buds like flocks to feed in air)
With living hues and odors plain and hill:

Wild Spirit, which art moving everywhere;
Destroyer and preserver; hear, oh, hear!

2

Thou on whose stream, mid the steep sky's commotion,   15
Loose clouds like earth's decaying leaves are shed,
Shook from the tangled boughs of Heaven and Ocean,

Angels of rain and lightning: there are spread
On the blue surface of thine aëry surge,
Like the bright hair uplifted from the head   20

Of some fierce Maenad, even from the dim verge
Of the horizon to the zenith's height,
The locks of the approaching storm. Thou dirge

Of the dying year, to which this closing night
Will be the dome of a vast sepulchre,   25
Vaulted with all thy congregated might

Of vapors, from whose solid atmosphere
Black rain, and fire, and hail will burst: oh, hear!

3

Thou who didst waken from his summer dreams
The blue Mediterranean, where he lay,   30
Lulled by the coil of his crystàlline streams,

Beside a pumice isle in Baiae's bay,
And saw in sleep old palaces and towers
Quivering within the wave's intenser day,

All overgrown with azure moss and flowers   35
So sweet, the sense faints picturing them! Thou
For whose path the Atlantic's level powers

Cleave themselves into chasms, while far below
The sea-blooms and the oozy woods which wear
The sapless foliage of the ocean, know   40

Thy voice, and suddenly grow gray with fear,
And tremble and despoil themselves: oh, hear!

4

If I were a dead leaf thou mightest bear;
If I were a swift cloud to fly with thee;
A wave to pant beneath thy power, and share   45

The impulse of thy strength, only less free
Than thou, O uncontrollable! If even
I were as in my boyhood, and could be

The comrade of thy wanderings over Heaven,
As then, when to outstrip thy skiey speed   50
Scarce seemed a vision; I would ne'er have striven

As thus with thee in prayer in my sore need.
Oh, lift me as a wave, a leaf, a cloud!
I fall upon the thorns of life! I bleed!

A heavy weight of hours has chained and bowed   55
One too like thee: tameless, and swift, and proud.

5

Make me thy lyre, even as the forest is:
What if my leaves are falling like its own!
The tumult of thy mighty harmonies

Will take from both a deep, autumnal tone,   60
Sweet though in sadness. Be thou, Spirit fierce,
My spirit! Be thou me, impetuous one!

Drive my dead thoughts over the universe
Like withered leaves to quicken a new birth!
And, by the incantation of this verse,   65

Scatter, as from an unextinguished hearth
Ashes and sparks, my words among mankind!
Be through my lips to unawakened earth

The trumpet of a prophecy! O, Wind,
If Winter comes, can Spring be far behind?   70

PERCY BYSSHE SHELLEY (*1792–1822*)

1. Show how the three things listed in section 4—wave, leaf, cloud—form the key motifs for sections 1, 2, and 3. How are all related to the wind? How are the three sections linked together, one leading into the next? Does the personal reference and application in section 5 have any links with the first sections? 2. Discuss the variety that Shelley uses in the tone and language of the ode. Is it always organic?

AN ODE FOR BEN JONSON

Ah Ben!
Say how, or when
Shall we thy guests
Meet at those lyric feasts
Made at the Sun,   5,
The Dog, the Triple Tun,
Where we such clusters had
As made us nobly wild, not mad;
And yet each verse of thine
Outdid the meat, outdid the frolic wine.   10,

My Ben!
Or come again,
Or send to us
Thy wit's great overplus;
But teach us yet   15,
Wisely to husband it,
Lest we that talent spend,
And having once brought to an end
That precious stock, the store
Of such a wit the world should have no more.   20

ROBERT HERRICK (*1591–1674*),

1. What does the poem itself tell about Ben Jonson and the life Herrick remembers? 2. Explain "lyric feasts," "wit's great overplus." 3. What is the stanza pattern (both rhyme and rhythm)?

Elegies

An *elegy* is a lament, or a song of sorrow. Some of the major elegies in English follow a classical pattern: a pastoral setting, shepherds who lament the loss of one of their number, the expression of personal grief, the mourning of all of nature, the universalizing of grief, and the consolation of a belief in immortality (see Milton's "Lycidas"). Other important elegies, such as,

Whitman's "When Lilacs Last in the Dooryard Bloom'd," emphasize the cosmic union of life and death, in the spirit of pastorals but without all their formal details. Some shorter elegies keep only the tradition of quiet mourning and the acceptance of death, as the personal loss blends into the universal meaning. Others simply memorialize the dead (see Dryden's "To the Memory of Mr. Oldham," Hopkins' "Felix Randal," Yeats's "In Memory of Major Robert Gregory"). In the following group, Gray's "Elegy Written in a Country Churchyard" is perhaps the most famous example of a generalized elegy. Jonson's "On My First Son" is an acutely personal poem.

ELEGY

WRITTEN IN A COUNTRY CHURCHYARD

The curfew tolls the knell of parting day,
   The lowing herd wind slowly o'er the lea,
The plowman homeward plods his weary way,
   And leaves the world to darkness and to me.

Now fades the glimmering landscape on the sight,   5
   And all the air a solemn stillness holds,
Save where the beetle wheels his droning flight,
   And drowsy tinklings lull the distant folds;

Save that from yonder ivy-mantled tower
   The moping owl does to the moon complain   10
Of such, as wand'ring near her secret bower,
   Molest her ancient solitary reign.

Beneath those rugged elms, that yew-tree's shade,
   Where heaves the turf in many a mold'ring heap,
Each in his narrow cell forever laid,   15
   The rude forefathers of the hamlet sleep.

The breezy call of incense-breathing morn,
   The swallow twitt'ring from the straw-built shed,
The cock's shrill clarion, or the echoing horn,
   No more shall rouse them from their lowly bed.   20

For them no more the blazing hearth shall burn,
   Or busy housewife ply her evening care:
No children run to lisp their sire's return,
   Or climb his knees the envied kiss to share.

Oft did the harvest to their sickle yield;   25
   Their furrow oft the stubborn glebe has broke;
How jocund did they drive their team afield!
   How bowed the woods beneath their sturdy stroke!

Let not Ambition mock their useful toil,
   Their homely joys, and destiny obscure;   30
Nor Grandeur hear with a disdainful smile
   The short and simple annals of the poor.

The boast of heraldry, the pomp of power,
   And all that beauty, all that wealth e'er gave,
Awaits alike th' inevitable hour: 35
   The paths of glory lead but to the grave.

Nor you, ye proud, impute to these the fault,
   If Mem'ry o'er their tomb no trophies raise,
Where through the long-drawn aisle and fretted vault
   The pealing anthem swells the note of praise.   40

Can storied urn or animated bust
   Back to its mansion call the fleeting breath?
Can Honor's voice provoke the silent dust,
   Or Flatt'ry sooth the dull, cold ear of Death?

Perhaps in this neglected spot is laid   45
   Some heart once pregnant with celestial fire;
Hands that the rod of empire might have swayed,
   Or waked to ecstasy the living lyre.

But Knowledge to their eyes her ample page,
   Rich with the spoils of time, did ne'er unroll;   50
Chill Penury repressed their noble rage,
   And froze the genial current of the soul.

Full many a gem of purest ray serene,
   The dark unfathomed caves of ocean bear:
Full many a flower is born to blush unseen,   55
   And waste its sweetness on the desert air.

Some village Hampden, that with dauntless breast
   The little tyrant of his fields withstood;
Some mute, inglorious Milton here may rest,
   Some Cromwell, guiltless of his country's blood.   60

Th' applause of listening senates to command,
   The threats of pain and ruin to despise,

To scatter plenty o'er a smiling land,
  And read their history in a nation's eyes,

Their lot forbade: nor circumscribed alone   65
  Their growing virtues, but their crimes confined;
Forbade to wade through slaughter to a throne,
  And shut the gates of mercy on mankind;

The struggling pangs of conscious truth to hide,
  To quench the blushes of ingenuous shame,   70
Or heap the shrine of Luxury and Pride
  With incense kindled at the Muse's flame.

Far from the madding crowd's ignoble strife,
  Their sober wishes never learned to stray;
Along the cool, sequestered vale of life   75
  They kept the noiseless tenor of their way.

Yet e'en these bones from insult to protect,
  Some frail memorial still erected nigh,
With uncouth rhymes and shapeless sculpture decked,
  Implores the passing tribute of a sigh.   80

Their name, their years, spelt by th' unlettered Muse,
  The place of fame and elegy supply;
And many a holy text around she strews,
  That teach the rustic moralist to die.

For who, to dumb forgetfulness a prey,   85
  This pleasing anxious being e'er resigned,
Left the warm precincts of the cheerful day,
  Nor cast one longing lingering look behind?

On some fond breast the parting soul relies,
  Some pious drops the closing eye requires;   90
E'en from the tomb the voice of Nature cries,
  E'en in our ashes live their wonted fires.

For thee who, mindful of the unhonored dead
  Dost in these lines their artless tale relate;
If chance, by lonely contemplation led,   95
  Some kindred spirit shall inquire thy fate,

Haply some hoary-headed swain may say,
  "Oft have we seen him at the peep of dawn
Brushing with hasty steps the dews away,
  To meet the sun upon the upland lawn.   100

"There at the foot of yonder nodding beech
  That wreathes its old fantastic roots so high,
His listless length at noontide would he stretch,
  And pore upon the brook that babbles by.

"Hard by yon wood, now smiling as in scorn,   105
  Mutt'ring his wayward fancies he would rove;
Now drooping, woeful-wan, like one forlorn,
  Or crazed with care, or crossed in hopeless love.

"One morn I missed him on the customed hill,
  Along the heath, and near his fav'rite tree;   110
Another came; nor yet beside the rill,
  Nor up the lawn, nor at the wood was he;

"The next, with dirges due, in sad array,
  Slow through the church-way path we saw him borne.
Approach and read (for thou canst read) the lay,   115
  Graved on the stone beneath yon agèd thorn."

THE EPITAPH

Here rests his head upon the lap of earth
  A youth to Fortune and to Fame unknown;
Fair Science frowned not on his humble birth,
  And Melancholy marked him for her own.   120

Large was his bounty, and his soul sincere;
  Heav'n did a recompense as largely send:
He gave to Mis'ry (all he had), a tear;
  He gained from Heav'n (twas all he wished) a friend.

No farther seek his merits to disclose,   125
  Or draw his frailties from their dread abode
(There they alike in trembling hope repose),
  The bosom of his Father and his God.

THOMAS GRAY (*1716–1771*)

1. Outline the poem by giving thematic subjects to the following sections: lines 1–16, 17–28, 29–44, 45–76, 77–92, 93–128. 2. Balance and contrast are particularly important in this poem. Give examples. 3. The point made in lines 65–76 is commonly overlooked. How does this modify the attitude expressed in the preceding stanzas? 4. Discuss this poem as either a revolutionary call to action or an expression of satisfaction with the status quo. 5. What is the general emotional tone of this elegy?

ON MY FIRST SON

Farewell, thou child of my right hand, and joy;
　My sin was too much hope of thee, loved boy.
Seven years thou wert lent to me, and I thee pay,
　Exacted by thy fate, on the just day.
O, could I lose all father, now. For why   5
　Will man lament the state he should envy?
To have so soon 'scaped world's and flesh's rage,
　And, if no other misery, yet age?
Rest in soft peace, and, askèd, say here doth lie
　Ben Jonson his [1] best piece of poetry.   10
For whose sake, henceforth, all his vows be such,
　As what he loves may never like too much.

BEN JONSON (*1572–1637*)

1. How does the poem reveal that the child is dead? 2. Explain "just day," "lose all father." 3. What idea gives some comfort? 4. Comment on the meaning of lines 9–10.

VARIATIONS

Certain other traditions in English poetry cross the boundaries of pure narrative or pure lyric and are distinguished by some emphasis in manner or content. We may say that a poem is *dramatic* or *didactic* or *satiric*—although one single example might have all three qualities and be a narrative as well. Other poems are marked primarily by their traditional content or poetic devices: We speak of *metaphysical* poems, or the *pastoral* tradition. There are, of course, other traditions, but these few familiar ones in poetry may illustrate something of its engaging variety.

Dramatic Poems

One type of poem is distinguished by its manner—the *dramatic* presentation of one or more speakers who tell a story or define a moment by letting us hear them talk. A dialogue between two or more persons is obviously a dramatic form. Many ballads are in dialogue ("Lord Randal," "Barbara Allen"). A less obvious form is the dramatic monologue, in which the poet speaks not

[1] *Ben Jonson his* Ben Jonson's

in his own voice but in that of an assumed identity. For example, Sir Thomas More creates the speech of a character, Davy the Dicer, who has lost his luck:

DAVY, THE DICER [1]

Long was I, Lady Luck, your serving-man,
And now have lost again all that I gat;
Wherefore, when I think on you now and than
And in my mind remember this and that,
Ye may not blame me though I beshrew your cat.   5
But, in faith, I bless you again, a thousand times,
For lending me now some leisure to make rhymes.

SIR THOMAS MORE (*1478–1535*)

Famous dramatic monologues are Browning's "My Last Duchess," Tennyson's "Ulysses," even Arnold's "Dover Beach." In these, a story is suggested and a character (perhaps several) revealed by what the speaker says. Among other examples, Burns's "To a Mouse" suggests both an incident and the sound of the speaker's voice. This kind of dramatic poem has a long history in English literature, from the curious "riddles" of Anglo-Saxon times (see "A Horn," here translated from the Old English) to the modern self-revealing soliloquies like Eliot's "The Love Song of J. Alfred Prufrock." A comparison of Prufrock with Chaucer's Troilus as he tells of his love will suggest the fascinating variety of the people who speak in poems.

An extension of the dramatic form is the lyric whose tone is of a person speaking to other persons. The language sounds direct from a living character, who may or may not be the poet himself. Donne's poetry usually has this dramatic (or acting) tone. Read some of his opening lines: "Go, and catch a falling star," "Batter my heart, three-personed God." These are spoken lines, addressed to someone who must hear. A poem like W. H. Auden's "Musée des Beaux Arts" is an especially skillful fusion of lyric

---

[1] 1. State the speaker and the one spoken to in "Davy, the Dicer." Suggest a possible scene and circumstances that would fit into the argument of the poem. 2. Sir Thomas More was in prison for political reasons when he wrote this poem. Would it be possible to trace personal references through the framework of the dramatic monologue? Explain.

and narrative elements presented in a dramatic form. Here a speaker in an art gallery meditates on an incident portrayed in a picture, and what art has revealed about the relation of tragedy to human life.

RIDDLE #14: A HORN

I was a warrior's weapon, once.
Now striplings have woven silver wires,
And gold, around me. I've been kissed by soldiers,
And I've called a field of laughing comrades
To war and death. I've crossed borders   5
On galloping steeds, and crossed the shining
Water, riding a ship. I've been filled
To the depth of my heart by girls with glittering
Bracelets, and I've lain along the bare
Cold planks, headless, plucked and worn.   10
They've hung me high on a wall, bright
With jewels and beautiful, and left me to watch
Their warriors drinking. Mounted troops
Have carried me out and opened my breast
To the swelling wind of some soldier's lips.   15
My voice has invited princes to feasts
Of wine, and has sung in the night to save
What savage thieves have stolen, driving them
Off into darkness. Ask my name.

translated from Old English by Burton Raffel

1. Who is the speaker? To whom is he speaking? 2. What is told of the life of the time? 3. What use of contrasts has been made in the poem? 4. The metrical system of Old English poetry is based on lines with four strong stresses and a regular use of alliteration. Analyze five or six lines of the poem to show how these elements appear.

THE COMPLAINT OF TROILUS

"O paleys,[1] whylom croune of houses alle,
Enlumined with sonne of alle blisse!
O ring, fro which the ruby is out-falle,
O cause of wo, that cause hast been of lisse! [2]
Yet, sin I may no bet, fayn wolde I kisse   5

---

[1] *paleys* palace   [2] *lisse* joy

Thy colde dores, dorste I for this route; [3]
And fare-wel shryne, of which the seynt is oute!"

．　　．　　．

Fro thennesforth he rydeth up and doun,
And every thing com him to remembraunce
As he rood forth by places of the toun   10
In whiche he whylom hadde al his plesaunce.
"Lo, yond saugh I myn owene lady daunce;
And in that temple, with hir eyen clere,
Me caughte first my righte lady dere.

And yonder have I herd ful lustily   15
My dere herte laughe, and yonder pleye
Saugh I hir ones eek ful blisfully.
And yonder ones to me gan she seye,
'Now goode swete, love me wel, I preye.'
And yond so goodly gan she me biholde,   20
That to the deeth myn herte is to hir holde.

And at that corner, in the yonder hous,
Herde I myn alderlevest [4] lady dere
So wommanly, with voys melodious,
Singen so wel, so goodly, and so clere,   25
That in my soule yet me thinketh I here
The blisful soun; and, in that yonder place,
My lady first me took un-to hir grace.

．　　．　　．

O sterre, of which I lost have al the light,
With herte soor wel oughte I to bewayle,   30
That ever derk in torment, night by night,
Toward my deeth with wind in stere I sayle;
For which the tenthe night if that I fayle
The gyding of thy bemes brighte an houre,
My ship and me Caribdis wol devoure."   35

from *Troilus and Criseyde* (V, l. 547 ff.)
GEOFFREY CHAUCER (*1340–1400*)

1. Describe the scene, the speaker, the situation. 2. What similarities
do you find in this poem (especially the last stanza) and the sonnets
by Spenser ("Like As a Ship," p. 65) and by Wyatt ("My Galley," p.
64)?

[3] *route* company   [4] *alderlevest* dearest

TO A MOUSE

ON TURNING HER UP IN HER NEST
WITH THE PLOUGH, NOVEMBER, 1785

Wee, sleekit, cow'rin', tim'rous beastie,
O what a panic's in thy breastie!
Thou need na start awa sae hasty,
    Wi' bickering brattle! [1]
I wad be laith to rin an' chase thee   5
    Wi' murd'ring pattle! [2]

I'm truly sorry man's dominion
Has broken Nature's social union,
An' justifies that ill opinion
    Which makes thee startle   10
At me, thy poor earth-born companion,
    An' fellow-mortal!

I doubt na, whiles, but thou may thieve;
What then? poor beastie, thou maun live!
A daimen-icker [3] in a thrave [4]   15
    'S a sma' request:
I'll get a blessin' wi' the lave,[5]
    And never miss 't!

Thy wee bit housie, too, in ruin!
Its silly wa's the win's are strewin'!   20
An' naething, now, to big a new ane,
    O' foggage [6] green!
An' bleak December's winds ensuin'
    Baith snell [7] an' keen!

Thou saw the fields laid bare and waste.   25
An' weary winter comin' fast,
An' cozie here, beneath the blast,
    Thou thought to dwell,
Till crash! the cruel coulter [8] past
    Out-thro' thy cell.   30

---

[1] *brattle* scamper   [2] *pattle* a plough-staff
[3] *daimen-icker* an occasional ear of corn
[4] *thrave* twenty-four sheaves of corn   [5] *lave* the rest
[6] *foggage* pasture   [7] *snell* biting   [8] *coulter* plowshare

That wee bit heap o' leaves an' stibble
Has cost thee mony a weary nibble!
Now thou's turn'd out, for a' thy trouble,
        But house or hald,[9]
To thole [10] the winter's sleety dribble,   35
        An' cranreuch [11] cauld!

But, Mousie, thou art no thy lane,
In proving foresight may be vain:
The best laid schemes o' mice an' men
        Gang aft a-gley,   40
An' lea'e us nought but grief an' pain
        For promis'd joy.

Still thou art blest compar'd wi' me!
The present only toucheth thee:
But oh! I backward cast my e'e   45
        On prospects drear!
An' forward tho' I canna see,
        I guess an' fear!

ROBERT BURNS (*1759–1796*)

1. Reconstruct the dramatic situation. 2. Is there any kind of organization or sense of direction in the meditation? 3. Does one get a strong sense of setting through use of detail?

MUSÉE DES BEAUX ARTS

About suffering they were never wrong,
The Old Masters: how well they understood
Its human position; how it takes place
While someone else is eating or opening a window or just walking
        dully along;
How, when the aged are reverently, passionately waiting   5
For the miraculous birth, there always must be
Children who did not specially want it to happen, skating
On a pond at the edge of the wood:
They never forgot
That even the dreadful martyrdom must run its course   10
Anyhow in a corner, some untidy spot
Where the dogs go on with their doggy life and the torturer's
        horse
Scratches its innocent behind on a tree.

[9] *hald* holding   [10] *thole* endure   [11] *cranreuch* hoarfrost

In Brueghel's *Icarus,* for instance: how everything turns away
Quite leisurely from the disaster; the ploughman may   15
Have heard the splash, the forsaken cry,
But for him it was not an important failure; the sun shone
As it had to on the white legs disappearing into the green
Water; and the expensive delicate ship that must have seen
Something amazing, a boy falling out of the sky,   20
Had somewhere to get to and sailed calmly on.

                                        W. H. AUDEN (*1907–*   )

1. Who is the speaker? Where is he? 2. In this poem there is a scene
within a scene. Explain. 3. Find, if you can, prints of "Icarus" and
other paintings by Breughel and point out details that Auden has used
in the poem. 4. Compare the theme of this poem with that of Gray's
"Elegy" (p. 72).

Satirical Poems

Another traditional type of poem, distinguished by its intention and manner, is *didactic.* It may be either a plain discourse
or a complex variation that may turn into satire. The poem of
discourse intends to instruct by communicating ideas directly,
without much imagery or incident. Interest is in the eloquence,
exactness, or wit of the language, occasionally in the turn or balance of ideas. In a sense, poetry of such direct discourse may have
as much dramatic play of events in the mind—even through abstractions—as image or story poems would have in a more objective way. For example, note that the following epigram, though
entirely in abstractions and in direct discourse, has some sharp
drama:

> Treason doth never prosper; what's the reason?
> For if it prosper, none dare call it treason.

                              SIR JOHN HARINGTON (*c.1561–1612*)

Poems like De Vere's "Were I a King" have no startling events:

> Were I a king, I could command content;
>   Were I obscure, unknown should be my cares;
> And were I dead, no thoughts should me torment,
>   Nor words, nor wrongs, nor loves, nor hopes, nor fears.
> A doubtful choice, of three things one to crave,   5
> A kingdom, or a cottage, or a grave.

          EDWARD DE VERE, EARL OF OXFORD (*1550–1604*)

Such poems state the issues in direct terms. They please not by the freshness of imagery or the excitement of incident but by the careful balance and fall of language and verse.

The tradition of *satire* is a variation of the "idea" or didactic poem. Satire is the criticism of faults and errors in human character and actions through ridicule. It may be achieved through exaggeration, such as using a ridiculously inflated style to describe trivialities. In *The Rape of the Lock* Pope tries to show the absurdities of some human values that make big things out of little: he uses the conventions of the heroic epic to describe the snipping of a lady's curl. Such adaptation of serious forms for trivial subjects is common enough as satire. Note how even the elegy has been used as satire on human values in John Gay's "An Elegy on a Lap Dog." See also Dryden's "Mac Flecknoe," which, in the more direct satirical style of personal lampoon and caricature, attacks persons, politics, and literary modes. Satire may also be achieved through verbal sarcasm and irony, which says the opposite of what is meant ("You are indeed a fine, upstanding citizen," said the Judge to the Thief). Stephen Crane's "War Is Kind" uses such reverse language. Irony takes on a more serious, cosmic meaning when circumstances (in the nature of things) are shown to be contradictory to expectation. See, for example, Hardy's "In Church." The epigram on treason quoted above has something of this same kind of cosmic irony. The style of satire, except for broad caricature, is often witty and intellectual, aiming at understanding and a sense of proportion gained through laughter, or at least a rueful smile. The point of satire is to communicate truth—a clear, rational view of a distorted subject.

AN ELEGY ON A LAP DOG

Shock's fate I mourn; poor Shock is now no more,
Ye Muses mourn, ye chamber-maids deplore.
Unhappy Shock! yet more unhappy Fair,
Doomed to survive thy joy and only care!
Thy wretched fingers now no more shall deck,   5
And tie the fav'rite ribband round his neck;
No more thy hand shall smooth his glossy hair,
And comb the wavings of his pendent ear.
Yet cease thy flowing grief, forsaken maid;
All mortal pleasures in a moment fade: 10

Our surest hope is in an hour destroyed,
And love, best gift of heaven, not long enjoyed.

Methinks I see her frantic with despair,
Her streaming eyes, wrung hands, and flowing hair;
Her Mechlen pinners rent the floor bestrow,   15
And her torn fan gives real signs of woe.
Hence Superstition, that tormenting guest,
That haunts with fancied fears the coward breast;
No dread events upon this fate attend,
Stream eyes no more, no more thy tresses rend.   20
Tho' certain omens oft forewarn a state,
And dying lions show the monarch's fate;
Why should such fears bid Celia's sorrow rise
For when a Lap-dog falls no lover dies.

Cease, Celia, cease; restrain thy flowing tears,   25
Some warmer passion will dispel thy cares.
In man you'll find a more substantial bliss,
More grateful toying and a sweeter kiss.

He's dead. Oh lay him gently in the ground!
And may his tomb be by this verse renowned: 30
Here Shock, the pride of all his kind, is laid,
Who fawned like man, but ne'er like man betrayed.

JOHN GAY (*1685–1732*)

1. What details carry out the idea of an elegy? 2. Is there any exaggeration used as a satirical device? 3. Does this satire on values in the eighteenth century have any pertinence today?

IN CHURCH

"And now to God the Father," he ends,
And his voice thrills up to the topmost tiles:
Each listener chokes as he bows and bends,
And emotion pervades the crowded aisles.
Then the preacher glides to the vestry-door,   5
And shuts it, and thinks he is seen no more.

The door swings softly ajar meanwhile,
And a pupil of his in the Bible class,
Who adores him as one without gloss or guile,
Sees her idol stand with a satisfied smile   10

And re-enact at the vestry-glass
Each pulpit gesture in deft dumb-show
That had moved the congregation so.

THOMAS HARDY (*1840–1928*)

1. What are the satirical, or ironical, qualities in this circumstance?
2. Are there implications beyond this particular character and situation?

RICHARD CORY

Whenever Richard Cory went down town,
We people on the pavement looked at him:
He was a gentleman from sole to crown,
Clean favored, and imperially slim.

And he was always quietly arrayed,   5
And he was always human when he talked;
But still he fluttered pulses when he said,
"Good-morning," and he glittered when he walked.

And he was rich—yes, richer than a king—
And admirably schooled in every grace: 10
In fine, we thought that he was everything
To make us wish that we were in his place.

So on we worked, and waited for the light,
And went without the meat, and cursed the bread;
And Richard Cory, one calm summer night,   15
Went home and put a bullet through his head.

EDWIN ARLINGTON ROBINSON (*1869–1935*)

1. Does this poem have ballad elements? 2. What specific details characterize Richard Cory? 3. What gives the last line its startling effect? How is the reversal prepared for? Is there any difference in the tone of the language in the last line?

WAR IS KIND

Do not weep, maiden, for war is kind.
Because your lover threw wild hands toward the sky
And the affrighted steed ran on alone,
Do not weep.
War is kind.   5

Hoarse, booming drums of the regiment,
Little souls who thirst for fight,
These men were born to drill and die.
The unexplained glory flies above them,
Great is the battle-god, great, and his kingdom—   10
A field where a thousand corpses lie.

Do not weep, babe, for war is kind.
Because your father tumbled in the yellow trenches,
Raged at his breast, gulped and died,
Do not weep.   15
War is kind.

Swift blazing flag of the regiment,
Eagle with crest of red and gold,
These men were born to drill and die.
Point for them the virtue of slaughter,   20
Make plain to them the excellence of killing
And a field where a thousand corpses lie.

Mother whose heart hung humble as a button
On the bright splendid shroud of your son,
Do not weep.   25
War is kind.

STEPHEN CRANE (*1871–1900*)

1. What words are to be taken ironically? Is Crane consistent? 2. Are the three visual scenes (in the passages of address to the maiden, the babe, and the mother) organic, or suitable to the persons addressed?

Metaphysical Poems

Becoming familiar with some traditions in poetry is like being initiated into the rituals of a club. A great many poems do take part in some carefully chosen habits of language and subject matter. Two of the most interesting are the traditions of metaphysical poetry and pastoral poetry.

Metaphysical poetry, in the modern sense of the term, is a tradition which begins in the seventeenth century with John Donne. It has two aspects: first, the use of intellectual, witty, philosophical ("above-the-physical"), scientific language for matters of emotion; and second, the use of startling, apparently unrelated elements in metaphors. The first point is made by William Drummond of Hawthornden in about 1630: Some men of late, he says, have "endeavored to abstract poetry to metaphysical ideas and scholastic quiddities" (see Donne's "Lecture upon the Shadow"), and by John Dryden in 1693: "[Donne] affects the metaphysics, not only in his satires, but in his amorous verses, where nature only should reign; and perplexes the minds of the fair sex with nice speculations of philosophy, when he should engage their hearts. . . ." For example, note the rather technical terms— *grammar, geometry,* and *astronomy* (instead of the more usual poetic *stars*)—applied to love and beauty in this passage from John Cleveland's "Mark Antony," a poem on the love of Venus:

> Mystical grammar of amorous glances;
> Feeling of pulses, the physic of love;
> Rhetorical courtings and musical dances;
> Numb'ring of kisses arithmetic prove;
> Eyes like astronomy;   5
> Straight-limbed geometry;
> In her art's ingeny
> Our wits were sharp and keen.
>   *Never Mark Antony*
>   *Dallied more wantonly*   10
>   *With the fair Egyptian Queen.*

JOHN CLEVELAND (*1613–1658*)

Donne, of course, does it much better in "A Valediction: Forbidding Mourning," and Andrew Marvell in "The Definition of Love" (p. 88).

The second point—the use of startling metaphor—is made by Samuel Johnson, writing (in his life of Cowley) of the metaphysical poets of the early seventeenth century: "[Their] wit may be considered as a kind of *discordia concors;* a combination of dissimilar images, or discovery of occult resemblances in things apparently unlike." One of the best examples is again in Donne's "Valediction," where an emotion (love) is represented by the compass, an instrument of cold, precise scientific knowledge. The metaphysical poets are difficult, intellectual, witty. They need to be examined carefully, because their terms are unexpected and unfamiliar. But, as Dr. Johnson concludes, in spite of their difficulty "To write on their plan it was at least necessary to read and think." Today we might call such poetry psychological, or scientific, or even "modern." At its worst, it is farfetched and confused with problems not worth the solving. At its best, it is complicated, richly involved, in the truest sense poetry of both the mind and the heart.

In the following examples of metaphysical poetry, the anonymous piece gives in simple form the themes treated more complexly by Donne and Marvell, whose poems are perhaps the classics of this form.

WE MUST NOT PART

We must not part as others do,
With sighs and tears, as we were two.
Though with these outward forms we part,
We keep each other in our heart.
What search hath found a being, where   5
I am not, if that thou be there?

True love hath wings, and can as soon
Survey the world, as sun and moon,
And everywhere our triumphs keep
Over absence, which makes others weep: 10
By which alone a power is given
To live on earth, as they in heaven.

ANONYMOUS (*before 1650*)

1. Trace the argument through carefully. 2. How do these lovers differ from ordinary lovers? 3. What is the meaning of the last line—how do "they" live in heaven?

THE DEFINITION OF LOVE

My love is of a birth as rare
As 'tis for object strange and high;
It was begotten by despair
Upon impossibility.

Magnanimous despair alone   5
Could show me so divine a thing,
Where feeble hope could ne'er have flown,
But vainly flapped its tinsel wing.

And yet I quickly might arrive
Where my extended soul is fixed,   10

But fate does iron wedges drive,
And always crowds itself betwixt.

For fate with jealous eye does see
Two perfect loves, nor lets them close;
Their union would her ruin be,   15
And her tyrannic power depose.

And therefore her decrees of steel
Us as the distant poles have placed,
Though love's whole world on us doth wheel,
Not by themselves to be embraced;   20

Unless the giddy heaven fall,
And earth some new convulsion tear,
And, us to join, the world should all
Be cramped into a planisphere.

As lines, so loves, oblique may well   25
Themselves in every angle greet;
But ours so truly parallel,
Though infinite, can never meet.

Therefore the love which us doth bind,
But fate so enviously debars,   30
Is the conjunction of the mind,
And opposition of the stars.

                        ANDREW MARVELL (*1621–1678*)

1. Point out the "scientific" details that help to give this poem its metaphysical tone. 2. What use is made of contrasts and oppositions? 3. Explain the last two lines. *Check meaning:* planisphere.

TO HIS COY MISTRESS *rhyme scheme*

Had we but world enough, and time,
This coyness, lady, were no crime.
We would sit down, and think which way
To walk, and pass our long love's day.
Thou by the Indian Ganges' side   5
Shouldst rubies find; I by the tide
Of Humber would complain. I would
Love you ten years before the Flood; *noun*
And you should, if you please, refuse
Till the conversion of the Jews.   10

My vegetable love should grow
Vaster than empires, and more slow.
An hundred years should go to praise
Thine eyes, and on thy forehead gaze;
Two hundred to adore each breast: 15
But thirty thousand to the rest;
An age at least to every part,
And the last age should show your heart.
For, lady, you deserve this state,
Nor would I love at lower rate.   20
    But at my back I always hear
Time's wingèd chariot hurrying near;
And yonder all before us lie
Deserts of vast eternity.
Thy beauty shall no more be found,   25
Nor in thy marble vault shall sound
My echoing song; then worms shall try
That long preserved virginity,
And your quaint honor turn to dust,
And into ashes all my lust.   30
The grave's a fine and private place,
But none, I think, do there embrace.
    Now therefore, while the youthful hue
Sits on thy skin like morning dew,
And while thy willing soul transpires   35
At every pore with instant fires,
Now let us sport us while we may;
And now, like am'rous birds of prey,
Rather at once our time devour,
Than languish in his slow-chapped power.   40
Let us roll all our strength, and all
Our sweetness, up into one ball;
And tear our pleasures with rough strife
Thorough the iron gates of life.
Thus, though we cannot make our sun   45
Stand still, yet we will make him run.

ANDREW MARVELL (*1621–1678*)

1. Outline the poem by summarizing the point of each of the three
paragraphs. Is there any logical arrangement in these sections? 2. Two
of the most famous lines are 21 and 22. What details make this an
especially chilling metaphor? 3. Discuss what is involved in the metaphors of "vegetable love" and "Time's wingèd chariot." 4. Explain the
contrast in the last two lines.

Pastoral Poems

The *pastoral* tradition began with the country scenes and characters of certain classical poets (Theocritus, Horace). But the rural scenes, the shepherds, and the idyllic life depicted soon became an allegory for some ideal life different from the common, more complex world. In Arcadia, the ideal pastoral setting of Greece, no storms blew and no grief lasted; life and man were simple, good, and virtuous. The conventions of the pastoral poem (as it was most popular in the late sixteenth century) included the shepherds, shepherdesses, and "nymphs," often called by type names such as Phyllis or Chloris or Corydon; fields, flowers, and rural settings; celebrations of spring and love, the whole archetypal pattern of death and rebirth, or the belief in the innocence and goodness of ideal man. One special form of pastoral poetry developed in the elegy (see p. 71). The pastoral poem (dialogue, lyric, or romance) is a kind of accepted shorthand for an ever-present "Garden of Eden," in which a ritual of human values can operate. Not all pastorals view the world in morning light. In the poems which follow, those by Breton and Marlowe do praise idealized simplicity. Those by Raleigh and Herrick, although using the pastoral devices, show a more sophisticated awareness of the dark.

OLDEN LOVE-MAKING

In time of yore when shepherds dwelt
   Upon the mountain rocks,
And simple people never felt
   The pain of lovers' mocks;
But little birds would carry tales   5
   'Twixt Susan and her sweeting,
And all the dainty nightingales
   Did sing at lovers' meeting:
Then might you see what looks did pass
   Where shepherds did assemble,   10
And where the life of true love was,
   When hearts could not dissemble.

Then yea and nay was thought an oath
   That was not to be doubted,
And when it came to faith and troth   15
   We were not to be flouted.

Then did they talk of curds and cream,
    Of butter, cheese, and milk;
There was no speech of sunny beam,
    Nor of the golden silk.   20
Then for a gift a row of pins,
    A purse, a pair of knives,
Was all the way that love begins;
    And so the shepherd wives.

But now we have so much ado,   25
    And are so sore aggrievèd,
That when we go about to woo
    We cannot be believèd.
Such choice of jewels, rings, and chains,
    That may but favor move;   30
And such intolerable pains
    Ere one can hit on love;
That if I still shall bide this life
    'Twixt love and deadly hate,
I will go learn the country life   35
    Or leave the lover's state.

NICHOLAS BRETON (*c.1545–c.1626*)

1. Select and explain the symbolical significance of the various pastoral
details in this poem. 2. What emotional values, if any, could these
details have for a modern reader?

THE PASSIONATE SHEPHERD TO HIS LOVE

Come live with me and be my love,
And we will all the pleasures prove
That hills and valleys, dales and fields,
Or woods or steepy mountain yields.

And we will sit upon the rocks,   5
And see the shepherds feed their flocks
By shallow rivers, to whose falls
Melodious birds sing madrigals.

And I will make thee beds of roses,
And a thousand fragrant posies;   10
A cap of flowers, and a kirtle
Embroider'd all with leaves of myrtle.

A gown made of the finest wool,
Which from our pretty lambs we pull;
Fair linèd slippers for the cold,   15
With buckles of the purest gold.

A belt of straw and ivy buds
With coral clasps and amber studs;
And if these pleasures may thee move,
Come live with me, and be my love.   20

The shepherd swains shall dance and sing
For thy delight each May morning:
If these delights thy mind may move,
Then live with me, and be my love.

CHRISTOPHER MARLOWE (*1564–1593*)

1. Show how the kind of gifts and the kind of pleasures are suitable
to a pastoral poem. 2. If the details are viewed allegorically, what might
they represent?

THE NYMPH'S REPLY TO THE SHEPHERD

If all the world and love were young,
And truth in every shepherd's tongue,
These pretty pleasures might me move
To live with thee and be thy love.

Time drives the flocks from field to fold   5
When rivers rage and rocks grow cold,
And Philomel becometh dumb;
The rest complains of cares to come.

The flowers do fade, and wanton fields
To wayward winter reckoning yields;   10
A honey tongue, a heart of gall,
Is fancy's spring, but sorrow's fall.

Thy gowns, thy shoes, thy beds of roses,
Thy cap, thy kirtle, and thy posies
Soon break, soon wither, soon forgotten,—   15
In folly ripe, in reason rotten.

Thy belt of straw and ivy buds,
Thy coral clasps and amber studs,
All these in me no means can move
To come to thee and be thy love.   20

But could youth last and love still breed,
Had joys no date nor age no need,
Then these delights my mind might move
To live with thee and be thy love.

SIR WALTER RALEIGH (*1552–1618*)

1. Here the theme of passing time is used again. Compare this poem
with "*Sic Vita*" (p. 8) and "To His Coy Mistress" (p. 89). 2. Is this
poem more realistic than Marlowe's "The Passionate Shepherd"? Is
it more true?

CORINNA'S GOING A-MAYING

Get up, get up for shame, the blooming morn
Upon her wings presents the god unshorn.
   See how Aurora throws her fair
   Fresh-quilted colors through the air;
   Get up, sweet slug-a-bed, and see   5
   The dew bespangling herb and tree.
Each flower has wept and bowèd toward the east
Above an hour since, yet you not dressed;
   Nay, not so much as out of bed?
   When all the birds have matins said   10
   And sung their thankful hymns, 'tis sin,
   Nay, profanation, to keep in,
Whenas a thousand virgins on this day
Spring, sooner than the lark, to fetch in May.

Rise, and put on your foliage, and be seen   15
To come forth like the springtime, fresh and green,
   And sweet as Flora. Take no care
   For jewels for your gown or hair;
   Fear not, the leaves will strew
   Gems in abundance upon you;   20
Besides, the childhood of the day has kept,
Against you come, some orient pearls unwept;
   Come and receive them while the light
   Hangs on the dew-locks of the night,
   And Titan on the eastern hill   25
   Retires himself, or else stands still
Till you came forth. Wash, dress, be brief in praying:
Few beads are best when once we go a-Maying.

Come, my Corinna, come; and coming, mark
How each field turns a street, each street a park   30
   Made green and trimmed with trees; see how
   Devotion gives each house a bough
   Or branch; each porch, each door, ere this,
   An ark, a tabernacle is,
Made up of white-thorn neatly interwove;   35
As if here were those cooler shades of love.
   Can such delights be in the street
   And open fields, and we not see 't?
   Come, we'll abroad; and let's obey
   The proclamation made for May,   40
And sin no more, as we have done, by staying;
But, my Corinna, come, let's go a-Maying.

There's not a budding boy or girl this day
But is got up, and gone to bring in May.
   A deal of youth, ere this, is come   45
   Back, and with white-thorn laden, home.
   Some have dispatched their cakes and cream
   Before that we have left to dream;
And some have wept, and wooed, and plighted troth,
And chose their priest, ere we can cast off sloth;   50
   Many a green-gown has been given,
   Many a kiss, both odd and even,
   Many a glance too has been sent
   From out the eye, love's firmament,
Many a jest told of the keys betraying   55
This night, and locks picked, yet we're not a-Maying.

Come, let us go while we are in our prime,
And take the harmless folly of the time.
   We shall grow old apace, and die
   Before we know our liberty.   60
   Our life is short, and our days run
   As fast away as does the sun;
And, as a vapor, or a drop of rain
Once lost, can ne'er be found again,
   So when or you or I are made   65
   A fable, song, or fleeting shade,
   All love, all liking, all delight
   Lies drowned with us in endless night.

Then while time serves, and we are but decaying,
Come, my Corinna, come, let's go a-Maying.   70

ROBERT HERRICK (*1591–1674*)

1. Point out all the uses of pagan and Christian imagery in the poem.
How can they be combined in one poem? Is either strain, pagan or
Christian, to be taken literally? 2. What *religious* attitude, neither pagan
nor Christian, may be at the heart of the poem? 3. Discuss the use of
contrasts and oppositions in the poem, especially in the last two lines.
4. Compare the theme with that of "To His Coy Mistress" (p. 89).

We have looked at some of the major types of poems, their
characteristics and relationships. There are, of course, other ways
to define and combine groups of poems. One might, for instance,
talk of "nature" poetry as a type, or more restrictively—of poems
about birds, or even poems about singing birds. Most of such
types and traditions the reader can find for himself, for one of
his pleasures in knowing poetry is that he can begin to see how
one poem connects with another. Some of the dimensions of a
poem can only be marked when it is studied as a part of a larger
world.

CHAPTER 3

POETRY AND JUDGMENT

NOW that we have explored the physical world inside the poem and examined the life the poem leads in the company of its kind, we may look homeward and examine our own relation to the poem—our complex attitudes toward poetry which lead to evaluation, analysis, and criticism. For we, too, have a "life" relationship with the poem—perhaps its most important dimension. Many poets have warned that the reader's creative role is as large and important as the poet's. Walt Whitman told his audience: "The reader will always have his or her part to do, just as much as I have had mine. I seek less to state or display any theme or thought, and more to bring you, reader, into the atmosphere of the theme or thought—there to pursue your own flight." In a very real sense, the poem depends on the reader for its very life. If the reader remains passive, uninvolved, the poem lies inert and bloodless on the page. If the reader participates, his imagination actively engaged, the poem rises pulsing with the full richness of life. The small child with a limp balloon that will not inflate itself first becomes frustrated and then bored, believing that balloons will not play with him. But the child who invests the living breath of his body to see the balloon grow large against his face and then cries out with joy as he bounces the balloon lightly in the air, has discovered the delights—as well as risks—of deep involvement.

One of the risks of involvement in poetry is that the reader must often make decisions and bring his judgment to bear upon the poem. Sometimes it may seem easier to avoid the whole thing and hide behind the barrier of some sweeping attitude—"I don't like poetry" or "modern poetry is incomprehensible." These attitudes are usually façades erected for convenience, without much thought, the materials borrowed from a friend or group. Like most of our prejudices, they are frequently constructed out of ignorance or fear.

We are concerned, however, only with those who are willing to live, and with the critical problems they may encounter. Like all of the vital things in life, poetry is full of uncertainties, its delights full of surprises, its deeper rewards bristling with ambiguities. Probably because of its uncertainties, poetry gathers about itself a cluster of critical questions that represent, in many instances, an uneasy search for the certainties of dogma: Do poems have morals? Can we judge a poem by its moral? How can we like a poem when it expresses a philosophy in which we don't believe? Who has the right to say what a poem means? Aren't all opinions equal in a democratic society, and doesn't one opinion as to what the poem means have as much validity as any other? How can we prove that one poem is better than another? Since we know what we like, don't we have as much right as anybody to call what we like *good*? Isn't it a mistake anyway to talk about good and bad poems—isn't it all simply a matter of taste?

All of us have, at one time or another, floundered around in these waters. The questions bring into focus important considerations of moral judgment, interpretive judgment, and value judgment. There are easy answers to the questions and easy ways of disposing of all these subjects. Many "authorities" and their various dogmas clamor for our allegiance, luring with their assurances of a ready anchor and safe harbor from every smashing wave or churning whirlpool. But we all know that in the vital matters of life, easy answers are suspect. So too in poetry. Honest answers are hard to find, but they are the only ones worth seeking. And we may discover in the search that even the honest answers—*especially* the honest answers—are not final, but tentative and complex, frequently puzzling and sometimes contradictory.

MORAL JUDGMENT

Poetry is as varied as people. What is true for one poem may not be true for another; what seems vital to one poet may appear trivial to many. Cautiousness is the rule, therefore, in making generalizations about poetry.

Some readers begin their mature exploration of poetry with the uneasy feeling that the key to a good poem, like the key to a respectable man, is morality. They are haunted by a generalization: a great poem has a great moral; to understand the poem, find the moral. And, according to some, who have no trouble recognizing their image in a mirror, the moral in the poem is merely a reflection of their own shining conviction.

It is not difficult to find the source of this idea. Nineteenth-century American poetry, especially that frequently found in the anthologies, is moralistic poetry, most (but not all) of it now considered predominantly shallow if sometimes competent. Two of the most admired poems of this kind are William Cullen Bryant's "To a Waterfowl" and Oliver Wendell Holmes's "The Chambered Nautilus" (see pp. 102–104). These poems display their "morals" with a flourish. In Bryant's "To a Waterfowl," the poet perceives the "lesson" that the same Being that guides the waterfowl also guides man. In Holmes's "The Chambered Nautilus," the poet receives the "message" that man's soul, like the organism of the multi-roomed shell, should build new and nobler temples throughout life. It is tempting to pause at this point and conclude: we have found the morals and they are good; therefore, these poems are good.

But this easy conclusion soon rings false. In the first place, finding the morals was simple because the poets used rather obvious signals to warn the reader that the morals were coming— "the lesson thou hast given," "the heavenly message brought by thee." These phrases flag the attention with all the subtlety of a neon sign. Other poets have avoided such signals, not because they were unaware of the virtues of lucidity and clarity, but because they were embarrassed by such heavy-handedness. Moreover, the morals, when examined outside the contexts of the poems and in the cold light of day, are really not very impressive. Almost any child might hit upon these same ideas or "truths." Indeed, there is a childlike innocence in the assumption that God guides a bird and must therefore guide man. Such an idea is not even very fresh or original—it has occurred to countless poets, theologians, and ordinary people.

But not just anyone could have written these poems. They are unique: no other poems in the language do just what they do. When we begin to examine a poem in detail—its images, its move-

ment, its diction—we gradually come to understand that we cannot make a sound judgment based solely on an isolated element,
an extracted and paraphrased moral, but must see the poem whole
and judge it intact, in all the complexity of its physical being,
in all the subtlety of its surface and subterranean strategy. A
poem works in the imagination by every picture and sound it
evokes, every word and combination of words, every pulse of its
rhythm. These elements are as vitally involved in judgment as
the generalizing statements to which they lead. In short, we
should judge a poem by its total behavior as well as by its assertion.

When we encounter poems like Bryant's or Holmes's—poems
that seem on the surface like philosophical discourse—we may
gain some distance in which to adjust our view if we pretend that
we are observing a drama in which a speaker is portrayed at a
moment of insight or perception. Does the dramatic action and
detail engage our imagination—does Bryant's waterfowl hold our
inner eye as it floats along the "crimson sky," does Holmes's chambered nautilus tease our curiosity as it lies on the seashore, its
"sunless crypt unsealed"? Do we see two solitary, meditative men
in physical settings which through sheer imaginative impact
sweep them on to an attitude or belief more felt than reasoned?
Once we are caught up in questions of this kind, the moralistic
statements seem to fade into and blend with their contexts. We
can say that the moral has a dramatic position in the poem. A
frequently useful analogy, if granted its limits, is the lyric poem
as a dramatic soliloquy. If sometimes we have trouble putting the
moral in its place, we might well step back and view the lyric as
a dramatic speech which reveals the character of the speaker at
a compelling moment of his life—like Hamlet's soliloquy, "To
be, or not to be," or Macbeth's "Tomorrow, and tomorrow, and
tomorrow." The dramatic setting for the poem might be supplied by the collaborating talents of reader and poet, who for the
moment join imaginations and produce an unwritten play as
backdrop for the few lines actually spoken.

If we take the dogmatic view and demand that poems have not
only morals but morals that can be readily detected and quoted,
we deny ourselves the pleasure of much of the most interesting,
fascinating, and enchanting poetry that has been written. Who
would want to reject, because he could not locate their morals,

Lewis Carroll's "nonsense" poem "Jabberwocky" or Edgar Allan Poe's melancholy lament "Annabel Lee" or Algernon Swinburne's "The Garden of Proserpine" (pp. 105, 106, 107)? Though these poems represent distinctive poetic types, they are similar in that all depend for effect largely on the *suggestion* of selected sound combinations and repetitions. We respond to these poems not with our moral understanding but with a complex of our emotional and imaginative being. The question of morality never seems relevant. In fact, if the reader delves far enough, he can find abundant material in these poems to engage the intellect both deeply and vigorously.

But perhaps the greatest argument against the moralistic approach to poetry is that, when rigidly and narrowly applied, it limits the reader to poetry which reflects his own bias, whether political, religious, or philosophical. If we turn into readers searching texts for confirmation of what we already *know* to be true, we have destroyed the zest which makes reading one of life's greatest adventures. It is as narcissistic as searching a series of mirrors for examples of beauty—and being satisfied with our multiple reflections.

Poetry does not demand our belief; it invites us to experience. We can best prepare for the experience by abandoning our prejudices, awakening our senses, and limbering our minds. We should not stop on the threshold of a poem when we sense that it is about to say something with which we cannot agree. If we must ask a question, it should not be, "Can I believe what this says?" but rather, "Is it dramatically valid for the speaker of the poem to assert his belief in the way he does?" And such a question can be intelligently posed only after the imaginative reconstruction of the dramatic situation of the speaker—What is the nature of his physical surroundings? What is his awareness of them? His response to them? What is his emotional state? Is he looking forward to action or regarding it in the past? Or is he experiencing an isolated moment of perception? What is the chain of responses and feelings that has led him to his particular insight?

When we cease engaging in argument and begin engaging in the experience—participating in the drama—we have taken the first full step, and perhaps the most important, in the judgment of poetry. Poetry may best be read not as argument inviting us to debate nor as explanation inviting us to understand, but as drama inviting our involvement. Our participation, our imaginative engagement, may result finally in modifying our belief, in deepening our awareness, or in heightening our perceptions, but these results may come from *any* experience of life whenever it is thoroughly absorbing and deeply felt.

We might test our ability to suspend our prejudices by examining a series of poems which seem to express widely varying views: two Christian poems, two non-Christian poems, two pessimistic poems suggesting a loss of faith, and two poems of pagan-like incantation and affirmation. Each of these poems has its individual perspective, its special validity, its unique effect. Henry Vaughan's "The World" is a symbolic expression of orthodox Christian faith, while Edward Taylor's "Housewifery" is an assertion of Calvinistic Puritanism. Ralph Waldo Emerson's "Brahma" is oriental in outlook, and William Cullen Bryant's "Thanatopsis" is, except perhaps for the closing lines, deistic. Matthew Arnold's "Dover Beach" represents a search for faith in human love, while Thomas Hardy's "The Darkling Thrush" portrays a cry for hope in the midst of despair. Stephen Spender's "I Think Continually of Those Who Were Truly Great" expresses a kind of pagan identification with the energies of nature, while E. E. Cummings' "anyone lived in a pretty how town" expresses a poignant reconciliation to the cyclic and repetitive nature of human life. Not one of these poems demands dogmatic belief before dramatic participation, moral acceptance before imaginative engagement. But each offers a valid experience for the venturesome reader willing to view the world from a corner other than his own (see pp. 110–118).

TO A WATERFOWL

Whither, midst falling dew,
While glow the heavens with the last steps of day,
Far, through their rosy depths, dost thou pursue
    Thy solitary way?

Vainly the fowler's eye   5
Might mark thy distant flight to do thee wrong,
As, darkly seen against the crimson sky,
    Thy figure floats along.

Seek'st thou the plashy brink
Of weedy lake, or marge of river wide,   10
Or where the rocking billows rise and sink
    On the chafed ocean-side?

There is a Power whose care
Teaches thy way along that pathless coast—
The desert and illimitable air—   15
    Lone wandering, but not lost.

All day thy wings have fanned,
At that far height, the cold, thin atmosphere,
Yet stoop not, weary, to the welcome land,
    Though the dark night is near.   20

And soon that toil shall end;
Soon shalt thou find a summer home, and rest,
And scream among thy fellows; reeds shall bend,
    Soon, o'er thy sheltered nest.

Thou'rt gone, the abyss of heaven   25
Hath swallowed up thy form; yet, on my heart
Deeply has sunk the lesson thou hast given,
    And shall not soon depart.

He who, from zone to zone,
Guides through the boundless sky thy certain flight,   30
In the long way that I must tread alone
    Will lead my steps aright.

WILLIAM CULLEN BRYANT (*1794–1878*)

Re-create in prose the precise dramatic situation of this poem, describing the probable physical location of the speaker, the time of day, the passage of time in the course of the poem, the scene actually viewed by the speaker as compared to the scenes he imagines, the mood of the speaker, and the character of the speaker as suggestd by his behavior in relating the bird's fate to his own.

THE CHAMBERED NAUTILUS

This is the ship of pearl, which, poets feign,
    Sails the unshadowed main,—
      The venturous bark that flings
On the sweet summer wind its purpled wings

In gulfs enchanted, where the Siren sings, 5
    And coral reefs lie bare,
Where the cold sea-maids rise to sun their streaming hair.

Its webs of living gauze no more unfurl;
    Wrecked is the ship of pearl!
    And every chambered cell, 10
Where its dim dreaming life was wont to dwell,
As the frail tenant shaped his growing shell,
    Before thee lies revealed,—
Its irised ceiling rent, its sunless crypt unsealed!

Year after year beheld the silent toil 15
    That spread his lustrous coil;
    Still, as the spiral grew,
He left the past year's dwelling for the new,
Stole with soft step its shining archway through,
    Built up its idle door, 20
Stretched in his last-found home, and knew the old no more.

Thanks for the heavenly message brought by thee,
    Child of the wandering sea,
    Cast from her lap, forlorn!
From thy dead lips a clearer note is born 25
Than ever Triton blew from wreathèd horn!
    While on mine ear it rings,
Through the deep caves of thought I hear a voice that sings:—

Build thee more stately mansions, O my soul,
    As the swift seasons roll! 30
    Leave thy low-vaulted past!
Let each new temple, nobler than the last,
Shut thee from heaven with a dome more vast,
    Till thou at length art free,
Leaving thine outgrown shell by life's unresting sea! 35

OLIVER WENDELL HOLMES (*1809–1894*)

1. Compare the narrative method of this poem with that of "To a Waterfowl." 2. What is the precise physical relationship of the speaker and shell when the poem opens, what does the speaker imagine and in what order, and how does his meditation lead to the analogy with which the poem concludes? How many relationships in the analogy may be listed? 3. Is the rhetorical force of the last stanza weakened in forcing emphasis on "Shut" by placing the word at the beginning of the third-from-the-last line?

JABBERWOCKY [1]

'Twas brillig, and the slithy toves
    Did gyre and gimble in the wabe;
All mimsy were the borogoves,
    And the mome raths outgrabe.

"Beware the Jabberwock, my son!   5
    The jaws that bite, the claws that catch!
Beware the Jubjub bird, and shun
    The frumious Bandersnatch!"

He took his vorpal sword in hand:
    Long time the manxome foe he sought—   10
So rested he by the Tumtum tree,
    And stood awhile in thought.

And as in uffish thought he stood,
    The Jabberwock, with eyes of flame,
Came whiffling through the tulgey wood,   15
    And burbled as it came!

One, two! One, two! And through and through
    The vorpal blade went snicker-snack!
He left it dead, and with its head
    He went galumphing back.   20

"And hast thou slain the Jabberwock?
    Come to my arms, my beamish boy!
O frabjous day! Callooh! Callay!"
    He chortled in his joy.

'Twas brillig, and the slithy toves   25
    Did gyre and gimble in the wabe;
All mimsy were the borogoves,
    And the mome raths outgrabe.

LEWIS CARROLL (*1832–1898*)

1. Can any statement that could conceivably be labeled a "moral" be formulated for this poem? 2. How is it that, although many of the words are unfamiliar, we are able to "understand" what is happening in the poem?

[1] From *Through the Looking Glass*. In it Alice says of the poem: "Somehow it seems to fill my head with ideas—only I don't exactly know what they are!"

ANNABEL LEE

It was many and many a year ago,
  In a kingdom by the sea,
That a maiden there lived whom you may know
  By the name of Annabel Lee;—
And this maiden she lived with no other thought   5
  Than to love and be loved by me.

She was a child and I was a child,
  In this kingdom by the sea,
But we loved with a love that was more than love—
  I and my Annabel Lee—   10
With a love that the wingèd seraphs of Heaven
  Coveted her and me.

And this was the reason that, long ago,
  In this kingdom by the sea,
A wind blew out of a cloud by night   15
  Chilling my Annabel Lee;
So that her highborn kinsmen came
  And bore her away from me,
To shut her up in a sepulchre
  In this kingdom by the sea.   20

The angels, not half so happy in Heaven,
  Went envying her and me:—
Yes! that was the reason (as all men know,
  In this kingdom by the sea)
That the wind came out of the cloud, chilling   25
  And killing my Annabel Lee.

But our love it was stronger by far than the love
  Of those who were older than we—
  Of many far wiser than we—
And neither the angels in Heaven above   30
  Nor the demons down under the sea,
Can ever dissever my soul from the soul
  Of the beautiful Annabel Lee:—

For the moon never beams without bringing me dreams
  Of the beautiful Annabel Lee;   35
And the stars never rise but I see the bright eyes
  Of the beautiful Annabel Lee;
And so, all the night-tide, I lie down by the side

Of my darling, my darling, my life and my bride,
  In her sepulchre there by the sea—   40
  In her tomb by the side of the sea.

                EDGAR ALLAN POE (*1809–1849*)

1. Can a "moral" be located in this poem? 2. Can a prose statement of the events of the poem be made without sounding absurd? 3. Read the poem aloud and listen to the poem's music. Wherein lies the magic of the poem? 4. Another version of the poem has "feel" for "see" in line 36; "sounding" for "side of the" in line 41. Which do you prefer? Give reasons for your judgment.

THE GARDEN OF PROSERPINE [1]

Here, where the world is quiet;
  Here, where all trouble seems
Dead winds' and spent waves' riot
  In doubtful dreams of dreams;
I watch the green field growing   5
For reaping folk and sowing,
For harvest-time and mowing,
  A sleepy world of streams.

I am tired of tears and laughter,
  And men that laugh and weep;   10
Of what may come hereafter
  For men that sow to reap:
I am weary of days and hours,
Blown buds of barren flowers,
Desires and dreams and powers   15
  And everything but sleep.

Here life has death for neighbor,
  And far from eye or ear
Wan waves and wet winds labor,
  Weak ships and spirits steer;   20
They drive adrift, and whither
They wot not who make thither;
But no such winds blow hither,
  And no such things grow here.

[1] Proserpine, whose mother was Demeter, goddess of the earth's fruitfulness, was carried away by Hades to rule as queen of the underworld—which would be her "garden."

No growth of moor or coppice,   25
  No heather-flower or vine,
But bloomless buds of poppies,
  Green grapes of Proserpine,
Pale beds of blowing rushes,
Where no leaf blooms or blushes   30
Save this whereout she crushes
  For dead men deadly wine.

Pale, without name or number,
  In fruitless fields of corn,
They bow themselves and slumber   35
  All night till light is born;
And like a soul belated,
In hell and heaven unmated,
By cloud and mist abated
  Comes out of darkness morn.   40

Though one were strong as seven,
  He too with death shall dwell,
Nor wake with wings in heaven,
  Nor weep for pains in hell;
Though one were fair as roses,   45
His beauty clouds and closes;
And well though love reposes,
  In the end it is not well.

Pale, beyond porch and portal,
  Crowned with calm leaves, she stands   50
Who gathers all things mortal
  With cold immortal hands;
Her languid lips are sweeter
Than love's who fears to greet her,
To men that mix and meet her   55
  From many times and lands.

She waits for each and other,
  She waits for all men born;
Forgets the earth her mother,
  The life of fruits and corn;   60
And spring and seed and swallow
Take wing for her and follow
Where summer song rings hollow
  And flowers are put to scorn.

There go the loves that wither,   65
   The old loves with wearier wings;
And all dead years draw thither,
   And all disastrous things;
Dead dreams of days forsaken,
Blind buds that snows have shaken,   70
Wild leaves that winds have taken,
   Red strays of ruined springs.

We are not sure of sorrow,
   And joy was never sure;
Today will die tomorrow;   75
   Time stoops to no man's lure;
And love, grown faint and fretful,
With lips but half regretful
Sighs, and with eyes forgetful
   Weeps that no loves endure.   80

From too much love of living,
   From hope and fear set free,
We thank with brief thanksgiving
   Whatever gods may be
That no life lives for ever;   85
That dead men rise up never;
That even the weariest river
   Winds somewhere safe to sea.

Then star nor sun shall waken,
   Nor any change of light: 90
Nor sound of waters shaken,
   Nor any sound or sight:
Nor wintry leaves nor vernal,
Nor days nor things diurnal;
Only the sleep eternal   95
   In an eternal night.

ALGERNON CHARLES SWINBURNE (*1837–1909*)

1. The music of this poem casts a kind of spell, lulling the reader and preparing him for a reversal of one of his usual attitudes—distaste for death. The next-to-last stanza is a "thanksgiving" for death. How have sound and sense made dramatic preparation for this conclusion? 2. Compare the use made of the myth in this poem with that in Lawrence's "Bavarian Gentians" (p. 30).

THE WORLD

I saw eternity the other night
Like a great ring of pure and endless light,
 All calm as it was bright;
And round beneath it, time in hours, days, years,
  Driv'n by the spheres,   5
Like a vast shadow moved, in which the world
 And all her train were hurled:
The doting lover in his quaintest strain
  Did there complain;
Near him his lute, his fancy, and his flights,   10
  Wit's hour delights,
With gloves and knots, the silly snares of pleasure,
  Yet his dear treasure,
All scattered lay, while he his eyes did pore
  Upon a flower.   15

The darksome statesman, hung with weights and woe,
Like a thick midnight fog moved there so slow
  He did not stay, nor go;
Condemning thoughts, like sad eclipses, scowl
  Upon his soul,   20
And clouds of crying witnesses without
  Pursued him with one shout;
Yet digged the mole, and lest his ways be found
  Worked underground,
Where he did clutch his prey, but One did see   25
  That policy;
Churches and altars fed him; perjuries
  Were gnats and flies;
It rained about him blood and tears, but he
  Drank them as free.   30

The fearful miser on a heap of rust
Sat pining all his life there, did scarce trust
  His own hands with the dust,
Yet would not place one piece above, but lives
  In fear of thieves.   35
Thousands there were as frantic as himself,
  And hugged each one his pelf:
The downright epicure placed heav'n in sense,
  And scorned pretense;

While others, slipped into a wide excess,   40
    Said little less;
The weaker sort slight trivial wares enslave,
    Who think them brave;
And poor despisèd truth sat counting by
    Their victory.   45

Yet some, who all this while did weep and sing,
And sing and weep, soared up into the ring;
    But most would use no wing.
O fools, said I, thus to prefer dark night
    Before true light,   50
To live in grots and caves, and hate the day
    Because it shows the way,
The way which from this dead and dark abode
    Leads up to God,
A way where you might tread the sun, and be   55
    More bright than he.
But as I did their madness so discuss,
    One whispered thus:
This ring the bridegroom did for none provide
    But for his bride.   60

HENRY VAUGHAN (*1622–1695*)

1. This poem is a somewhat conventional Christian commentary on the world. What makes it unusual? 2. What is the dramatic order of the poem as suggested in the opening line? 3. Can you justify the division of the poem into four stanzas and the present arrangement of the stanzas?

HOUSEWIFERY

Make me, O Lord, Thy spinning-wheel complete.
    Thy holy Word my distaff make for me;
Make mine affections Thy swift flyers neat;
    And make my soul Thy holy spool to be;
    My conversation make to be Thy reel,   5
And reel the yarn thereon spun of Thy wheel.

Make me Thy loom then; knit therein this twine;
    And make Thy Holy Spirit, Lord, wind quills.
Then weave the web Thyself. The yarn is fine.
    Thine ordinances make my fulling mills.   10

Then dye the same in heavenly colors choice,
All pinked with varnished flowers of paradise.

Then clothe therewith mine understanding will,
Affections, judgment, conscience, memory,
My words and actions, that their shine may fill   15
My ways with glory and Thee glorify.
Then mine apparel shall display before Ye
That I am clothed in holy robes for glory.

EDWARD TAYLOR (*c.1645–1729*)

1. Does this poem, in expressing the sentiment of an American Calvinist,
differ in tone from Henry Vaughan's "The World"? 2. Is it possible to
detect the doctrine of "innate depravity" or predestination in the Taylor
poem? 3. Does our interest in "Housewifery" as a poem center in its
doctrine or its metaphor? 4. Trace the extent of the elaboration of the
central metaphor.

BRAHMA

If the red slayer think he slays,
    Or if the slain think he is slain,
They know not well the subtle ways
    I keep, and pass, and turn again.

Far or forgot to me is near;   5
    Shadow and sunlight are the same;
The vanquished gods to me appear;
    And one to me are shame and fame.

They reckon ill who leave me out;
    When me they fly, I am the wings;   10
I am the doubter and the doubt,
    And I the hymn the Brahmin sings.

The strong gods pine for my abode,
    And pine in vain the sacred Seven;
But thou, meek lover of the good!   15
    Find me, and turn thy back on heaven.

RALPH WALDO EMERSON (*1803–1882*)

1. How do the ideas of this poem differ from common Christian belief?
2. What is the meaning of the title and how is it related to the poem?
3. How is the paradox of the last two lines prepared for in the detail
of the preceding stanzas?

THANATOPSIS

To him who in the love of Nature holds
Communion with her visible forms, she speaks
A various language; for his gayer hours
She has a voice of gladness, and a smile
And eloquence of beauty, and she glides   5
Into his darker musings, with a mild
And healing sympathy, that steals away
Their sharpness, ere he is aware. When thoughts
Of the last bitter hour come like a blight
Over thy spirit, and sad images   10
Of the stern agony, and shroud, and pall,
And breathless darkness, and the narrow house,
Make thee to shudder, and grow sick at heart;—
Go forth, under the open sky, and list
To Nature's teachings, while from all around—   15
Earth and her waters, and the depths of air—
Comes a still voice—Yet a few days, and thee
The all-beholding sun shall see no more
In all his course; nor yet in the cold ground,
Where thy pale form was laid, with many tears,   20
Nor in the embrace of ocean, shall exist
Thy image. Earth, that nourished thee, shall claim
Thy growth, to be resolved to earth again,
And, lost each human trace, surrendering up
Thine individual being, shalt thou go   25
To mix for ever with the elements,
To be a brother to the insensible rock
And to the sluggish clod, which the rude swain
Turns with his share, and treads upon. The oak
Shall send his roots abroad, and pierce thy mold.   30

Yet not to thine eternal resting-place
Shalt thou retire alone, nor couldst thou wish
Couch more magnificent. Thou shalt lie down
With patriarchs of the infant world—with kings,
The powerful of the earth—the wise, the good,   35
Fair forms, and hoary seers of ages past,
All in one mighty sepulcher. The hills
Rock-ribbed and ancient as the sun,—the vales
Stretching in pensive quietness between;
The venerable woods—rivers that move   40

In majesty, and the complaining brooks
That make the meadows green; and, poured round all,
Old Ocean's gray and melancholy waste,—
Are but the solemn decorations all
Of the great tomb of man. The golden sun,   45
The planets, all the infinite host of heaven,
Are shining on the sad abodes of death,
Through the still lapse of ages. All that tread
The globe are but a handful to the tribes
That slumber in its bosom.—Take the wings   50
Of morning, pierce the Barcan wilderness,
Or lose thyself in the continuous woods
Where rolls the Oregon, and hears no sound,
Save his own dashings—yet the dead are there:
And millions in those solitudes, since first   55
The flight of years began, have laid them down
In their last sleep—the dead reign there alone.
So shalt thou rest, and what if thou withdraw
In silence from the living, and no friend
Take note of thy departure? All that breathe   60
Will share thy destiny. The gay will laugh
When thou art gone, the solemn brood of care
Plod on, and each one as before will chase
His favorite phantom; yet all these shall leave
Their mirth and their employments, and shall come   65
And make their bed with thee. As the long train
Of ages glides away, the sons of men,
The youth in life's green spring, and he who goes
In the full strength of years, matron and maid,
The speechless babe, and the gray-headed man—   70
Shall one by one be gathered to thy side,
By those, who in their turn shall follow them.

So live, that when thy summons comes to join
The innumerable caravan, which moves
To that mysterious realm, where each shall take   75
His chamber in the silent halls of death,
Thou go not, like the quarry-slave at night,
Scourged to his dungeon, but, sustained and soothed
By an unfaltering trust, approach thy grave,
Like one who wraps the drapery of his couch   80
About him, and lies down to pleasant dreams.

          WILLIAM CULLEN BRYANT (*1794–1878*)

1. How do the last nine lines of this poem differ from the rest? 2. In what sense is the poem deistic? In what sense Christian? 3. Relate the imagery of the poem to the consolation being offered for death.

DOVER BEACH

The sea is calm tonight.
The tide is full, the moon lies fair
Upon the straits;—on the French coast the light
Gleams and is gone; the cliffs of England stand,
Glimmering and vast, out in the tranquil bay.   5
Come to the window, sweet is the night-air!
Only, from the long line of spray
Where the sea meets the moon-blanched land,
Listen! you hear the grating roar
Of pebbles which the waves draw back, and fling,   10
At their return, up the high strand,
Begin, and cease, and then again begin,
With tremulous cadence slow, and bring
The eternal note of sadness in.

Sophocles long ago   15
Heard it on the Aegean, and it brought
Into his mind the turbid ebb and flow
Of human misery; we
Find also in the sound a thought,
Hearing it by this distant northern sea.   20

The Sea of Faith
Was once, too, at the full, and round earth's shore
Lay like the folds of a bright girdle furled.
But now I only hear
Its melancholy, long, withdrawing roar,   25
Retreating, to the breath
Of the night-wind, down the vast edges drear
And naked shingles of the world.

Ah, love, let us be true
To one another! for the world, which seems   30
To lie before us like a land of dreams,
So various, so beautiful, so new,
Hath really neither joy, nor love, nor light,
Nor certitude, nor peace, nor help for pain;
And we are here as on a darkling plain   35

Swept with confused alarms of struggle and flight,
Where ignorant armies clash by night.

MATTHEW ARNOLD (*1822–1888*)

1. Analyze the poem as a short drama with setting, characters, action.
2. Characterize as fully as you can the speaker and the person spoken
to. 3. In what sense is the poem non-Christian? 4. This poem is frequently linked to Darwin (whose *Origin of the Species* appeared in
1859). Explain.

THE DARKLING THRUSH

I leant upon a coppice gate
　　When Frost was spectre-gray,
And Winter's dregs made desolate
　　The weakening eye of day.
The tangled bine-stems scored the sky　　　5
　　Like strings of broken lyres,
And all mankind that haunted nigh
　　Had sought their household fires.

The land's sharp features seemed to be
　　The Century's corpse outleant,　　　10
His crypt the cloudy canopy,
　　The wind his death-lament.
The ancient pulse of germ and birth
　　Was shrunken hard and dry,
And every spirit upon earth　　　15
　　Seemed fervourless as I.

At once a voice arose among
　　The bleak twigs overhead
In a full-hearted evensong
　　Of joy illimited;　　　20
An aged thrush, frail, gaunt, and small,
　　In blast-beruffled plume,
Had chosen thus to fling his soul
　　Upon the growing gloom.

So little cause for carolings　　　25
　　Of such ecstatic sound
Was written on terrestrial things
　　Afar or nigh around,

That I could think there trembled through
  His happy good-night air   30
Some blessed Hope, whereof he knew
  And I was unaware.

THOMAS HARDY (*1840–1928*)

1. Is this a poem of pessimism or of hope? 2. Could this poem be
called Christian, deistic, or neither? 3. Trace the dramatic action of the
poem, showing how setting especially determines the tone of the poem.

I THINK CONTINUALLY OF THOSE

I think continually of those who were truly great.
Who, from the womb, remembered the soul's history
Through corridors of light where the hours are suns
Endless and singing. Whose lovely ambition
Was that their lips, still touched with fire,   5
Should tell of the Spirit clothed from head to foot in song.
And who hoarded from the Spring branches
The desires falling across their bodies like blossoms.

What is precious is never to forget
The essential delight of the blood drawn from ageless springs   10
Breaking through rocks in worlds before our earth.
Never to deny its pleasure in the morning simple light
Nor its grave evening demand for love.
Never to allow gradually the traffic to smother
With noise and fog the flowering of the spirit.   15

Near the snow, near the sun, in the highest fields
See how these names are fêted by the waving grass
And by the streamers of white cloud
And whispers of wind in the listening sky.
The names of those who in their lives fought for life   20
Who wore at their hearts the fire's centre.
Born of the sun they travelled a short while towards the sun,
And left the vivid air signed with their honor.

STEPHEN SPENDER (*1909–*   )

1. Is this poem pagan or Christian, or neither? 2. How do the "truly
great" differ from the conventionally great, in both their greatness and
the way in which they are memorialized?

ANYONE LIVED IN A PRETTY HOW TOWN

anyone lived in a pretty how town
(with up so floating many bells down)
spring summer autumn winter
he sang his didn't he danced his did.

Women and men(both little and small)   5
cared for anyone not at all
they sowed their isn't they reaped their same
sun moon stars rain

children guessed(but only a few
and down they forgot as up they grew   10
autumn winter spring summer)
that noone loved him more by more

when by now and tree by leaf
she laughed his joy she cried his grief
bird by snow and stir by still   15
anyone's any was all to her

someones married their everyones
laughed their cryings and did their dance
(sleep wake hope and then)they
said their nevers they slept their dream   20

stars rain sun moon
(and only the snow can begin to explain
how children are apt to forget to remember
with up so floating many bells down)

one day anyone died i guess   25
(and noone stooped to kiss his face)
busy folk buried them side by side
little by little and was by was

all by all and deep by deep
and more by more they dream their sleep   30
noone and anyone earth by april
wish by spirit and if by yes.

Women and men(both dong and ding)
summer autumn winter spring
reaped their sowing and went their came   35
sun moon stars rain

E. E. CUMMINGS (*1894–*   )

1. What is the central narrative of this poem? Can it be related to Spender's "I Think Continually of Those"? How is anonymity important to both poems? 2. Does the "chanting" quality suggest a pagan or a Christian view, or neither? 3. Does a fundamental gap in point of view separate Henry Vaughan's "The World" from E. E. Cummings' "anyone lived in a pretty how town"? 4. Relate the technique of "anyone lived" to the technique of Lewis Carroll's "Jabberwocky."

INTERPRETIVE JUDGMENT

In talking about the morals of poems, we have raised a host of questions about the *meaning* of poetry and what we have in mind when we say a poem *means*. Perhaps next to the error of moral judgment of poetry (the heresy of the didactic) comes the error of interpretive judgment (or the heresy of paraphrase). The reader substitutes a prose interpretation of the poem (its "meaning") for the poem and proceeds to judge not the poem but its assumed equivalent. This procedure is roughly like judging a car by its stripped chassis or by a blurred impression lingering on the retina after the vehicle has sped by. In reality, we should ride in the car itself, experiencing firsthand the quality of its ride and the nature of its movement toward its destination.

Perhaps Archibald MacLeish has made the most vivid statement of the unparaphrasable nature of poetry:

ARS POETICA

A poem should be palpable and mute
As a globed fruit,

Dumb
As old medallions to the thumb,

Silent as the sleeve-worn stone   5
Of casement ledges where the moss has grown—

A poem should be wordless
As the flight of birds

*

A poem should be motionless in time
As the moon climbs,   10

Leaving, as the moon releases
Twig by twig the night-entangled trees,

Leaving, as the moon behind the winter leaves,
Memory by memory the mind—

A poem should be motionless in time   15
As the moon climbs.

*

A poem should be equal to:
Not true.

For all the history of grief
An empty doorway and a maple leaf.   20

For love
The leaning grasses and two lights above the sea—

A poem should not mean
But be.

ARCHIBALD MACLEISH (*1892*–   )

As soon as we have finished reading this poem, we realize that
it contains a basic contradiction—it "means" at the same time
that it says that "a poem should not mean." Inevitably the question arises: What is the meaning of *mean*? There is a sense in
which all poems "mean," but there is also a sense in which no
true poem "means." When MacLeish says a poem "should not
mean," he is simply saying that the essence of poetry exists not
in statement or argument, but in the *embodiment,* in what is left
out when the poem is reduced to prose. We all know that poems
certainly do *mean* in the sense that they are constructions in language requiring our understanding, and therefore our interpretation, if we are to experience them fully. In spite of MacLeish's
poem, we may and must talk about the meaning of poems. But
we should never assume that the meaning as we distill it and talk
about it is in some mysterious way the poem itself—or even the
main purpose or *raison d'être* of the poem. As a ready-made experiment, let us throw out the globed fruit, old medallions, and
the flight of birds from MacLeish's poem and leave only the final
assertion—"A poem should not mean/But be." In removing the
"unnecessary," the seemingly superfluous, we end up with the
poetic essence not in hand but in the discard.

MacLeish's contemporary view is not really far removed from
Alexander Pope's eighteenth-century statement, in "An Essay on

Criticism" ("poetry" may be substituted for "Wit" in the opening lines):

> True Wit is Nature to advantage dressed,
> What oft was thought, but ne'er so well expressed.

Poetry does have meaning, but the poetry exists not so much in the meaning as in those intangible elements which sharpen and deepen it, charging it with the force of life itself. Poetry is breath filling the lungs and blood pulsing in the veins: these are seemingly insignificant, immaterial substances in themselves; but withdraw them, and though the body seems the same, it dies. For example, take Shakespeare's

> Golden lads and girls all must,
> As chimney-sweepers, come to dust.

The meaning is clear and familiar—all youths must eventually die, regardless of their beauty or their status. We can compare this paraphrase with the original and decide at once which one has the poetry. Shakespeare's couplet does have meaning, but the magic quality, the *poetic* quality—that combustion which sets off a bright explosion or a steady glow illuminating the imagination—is destroyed in the paraphrase. The original quickens to renewed life what lies buried in the sublevels of consciousness. W. H. Auden suggested this elusive nature of poetry when he said that a true poet is not one who has important things to say but one who likes "hanging around" words to hear what *they* have to say.

Once we have firmly in mind the genuine nature of meaning in poetry, once we realize that poems have meanings but that meanings are not poems, we are ready to attempt useful interpretation of poetry. At this point we may frequently become frustrated and annoyed, frustrated because interpretation of complex poetry is difficult, annoyed because our interpretations are challenged. We might in desperation even invoke the democratic nature of American society in our defense, arguing that "all interpretations are equal" and claiming an inalienable right to our "opinion."

But though interpreting poems is far different from solving mathematical problems, with answers in the back of the book, the skill is still a far cry from being "just a matter of opinion."

Although pat answers do not appear even in the back of the teacher's book, many usable answers appear in the text of the poem. Final authority for interpretation rests not with majority opinion, not with the teacher, not with the nationally acclaimed critic, but with the text. Of course experience counts for much in this as in any other field; the experienced teacher or the seasoned critic will, therefore, have an edge on the inexperienced reader.

But when we go to the ultimate authority, the text, we do not expect simple answers. Words are sometimes ambiguous, frequently rich in suggestion; and all the ambiguity and suggestiveness are ultimately involved in the meaning. It is quite possible, and indeed it frequently happens, that several interpretations, all somewhat different but not mutually exclusive, illuminate different aspects and various segments of the poem. We may similarly view a painting or piece of sculpture in a number of lightings, from a variety of perspectives. It is, indeed, rare that any interpretation is so exhaustive or so comprehensive that nothing more can be discovered or added. But in spite of this seeming multiplicity of meaning, debates over a poem's basic core, its central direction, are rare. Most controversies over interpretation seem to hover about the periphery of the poem. We should avoid both an extreme rigidity in interpretation of poetry, which allows only a very narrow and limited meaning, and an extreme looseness in interpretation, which allows a poem to mean all things to all readers.

Although the charge is frequently made that modern poetry is difficult to read (and it does seem sometimes to present unusual obscurities), the truth is that every period has produced poetry that presents problems in interpretation. Below are printed a number of poems from widely separated periods, offering a variety of kinds and levels of difficulty for the reader. Chaucer's fourteenth-century masterpiece, *The Canterbury Tales*, presents a surface difficulty for modern readers—the language changes of five hundred years. This barrier can be overcome by learning a few obsolete words and by reading the lines aloud, pronouncing every syllable (including the final *e*) just as the spelling indicates. The seventeenth-century poems, George Herbert's "The Pulley" and Andrew Marvell's "The Garden," require insight into religious allegory and some attention to linguistic levity and verbal play, particularly punning and ingeniously extended comparisons that stretch the language to its limits (see the discussion of metaphysical poetry in Chapter 2, pp. 86–88). Two nineteenth-century poems, Ralph Waldo Emerson's "The Sphinx" and Percy Bysshe Shelley's "To a Skylark," demand some insight into New England transcendentalism and some understanding of Romantic Platonic idealism; in addition, they call for comprehension of their intricate symbolism. The two modern poems present two kinds of difficulties: Wallace Stevens' "Thirteen Ways of Looking at a Blackbird" is understandable in its separate details but puzzling as to its total meaning; Hart Crane's "To Brooklyn Bridge" is clearer in its total meaning than in its individual phrases and clauses. Taking a cue from the Stevens' title, we might try looking at all these poems in a number of different ways to see how much relevant and valid meaning we can discover.

PROLOGUE TO *THE CANTERBURY TALES*

Whan that Aprille with hise shoures soote [1]
The droghte of March hath perced to the roote,
And bathed every veyne in swich licour [2]
Of which vertu engendred is the flour;
Whan Zephirus eek with his swete breeth   5
Inspired hath in every holt and heeth
The tendre croppes, and the yonge sonne
Hath in the Ram his halfe cours yronne;
And smale foweles maken melodye,
That slepen al the nyght with open eye—   10
So priketh hem nature in hir corages;
Thanne longen folk to goon on pilgrimages,
And palmeres [3] for to seken straunge strondes
To ferne halwes,[4] kowthe in sondry londes;
And specially from every shires ende   15
Of Engelond to Caunterbury they wende,
The hooly, blisful martir for to seke
That hem hath holpen whan that they were seeke.

· · · · · · · · · · · ·

GEOFFREY CHAUCER (*1340–1400*)

[1] *soote* sweet   [2] *licour* moisture   [3] *palmeres* pilgrims   [4] *halwes* shrines

1. These introductory lines merely give the setting for later character sketches, dialogues, and stories. State exactly the setting, the time, the situation. 2. What details help to establish a tone of eagerness and expectation? 3. What parts do spring and religious devotion play in the pilgrimage?

THE PULLEY

When God at first made man,
Having a glass of blessings standing by,
Let us, said he, pour on him all we can.
Let the world's riches, which dispersèd lie,
    Contract into a span.   5

So strength first made a way,
Then beauty flowed, then wisdom, honor, pleasure.
When almost all was out, God made a stay,
Perceiving that alone of all his treasure
    Rest in the bottom lay.   10

For if I should, said he,
Bestow this jewel also on my creature,
He would adore my gifts instead of me,
And rest in nature, not the God of nature;
    So both should losers be.   15

Yet let him keep the rest,
But keep them with repining restlessness.
Let him be rich and weary, that at least,
If goodness lead him not, yet weariness
    May toss him to my breast.   20

GEORGE HERBERT (*1593–1633*)

1. Show how the "glass" introduced in line 2 is used consistently throughout. 2. Show how the poem turns on a pun. Who is the speaker in the poem and what is the effect of his punning? 3. How is the title related to the poem? 4. Compare this poem with Henry Vaughan's "The World": both are religious but the wit of the language play gives a special tone to "The Pulley."

THE GARDEN

How vainly men themselves amaze
To win the palm, the oak, or bays,
And their uncessant labors see

Crowned from some single herb or tree,
Whose short and narrow vergèd shade   5
Does prudently their toils upbraid;
While all flowers and all trees do close
To weave the garlands of repose.

Fair quiet, have I found thee here,
And innocence, thy sister dear!   10
Mistaken long, I sought you then
In busy companies of men;
Your sacred plants, if here below,
Only among the plants will grow.
Society is all but rude,   15
To this delicious solitude.

No white nor red was ever seen
So am'rous as this lovely green.
Fond lovers, cruel as their flame,
Cut in these trees their mistress' name;   20
Little, alas, they know or heed
How far these beauties hers exceed!
Fair trees! wheres'e'er your barks I wound,
No name shall but your own be found.

When we have run our passion's heat,   25
Love hither makes his best retreat.
The gods that mortal beauty chase,
Still in a tree did end their race:
Apollo hunted Daphne so,
Only that she might laurel grow;   30
And Pan did after Syrinx speed,
Not as a nymph, but for a reed.

What wond'rous life is this I lead!
Ripe apples drop about my head;
The luscious clusters of the vine   35
Upon my mouth do crush their wine;
The nectarine and curious peach
Into my hands themselves do reach;
Stumbling on melons as I pass,
Insnared with flowers, I fall on grass.   40

Meanwhile the mind from pleasure less
Withdraws into its happiness;
The mind, that ocean where each kind
Does straight its own resemblance find,

Yet it creates, transcending these,   45
Far other worlds and other seas,
Annihilating all that's made
To a green thought in a green shade.

Here at the fountain's sliding foot,
Or at some fruit-tree's mossy root,   50
Casting the body's vest aside,
My soul into the boughs does glide;
There like a bird it sits and sings,
Then whets, then combs its silver wings;
And till prepared for longer flight,   55
Waves in its plumes the various light.

Such was that happy garden-state,
While man there walked without a mate;
After a place so pure and sweet,
What other help could yet be meet!   60
But 'twas beyond a mortal's share
To wander solitary there;
Two paradises 'twere, in one,
To live in paradise alone.

How well the skillful gard'ner drew   65
Of flowers and herbs this dial new,
Where, from above, the milder sun
Does through a fragrant zodiac run;
And as it works, th' industrious bee
Computes its time as well as we.   70
How could such sweet and wholesome hours
Be reckoned but with herbs and flowers?

ANDREW MARVELL (*1621–1678*)

1. What is the paradox posed in the opening stanza? 2. What is the "green thought" in the last line of stanza six (lines 41–48)? 3. What are the two paradises in line 63? 4. Can you reconstruct the kind of life the speaker had in society from his meditation in his garden? *Identify:* Apollo, Daphne, Pan, Syrinx.

THE SPHINX

The Sphinx is drowsy,
    Her wings are furled:
Her ear is heavy,
    She broods on the world.

"Who'll tell me my secret,   5
     The ages have kept?—
I awaited the seer
     While they slumbered and slept:—

"The fate of the man-child,
     The meaning of man;   10
Known fruit of the unknown;
     Daedalian plan;
Out of sleeping a waking,
     Out of waking a sleep;
Life death overtaking;   15
     Deep underneath deep?

"Erect as a sunbeam,
     Upspringeth the palm;
The elephant browses,
     Undaunted and calm;   20
In beautiful motion
     The thrush plies his wings;
Kind leaves of his covert,
     Your silence he sings.

"The waves, unashamèd,   25
     In difference sweet,
Play glad with the breezes,
     Old playfellows meet;
The journeying atoms,
     Primordial wholes,   30
Firmly draw, firmly drive,
     By their animate poles.

"Sea, earth, air, sound, silence,
     Plant, quadruped, bird,
By one music enchanted,   35
     One deity stirred,—
Each the other adorning,
     Accompany still;
Night veileth the morning,
     The vapor the hill.   40

"The babe by its mother
     Lies bathèd in joy;
Glide its hours uncounted,—
     The sun is its toy;
Shines the peace of all being,   45
     Without cloud, in its eyes;

And the sum of the world
  In soft miniature lies.

"But man crouches and blushes,
  Absconds and conceals;   50
He creepeth and peepeth,
  He palters and steals;
Infirm, melancholy,
  Jealous glancing around,
An oaf, an accomplice,   55
  He poisons the ground.

"Out spoke the great mother,
  Beholding his fear;—
At the sound of her accents
  Cold shuddered the sphere:—   60
'Who has drugged my boy's cup?
  Who has mixed my boy's bread?
Who, with sadness and madness,
  Has turned my child's head?' "

I heard a poet answer   65
  Aloud and cheerfully,
"Say on, sweet Sphinx! thy dirges
  Are pleasant songs to me.
Deep love lieth under
  These pictures of time;   70
They fade in the light of
  Their meaning sublime.

"The fiend that man harries
  Is love of the Best;
Yawns the pit of the Dragon,   75
  Lit by rays from the Blest.
The Lethe of Nature
  Can't trance him again,
Whose soul sees the perfect,
  Which his eyes seek in vain.   80

"To vision profounder,
  Man's spirit must dive;
His aye-rolling orb
  At no goal will arrive;
The heavens that now draw him   85
  With sweetness untold,
Once found,—for new heavens,
  He spurneth the old.

"Pride ruined the angels,
    Their shame them restores;   90
Lurks the joy that is sweetest
    In stings of remorse.
Have I a lover
    Who is noble and free?—
I would he were nobler   95
    Than to love me.

"Eterne alternation
    And follows, now flies;
And under pain, pleasure,—
    Under pleasure, pain lies.   100
Love works at the centre,
    Heart-heaving alway;
Forth speed the strong pulses
    To the borders of day.

"Dull Sphinx, Jove keep thy five wits;   105
    Thy sight is growing blear;
Rue, myrrh and cummin for the Sphinx,
    Her muddy eyes to clear!"
The old Sphinx bit her thick lip,—
    Said, "Who taught thee me to name?   110
I am thy spirit, yoke-fellow;
    Of thine eye I am eyebeam.

"Thou art the unanswered question;
    Couldst see thy proper eye,
Alway it asketh, asketh;   115
    And each answer is a lie.
So take thy quest through nature,
    It through thousand natures ply;
Ask on, thou clothed eternity;
    Time is the false reply."   120

Uprose the merry Sphinx,
    And crouched no more in stone;
She melted into purple cloud,
    She silvered in the moon;
She spired into a yellow flame;   125
    She flowered in blossoms red;
She flowed into a foaming wave:
    She stood Monadnoc's head.

Thorough a thousand voices
    Spoke the universal dame;   130

"Who telleth one of my meanings
Is master of all I am."

RALPH WALDO EMERSON (*1803–1882*)

1. What is the question posed by the sphinx? What is the nature of the poet's answer? And what does the reply of the sphinx signify? 2. Readers have always been teased by the meaning of this poem. Emerson wrote in his notebooks (1859): "I have often been asked the meaning of the 'Sphinx.' It is this,—The perception of identity unites all things and explains one by another, and the most rare and strange is equally facile as the most common. But if the mind live only in particulars, and see only differences (wanting the power to see the whole—all in each), then the world addresses to this mind a question it cannot answer, and each new fact tears it in pieces, and it is vanquished by the distracting variety." How may this explanation be related to the details and drama of the poem?

TO A SKYLARK

Hail to thee, blithe Spirit!
   Bird thou never wert,
That from Heaven, or near it,
   Pourest thy full heart
In profuse strains of unpremeditated art.   5

Higher still and higher
   From the earth thou springest
Like a cloud of fire;
   The blue deep thou wingest,
And singing still dost soar, and soaring ever singest.   10

In the golden lightning
   Of the sunken sun,
O'er which clouds are bright'ning,
   Thou dost float and run;
Like an unbodied joy whose race is just begun.   15

The pale purple even
   Melts around thy flight;
Like a star of Heaven
   In the broad daylight
Thou art unseen, but yet I hear thy shrill delight,   20

Keen as are the arrows
   Of that silver sphere,

Whose intense lamp narrows
  In the white dawn clear,
Until we hardly see—we feel that it is there.   25

All the earth and air
  With thy voice is loud,
As, when night is bare,
  From one lonely cloud
The moon rains out her beams, and Heaven is overflowed.   30

What thou art we know not;
  What is most like thee?
From rainbow clouds there flow not
  Drops so bright to see
As from thy presence showers a rain of melody.   35

Like a Poet hidden
  In the light of thought,
Singing hymns unbidden,
  Till the world is wrought
To sympathy with hopes and fears it heeded not: 40

Like a high-born maiden
  In a palace-tower,
Soothing her love-laden
  Soul in secret hour
With music sweet as love, which overflows her bower: 45

Like a glow-worm golden
  In a dell of dew,
Scattering unbeholden
  Its aëreal hue
Among the flowers and grass, which screen it from the view!   50

Like a rose embowered
  In its own green leaves,
By warm winds deflowered,
  Till the scent it gives
Makes faint with too much sweet those heavy-wingèd thieves: 55

Sound of vernal showers
  On the twinkling grass,
Rain-awakened flowers,
  All that ever was
Joyous, and clear, and fresh, thy music doth surpass: 60

Teach us, Sprite or Bird,
   What sweet thoughts are thine:
I have never heard
   Praise of love or wine
That panted forth a flood of rapture so divine.   65

Chorus Hymeneal,
   Or triumphal chaunt,
Matched with thine, would be all
   But an empty vaunt,
A thing wherein we feel there is some hidden want.   70

What objects are the fountains
   Of thy happy strain?
What fields, or waves, or mountains?
   What shapes of sky or plain?
What love of thine own kind? what ignorance of pain?   75

With thy clear keen joyance
   Languor cannot be:
Shadow of annoyance
   Never came near thee:
Thou lovest—but ne'er knew love's sad satiety.   80

Waking or asleep,
   Thou of death must deem
Things more true and deep
   Than we mortals dream,
Or how could thy notes flow in such a crystal stream?   85

We look before and after,
   And pine for what is not:
Our sincerest laughter
   With some pain is fraught;
Our sweetest songs are those that tell of saddest thought.   90

Yet if we could scorn
   Hate, and pride, and fear;
If we were things born
   Not to shed a tear,
I know not how thy joy we ever should come near.   95

Better than all measures
   Of delightful sound,
Better than all treasures
   That in books are found,
Thy skill to poet were, thou scorner of the ground!   100

Teach me half the gladness
  That thy brain must know,
Such harmonious madness
  From my lips would flow
The world should listen then—as I am listening now.   105

PERCY BYSSHE SHELLEY (*1792–1822*)

1. What does the bird symbolize for the speaker? 2. Lines 86–90 are widely quoted. How are they prepared for and related to their context? 3. Compare this poem with William Cullen Bryant's "To a Waterfowl." How do the birds of the two poems differ as symbols?

THIRTEEN WAYS OF LOOKING AT A BLACKBIRD

1

Among twenty snowy mountains,
The only moving thing
Was the eye of the blackbird.

2

I was of three minds,
Like a tree   5
In which there are three blackbirds.

3

The blackbird whirled in the autumn winds.
It was a small part of the pantomime.

4

A man and a woman
Are one.   10
A man and a woman and a blackbird
Are one.

5

I do not know which to prefer,
The beauty of inflections
Or the beauty of innuendoes,   15
The blackbird whistling
Or just after.

6

Icicles filled the long window
With barbaric glass.

The shadow of the blackbird   20
Crossed it, to and fro.
The mood
Traced in the shadow
An indecipherable cause.

7

O thin men of Haddam,   25
Why do you imagine golden birds?
Do you not see how the blackbird
Walks around the feet
Of the women about you?

8

I know noble accents   30
And lucid, inescapable rhythms;
But I know, too,
That the blackbird is involved
In what I know.

9

When the blackbird flew out of sight,   35
It marked the edge
Of one of many circles.

10

At the sight of blackbirds
Flying in a green light,
Even the bawds of euphony   40
Would cry out sharply.

11

He rode over Connecticut
In a glass coach.
Once, a fear pierced him,
In that he mistook   45
The shadow of his equipage
For blackbirds.

12

The river is moving.
The blackbird must be flying.

13

It was evening all afternoon.   50
It was snowing
And it was going to snow.
The blackbird sat
In the cedar-limbs.

WALLACE STEVENS (*1879–1955*)

1. Stevens concludes his poem "Of Modern Poetry":

It must
Be the finding of a satisfaction, and may
Be of a man skating, a woman dancing, a woman
Combing. The poem of the act of the mind.

For Stevens, modern poetry, *his* poetry, seems to be "The poem of the
mind in the act of finding/ What will suffice." How do these statements
suggest a special, nonrational way of reading Stevens' poems? 2. Show
how the thirteen stanzas of "Looking at a Blackbird" are sharply etched
examples of intense imaginative perception. 3. Explore the possible
interrelation of these stanzas. Could they be scrambled, or do they
have some order, obvious or latent? 4. Does the blackbird develop as a
symbol as does Shelley's skylark? Or is it something more than a mere
bird but not so rigid as a symbol?

TO BROOKLYN BRIDGE

How many dawns, chill from his rippling rest
The seagull's wings shall dip and pivot him,
Shedding white rings of tumult, building high
Over the chained bay waters Liberty—

Then, with inviolate curve, forsake our eyes   5
As apparitional as sails that cross
Some page of figures to be filed away;
—Till elevators drop us from our day . . .

I think of cinemas, panoramic sleights
With multitudes bent toward some flashing scene   10
Never disclosed, but hastened to again,
Foretold to other eyes on the same screen;

And Thee, across the harbor, silver-paced
As though the sun took step of thee, yet left
Some motion ever unspent in thy stride,—   15
Implicitly thy freedom staying thee!

Out of some subway scuttle, cell or loft
A bedlamite speeds to thy parapets,
Tilting there momently, shrill shirt ballooning,
A jest falls from the speechless caravan.   20

Down Wall, from girder into street noon leaks,
A rip-tooth of the sky's acetylene;
All afternoon the cloud-flown derricks turn . . .
Thy cables breathe the North Atlantic still.

And obscure as that heaven of the Jews,   25
Thy guerdon . . . Accolade thou dost bestow
Of anonymity time cannot raise:
Vibrant reprieve and pardon thou dost show.

O harp and altar, of the fury fused,
(How could mere toil align thy choiring strings!)   30
Terrific threshold of the prophet's pledge,
Prayer of pariah, and the lover's cry,—

Again the traffic lights that skim thy swift
Unfractioned idiom, immaculate sigh of stars,
Beading thy path—condense eternity: 35
And we have seen night lifted in thine arms.

Under thy shadow by the piers I waited;
Only in darkness is thy shadow clear.
The City's fiery parcels all undone,
Already snow submerges an iron year . . .   40

O Sleepless as the river under thee,
Vaulting the sea, the prairies' dreaming sod,
Unto us lowliest sometime sweep, descend
And of the curveship lend a myth to God.

HART CRANE (*1899–1932*)

This poem is addressed to Brooklyn Bridge, a kind of invocation suggesting that the bridge is to fill the role of a muse (the poem stands at
the beginning of Crane's masterpiece, *The Bridge*). 1. Trace the progression of the time of day through the poem, and show the various
roles of the bridge. 2. In line 34, what are some possible meanings of
"unfractioned idiom"? 3. What is meant, in the last stanza, by the
speaker's request of the sleepless bridge that it "lend a myth to God"?
4. Compare the symbolism of the bridge in this poem with that of the
ferry in Walt Whitman's "Crossing Brooklyn Ferry."

VALUE JUDGMENT

In the reading of poetry, the final act of judgment is the value judgment, the consideration as to whether a particular poem is good or bad. Actually, the two categories are misleading: our vocabulary is deficient in that it does not supply a variety of terms that would allow for many levels of success and many kinds of failure. It is the mark of the experienced critic to avoid clumsy and inept value-terms and to discover those qualifications and extensions, reservations and expansions, which ferret out the unique success or failure, partial or total, of each individual poem.

In making value judgments, the reader has a large measure of assistance from time, the severest and most impersonal of critics. Time plays a large role in sifting and sorting through all art, separating the lasting from the ephemeral, frequently reversing an age's biased evaluation of its own poets. But time in this role is nothing more than the cumulative and complexly interrelated judgments of readers and critics through succeeding periods. Its authority comes from its massiveness and weight, but its methods are essentially no different from those of the individual critic.

The student who is just starting the serious study of poetry is usually confronted with an anthology filled with the best poetry in the English and American tradition. He seldom sees a truly bad poem. If he is a diligent seeker, however, he does not have to look far—no farther, indeed, than the local newspaper, which usually carries a daily "inspirational" or "patriotic" poem. Newspaper versifiers are generally bad poets who never write any good poetry, even by accident. The anthologies are filled with good poets who occasionally turned out bad poems. Henry Wadsworth Longfellow no longer has the reputation he once had, though some of his poems, such as his sonnets, are still considered first-rate. A Longfellow poem that was once universally admired now serves frequently as an example of poetry at its weakest:

A PSALM OF LIFE

Tell me not, in mournful numbers,
   Life is but an empty dream!—
For the soul is dead that slumbers,
   And things are not what they seem.

Life is real! Life is earnest!   5
  And the grave is not its goal;
Dust thou art, to dust returnest,
  Was not spoken of the soul.

Not enjoyment, and not sorrow,
  Is our destined end or way;   10
But to act, that each to-morrow
  Find us farther than to-day.

Art is long, and Time is fleeting,
  And our hearts, though stout and brave,
Still, like muffled drums, are beating   15
  Funeral marches to the grave.

In the world's broad field of battle,
  In the bivouac of Life,
Be not like dumb, driven cattle!
  Be a hero in the strife!   20

Trust no Future, howe'er pleasant!
  Let the dead Past bury its dead!
Act,—act in the living Present!
  Heart within, and God o'erhead!

Lives of great men all remind us   25
  We can make our lives sublime,
And, departing, leave behind us
  Footprints on the sands of time;

Footprints, that perhaps another,
  Sailing o'er life's solemn main,   30
A forlorn and shipwrecked brother,
  Seeing, shall take heart again.

Let us, then, be up and doing,
  With a heart for any fate;
Still achieving, still pursuing,   35
  Learn to labor and to wait.

HENRY WADSWORTH LONGFELLOW (*1807–1882*)

Interpretation of this poem presents a number of difficulties. A
slumbering soul is said to be a dead soul in the first stanza, yet the
second asserts that souls cannot die. In the second stanza, it is
asserted that the grave is not the goal of life. Yet in the fourth

stanza we are told that our hearts are beating "funeral marches to the grave." In the fifth stanza we are asked to envision "dumb, driven cattle" on, of all places, a field of battle. And in the seventh stanza we are given footprints in sand (usually washed away within a few hours) as a token of a great man's lasting mark that will guide others who come after. Once the reader has worked through all these difficulties, put down here at random, he might ponder what "real" and "earnest" mean when the poet cries out "Life is real! Life is earnest!" He may, indeed, have encountered impenetrable obscurities!

Lest Longfellow seem a special case, however, let us look at another poet's indiscretion. In the same year that he wrote one of his best works, "To a Skylark," Percy Bysshe Shelley wrote the following poem:

DEATH

I

Death is here and death is there,
Death is busy everywhere,
All around, within, beneath,
Above is death—and we are death.

II

Death has set his mark and seal   5
On all we are and all we feel,
On all we know and all we fear,

. . . .

III

First our pleasures die—and then
Our hopes, and then our fears—and when   10
These are dead, the debt is due,
Dust claims dust—and we die too.

IV

All things that we love and cherish,
Like ourselves must fade and perish;
Such is our rude mortal lot—   15
Love itself would, did they not.

PERCY BYSSHE SHELLEY (*1792–1822*)

We do not know what has become of the last line of the second stanza, but we may rest assured that its loss will not plunge the world into grief. It is impossible to read the opening stanza without lapsing into a singsong, bumpily merry rhythm. And this joyful, juvenile meter, coupled with the nursery-rhyme level of language (as exemplified in "here," "there," and "everywhere"), seems spectacularly inappropriate to the subject of death. Indeed, the poem opens on such a jarring, incongruous note that the reader might well expect his leg is being pulled, but by the last stanza he realizes that the poet has been deadly serious—and has seriously failed. The poem consists rather largely of direct statement rather than experience, of assertion rather than drama, and fails to involve the reader or to engage his imagination.

Much more frequent for the serious reader than sorting good from bad poems, however, will be the task of discovering the redeeming qualities which have caused an otherwise weak poem to survive or of discovering the defects that mar an otherwise fine poem. As we move from the black and white of extreme contrasts into this "gray" area, it is not surprising that argument becomes more intense and opinion more violent. Such are the results wherever answers are provisional and conclusions tentative. But difficulty and uncertainty are the rule, not the exception, in most rewarding experiences of life, and should not frighten one from the attempt to make judgments. Indeed it is the ability to be intelligent in just such areas that is the mark of the educated man. Anyone can tell black from white, but it takes a cultivated sight to detect the subtle shadings that distinguish one gray from another.

Specific approaches to poems and methods of analysis are dealt with in the succeeding chapter. But we might, before adopting any methodology, turn a fresh and uncommitted eye on a few poems for evaluation. And since Longfellow and Shelley have furnished examples of bad poems, it is perhaps only fair to begin by examining two of their more successful poems. Is it possible to apply the criteria used in describing the failure of "A Psalm of Life" and "Death" to two of their admired poems, "Chaucer" and "Ozymandias," in order to get at the quality and measure of their success? As we noted a lack of harmony among the various vital elements in the one instance, can we point to the harmonious working together of the elements in the other? And these two sonnets are followed by additional poems, which, though not masterpieces, still have redeeming qualities that make them memorable and worthy of attention. Sidney Lanier's "Song of the Chattahoochee" is far from the highest levels of excellence, but there is nevertheless an element in it that commands respect: the brilliant technical manipulation of the sounds in relation to meaning. Edgar Allan Poe's "Ulalume" has inspired controversy as to both its meaning and its value; can we take what it offers as a mood-poem and a technical tour de force and be satisfied with nothing more? Dante Gabriel Rossetti's "The Blessed Damozel" seems a strange combination of vagueness and vividness; does its striking imagery underscore or dominate the poem's feeling? Rudyard Kipling's "Danny Deever" is clearly limited in its intention and depth; but what elements of refrain and rhythm make reading it a memorable experience? Perhaps in looking at these poems we shall raise more questions than we can answer. But it is the beginning of wisdom to discover and pose the relevant questions that ultimately lead to meaningful answers.

For an example of a critical essay which analyzes both the virtues and faults of a poem, see Charles R. Anderson on Emily Dickinson's "My Life Had Stood—a Loaded Gun," pp. 618–621.

CHAUCER

An old man in a lodge within a park;
The chamber walls depicted all around
With portraitures of huntsman, hawk, and hound,
And the hurt deer. He listeneth to the lark,
Whose song comes with the sunshine through the dark   5
Of painted glass in leaden lattice bound;
He listened and he laugheth at the sound,
Then writeth in a book like any clerk.
He is the poet of the dawn, who wrote
The Canterbury Tales, and his old age   10
Made beautiful with song; and as I read
I hear the crowing cock, I hear the note
Of lark and linnet, and from every page
Rise odors of ploughed field or flowery mead.

HENRY WADSWORTH LONGFELLOW (*1807–1882*)

1. How do the first eight lines differ from the last six in point of view?
2. How do the details combine to give a vivid impression of Chaucer as a writer? 3. Do you see any defects?

OZYMANDIAS

I met a traveller from an antique land
Who said: Two vast and trunkless legs of stone
Stand in the desert . . . Near them, on the sand,
Half sunk, a shattered visage lies, whose frown,
And wrinkled lip, and sneer of cold command,   5
Tell that its sculptor well those passions read
Which yet survive (stamped on these lifeless things),
The hand that mocked them and the heart that fed:
And on the pedestal these words appear:
"My name is Ozymandias, king of kings: 10
Look on my works, ye Mighty, and despair!"
Nothing beside remains. Round the decay
Of that colossal wreck, boundless and bare
The lone and level sands stretch far away.

PERCY BYSSHE SHELLEY (*1792–1822*)

1. Does the structure of this poem underscore its tone? Note the emphasis given to the words ending the last four lines. 2. What kind of a man was Ozymandias? Is his characterization convincing or does it tend to be a stereotype? Would the theme of the poem be altered radically if Ozymandias were presented as a benevolent or enigmatic ruler?

SONG OF THE CHATTAHOOCHEE

Out of the hills of Habersham,
Down the valleys of Hall,
I hurry amain to reach the plain,
Run the rapid and leap the fall,
Split at the rock and together again,   5
Accept my bed, or narrow or wide,
And flee from folly on every side
With a lover's pain to attain the plain
Far from the hills of Habersham,
Far from the valleys of Hall.   10

All down the hills of Habersham,
All through the valleys of Hall,

The rushes cried *Abide, abide,*
The willful waterweeds held me thrall,
The laving laurel turned my tide, 15
The ferns and the fondling grass said *Stay,*
The dewberry dipped for to work delay,
And the little reeds sighed *Abide, abide,*
    Here in the hills of Habersham,
    Here in the valleys of Hall. 20

High o'er the hills of Habersham,
    Veiling the valleys of Hall,
The hickory told me manifold
Fair tales of shade, the poplar tall
Wrought me her shadowy self to hold, 25
The chestnut, the oak, the walnut, the pine,
Overleaning, with flickering meaning and sign,
Said, *Pass not, so cold, these manifold*
    Deep shades of the hills of Habersham,
    These glades in the valleys of Hall. 30

And oft in the hills of Habersham,
    And oft in the valleys of Hall,
The white quartz shone, and the smooth brook-stone
Did bar me of passage with friendly brawl,
And many a luminous jewel lone 35
—Crystals clear or a-cloud with mist,
Ruby, garnet and amethyst—
Made lures with the lights of streaming stone
    In the clefts of the hills of Habersham,
    In the beds of the valleys of Hall. 40

But oh, not the hills of Habersham,
    And oh, not the valleys of Hall
Avail: I am fain for to water the plain.
Downward the voices of Duty call—
Downward, to toil and be mixed with the main, 45
The dry fields burn, and the mills are to turn,
And a myriad flowers mortally yearn,
And the lordly main from beyond the plain
    Calls o'er the hills of Habersham,
    Calls through the valleys of Hall. 50

SIDNEY LANIER (*1842–1881*)

1. Analyze the organization of the sounds of these stanzas to discover
how the impression of running water is created. 2. Read the poem

carefully for its allegorical meaning, as suggested by the "voices of Duty" of the last stanza. 3. Is the poem as subtle in the handling of its theme as in its technical execution?

ULALUME

The skies they were ashen and sober;
　　The leaves they were crispèd and sere—
　　The leaves they were withering and sere:
It was night, in the lonesome October
　　Of my most immemorial year:　　　　　　　　　　5
It was hard by the dim lake of Auber,
　　In the misty mid region of Weir—
It was down by the dank tarn of Auber,
　　In the ghoul-haunted woodland of Weir.

Here once, through an alley Titanic,　　　　　　　10
　　Of cypress, I roamed with my Soul—
　　Of cypress, with Psyche, my Soul.
These were days when my heart was volcanic
　　As the scoriac rivers that roll—
　　As the lavas that restlessly roll　　　　　　　15
Their sulphurous currents down Yaanek
　　In the ultimate climes of the Pole—
That groan as they roll down Mount Yaanek
　　In the realms of the Boreal Pole.

Our talk had been serious and sober,　　　　　　20
　　But our thoughts they were palsied and sere—
　　Our memories were treacherous and sere;
For we knew not the month was October,
　　And we marked not the night of the year
　　(Ah, night of all nights in the year!)—　　　　25
We noted not the dim lake of Auber
　　(Though once we have journeyed down here)—
We remembered not the dank tarn of Auber,
　　Nor the ghoul-haunted woodland of Weir.

And now, as the night was senescent　　　　　　30
　　And star-dials pointed to morn—
　　As the star-dials hinted of morn—
At the end of our path a liquescent
　　And nebulous lustre was born,
Out of which a miraculous crescent　　　　　　35
　　Arose with a duplicate horn—

Astarte's bediamonded crescent
   Distinct with its duplicate horn.

And I said: "She is warmer than Dian;
   She rolls through an ether of sighs— 40
   She revels in a region of sighs.
She has seen that the tears are not dry on
   These cheeks, where the worm never dies,
And has come past the stars of the Lion,
   To point us the path to the skies— 45
   To the Lethean peace of the skies—
Come up, in despite of the Lion,
   To shine on us with her bright eyes—
Come up through the lair of the Lion,
   With love in her luminous eyes." 50

But Psyche, uplifting her finger,
   Said: "Sadly this star I mistrust—
   Her pallor I strangely mistrust:
Ah, hasten!—ah, let us not linger!
   Ah, fly!—let us fly!—for we must." 55
In terror she spoke, letting sink her
   Wings till they trailed in the dust—
In agony sobbed, letting sink her
   Plumes till they trailed in the dust—
   Till they sorrowfully trailed in the dust. 60

I replied: "This is nothing but dreaming:
   Let us on by this tremulous light!
   Let us bathe in this crystalline light!
Its Sibyllic splendor is beaming
   With Hope and in Beauty to-night:— 65
See!—it flickers up the sky through the night!
Ah, we safely may trust to its gleaming,
   And be sure it will lead us aright—
We safely may trust to a gleaming
   That cannot but guide us aright, 70
   Since it flickers up to Heaven through the night."

Thus I pacified Psyche and kissed her,
   And tempted her out of her gloom—
   And conquered her scruples and gloom;
And we passed to the end of the vista, 75
   But were stopped by the door of a tomb—
   By the door of a legended tomb;

And I said: "What is written, sweet sister,
  On the door of this legended tomb?"
  She replied—"Ulalume—Ulalume!—   80
  'Tis the vault of thy lost Ulalume!"

Then my heart it grew ashen and sober
  As the leaves that were crispèd and sere—
  As the leaves that were withering and sere;
And I cried: "It was surely October   85
  On *this* very night of last year
  That I journeyed—I journeyed down here!—
  That I brought a dread burden down here—
  On this night of all nights in the year,
  Ah, what demon has tempted me here?   90
Well I know, now, this dim lake of Auber—
  This misty mid region of Weir—
Well I know, now, this dank tarn of Auber,
  This ghoul-haunted woodland of Weir."

Said we, then—the two, then: "Ah, can it   95
  Have been that the woodlandish ghouls—
  The pitiful, the merciful ghouls—
To bar up our way and to ban it
  From the secret that lies in these wolds—
  From the thing that lies hidden in these wolds—   100
Have drawn up the spectre of a planet
  From the limbo of lunary souls—
This sinfully scintillant planet
  From the Hell of the planetary souls?"

EDGAR ALLAN POE (1809–1849)

1. In this poem Poe is trying to weave a web of tone-magic; analyze the sounds, the rhyme, and the rhythm; and speculate on how they relate to the peculiar effect the poem has when read aloud. 2. The poem seems to have an allegorical intent—can you work out any kind of consistent allegorical meaning? Try applying theories of modern psychology, concepts of the conscious and unconscious, to a psychological reading of the poem. 3. Does the last stanza seem to be unnecessary? (Poe did not always print it with the poem.)

THE BLESSED DAMOZEL

The blessed damozel leaned out
  From the gold bar of Heaven;

Her eyes were deeper than the depth
  Of waters stilled at even;
She had three lilies in her hand,   5
  And the stars in her hair were seven.

Her robe, ungirt from clasp to hem,
  No wrought flowers did adorn,
But a white rose of Mary's gift,
  For service meetly worn;   10
Her hair that lay along her back
  Was yellow like ripe corn.

Herseemed she scarce had been a day
  One of God's choristers;
The wonder was not yet quite gone   15
  From that still look of hers;
Albeit, to them she left, her day
  Had counted as ten years.

(To one it is ten years of years.
    . . . Yet now, here in this place,   20
Surely she leaned o'er me—her hair
  Fell all about my face. . . .
Nothing: the autumn-fall of leaves.
  The whole year sets apace.)

It was the rampart of God's house   25
  That she was standing on;
By God built over the sheer depth
  In which is Space begun;
So high, that looking downward thence
  She scarce could see the sun.   30

It lies in Heaven, across the flood
  Of ether, as a bridge.
Beneath, the tides of day and night
  With flame and darkness ridge
The void, as low as where this earth   35
  Spins like a fretful midge.

Around her, lovers, newly met
  'Mid deathless love's acclaims,
Spoke evermore among themselves,
  Their heart-remembered names;   40
And the souls mounting up to God,
  Went by her like thin flames.

And still she bowed herself and stooped
    Out of the circling charm;
Until her bosom must have made   45
    The bar she leaned on warm,
And the lilies lay as if asleep
    Along her bended arm.

From the fixed place of Heaven she saw
    Time like a pulse shake fierce   50
Through all the worlds. Her gaze still strove
    Within the gulf to pierce
Its path; and now she spoke as when
    The stars sang in their spheres.

The sun was gone now; the curled moon   55
    Was like a little feather
Fluttering far down the gulf; and now
    She spoke through the still weather.
Her voice was like the voice the stars
    Had when they sang together.   60

(Ah sweet! Even now, in that bird's song,
    Strove not her accents there,
Fain to be hearkened? When those bells
    Possessed the mid-day air,
Strove not her steps to reach my side   65
    Down all the echoing stair?)

"I wish that he were come to me,
    For he will come," she said.
"Have I not prayed in Heaven?—on earth,
    Lord, Lord, has he not prayed?   70
Are not two prayers a perfect strength?
    And shall I feel afraid?

"When round his head the aureole clings,
    And he is clothed in white,
I'll take his hand and go with him   75
    To the deep wells of light;
As unto a stream we will step down,
    And bathe there in God's sight.

"We two will stand beside that shrine,
    Occult, withheld, untrod,   80
Whose lamps are stirred continually
    With prayer sent up to God;

And see our old prayers granted, melt
  Each like a little cloud.

"We two will lie i' the shadow of   85
  That living mystic tree
Within whose secret growth the Dove
  Is sometimes felt to be.
While every leaf that His plumes touch
  Saith His Name audibly.   90

"And I myself will teach to him,
  I myself, lying so,
The songs I sing here; which his voice
  Shall pause in, hushed and slow,
And find some knowledge at each pause,   95
  Or some new thing to know."

(Alas! we two, we two, thou say'st!
  Yea, one wast thou with me
That once of old. But shall God lift
  To endless unity   100
The soul whose likeness with thy soul
  Was but its love for thee?)

"We two," she said, "will seek the groves
  Where the lady Mary is,
With her five handmaidens, whose names   105
  Are five sweet symphonies,
Cecily, Gertrude, Magdalen,
  Margaret and Rosalys.

"Circlewise sit they, with bound locks
  And foreheads garlanded;   110
Into the fine cloth white like flame
  Weaving the golden thread,
To fashion the birth-robes for them
  Who are just born, being dead.

"He shall fear, haply, and be dumb: 115
  Then will I lay my cheek
To his, and tell about our love,
  Not once abashed or weak:
And the dear Mother will approve
  My pride, and let me speak.   120

"Herself shall bring us, hand in hand,
  To Him round whom all souls

Kneel, the clear-ranged unnumbered heads
  Bowed with their aureoles:
And angels, meeting us, shall sing   125
  To their citherns and citoles.

"There will I ask of Christ the Lord
  Thus much for him and me:—
Only to live as once on earth
  With Love,—only to be,   130
As then awhile, for ever now
  Together, I and he."

She gazed, and listened, and then said,
  Less sad of speech than mild,—
"All this is when he comes." She ceased.   135
  The light thrilled towards her, filled
With angels in strong level flight.
  Her eyes prayed, and she smiled.

(I saw her smile.) But soon their path
  Was vague in distant spheres: 140
And then she cast her arms along
  The golden barriers,
And laid her face between her hands,
  And wept. (I heard her tears.)

DANTE GABRIEL ROSSETTI (1828–1882)

1. What is the basic situation in the poem? 2. Examine closely the imagery of the stanzas in which the blessed damozel imagines her lover's entry into heaven to be by her side: What kind of life does she envision them living? 3. Is the poem entirely persuasive in evoking the strong feelings in the reader that are expressed in the poem? 4. Are all of the stanzas equally effective, or are some lines marred by some slight clumsiness of execution (for example, line 45: "Until her bosom must have made")?

DANNY DEEVER

"What are the bugles blowin' for?" said Files-on-Parade.
"To turn you out, to turn you out," the Color-Sergeant said.
"What makes you look so white, so white?" said Files-on-Parade.
"I'm dreadin' what I've got to watch," the Color-Sergeant said.
  For they're hangin' Danny Deever, you can 'ear the Dead
    March play,   5

The regiment's in 'ollow square—they're hangin' him today;
They've taken of his buttons off an' cut his stripes away,
An' they're hangin' Danny Deever in the mornin'.

"What makes the rear-rank breathe so 'ard?" said Files-on-Parade.
"It's bitter cold, it's bitter cold," the Color-Sergeant said.   10
"What makes the front-rank man fall down?" says Files-on-Parade.
"A touch 'o sun, a touch 'o sun," the Color-Sergeant said.
    They are hangin' Danny Deever, they are marchin' of 'im
        round,
    They 'ave 'alted Danny Deever by 'is coffin on the ground;
    An' 'e'll swing in 'arf a minute for a sneakin' shootin' hound—
    O they're hanging' Danny Deever in the mornin'!   16

" 'Is cot was right-'and cot to mine," said Files-on-Parade.
" 'E's sleepin' out an' far to-night," the Color-Sergeant said.
"I've drunk 'is beer a score o' times," said Files-on-Parade.
" 'E's drinkin' bitter beer alone," the Color-Sergeant said.   20
    They are hangin' Danny Deever, you must mark 'im to 'is place,
    For 'e shot a comrade sleepin'—you must look 'im in the face;
    Nine 'undred of 'is county an' the regiment's disgrace,
    While they're hangin' Danny Deever in the mornin'.

"What's that so black agin the sun?" said Files-on-Parade.   25
"It's Danny fightin' 'ard for life," the Color-Sergeant said.
"What's that that whimpers over'ead?" said Files-on-Parade.
"It's Danny's soul that's passin' now," the Color-Sergeant said.
    For they're done with Danny Deever, you can 'ear the quickstep
        play,
    The regiment's in column, an' they're marchin' us away;   30
    Ho! the young recruits are shakin', an' they'll want their beer
        to-day,
    After hangin' Danny Deever in the mornin'.

                                    RUDYARD KIPLING (*1865–1936*)

1. How is this potentially sentimental subject rendered unsentimental?
Assess particularly the role of the refrain, the repetition, and the
rhythm. Danny's crime is covered and dismissed in one line in the third
stanza; why is not more made of it? 2. Compare the effect of the
sustained rhythmical pattern in this poem with that in Poe's "Ulalume."

CHAPTER 4
APPROACHES TO POEMS

AS we become increasingly aware of the many dimensions of poetry, we discover that there is a vast body of material written on the subject, on poets, and on individual poems. If we explore this secondary material, we quickly learn that there are many, many approaches to poems, and most of these paths lead to some lookout that presents a useful perspective. As poetry is multi-dimensional, so there are many kinds of understanding, and any approach that contributes to understanding has its own excuse for being.

Our gradual understanding and comprehension of a poem may be likened to our developing and deepening acquaintanceship with a person. The first stage in a friendship is usually our coming to know and appreciate a person as he is *in himself,* his characteristics, his individuality, his behavior—all of which help us to formulate some kind of judgment. Gradually our acquaintanceship might extend itself to a knowledge of the life, or biography, of the individual, and we have glimpses of his character or behavior at earlier ages. And finally, the acquaintanceship might deepen as we become familiar with the individual's parents, relatives, ancestry, the region of the country where he grew up, the cultural and social milieu which he unconsciously assimilated and which helped to make him what he presently is.

Our acquaintanceship with a poem might well develop through similar stages. First we might come to know the poem as it is in and of itself; and in doing so we might work out, unwritten or elaborately composed, such aids as a summary, a précis, a paraphrase, an explication, an exegesis, or a critical analysis. We might deepen our understanding by reviewing the life of the poem—

should we be so fortunate as to have earlier versions which the author worked out and subsequently abandoned. And, finally, we might broaden our understanding by viewing the poem in a context larger than itself, involving its author, its time, its milieu, its tradition. These perspectives on a poem might conveniently be grouped under two titles: "Poem in Profile" and "Poem in History."

POEM IN PROFILE

The only place to begin in the reading of poetry or the reading of a poet is with a single, isolated, independent poem. There is, indeed, no way of reading *a poet* or of reading *poetry* except through extensive reading of separate, individual poems. And each poem presents a unique set of critical problems. These points are worth emphasizing because they are easily forgotten in the impatience that is sometimes aroused by the prolonged examination of a single, simple poem. If we would know the geography of the landscape, we must study the hill, the lake, the meadow. If we would know the history of the century, we must read its days and hours.

A poem, as a work of art, proclaims to the world that it is independent, whole, and self-contained, and ready to meet the reader alone without assistance. The reader should seek an encounter with the poem without an alien presence. Both poem and reader hope that out of the lonely rendezvous will develop an intimacy that will last beyond the moment. If chill dominates warmth in the encounter, we may assume that one of the participants was unprepared.

There are a number of ways of talking about a poem on the terms it alone presents. On the very simplest level, we may write a *summary,* or *précis,* by reducing the meaning to its briefest prose statement. Such an exercise is obviously of limited value, precisely because it captures and preserves only the bare substance of what is said in the poem, its nonpoetic part. But the process has its value, not only in sharpening the understanding, but in compelling the imagination to entertain alternatives, however dreary, to the seemingly eternal and fixed words on the page. If nothing else, by its very cramped and faded reflection of the original, the summary surprises the eyes into seeing the real poem

anew. For example, read the following untitled poem by Emily
Dickinson:

> The Bustle in a House
> The Morning after Death
> Is solemnest of industries
> Enacted upon Earth,—
>
> The Sweeping up the Heart,   5
> And putting Love away
> We shall not want to use again
> Until Eternity.

A possible summary: One of the most difficult of all tasks in life
is the emotional adjustment following the loss through death
of someone close.

If a summary is like the bruised rind of an orange from which
all the golden juices have been squeezed, a *paraphrase* is like a
black-and-white photograph of a brilliant masterpiece of art. It
is a detailed prose restatement of the poem, longer than the summary (and sometimes longer than the poem), closely following the
original and attempting to convey as nearly as possible the full
meaning. The danger of judging a poem by a paraphrase would
parallel the danger of judging a masterpiece by a black-and-white,
slightly blurred reproduction. If such dangers are studiously
avoided, the paraphrase might well serve many valuable purposes,
among them the clarification of what appear to be vague or ambiguous passages—or it might make clear that the vagueness and
ambiguity are intentional. But above all, in its line-by-line prose
rendering of a poem, a paraphrase throws into bold relief the
brilliant poetic texture of the original. A paraphrase contributes
most when it demonstrates that it cannot compete with the original in splendor, but that it can make up for its dullness in its
fidelity, or accuracy. It cannot copy: it must be the same, yet different throughout. Emily Dickinson's poem might be paraphrased:
On the day after the death of a beloved relative, the soberest activity in the home (the soberest, in fact, in the world) is the dis-
position of the affections which have lost their object and which
will be superfluous until a spiritual reunion outside time is ef-
fected.

An *explication* (exegesis) does not try to embody or embrace
the entire poem, but clarifies with its explanations the opaque

passages or the intricate syntax. It gives a general idea, interprets selected passages, shows the function of details. Its danger is not that it might be substituted for the original (as with the summary or paraphrase), but that the poem itself might be lost or forgotten in all the attention given to its problems. Therefore, a good balance for the study of an explication is to go back and read the whole poem again. If the account has been good; if it has cleared up the metaphorical, linguistic, or intellectual difficulties; if it has revealed qualities not apparent in casual reading—then the experience of the poem will be more complete and vivid than before. The pleasure of the explication is to dart beams of light into the dark corners of the poem. Its great virtue is in brightening the corner where the reader is, if he happens to find himself enveloped in shadows or is even standing in his own shadow. But explication is pointless when it tells us what we already know. An explication of Emily Dickinson's poem would raise such questions as: How can a *bustle* in the home be described as *industry*? How can an industry be *enacted*? What is actually meant by *sweeping up the heart* and *putting love away*? What does the final word, *eternity,* mean in the context of the poem? Although some of these questions might be answered in the summary or paraphrase, they would not be the center of focus as they would in the explication.

These approaches to poems—summary, paraphrase, explication—have in common their willingness to leave the poem intact and indivisible, and their effort to comprehend or illuminate meaning. They concentrate on a close examination of the text of a poem. Explication, particularly, has been the method of what has been called the "new criticism," the work of critic-scholars who in recent years have developed the technique of studying a poem by detailed analysis of its language and imagery, and how they function within the given lines. This method may also be grouped with others more comprehensive and varied under the general term *critical analysis,* which suggests that the poem is studied analytically, with critical (or evaluative) conclusions.

Every thoughtful consideration of a poem involves in some way the process of *analysis,* or the careful examination of the whole and the definition of all the parts and their relationships. The intention of analysis is to answer the question: How does this poem, complete and self-contained, come to be what it is and do what it does; how do the parts come together to make this whole? Behind the face of the watch lie the delicately and intricately meshed parts, some of them microscopic, some of them nakedly visible, some moving rhythmically, some quietly supporting, all contributing to the shifting posture of the hands on the face. The analyst is interested in more than merely the hour or the minute. Although he wants to know the time, he wants even more to know of time's creation.

Before we study the ways of analysis, we need to look at one misconception about it. There is a romantic notion abroad that analysis destroys the object it would examine. "Why tear it apart?" some say. But we must emphasize not the act of "tearing apart" but the act of "coming to know"—as sharper glasses reveal the lines of a leaf or as friendship may grow deeper with knowledge. There is no need to murder a poem in order to display its parts; there is no need to kill it in order to discover its components. No doubt some poems have been mangled by clumsy critics. But a really good poem is made of the tough stuff of eternity and can survive many a massacre. Good poetic analysis is a kind of magic, the critic becoming a miniature creator; he takes apart the living poem, observes the very sources of life, and then, in a final creative act, restores the parts to a living whole, its vitality renewed. Through sympathetic insight and perception, the analyst rekindles and rejuvenates, seeks the springs of life only to set the streams flowing to the full again. The true analyst is not the Death-Deliverer but the Life-Bringer.

The first step in analysis is not the separation into parts but the comprehension of the whole. The watch must be known in its function of time-sayer before its mechanism will meaningfully reveal its intricate design. In an attempt to get at the whole of the Emily Dickinson poem, we might say: "The Bustle in a House" captures and evokes that sense of quiet grief following the death of someone near, an emotion neither profound nor shallow, but held in delicate and poignant balance between the keenly felt loss from the household and the assurance of ultimate spiritual reunion. This is one way of formulating what the poem is and does. Any such statement is likely to seem woefully inadequate, especially in view of the ungainliness of language in describing the subtleties of the emotions. Only the strategy of poetry can defeat the crudeness of language.

Once we have grasped the poem in its wholeness, we may profitably begin an exploration of the elements that have merged to make up its magnetism. No one can list all the possible parts of a poem: they are multitudinous, and in any specific poem, they are in unique arrangement. Each poem must, therefore, determine the nature of its own analysis. Perhaps in one poem the dominant component will be imagery or diction; while in another, the most striking element will be rhythm, or character, or action.

The analysis of Emily Dickinson's poem might proceed with an examination of the imagery, particularly the use throughout, after the reference in the opening line to the domestic "bustle" of a housekeeper's activities ("sweeping," "putting away"). An assessment might be made of the contribution of the slightly distorted rhyme of both stanzas (Death / Earth — away / Eternity) to the emotional tension central to the poem. Some consideration might be given to the stanzaic form which permits the emphasis of concluding the first stanza with "Earth," the last with "Eternity." The key juxtaposition of these words suggests that the progression or movement of the poem might well be defined and traced. These are only a few of the elements which affect and shape the total poem, making it what it uniquely is.

In the "critical" side of the critical analysis, judgment and evaluation are emphasized. Such criticism tries to draw conclusions about the success or failure of the poem, the kind of life it has, and the possibilities of its experience for those who read it. Easy criticism may begin with a personal preference, "I like this poem," or with a sweeping generalization, "This poem is wonderful." But such innocent statements usually bubble up from an unexamined and sometimes irrelevant response—perhaps a character in a poem reminds someone of his favorite aunt. Mature criticism must inevitably be involved with analysis, either intellectualized or intuitive. In effect, analysis and criticism may proceed simultaneously. It would, indeed, be difficult, in defining the relationship of an image to the rest of the poem, to avoid at the same time evaluating that relationship in an estimate of its contribution, its relevance or irrelevance. In Emily Dickinson's poem, for example, we may note not only the function and consistency of the housekeeping imagery but also how it relates to the poem's dominant tone of emotional restraint.

A critical analysis, then, as the words suggest, is merely a work of judgment and evaluation in which the conclusions are supported by close observations. In such a synthesis the critic has a good bit of latitude in formulating his judgment of a poem. He can demonstrate at length the way in which rhythm reinforces sense in Sidney Lanier's "Song of the Chattahoochee" (p. 142), but at the same time he can show how tarnished diction mars the emotional and thematic quality. He can explain how diction builds mood in Edgar Allan Poe's "Ulalume" (p. 144), but at the same time describe how the regularity of the rhythm gives a hollow ring to the poem's serious music. In short, in a critical analysis the critic may get at, without excessive oversimplification, the complex combination of strengths and weaknesses that make up most poems.

It is rare that commentary on a poem is strictly limited in form to a summary, paraphrase, explication, or critical analysis. The reader-turned-critic must let the poem speak to him with its individual voice, telling him what needs to be revealed or explored. While a summary may be sufficient in one instance, a critical analysis may be called for in another. And each study will be individual. Different poems demand different approaches. Some invite more comment and analysis than others, tempting the pedant to evaluate a poem by counting the words of its critics. It is nonsense, of course, to ignore a lucid poem because it needs no explication or to elevate an obscure verse because of the complexity of its analysis. But perhaps the most immediate danger is the substitution of the commentary for the verse, the prose for the poem. The final ritual act of any critical approach must be a return to the isolated and uncluttered poem, the criticism's only source of life, to participate again in its particularized-universalized experience.

Although the "Poem in Profile" offers many surfaces and shapes to the reader's view, there are still more and varied ways of seeing. One of these, which takes the reader back to the time of the poem's conception, yet not beyond its organic limits, is the poem's biography, the record of the several stages of its growth. Because of the many mysteries in and around the creative process, even the smallest glimpse of it cannot help being of some consequence to the genuinely curious. Reconstructing the complete life of a poem, however, is as difficult—indeed, as impossible—as reconstructing the complete life of a person. For some poems we have early versions, and sometimes some enlightening comment by the author. But lost forever are the versions that the poem went through before poet ever put pen to paper.

If we recognize the inevitable fragmentary quality of the "biographical" materials which survive for any individual poem, we shall necessarily be cautious in formulating from these materials any generalization about its growth or development. But we may analyze a poet's revisions and discover that they were made for many reasons: to clarify meaning, to strengthen metaphor, to improve rhythm, to sharpen language, or to harmonize sound. To view a poem in intermediate drafts is sometimes to see for the first time the particular problems of art and craft the poet confronted—and to observe the nature of his solutions. We have this privilege only in a limited number of cases; but it is worthwhile to look at an example or two, if for no other reason than to get over the impression we sometimes have that the poems we read somehow sprang to full-blown life just as they appear on the printed page. Some of our illusions may be amended, our conceptions corrected, when we know the difficulty the poet encountered and overcame in bringing a poem to full and independent life. It is important to see graphically that poetry is not all exhilaration and inspiration but also a large measure of trial and error, sweat and toil.

In the examples which follow, we observe Walt Whitman at work, going back to a poem some time after it was written, extracting a single metaphor, and composing an almost entirely new poem out of it; and we observe Emily Dickinson at work, changing words and phrases, polishing and tightening. In examining the early and finished versions, we should raise questions as to why the poet made the changes and whether they improved the poem. These questions will not have definitive answers, nor will the answers be of service to the poets; but the questions can bring into focus central problems of craft, and the answers, though speculative, can deepen the reader's awareness of the nature of poetry.

A NOISELESS PATIENT SPIDER

The Soul, reaching, throwing out for love,
As the spider, from some little promontory, throwing out filament
    after filament, tirelessly out of itself, that one at least may
    catch and form a link, a bridge, a connection
O I saw one passing along, saying hardly a word—yet full of love
    I detected him, by certain signs
O eyes wishfully turning! O silent eyes!
For then I thought of you oer the world   5
O latent oceans, fathomless oceans of love!
O waiting oceans of love! yearning and fervid! and of you sweet
    souls perhaps in the future, delicious and long:
But Dead, unknown on the earth—ungiven, dark here, unspoken,
    never born:
You fathomless latent souls of love—you pent and unknown
    oceans of love!

A noiseless patient spider,
I mark'd where on a little promontory it stood isolated,
Mark'd how to explore the vacant vast surrounding,
It launch'd forth filament, filament, filament, out of itself,
Ever unreeling them, ever tirelessly speeding them.   5

And you O my soul where you stand,
Surrounded, detached, in measureless oceans of space,
Ceaselessly musing, venturing, throwing, seeking the spheres to
    connect them,
Till the bridge you will need be form'd, till the ductile anchor
    hold,
Till the gossamer thread you fling catch somewhere, O my soul.   10

WALT WHITMAN (*1819–1892*)

POEM 609

1862 VERSION		1872 VERSION
I—Years had been—from Home—	1	I Years had been from Home
And now—before the Door—	2	And now before the Door

1862 VERSION		1872 VERSION
I dared not *open*—lest a face	3	I dared not *enter,* lest a face
I never saw before	4	I never saw before
Stare *vacant* into mine—	5	Stare *stolid* into mine (or "horrid")
And ask my Business there—	6	And ask my Business there—
My Business—*just* a Life I left—	7	"My Business *but* a Life I left
Was such—*still dwelling* there?	8	Was such *remaining* there?"
I *fumbled at my nerve*—	9	I *leaned upon the Awe*—
I *scanned the Windows o'er*—	10	I *lingered with Before*—
The *Silence*—like an Ocean rolled—	11	The *Second* like an Ocean rolled
And broke against my Ear—	12	And broke against my ear—
I laughed a *Wooden* laugh—	13	I laughed a *crumbling* Laugh
That I—could fear a Door—	14	That I could fear a Door
Who *Danger—and the Dead—had faced*—	15	Who *Consternation compassed*
But never *shook*—before—	16	And never *winced* before.
I fitted to the Latch—*my Hand*—	17	I fitted to the Latch
With trembling care—	18	*My Hand,* with trembling care
Lest back the Awful Door should spring—	19	Lest back the awful Door should spring
And leave me—in the Floor—	20	And leave me in the Floor—
I moved my fingers off, *as cautiously as Glass*—	21	*Then* moved my Fingers off
	22	*As cautiously as Glass*
And held my Ears—and like a Thief	23	And held my ears, and like a Thief
Stole—gasping—from the House.	24	*Fled* gasping from the House—

8. still dwelling there   Remaining there
12. broke   smote—
16. shook   quaked—
23. Stole   fled

EMILY DICKINSON (*1830–1886*)

Under the 1862 version are alternate word choices which Emily Dickinson listed for her later use. She selected only two of these in her 1872 version, but she changed a great many more words and phrases, indicated by italics. Even in the later version, she listed an alternate choice for a word in line 5. As this poem was not published in her lifetime, she never indicated her final choice between *stolid* and *horrid.*

All the ways of viewing a poem can be used by the reader-critic in unlimited combinations. Explication, for example, may determine the full interpretation of a line by referring to an author's early versions and revisions. Critical analysis may include some paraphrase, some explication. And all critical judgments of a poem may involve the poem's relationship with others. We need now to look at the dimensions of the poem as it appears in history.

POEM IN HISTORY

Although we read poems singly, seldom do they come alone. Frequently we speak of "Browning" or "Eliot," by which we mean the poet's entire body of work—or the major poems which have come to be universally identified as his characteristic work. We also speak more frequently of a poet's than of a poem's themes. This book has been designed to concentrate on a limited number of major poets in order that the reader will not feel that he is merely skimming over a multitude of poets and poems but, rather, that he is diving to some depth and surfacing with some lasting impressions about the characteristic style, manner, technique, craft, ideas, and themes of the great poets of the English language.

When we emerge from a single poem, then, one of the first

places we are likely to go is to other poems of the same poet. And of course our understanding and appreciation will not be confined to isolated poems but will be in some way cumulative, expanding with the breadth of our knowledge of any one poet. A poet's poems illuminate one another, as ideas reappear and themes recur. And invariably our appreciation is sharpened as we become familiar with a poet's work and begin to recognize the tone of voice in lines of verses even before we spot the author's name. Every great poet signs his work with the signature of his style.

As we become immersed in the work of a poet, familiar with the ring of his phrase and the tone of his voice, we begin to trace the special configuration of his poetry: we may define a recurring theme or follow a repeated image or sketch a reappearing form. As we read Shakespeare's sonnets, we cannot help but notice the obsessive concern for time and its passing—"When I do count the clock that tells the time;" "Devouring Time, blunt thou the lion's paws." Our curiosity might well lead us to investigate systematically the various patterns of Shakespeare's attitude toward time; we might find that he was doing no more than following the conventions of the sonnet sequences of his day, or we might find that he invested an ancient theme with an individual accent.

Like Shakespeare in his sonnets, Emily Dickinson in her multitude of brief lyrics introduced only a few major themes. As we read her poetry, perhaps we will become fascinated with her uses of nature—a bird in "Hope is the thing with feathers"; the fly in "I heard a Fly buzz—when I died"; the horse in "I like to see it lap the Miles"; the snake in "A narrow Fellow in the Grass"; and the mushroom in "The Mushroom is the Elf of Plants." If we see anew, because of Emily, the teeming world of nature, we might well wish to trace more fully the vision of it in her poetry. Or as we read deeply into the poetry of Robert Frost, we might perceive (as one critic has) that the image of the dark woods, so simply introduced and described in "Stopping by Woods on a Snowy Evening," recurs throughout the poetry and takes on, as it recurs, a complexity and depth of meaning that the casual reader could not guess. To peer long into the dark woods of Frost, whenever they recur, is to explore the depths beneath the simple surface of his poetry.

But of course, beyond the poem and the poetry lies the world with all its wonders, and frequently the poem links with the "outside" world in remarkable ways. First and foremost is the author, the parent of the poem, the individual man or woman who struggled to give it birth, disciplined and shaped it until it was ready to meet the world on its own terms and merit. Some poems, like people, have closer ties with their origins than others. To know them well or deeply, we discover that we must know something of their continuing relationship with their author. Other poems seem to have severed relationship with their authors, going forth entirely on their own and asserting their independence before the world. These poems might even go so far as to mislead the reader about their authors, to drop hints and clues that confuse and deceive (as in a dramatic monologue).

There was a time when all criticism was predominantly biographical criticism—a poem was considered "explained" when it was fitted, with some narrative detail, into the life of the poet. Sometimes this kind of criticism became embarrassingly circular. It is not difficult to realize why. Consider, for a moment, the apparently personal, deeply symbolic poem "Ulalume," by Edgar Allan Poe. A perceptive reader could easily construct a theory that the poem grew out of a specific tragic love affair, and if he is also imaginative he could describe the experience with some embellishments, tentatively date it, toss around some names in speculation as to the individual person involved with the poet. Were this account to be presented in vivid and memorable terms, its primary origins in speculation might soon be forgotten, and it could easily come to pass for fact. The next step seems inevitable. A critic, coming from the biographical account to the poem, will decide that the love affair of the poet clarifies the entire meaning of the poem, and will read the poem in the light of it, not realizing that he is using reflected light, much like turning the moon on the sun to light its shadows. There is always the danger in biographical criticism of traveling this full circle.

The old biographical criticism has turned up in the twentieth century in modern dress. The major difference is the displacement of the interest in external event by a fascination for the internal disorder. Some critics have gone so far as to consider all art one or another form of neurosis, a symptom of emotional sickness in the author. They assume that every poem derives from the disturbed psyche of the poet. Following poems to their origins, critics gape into the minds and emotions of the artists, revealing what they consider the "sick" sources of image and idea. One notion widely current is that no art can be produced except by a wounded psyche (for an account of the antiquity of this notion, see Edmund Wilson's *"Philoctetes:* The Wound and the Bow").

Such an extreme view has not, however, produced an impressive body of influential criticism. Most sensitive readers are repelled by its morbidity at the same time that they are fascinated by its ingenuity. But there is hardly a modern reader or critic who can claim not to have been influenced by Freud and the new psychology. Before psychology was ever a science, poetry was discovering and dramatizing some of its fundamental principles. It is not surprising, then, to find psychology contributing to criticism some words for its vocabulary and some points of departure for its investigations. The most valuable psychological approaches are not those based on the cynical assumption that art is neurosis, but on the demonstrable assumption that art often anticipates or embraces the truths of psychology. T. S. Eliot's "The Love Song of J. Alfred Prufrock" needs to be read not as a revelation of the author's psychic state but as the dramatic portrayal of the psychic state of a man agonizingly paralyzed as two voices within him urge contrary actions. Much more than an inadvertent revelation of Eliot, "Prufrock" becomes by symbolic extension an incisive comment on the dilemma and doom of modern, civilized man.

Although it is probably true that the more a poem is dependent on its author the less likely it is to survive his death, it is also true that elementary knowledge of biographical fact frequently clears up an obscure element in a poem or brings it into a different, if not clearer, focus. Biography probably does not deepen our understanding of the *essential* poem, but it can broaden our awareness of the poem's many existences. Knowledge of Milton's own blindness adds poignance if not meaning to his sonnets "On His Blindness," and "To Mr. Cyriack Skinner Upon his Blindness." Some awareness of Milton's relationship with Edward King, his young "Lycidas" who died by drowning, adds another dimension to our response to the poem. But on the other hand, we cannot conclude that Shakespeare's sonnets are diminished in any way by the inability of the scholars to identify the young man or the dark lady to whom they are addressed. Both have their sufficient—indeed immortal—existence within the poems. A bit of common sense should assist us in evaluating the relevance of biography in the reading of poetry. We should neither toss it all out nor drag it all in: rather, we should pause and say to ourselves, "Well, let's see. . . ."

Along with biography, literary history once dominated scholarship in letters. Some critics believed that biography and history together could entirely "explain" a work of art, casting light on all its origins and thus making its total meaning clear. The great nineteenth-century French writer Hippolyte Taine wrote a massive history of English literature using the methods of a scientist, repeatedly demonstrating his theory that any work of literature was determined and accounted for by three elements— race, milieu, and moment. By reconstructing and assessing these elements for any given work, Taine believed that he could entirely explain the work. Although few critics adopted Taine's deterministic theories, his influence has persisted into the twentieth century in many forms of historical scholarship.

Somewhat in the tradition of Taine, the twentieth-century American Vernon Parrington produced his masterwork, *Main Currents of American Thought,* out of his theory that literature can best be understood in its social, economic, and political context. Like Taine, Parrington tended to ignore individuality and genius and to emphasize historical factors in criticizing works of literature. But Parrington did not carry his approach to the extremes of some of the Marxist critics who were particularly active during the 1930's. They proclaimed that all literature was but a reflection of the social class that produced it and that criticism could deal with it only by analyzing its sometimes direct, sometimes subtle involvement with the class struggle and economic conflict.

Although there has been a revolution in critical theory since these beliefs were widely held, historical scholarship is still a very much respected branch of literary study. No one now would agree that such scholarship explains all, but all would agree that historical criticism frequently leads to fuller comprehension and appreciation of a work of art. Literary history continues to be written today and is valuable in placing poets in a clear historical perspective. Such perspective is an important accompaniment to, but not a substitute for, critical analysis of the work itself. Much historical scholarship is devoted to the tracing of sources, whether in the biography of the poet, in the books that he read, in the culture in which he was immersed, or in the poets who preceded him. This approach to poetry presumes the poem to have the shape and mystery of an iceberg, the published lines revealing much less of the creative act than remains hidden. In diving beneath the surface of the waters and exploring the contour and texture of the concealed foundation of the poem, the critic throws light on the creative process as well as on the poem. But if he has dived deep, he knows very well that the mass that lies beneath the water is much too immense ever to be held up to view in its entirety.

Historical scholarship can deal with matters of wide scope. It can trace the evolution of a literary form, such as free verse, the sonnet, or the heroic couplet, frequently revealing significant relationships between an art form and the society which produced or perfected it. Or the historical approach can limit itself to a small matter, such as investigation of the method of playing the card game of ombre in the eighteenth century, a game that figures importantly in Pope's *Rape of the Lock.* The characteristic critical-historical essay of today, however, is not narrow in its approach. It is more likely than not to represent in its method a synthesis of the old and the new, weaving together in illuminating patterns both textual analysis and biographical fact, analytical commentary and historical perspective. Ideally, it is eclectic criticism, bound by no dogma, receptive to all insight, fearful of distortion, its one main aim to illuminate.

The newest direction criticism seems to be taking is toward myth and archetype, along paths that appear to run parallel to the traditionally historical. Literature's partiality to Greek mythology and the Christian traditions and themes has long been known and noted. But mythic and archetypal criticism seeks to go beyond mere identification of mythological heroes and events. It studies the basic and universal patterns from which the individual myths are cut, and determines meaning and symbolism in relation to them. For example, the themes of many poems are from the archetype of rebirth (and the reborn god), which seems to fill a deeply psychic human need and offers a human, or divine, parallel to nature's renewal of itself each spring. The archetype is a basic, recurring, elemental pattern, whose origins lie mysteriously deep in the human mind and obscurely remote in human prehistory. The pattern it offers is familiar not because we know mythology but because we are human and are born with instinctual human knowledge within us. Thus the myth merely dramatizes what we as humans already know, but which we often do not know that we know. Archetypes and their myths tend to engage imaginatively those experiences most deeply imprinted on the human psyche—the cyclic patterns of all existence: birth, union, death, rebirth. But closely related in man's imagination are the cyclic units of time: night and day, twilight and dawn, summer and winter, autumn and spring. And out of his deepest physical nature man projects (and myth reflects) his own sexual drama in the universe, dividing it into the male and female principles, seeing the earth as feminine, the heavens as masculine, and a whole series of related dualities: land and sea, city and country, night and day.

The archetypal critic may believe that the source of these recurring patterns lies in Jung's collective unconscious, a racial memory which is the individual's birthright as a human and which constitutes his psychic link of "shared" experience with all the other humans that have ever lived. Or the critic may believe that their origins are obscurely psychological and cultural, that the patterns originate spontaneously in every individual because of the fundamental nature of his being and mind, and that they are reflected and perpetuated in his culture in the most subtle and pervasive ways. But whatever their origins, the presence of these patterns in a poem suggests connections with other works of other times, leading back, back in time, into the dimly receding past to the earliest examples, suggesting both a greater continuity and a deeper significance, both cultural and psychic, than conventional historical criticism has ever done. Thus archetypal criticism attempts to isolate and identify that element, sometimes buried in a work like an ancient fossil in bedrock, which strikes the most sensitive, vulnerable, and profound chords of response in both a society and an individual.

Criticism is, in brief, the thoughtful consideration of a poem. Its first responsibility is to understand; its end is to evaluate. If we look objectively at the many possible ways of examining a poem profitably, we might well conclude that much time is wasted in argument over the superiority or inferiority of a particular "critical system." The difference between "systems" is not so much in quality as in perspective. If we imagine the poem a physical object with many dimensions and the critical approach an act of observing, we might well contend that to see the object "fully" it must be seen not only up close where it is magnified (examination of the diction of a poem), and not only from a long distance where it is dwarfed by its surroundings (putting the poem in historical setting or connecting it with its archetypal forebears), but also from an infinite number of intermediate points. The critic, or the student, should not make the mistake of believing that his singular perspective, no matter how illuminating, is the *only* useful way of seeing the poem. Its other dimensions will require other ways of seeing.

And for the beginning student of poetry, surely, or for any reader, for that matter, the best initial perspective is near the poem, where the language appears large and engaging, and where all understanding must begin. Indeed, if the reader is to become deeply involved, as he must if he seeks a lasting experience with the poem, he must accept the poem's bid to enter, to step inside and participate in the physical life of the poem, listening to its music, observing its shifting colors, feeling its shape and form. If this experience proves genuinely moving and is vividly felt after the reader emerges from the poem, then he is ready to see the poem from other perspectives and to attempt the measure of its other dimensions.

Further Reading

For major examples of various approaches to poetry, not always in "pure" form, see the essays reprinted in this book:

POEM IN PROFILE

Summary: W. H. Gardner's synopsis of "The Wreck of the Deutschland"; Northrop Frye, "Blake's 'The Mental Traveller' "; Gerard Manley Hopkins on his own "The Wreck of the Deutschland."

Paraphrase: John L. Sweeney, "A Paraphrase of John Donne in Basic English"; C. M. Bowra, "Blake's 'The Sick Rose' and 'Ah! Sun-flower.' "

Explication: Elisabeth Schneider, "Hopkins' 'The Windhover' "; Hallett Smith, "Time and Beauty in Shakespeare: Sonnets 18 and 55"; Helen Darbishire on "Milton's Poetic Language" in "Lycidas"; Derek Stanford, "Motifs in Dylan Thomas' 'Fern Hill.' "

Critical Analysis: Elder Olson's commentary on Yeats's "Sailing to Byzantium"; Wallace Cable Brown on Dryden, "The Structure of 'To the Memory of Mr. Oldham'"; E. M. W. Tillyard on the levels of meaning in Coleridge's "The Rime of the Ancient Mariner"; Charles R. Anderson on the failure of Emily Dickinson's "My Life had Stood— a Loaded Gun." Essays which involve more than criticism through analysis, but which have something of the nature of the critical analysis, are: Richard H. Fogle on Coleridge, "The Romantic Unity of 'Kubla Khan'"; John T. Ogilvie on Frost's "Stopping by Woods on a Snowy Evening" in "From Woods to Stars: A Pattern of Imagery in Robert Frost's Poetry"; and Harvey Gross on Eliot, "'Gerontion' and the Meaning of History."

A Poet's Revisions: Oliver Evans, "The Making of a Poem: Dylan Thomas' 'Do Not Go Gentle into That Good Night'"; Helen Darbishire on "Lycidas" in "Milton's Poetic Language."

POEM IN HISTORY

Poet's Total Work: James E. Miller, Jr., "The Mysticism of Whitman"; John T. Ogilvie, "From Woods to Stars; A Pattern of Imagery in Robert Frost's Poetry"; Edward Hubler's general discussion of "Shakespeare's Sonnets."

Biographical Criticism: George Saintsbury on "Tennyson"; Bernice Slote on Keats in "Of Chapman's Homer and Other Books."

Psychological Criticism: Roy P. Basler, "Blake's 'The Tyger.'"

Historical Criticism: George Saintsbury on the historical background of "Tennyson"; John D. Rea on a possible historical source for the Duke in Browning's "My Last Duchess"; Lytton Strachey on the historical development of a literary form in "Pope and the Heroic Couplet." Other essays combine the analytical with the historical approaches: Richard Fogle on the historical milieu and structure of Coleridge's poem in "The Romantic Unity of 'Kubla Khan'"; Bernice Slote on the geographical conditions of composition of Wordsworth's "Tintern Abbey" in "The Case of the Missing Abbey"; Harvey Gross on the cultural and intellectual concepts of history in an Eliot poem in "'Gerontion' and the Meaning of History."

Archetypal Criticism: Richard P. Adams, "The Archetypal Pattern of Death and Rebirth in Milton's *Lycidas*." The student who wants to investigate the archetypal approach more deeply should consult Maud Bodkin, *Archetypal Patterns in Poetry* (1934), and Northrop Frye, *Anatomy of Criticism* (1957).

Suggested Problems

1. Discuss "Ozymandias" (p. 142) and "Dover Beach" (p. 115) individually in these ways:

   (*a*) as expressions of universal truths, applicable today as well as at the time they were written.

   (*b*) as poems referring to the author's own historical point of view—

what might Shelley and Arnold have had particularly in mind, in the time in which they lived?

Explain how you might combine these interpretations (*a* and *b*) in order to understand the poem as completely as possible.

2. "The Garden of Proserpine" (p. 107) and "O My Luve Is Like a Red, Red Rose" (p. 3) have both been taken at one time for autobiography, but scholars have found that Swinburne's poem has definite literary sources and that Burns's poem is one of many songs collected from the Scottish people. Omitting autobiographical considerations, suggest as many approaches to a study of these two poems as you can.

3. Discuss Herrick's poems "To the Virgins" (p. 57) and "Corinna's Going a-Maying" (p. 94) in these four ways:

(*a*) as two poems by the same author, presumably revealing something about his themes, ideas, techniques, habits.

(*b*) as poems in the *carpe diem* ("seize the day while you may") tradition. Are there other poems in this same tradition that you could bring into a comparison?

(*c*) as poems in relation to Herrick's life and the time in which he lived.

(*d*) as poems in relation to archetype and myth.

4. Choose any poem in Chapters 1–3 and approach it in these various ways:

(*a*) Write a summary of it.

(*b*) Write a paraphrase of it.

(*c*) Write an explication of it.

(*d*) Write a brief study of (1) its form, (2) its language, (3) its theme.

(*e*) State specifically four or five subjects that might be emphasized in various critical analyses of the poem.

(*f*) Write one critical analysis of the poem.

5. What poems in Chapters 1–3 might be profitably studied in relation to the following:

(*a*) the type or tradition to which the poem belongs

(*b*) other works of the poet

(*c*) the author's life

(*d*) the period in which the poem was written

(*e*) archetype and myth

(*f*) some knowledge of psychology

(*g*) its sources

(*h*) its metaphors

(*i*) its language

(*j*) its sound, rhythm, and music

(*k*) its idea

(*l*) its pattern or structure

PART II

THE

HORIZONTAL VIEW

WILLIAM SHAKESPEARE

[1564-1616]

WILLIAM SHAKESPEARE, one of three children born to a prosperous Stratford-on-Avon businessman and city father, grew up with a good education which included glimpses into other worlds through the London dramatic companies that toured the country. Sometime between 1582 and 1585, he married Anne Hathaway and had three children—Susanna and the twins Hamnet and Judith. Tradition is that he was also a schoolmaster—but it is certain that by 1592 he was in London, a successful dramatist. His first long poem, *Venus and Adonis* (1593), was a best-seller. By 1594, Shakespeare was a shareholder in and chief dramatist for the Lord Chamberlain's Company, which was later to occupy the new and popular theater, the Globe. For twenty years Shakespeare wrote for the London stage. In the decade of 1590–1600 appeared the chronicle histories (like *Henry V*) and romantic comedies (like *A Midsummer Night's Dream* and *Twelfth Night*). Between 1601 and 1611 came the tragedies (like *Hamlet, King Lear, Othello, Macbeth*), the satirical comedies (like *Troilus and Cressida*), and the poetic tragicomedies (like *The Tempest*). In the early 1590's, Shakespeare had written a series of more than a hundred and fifty sonnets for himself and his friends. These were published in 1609. In London, Shakespeare was by all reports famous, brilliant, and successful; but at the age of 47, he completed the circle of his life and retired to a large house in the country town where he had been born. His complete work was collected and published only after his death, in the folio edition of 1623. Shakespeare's true monument is what he calls (in Sonnet 55) "this powerful rhyme."

Introductory Readings

EDITION: *The Complete Works of Shakespeare*, ed. George Lyman Kittredge, 1 vol. (1936). BIOGRAPHY: J. Q. Adams, *A Life of William Shakespeare* (1923); J. Dover Wilson, *The Essential Shakespeare* (1932). CRITICISM: *A Companion to Shakespeare Studies*, ed. Harley Granville-Barker and G. B. Harrison (1934); G. B. Harrison, *Introducing Shakespeare* (1947); A. C. Bradley, *Shakespearean Tragedy* [on the plays] (1949); M. C. Bradbrook, *Shakespeare and Elizabethan Poetry* (1951); Edward Hubler, *The Sense of Shakespeare's Sonnets* (1952); Thomas Marc Parrott, *William Shakespeare, A Handbook* (rev. ed., 1955).

SONNETS [1]

12

When I do count the clock that tells the time
And see the brave day sunk in hideous night,
When I behold the violet past prime
And sable curls all silvered o'er with white;
When lofty trees I see barren of leaves,   5
Which erst [2] from heat did canopy the herd,
And summer's green all girded up in sheaves,
Borne on the bier with white and bristly beard—
Then of thy beauty do I question make,
That thou among the wastes of time must go,   10
Since sweets and beauties do themselves forsake
And die as fast as they see others grow,
    And nothing 'gainst Time's scythe can make defense
    Save breed, to brave him [3] when he takes thee hence.

15

When I consider everything that grows
Holds in perfection but a little moment,
That this huge stage presenteth naught but shows
Whereon the stars in secret influence comment; [1]
When I perceive that men as plants increase,   5
Cheerèd and checked even by the selfsame sky,
Vaunt in their youthful sap, at height decrease,
And wear [2] their brave [3] state out of memory—

---

[1] Critical comment on the Sonnets appears on p. 196.
[2] *erst* formerly   [3] *to brave him* to defy him (time)

---

[1] *comment* contrive   [2] *wear* consume   [3] *brave* handsome

Then the conceit [4] of this inconstant stay
Sets you most rich in youth before my sight,   10
Where wasteful Time debateth with Decay
To change your day of youth to sullied night;
   And, all in war with Time for love of you,
   As he takes from you, I engraft [5] you new.

17

Who will believe my verse in time to come
If it were filled with your most high deserts?
Though yet, heaven knows, it is but as a tomb
Which hides your life and shows not half your parts.
If I could write the beauty of your eyes   5
And in fresh numbers number all your graces,
The age to come would say, "This poet lies!
Such heavenly touches ne'er touched earthly faces."
So should my papers, yellowed with their age,
Be scorned, like old men of less truth than tongue,   10
And your true rights be termed a poet's rage
And stretchèd meter of an antique song.
   But were some child of yours alive that time,
   You should live twice—in it, and in my rhyme.

18 [1]

Shall I compare thee to a summer's day?
Thou art more lovely and more temperate.
Rough winds do shake the darling buds of May,
And summer's lease hath all too short a date.
Sometime too hot the eye of heaven shines,   5
And often is his gold complexion dimmed;
And every fair from fair sometime declines,
By chance, or nature's changing course untrimmed,[2]
But thy eternal summer shall not fade
Nor lose possession of that fair thou owest,[3]   10
Nor shall Death brag thou wander'st in his shade
When in eternal lines to time thou grow'st.
   So long as men can breathe or eyes can see,
   So long lives this, and this gives life to thee.

[4] *conceit* thought
[5] *engraft* graft (enhance the beauty by immortalizing it in poetry)

---

[1] Critical comment on this poem appears on p. 199.
[2] *untrimmed* reduced   [3] *owest* own

19

Devouring Time, blunt thou the lion's paws
And make the earth devour her own sweet brood.
Pluck the keen teeth from the fierce tiger's jaws
And burn the long-lived phoenix in her blood.
Make glad and sorry seasons as thou fleet'st,   5
And do whate'er thou wilt, swift-footed Time,
To the wide world and all her fading sweets;
But I forbid thee one most heinous crime:
O, carve not with thy hours my love's fair brow,
Nor draw no lines there with thine antique pen;   10
Him in thy course untainted do allow
For beauty's pattern to succeeding men.
    Yet do thy worst, old Time! Despite thy wrong,
    My love shall in my verse ever live young.

27

Weary with toil, I haste me to my bed,
The dear repose for limbs with travel tired;
But then begins a journey in my head
To work my mind when body's work's expired.
For then my thoughts, from far where I abide,   5
Intend a zealous pilgrimage to thee,
And keep my drooping eyelids open wide,
Looking on darkness which the blind do see;
Save that my soul's imaginary sight
Presents thy shadow [1] to my sightless view,   10
Which, like a jewel hung in ghastly night,
Makes black night beauteous and her old face new.
    Lo, thus by day my limbs, by night my mind,
    For thee, and for myself, no quiet find.

29

When, in disgrace with fortune and men's eyes,
I all alone beweep my outcast state,
And trouble deaf heaven with my bootless [1] cries,
And look upon myself, and curse my fate,
Wishing me like to one more rich in hope,   5

[1] *shadow* image
-----
[1] *bootless* useless

Featured like him, like him with friends possessed,
Desiring this man's art, and that man's scope,
With what I most enjoy contented least;
Yet in these thoughts myself almost despising,
Haply I think on thee, and then my state,   10
Like to the lark at break of day arising
From sullen earth, sings hymns at heaven's gate;
    For thy sweet love remembered such wealth brings
    That then I scorn to change my state with kings.

30

When to the sessions of sweet silent thought
I summon up remembrance of things past,
I sigh the lack of many a thing I sought
And with old woes new wail my dear time's waste.
Then can I drown an eye, unused to flow,   5
For precious friends hid in death's dateless [1] night,
And weep afresh love's long since canceled [2] woe,
And moan th' expense [3] of many a vanished sight.
Then can I grieve at grievances foregone,
And heavily from woe to woe tell [4] o'er   10
The sad account of fore-bemoanèd moan,
Which I new pay as if not paid before.
    But if the while I think on thee, dear friend,
    All losses are restored and sorrows end.

55 [1]

Not marble nor the gilded monuments
Of princes, shall outlive this powerful rhyme;
But you shall shine more bright in these contents [2]
Than unswept stone, besmeared with sluttish time.
When wasteful war shall statues overturn,   5
And broils root out the work of masonry,
Nor Mars his sword nor war's quick fire shall burn
The living record of your memory.
'Gainst death and all-oblivious enmity
Shall you pace forth. Your praise shall still find room   10

---

[1] *dateless* endless   [2] *canceled* discharged because already paid
[3] *expense* loss   [4] *tell* count

---

[1] Critical comment on this poem appears on p. 199.
[2] *these contents* contents of these poems

Even in the eyes of all posterity
That wear this world out to the ending doom.
So, till the judgment that yourself arise,
You live in this, and dwell in lovers' eyes.

65

Since brass, nor stone, nor earth, nor boundless sea,
But sad mortality o'ersways their power,
How with this rage shall beauty hold a plea,
Whose action is no stronger than a flower?
O, how shall summer's honey breath hold out   5
Against the wrackful siege of batt'ring days,
When rocks impregnable are not so stout,
Nor gates of steel so strong, but Time decays?
O fearful meditation! Where, alack,
Shall Time's best jewel from Time's chest lie hid?   10
Or what strong hand can hold his swift foot back?
Or who his spoil of beauty can forbid?
    O, none, unless this miracle have might,
    That in black ink my love may still shine bright.

73

That time of year thou mayst in me behold
When yellow leaves, or none, or few, do hang
Upon those boughs which shake against the cold,
Bare ruined choirs where late the sweet birds sang.
In me thou see'st the twilight of such day   5
As after sunset fadeth in the west,
Which by-and-by [1] black night doth take away,
Death's second self, that seals up all in rest.
In me thou see'st the glowing of such fire
That on the ashes of his youth doth lie,   10
As the deathbed whereon it must expire,
Consumed with that which it was nourished by.
    This thou perceiv'st, which makes thy love more strong,
    To love that well which thou must leave ere long.

97

How like a winter hath my absence been
From thee, the pleasure of the fleeting year!

---

[1] *by-and-by* shortly

What freezings have I felt, what dark days seen!
What old December's bareness everywhere!
And yet this time removed was summer's time,   5
The teeming autumn, big with rich increase,
Bearing the wanton [1] burden of the prime,[2]
Like widowed wombs after their lords' decease.
Yet this abundant issue seemed to me
But hope of orphans and unfathered fruit;   10
For summer and his pleasures wait on thee,
And, thou away, the very birds are mute;
   Or, if they sing, 'tis with so dull a cheer
   That leaves look pale, dreading the winter's near.

98

From you have I been absent in the spring,
When proud-pied [1] April, dressed in all his trim,
Hath put a spirit of youth in everything,
That heavy [2] Saturn laughed and leaped with him;
Yet nor the lays [3] of birds, nor the sweet smell   5
Of different flowers in odor and in hue,
Could make me any summer's story tell,
Or from their proud lap pluck them where they grew;
Nor did I wonder at the lily's white,
Nor praise the deep vermilion in the rose: 10
They were but sweet, but figures of delight,
Drawn after you, you pattern of all those.
   Yet seemed it winter still, and, you away,
   As with your shadow I with these did play.

106

When in the chronicle of wasted time
I see descriptions of the fairest wights,[1]
And beauty making beautiful old rhyme
In praise of ladies dead and lovely knights,
Then, in the blazon of sweet beauty's best,   5
Of hand, of foot, of lip, of eye, of brow,
I see their antique pen would have expressed
Even such a beauty as you master now.

[1] *wanton* luxuriant   [2] *prime* young (fertile) manhood of the year

[1] *proud-pied* beautifully dappled   [2] *heavy* morose
[3] *lays* songs

[1] *wights* persons

So all their praises are but prophecies
Of this our time, all you prefiguring;   10
And, for they looked but with divining eyes,
They had not skill enough your worth to sing.
   For we, which now behold these present days,
   Have eyes to wonder, but lack tongues to praise.

107

Not mine own fears, nor the prophetic soul
Of the wide world, dreaming on things to come,
Can yet the lease [1] of my true love control,
Supposed as forfeit to a confined [2] doom.
The mortal moon hath her eclipse endured,   5
And the sad augurs mock their own presage; [3]
Incertainties now crown themselves assured,
And peace proclaims olives of endless age.
Now with the drops of this most balmy time
My love looks fresh, and Death to me subscribes,   10
Since, spite of him, I'll live in this poor rhyme
While he insults o'er dull and speechless tribes;
   And thou in this shalt find thy monument
   When tyrants' crests and tombs of brass are spent.

116

Let me not to the marriage of true minds
Admit impediments. Love is not love
Which alters when it alteration finds
Or bends with the remover [1] to remove.
O, no! it is an ever-fixèd mark   5
That looks on tempests and is never shaken;
It is the star to every wand'ring bark,
Whose worth 's unknown, although his height be taken.
Love's not Time's fool, though rosy lips and cheeks
Within his bending sickle's compass come.   10
Love alters not with his brief hours and weeks,
But bears it out even to the edge of doom.
   If this be error, and upon me proved,
   I never writ, nor no man ever loved.

[1] *lease* lifetime   [2] *confined* early
[3] *sad augurs mock their own presage* those who made gloomy prophecies
mock their own predictions

[1] *remover* one of fickle affections

127

In the old age [1] black was not counted fair,
Or if it were, it bore not beauty's name;
But now is black beauty's successive heir,
And beauty slandered with a bastard shame;
For since each hand hath put on nature's power,   5
Fairing the foul [2] with art's false borrowed face,
Sweet beauty hath no name, no holy bower,
But is profaned, if not lives in disgrace.
Therefore my mistress' brows are raven black,
Her eyes so suited, and they mourners seem   10
At such who, not born fair, no beauty lack,
Sland'ring creation with a false esteem.
    Yet so they mourn, becoming of their woe,
    That every tongue says beauty should look so.

129

Th' expense [1] of spirit in a waste of shame
Is lust in action; and till action, lust
Is perjured, murd'rous, bloody, full of blame,
Savage, extreme, rude, cruel, not to trust;
Enjoyed no sooner but despisèd straight;   5
Past reason hunted, and no sooner had,
Past reason hated, as a swallowed bait
On purpose laid to make the taker mad;
Mad in pursuit, and in possession so;
Had, having, and in quest to have, extreme;   10
A bliss in proof [2]—and proved, a very woe;
Before, a joy proposed; behind, a dream.
    All this the world well knows, yet none knows well
    To shun the heaven that leads men to this hell.

130

My mistress' eyes are nothing like the sun;
Coral is far more red than her lips' red.

[1] *old age* age of chivalry
[2] *Fairing the foul* making beautiful the ugly (of the black) by use of cosmetics

[1] *expense* expenditure   [2] *in proof* during the act

If snow be white, why then her breasts are dun;
If hairs be wires, black wires grow on her head.
I have seen roses damasked,[1] red and white,　　5
But no such roses see I in her cheeks;
And in some perfumes is there more delight
Than in the breath that from my mistress reeks.
I love to hear her speak, yet well I know
That music hath a far more pleasing sound.　　10
I grant I never saw a goddess go:
My mistress, when she walks, treads on the ground.
　　And yet, by heaven, I think my love as rare
　　As any she [2] belied with false compare.

146

Poor soul, the center of my sinful earth,[1]
My sinful earth,[2] these rebel powers that thee array,
Why dost thou pine within and suffer dearth,
Painting thy outward walls so costly gay?
Why so large cost, having so short a lease,　　5
Dost thou upon thy fading mansion spend?
Shall worms, inheritors of this excess,
Eat up thy charge? is this thy body's end?
Then, soul, live thou upon thy servant's loss,[3]
And let that pine to aggravate [4] thy store;　　10
　　And Death once dead, there's no more dying then.
Buy terms divine in selling hours of dross;
Within be fed, without be rich no more.
　　So shalt thou feed on Death, that feeds on men,

147

My love is as a fever, longing still [1]
For that which longer nurseth the disease,
Feeding on that which doth preserve the ill,
Th' uncertain sickly appetite to please.
My reason, the physician to my love,　　5
Angry that his prescriptions are not kept,

---

[1] *damasked* mingled　　　[2] *any she* any woman

---

[1] *sinful earth* body
[2] *my sinful earth* In the first printing of the sonnets, these three words were repeated by mistake from the preceding line. Two syllables are needed. Some suggestions by editors are "Fool'd by" and "Feeding."
[3] *thy servant's loss* thy body's loss　　　[4] *aggravate* increase

---

[1] *still* always

Hath left me, and I desperate now approve [2]
Desire is death, which physic did except.
Past cure I am, now reason is past care,
And frantic-mad with evermore unrest;   10
My thoughts and my discourse as madmen's are,
At random from the truth vainly expressed;
    For I have sworn thee fair, and thought thee bright,
    Who art as black as hell, as dark as night.

SONGS FROM THE PLAYS

WHO IS SILVIA?

Who is Silvia? what is she,
    That all our swains commend her?
Holy, fair, and wise is she;
    The heavens such grace did lend her,
That she might admired be.   5

Is she kind as she is fair?
    For beauty lives with kindness.
Love doth to her eyes repair,
    To help him of his blindness,
And being helped, inhabits there.   10

Then to Silvia let us sing
    That Silvia is excelling;
She excels each mortal thing
    Upon the dull earth dwelling.
To her let us garlands bring.   15

MUSICIANS. *The Two Gentlemen of Verona* (**IV,** ii)

DIALOGUE IN PRAISE OF THE OWL
AND THE CUCKOO

SPRING.   When daisies pied,[1] and violets blue,
    And lady-smocks all silver white,
    And cuckoo-buds of yellow hue,
    Do paint the meadows with delight—
    The cuckoo then on every tree   5
    Mocks [2] married men, for thus sings he,
    Cuckoo.

[2] *approve* learn that

[1] *pied* many-colored
[2] *Mocks* (because he suggests cuckoldry, unfaithful wives)

Cuckoo, cuckoo: O word of fear,
Unpleasing to a married ear.

When shepherds pipe on oaten straws,   10
And merry larks are ploughmen's clocks;
When turtles tread,³ and rooks and daws,
And maidens bleach their summer smocks—
The cuckoo then on every tree
Mocks married men, for thus sings he,   15
Cuckoo.
Cuckoo, cuckoo: O word of fear,
Unpleasing to a married ear.

WINTER. When icicles hang by the wall,
And Dick the shepherd blows his nail,⁴   20
And Tom bears logs into the hall,
And milk comes frozen home in pail;
When blood is nipped and ways be foul—
Then nightly sings the staring owl,
To-whit, to-who: 25
    A merry note,
    While greasy Joan doth keel ⁵ the pot.

When all aloud the wind doth blow,
And coughing drowns the parson's saw,⁶
And birds sit brooding in the snow,   30
And Marian's nose looks red and raw;
When roasted crabs ⁷ hiss in the bowl—
Then nightly sings the staring owl,
To-whit, to-who:
    A merry note,   35
    While greasy Joan doth keel the pot.

PLAYERS, INTRODUCED BY DON ADRIANO DE ARMADO
Love's Labour's Lost (V, ii)

TELL ME WHERE IS FANCY BRED

Tell me where is fancy ¹ bred,
Or in the heart, or in the head:
How begot, how nourishèd.
Reply, reply.

---

³ *turtles tread* turtledoves mate
⁴ *blows his nail* blows on his fingers to warm them   ⁵ *keel* stir to cool
⁶ *saw* moral saying   ⁷ *crabs* crab apples

¹ *fancy* love

It is engendered in the eyes,   5
With gazing fed; and fancy dies,
In the cradle where it lies:
Let us all ring fancy's knell.
I'll begin it:
Ding, dong, bell.   10
[ALL.] Ding, dong, bell.

PORTIA AND ATTENDANTS. *The Merchant of Venice* (III, ii)

SIGH NO MORE, LADIES

Sigh no more, ladies, sigh no more,
   Men were deceivers ever;
One foot in sea, and one on shore,
   To one thing constant never.
         Then sigh not so,   5
         But let them go,
   And be you blithe and bonny,
Converting all your sounds of woe,
   Into hey nonny nonny.

Sing no more ditties, sing no moe,   10
   Of dumps ¹ so dull and heavy;
The fraud of men was ever so,
   Since summer first was leavy.²
         Then sigh not so,
         But let them go,   15
   And be you blithe and bonny,
Converting all your sounds of woe,
   Into hey nonny nonny.

BALTHASAR. *Much Ado About Nothing* (II, iii)

BLOW, BLOW, THOU WINTER WIND

Blow, blow, thou winter wind,
Thou art not so unkind, as man's ingratitude.
Thy tooth is not so keen, because thou art not seen,
   Although thy breath be rude.
Heigh ho, sing heigh ho, unto the green holly,   5
Most friendship is feigning, most loving mere folly.
      Then heigh ho, the holly,
      This life is most jolly.

¹ *dumps* depressions   ² *leavy* full of leaves

Freeze, freeze, thou bitter sky
That dost not bite so nigh as benefits forgot.   10
Though thou the waters warp, thy sting is not so sharp,
    As friend remembered not.
Heigh ho, sing heigh ho, unto the green holly,
Most friendship is feigning, most loving mere folly.
    Then heigh ho, the holly,   15
    This life is most jolly.

AMIENS. As You Like It (II, vii)

O MISTRESS MINE

O mistress mine, where are you roaming?
O stay and hear, your true love's coming,
That can sing both high and low.
Trip no further, pretty sweeting.
Journeys end in lovers meeting,   5
Every wise man's son doth know.

What is love? 'Tis not hereafter;
Present mirth hath present laughter.
What's to come is still unsure.
In delay there lies no plenty;   10
Then come kiss me, sweet and twenty:
Youth's a stuff will not endure.

CLOWN. Twelfth Night (II, iii)

COME AWAY DEATH

Come away,[1] come away death,
And in sad cypress let me be laid.
Fly away, fly away breath,
I am slain by a fair cruel maid.
    My shroud of white, stuck all with yew, O prepare it.   5
    My part [2] of death no one so true did share it.

Not a flower, not a flower sweet
On my black coffin, let there be strown.
Not a friend, not a friend greet
My poor corpse, where my bones shall be thrown.   10
    A thousand thousand sighs to save, lay me O where
    Sad true lover never find my grave, to weep there.

CLOWN. Twelfth Night (II, iv)

[1] *come away* come here   [2] *part* share

THE WIND AND THE RAIN [1]

When that I was and a little tiny boy,
  With hey, ho, the wind and the rain,
A foolish thing was but a toy,
  For the rain it raineth every day.

But when I came to man's estate, 5
  With hey, ho, the wind and the rain,
'Gainst knaves and thieves men shut their gate,
  For the rain it raineth every day.

But when I came, alas, to wive,
  With hey, ho, the wind and the rain, 10
By swaggering could I never thrive,
  For the rain it raineth every day.

But when I came unto my beds,
  With hey, ho, the wind and the rain,
With tosspots [2] still had drunken heads, 15
  For the rain it raineth every day.

A great while ago the world begun,
  With hey, ho, the wind and the rain;
But that's all one, our play is done,
  And we'll strive to please you every day. 20

CLOWN. *Twelfth Night* (V, i)

TAKE, OH TAKE THOSE LIPS AWAY

Take, oh take those lips away
  That so sweetly were forsworn;
And those eyes: the break of day,
  Lights that do mislead the morn;
But my kisses bring again, bring again, 5
Seals of love, but sealed in vain, sealed in vain.

BOY. *Measure for Measure* (IV, i)

HARK, HARK, THE LARK

Hark, hark, the lark at heaven's gate sings,
  And Phoebus [1] gins arise,

[1] This song by the Clown concludes the play.   [2] *toss-pots* drunkards

[1] *Phoebus* the sun

His steeds to water at those springs [2]
   On chaliced [3] flowers that lies;
And winking Mary-buds [4] begin to ope their golden eyes.   5
With every thing that pretty is, my lady sweet, arise:
   Arise, arise.

                           MUSICIANS. *Cymbeline* (II, iii)

FEAR NO MORE

GUID.   Fear no more the heat o' the sun,
         Nor the furious winter's rages;
         Thou thy worldly task hast done,
         Home art gone, and ta'en thy wages.
         Golden lads and girls all must,   5
         As chimney-sweepers come to dust.

ARVI.   Fear no more the frown o' the great,
         Thou art past the tyrant's stroke.
         Care no more to clothe and eat;
         To thee the reed is as the oak.   10
         The scepter, learning, physic,[1] must
         All follow this and come to dust.

GUID.   Fear no more the lightning flash.
ARVI.   Nor th'all-dreaded thunderstone.[2]
GUID.   Fear not slander, censure rash.   15
ARVI.   Thou hast finished joy and moan.
BOTH.   All lovers young, all lovers must,
         Consign [3] to thee and come to dust.

GUID.   No exorciser harm thee,
ARVI.   Nor no witchcraft charm thee.   20
GUID.   Ghost unlaid forbear thee.
ARVI.   Nothing ill come near thee.
BOTH.   Quiet consummation have,
         And renownèd be thy grave.

       GUIDERIUS AND ARVIRAGUS. *Cymbeline* (IV, ii)

---

[2] *springs* the dew   [3] *chaliced* cup-shaped   [4] *Mary-buds* marigolds

---

[1] *physic* the art of healing (all science)   [2] *thunderstone* thunderbolt
[3] *Consign to thee* submit as you do

FULL FATHOM FIVE

ARIEL. Full fathom five thy father lies;
Of his bones are coral made.
Those are pearls that were his eyes;
Nothing of him that doth fade,
But doth suffer a sea-change   5
Into something rich, and strange.
Sea-nymphs hourly ring his knell.
[VOICES IN UNDERSONG] Ding, dong.
ARIEL. Hark now I hear them, ding-dong bell.

ARIEL. *The Tempest* (I, ii)

WHERE THE BEE SUCKS

Where the bee sucks, there suck I;
In a cowslip's bell I lie;
There I couch when owls do cry.
On the bat's back I do fly
After summer merrily.   5
Merrily, merrily, shall I live now,
Under the blossom that hangs on the bough.

ARIEL. *The Tempest* (V, i)

LINES FROM THE PLAYS

LET'S TALK OF GRAVES

Let's talk of graves, of worms, and epitaphs,
Make dust our paper and with rainy eyes
Write sorrow on the bosom of the earth.
Let's choose executors and talk of wills.
And yet not so, for what can we bequeath   5
Save our deposèd bodies to the ground?
Our lands, our lives, and all are Bolingbroke's,
And nothing can we call our own but death
And that small model of the barren earth
Which serves as paste and cover to our bones.   10
For God's sake let us sit upon the ground
And tell sad stories of the death of kings:
How some have been deposed, some slain in war,

Some haunted by the ghosts they have deposed,
Some poisoned by their wives, some sleeping killed— 15
All murthered; for within the hollow crown
That rounds the mortal temples of a king
Keeps Death his court; and there the antic sits,
Scoffing his state and grinning at his pomp,
Allowing him a breath, a little scene, 20
To monarchize, be feared, and kill with looks;
Infusing him with self and vain conceit,
As if this flesh which walls about our life
Were brass impregnable; and humored thus,
Comes at the last, and with a little pin 25
Bores through his castle wall, and farewell king!

KING RICHARD. *Richard II* (III, ii)

THE LUNATIC, THE LOVER, AND THE POET

The lunatic, the lover, and the poet
Are of imagination all compact.
One sees more devils than vast hell can hold:
That is the madman. The lover, all as frantic,
Sees Helen's beauty in a brow of Egypt. 5
The poet's eye, in a fine frenzy rolling,
Doth glance from heaven to earth, from earth to heaven;
And as imagination bodies forth
The forms of things unknown, the poet's pen
Turns them to shapes, and gives to airy nothing 10
A local habitation, and a name.

THESEUS. *A Midsummer Night's Dream* (V, i)

ALL THE WORLD'S A STAGE

All the world's a stage,
And all the men and women merely players.
They have their exits and their entrances,
And one man in his time plays many parts,
His acts being seven ages. At first the infant, 5
Mewling ¹ and puking in the nurse's arms.
Then the whining schoolboy, with his satchel
And shining morning face, creeping like snail
Unwillingly to school. And then the lover,

¹ *mewling* squalling

Sighing like furnace, with a woeful ballad   10
Made to his mistress' eyebrow. Then a soldier,
Full of strange oaths and bearded like the pard,[2]
Jealous in honor, sudden and quick in quarrel,
Seeking the bubble reputation
Even in the cannon's mouth. And then the justice,   15
In fair round belly with good capon lined,
With eyes severe and beard of formal cut,
Full of wise saws [3] and modern instances,[4]
And so he plays his part. The sixth age shifts
Into the lean and slippered Pantaloon [5]   20
With spectacles on nose and pouch on side,
His youthful hose, well saved, a world too wide
For his shrunk shank, and his big manly voice,
Turning again toward childish treble, pipes
And whistles in his sound. Last scene of all,   25
That ends this strange eventful history,
Is second childishness and mere oblivion,
Sans [6] teeth, sans eyes, sans taste, sans everything.

JACQUES. *As You Like It* (II, vii)

TO BE, OR NOT TO BE

To be, or not to be—that is the question:
Whether 'tis nobler in the mind to suffer
The slings and arrows of outrageous fortune,
Or to take arms against a sea of troubles,
And by opposing end them. To die, to sleep—   5
No more; and by a sleep, to say we end
The heartache and the thousand natural shocks
That flesh is heir to? 'Tis a consummation
Devoutly to be wished. To die, to sleep;
To sleep—perchance to dream. Aye, there's the rub,   10
For in that sleep of death what dreams may come
When we have shuffled [1] off this mortal coil [2]
Must give us pause. There's the respect
That makes calamity of so long life.

[2] *pard* leopard   [3] *saws* sayings
[4] *modern instances* commonplace proverbs
[5] *Pantaloon* old dotard; a stock character in the Italian *commedia del' arte*
(the Harlequin plays)
[6] *Sans* without

[1] *shuffled* cast   [2] *coil* turmoil

For who would bear the whips and scorns of time,   15
The oppressor's wrong, the proud man's contumely,
The pangs of disprized [3] love, the law's delay,
The insolence of office, and the spurns
That patient merit of the unworthy takes,
When he himself might his quietus make   20
With a bare bodkin? Who would fardels [4] bear,
To grunt and sweat under a weary life,
But that the dread of something after death,
The undiscovered country from whose bourn
No traveler returns, puzzles the will,   25
And makes us rather bear those ills we have
Than fly to others that we know not of?
Thus conscience does make cowards of us all,
And thus the native hue of resolution
Is sicklied o'er with the pale cast of thought;   30
And enterprises of great pitch and moment,
With this regard their currents turn awry
And lose the name of action.

HAMLET. *Hamlet* (III, i)

TO-MORROW, AND TO-MORROW

To-morrow, and to-morrow, and to-morrow,
Creeps in this petty pace from day to day
To the last syllable of recorded time;
And all our yesterdays have lighted fools
The way to dusty death. Out, out, brief candle!   5
Life's but a walking shadow, a poor player,
That struts and frets his hour upon the stage,
And then is heard no more. It is a tale
Told by an idiot, full of sound and fury,
Signifying nothing.   10

MACBETH. *Macbeth* (V, v)

CLEOPATRA: THE BARGE SHE SAT IN

The barge she sat in, like a burnished throne,
Burned on the water. The poop was beaten gold,
Purple the sails, and so perfumèd that

[3] *disprized* the word used in the *First Folio* (1623). "Despised" (*Second Quarto*, 1604–05) is chosen by some editors.
[4] *fardels* burdens

The winds were lovesick with them. The oars were silver,
Which to the tune of flutes kept stroke and made   5
The water which they beat to follow faster,
As amorous of their strokes. For her own person,
It beggared all description. She did lie
In her pavilion, cloth-of-gold of tissue,[1]
O'er-picturing that Venus where we see   10
The fancy outwork nature. On each side her
Stood pretty dimpled boys, like smiling Cupids,
With divers-colored fans, whose wind did seem
To glow [2] the delicate cheeks which they did cool,
And what they undid did.   15

ENOBARBUS. *Antony and Cleopatra* (II, ii)

OUR REVELS NOW ARE ENDED

Our revels now are ended. These our actors,
As I foretold you, were all spirits and
Are melted into air, into thin air;
And, like the baseless fabric of this vision,
The cloud-capped towers, the gorgeous palaces,   5
The solemn temples, the great globe itself,
Yea, all which it inherit, shall dissolve,
And, like this insubstantial pageant faded,
Leave not a rack [1] behind. We are such stuff
As dreams are made on, and our little life   10
Is rounded with a sleep.

PROSPERO. *The Tempest* (IV, i)

CRITICISM

The following critical selections illustrate two general approaches to poems: the wide "horizontal" view of a poet's work and the close "vertical" look at the text of a poem. "Shakespeare's Sonnets" presents the poems in their historical position, in their relation to each other as they form a pattern in the series, and in their relation to the author. In the second essay, Hallett Smith discusses Sonnets 18 and 55, noting words, sounds, and patterns

---

[1] *tissue* cloth interwoven with gold
[2] *glow* used by most editors to fit the sense, although the *First Folio* has "glove"

---

[1] *rack* cloud

within the poem. But even here, the two sonnets are placed in a larger context—the themes characteristic of Shakespeare.

Shakespeare's Sonnets [1]

EDWARD HUBLER

[*Shake-speares Sonnets* was printed in 1609 for a Thomas Thorpe, probably without Shakespeare's knowledge.]

Although the volume of sonnets was not printed until 1609, two of them, numbers 138 and 144, were printed in *The Passionate Pilgrim*, 1599. In 1598, while listing and commenting on Shakespeare's works in his *Palladis Tamia: Wits Treasury*, Francis Meres mentioned Shakespeare's "sugred sonnets among his private friends," indicating that, according to a custom of the time, Shakespeare's sonnets were circulating in manuscript. An Elizabethan gentleman who did not wish to descend to what he took to be the vulgarity of print could gain a reputation as a poet by giving manuscript copies of his poems to his friends, who, if they liked them, could give copies to their friends, and so on. In this manner a writer's reputation could be established without publication, and this is one of the means Shakespeare took to gain the name of poet. It is not known how many of the sonnets were so circulating, and it is possible that some of the sonnets we now have were written after 1598; but the probability is that they were all written in the early 1590's. . . .

Sonnets 1–126 are addressed to or concerned with a young man whom the poet addresses in terms of affection and esteem. Sonnets 127–152 are addressed to or concerned with a young woman, who because of her black hair and swarthy complexion, has come to be known as the Dark Lady. Sonnets 153–154 are free translations of a fifth-century A.D. Greek poem and have no connection with the sonnets of the first two groups except a common authorship. Although Elizabethan sonnet sequences are not narrative poems, the reader discerns reflections of a story in the first two groups of Shakespeare's sonnets. They tell of four people: Shakespeare, who speaks in the first person, the young man, the Dark Lady, and another poet. The young man is handsome, of good family, and, at least in the beginning, the possessor of boundless

[1] By permission from *Shakespeare's Songs and Poems*, ed. Edward Hubler. (Copyright, 1959. McGraw-Hill Book Company, Inc.)

virtues. He is told that youth and beauty are brief, that father-hood is a duty to himself and to the world (the same arguments are used in *Venus and Adonis*), and that his qualities must be preserved in the immortality which children can bestow. Shake-speare then promises to immortalize the young man in verses which will never die. After a while other poets began addressing poems to the young man, and one of them, a poet of more power than the rest, came to be regarded by Shakespeare as something of a rival. He is often referred to as the Rival Poet. Sometime after the friendship with the young man began, Shakespeare acquired a mistress, a woman younger than he, attractive with an unfashionable beauty, and with no moral principles whatso-ever. The relationship between them had not a glimmer of ro-mance, and in time the poet came to recognize it as a sexual enslavement, but not until the lady had seduced the young friend and maintained a liaison with him for some time. Finding this triangular relationship increasingly unbearable, Shakespeare re-solved the problem by rejecting the lady. Such is the story re-flected in the sonnets. . . .

The 1609 Quarto is the only edition of the sonnets to be pub-lished during Shakespeare's lifetime, and all later editions de-rive from it. In 1640 the sonnets were reprinted by John Benson in a small octavo volume entitled *Poems: Written by Wil. Shake-speare. Gent.* The volume is a dishonest venture in publishing. Benson did not own the copyright. He scrambled the order of the sonnets, interspersing them with other poems by Shakespeare and other poets. He gave the sonnets descriptive titles which are often inept, and he changed the pronouns in some of the son-nets addressed to the young man, making them appear to be ad-dressed to a woman. But he did correct, by conjectural emenda-tion, some of the errors in the text of the 1609 Quarto. . . .

In a preface addressed to the reader Benson describes the poems as "seren, cleere amd eligantly plaine, such gentle straines as shall recreate and not perplexe your braine, no intricate or cloudy stuffe to puzzell intellect, but perfect eloquence. . . ." And ever since then there have been critics to praise the sonnets for their simplicity, although some of them are in fact among the most difficult poems in the language. Shakespeare has, of course, his simplicities. In Sonnet 66 he makes a list of the things which discourage him most, and one of them is "simple truth miscall'd simplicity." He saw things as they were, and his sophistication did not compel him to condescend to the commonplace. Things sometimes become clichés because they are true, and they are to be recognized as truth. Nowhere in his works is there any avoidance of this. He could be disarmingly simple where other writers would not dare to be, as in the "Good-night, sweet prince" speech in *Hamlet,* and many of the memorable passages in the sonnets are characterized by their unobtrusive melody, easy grace, and simplicity of statement. He always wrote with an unmatchable freshness on nature's morning loveliness and her plenitude, subjects to which he constantly took an unequivocal attitude, but the dominant mode of his mature work is complexity, and this first emerges fully in the sonnets. He saw all aspects of things, and they stand together in his works without canceling each other out. . . .

The sonnets abound in irony and paradox, which are the manifestations of Shakespeare's awareness of his own multiplicity, an awareness he was later to confer upon Hamlet. And this is, of course, the awareness of the dramatist, for the most interesting dramatic choice is not between right and wrong but between two rights or two wrongs, or between things which are neither wholly right nor wholly wrong.

The sonnets are Shakespeare's lyric expressions of the perceptions later to find dramatic expression in the plays of his maturity—his perceptions of friendship, of love and lust, of growth through experience, of sin and expiation, of mutability, plenitude, and the knowledge of good and evil. They begin with a concern for physical beauty and exhortations to preserve it in such immortality as children can bestow, and in the promises to eternize beauty in poetry. In later sonnets mortality is found to be tainted with something more ghastly than mutability, and in this view the power of "sinful earth" to recreate itself does not console. At the close of the sonnets the body is rejected that the soul may live. At no point in the sonnets, or in the later works, is the concern for physical beauty abandoned. It is not that as Shakespeare grew older he came to love beauty less; it is rather that he had come to love other things as much, moral beauty among them. And this, too, is in the sonnets, which are a foreshadowing of the course his career as artist was to take. The best of the sonnets are in themselves perfect lyric realizations of the perceptions which were not actualized in his plays until a later time.

Time and Beauty in Shakespeare: Sonnets 18 and 55 [1]

HALLETT SMITH

There is much in Shakespeare's sonnets on the theme of the conflict between time and beauty. The cycle opens with a series which pleads with a fair young man to marry and beget children so that his beauty may not perish with him but may survive through "breed." This leads very soon to the introduction of another means of defying time and death—poetry. In its simplest form, this theme may be handled rhetorically, with some satisfactory image such as that of nature, flowers, the spring, readily associated with youth. A good example is No. 18, "Shall I compare thee to a summer's day?" The poet counters the light and delicate effects, achieved largely through imagery, in the first eight lines, by an insistent and sonorous metrical effect in the line which marks the turn of thought. The fragility and temporary quality of physical beauty, which is the idea of the first eight lines, is not allowed to overwhelm the bright and lovely aspects of it; the two are evoked equally, one by statement and the other by illustrations and images. The gaiety that is injected by the refused or qualified comparison in the first two lines is carried through, to swell into the confident tone of the last six lines. The "fair" becomes an abstract idea, but its concreteness is supported by the darling buds of May, the gold complexion of the sun, and, by implication throughout, the youth of the one addressed. The recurrence of And . . . and . . . and, but . . . nor . . . nor . . . so . . . so . . . at the beginning of lines gives the verse a rapidity of movement; the word "Rough" in line 3 is the only strong accent to begin a line. Moreover, the rhetorical pattern is carried on by this process, so we have the impression of smooth, quick, effortless persuasion, fitted to the lighthearted character of the poem.

Time is not usually treated so lightheartedly, however. Sonnet

[1] Extracted from Hallett Smith, *Elizabethan Poetry* (Harvard University Press, 1952).

55 is an example of the treatment of time in a tone of solemn dignity. The poem is extraordinarily rich in texture of sound combinations, and a detailed analysis would reveal how subtly the sound effects reinforce the imagery. But, at the risk of making explicit what should remain implicit, we must examine the nature of the metaphorical thinking in this sonnet, if only to show how different it is from Spenser's *Amoretti* 69, which also uses the commonplace of poetry as a monument or memorial.[2] In the first quatrain [of Shakespeare's Sonnet] there is a competition regarding the brightness of material things, specifically monuments, and the memory of "you" embodied in these poems. The word "gilded" implies no disrespect for princes' monuments; it is a way of introducing brightness and color which the marble failed to do. By line 4 the poet has turned to deprecation of gravestones and has a homely image for them. The key or principle of all this is the idea of brightness. Why "sluttish" time? Because "unswept stone" suggests a negligent housemaid, too lazy to sweep. "Unswept stone, besmear'd with sluttish time" has therefore a transferred epithet in it, and the line resolves two modes of considering time and gravestones: the aristocratic connotations of the first line of the sonnet are destroyed by the association with "unswept" and "sluttish," and simultaneously the contrast of brightness between poetry and stone is insisted upon.

The programmatic or imitative quality of the second quatrain is obvious; the movement and the sound texture together mimic the violence and disorder of war and civil strife ("broils"). The speed and violence of the destruction are conveyed rhetorically by the suspended subject, "Mars his sword," which has no verb, or rather, is joined with "war's quick fire" in

[2] The editors add here the text of Spenser's *Amoretti* 69:

The famous warriors of the antique world
Used trophies to erect in stately wise,
In which they would the records have enrolled
Of their great deeds and valorous emprise.
What trophy then shall I most fit devise,
In which I may record the memory
Of my love's conquest, peerless beauty's prize,
Adorned with honor, love, and chastity?
Even this verse, vowed to eternity,
Shall be thereof immortal monument,
And tell her praise to all posterity,
That may admire such world's rare wonderment:
The happy purchase of my glorious spoil,
Gotten at last with labor and long toil.

the act, impossible for it, of burning. The rhythmical turbulence of the ten monosyllables in line 7 is quieted by the simplicity and calmness of the eighth line, and there is a curious connection between "living" and the ambiguity in the meaning of "quick."

The third quatrain begins with another transferred epithet, or rather a hysteron proteron: "all-oblivious enmity" should be, in prose, "all-inimical oblivion," but the transfer has accomplished something by emphasizing the antagonism of time and forgetfulness. It is a semi-personification. Furthermore, the tenth line has in it a dim suggestion of the aristocratic atmosphere of line 1; the pacing forth is like the entry of a nobleman into a crowded place, and room is made for him. If this impression is really there and is not a mere critic's fancy, then some sort of revolution has taken place in the sonnet by which princes, represented in their gilded monuments, are deposed to the level of sluts, but "you," celebrated only by poetry, pace forth as the new cynosure. At any rate, the person addressed will find his place "in the eyes" of posterity; the sense is double: posterity will read the poems, and the eyes of posterity are in some sense the final repository of fame. This is made clearer and more explicit in the fourteenth line. Posterity "that wear this world out to the ending doom" is somewhat more complex than "bears it out even to the edge of doom" in No. 116; as time, war, and broils wear out the physical monuments on the earth, so posterity wears out the world itself. The universal character of the enmity of time is again suggested. The "ending doom" here is also taken seriously, for the figure of the couplet includes an actual judgment day. The powerful rhyme which outlives marble and the gilded monuments of princes is coextensive with posterity, and this makes the introduction to the couplet a logical one: *So,* till the judgment . . .

It should be observed that the first twelve lines are all in the future; the word "shall" occurs six times. The continuing present of the couplet is therefore very strong by contrast: "So, till . . . You *live* in this and *dwell* in lovers' eyes." The contrasts in the sonnet's statement, between permanence and change, destruction and survival, frailty and power, are thus strengthened by the grammatical structure as well as by the metaphorical thought.

JOHN DONNE

[1572?-1631]

JOHN DONNE was a Londoner, a student of theology and law, a traveler, and (briefly) a sea-adventurer. At one point in his youth, he turned from Catholicism to Protestantism. From 1598 to 1615 (when he was past forty), his life was a series of clerical jobs, poems for patrons, and the hazards of supporting a large family (in 1601 he had eloped with Anne More, the niece of his employer, and had been briefly imprisoned for it). In 1615, however, he was ordained in the Church of England. He became a great preacher, and in 1621 was made Dean of St. Paul's. He wrote essays, sermons, poetry; the 1624 *Devotions upon Emergent Occasions* contains the now-familiar passage, "No man is an island. . . ." His poetry was first collected in the posthumous volume of 1633—*Poems, by J. D.*

Donne is considered by many to be a "modern" poet. Both passionate and intellectual, with the shock of unusual language and the direct human voice, he has been one of the strongest influences on twentieth-century poetry. The story of his poetry goes from young Jack Donne—lover and man-of-the-world—to Dr. John Donne of the dark, intricate voice—minister, Dean of St. Paul's, and finally, a man against death. It is, in his own phrase, "a progress of the soul."

Introductory Readings

EDITION: *The Poems of John Donne*, ed. Sir H. J. C. Grierson, 2 vols. (1912); 1 vol. (1933). BIOGRAPHY: Sir Edmund Gosse, *The Life and Letters of John Donne*, 2 vols. (1899). CRITICISM: George Williamson, *The Donne Tradition* (1930); *A Garland for John Donne, 1631–1931*, ed. Theodore Spencer (1932); Joan Bennett, *Four Metaphysical Poets* (rev. ed., 1953); Clay Hunt, *Donne's Poetry* (1954); Frank Kermode, *John Donne* (1957).

THE GOOD-MORROW

I wonder, by my troth, what thou and I
Did, till we loved? were we not weaned till then?
But sucked on country pleasures, childishly?
Or snorted [1] we in the seven sleepers' den? [2]
'Twas so; but this, all pleasures fancies be.   5
If ever any beauty I did see,
Which I desired, and got, 'twas but a dream of thee.

And now good morrow to our waking souls,
Which watch not one another out of fear;
For love, all love of other sights controls,   10
And makes one little room, an every where.
Let sea-discoverers to new worlds have gone,
Let maps to other, worlds on worlds have shown,
Let us possess one world, each hath one, and is one.

My face in thine eye, thine in mine appears,   15
And true plain hearts do in the faces rest;
Where can we find two better hemispheres
Without sharp North, without declining West?
Whatever dies, was not mixed equally;
If our two loves be one, or, thou and I   20
Love so alike, that none do slacken, none can die.

SONG: [1] GO, AND CATCH A FALLING STAR

Go, and catch a falling star,
    Get with child a mandrake root, [2]
Tell me, where all past years are,
    Or who cleft the Devil's foot,
Teach me to hear mermaids singing,   5
Or to keep off envy's stinging,
        And find
        What wind
Serves to advance an honest mind.

---

[1] *snorted* slept heavily, snoring
[2] *seven sleepers' den* cave in which seven Christians of Ephesus were walled
up; they slept from A.D. 250 to 479.

---

[1] *Song* Donne's "Songs and Sonnets" were no doubt set to music. For the air
of this song, see Grierson, ed., Donne's *Poetical Works*, II, 54–55.
[2] *mandrake root* a plant whose root is thought to resemble the human form

If thou be'st born to strange sights,   10
   Things invisible to see,
Ride ten thousand days and nights,
   Till age snow white hairs on thee;
Thou, when thou return'st, wilt tell me
All strange wonders that befell thee,   15
     And swear
     No where
Lives a woman true, and fair.

If thou find'st one, let me know;
   Such a pilgrimage were sweet.   20
Yet do not, I would not go,
   Though at next door we might meet,
Though she were true, when you met her,
And last, till you write your letter,
     Yet she   25
     Will be
False, ere I come, to two, or three.

THE SUN RISING

Busy old fool, unruly Sun,
   Why dost thou thus,
Through windows, and through curtains, call on us?
Must to thy motions lovers' seasons run?
     Saucy pedantic wretch, go chide   5
     Late schoolboys and sour prentices,[1]
   Go tell Court huntsmen that the King will ride,
   Call country ants to harvest offices;
Love, all alike, no season knows, nor clime,
Nor hours, days, months, which are the rags of time.   10

     Thy beams, so reverend and strong
     Why should'st thou think?
I could eclipse and cloud them with a wink,
But that I would not lose her sight so long:
     If her eyes have not blinded thine,   15
     Look, and tomorrow late, tell me,
   Whether both the Indias of spice and mine [2]
   Be where thou left'st them, or lie here with me.

---

[1] *prentices* apprentices
[2] *spice and mine* spice from the East Indies; mines of gold in the West Indies

Ask for those Kings whom thou saw'st yesterday,
And thou shalt hear, All here in one bed lay.   20

    She's all States, and all Princes, I,
      Nothing else is.
Princes do but play us; compared to this,
All honor's mimic; all wealth alchemy.[3]
     Thou sun art half as happy as we,   25
      In that the world's contracted thus;
   Thine age asks ease, and since thy duties be
   To warm the world, that's done in warming us.
Shine here to us, and thou art every where;
This bed thy center is, these walls, thy sphere.   30

THE INDIFFERENT

I can love both fair and brown,
Her whom abundance melts, and her whom want betrays,
Her who loves loneness best, and her who masks and plays,
Her whom the country formed, and whom the town,
Her who believes, and her who tries,   5
Her who still weeps with spongy eyes,
And her who is dry cork and never cries;
I can love her, and her, and you and you;
I can love any, so she be not true.

Will no other vice content you?   10
Will it not serve your turn to do, as did your mothers?
Or have you all old vices spent, and now would find out others?
Or doth a fear, that men are true, torment you?
O, we are not, be not you so;
Let me, and do you, twenty know.   15
Rob me, but bind me not, and let me go.
Must I, who came to travail thorough you,
Grow your fixed subject, because you are true?

Venus heard me sigh this song,
And by love's sweetest part, variety, she swore   20
She heard not this till now, and that it should be so no more.
She went, examined, and returned ere long,
And said, alas, Some two or three
Poor heretics in love there be,
Which think to 'stablish dangerous constancy.   25

---

[3] *alchemy* false glitter, artificial gold

But I have told them, Since you will be true,
You shall be true to them, who're false to you.

THE CANONIZATION [1]

For God's sake hold your tongue, and let me love,
  Or chide my palsy, or my gout,
My five gray hairs, or ruined fortune flout,
    With wealth your state, your mind with arts improve,
      Take you a course, get you a place,   5
      Observe his Honor, or his Grace,
Or the King's real, or his stampèd face [2]
    Contemplate; what you will, approve,
    So you will let me love.

Alas, alas, who's injured by my love?   10
  What merchant's ships have my sighs drowned?
Who says my tears have overflowed his ground?
    When did my colds a forward spring remove?
      When did the heats which my veins fill
      Add one more [3] to the plaguey bill? [4]   15
Soldiers find wars, and lawyers find out still
    Litigious men, which quarrels move,
    Though she and I do love.

Call us what you will, we are made such by love;
  Call her one, me another fly,   20
We're tapers too, and at our own cost die,
    And we in us find th' eagle and the dove.
      The phoenix [5] riddle hath more wit
      By us; we two being one, are it.
So to one neutral thing both sexes fit;   25
    We die and rise the same, and prove
    Mysterious by this love.

We can die by it, if not live by love;
  And if unfit for tombs and hearse
Our legend be, it will be fit for verse;   30
    And if no piece of chronicle [6] we prove,

[1] *canonization* the process of declaring a person a saint after death
[2] *stamped face* face on money
[3] *more* "man," according to some Donne manuscripts
[4] *plaguey bill* list of those who are plague-stricken
[5] *phoenix* legendary bird that burned and arose again from his own ashes
[6] *chronicle* history

We'll build in sonnets pretty rooms;
  As well a well-wrought urn becomes
The greatest ashes, as half-acre tombs,
  And by these hymns, all shall approve   35
    Us *canonized* for love:

And thus invoke us: "You whom reverend love
  Made one another's hermitage; [7]
You, to whom love was peace, that now is rage;
  Who did the whole world's soul contract, and drove   40
    Into the glasses of your eyes
    (So made such mirrors and such spies,
That they did all to you epitomize)
  Countries, towns, courts: Beg from above
  A pattern of your love!"   45

THE TRIPLE FOOL

    I am two fools, I know,
  For loving, and for saying so
    In whining poetry;
But where's that wise man that would not be I,
    If she would not deny?   5
Then as th' earth's inward, narrow, crooked lanes
Do purge sea water's fretful salt away,
    I thought, if I could draw my pains
Through rhyme's vexation, I should them allay.
Grief brought to numbers cannot be so fierce,   10
For, he tames it, that fetters it in verse.

    But when I have done so,
  Some man, his art and voice to show,
    Doth set [1] and sing my pain,
And by delighting many, frees again   15
    Grief, which verse did restrain.
To love and grief tribute of verse belongs,
But not of such as pleases when 'tis read;
    Both are increasèd by such songs:
For both their triumphs so are publishèd,   20
And I, which was two fools, do so grow three;
Who are a little wise, the best fools be.

[7] *hermitage* refuge away from others

[1] *set* place in a musical setting

A FEVER

Oh do not die, for I shall hate
    All women so, when thou art gone,
That thee I shall not celebrate,
    When I remember, thou wast one.

But yet thou canst not die, I know;   5
    To leave this world behind, is death,
But when thou from this world wilt go,
    The whole world vapors with thy breath.

Or if, when thou, the world's soul, goest,
    It stay, 'tis but thy carcass then;   10
The fairest woman, but thy ghost;
    But corrupt worms, the worthiest men.

O wrangling schools, that search what fire
    Shall burn this world,[1] had none the wit
Unto this knowledge to aspire,   15
    That this her fever might be it?

And yet she cannot waste by this,
    Nor long bear this torturing wrong,
For much corruption needful is
    To fuel such a fever long.   20

These burning fits but meteors be,
    Whose matter in thee is soon spent.
Thy beauty and all parts, which are thee,
    Are unchangeable firmament.

Yet 'twas of my mind, seising [2] thee,   25
    Though it in thee cannot persever.
For I had rather owner be
    Of thee one hour, than all else ever.

THE ANNIVERSARY

All kings, and all their favorites,
    All glory of honors, beauties, wits,
The sun itself, which makes times,[1] as they pass,

[1] *O wrangling schools . . . world* (ll. 13–14) referring to many ancient
prophecies that the world would be destroyed by fire
[2] *seising* taking possession, as of lands or property

[1] *times* periods of time, such as seasons

Is elder by a year, now, than it was
When thou and I first one another saw: 5
All other things to their destruction draw,
    Only our love hath no decay;
This, no tomorrow hath, nor yesterday,
Running it never runs from us away,
But truly keeps his first, last, everlasting day.   10

    Two graves must hide thine and my corse.
    If one might, death were no divorce:
Alas, as well as other princes, we
(Who prince enough in one another be)
Must leave at last in death, these eyes, and ears,   15
Oft fed with true oaths, and with sweet salt tears;
    But souls where nothing dwells but love
(All other thoughts being inmates) [2] then shall prove
This, or a love increasèd there above,
When bodies to their graves, souls from their graves remove.   20

    And then we shall be throughly blest,
    But we no more than all the rest; [3]
Here upon earth, we are kings, and none but we
Can be such kings, nor of such subjects be.
Who is so safe as we? where none can do   25
Treason to us, except one of us two.
    True and false fears let us refrain,
Let us love nobly, and live, and add again
Years and years unto years, till we attain
To write threescore: this is the second of our reign.   30

TWICKENHAM GARDEN [1]

Blasted with sighs, and surrounded [2] with tears,
    Hither I come to seek the spring,
    And at mine eyes, and at mine ears,
Receive such balms, as else cure everything;
    But O, self-traitor, I do bring   5
The spider love, which transubstantiates [3] all,
    And can convert manna to gall;

[2] *inmates* temporary lodgers or strangers
[3] *But . . . rest* "But we will be no more blest or content than all the rest in Heaven are blest."

---

[1] *Twickenham* home of the Countess of Bedford, friend and patron of Donne
[2] *surrounded* overflowed   [3] *transubstantiates* changes forms

And that this place may thoroughly be thought
   True Paradise, I have the serpent brought.

'Twere wholesomer for me, that winter did   10
   Benight the glory of this place,
   And that a grave frost did forbid
These trees to laugh, and mock me to my face;
   But that I may not this disgrace
Endure, nor yet leave loving, Love let me   15
   Some senseless piece of this place be;
Make me a mandrake, so I may groan here,[4]
   Or a stone fountain weeping out my year.

Hither with crystal vials, lovers come,
   And take my tears, which are love's wine,   20
   And try your mistress' tears at home,
For all are false, that taste not just like mine;
   Alas, hearts do not in eyes shine,
Nor can you more judge woman's thoughts by tears,
   Than by her shadow, what she wears.   25
O perverse sex, where none is true but she,
   Who's therefore true, because her truth kills me.

THE BAIT [1]

Come live with me, and be my love,
And we will some new pleasures prove
Of golden sands, and crystal brooks,
With silken lines, and silver hooks.

There will the river whispering run   5
Warmed by thine eyes more than the sun,
And there th' enamored fish will stay,
Begging themselves they may betray.

When thou wilt swim in that live bath,
Each fish, which every channel hath,   10
Will amorously to thee swim,
Gladder to catch thee, than thou him.

If thou, to be so seen, be'st loath,
By sun, or moon, thou dark'nest both,

[4] *mandrake . . . here* According to legend, the mandrake plant would shriek or howl when torn out of the earth.

[1] Compare with Marlowe's "The Passionate Shepherd to His Love" (p. 92). The original lute music for "The Bait" is in Grierson, ed., Donne's *Poetical Works*, II, 57.

And if myself have leave to see,   15
I need not their light, having thee.

Let others freeze with angling reeds,
And cut their legs, with shells and weeds,
Or treacherously poor fish beset,
With strangling snare, or windowy net: 20

Let coarse bold hands, from slimy nest
The bedded fish in banks out-wrest,
Or curious traitors, sleave silk flies,
Bewitch poor fishes' wand'ring eyes.

For thee, thou need'st no such deceit,   25
For thou thyself art thine own bait;
That fish, that is not catched thereby,
Alas, is wiser far than I.

THE BROKEN HEART

He is stark mad, whoever says,
    That he hath been in love an hour,
Yet not that love so soon decays,
    But that it can ten in less space devour;
Who will believe me, if I swear   5
That I have had the plague a year?
    Who would not laugh at me, if I should say,
    I saw a flask of powder burn a day?

Ah, what a trifle is a heart,
    If once into Love's hands it come!   10
All other griefs allow a part
    To other griefs, and ask themselves but some;
They come to us, but us Love draws,
He swallows us, and never chaws; [1]
    By him, as by chained shot, whole ranks do die; 15
    He is the tyrant pike,[2] our hearts the fry.[3]

If 'twere not so, what did become
    Of my heart, when I first saw thee?
I brought a heart into the room,
    But from the room, I carried none with me: 20
If it had gone to thee, I know
Mine would have taught thine heart to show

---

[1] *chaws* chews   [2] *tyrant pike* voracious large fish   [3] *fry* small fish

> More pity unto me: but Love, alas,
>   At one first blow did shiver it as glass.
>
> Yet nothing can to nothing fall,   25
>   Nor any place be empty quite;
> Therefore I think my breast hath all
>   Those pieces still, though they be not unite;
> And now as broken glasses show
> A hundred lesser faces, so   30
>   My rags of heart can like, wish, and adore,
>   But after one such love, can love no more.

A VALEDICTION: FORBIDDING MOURNING [1]

> As virtuous men pass mildly away,
>   And whisper to their souls, to go,
> Whilst some of their sad friends do say,
>   The breath goes now, and some say, no:
>
> So let us melt, and make no noise,   5
>   No tear-floods, nor sigh-tempests move;
> 'Twere profanation of our joys
>   To tell the laity our love.
>
> Moving of th' earth brings harms and fears,
>   Men reckon what it did and meant;   10
> But trepidation of the spheres,
>   Though greater far, is innocent.[2]
>
> Dull sublunary [3] lovers' love
>   (Whose soul is sense) cannot admit
> Absence, because it doth remove   15
>   Those things which elemented [4] it.
>
> But we by a love, so much refined,
>   That ourselves know not what it is,
> Inter-assurèd of the mind,
>   Care less, eyes, lips, and hands to miss.   20
>
> Our two souls therefore, which are one,
>   Though I must go, endure not yet

[1] *A Valediction* given by Donne to his wife when he went on a trip to the Continent in 1612

[2] *Moving . . . innocent* (ll. 9–12) passing changes in the earth contrasted with the seasonal changes caused, according to Ptolemaic astronomy, by movements of the heavenly spheres which surrounded the earth

[3] *sublunary* under the moon, or earthly   [4] *elemented* composed

A breach, but an expansión,
  Like gold to airy thinness beat.

If they be two, they are two so   25
  As stiff twin compasses are two;
Thy soul the fixed foot, makes no show
  To move, but doth if th' other do.

And though it in the center sit,
  Yet when the other far doth roam,   30
It leans, and hearkens after it,
  And grows erect, as that comes home.

Such wilt thou be to me, who must
  Like the other foot, obliquely run;
Thy firmness makes my circle just,   35
  And makes me end, where I begun.

THE ECSTASY [1]

Where, like a pillow on a bed,
  A pregnant bank swelled up, to rest
The violet's reclining head,
  Sat we two, one another's best.
Our hands were firmly cemented   5
  With a fast balm, which thence did spring,
Our eye-beams twisted, and did thread
  Our eyes upon one double string;
So t' intergraft our hands, as yet
  Was all the means to make us one,   10
And pictures in our eyes to get
  Was all our propagation.
As 'twixt two equal armies, fate
  Suspends uncertain victory,
Our souls (which to advance their state,   15
  Were gone out) hung 'twixt her and me.
And whilst our souls negotiate there,
  We like sepulchral statues lay;
All day, the same our postures were,
  And we said nothing, all the day.   20

[1] *Ecstasy* In order to define the union of love in body and soul, Donne uses the Neoplatonic idea of "ecstasy"—a mystical state of suspension in which the soul, freed from the body, contemplates and desires to merge with the perfection of God.

JOHN DONNE

If any, so by love refined,
    That he soul's language understood,
And by good love were grown all mind,
    Within convenient distance stood,
He (though he knew not which soul spake,   25
    Because both meant, both spake the same)
Might thence a new concoction take,
    And part far purer than he came.
This ecstasy doth unperplex   30
    (We said) and tell us what we love:
We see by this, it was not sex,
    We see, we saw not what did move:
But as all several souls contain
    Mixture of things, they know not what,   35
Love, these mixed souls doth mix again,
    And makes both one, each this and that.
A single violet transplant,
    The strength, the color, and the size
(All which before was poor, and scant)   40
    Redoubles still, and multiplies.
When love, with one another so
    Interinanimates two souls,
That abler soul, which thence doth flow,
    Defects of loneliness controls.
We then, who are this new soul, know,   45
    Of what we are composed, and made,
For, th' atomies [2] of which we grow,
    Are souls, whom no change can invade.
But O alas, so long, so far
    Our bodies why do we forbear?   50
They're ours, though they're not we: we are
    The intelligences, they the sphere.
We owe them thanks, because they thus,
    Did us, to us, at first convey,
Yielded their forces, sense, to us,   55
    Nor are dross [3] to us, but allay.[4]
On man heaven's influence works not so,
    But that it first imprints the air,
So soul into the soul may flow,
    Though it to body first repair.   60
As our blood labors to beget
    Spirits, as like souls as it can,

[2] *atomies* atoms, or minute parts   [3] *dross* impure worthless matter
[4] *allay* alloy; mixed with a baser metal

Because such fingers need to knit
    That subtle knot, which makes us man: [5]
So must pure lovers' souls descend   65
    T' affections, and to faculties,
Which sense may reach and apprehend,
    Else a great prince in prison lies.
To our bodies turn we then, that so
    Weak men on love revealed may look;   70
Love's mysteries in souls do grow,
    But yet the body is his book.
And if some lover, such as we,
    Have heard this dialogue of one,
Let him still mark us, he shall see   75
    Small change, when we're to bodies gone.

LOVE'S DEITY [1]

I long to talk with some old lover's ghost,
    Who died before the god of love was born:
I cannot think that he, who then loved most,
    Sunk so low, as to love one which did scorn.
But since this god produced a destiny,   5
And that vice-nature,[2] custom, lets it be;
    I must love her, that loves not me.

Sure, they which made him god, meant not so much,
    Nor he in his young godhead practiced it;
But when an even flame two hearts did touch,   10
    His office was indulgently to fit
Actives to passives. Correspondency
Only his subject was; it cannot be
    Love, till I love her, that loves me.

But every modern god will now extend   15
    His vast prerogative, as far as Jove.
To rage, to lust, to write to, to commend,
    All is the purlieu [3] of the god of love.
Oh were we wakened by this tyranny
To ungod this child again, it could not be   20
    I should love her, who loves not me.

---

[5] *As . . . man* (ll. 61–64) In Donne's biology, Spirits were of the brain (natural), heart (vital), and liver (animal). Transmitted through the blood, they joined body and soul and gave life.

---

[1] Critical comment on this poem appears on p. 225.
[2] *vice-nature* secondary nature   [3] *purlieu* domain

Rebel and atheist too, why murmur I,
    As though I felt the worst that love could do?
Love might make me leave loving, or might try
    A deeper plague, to make her love me too,   25
Which, since she loves before, I'm loath to see;
Falsehood is worse than hate; and that must be,
    If she whom I love, should love me.

THE FUNERAL

Whoever comes to shroud me, do not harm
    Nor question much
That subtle wreath of hair [1] about mine arm;
The mystery, the sign you must not touch,
    For 'tis my outward soul,   5
Viceroy to that, which then to heaven being gone,
    Will leave this to control,
And keep these limbs, her provinces, from dissolution.

For if the sinewy thread my brain lets fall
    Through every part,   10
Can tie those parts, and make me one of all;
Those hairs which upward grew, and strength and art
    Have from a better brain,
Can better do't; except she meant that I
    By this should know my pain,   15
As prisoners then are manacled, when they're condemned to die.

Whate'er she meant by it, bury it with me,
    For since I am
Love's martyr, it might breed idolatry
If into others' hands these reliques came;   20
    As 'twas humility
To afford [2] to it all that a soul can do,
    So, 'tis some bravery,
That since you would have none of me, I bury some of you.

THE COMPUTATION

For the first twenty years, since yesterday,
I scarce believed, thou couldst be gone away;

[1] *wreath of hair* a bracelet woven of the loved one's hair. Such tokens were
sometimes spoken of as religious "reliques," symbols of sacred influence.
[2] *afford* give

For forty more, I fed on favors past,
  And forty on hopes, that thou wouldst, they might last.
Tears drowned one hundred, and sighs blew out two,   5
  A thousand, I did neither think, nor do,
  Or not divide, all being one thought of you;
  Or in a thousand more, forgot that too.
Yet call not this long life; but think that I
Am, by being dead, immortal. Can ghosts die?   10

A LECTURE UPON THE SHADOW

Stand still, and I will read to thee
A lecture, love, in love's philosophy.
    These three hours that we have spent,
    Walking here, two shadows went
Along with us, which we ourselves produced;   5
But, now the sun is just above our head,
      We do those shadows tread;
      And to brave clearness all things are reduced.
So whilst our infant loves did grow,
Disguises did, and shadows, flow,   10
From us, and our cares; but, now 'tis not so.

That love hath not attained the high'st degree,
Which is still diligent lest others see.

Except our loves at this noon stay,
We shall new shadows make the other way.   15
    As the first were made to blind
    Others, these which come behind
Will work upon ourselves, and blind our eyes.
If our loves faint, and westwardly decline,
      To me thou, falsely, thine,   20
      And I to thee mine actions shall disguise.
    The morning shadows wear away,
    But these grow longer all the day,
    But oh, love's day is short, if love decay.

Love is a growing, or full constant light;   25
And his first minute, after noon, is night.

EPIGRAM: A BURNT SHIP

Out of a fired ship, which, by no way
But drowning, could be rescued from the flame,

Some men leaped forth, and ever as they came
Near the foe's ships, did by their shot decay;
So all were lost, which in the ship were found,   5
    They in the sea being burnt, they in the burnt ship drowned.

ELEGY IX

THE AUTUMNAL [1]

No spring, nor summer beauty hath such grace,
    As I have seen in one autumnal face.
Young beauties force our love, and that's a rape;
    This doth but counsel, yet you cannot 'scape.
If 'twere a shame to love, here 'twere no shame;   5
    Affection here takes Reverence's name.
Were her first years the Golden Age? That's true,
    But now she's gold oft tried, and ever new.
That was her torrid and inflaming time;
    This is her tolerable tropic clime.   10
Fair eyes! Who asks more heat than comes from hence,
    He in a fever wishes pestilence.
Call not these wrinkles, graves; if graves they were,
    They were Love's graves; for else he is nowhere.
Yet lies not Love dead here, but here doth sit   15
    Vowed to this trench, like an anchorite.
And here, till hers, which must be his death, come,
    He doth not dig a grave, but build a tomb.
Here dwells he; though he sojourn ev'rywhere,
    In Progress, yet his standing house is here,   20
Here, where still evening is; not noon, nor night;
    Where no voluptuousness, yet all delight.
In all her words, unto all hearers fit,
    You may at revels, you at council, sit.
This is Love's timber, youth his underwood;   25
    There he, as wine in June, enrages blood,
Which then comes seasonabliest, when our taste
    And appetite to other things, is past.
Xerxes' strange Lydian love, the platan tree,
    Was loved for age, none being so large as she,[2]   30

---

[1] Written to the Lady Herbert, afterwards Lady Danvers, before 1609. She was a little more than forty, Donne about eight years younger.
[2] *Xerxes . . . she* (ll. 29-30) On his march to Greece, Xerxes decorated a large and beautiful plane tree in Lydia with gold ornaments, left it to a guardian.

Or else because, being young, nature did bless
   Her youth with age's glory, barrenness.
If we love things long sought, age is a thing
   Which we are fifty years in compassing;
If transitory things, which soon decay,   35
   Age must be loveliest at the latest day.
But name not winter faces, whose skin's slack;
   Lank, as an unthrift's purse; but a soul's sack;
Whose eyes seek light within, for all here's shade;
   Whose mouths are holes, rather worn out, than made;   40
Whose every tooth to a several place is gone,
   To vex their souls at resurrectión;
Name not these living death's-heads unto me,
   For these, not ancient, but ántique be.
I hate extremes; yet I had rather stay   45
   With tombs than cradles, to wear out a day.
Since such love's natural lation [3] is, may still
   My love descend, and journey down the hill,
Not panting after growing beauties, so,
   I shall ebb on with them, who homeward go.   50

HOLY SONNETS

7

At the round earth's imagined corners, blow
Your trumpets, angels, and arise, arise
From death, you numberless infinities
Of souls, and to your scattered bodies go,
All whom the flood did, and fire shall o'erthrow,   5
All whom war, dearth, age, agues, tyrannies,
Despair, law, chance, hath slain, and you whose eyes
Shall behold God, and never taste death's woe.
But let them sleep, Lord, and me mourn a space,
For, if above all these, my sins abound,   10
'Tis late to ask abundance of thy grace,
When we are there; here on this lowly ground,
Teach me how to repent; for that's as good
As if thou hadst sealed my pardon, with thy blood.

---

[3] *lation* in astrology, "local motion," or the motion of a body from one place to another

10

Death be not proud, though some have callèd thee
Mighty and dreadful, for thou art not so,
For those whom thou think'st thou dost overthrow,
Die not, poor Death, nor yet canst thou kill me.
From rest and sleep, which but thy pictures be,   5
Much pleasure, then from thee much more must flow,
And soonest our best men with thee do go,
Rest of their bones, and soul's delivery.
Thou art slave to fate, chance, kings, and desperate men,
And dost with poison, war, and sickness dwell,   10
And poppy, or charms can make us sleep as well,
And better than thy stroke; why swell'st thou then?
One short sleep past, we wake eternally,
And death shall be no more; Death, thou shalt die.

14

Batter my heart, three-personed God; for you
As yet but knock, breathe, shine, and seek to mend;
That I may rise and stand, o'erthrow me and bend
Your force, to break, blow, burn, and make me new.
I, like an usurped town to another due,   5
Labor to admit you, but oh, to no end;
Reason your viceroy in me, me should defend,
But is captíved, and proves weak or untrue.
Yet dearly I love you, and would be lovèd fain,
But am betrothed unto your enemy: 10
Divorce me, untie, or break that knot again,
Take me to you, imprison me, for I,
Except you enthrall me, never shall be free,
Nor ever chaste, except you ravish me.

GOOD FRIDAY, 1613. RIDING WESTWARD [1]

Let man's soul be a sphere, and then, in this,
The intelligence that moves,[2] devotion is,

---

[1] Notations on two manuscript copies of this poem: "Mr. J. Dun goeing from Sir H. G. on good friday sent him back this meditation on the way."/ "Riding to Sr Edward Harbert in Wales."
[2] *intelligence that moves* An angel or intelligence moves each sphere (Raphael —the sun, Gabriel—the moon, and so on).

And as the other spheres, by being grown
Subject to foreign motions, lose their own,
And being by others hurried every day,   5
Scarce in a year their natural form obey:
Pleasure or business, so, our souls admit
For their first mover, and are whirled by it.
Hence is't, that I am carried towards the west
This day, when my soul's form bends toward the east.   10
There I should see a Sun, by rising set,
And by that setting endless day beget;
But that Christ on this cross, did rise and fall,
Sin had eternally benighted all.
Yet dare I almost be glad, I do not see   15
That spectacle of too much weight for me.
Who sees God's face, that is self life, must die;
What a death were it then to see God die?
It made his own lieutenant, nature, shrink;
It made his footstool crack, and the sun wink.   20
Could I behold those hands which span the poles,
And tune all spheres at once, pierced with those holes?
Could I behold that endless height, which is
Zenith to us, and our antipodes,
Humbled below us? or that blood which is   25
The seat of all our souls, if not of his,
Made dirt of dust, or that flesh which was worn
By God, for his apparel, ragged and torn?
If on these things I durst not look, durst I
Upon his miserable mother cast mine eye,   30
Who was God's partner here, and furnished thus
Half of that sacrifice, which ransomed us?
Though these things, as I ride, be from mine eye,
They're present yet unto my memory,
For that looks towards them; and thou look'st towards me,   35
O Saviour, as thou hang'st upon the tree;
I turn my back to thee, but to receive
Corrections, till thy mercies bid thee leave.
O think me worth thine anger, punish me,
Burn off my rusts, and my deformity,   40
Restore thine image, so much, by thy grace,
That thou may'st know me, and I'll turn my face.

A HYMN TO CHRIST [1]

AT THE AUTHOR'S LAST GOING INTO GERMANY

In what torn ship soever I embark,
That ship shall be my emblem of thy ark;
What sea soever swallow me, that flood
Shall be to me an emblem of thy blood;
Though thou with clouds of anger do disguise   5
Thy face, yet through that mask I know those eyes,
  Which, though they turn away sometimes,
   They never will despise.

I sacrifice this island unto thee,
And all whom I loved there, and who loved me;   10
When I have put our seas 'twixt them and me,
Put thou thy sea [2] betwixt my sins and thee.
As the tree's sap doth seek the root below
In winter, in my winter now I go
  Where none but thee, th' eternal root   15
   Of true Love I may know.

Nor thou nor thy religion dost control,
The amorousness of an harmonious soul,
But thou wouldst have that love thyself. As thou
Art jealous, Lord, so I am jealous now;   20
Thou lov'st not, till from loving more, thou free
My soul. Whoever gives, takes liberty.
  O, if thou car'st not whom I love
   Alas, thou lov'st not me.

Seal then this bill of my divorce to all   25
On whom those fainter beams of love did fall;
Marry those loves which in youth scattered be
On fame, wit, hopes (false mistresses) to thee.
Churches are best for prayer, that have least light:
To see God only, I go out of sight: 30
  And to 'scape stormy days, I choose
   An everlasting night.

[1] *A Hymn to Christ* "At his going with my Lord of Doncaster [into Germany] 1619"

[2] *sea* the blood of Christ. From Donne's farewell sermon before his trip to Germany (April 18, 1619): ". . . and Christ Jesus remember us all in his Kingdome, to which, though we must sail through a sea, it is the sea of his blood, where no soul suffers shipwrack."

HYMN TO GOD MY GOD, IN MY SICKNESS [1]

Since I am coming to that holy room,
  Where, with thy choir of saints for evermore,
I shall be made thy music; as I come
    I tune the instrument here at the door,
    And what I must do then, think here before.   5

Whilst my physicians by their love are grown
  Cosmographers, and I their map, who lie
Flat on this bed, that by them may be shown
    That this is my Southwest discovery [2]
    Per fretum febris,[3] by these straits to die,   10

I joy, that in these straits, I see my West;
  For, though their currents yield return to none,
What shall my West hurt me? As West and East
    In all flat maps (and I am one) are one,
    So death doth touch the resurrectión.   15

Is the Pacific Sea my home? Or are
  The Eastern riches? Is Jerusalem?
Anyan,[4] and Magellan, and Gibraltar,
    All straits, and none but straits, are ways to them,
    Whether where Japhet dwelt, or Cham or Shem.[5]   20

We think that Paradise and Calvary,
  Christ's cross and Adam's tree, stood in one place.
Look Lord, and find both Adams met in me;
    As the first Adam's sweat surrounds my face,
    May the last Adam's blood my soul embrace.   25

So, in his purple wrapped, receive me Lord,
  By these his thorns give me his other crown;
And as to others' souls I preached thy word,
    Be this my text, my sermon to mine own,
    Therefore that he may raise, the Lord throws down.   30

[1] Written March 23, 1631, eight days before Donne's death
[2] *Southwest discovery* Straits of Magellan
[3] *per fretum febris* through the strait of fever   [4] *Anyan* Bering Strait
[5] *Japhet, Cham, Shem* sons of Noah whose descendants inhabited Europe
(Japhet), Africa (Cham or Ham), and Asia or the eastern Mediterranean
(Shem)

A HYMN TO GOD THE FATHER [1]

1

Wilt thou forgive that sin where I begun,
    Which is my sin, though it were done before?
Wilt thou forgive that sin; through which I run,
    And do run still: though still I do deplore?
        When thou hast done, thou hast not done,   5
            For I have more.

2

Wilt thou forgive that sin which I have won
    Others to sin? and, made my sin their door?
Wilt thou forgive that sin which I did shun
    A year, or two: but wallowed in, a score?   10
        When thou hast done, thou hast not done,
            For I have more.

3

I have a sin of fear, that when I have spun
    My last thread, I shall perish on the shore;
Swear by thy self that at my death thy son   15
    Shall shine as he shines now, and heretofore;
        And, having done that, thou hast done,
            I fear no more.

CRITICISM

The following essay recognizes the limited use of paraphrase in
the interpretation of a poem (see the discussion in Chapter 4,
pp. 154–155), but it uses that very limitation to show the difference between prose sense and poetic meaning. The writer considers details of language but little of imagery and metaphor.
Neither does he attempt to characterize Donne or Donne's work,
or consider the origins of the poem.

[1] Donne is said to have had this poem set to music and sung often at St.
Paul's. For the music, see Grierson, ed., Donne's *Poetical Works*, II, 252–253.

A Paraphrase of John Donne in Basic English [1]

JOHN L. SWEENEY

A good poem is not susceptible of paraphrase—at any rate of paraphrase such as Empson made of Haldane's prose. Coleridge recognized this resistance axiomatically when he said: "Whatever lines can be translated into other words of the same language without diminution of their significance either in sense or association, or any worthy feeling, are so far vicious in diction." Certain sides of the sense in which words are used in a poem may be examined, and a limited view of that "allusiveness" which, according to T. S. Eliot,[2] is in the nature of words, may be recorded in Basic.[3] But there can never be a reconstruction of these separate elements into a total equivalent of the poem. Operating as a poem these elements are inseparable; separately they are inoperable as a poem. Basic paraphrase can be properly applied to a poem only with the understanding that a reproduction of the poem by this technique is impossible and should not be attempted. A very crude copy of certain aspects of the poem is the most that can be expected. But, as William Empson has said: "The copy that you do in Basic is not important; it would be truer to say that the important thing is to see why the Basic copy is wrong. It is the starting point of thought about how the details in poetry get their effect, and what the effect is. And after all this is important for poetry, because if we are not able to get their effect we are not reading poetry at all." The Basic version of a poem may be made in prose or verse. One objection to verse paraphrase is the uncongenial character of Basic if rhyme is required. Another is that the problems of versification may distract from the business of interpretation. But a verse paraphrase will be more effective than prose in sharpening an awareness of "how details in poetry get their effect." The inevitable differences between the form of the original and the form used in the Basic version will help to focus attention on the formal

[1] A portion of John L. Sweeney's essay, "Basic in Reading," first published in *The Kenyon Review*, V (Winter, 1943).
[2] The W. P. Ker Memorial lecture, *The Music of Poetry*, given at the University of Glasgow, February, 1942.
[3] *Basic* Basic English, which uses a simplified vocabulary of 850 words.— *Editors' note.*

and sensuous aspects of the poem. Whatever insight results from this attention is not simply an added nicety, a pleasurable but superfluous experience. It is essential. For an examination of the sense in which a poet is using his words cannot be intelligently pursued without a concurrent sensuous apprehension of the architecture of his lines.

Let us take, for example, a moderately intricate poem, and subject the opening stanza to the process of Basic paraphrase, first in prose and then in verse. The poem is *Love's Deitie* by John Donne.

> I long to talke with some old lovers ghost,
>   Who dyed before the god of Love was borne:
> I cannot thinke that hee, who then lov'd most,
>   Sunke so low, as to love one which did scorne.
> But since this god produc'd a destinie,
> And that vice-nature, custome, lets it be;
>   I must love her, that loves not mee.

A paraphrase in prose might go something like this. "It would give me great pleasure and comfort to have a talk with some old-time lover whose death took place before the birth of that power which is now ruling over our ways of love. I am certain that he, who in those days was most deeply in love, would not have put such a low value on his love as to give it to someone who had no respect for it—and let his love be laughed at and looked down upon. A man has a very low opinion of himself who puts such a low value on his love. The old-time lover would not have come to this. But because this new government has given us a fixed design controlling the ways of love and because something unnatural in man lets it be so—something which has taken the place of natural impulses and keeps them in its grip—I have to go on loving a woman who has no love for me."

And the argument to justify the paraphrase:

"Clearly the writer of these lines has at heart a desire for something more material than talk with an old, dead lover. But he gets a deeper and more delicate effect by opening with this understatement. His true desire will come out with force in the development of his protest against the new order of love. After the first four lines no more is said about the old lover. It would seem that he was put there for the purpose of getting the idea of desire into the picture, and of starting a comparison between the ways of love in the old and in the new order. The change from the old to the new came with the new birth of Love's ruler. A different view was taken of love. Harmony was no longer its keynote. These points come out later, but they are important in reading the opening verses. This birth of Love is the new birth of Eros. Donne is talking about the turn—said to have come at the time of the Troubadours—from the idea of love as an experience of body and mind uniting the equal desires of lovers, to the idea of a love in which the lover, burning with desire, was forever kept at a distance and the loved one ever said 'no.' Probably there would have been some pleasure or comfort in a heart-to-heart talk about the troubles of love with a serious representative of the old order. The fact that the old lover was a *serious* lover is important. It gives the writer a chance to say quietly that he is as serious a lover in his day and way as the old lover was in his. This does not come out as a flat statement but as a suggestion dropped between 'hee' and 'then' in the third line. The words *lov'd most* are certainly to be taken as 'most deeply in love' and *not* as 'in love with most women.' In the words *sunke so low* there is the idea of a falling off in self-respect, and *scorne* here is the same sort as that in Shakespeare's 'Scorn at first makes after love the more.' *Destiny* generally is a design of events with an outcome fixed and made certain by the higher powers. Man has no control over it. *Destiny,* as used here, has been fixed by the ruler of Love so it is *destiny* controlling the ways of love and lovers. The sense in which *custom* (the common way of doing things) is to be taken, is given as *vice-nature. Vice* when joined with another word is the sign for 'in place of.' So *custom* is something which takes the place of natural impulses. *Vice* may be taken in two other senses, that of 'wrongdoing' and 'grip.' Back of the words *vice-nature* there may possibly be a suggestion that under these circumstances, unnatural acts take the place of love, as well as the idea of man being in the grip of *custom.*" These are the points which the very character of Basic leads one to stress in a prose version.

A possible verse paraphrase of this stanza would be as follows:

> Talk with some old lover
> Dead before Love came to be
> Would do my poor heart good. For he
> As full of love when living as I am now
> Would not have done what I have done,
> Have given love to an unkind, unloving one.

> But as this ruler Love has made things so,
> And ways of men have not till now said 'no,'
> No other way I see
> But give my love to one
> Who has no love for me.

It is immediately evident that only the surface of the poem has been touched. None of Donne's density is present; the flow is even, without eddy, monotonous. A harpsichord has been exchanged for a penny whistle. Even the dullest ear will note the difference between this slack, depleted rhythm and the deep discursive sigh of the original. The technical aspects of poetic construction emerge for discussion, again and again, as the comparison reveals now the peculiar power of alliteration, now a purposeful pattern of internal rhyme. In the paraphrase Donne's exquisitely alliterated opening is sacrificed to the exigencies of Basic and much of its force is lost in displacing the first person singular. But a valid first level sense of the lines is preserved, a thin outer film of meaning. This is accomplished not by equivalents but by a rephrasing which puts "longing" into words, and expresses the lover's need by the adjective "poor." The same procedure is followed in the next sentence. "Then" refers to the time before the god of Love was born, that is, the time when the old lover was alive and "lov'd most." The unlikely ambiguity of "most" is avoided by the phrase "full of love," but the significant emphasis of "hee" and "then" with its implication that "it is I who now loves most" is reduced to the words "as I am now." The self-accusatory tone is feebly reproduced in the fifth line of the paraphrase, and the lov'd one's "scorne," in the next, is sorted into "unkind" and "unloving." The full force of "vice-nature" is lost but the sense of "custom," indifferent or conniving, is kept. The compulsive "must" of the final line is limply paraphrased into an apparent absence of alternative. The Basic version gives a total impression of flaccid construction, and expression lacking edge. It is from that impression that an investigation of the excellences or infirmities of the poem may proceed. And for this task the student is equipped with a justifiable comparison on which to exercise his judgment—as justifiable, certainly, as the more usual juxtaposition of two unrelated poems whose only common characteristic is that both are required reading in a literature course.

JOHN MILTON

[1608-1674]

JOHN MILTON was—intellectually and creatively—a giant of his century and is second only to Shakespeare in English poetry. His preparation for a life of both literary and political activity was quiet but thorough. Born to a cultured London family (his father a musician and composer), he was educated in the classical, humanistic, and liberal traditions at St. Paul's school; at Christ's College, Cambridge; and in some years of private study and writing. In 1638 he visited Galileo in Italy, returned to teach a few years in London, and began planning a major poem or drama on the theme of man's fall. As a political man, he joined the cause of the Puritans and Parliament against Charles I and wrote a number of controversial pamphlets on reformation (1641), divorce (1643), education (1644), and censorship (*Areopagitica*, 1644). During the early 1640's, also, Milton began a stormy marriage with Mary Powell, the first of his three wives and mother of his three daughters. After the execution of Charles I in 1649, Milton joined Cromwell's government as Latin Secretary, working until he became totally blind in 1652. On the restoration of Charles II in 1660, he retired to complete *Paradise Lost* (1667), wrote his final poems of 1671, *Paradise Regained* and *Samson Agonistes.*

Milton's great prose work was the *Areopagitica*, still the most eloquent modern argument for intellectual freedom and individual responsibility. His major fame, of course, rests on *Paradise Lost*, the epic of man's creation and fall. In it the blind poet imagined a universe of brilliant contrasts—Heaven, Hell, and Paradise between. Man, God, and Angels play out a cosmic drama.

Introductory Readings

EDITION: *The Student's Milton,* ed. F. A. Patterson (rev. ed., 1939); *The Poetical Works of John Milton,* ed. Helen Darbishire (1955); BIOGRAPHY: *The Early Lives of Milton,* ed. Helen Darbishire (1932); James Holly Hanford, *John Milton, Englishman* (1949). CRITICISM: E. M. W. Tillyard, *Milton* (1930); James Holly Hanford, *A Milton Handbook* (4th ed., 1946); *Milton Criticism: Selections from Four Centuries,* ed. James Thorpe (1950); Rosemond Tuve, *Images and Themes in Five Poems by Milton* (1957). See also, *John Milton, Poems in English with Illustrations by William Blake,* ed. Geoffrey Keynes (1926).

ON TIME [1]

Fly envious Time, till thou run out thy race,
Call on the lazy leaden-stepping hours,
Whose speed is but the heavy plummet's [2] pace;
And glut thyself with what thy womb [3] devours,
Which is no more than what is false and vain,   5
And merely mortal dross;
So little is our loss,
So little is thy gain.
For whenas each thing bad thou hast entombed,
And last of all, thy greedy self consumed,   10
Then long Eternity shall greet our bliss
With an individual [4] kiss;
And Joy shall overtake us as a flood,
When every thing that is sincerely good
And perfectly divine,   15
With Truth, and Peace, and Love shall ever shine
About the supreme throne
Of him, t'whose happy-making sight alone,
When once our heav'nly-guided soul shall climb,
Then all this earthy grossness quit,   20
Attired with stars, we shall for ever sit,
     Triumphing over Death, and Chance, and thee O Time.

ON SHAKESPEARE

What needs my Shakespeare for his honored bones,
The labor of an age in piled stones,

[1] *On Time* Milton wrote as his first heading, "set on a clock case."
[2] *plummet* weight moving the works of a clock   [3] *womb* belly
[4] *individual* indivisible

Or that his hallowed reliques should be hid
Under a star-ypointing [1] pyramid?
Dear son of memory,[2] great heir of Fame,   5
What need'st thou such weak witness of thy name?
Thou in our wonder and astonishment
Hast built thyself a live-long monument.
For whilst to the shame of slow-endeavoring art,
Thy easy numbers flow, and that each heart   10
Hath from the leaves of thy unvalued [3] book,
Those Delphic [4] lines with deep impression took,
Then thou our fancy of itself bereaving,
Dost make us marble with too much conceiving;
And so sepulchered in such pomp dost lie,   15
That kings for such a tomb would wish to die.

1630

TO THE NIGHTINGALE

O Nightingale, that on yon bloomy spray
  Warblest at eve, when all the woods are still,
  Thou with fresh hope the lover's heart dost fill,
  While the jolly hours lead on propitious May,
Thy liquid notes that close the eye of day,   5
  First heard before the shallow cuckoo's bill,[1]
  Portend success in love; O if Jove's will
  Have linked that amorous power to thy soft lay,
Now timely sing, ere the rude bird of hate
  Foretell my hopeless doom in some grove nigh   10
  As thou from year to year hast sung too late
For my relief, yet hadst no reason why:
  Whether the Muse, or Love call thee his mate,
  Both them I serve, and of their train am I.

ON HIS HAVING ARRIVED AT THE AGE OF
TWENTY-THREE

How soon hath Time, the subtle thief of youth,
Stol'n on his wing my three and twentieth year!

[1] *star-ypointing* The *y* merely suggests an obsolete spelling.
[2] *son of memory* The Muses are daughters of Memory and Zeus; thus Milton makes Shakespeare brother of the Muses.
[3] *unvalued* invaluable   [4] *Delphic* inspired by the god of Delphi, Apollo

[1] *cuckoo's bill* The cuckoo was traditionally associated with lewdness, the nightingale with genuine love.

My hasting days fly on with full career,
But my late spring no bud or blossom shew'th.
Perhaps my semblance might deceive the truth,   5
That I to manhood am arrived so near,
And inward ripeness doth much less appear,
That some more timely-happy spirits endu'th.
Yet be it less or more, or soon or slow,
It shall be still [1] in strictest measure even   10
To that same lot, however mean or high,
Toward which Time leads me, and the will of Heaven;
All is, if I have grace to use it [2] so,
As ever in my great task-Master's eye.

LYCIDAS [1]

Yet once more, O ye laurels, and once more,
Ye myrtles brown, with ivy never sere,
I come to pluck your berries harsh and crude,
And with forced fingers rude
Shatter your leaves before the mellowing year.   5
Bitter constraint, and sad occasion dear,
Compels me to disturb your season due:
For Lycidas is dead, dead ere his prime
Young Lycidas, and hath not left his peer.
Who would not sing for Lycidas? he well knew   10
Himself to sing, and build the lofty rhyme.
He must not float upon his watery bier
Unwept, and welter [2] to the parching wind,
Without the meed of some melodious tear.
   Begin then, Sisters of the sacred well [3]   15
That from beneath the seat of Jove doth spring,
Begin, and somewhat loudly sweep the string.
Hence with denial vain, and coy [4] excuse;

---

[1] *still* always   [2] *it* refers back to "inward ripeness"

---

[1] Critical comment on this poem appears on pp. 257 and 262.
   Milton explained: *"In this Monody the Author bewails a learned Friend,
unfortunately drown'd in his passage from* Chester *on the* Irish *Sea, 1637.
And by occasion foretells the ruine of our corrupted Clergie then in their
height."* The friend was Edward King, a Cambridge classmate. *Lycidas* is the
name of one of Vergil's shepherds.
[2] *welter* toss about
[3] *Sisters of the sacred well* the Muses of the Pierian Spring, origin of poetic
inspiration at the foot of Mount Olympus.
[4] *coy* modest

So may some gentle Muse
With lucky words favor my destined urn,   20
And as he passes turn,
And bid fair peace be to my sable shroud.
For we were nursed upon the self-same hill,
Fed the same flock, by fountain, shade, and rill.
   Together both, ere the high lawns [5] appeared   25
Under the opening eyelids of the morn,
We drove afield, and both together heard
What time the gray-fly winds [6] her sultry horn,
Battening [7] our flocks with the fresh dews of night,
Oft till the star that rose, at evening, bright   30
Toward Heaven's descent had sloped his westering wheel.
Meanwhile the rural ditties were not mute,
Tempered to the oaten flute;
Rough Satyrs danced, and Fauns with cloven heel
From the glad sound would not be absent long,   35
And old Damoetas [8] loved to hear our song.
  But O the heavy change, now thou art gone,
Now thou art gone, and never must return!
Thee, Shepherd, thee the woods, and desert caves,
With wild thyme and the gadding [9] vine o'ergrown,   40
And all their echoes mourn.
The willows, and the hazel copses green,
Shall now no more be seen,
Fanning their joyous leaves to thy soft lays.
As killing as the canker [10] to the rose,   45
Or taint-worm to the weanling [11] herds that graze,
Or frost to flowers, that their gay wardrobe wear,
When first the white-thorn blows;
Such, Lycidas, thy loss to shepherd's ear.
   Where were ye, Nymphs, when the remorseless deep   50
Closed o'er the head of your loved Lycidas?
For neither were ye playing on the steep,
Where your old Bards, the famous Druids,[12] lie,
Nor on the shaggy top of Mona [13] high,
Nor yet where Deva [14] spreads her wizard stream.   55

[5] *lawns* meadows   [6] *winds* blows   [7] *Battening* fattening
[8] *Damoetas* a shepherd, possibly a Cambridge tutor   [9] *gadding* straggling
[10] *canker* cankerworm   [11] *weanling* just weaned
[12] *Druids* in ancient Celtic religion, the priests and poets
[13] *Mona* the Isle of Anglesey, the northwestern county of Wales
[14] *Deva* the river Dee, pouring into the Irish Sea near Chester, where King
began his last sea-trip

Ay me! I fondly [15] dream!
Had ye been there . . . for what could that have done?
What could the Muse herself that Orpheus bore,[16]
The Muse herself, for her enchanting son
Whom universal nature did lament,   60
When by the rout that made the hideous roar,
His gory visage down the stream was sent,
Down the swift Hebrus to the Lesbian shore?
    Alas! what boots [17] it with uncessant [18] care
To tend the homely slighted shepherd's trade,[19]   65
And strictly meditate the thankless Muse?
Were it not better done as other use,
To sport with Amaryllis in the shade,
Or with the tangles of Neaera's hair? [20]
Fame is the spur that the clear spirit doth raise   70
(That last infirmity of noble mind)
To scorn delights, and live laborious days;
But the fair guerdon [21] when we hope to find,
And think to burst out into sudden blaze,
Comes the blind Fury [22] with the abhorrèd shears,   75
And slits the thin-spun life. "But not the praise,"
Phoebus [23] replied, and touched my trembling ears:
"Fame is no plant that grows on mortal soil,
Nor in the glistering foil [24]
Set off to the world, nor in broad rumor lies,   80
But lives and spreads aloft by those pure eyes
And perfect witness of all-judging Jove;
As he pronounces lastly on each deed,
Of so much fame in Heaven expect thy meed."
    O fountain Arethuse,[25] and thou honored flood,   85
Smooth-sliding Mincius,[26] crowned with vocal reeds,
That strain I heard was of a higher mood;
But now my oat [27] proceeds,

[15] *fondly* foolishly
[16] *the Muse herself that Orpheus bore* Calliope herself could not have helped her son Orpheus as he was torn to pieces by the Thracian women, who cast his head into the Hebrus.
[17] *boots* profits   [18] *uncessant* unceasing   [19] *shepherd's trade* poet's craft
[20] *Amaryllis, Nearera* fun-loving shepherdesses   [21] *guerdon* reward
[22] *blind fury* the Fate, Atropos, who cuts the threads of men's lives
[23] *Phoebus* Apollo, god of poetic inspiration
[24] *glistering foil* glittering setting for a gem
[25] *fountain Arethuse* a fountain in Sicily figuring in traditional pastoral poetry
[26] *Mincius* an Italian (Lombard) river mentioned by Vergil
[27] *oat* oaten flute, song; see l. 33

And listens to the Herald of the Sea,
That came in Neptune's plea.[28]   90
He asked the waves, and asked the felon winds,
What hard mishap hath doomed this gentle swain?
And questioned every gust of rugged wings
That blows from off each beakèd promontory;
They knew not of his story,   95
And sage Hippotades [29] their answer brings,
That not a blast was from his dungeon strayed;
The air was calm, and on the level brine
Sleek Panope [30] with all her sisters played.
It was that fatal and perfidious bark,   100
Built in the eclipse, and rigged with curses dark,
That sunk so low that sacred head of thine.
    Next Camus,[31] reverend sire, went footing slow,
His mantle hairy, and his bonnet sedge,
Inwrought with figures dim, and on the edge   105
Like to that sanguine flower [32] inscribed with woe.
"Ah! who hath reft" (quoth he) "my dearest pledge?"
Last came, and last did go,
The Pilot of the Galilean lake; [33]
Two massy keys he bore of metals twain   110
(The golden opes, the iron shuts amain).
He shook his mitered locks, and stern bespake:
"How well could I have spared for thee, young swain,
Enow of such as for their bellies' sake
Creep and intrude, and climb into the fold!   115
Of other care they little reckoning make,
Than how to scramble at the shearers' feast,
And shove away the worthy bidden guest;
Blind mouths! that scarce themselves know how to hold
A sheep-hook, or have learned aught else the least   120
That to the faithful herdman's art belongs!
What recks it them? What need they? They are sped;
And when they list, their lean and flashy songs

[28] *Herald of the Sea . . . Neptune's plea* Triton, son of Neptune, appears in defense of his father.
[29] *Hippotades* Aeolus, god of the winds   [30] *Panope* a Nereid, or sea nymph
[31] *Camus* god of the Cambridge river Cam, here personified as wearing the traditional academic robe whose dark color is relieved by the crimson hyacinth
[32] *sanguine flower,* hyacinth, woeful because derived from the blood of Hyacinth whom Apollo accidentally killed
[33] *Pilot of the Galilean lake* St. Peter, from whose boat Christ preached, to whom were given the keys of the kingdom, and who as first bishop wears a miter

Grate on their scrannel [34] pipes of wretched straw;
The hungry sheep look up, and are not fed,   125
But swoln with wind, and the rank mist they draw,
Rot inwardly, and foul contagion spread;
Besides what the grim wolf with privy paw
Daily devours apace, and nothing said,
But that two-handed engine [35] at the door   130
Stands ready to smite once, and smite no more."
    Return, Alpheus,[36] the dread voice is past
That shrunk thy streams; return, Sicilian Muse,
And call the vales, and bid them hither cast
Their bells, and flowerets of a thousand hues.   135
Ye valleys low, where the mild whispers use
Of shades and wanton winds and gushing brooks,
On whose fresh lap the swart star [37] sparely looks,
Throw hither all your quaint enameled eyes,
That on the green turf suck the honied showers,   140
And purple all the ground with vernal flowers.
Bring the rathe [38] primrose that forsaken dies,
The tufted crow-toe, and pale jessamine,
The white pink, and the pansy freaked with jet,
The glowing violet,   145
The musk-rose, and the well-attired woodbine,
With cowslips wan that hang the pensive head,
And every flower that sad embroidery wears.
Bid amaranthus all his beauty shed,
And daffadillies fill their cups with tears,   150
To strew the laureate hearse [39] where Lycid lies.
For so to interpose a little ease,
Let our frail thoughts dally with false surmise.
Ay me! whilst thee the shores and sounding seas
Wash far away, where'er thy bones are hurled,   155
Whether beyond the stormy Hebrides,[40]
Where thou perhaps under the whelming tide
Visit'st the bottom of the monstrous world;
Or whether thou, to our moist vows denied,
Sleep'st by the fable of Bellerus old,[41]   160

[34] *scrannel* feeble   [35] *two-handed engine* sword of Divine Justice
[36] *Alpheus* Sicilian river traditionally associated with the pastoral
[37] *swart star* Sirius, the Dog Star, who blights flowers   [38] *rathe* early
[39] *hearse* bier   [40] *Hebrides* islands west of northern Scotland
[41] *Bellerus* Land's End in Cornwall

Where the great vision of the guarded Mount [42]
Looks toward Namancos and Bayona's hold; [43]
Look homeward, Angel, now, and melt with ruth; [44]
And, O ye dolphins, waft the hapless youth.
 Weep no more, woeful shepherds, weep no more,   165
For Lycidas, your sorrow, is not dead,
Sunk though he be beneath the watery floor;
So sinks the day-star [45] in the ocean bed,
And yet anon repairs his drooping head,
And tricks [46] his beams, and with new-spangled ore   170
Flames in the forehead of the morning sky:
So Lycidas sunk low, but mounted high,
Through the dear might of him that walked the waves,
Where, other groves and other streams along,
With nectar pure his oozy locks he laves,   175
And hears the unexpressive [47] nuptial song,
In the blest kingdoms meek of joy and love.
There entertain him all the Saints above,
In solemn troops, and sweet societies
That sing, and singing in their glory move,   180
And wipe the tears for ever from his eyes.
Now, Lycidas, the shepherds weep no more;
Henceforth thou art the Genius [48] of the shore,
In thy large recompense, and shalt be good
To all that wander in that perilous flood.   185
 Thus sang the uncouth swain [49] to the oaks and rills,
While the still morn went out with sandals gray;
He touched the tender stops of various quills,
With eager thought warbling his Doric [50] lay.
And now the sun had stretched out all the hills,   190
And now was dropped into the western bay;
At last he rose, and twitched [51] his mantle blue:
To-morrow to fresh woods, and pastures new.

---

[42] *guarded Mount* St. Michael's Mount (off Cornwall) which looks toward Spain
[43] *Namancos* and *Bayona* strongholds in Spain.   [44] *ruth* pity
[45] *day-star* sun   [46] *tricks* adorns   [47] *unexpressive* inexpressible
[48] *Genius* guardian spirit
[49] *uncouth swain* rustic and unlearned poet (Milton himself)
[50] *Doric* the Greek dialect used in pastorals
[51] *twitched* threw around him

ON THE LATE MASSACRE IN PIEMONT

Avenge O Lord thy slaughtered Saints,[1] whose bones
  Lie scattered on the Alpine mountains cold;
  Ev'n them who kept thy truth so pure of old
  When all our fathers worshipped stocks and stones
Forget not: in thy book record their groans   5
  Who were thy sheep, and in their ancient fold
  Slain by the bloody Piemontese that rolled
  Mother with infant down the rocks. Their moans
The vales redoubled to the hills, and they
  To Heav'n. Their martyred blood and ashes sow   10
  O'er all the Italian fields where still doth sway
The triple tyrant: [2] that from these may grow
  A hundredfold, who, having learnt thy way,
  Early may fly the Babylonian woe.[3]

ON HIS BLINDNESS

When I consider how my light is spent,[1]
  Ere half my days, in this dark world and wide,
  And that one talent [2] which is death to hide
  Lodged with me useless, though my soul more bent
To serve therewith my Maker, and present   5
  My true account, lest he returning chide,
  "Doth God exact day-labor, light denied?"
  I fondly [3] ask. But Patience, to prevent
That murmur, soon replies, "God doth not need
  Either man's work or his own gifts; who best   10
  Bear his mild yoke, they serve him best. His State
Is Kingly. Thousands [4] at his bidding speed
  And post o'er land and ocean without rest;
  They also serve who only stand and wait." [5]

---

[1] *slaughtered Saints* the Waldenses, Protestants of the section of northern Italy called in Italian, Piemonte; in English, Piedmont. They were massacred by Italian soldiers on April 24, 1655.
[2] *triple tyrant* the Pope   [3] *Babylonian woe* misery spread by Papal Court

---

[1] *light is spent* Milton became totally blind at age 42.
[2] *talent* a unit of money as well as an ability (See the parable of the servant who neglected his Lord's talent, Matt. 25:24–30.)
[3] *fondly* foolishly   [4] *Thousands* the heavenly angels
[5] *They . . . wait* the angels who stand by ready for any heavenly assignment

TO MR. LAWRENCE

Lawrence,[1] of virtuous father virtuous son,
   Now that the fields are dank, and ways are mire,
   Where shall we sometimes meet, and by the fire
   Help waste a sullen day, what may be won
From the hard season gaining? Time will run   5
   On smoother, till Favonius [2] re-inspire
   The frozen earth, and clothe in fresh attire
   The lily and rose, that neither sowed nor spun.
What neat repast shall feast us, light and choice,
   Of Attic [3] taste, with wine, whence we may rise   10
   To hear the lute well touched, or artful voice
Warble immortal notes and Tuscan [4] air?
   He who of those delights can judge, and spare
   To interpose them oft, is not unwise.

TO MR. CYRIACK SKINNER UPON HIS BLINDNESS

Cyriack, this three years' day these eyes, though clear
   To outward view of blemish or of spot,
   Bereft of light their seeing have forgot;
   Nor to their idle orbs doth sight appear
Of sun or moon or star throughout the year,   5
   Or man or woman. Yet I argue not
   Against Heaven's hand or will, nor bate a jot
   Of heart or hope; but still bear up and steer
Right onward. What supports me, dost thou ask?
   The conscience,[1] friend, to have lost them overplied   10
   In Liberty's defense, my noble task,
Of which all Europe talks from side to side.
   This thought might lead me through the world's vain mask,
   Content though blind, had I no better guide.

---

[1] *Lawrence* The son, Edward, was Milton's friend, and the father, Henry, was Cromwell's Lord President of the Council.
[2] *Favonius* Zephyrus, west wind
[3] *Attic* Greek, Athenian (traditionally delicate banquets)
[4] *Tuscan* Italian, Florentine

---

[1] *conscience* consciousness

ON HIS DECEASED WIFE

Methought I saw my late espoused saint [1]
  Brought to me like Alcestis [2] from the grave,
  Whom Jove's great son [3] to her glad husband gave,
  Rescued from death by force, though pale and faint.
Mine as whom washed from spot of child-bed taint   5
  Purification in the old Law [4] did save,
  And such, as yet once more I trust to have
  Full sight of her in Heaven without restraint,
Came vested all in white, pure as her mind.
  Her face was veiled; yet to my fancied sight   10
  Love, sweetness, goodness, in her person shined
So clear as in no face with more delight.
  But O as to embrace me she inclined,
  I waked, she fled, and day brought back my night.

PARADISE LOST

IN TWELVE BOOKS

[INVOCATION] Book I, lines 1–26

Of man's first disobedience, and the fruit
Of that forbidden tree, whose mortal taste
Brought death into the world, and all our woe,
With loss of Eden, till one greater man
Restore us, and regain the blissful seat,   5
Sing Heav'nly Muse, that on the secret top
Of Oreb, or of Sinai,[1] didst inspire
That shepherd, who first taught the chosen seed,
In the beginning how the heav'ns and earth
Rose out of chaos; or if Sion hill   10
Delight thee more, and Siloa's [2] brook that flowed
Fast by the oracle of God, I thence

[1] *espoused saint* Milton's second wife, Katharine Woodcock, died in February, 1658, several months after childbirth.
[2] *Alcestis* Admetus' wife who (in Euripides' *Alcestis*) is brought back alive from the underworld by Hercules.
[3] *Jove's great son* Hercules
[4] *the old Law* the old Levitical law prescribing the ritual of cleansing women after childbirth

[1] *Heav'nly Muse . . . Oreb, or of Sinai* the Spirit which spoke to Moses on the mountain
[2] *Sion, Siloa* sacred places in Jerusalem

Invoke thy aid to my advent'rous song,
That with no middle flight intends to soar
Above th' Aonian [3] mount, while it pursues   15
Things unattempted yet in prose or rhyme.
And chiefly thou, O Spirit,[4] that dost prefer
Before all temples the upright heart and pure,
Instruct me, for thou know'st; thou from the first
Wast present, and with mighty wings outspread   20
Dove-like sat'st brooding on the vast abyss
And mad'st it pregnant: What in me is dark
Illumine, what is low raise and support;
That to the height of this great argument
I may assert eternal providence,   25
And justify the ways of God to men.

The serpent (Satan) who caused man to lose Eden was once an
archangel who warred against God and with his crew was thrown
flaming into chaos.

[FALLEN ANGELS] Book I, lines 50–67

Nine times the space that measures day and night   [50]
To mortal men, he with his horrid crew
Lay vanquished, rolling in the fiery gulf,
Confounded though immortal: But his doom
Reserved him to more wrath; for now the thought   5
Both of lost happiness and lasting pain   [55]
Torments him; round he throws his baleful eyes
That witnessed huge affliction and dismay
Mixed with obdurate pride and steadfast hate:
At once as far as angels' ken [1] he views   10
The dismal situation waste and wild: [60]
A dungeon horrible, on all sides round
As one great furnace flamed, yet from those flames
No light, but rather darkness visible
Served only to discover sights of woe,   15
Regions of sorrow, doleful shades, where peace   [65]
And rest can never dwell, hope never comes
That comes to all, but torture without end. . . .

Satan, with unchanged pride, led his companions from the burn-
ing lake to the land.

[3] *Aonian* home of the Muses, Helicon mountain
[4] *Spirit* the Holy Spirit that aided in creation

[1] *angels' ken* angels' sight

[SATAN'S SPEECH] Book I, lines 249–263

        Farewell happy fields
Where joy for ever dwells: Hail horrors, hail   [250]
Infernal world, and thou profoundest Hell,
Receive thy new possessor: one who brings
A mind not to be changed by place or time.   5
The mind is its own place, and in itself
Can make a Heav'n of Hell, a Hell of Heav'n.   [255]
What matter where, if I be still the same,
And what I should be, all but less than he
Whom thunder hath made greater? Here at least   10
We shall be free; th' Almighty hath not built
Here for his envy, will not drive us hence: [260]
Here we may reign secure, and in my choice
To reign is worth ambition though in Hell:
Better to reign in Hell, than serve in Heav'n.   15

The legions of Satan built a kingdom in Hell, and determined to
take revenge on God's new creation. Satan went through chaos in
search of the world and man. In Heaven, a council of God and
angels foresaw man's fall but also the ultimate victory of good.
Satan flew through the universe, at last arrived at the Garden of
Eden, and in the shape of a cormorant sat on the Tree of Life to
look about him.

[EDEN] Book IV, lines 246–268

               Thus was this place,
A happy rural seat of various view;
Groves whose rich trees wept odorous gums and balm,
Others whose fruit burnished with golden rind
Hung amiable,[1] Hesperian fables [2] true,   [250] 5
If true, here only, and of delicious taste.
Betwixt them lawns, or level downs, and flocks
Grazing the tender herb, were interposed,
Or palmy hillock, or the flowery lap
Of some irriguous [3] valley spread her store,   [255] 10
Flowers of all hue, and without thorn the rose.
Another side, umbrageous grots and caves

[1] *amiable* beautiful
[2] *Hesperian fables* in Greek mythology, the garden of the Hesperides in
which grew golden apples
[3] *irriguous* well-watered

Of cool recess, o'er which the mantling vine
Lays forth her purple grape, and gently creeps
Luxuriant; meanwhile murmuring waters fall   [260]   15
Down the slope hills, dispersed, or in a lake,
That to the fringèd bank with myrtle crowned,
Her crystal mirror holds, unite their streams.
The birds their choir apply;⁴ airs, vernal airs,
Breathing the smell of field and grove, attune   [265]   20
The trembling leaves, while universal Pan
Knit with the Graces and the Hours in dance
Led on the eternal spring.

The Fiend watched the man and woman in the Garden. He learned that the Tree of Knowledge was forbidden to them, on penalty of death. And he heard Eve tell Adam of their first meeting:

[EVE'S SPEECH TO ADAM] Book IV, lines 449–477

That day I oft remember, when from sleep
I first awaked, and found myself reposed   [450]
Under a shade on flowers, much wond'ring where
And what I was, whence thither brought, and how.
Not distant far from thence a murmuring sound   5
Of waters issued from a cave and spread
Into a liquid plain, then stood unmoved   [455]
Pure as th' expanse of Heav'n; I thither went
With unexperienced thought, and laid me down
On the green bank, to look into the clear   10
Smooth lake, that to me seemed another sky.
As I bent down to look, just opposite   [460]
A shape within the wat'ry gleam appeared
Bending to look on me. I started back,
It started back, but pleased I soon returned,   15
Pleased it returned as soon with answering looks
Of sympathy and love; there I had fixed   [465]
Mine eyes till now, and pined with vain desire,
Had not a voice thus warned me, "What thou seest,
What there thou seest fair creature is thyself,   20
With thee it came and goes: but follow me,
And I will bring thee where no shadow stays   [470]
Thy coming, and thy soft embraces, he
Whose image thou art, him thou shalt enjoy
⁴ *apply* contribute

Inseparably thine, to him shalt bear   25
Multitudes like thyself, and thence be called
Mother of human race." What could I do,   [475]
But follow straight, invisibly thus led?
Till I espied thee, fair indeed and tall. . . .

*Adam and Eve, enjoying their Paradise, were protected by Gabriel
and other angels, who found Satan tempting the woman in a
dream and threw him out of the Garden. God then sent Raphael
to warn the man and woman and tell them of the time when
Satan (then an archangel) rebelled, and there was war in Heaven.
Raphael described the violent battles, and how at last the Son of
God spoke to his army:*

[WAR IN HEAVEN] Book VI, lines 801–892

" 'Stand still in bright array ye saints, here stand
Ye angels armed, this day from battle rest;
Faithful hath been your warfare, and of God
Accepted, fearless in his righteous cause,
And as ye have received, so have ye done   [805]   5
Invincibly; but of this cursèd crew
The punishment to other hand belongs;
Vengeance is his, or whose he sole appoints;
Number to this day's work is not ordained
Nor multitude, stand only and behold   [810]   10
God's indignation on these godless poured
By me; not you but me they have despised,
Yet envied; against me is all their rage,
Because the Father t' whom in Heav'n supreme
Kingdom and power and glory appertains,   [815]   15
Hath honored me according to his will.
Therefore to me their doom he hath assigned;
That they may have their wish, to try with me
In battle which the stronger proves, they all,
Or I alone against them, since by strength   [820]   20
They measure all, of other excellence
Not emulous, nor care who them excels;
Nor other strife with them do I vouchsafe.'
So spake the Son, and into terror changed
His count'nance too severe to be beheld,   [825]   25
And full of wrath bent on his enemies.
At once the four spread out their starry wings
With dreadful shade contiguous, and the orbs

Of his fierce chariot rolled, as with the sound
Of torrent floods, or of a numerous host.   [830]   30
He on his impious foes right onward drove,
Gloomy as night; under his burning wheels
The steadfast empyrean shook throughout,
All but the throne itself of God. Full soon
Among them he arrived, in his right hand   [835]   35
Grasping ten thousand thunders, which he sent
Before him, such as in their souls infixed
Plagues; they, astonished, all resistance lost,
All courage; down their idle weapons dropped;
O'er shields and helms and helmed heads he rode,   [840]   40
Of thrones and mighty seraphim prostrate,
That wished the mountains now might be again
Thrown on them as a shelter from his ire.
Nor less on either side tempestuous fell
His arrows, from the fourfold-visaged four,   [845]   45
Distinct with eyes, and from the living wheels,
Distinct alike with multitude of eyes;
One spirit in them ruled, and every eye
Glared lightning, and shot forth pernicious fire
Among th' accursed, that withered all their strength,   [850]   50
And of their wonted vigor left them drained,
Exhausted, spiritless, afflicted, fall'n.
Yet half his strength he put not forth, but checked
His thunder in mid-volley, for he meant
Not to destroy, but root them out of Heav'n: [855]   55
The overthrown he raised, and as a herd
Of goats or timorous flock together thronged,
Drove them before him thunderstruck, pursued
With terrors and with furies to the bounds
And crystal wall of Heav'n, which op'ning wide,   [860]   60
Rolled inward, and a spacious gap disclosed
Into the wasteful deep; the monstrous sight
Struck them with horror backward, but far worse
Urged them behind; headlong themselves they threw
Down from the verge of Heav'n; eternal wrath   [865]   65
Burned after them to the bottomless pit.
    Hell heard th' unsufferable noise, Hell saw
Heav'n ruining from Heav'n, and would have fled
Affrighted; but strict fate had cast too deep
Her dark foundations, and too fast had bound.   [870]   70
Nine days they fell; confounded Chaos roared,
And felt tenfold confusion in their fall

Through his wild anarchy, so huge a rout
Encumbered him with ruin: Hell at last
Yawning received them whole, and on them closed,   [875]   75
Hell their fit habitation fraught with fire
Unquenchable, the house of woe and pain.
Disburdened Heav'n rejoiced, and soon repaired
Her mural breach,[1] returning whence it rolled.
Sole victor from th' expulsion of his foes   [880]   80
Messiah his triumphal chariot turned:
To meet him all his saints, who silent stood
Eye witnesses of his almighty acts,
With jubilee advanced; and as they went,
Shaded with branching palm, each order bright   [885]   85
Sung triumph, and him sung victorious King,
Son, Heir, and Lord, to him dominion giv'n,
Worthiest to reign: he, celebrated, rode
Triumphant through mid Heav'n, into the courts
And temple of his mighty Father throned   [890]   90
On high: who into glory him received,
Where now he sits at the right hand of bliss."

*Raphael told then of the creation of the world and man, and
Adam recalled his own first days in Paradise, talked of the relationship of God and man, of perfection and knowledge. So the
counsels of Raphael ended.*

*That night, Satan returned as a mist into the Garden and en-
tered into the body of the sleeping serpent. In the morning, he
found Eve alone, and said to himself that he would cause her ruin.*

[EVE'S TEMPTATION AND FALL] Book IX, lines 494–792

So spake the Enemy of mankind, enclosed
In serpent, inmate bad, and toward Eve   [495]
Addressed his way, not with indented wave,
Prone on the ground, as since, but on his rear,
Circular base of rising folds, that towered   5
Fold above fold a surging maze, his head
Crested aloft, and carbuncle [1] his eyes;   [500]
With burnished neck of verdant gold, erect
Amidst his circling spires, that on the grass
Floated redundant. Pleasing was his shape,   10
And lovely, never since of serpent kind

---

[1] *mural breach* breach in the walls

---

[1] *carbuncle* ruby-colored

Lovelier, not those that in Illyria changed, [505]
Hermione and Cadmus,[2] or the god
In Epidaurus; [3] nor to which transformed
Ammonian Jove, or Capitoline was seen, 15
He with Olympias, this with her who bore
Scipio, the height of Rome.[4] With tract [5] oblique [510]
At first, as one who sought access, but feared
To interrupt, sidelong he works his way.
As when a ship by skillful steersman wrought 20
Nigh river's mouth or foreland, where the wind
Veers oft, as oft so steers, and shifts her sail; [515]
So varied he, and of his tortuous train
Curled many a wanton wreath in sight of Eve,
To lure her eye; she busied heard the sound 25
Of rustling leaves, but minded not, as used
To such disport before her through the field [520]
From every beast, more duteous at her call
Than at Circean call [6] the herd disguised.
He bolder now, uncalled before her stood; 30
But as in gaze admiring. Oft he bowed
His turret crest, and sleek enameled neck, [525]
Fawning, and licked the ground whereon she trod.
His gentle dumb expression turned at length
The eye of Eve to mark his play; he glad 35
Of her attention gained, with serpent tongue
Organic, or impulse of vocal air, [530]
His fraudulent temptation thus began.
    "Wonder not, sovereign mistress, if perhaps
Thou canst, who art sole wonder; much less arm 40
Thy looks, the heav'n of mildness, with disdain,
Displeased that I approach thee thus and gaze [535]
Insatiate, I thus single, nor have feared
Thy awful brow, more awful thus retired.
Fairest resemblance of thy Maker fair, 45
Thee all things living gaze on, all things thine

---

[2] *in Illyria changed,/ Hermione and Cadmus* In Ovid, Cadmus of Thebes and his wife requested to be changed into serpents.
[3] *the God/ In Epidaurus* Aesculapius, god of medicine, in the guise of a serpent in his temple in Epidaurus
[4] *Ammonian Jove . . . Rome* Both Jupiter Ammon and Jupiter Capitolinus became serpents to beget children: the first, Alexander on Olympias; the second, Scipio Africanus.
[5] *tract* path
[6] *Circean call* the commanding call of Circe to the men she had changed into animals

By gift, and thy celestial beauty adore   [540]
With ravishment beheld, there best beheld
Where universally admired; but here
In this enclosure wild, these beasts among,   50
Beholders rude, and shallow to discern
Half what in thee is fair, one man except,   [545]
Who sees thee? (and what is one?) who shouldst be seen
A goddess among gods, adored and served
By angels numberless, thy daily train."   55
    So glozed [7] the Tempter, and his proem [8] tuned;
Into the heart of Eve his words made way,   [550]
Though at the voice much marveling; at length
Not unamazed she thus in answer spake:
    "What may this mean? Language of man pronounced   60
By tongue of brute, and human sense expressed?
The first at least of these I thought denied   [555]
To beasts, whom God on their creation-day
Created mute to all articulate sound;
The latter I demur,[9] for in their looks   65
Much reason, and in their actions oft appears.
Thee, Serpent, subtlest beast of all the field   [560]
I knew, but not with human voice endued;
Redouble then this miracle, and say,
How cam'st thou speakable of mute, and how   70
To me so friendly grown above the rest
Of brutal kind, that daily are in sight?   [565]
Say, for such wonder claims attention due."
    To whom the guileful Tempter thus replied:
"Empress of this fair world, resplendent Eve,   75
Easy to me it is to tell thee all
What thou commandst, and right thou shouldst be
      obeyed.   [570]
I was at first as other beasts that graze
The trodden herb, of abject thoughts and low,
As was my food, nor aught but food discerned   80
Or sex, and apprehended nothing high:
Till on a day roving the field, I chanced   [575]
A goodly tree far distant to behold,
Loaden with fruit of fairest colors mixed,
Ruddy and gold. I nearer drew to gaze;   85
When from the boughs a savory odor blown,
Grateful to appetite, more pleased my sense   [580]

---

[7] *glozed* flattered   [8] *proem* prologue   [9] *demur* question

Than smell of sweetest fennel or the teats
Of ewe or goat dropping with milk at even,
Unsucked of lamb or kid, that tend their play.   90
To satisfy the sharp desire I had
Of tasting those fair apples, I resolved   [585]
Not to defer; hunger and thirst at once,
Powerful persuaders, quickened at the scent
Of that alluring fruit, urged me so keen.   95
About the mossy trunk I wound me soon,
For high from ground the branches would require   [590]
Thy utmost reach or Adam's. Round the tree
All other beasts that saw, with like desire
Longing and envying stood, but could not reach.   100
Amid the tree now got, where plenty hung
Tempting so nigh, to pluck and eat my fill   [595]
I spared not, for such pleasure till that hour
At feed or fountain never had I found.
Sated at length, erelong I might perceive   105
Strange alteration in me, to degree
Of reason in my inward powers, and speech   [600]
Wanted not long, though to this shape retained.
Thenceforth to speculations high or deep
I turned my thoughts, and with capacious mind   110
Considered all things visible in Heav'n,
Or Earth, or Middle,[10] all things fair and good;   [605]
But all that fair and good in thy divine
Semblance, and in thy beauty's heav'nly ray
United I beheld; no fair [11] to thine   115
Equivalent or second, which compelled
Me thus, though importune perhaps, to come   [610]
And gaze, and worship thee of right declared
Sovereign of creatures, universal dame."
  So talked the spirited sly Snake; and Eve   120
Yet more amazed unwary thus replied:
  "Serpent, thy overpraising leaves in doubt   [615]
The virtue of that fruit, in thee first proved.
But say, where grows the tree, from hence how far?
For many are the trees of God that grow   125
In Paradise, and various, yet unknown
To us; in such abundance lies our choice   [620]
As leaves a greater store of fruit untouched,
Still hanging incorruptible, till men

[10] *Middle* air   [11] *fair* beauty

Grow up to their provision, and more hands   130
Help to disburden nature of her birth."
   To whom the wily Adder, blithe and glad: [625]
"Empress, the way is ready, and not long,
Beyond a row of myrtles, on a flat,
Fast by a fountain, one small thicket past   135
Of blowing [12] myrrh and balm; if thou accept
My conduct, I can bring thee thither soon."   [630]
   "Lead then," said Eve. He leading swiftly rolled
In tangles, and made intricate seem straight,
To mischief swift. Hope elevates, and joy   140
Brightens his crest: as when a wandering fire,
Compact of unctuous vapor, which the night   [635]
Condenses, and the cold environs round,
Kindled through agitation to a flame,
Which oft, they say, some evil spirit attends,   145
Hovering and blazing with delusive light,
Misleads th' amazed night-wanderer from his way   [640]
To bogs and mires, and oft through pond or pool,
There swallowed up and lost, from succor far.
So glistered the dire Snake, and into fraud   150
Led Eve our credulous mother, to the tree
Of prohibition, root of all our woe;   [645]
Which when she saw, thus to her guide she spake:
   "Serpent, we might have spared our coming hither,
Fruitless to me, though fruit be here to excess,   155
The credit of whose virtue rest with thee,
Wondrous indeed, if cause of such effects.   [650]
But of this tree we may not taste nor touch;
God so commanded, and left that command
Sole daughter of his voice; the rest, we live   160
Law to ourselves, our reason is our law."
   To whom the Tempter guilefully replied: [655]
"Indeed? hath God then said that of the fruit
Of all these garden trees ye shall not eat,
Yet lords declared of all in Earth or air?"   165
   To whom thus Eve yet sinless: "Of the fruit
Of each tree in the garden we may eat,   [660]
But of the fruit of this fair tree amidst
The garden, God hath said, 'Ye shall not eat
Thereof, nor shall ye touch it, lest ye die.' "   170
   She scarce had said, though brief, when now more bold
The Tempter, but with show of zeal and love   [665]

[12] *blowing* blooming

To man, and indignation at his wrong,
New part puts on, and as to passion moved,
Fluctuates disturbed, yet comely, and in act   175
Raised, as of some great matter to begin.
As when of old some orator renowned   [670]
In Athens or free Rome, where eloquence
Flourished, since mute, to some great cause addressed,
Stood in himself collected, while each part,   180
Motion, each act won audience ere the tongue,
Sometimes in height [13] began, as no delay   [675]
Of preface brooking through his zeal of right:
So standing, moving, or to height upgrown
The Tempter all impassioned thus began: 185
    "O sacred, wise, and wisdom-giving plant,
Mother of science,[14] now I feel thy power   [680]
Within me clear, not only to discern
Things in their causes, but to trace the ways
Of highest agents, deemed however wise.   190
Queen of this universe, do not believe
Those rigid threats of death; ye shall not die: [685]
How should ye? by the fruit? it gives you life
To knowledge; by the threat'ner? look on me,
Me who have touched and tasted, yet both live,   195
And life more perfect have attained than fate
Meant me, by venturing higher than my lot.   [690]
Shall that be shut to man, which to the beast
Is open? or will God incense his ire
For such a petty trespass, and not praise   200
Rather your dauntless virtue, whom the pain
Of death denounced,[15] whatever thing death be,   [695]
Deterred not from achieving what might lead
To happier life, knowledge of good and evil?
Of good, how just? of evil, if what is evil   205
Be real, why not known, since easier shunned?
God therefore cannot hurt ye, and be just;   [700]
Not just, not God; not feared then, nor obeyed:
Your fear itself of death removes the fear.
Why then was this forbid? Why but to awe,   210
Why but to keep ye low and ignorant,
His worshipers; he knows that in the day   [705]
Ye eat thereof, your eyes that seem so clear,
Yet are but dim, shall perfectly be then

[13] *height* at the height of his argument   [14] *science* knowledge
[15] *denounced* threatened

Opened and cleared, and ye shall be as gods,   215
Knowing both good and evil as they know.
That ye should be as gods, since I as man,   [710]
Internal man,[16] is but proportion meet,
I of brute human, ye of human gods.
So ye shall die perhaps, by putting off   220
Human, to put on gods, death to be wished,
Though threatened, which no worse than this can bring. [715]
And what are gods that man may not become
As they, participating godlike food?
The gods are first, and that advantage use   225
On our belief, that all from them proceeds;
I question it, for this fair Earth I see,   [720]
Warmed by the sun, producing every kind,
Them nothing. If they all things, who enclosed
Knowledge of good and evil in this tree,   230
That whoso eats thereof, forthwith attains
Wisdom without their leave? and wherein lies   [725]
Th' offense, that man should thus attain to know?
What can your knowledge hurt him, or this tree
Impart against his will if all be his?   235
Or is it envy, and can envy dwell
In heav'nly breasts? These, these and many more   [730]
Causes import [17] your need of this fair fruit.
Goddess humane, reach then, and freely taste."
    He ended, and his words replete with guile   240
Into her heart too easy entrance won.
Fixed on the fruit she gazed, which to behold   [735]
Might tempt alone, and in her ears the sound
Yet rung of his persuasive words, impregned [18]
With reason, to her seeming, and with truth;   245
Meanwhile the hour of noon drew on, and waked
An eager appetite, raised by the smell   [740]
So savory of that fruit, which with desire,
Inclinable now grown to touch or taste,
Solicited her longing eye; yet first   250
Pausing a while, thus to herself she mused:
    "Great are thy virtues, doubtless, best of fruits,   [745]
Though kept from man, and worthy to be admired,
Whose taste, too long forborne, at first assay [19]
Gave elocution to the mute, and taught   255
The tongue not made for speech to speak thy praise.

[16] *Internal man* like man inside, intellectually (but not in appearance)
[17] *import* prove   [18] *impregned* impregnated   [19] *assay* try

Thy praise he also who forbids thy use,   [750]
Conceals not from us, naming thee the Tree
Of Knowledge, knowledge both of good and evil;
Forbids us then to taste, but his forbidding   260
Commends thee more, while it infers the good
By thee communicated, and our want;   [755]
For good unknown, sure is not had, or had
And yet unknown, is as not had at all.
In plain then, what forbids he but to know,   265
Forbids us good, forbids us to be wise?
Such prohibitions bind not. But if death   [760]
Bind us with after-bands, what profits then
Our inward freedom? In the day we eat
Of this fair fruit, our doom is, we shall die.   270
How dies the Serpent? He hath eat'n and lives,
And knows, and speaks, and reasons, and discerns,   [765]
Irrational till then. For us alone
Was death invented? or to us denied
This intellectual food, for beasts reserved?   275
For beasts it seems: yet that one beast which first
Hath tasted, envies not, but brings with joy   [770]
The good befall'n him, author unsuspect,[20]
Friendly to man, far from deceit or guile.
What fear I then, rather what know to fear   280
Under this ignorance of good and evil,
Of God or death, of law or penalty?   [775]
Here grows the cure of all, this fruit divine,
Fair to the eye, inviting to the taste,
Of virtue to make wise: what hinders then   285
To reach, and feed at once both body and mind?"
   So saying, her rash hand in evil hour   [780]
Forth reaching to the fruit, she plucked, she eat:
Earth felt the wound, and nature from her seat
Sighing through all her works gave signs of woe,   290
That all was lost. Back to the thicket slunk
The guilty Serpent, and well might, for Eve   [785]
Intent now wholly on her taste, naught else
Regarded; such delight till then, as seemed,
In fruit she never tasted, whether true   295
Or fancied so, through expectation high
Of knowledge, nor was godhead from her thought.   [790]
Greedily she engorged without restraint,
And knew not eating death.
[20] *author unsuspect* an authority reliable

*Eve gave the fruit to Adam, who ate not in ignorance but in love,
so that he would not be parted from her. But their disaster was
soon clear: Sin and Death entered the World, and though God
told of the great victory of his Son, he ordered Adam and Eve out
of Paradise. First, the Angel Michael showed Adam the future,
and taught him the way:
Adam said,*

[EXIT FROM EDEN] Book XII, lines 561–649

"Henceforth I learn, that to obey is best,
And love with fear the only God, to walk
As in his presence, ever to observe
His providence, and on him sole depend,
Merciful over all his works, with good   [565]   5
Still overcoming evil, and by small
Accomplishing great things, by things deemed weak
Subverting worldly strong, and worldly wise
By simply meek; that suffering for truth's sake
Is fortitude to highest victory;   [570]   10
And to the faithful, death the gate of life;
Taught this by his example whom I now
Acknowledge my redeemer ever blest."
     To whom thus also the angel last replied:
"This having learned, thou hast attained the sum   [575]   15
Of wisdom; hope no higher, though all the stars
Thou knewst by name, and all th' ethereal powers,
All secrets of the deep, all nature's works,
Or works of God in Heav'n, Air, Earth, or Sea,
And all the riches of this world enjoyedst,   [580]   20
And all the rule, one empire; only add
Deeds to thy knowledge answerable, add faith,
Add virtue, patience, temperance, add love,
By name to come called charity, the soul
Of all the rest: then wilt thou not be loath   [585]   25
To leave this Paradise, but shalt possess
A paradise within thee, happier far.
Let us descend now therefore from this top
Of speculation; [1] for the hour precise
Exacts our parting hence; and see the guards,   [590]   30
By me encamped on yonder hill, expect
Their motion, at whose front a flaming sword,
In signal of remove, waves fiercely round;

---

[1] *speculation* looking out

We may no longer stay: go, waken Eve;
Her also I with gentle dreams have calmed   [595]   35
Portending good, and all her spirits composed
To meek submission: thou at season fit
Let her with thee partake what thou hast heard,
Chiefly what may concern her faith to know,
The great deliverance by her seed to come   [600]   40
(For by the woman's seed) on all mankind,
That ye may live, which will be many days,
Both in one faith unanimous though sad,
With cause for evils past, yet much more cheered
With meditation on the happy end."   [605]   45
    He ended, and they both descend the hill;
Descended, Adam to the bower where Eve
Lay sleeping ran before, but found her waked;
And thus with words not sad she him received:
    "Whence thou returnst, and whither wentst, I know; [610]   50
For God is also in sleep, and dreams advise,
Which he hath sent propitious, some great good
Presaging, since with sorrow and heart's distress
Wearied I fell asleep: but now lead on;
In me is no delay; with thee to go,   [615]   55
Is to stay here; without thee here to stay,
Is to go hence unwilling; thou to me
Art all things under Heav'n, all places thou,
Who for my willful crime art banished hence.
This further consolation yet secure   [620]   60
I carry hence: though all by me is lost,
Such favor I unworthy am vouchsafed,
By me the promised seed shall all restore."
    So spake our mother Eve, and Adam heard
Well pleased, but answered not; for now too nigh   [625]   65
The archangel stood, and from the other hill
To their fixed station, all in bright array
The cherubim descended; on the ground
Gliding meteorous, as ev'ning mist
Ris'n from a river o'er the marish ² glides,   [630]   70
And gathers ground fast at the laborer's heel
Homeward returning. High in front advanced,
The brandished sword of God before them blazed
Fierce as a comet; which with torrid heat,
And vapor as the Libyan air adust,³   [635]   75

---

² *marish* marsh   ³ *Libyan air adust* hot Sahara wind

Began to parch that temperate clime; whereat
In either hand the hastning angel caught
Our lingering parents, and to th' eastern gate
Led them direct, and down the cliff as fast
To the subjected plain; then disappeared.   [640]   80
They looking back, all th' eastern side beheld
Of Paradise, so late their happy seat,
Waved over by that flaming brand, the gate
With dreadful faces thronged and fiery arms:
Some natural tears they dropped, but wiped them soon; [645]   85
The world was all before them, where to choose
Their place of rest, and providence their guide:
They hand in hand with wand'ring steps and slow,
Through Eden took their solitary way.

THE END

CRITICISM

Two essays on "Lycidas" may be compared here for their quite
different approaches to the poem. Helen Darbishire in "Milton's
Poetic Language" concentrates on the language of the poem:
what it reveals about Milton's skill as a poet and about his intention in the poem. But she is also relating "Lycidas" (through
its language) to a larger field—the conventions and tone of the
pastoral elegy (see the discussion of elegy and pastoral poetry in
Chapter 2, pp. 71, 91). Richard P. Adams also looks at "Lycidas" as a pastoral elegy, but he combines this approach with
the tracing of the archetypal pattern of death and rebirth in the
poem (see the discussion of archetypal criticism in Chapter 4,
pp. 167–168). Note also that Miss Darbishire has studied manuscripts of "Lycidas" and is able to comment on the poem's composition (compare the "biographies" of the Whitman and Dickinson poems, Chapter 4, pp. 160–162). While her essay stays almost entirely with the poem, and is even restricted to particular
lines and passages, the following essay on "Lycidas" and archetypal patterns goes often to relationships with other figures,
stories, and myths. Neither essay says much of the personal side
of the poem. Do critics study "Lycidas" primarily in terms of
pastoral elegy or archetypes? To compare what other critics have
done with the poem, see also John Crowe Ransom's "A Poem
Nearly Anonymous" (*The World's Body,* 1938); Rosemond

Tuve's "Theme, Pattern, and Imagery in *Lycidas*" (*Images and Themes in Five Poems by Milton*, 1957); and John Edward Hardy's "Lycidas" (*Kenyon Review*, 1945).

Milton's Poetic Language [1]

HELEN DARBISHIRE

Milton was by instinct first, and then by trained habit, a craftsman. It is our luck to be able to watch him at work in some of his early poems, for they are preserved in a manuscript which he used as a kind of work-book [now in the Library of Trinity College, Cambridge]. The most interesting glimpses of his handling of language are to be got in the pages of *Lycidas* and *Comus*. First consider the decorum of his language in *Lycidas*. Milton inevitably conceives *Lycidas* in the form of the classical elegy. The general character of the decorum is decreed by the tradition of the pastoral, which passed from Greek poetry to Latin, thence into Italian, French and English; taking in, in the medieval period, a fresh strand through the obvious usefulness of its imagery of sheep and shepherds for satire on the clergy and the Church. Milton weaves in all the strands in *Lycidas* in a manner triumphantly his own. It is no set piece: and it has a particular, a living decorum of style to fit his subject, this lament for a young man of high character destined for the Church, cruelly cut off in his promise. He wants sheer beauty, like the beauty of Theocritus's lament for Adonis; he wants the monumental quality, the reverberating prophetic note of Virgil's eclogue on the dead Daphnis; he wants the simple feeling that can only come home to the heart through English phrases and cadences; and for the true pastoral setting he wants some touches of the rusticity of simple country speech.

The words he calls into play, the idioms, the constructions, answer his needs.

The Greek word *amaranthus,* as beautiful in sound as in meaning, sets the key to lines which could only be composed by one whose ears are filled with the melody of Greek poetry:

[1] A portion of Helen Darbishire's essay, "Milton's Poetic Language," first published in *Essays and Studies of the English Association, 1957* (John Murray, 1957).

> Bid *Amaranthus* all his beauty shed
> And daffadillies fill their cups with tears
> To strew the Laureat hearse where *Lycid* lies.

From Latin poetry he learnt the art of masterly close phrasing which sets each chosen word in its right place, like stones in a mosaic, thus:

> To tend the homely slighted Shepherds trade,
> And strictly meditate the thankles Muse.

"To meditate the muse" is not English; the phrase is Virgilian, *meditare musam*. Yet in its weight, compression and severe dignity as Milton puts his stamp upon it, it is final.

English poetry and natural English speech are there too, when the sense demands an English background and associations. His friend is dead, and the Spring will come and the countryside will be without him:

> As killing as the Canker to the Rose
> Or Taint-worm to the weanling Herds that graze
> Or Frost to Flowers that their gay wardrop wear
> When first the Whitethorn blows;
> Such, *Lycidas,* thy loss to Shepherds ear.

The last line echoes *A Midsummer Night's Dream:*

> More tunable than lark to Shepherd's ear;

and the image of the canker and the rose and the words "When first the whitethorn blows" bring back Shakespeare's

> as the most forward bud
> Is eaten by the canker ere its blows.

Taint-worm and *weanling* belong to English country speech. And throughout *Lycidas* the rustic flavour is tasted in such scattered words as these: the *uncouth* swain, *swart* star, *rugged* wings.

There is one passage in the poem where this general character of the language with its sustained beauty, dignity and rustic grace changes, and a new decorum is obeyed. This is St. Peter's angry burst of invective against the Church in Milton's day:

> He shook his Miter'd locks, and stern bespake:
> How well could I have spar'd for thee young swain,
> Anow of such as for their bellies sake,
> Creep and intrude and climb into the fold!
> Of other care they little reck'ning make

Than how to scramble at the shearer's feast,
And shove away the worthy bidden guest
Blind mouthes! that scarce themselves know how to hold
A Sheep-hook, or have learn'd ought els the least
That to the faithful Herdmans art belongs!
What recks it them? What need they? They are sped;
And when they list, their lean and flashy songs
Grate on their scrannel pipes of wretched straw;
The hungry Sheep look up, and are not fed,
But swoln with wind, and the rank mist they draw,
Rot inwardly, and foul contagion spread.

Here a harsh and ugly strain is matched by vocabulary and idiom. "Anow of such," "for their bellies sake," "shove away," "lean and flashy songs," "grate on their scrannel pipes": these phrases belong to rough, unlettered speech, as do the ugly monosyllables that crowd into the last lines: *swoln, rank, rot, foul.* "Scrannel," according to the Oxford Dictionary, is a nonce-word, Milton its apparent author. But in fact it is a dialect word, and you can still hear talk in Lancashire of an "owd 'ooman wi' *a scrannel voice."* Milton follows Spenser, who in his *Shepherds Calendar* chose as his medium for satire a harsh, rustic speech, sprinkled with dialect forms.

Dr. Johnson did not admire *Lycidas,* and as we all remember called its numbers unpleasing, its diction *harsh.* Is it? If you isolate the phrases, it certainly is: *blind mouths* is a harsh phrase. How can a mouth, blind or not, hold a sheephook? *Melodious tear* is strange unless we remember the common Elizabethanism of *tear* for *lament.* To make a tear vocal had become a simple literary convention. We accept *Tears of the Muses.* But if you would be reminded of how badly the convention could be used, here is a sample of the elegy by Cleveland which stands immediately before *Lycidas* in the little Cambridge book of *Obsequies to the memorie of Mr. Edward King:*

> I like not tears in tune: nor will I prise
> His artificial grief that scannes his eyes;
> Mine weep down pious beads: but why should I
> Confine them to the Muses Rosarie?
> I am no Poet here; my penn's the spout
> Where the rain water of my eyes run out,
> In pitie of that name, whose fate we see
> Thus copied out in grief's Hydrographie.

There's language for you!

"I like not tears in tune," he says, but neither do we when Cleveland sheds them. We cannot care for his tuneful tears or his tearful tune: whereas Milton's *melodious tear* we welcome with delight: "Without the meed of some melodious tear." How much does our pleasure in the phrase owe to the beauty of its sound, its perfect rightness in its context? Milton took especial care with his epithets, their sound as well as their sense: we see this again and again in his manuscript.

> Under the opening eyelids of the morn
> We drove afield . . .

That sounds precisely right. But Milton first wrote "under the *glimmering* eyelids," a much more arresting epithet, not only giving a clear note of the time, but a subtle suggestion of the effect of the early morning light. For myself I cannot help connecting those "glimmering eyelids of the morn" with the "twinckling eyelids" of Pastorella in Spenser's haunting stanza, full of the imagery of light, in Book VI of the *Faerie Queene*. She seems to be dying, but is just alive:

> Her lovely light was dimmèd and decayd
> With cloud of death upon her eyes displayed:
> Yet did the cloud make even that dimmed light
> Seem much more lovely in that darknesse layd
> And 'twixt the twinckling of her eyelids bright
> To sparke out little beams, like starres in foggie night.

However that may be, "the glimmering eyelids of the morn" carry the subtle suggestion of light a little further than Milton wants in his simple statement of the two young shepherds setting out at dawn. So he substitutes an inherited poetic phrase which gives him the vigorous sound he needs—the right broad vowel in *opening*. His sensitive ear insisted on a similar change in a line in *Comus:*

> Thou *hovering* angel girt with golden wings . . .

He first wrote *"flittering* angel," but rejected the thin-sounding "flittering" (as too bat-like, perhaps?).

There is one vital passage in this manuscript of *Lycidas* where composition is going on. This is so remarkable a lesson in a craftsman's handling of language that I cannot pass it by. It begins:

What could the muse herself that Orpheus bore . . .

Milton first wrote:

> What could the golden-hayrd Calliope
> for her enchanting son
> When she beheld (the gods far-sighted be)
> His goarie scalp rowle down the Thracian lee . . .

Then he crossed out the two last lines and wrote:

> Whom universal nature might lament
> and heaven and hell deplore
> When his divine head down the stream was sent
> down the swift Hebrus to the Lesbian shore . . .

Again he was dissatisfied. The scene asserted itself in fuller life, and he wrote:

> When *by the rout that made the hideous roar*
> his goarie visage down the stream was sent . . .

And returning to the opening passage with a deeper sense of its import, he abandoned the golden-hayrd Calliope, and wrote:

> What could the Muse herself that Orpheus bore
> The Muse herself for her enchanting son
> Whom universal nature did lament . . .

Following him through the successive versions we glimpse that intense and arduous activity that belongs to artistic genius. The first version seems unsatisfying only after reading the final one. Gone is "the golden-haired Calliope," but with what glorious compensation in the solemn, rhythmic entry of "The Muse herself." Calliope no longer scans the distant stream for the gory scalp that moves down it; but a new delight of contrast appeases the imagination in the rushing in of the noisy turbulent rout— "the rout that made the hideous roar" (every word precisely right in sound and suggestion)—upon the serene, grave beauty of the opening and closing lines. The central feeling deepens, and charges every word and cadence. The most significant alteration, where all is significant and exciting, is to me that which exchanges a phrase truly poetical, "the golden-haired Calliope," for words which seem to reduce language to its barest elements:

> What could the Muse herself that Orpheus bore?

Only a great poet can do this.

The Archetypal Pattern of Death and Rebirth in Milton's "Lycidas" [1]

RICHARD P. ADAMS

It has been made increasingly evident by critics in recent years that the drowning of Edward King was the occasion, rather than the subject, of *Lycidas*. Milton's concern was generally with the life, death, and resurrection of the dedicated poet, and specifically with his own situation at the time. From this premise it follows that there are no digressions in the poem and that the form and traditions of pastoral elegy are entirely appropriate to its intentions.

Every serious poet must at some time come to an emotional realization of the length of art and the shortness of life. He, more than most men, desires immortality, which he tries to achieve in his works, to leave, as Milton said, "something so written to after-times, as they should not willingly let it die." It is an appalling thought that he may die himself before his work is done, and this thought may be most sharply imposed upon him by the death of a friend or acquaintance who is also a poet of some worth or promise. Such an event is likely to be felt as an impelling occasion to find some way of reconciling the desire for immortality with the certainty of death. Many poets, from Moschus or (whoever wrote the *Lament for Bion*) to Matthew Arnold, have used for this purpose the conventions of pastoral elegy as established by Theocritus in his *Lament for Daphnis*. They have made additions and modifications, but the continuity of the traditional form remains unbroken. Milton chose it because he considered it an appropriate vehicle for the expression of his feelings. The result renders any apology absurd.

The conventions of pastoral elegy were appropriate because they had been hammered out over the centuries by poets concerned, as Milton was, with the problem and the mystery of death. In the cultural medium of their origin, the Hellenistic world of the third century B.C., the most popular solutions of the problem of death were expressed in the rituals of various fertility cults. It is therefore not surprising to find that Adonis

[1] Reprinted from PMLA, LXIV (March, 1949).

appeared in the *Fifteenth* and *Thirtieth Idylls* of Theocritus and that Bion's pastoral elegy was a *Lament for Adonis.* Similarly, in the *Lament for Bion,* a long list of mourners was capped by the statement that "Cypris loves thee far more than the kiss wherewith she kissed the dying Adonis." Analogies between the conventions of fertility ritual and those of pastoral elegy are numerous and obvious, and some of them at least were clearly seen by Milton, who used them to reinforce the imagery of *Lycidas.* He also used appropriate Christian materials and some references to mediæval history and legend where they matched his pattern.

The result is a remarkably tight amalgam of death-and-rebirth imagery, drawn from a more than catholic variety of sources. It is far from being merely eclectic, however. Each individual image and reference has its immediate purpose and its relevancy to the form of the whole.

The emotional pattern of the poem consists of a two-fold movement. First it goes from the announcement of the friend's death downward through various expressions of sorrow to despair; then comfort is offered, and the sequence reverses itself until the conclusion is reached in heavenly joy. It is the conventional pattern of pastoral elegy, at least from the time of Virgil, and it is at the same time the pattern of Milton's feeling about death at the time he wrote *Lycidas.* There is no mystery or contradiction in the facts that *Lycidas* is one of the most richly traditional and conventional of all pastoral elegies, and that it is at the same time one of the most intensely personal in its expression of the poet's emotion. The two things do not conflict; they work together and reinforce each other. This effect can be demonstrated by an examination of individual images in relation to the overall pattern.

The opening invocation exposes a vein of death-and-rebirth imagery concerned with various forms of vegetation. The laurel, the myrtle, and the ivy are evergreens. Besides being emblems of poetry they are symbols of immortality generally, in contrast to deciduous plants. All of them have been held sacred to fertility gods and demigods. Adonis, in one version of his myth, was born out of a myrtle tree. The laurel was supposed to have been a sweetheart of Apollo transformed into a tree to escape his pursuit. The ivy was sacred to Dionysus.

The transformation by some deity of a mortal into a plant or flower was a favorite symbol of immortality in the classical myths. It is recalled in Milton's reference to "that sanguine flower inscrib'd with woe" (l. 106); that is, the hyacinth, which sprang from the blood of a young prince of Amyclae beloved and accidentally killed by Apollo, just as the rose (l. 45) was said to have sprung from the blood of Adonis and the violet (l. 145) from that of Attis, the fertility demigod of Phrygia. The amaranth (*Amaranthus*, l. 149) was also a symbol of immortality; its Greek root, coined for the purpose, meant "unfading." In *Paradise Lost* Milton spoke of it as

> Immortal Amarant, a Flour which once
> In Paradise, fast by the Tree of Life
> Began to bloom. . . . [III, 354-356]

These specific references are of course in addition to the general applications of the annual cycle of blighted and reviving vegetation. The ritual observances in the fertility cults were designed partly to assist in the completion of the cycle, the revival of the demigod being accompanied by a sympathetic revival of fertility in plants and animals. In this connection the pathetic fallacy, one of the most persistent of the conventions of pastoral elegy, is no fallacy at all but a perfectly logical aspect of the ritual. In pastoral elegy, however, the application is often reversed, as it is in *Lycidas,* so that flowers, and vegetation generally, symbolize the promise of rebirth for the poet's friend as well as the mourning for his death.

The fact that King died by drowning perhaps fortuitously but nonetheless effectively opened up to Milton a much larger range of death-and-rebirth imagery, which he exploited with his usual thoroughness. No less than fifty lines, out of a total of 193, are concerned with water in one way or another. Water was of course a prime symbol of fertility in all the ancient cults, for reasons that Milton seems to recognize in connection with his flowers, which grow near "gushing brooks" (l. 137) and which "suck the honied showres" (l. 140). By the same association, the two friends had gone out "by fountain, shade, and rill" (l. 24), "Batt'ning our flocks with the fresh dews of night" (l. 29). He himself sang "to th'Okes and rills" (l. 186). Several references involving water are specifically to themes of death and rebirth, one of the most definite being the legend of Alpheus and Arethusa (ll. 132–133), to which Milton had referred in *Arcades:*

> Divine *Alpheus,* who by secret sluse,
> Stole under Seas to meet his *Arethuse.* . . . [30–31]

The nymph herself, transformed into a fountain, is a symbol of immortality in much the same sense as the rose, the violet, and the hyacinth. Milton's personification of Cambridge University as the River Cam (*Camus,* l. 103) is in harmony, and St. Peter as "The Pilot of the *Galilean* lake" (l. 109) is nearly related. This reference emphasizes the pattern of death and rebirth in two specific connections, the story of Peter's walk on the water, beginning to sink and being raised by Christ, and the fact that he was the keeper of the keys. The first item is reserved, while the second is developed immediately:

> Two massy Keyes he bore of metals twain,
> (The Golden opes, the Iron shuts amain) [110–111]

Milton goes to some length to show that water, the principle of life, is not responsible for the death of Lycidas. Triton ("the Herald of the Sea," l. 96) testifies that the winds were at home and that the Nereids ("Sleek *Panope* with all her sisters," l. 99) were attending to their duty as protectresses of ships and sailors. The blame is put finally on the man-made ship which, in defiance of the powers of nature, had been "Built in th'eclipse, and rigg'd with curses dark" (l. 101).

For some reason the descent into water which is often a feature of death-and-rebirth cycles is, if not often, at least sometimes associated with the dragon-fight theme, especially in North European mythology. Beowulf's fight with Grendel's mother in the cave under the mere is perhaps the most familiar example. Milton did not know *Beowulf,* but he paralleled the incident in *Lycidas:*

> Where thou perhaps under the whelming tide
> Visit'st the bottom of the monstrous world;
> Or whether thou to our moist vows deny'd,
> Sleep'st by the fable of *Bellerus* old,
> Where the great vision of the guarded Mount
> Looks toward *Namancos* and *Bayona's* hold. . . . [157–163]

The parallel is complete if the word "monstrous" is interpreted to mean "full of monsters." There is no uncertainty about the references to Corineus, the slayer of Gogmagog, and to St. Michael, the dragon fighter par excellence of Christian tradition. The appeal to the dolphins to "waft the haples youth" (l. 164) follows naturally. It may refer to the story of Palaemon, whose body was carried ashore by dolphins, or to that of Arion, who was saved by them from drowning, or both. Ovid told a somewhat similar story of Bacchus, to which Milton referred in *Comus* (ll. 48–49).

The descent into and re-emergence from water is specifically related by Milton to the setting and rising of the sun [2] as a symbol of death and rebirth.

> Weep no more, woful Shepherds weep no more,
> For *Lycidas* your sorrow is not dead,
> Sunk though he be beneath the watry floar,
> So sinks the day-star in the Ocean bed,
> And yet anon repairs his drooping head,
> And tricks his beams, and with new spangled Ore,
> Flames in the forehead of the morning sky:
> So *Lycidas* sunk low, but mounted high,
> Through the dear might of him that walk'd the waves. . . . [165–173]

Besides respecifying and reinforcing the reference to St. Peter's adventure (l. 109) this passage coordinates two accounts of the sun's journey from rising to setting. The first of these represents in parallel the life of the two friends at Cambridge (ll. 25–31), and the second represents the life of the surviving poet:

> Thus sang the uncouth Swain to th'Okes and rills,
> While the still morn went out with Sandals gray,
> He touch'd the tender stops of various Quills,
> With eager thought warbling his *Dorick* lay:
> And now the Sun had stretch'd out all the hills,
> And now was dropt into the Western Bay;
> At last he rose, and twitch'd his Mantle blew:
> To morrow to fresh Woods, and Pastures new. [186–193]

[2] For the present interpretation it makes little difference whether the term "day-star" is taken to mean the sun itself or whether, as seems likely, it refers to Hesperus and Lucifer (Jerram, p. 85). If the day-star is not the sun, it accompanies the sun in its death-and-rebirth journey under the ocean. In this connection, it is interesting and perhaps significant that Selden remarked of the mourning and rejoicing in the cult of Thammuz, "Those who first instituted these laments were not thinking of anything but the approach and departure of the sun, which they mourned at one time as something lost, and which they customarily received with happy auguries after it was reborn" (*De Diis Syriis*, p. 246).

These passages render in a very striking way the pattern of life, death, and rebirth with which the poem as a whole is concerned.

The last quotation recalls the fact that Milton was expressing his own feelings in *Lycidas,* and not any abstract or general or public sorrow. The personal note established in the first five lines is maintained throughout. It is struck again in the passage where he puts himself in the dead man's place (ll. 19–22), hoping that "some gentle Muse" will turn aside to confer on him the immortality which he is giving King. He deliberately takes to himself here the emotional experience of death and, at least by implication, of rebirth.

The nadir of the movement from life through death to resurrection follows logically by way of the reference to Orpheus, in which death is presented as final. The reference expands in at least three directions, two of which are exploited. Orpheus's descent into the underworld and not-quite-successful effort to rescue Eurydice is the most obvious, and perhaps for that reason the one that Milton neglects. The death of Orpheus at the hands of the Bacchanals, his dismemberment, and the journey of his head to Lesbos are the things that occupy Milton's attention first. The parallels between this event and the deaths of Adonis, Attis, Osiris, and other fertility demigods have been pointed out by modern scholars.[3] The facts that he was a singer, i.e., a poet, that he died a violent death, that his head was thrown into the water, and that his mother Calliope, the muse of epic poetry, mourned his death made him sufficiently adaptable to the general pattern of pastoral elegy and to Milton's treatment. The third direction gives Milton, in the "digression" on fame, most scope for the expression of his personal feelings, both of despair and of hope. Identifying himself with Orpheus as before with King, he asks what is the use of casting his pearls before the swine by whom the god is killed, to whom he has paid his respects in *Comus* and whom he is about to attack in the passage on the corrupt clergy. Then Phoebus, the patron of Orpheus, repre-

---

[3] Frazer, II, 99. Milton was undoubtedly familiar with the custom of throwing a vase woven of papyrus, with letters inside, into the sea at Alexandria, whence it floated to Byblos. There the women, who had been mourning the death of Adonis, received it with rejoicing as the reborn demigod. This ritual is described by Lucian (*De Dea Syrea,* vii) and cited from Lucian by Selden (*De Diis Syriis,* pp. 242–243), who particularly emphasizes the fact that the vase was called "a papyrus head."

senting Milton's patron Christ, promises him his final reward in Heaven.

Such are the means by which Milton in *Lycidas* interrelated elements from the fertility cults, the tradition of pastoral elegy, the Christian religion, and his own past with the purpose and most richly the effect of rendering his present emotion. Such, by the same token, is the meaning of the phrase "With eager thought," and such again is the promise of "fresh Woods, and Pastures new."

JOHN DRYDEN

[1631-1700]

JOHN DRYDEN came from a Puritan family in Northampton-
shire. After attending school in London and graduating from
Trinity College, Cambridge (1654), he plunged into the public
literary life that made him one of the century's most influential
writers—dramatist, satirist, pamphleteer. He had a chameleon-
like career. His 1659 poem in memory of Cromwell ("Heroic
Stanzas") was followed in 1660 by "Astraea Redux," a poem on
the "Happy Restoration" of Charles II; and by Dryden's shift
from Puritan to Royalist and Tory. Dryden began in 1664 to
write for the stage, developing a style of poetic drama in rhymed
verse. Some of his important plays are *The Conquest of Granada*
(1672) and *All for Love* (1678). His *Essay of Dramatic Poesy* appeared in 1668. In 1681 Dryden began a brilliant series of poetic
satires that took him into the violent arena of literary, political,
and religious disputes: "Absalom and Achitophel" (1681), "The
Medall" (1682), "Mac Flecknoe" (1682). *Religio Laici* (1682) attacked the Papists; but a few years later Dryden was converted
to Catholicism, was made Poet Laureate, and wrote *The Hind
and the Panther*, more favorable to the Roman Church. In his
last years he turned to the quieter world of translations from the
classics—Vergil, Ovid, Boccaccio, Chaucer. Dryden could do
many things. His satires, though bound in by close references to
their own time, still exhibit a master of cutting wit in action.
Perhaps more important, his originality and skill in handling
the language and rhythms of English verse made him the teacher
of many poets who came after.

Introductory Readings

EDITION: *The Poems of John Dryden*, ed. James Kinsley, 4 vols. (1958);
The Songs of John Dryden [with music], ed. Cyrus Lawrence Day (1932).

Biography: George Saintsbury, *Dryden* (1881); George R. Noyes, ed., "Biographical Sketch" in *The Poetical Works of Dryden* (rev. ed., 1950). Criticism: Mark Van Doren, *John Dryden, A Study of His Poetry* (1946); T. S. Eliot, *John Dryden, the Poet, the Dramatist, the Critic* (1932); L. I. Bredvold, *The Intellectual Milieu of John Dryden* (1934); Bonamy Dobrée, *John Dryden* (1956).

SONGS FROM THE PLAYS

YOU CHARMED ME NOT

You charmed me not with that fair face,
   Though it was all divine:
To be another's is the grace
   That makes me wish you mine.
The gods and Fortune take their part   5
   Who like young monarchs fight,
And boldly dare invade that heart
   Which is another's right.
First, mad with hope, we undertake
   To pull up every bar;   10
But, once possessed, we faintly make
   A dull defensive war.
Now every friend is turned a foe,
   In hope to get our store;
And passion makes us cowards grow,   15
   Which made us brave before.

WILDBLOOD. *An Evening's Love* (II, i)

CALM WAS THE EVEN

1

Calm was the even, and clear was the sky,
   And the new-budding flowers did spring,
When all alone went Amyntas and I
   To hear the sweet nightingale sing;
I sat, and he laid him down by me;   5
   But scarcely his breath he could draw;
For when with a fear he began to draw near,
   He was dashed with A ha ha ha ha!

2

He blushed to himself, and lay still for a while,
   And his modesty curbed his desire;   10

But straight I convinced all his fear with a smile,
  Which added new flames to his fire.
O Sylvia, said he, you are cruel,
  To keep your poor lover in awe;
Then once more he pressed with his hand to my breast,   15
But was dashed with A ha ha ha ha.

3

I knew 'twas his passion that caused all his fear;
  And therefore I pitied his case:
I whispered him softly there's nobody near,
  And laid my cheek close to his face: 20
But as he grew bolder and bolder,
  A shepherd came by us and saw;
And just as our bliss we began with a kiss,
  He laughed out with A ha ha ha ha.

BEATRIX. *An Evening's Love* (IV, i)

WHEREVER I AM

1

Wherever I am, and whatever I do;
  My Phillis is still in my mind:
When angry I mean not to Phillis to go,
  My feet of themselves the way find:
Unknown to myself I am just at her door,   5
And when I would rail, I can bring out no more,
  Than Phillis too fair and unkind!

2

When Phillis I see, my heart bounds in my breast,
  And the love I would stifle is shown:
But asleep, or awake, I am never at rest   10
  When from my eyes Phillis is gone!
Sometimes a sad dream does delude my sad mind,
But, alas, when I wake and no Phillis I find
  How I sigh to myself all alone.

3

Should a king be my rival in her I adore   15
  He should offer his treasure in vain:
O let me alone to be happy and poor,
  And give me my Phillis again:
Let Phillis be mine, and for ever be kind,

I could to a desert with her be confined,   20
And envy no monarch his reign.

4

Alas, I discover too much of my love,
And she too well knows her own power!
She makes me each day a new martyrdom prove,
And makes me grow jealous each hour: 25
But let her each minute torment my poor mind
I had rather love Phillis both false and unkind,
Than ever be freed from her power.

ABDALLA. *The Conquest of Granada,* Part I (IV, ii)

DRAMATIC SELECTIONS

SIR FOPLING FLUTTER [1]

Most modern wits, such monstrous fools have shown,
They seemed not of heav'n's making but their own.
Those nauseous harlequins in farce may pass,
But there goes more to a substantial ass!
Something of man must be exposed to view,   5
That, gallants, it may more resemble you:
Sir Fopling is a fool so nicely writ,
The ladies would mistake him for a wit;
And when he sings, talks loud, and cocks, would cry:
"Ay, now methinks he's pretty company,   10
So brisk, so gay, so traveled, so refined!
As he took pains to graff [2] upon his kind."
True fops help nature's work, and go to school,
To file and finish god-a'mighty's fool.
Yet none Sir Fopling him, or him can call;   15
He's knight o'th' shire, and represents ye all.
From each he meets, he culls what e'er he can;
Legion's his name, a people in a man.
His bulky folly gathers as it goes,
And, rolling o'er you, like a snowball grows.   20
His various modes from various fathers follow;
One taught the toss, [3] and one the new French wallow. [4]

---

[1] Dryden's Epilogue written for Sir George Etherege's play, *The Man of
Mode; or, Sir Fopling Flutter* (1676)
[2] *graff* graft   [3] *toss* throwing the head up and shaking wig-hair back
[4] *French wallow* a rolling walk

His sword-knot, this; his cravat, this designed;
And this, the yard long snake [5] he twirls behind.
From one the sacred periwig he gained,   25
Which wind ne'er blew, nor touch of hat profaned.
Another's diving bow he did adore,
Which with a shog [6] casts all the hair before,
Till he with full decorum brings it back,
And rises with a water-spaniel shake.   30
As for his songs (the ladies' near delight)
Those sure he took from most of you who write.
Yet every man is safe from what he feared,
For no one fool is hunted from the herd.

PROLOGUE AND EPILOGUE TO *ALL FOR LOVE* [1]

PROLOGUE

What flocks of critics hover here to-day,
As vultures wait on armies for their prey,
All gaping for the carcass of a play!
With croaking notes they bode some dire event,
And follow dying poets by the scent.   5
Ours gives himself for gone; y' have watched your time!
He fights this day unarmed; without his rhyme.
And brings a tale which often has been told;
As sad as Dido's,[2] and almost as old.
His hero, whom you wits his bully call,   10
Bates of his mettle, and scarce rants at all:
He's somewhat lewd, but a well-meaning mind;
Weeps much, fights little, but is wondrous kind.
In short, a pattern, and companion fit,
For all the keeping Tonies [3] of the pit.[4]   15
I could name more: a wife, and mistress too;
Both (to be plain) too good for most of you:
The wife well-natured, and the mistress true.
   Now, poets, if your fame has been his care,
Allow him all the candor you can spare.   20

[5] *snake* tail attached to a wig   [6] *shog* shake

---

[1] The tragedy of *All for Love; or, The World Well Lost,* is a variation on
the theme of Shakespeare's *Antony and Cleopatra,* written in Shakespearean
blank verse. It was acted in 1677, published the following year.
[2] *Dido* loved and left by Aeneas in Carthage
[3] *Tonies* short for Antony, a simpleton
[4] *pit* the ground floor of a theater, what is now called the orchestra

A brave man scorns to quarrel once a day;
Like Hectors,[5] in at every petty fray.
Let those find fault whose wit's so very small,
They've need to show that they can think at all;
Errors like straws upon the surface flow;   25
He who would search for pearls must dive below.
Fops [6] may have leave to level all they can,
As pigmies would be glad to lop a man.
Half-wits are fleas; so little and so light;
We scarce could know they live, but that they bite.   30
But, as the rich, when tired with daily feasts,
For change, become their next poor tenant's guests,
Drink hearty draughts of ale, from plain brown bowls,
And snatch the homely rasher from the coals:
So you, retiring from much better cheer,   35
For once, may venture to do penance here.
And since that plenteous autumn now is past,
Whose grapes and peaches have indulged your taste,
Take in good part, from our poor poet's board,
Such riveled [7] fruits as winter can afford.   40

EPILOGUE

Poets, like disputants, when reasons fail,
Have one sure refuge left—and that's to rail.
Fop, coxcomb, fool, are thundered through the pit;
And this is all their equipage of wit.
We wonder how the devil this diff'rence grows,   45
Betwixt our fools in verse, and yours in prose:
For, 'faith, the quarrel rightly understood,
'T is civil war with their own flesh and blood.
The threadbare author hates the gaudy coat,
And swears at the gilt coach, but swears afoot: 50
For 't is observed of every scribbling man,
He grows a fop as fast as e'er he can;
Prunes up,[8] and asks his oracle, the glass,
If pink or purple best become his face.
For our poor wretch, he neither rails nor prays;   55
Nor likes your wit just as you like his plays;
He has not yet so much of Mr. Bayes.[9]

---

[5] *Hectors* brash, daring fellows   [6] *fops* silly persons
[7] *riveled* wrinkled, shrunken
[8] *Prunes up* as birds dress their feathers with their bills
[9] *Mr. Bayes* the character of a fashionable poet, representing Dryden (who as Poet Laureate wore the crown of bay), in a satirical play, *The Rehearsal* (1671), by George Villiers, Duke of Buckingham

He does his best; and, if he cannot please,
Would quietly sue out his *writ of ease*.[10]
Yet, if he might his own grand jury call,   60
By the fair sex he begs to stand or fall.
Let Caesar's pow'r the men's ambition move,
But grace you him who lost the world for love!
Yet if some antiquated lady say,
The last age is not copied in his play;   65
Heav'n help the man who for that face must drudge,
Which only has the wrinkles of a judge.
Let not the young and beauteous join with those;
For should you raise such numerous hosts of foes,
Young wits and sparks he to his aid must call;   70
'T is more than one man's work to please you all.

OTHER POEMS

MAC FLECKNOE [1]

OR, A SATIRE UPON THE TRUE-BLUE-PROTESTANT POET T. S.

All human things are subject to decay,
And, when fate summons, monarchs must obey.
This Flecknoe found, who, like Augustus, young
Was called to empire, and had governed long;
In prose and verse, was owned, without dispute,   5
Through all the realms of *Nonsense,* absolute.
This aged prince, now flourishing in peace,
And blest with issue of a large increase,
Worn out with business, did at length debate
To settle the succession of the State;   10
And pond'ring which of all his sons was fit
To reign, and wage immortal war with wit,
Cried: " 'T is resolved; for nature pleads that he
Should only rule, who most resembles me.

[10] *writ of ease* certificate of discharge from employment

[1] *Mac Flecknoe* one of a series of satires in the political and literary feuds of
Dryden and his contemporaries. In "Mac Flecknoe," Dryden (a Tory) attacks
his former friend, the Whig dramatist Thomas Shadwell (c.1641–1692).
The poem had been preceded by Shadwell's support of the Duke of Buckingham and his play, *The Rehearsal,* in which the character of John Bayes
was a parody of Dryden; Dryden's satires "Absalom and Achitophel" and
"The Medal"; and Shadwell's "The Medal of John Bayes." "Mac Flecknoe,"
made public in 1682, was a personal and literary lampoon of Shadwell,
showing him as the heir to the talents of Richard Flecknoe, a recently
deceased minor Irish dramatist, famed for his dullness and stupidity.

Sh—— alone my perfect image bears,   15
Mature in dullness from his tender years.
Sh—— alone, of all my sons, is he
Who stands confirmed in full stupidity.
The rest to some faint meaning make pretense,
But Sh—— never deviates into sense.   20
Some beams of wit on other souls may fall,
Strike through, and make a lucid interval;
But Sh——'s genuine night admits no ray,
His rising fogs prevail upon the day.
Besides, his goodly fabric fills the eye,   25
And seems designed for thoughtless majesty:
Thoughtless as monarch oaks, that shade the plain,
And, spread in solemn state, supinely reign.
Heywood and Shirley ² were but types of thee,
Thou last great prophet of tautology.   30
Even I, a dunce of more renown than they,
Was sent before but to prepare thy way;
And coarsely clad in Norwich drugget ³ came
To teach the nations in thy greater name.
My warbling lute, the lute I whilom strung   35
When to King John of Portugal I sung,
Was but the prelude to that glorious day,
When thou on silver Thames didst cut thy way,
With well-timed oars before the royal barge,
Swelled with the pride of thy celestial charge;   40
And big with hymn, commander of a host,
The like was ne'er in Epsom blankets ⁴ tossed.
Methinks I see the new Arion ⁵ sail,
The lute still trembling underneath thy nail.
At thy well-sharpened thumb from shore to shore   45
The treble squeaks for fear, the basses roar;
Echoes from Pissing-Alley,⁶ Sh—— call,
And Sh—— they resound from Aston Hall.⁷
About thy boat the little fishes throng,
As at the morning toast that floats along.   50

² *Heywood* and *Shirley* Thomas Heywood (d. 1650?), James Shirley (d. 1666),
prolific Elizabethan dramatists
³ *Norwich drugget* coarse woolen cloth
⁴ *Epsom blankets* Shadwell had a play *Epsom Wells*
⁵ *Arion* Greek musician (*c.*700 B.C.) who saved himself from robbers at sea by
riding to land on dolphins attracted to the music of his lyre
⁶ *Pissing Alley* a narrow London street
⁷ *Aston Hall* not identified

Sometimes as prince of thy harmonious band
Thou wield'st thy papers in thy threshing hand.
St. André's [8] feet ne'er kept more equal time,
Not ev'n the feet of thy own *Psyche's* [9] rhyme;
Though they in number as in sense excel: 55
So just, so like tautology they fell,
That, pale with envy, Singleton [10] forswore
The lute and sword,[11] which he in triumph bore,
And vowed he ne'er would act Villerius [12] more."
Here stopped the good old sire, and wept for joy   60
In silent raptures of the hopeful boy.[13]
All arguments, but most his plays, persuade,
That for anointed dullness he was made.
    Close to the walls which fair Augusta [14] bind
(The fair Augusta much to fears inclined),   65
An ancient fabric, raised t' inform the sight,
There stood of yore, and Barbican [15] it hight: [16]
A watchtower once; but now, so fate ordains,
Of all the pile an empty name remains.
From its old ruins brothel-houses rise,   70
Scenes of lewd loves, and of polluted joys,
Where their vast courts the mother-strumpets keep,
And, undisturbed by watch, in silence sleep.
Near these a Nursery [17] erects its head,
Where queens are formed, and future heroes bred;   75
Where unfledged actors learn to laugh and cry,
Where infant punks their tender voices try,
And little Maximins [18] the gods defy.
Great Fletcher never treads in buskins here,
Nor greater Jonson [19] dares in socks appear.   80
But gentle Simkin [20] just reception finds
Amidst this monument of vanished minds:
Pure clinches, the suburbian Muse affords;

[8] *St. André* a famous French dancing-master   [9] *Psyche* opera by Shadwell
[10] *Singleton* one of the king's musicians
[11] *lute and sword* duel with lutes instead of swords in *The Rehearsal*
[12] *Villerius* character in Davenant's *Siege of Rhodes,* where part of the dialogue is in recitative
[13] *boy* Shadwell   [14] *Augusta* the old name of London
[15] *Barbican* a street in London   [16] *hight* was called
[17] *Nursery* theater school erected in 1664
[18] *Maximin* ranting hero of Dryden's play, *Tyrannic Love*
[19] *Fletcher, Jonson* John Fletcher (d. 1625) and Ben Jonson (d. 1637), Elizabethan dramatists
[20] *Simkin* simpleton. Variations of the character appear in a number of plays.

And Panton [21] waging harmless war with words.
Here Flecknoe, as a place to fame well known,   85
Ambitiously designed his Sh——'s throne.
For ancient Dekker [22] prophesied long since,
That in this pile should reign a mighty prince,
Born for a scourge of wit, and flail of sense;
To whom true dullness should some *Psyches* owe,   90
But worlds of *Misers* from his pen should flow;
Humorists and *Hypocrites* it should produce,
Whole Raymond families, and tribes of Bruce.[23]
    Now Empress Fame had published the renown
Of Sh——'s coronation through the town.   95
Roused by report of Fame, the nations meet,
From near Bunhill, and distant Watling Street.[24]
No Persian carpets spread th' imperial way,
But scattered limbs of mangled poets lay:
From dusty shops neglected authors come,   100
Martyrs of pies, and relics of the bum.
Much Heywood, Shirley,[25] Ogleby [26] there lay,
But loads of Sh—— almost choked the way.
Bilked [27] stationers for yeomen stood prepared,
And Herringman [28] was captain of the guard.   105
The hoary prince in majesty appeared,
High on a throne of his own labors reared.
At his right hand our young Ascanius [29] sate,
Rome's other hope, and pillar of the State.
His brows thick fogs, instead of glories, grace,   110
And lambent dullness played around his face.
As Hannibal did to the altars come,
Sworn by his sire a mortal foe to Rome;
So Sh—— swore, nor should his vow be vain,
That he till death true dullness would maintain;   115
And in his father's right, and realm's defense,
Ne'er to have peace with wit, nor truce with sense.
The king himself the sacred unction made,

[21] *Panton* a farcical character, perhaps a punster
[22] *Dekker* Thomas Dekker (d. 1632), satirized by Jonson in *Poetaster*
[23] *Misers . . . , Bruce* references to Shadwell's early plays
[24] *Bun-Hill, Watling Street* widely separated places in London
[25] *Heywood, Shirley* see note 2
[26] *Ogleby* John Ogleby (d. 1676), known as a bad poet
[27] *Bilked* defrauded (with bad poetry)
[28] *Herringman* Henry Herringman (d. 1678), bookseller and publisher who both employed and published Dryden
[29] *Ascanius* son of Aeneas

As king by office, and as priest by trade.
In his sinister hand, instead of ball,   120
He placed a mighty mug of potent ale;
Love's Kingdom [30] to his right he did convey,
At once his sceptre, and his rule of sway;
Whose righteous lore the prince had practiced young,
And from whose loins recorded *Psyche* sprung.   125
His temples, last, with poppies were o'erspread,
That nodding seemed to consecrate his head.
Just at that point of time, if fame not lie,
On his left hand twelve reverend owls did fly.
So Romulus, 't is sung, by Tiber's brook,   130
Presage of sway from twice six vultures took.
Th'admiring throng loud acclamations make,
And omens of his future empire take.
The sire then shook the honors of his head,
And from his brows damps of oblivion shed   135
Full on the filial dullness: long he stood,
Repelling from his breast the raging god;
At length burst out in this prophetic mood:
  "Heavens bless my son, from Ireland let him reign
To far Barbadoes on the western main;   140
Of his dominion may no end be known,
And greater than his father's be his throne.
Beyond *Love's Kingdom* let him stretch his pen!"
He paused, and all the people cried, "Amen."
Then thus continued he: "My son, advance   145
Still in new impudence, new ignorance.
Success let others teach, learn thou from me
Pangs without birth, and fruitless industry.
Let *Virtuosos* [31] in five years be writ;
Yet not one thought accuse thy toil of wit.   150
Let gentle George [32] in triumph tread the stage,
Make Dorimant betray, and Loveit rage;
Let Cully, Cockwood, Fopling,[33] charm the pit,
And in their folly shew the writer's wit.
Yet still thy fools shall stand in thy defense,   155
And justify their author's want of sense.
Let 'em be all by thy own model made
Of dullness, and desire no foreign aid:

[30] *Love's Kingdom* play by Flecknoe
[31] *Virtuoso* play by Shadwell satirizing the Royal Society
[32] *George* George Etherege, writer of comedies, admired by Dryden
[33] *Dorimant . . . Fopling* various allusions to Etherege's plays

That they to future ages may be known,
Not copies drawn, but issue of thy own.   160
Nay, let thy men of wit too be the same,
All full of thee, and differing but in name;
But let no alien S—dl—y [34] interpose,
To lard with with thy hungry *Epsom* prose.
And when false flowers of rhetoric thou wouldst cull,   165
Trust nature, do not labor to be dull;
But write thy best, and top; and in each line,
Sir Formal's [35] oratory will be thine.
Sir Formal, though unsought, attends thy quill,
And does thy northern dedications [36] fill.   170
Nor let false friends seduce thy mind to fame,
By arrogating Jonson's hostile name.
Let father Flecknoe fire thy mind with praise,
And uncle Ogleby thy envy raise.
Thou art my blood, where Jonson has no part;   175
What share have we in nature or in art?
Where did his wit on learning fix a brand,
And rail at arts he did not understand?
Where made he love in Prince Nicander's [37] vein,
Or swept the dust in *Psyche's* humble strain?   180
Where sold he bargains, 'whip-stitch, kiss my arse,'
Promised a play and dwindled to a farce?
When did his Muse from Fletcher scenes purloin,
As thou whole Eth'rege dost transfuse to thine?
But so transfused, as oil on waters flow,   185
His always floats above, thine sinks below.
This is thy province, this thy wondrous way,
New humors to invent for each new play:
This is that boasted bias of thy mind,
By which one way, to dullness, 't is inclined;   190
Which makes thy writings lean on one side still,
And in all changes that way bends thy will.
Nor let thy mountain-belly [38] make pretense
Of likeness; thine 's a tympany [39] of sense.
A tun of man in thy large bulk is writ,   195

[34] *S-dl-y* Sir Charles Sedley, poet, dramatist, friend of Dryden
[35] *Sir Formal* Sir Formal Trifle, character in *The Virtuoso*
[36] *northern dedications* Shadwell's dedications of plays to the Duke of New-castle, in the north of England
[37] *Prince Nicander* character in Shadwell's *Psyche*
[38] *mountain-belly* Shadwell was a big man.
[39] *tympany* swelling of the body

But sure thou 'rt but a kilderkin [40] of wit.
Like mine, thy gentle numbers feebly creep;
Thy tragic Muse gives smiles, thy comic sleep.
With whate'er gall thou sett'st thyself to write,
Thy inoffensive satires never bite.   200
In thy felonious heart, though venom lies,
It does but touch thy Irish pen, and dies.
Thy genius calls thee not to purchase fame
In keen iambics,[41] but mild anagram.
Leave writing plays, and choose for thy command   205
Some peaceful province in acrostic land.
There thou may'st wings display and altars [42] raise,
And torture one poor word ten thousand ways.
Or, if thou wouldst thy diff'rent talents suit,
Set thy own songs, and sing them to thy lute."   210
    He said; but his last words were scarcely heard,
For Bruce and Longvil had a trap prepared,
And down they sent the yet declaiming bard.
Sinking he left his drugget robe behind,
Borne upwards by a subterranean wind.   215
The mantle fell to the young prophet's part,
With double portion of his father's art.

TO THE MEMORY OF MR. OLDHAM [1]

Farewell, too little, and too lately known,
Whom I began to think and call my own;
For sure our souls were near allied, and thine
Cast in the same poetic mold with mine.
One common note on either lyre did strike,   5
And knaves and fools we both abhorred alike.
To the same goal did both our studies drive;
The last set out the soonest did arrive.
Thus Nisus [2] fell upon the slippery place,
While his young friend performed and won the race.   10
O early ripe! to thy abundant store
What could advancing age have added more?

---

[40] *kilderkin* small cask   [41] *iambics* sometimes used as a term for satire
[42] *wings, altars* poems printed in visual patterns such as a wing, a cross, etc.

---

[1] Critical comment on this poem appears on p. 289. John Oldham, a promising satirist, died December 9, 1683, aged 30. This poem was prefixed to the
edition of Oldham's works, *Remains in Verse and Prose*, 1684.
[2] *Nisus* a Trojan runner who fell in a race which was then won by his
friend Euralyus

It might (what nature never gives the young)
Have taught the numbers [3] of thy native tongue.
But satire needs not those, and wit will shine   15
Through the harsh cadence of a rugged line.
A noble error, and but seldom made,
When poets are by too much force betrayed.
Thy generous fruits, though gathered ere their prime,
Still shewed a quickness; and maturing time   20
But mellows what we write to the dull sweets of rhyme.
Once more, hail and farewell; farewell, thou young,
But ah too short, Marcellus [4] of our tongue;
Thy brows with ivy, and with laurels bound;
But fate and gloomy night encompass thee around.   25

A SONG FOR ST. CECILIA'S DAY, 1687 [1]

I

From harmony, from heav'nly harmony
    This universal frame began.
    When Nature underneath a heap
        Of jarring atoms lay,
    And could not heave her head,   5
The tuneful voice was heard from high,
    "Arise, ye more than dead."
Then cold, and hot, and moist, and dry,
In order to their stations leap,
        And Music's pow'r obey.   10
From harmony, from heav'nly harmony
    This universal frame began:
    From harmony to harmony

Through all the compass of the notes it ran,
The diapason closing full in Man.   15

---

[3] *numbers* metrics, poetry
[4] *Marcellus* nephew of Augustus. He died at 20, was praised by Vergil in the
Aeneid, VI.

---

[1] *St. Cecilia's Day* November 22, the Feast of St. Cecilia, martyr of the second
century and legendary patroness of music, was celebrated by concerts. Dryden's
ode was set to music by Giovanni Battista Draghi for the concert of 1687.
See also Dryden's "Alexander's Feast" (1697), another ode for St. Cecilia's
Day.

II

What passion cannot Music raise and quell!
    When Jubal [2] struck the corded shell,
    His list'ning brethren stood around,
    And, wond'ring, on their faces fell
    To worship that celestial sound.   20
Less than a god they thought there could not dwell
      Within the hollow of that shell
      That spoke so sweetly and so well.
What passion cannot Music raise and quell!

III

    The Trumpet's loud clangor   25
      Excites us to arms
    With shrill notes of anger
      And mortal alarms.
    The double double double beat
      Of the thund'ring Drum   30
Cries, "Hark! the foes come;
Charge, charge, 't is too late to retreat."

IV

    The soft complaining Flute
    In dying notes discovers
    The woes of hopeless lovers,   35
Whose dirge is whispered by the warbling Lute.

V

    Sharp Violins proclaim
Their jealous pangs, and desperation,
Fury, frantic indignation,
Depth of pains, and height of passion,   40
    For the fair, disdainful dame.

VI

    But oh! what art can teach,
    What human voice can reach,
The sacred Organ's praise?
    Notes inspiring holy love,   45
Notes that wing their heav'nly ways
    To mend the choirs above.

[2] *Jubal* descendant of Cain, said to have invented such musical instruments as the harp, organ, lyre, flute

VII

Orpheus could lead the savage race;
And trees unrooted left their place,
   Sequacious ³ of the lyre: 50
But bright Cecilia raised the wonder higher;
When to her Organ vocal breath was giv'n,
An angel heard, and straight appeared,
   Mistaking earth for heav'n.

GRAND CHORUS

As from the pow'r of sacred lays   55
   The spheres began to move,
And sung the great Creator's praise
   To all the blest above;
So, when the last and dreadful hour
This crumbling pageant shall devour,   60
The Trumpet shall be heard on high,
The dead shall live, the living die,
And Music shall untune the sky.

RONDELAY ¹

1

   Chloe found Amyntas lying
      All in tears, upon the plain;
   Sighing to himself, and crying:
      Wretched I, to love in vain!
   Kiss me, Dear, before my dying;   5
      Kiss me once, and ease my pain!

2

   Sighing to himself, and crying
      Wretched I, to love in vain:
   Ever scorning, and denying
      To reward your faithful swain: 10
   Kiss me, Dear, before my dying;
      Kiss me once, and ease my pain!

³ *sequacious* desiring to follow

¹ *Rondelay* a song with a recurring line, or refrain

3

Ever scorning, and denying
  To reward your faithful swain;
Chloe, laughing at his crying,   15
  Told him that he loved in vain:
Kiss me, Dear, before my dying;
  Kiss me once, and ease my pain!

4

Chloe, laughing at his crying,
  Told him that he loved in vain: 20
But repenting, and complying,
  When he kissed, she kissed again:
Kissed him up, before his dying;
  Kissed him up, and eased his pain.

THE SECULAR MASQUE [1]

Enter JANUS.[2]

JANUS: Chronos,[3] Chronos, mend thy pace;
  An hundred times the rolling sun
  Around the radiant belt has run
  In his revolving race.
  Behold, behold, the goal in sight;   5
  Spread thy fans, and wing thy flight.

Enter CHRONOS, *with a scythe in his hand, and a great globe on his back, which he sets down at his entrance.*

CHRONOS: Weary, weary of my weight,
  Let me, let me drop my freight,
  And leave the world behind.

[1] An after-piece to an alteration of Fletcher's *The Pilgrim*, played for Dryden's benefit in April 1700. Dryden died May 1, 1700, according to one authority (William Egerton, 1731), the third night of the play. The printed version of *The Pilgrim* (June 18, 1700) closed with the Governor's speech: "I hope, before you go, sir, you'll share with us an entertainment of the late great poet of our age prepar'd to celebrate this day. Let the masque begin." Dryden's *Masque,* a play with music and spectacle, of course celebrates the beginning of a new century. In Dryden's age, March 25 was considered the beginning of the new year.
[2] *Janus* god of beginnings, whose two faces looked in opposite ways
[3] *Chronos* Cronus, the same as Saturn, later identified with Time and the revolution of the year. He is represented as an old man carrying a scythe with a serpent and holding a child in his left hand.

I could not bear   10
Another year,
The load of human-kind.

Enter MOMUS [4] *laughing.*

MOMUS: Ha! ha! ha! Ha! ha! ha! well hast thou done,
           To lay down thy pack,
           And lighten thy back.   15
           The world was a fool, e'er since it begun,
           And since neither Janus, nor Chronos, nor I,
               Can hinder the crimes,
               Or mend the bad times,
           'Tis better to laugh than to cry.   20

CHORUS OF
ALL THREE: *'Tis better to laugh than to cry.*

JANUS: Since Momus comes to laugh below,
               Old Time, begin the show,
           That he may see, in every scene,
           What changes in this age have been.   25

CHRONOS: Then, goddess of the silver bow, begin.

Horns, or hunting-music within. Enter DIANA.[5]

DIANA: With horns and with hounds I waken the day,
           And hie to my woodland walks away;
           I tuck up my robe, and am buskined [6] soon,
           And tie to my forehead a waxing moon.   30
           I course the fleet stag, unkennel the fox,
           And chase the wild goats o'er summits of rocks;
           With shouting and hooting we pierce through the
               sky,
           And Echo turns hunter, and doubles the cry.

CHORUS OF
ALL: *With shouting and hooting, we pierce through the*
               sky,   35
            And Echo turns hunter, and doubles the cry.

JANUS: Then our age was in its prime,
CHRONOS: Free from rage,
DIANA: ———— And free from crime.

[4] *Momus* god of pleasantry, who laughed at the other gods in whatever they
did. He is identified with comedy.
[5] *Diana* goddess of the chase; the moon   [6] *buskined* wearing high boots

MOMUS: A very merry, dancing, drinking, 40
    Laughing, quaffing, and unthinking time.

CHORUS OF
ALL: *Then our age was in its prime,*
   Free from rage, and free from crime.
   A very merry, dancing, drinking,
   Laughing, quaffing, and unthinking time. 45

Dance of DIANA'S *Attendants.*
Enter MARS.[7]

MARS: Inspire the vocal brass, inspire;
   The world is past its infant age:
    Arms and honor,
    Arms and honor,
   Set the martial mind on fire, 50
   And kindle manly rage.
   Mars has looked the sky to red;
   And Peace, the lazy good, is fled.
   Plenty, Peace, and Pleasure fly;
    The sprightly green 55
   In woodland-walks no more is seen;
   The sprightly green has drunk the Tyrian [8] dye.

CHORUS OF
ALL: *Plenty, Peace, &c.*

MARS: Sound the trumpet, beat the drum,
   Through all the world around; 60
   Sound a reveille, sound, sound,
    The warrior-god is come.

CHORUS OF
ALL: *Sound the trumpet, &c.*

MOMUS: Thy sword within the scabbard keep,
    And let mankind agree; 65
   Better the world were fast asleep,
    Than kept awake by thee.
   The fools are only thinner,
    With all our cost and care;
   But neither side a winner, 70
    For things are as they were.

CHORUS OF
ALL: *The fools are only, &c.*

[7] *Mars* god of war   [8] *Tyrian* bluish-red or purple

Enter VENUS.[9]

VENUS:	Calms appear, when storms are past;
	Love will have his hour at last:
	Nature is my kindly care; 75
	Mars destroys, and I repair;
	Take me, take me, while you may,
	Venus comes not ev'ry day.

CHORUS OF
ALL: *Take her, take her, &c.*

CHRONOS: The world was then so light,   80
           I scarcely felt the weight;
           Joy ruled the day, and Love the night.
           But since the Queen of Pleasure left the ground,
               I faint, I lag,
                   And feebly drag   85
           The pond'rous orb around.

MOMUS: All, all, of a piece throughout:
Pointing to
DIANA: Thy chase had a beast in view;
to MARS: Thy wars brought nothing about;
to VENUS: Thy lovers were all untrue.   90
JANUS: 'Tis well an old age is out.
CHRONUS: And time to begin a new.

CHORUS OF
ALL: *All, all, of a piece throughout;*
           Thy chase had a beast in view;
           Thy wars brought nothing about;   95
           Thy lovers were all untrue.
           'Tis well an old age is out,
           And time to begin a new.

Dance of huntsmen, nymphs, warriors, and lovers.

CRITICISM

The following essay is confined to an analysis of the structure of a poem. The parts of one poem can be separated and described, just as the sections of Shakespeare's sonnet cycle can be outlined (see p. 196). Compare also this prose statement of the contents of

[9] *Venus* goddess of love

Dryden's poem with the paraphrase of Donne's "Love's Deity" (pp. 225–228). The reader may also think of many approaches to Dryden's poem that may yet be tried: the historical and personal situation; the verse form and music; the language of the poem; the kind of elegy it is, as compared with others; and the full implications of certain lines or phrases.

The Structure of "To the Memory of Mr. Oldham" [1]

WALLACE CABLE BROWN

The usual criticism is that [didactic] poetry tends to be too mechanical in structure—too lacking in not only beginning, middle, and end, but in a central core to which the parts are organically related. Obviously there are many poorly-constructed didactic poems—more perhaps than of any other kind, for the didactic poem, like the heroic couplet, is one of the easiest to write and one of the hardest to write well. But the analysis of most well-written didactic poems will, I believe, show that nothing inherent in the type makes them structurally weak. As an example, let us consider Dryden's elegy "To the Memory of Mr. Oldham."

This poem of 25 lines is logically divided into two main parts of almost equal length and a short conclusion—the first ten, the second eleven, and the last four lines. The subject of the first part is that Dryden and Oldham are poetic brothers; and this for four reasons: (1) spiritually they are "near allied," (2) they use the same verse form, (3) they treat the same themes in the same satiric way, and (4) their purpose in writing is the same. The second part asserts that, although Oldham died young, his poetic achievements are so great that longer life would have added little to them. This part also contains four sub-divisions: (1) longer life might have improved Oldham's "numbers," that is, his versification, (2) but, being a satirist, he really doesn't need harmonious numbers, (3) anyway this is a "noble errour," a kind of virtue in disguise, and (4) Oldham's poetry, though premature, is nevertheless the work of genius. The last part recalls the

---

[1] A portion of Wallace Cable Brown's essay, "The 'Heresy' of the Didactic," first published in the *University of Kansas City Review*, XI (Spring, 1945).

beginning, with the emphasis on "farewell," and concludes with appropriate elegaic compliments.

The opening exclamation of the second part (line 11) includes in its meaning the idea of the first line of the poem, thus knitting the parts more closely together. And of course the opening line of the conclusion (line 22) practically repeats this first line, which gives the poem a compact circular structure. Finally, the element of suspense is maintained throughout the poem by not resolving the hint of death in the first line until the very end— "But fate and gloomy night encompass thee around."

This analysis reveals the solid precise thought structure of the elegy. The accompanying emotional meanings are no less precise and powerful. Each of the three parts, for example, is introduced with a strong lyrical note, in which the music echoes and reinforces the feeling (lines 1, 11, and 22). The one triplet comes at a crucial and climactic point (just before the short conclusion), and, by expressing the most powerful emotion thus far, prepares for the exclamations that follow. Individual lines and groups of lines, by themselves and in context, also denote a wide variety of strong but modulated feeling:

> For sure our souls were near allied, and thine
> Cast in the same poetic mould with mine.
> And knaves and fools we both abhorred alike.
> What could advancing age have added more?
> But satire needs not those, and wit will shine
> Through the harsh cadence of a rugged line.
> Thy generous fruits, though gathered ere their prime,
> Still showed a quickness; and maturing time
> But mellows what we write to the dull sweets of rhyme.

The poem, of course, presents a well-marked beginning, middle, and end. It has a central core of thought and feeling that may be described as critical admiration, to which all the images and incidental statements are organically related. In structure, in execution within the structure, and as a didactic poem, this elegy merits the praise which Mr. Eliot has given it: "From the perfection of such an elegy we cannot detract; the lack of nebula is compensated by the satisfying completeness of the statement." Along with "The Vanity of Human Wishes," Gray's "Elegy," the conclusion of "The Dunciad," and a handful of other poems, it represents what can be done with a kind of poetry too little appreciated today.

ALEXANDER POPE

[1688-1744]

ALEXANDER POPE was born into a prosperous London Catholic family that early removed to Windsor Forest. From childhood on, he composed poems modeled on classical forms. By 1705, when he was only 17, he had entered the London literary and social world, and he rose quickly to a favored position. Every few years a book of poetry would come out—*Pastorals* (1709), *An Essay on Criticism* (1711), *Windsor-Forest* (1713), *The Rape of the Lock* (in two versions, 1712 and 1714), and in 1717 his first collected volume of *Works*. After 1719 Pope lived at Twickenham on an estate on the Thames—social, famous, and rich. His fortune came principally from translations of Homer's *Iliad* (1715–1720) and *Odyssey* (1725–1726). Later poems included *The Dunciad* (1728–1743), a satirical piece of social criticism sometimes called Pope's masterpiece, and *An Essay on Man* (1733–1734). Pope never married, but was the center of an admiring circle of friends and was especially fond of Lady Mary Wortley Montagu and Martha and Teresa Blount. He was a popular, successful poet, the acknowledged literary dictator of his own time and the unexcelled delineator of eighteenth-century mores and morality. In his hands the heroic couplet became a balanced rapier, very sharp on both edges. He had a talent for saying the inevitable, so that some of his lines have become almost idiomatic in the English language.

Introductory Readings

EDITION: *The Twickenham Edition of the Poems,* general ed. John Butt, 6 vols. (1939–1954). LETTERS: *The Correspondence,* ed. George Sherburn, 5 vols. (1956). BIOGRAPHY: W. J. Courthope, "The Life of Pope," in vol. V of Pope's *Works,* ed. Elwin and Courthope (1871–1889); Edith Sitwell,

Alexander Pope (1930); Bonamy Dobrée *Alexander Pope* (1951). CRITICISM: Geoffrey Tillotson, *On the Poetry of Pope* (2nd ed., 1950).

ODE ON SOLITUDE [1]

Happy the man, whose wish and care
    A few paternal acres bound,
Content to breathe his native air,
        In his own ground.

Whose herds with milk, whose fields with bread,   5
    Whose flocks supply him with attire,
Whose trees in summer yield him shade,
        In winter fire.

Blest, who can unconcern'dly find
    Hours, days, and years slide soft away,   10
In health of body, peace of mind,
        Quiet by day;

Sound sleep by night; study and ease
    Together mixed; sweet recreation,
And innocence, which most does please,   15
        With meditation.

Thus let me live, unseen, unknown,
    Thus unlamented let me die,
Steal from the world, and not a stone
        Tell where I lie.   20

EPISTLE TO MISS BLOUNT

ON HER LEAVING THE TOWN, AFTER THE CORONATION [1]

As some fond virgin, whom her mother's care
Drags from the town to wholesome country air,
Just when she learns to roll a melting eye,
And hear a spark, yet think no danger nigh—
From the dear man unwilling she must sever,   5
Yet takes one kiss before she parts for ever:

[1] *Ode on Solitude* according to Pope, written at the age of twelve; later revised

[1] *Coronation* George I, on October 20, 1714

Thus from the world fair Zephalinda [2] flew,
Saw others happy, and with sighs withdrew;
Not that their pleasures caused her discontent;
She sighed not that they stayed, but that she went.   10
　　She went, to plain work [3] and to purling brooks,
Old-fashioned halls, dull aunts, and croaking rooks:
She went from op'ra, park, assembly, play,
To morning walks, and prayers three hours a day;
To part her time 'twixt reading and bohea,[4]   15
To muse, and spill her solitary tea;
Or o'er cold coffee trifle with the spoon,
Count the slow clock, and dine exact at noon;
Divert her eyes with pictures in the fire,
Hum half a tune, tell stories to the squire;   20
Up to her godly garret after sev'n,
There starve and pray, for that's the way to Heav'n.
　　Some squire, perhaps, you take delight to rack,[5]
Whose game is whisk,[6] whose treat a toast in sack; [7]
Who visits with a gun, presents you birds,   25
Then gives a smacking buss, and cries—No words!
Or with his hound comes hollowing from the stable,
Makes love with nods, and knees beneath a table;
Whose laughs are hearty, though his jests are coarse,
And loves you best of all things—but his horse.   30
　　In some fair ev'ning, on your elbow laid,
You dream of triumphs in the rural shade;
In pensive thought recall the fancied scene,
See coronations rise on ev'ry green;
Before you pass th' imaginary sights   35
Of lords, and earls, and dukes, and gartered knights,
While the spread fan o'ershades your closing eyes;
Then give one flirt, and all the vision flies.
Thus banish sceptres, coronets, and balls,
And leave you in lone woods, or empty walls.   40
　　So when your slave, at some dear, idle time,
(Not plagued with headaches, or the want of rhyme)

---

[2] *Zephalinda* Teresa Blount. Pope was attentive to both Teresa and her younger sister Martha. After about 1718 he was attached to Martha, leaving her most of his estate.
[3] *plain work* sewing, the opposite of fancywork   [4] *bohea* black tea
[5] *rack* torture
[6] *whisk* whist (opposed to society's favorite card game, ombre)
[7] *sack* a dry white wine

Stands in the streets, abstracted from the crew,
And while he seems to study, thinks of you;
Just when his fancy paints your sprightly eyes,   45
Or sees the blush of soft Parthenia [8] rise,
Gay [9] pats my shoulder, and you vanish quite,
Streets, chairs, and coxcombs [10] rush upon my sight;
Vexed to be still in town, I knit my brow,
Look sour, and hum a tune — — as you may now.   50

THE RAPE OF THE LOCK [1]

AN HEROI-COMICAL POEM

Nolueram, Belinda, tuos violare capillos;
Sed juvat, hoc precibus me tribuisse tuis.[2]—MARTIAL

TO MRS. ARABELLA FERMOR

MADAM,—It will be in vain to deny that I have some regard for this piece, since I dedicate it to you. Yet you may bear me witness, it was intended only to divert a few young ladies, who have good sense and good humor enough to laugh not only at their sex's little unguarded follies, but at their own. But as it was communicated with the air of a secret, it soon found its way into the world. An imperfect copy having been offered to a bookseller, you had the good nature for my sake to consent to the publication of one more correct: this I was forced to before I had executed half my design, for the machinery was entirely wanting to complete it.

The machinery, Madam, is a term invented by the critics, to signify that part which the deities, angels, or daemons are made to act in a poem: for the ancient poets are in one respect like many modern ladies: let an action be never so trivial in itself, they always make it appear of the utmost importance. These machines I determined to raise on a very new and odd foundation, the Rosicrucian doctrine of spirits.

[8] *Parthenia* Martha Blount
[9] *Gay* the poet and playwright John Gay (1685–1732), who wrote *The Beggars'*
Opera
[10] *coxcombs* vain, conceited fellows

---

[1] *The Rape of the Lock* was written at the suggestion of John Caryll in an effort to end a quarrel between the families of Miss Arabella Fermor and Lord Petre, who did cut off a lock of her hair. The first version of the poem was in two cantos, written in 1711 and printed anonymously in 1712. In 1714 Pope published an expanded version of five cantos under his name.
[2] *Nolueram . . . tuis* I was reluctant, Belinda, to violate your locks, but I am glad to have granted this to your prayers.

I know how disagreeable it is to make use of hard words before a lady; but 'tis so much the concern of a poet to have his works understood, and particularly by your sex, that you must give me leave to explain two or three difficult terms.

The Rosicrucians are a people I must bring you acquainted with. The best account I know of them is in a French book called *Le Comte de Gabalis*, which, both in its title and size is so like a novel that many of the fair sex have read it for one by mistake. According to these gentlemen, the four elements are inhabited by spirits, which they call sylphs, gnomes, nymphs and salamanders. The gnomes, or daemons of earth, delight in mischief; but the sylphs, whose habitation is in the air, are the best-conditioned creatures imaginable. For they say, any mortals may enjoy the most intimate familiarities with these gentle spirits, upon a condition very easy to all true adepts, an inviolate preservation of chastity.

As to the following cantos, all the passages of them are as fabulous as the vision at the beginning, or the transformation at the end; (except the loss of your hair, which I always mention with reverence). The human persons are as fictitious as the airy ones; and the character of Belinda, as it is now managed, resembles you in nothing but in beauty.

If this poem had as many graces as there are in your person, or in your mind, yet I could never hope it should pass through the world half so uncensured as you have done. But let its fortune be what it will, mine is happy enough, to have given me this occasion of assuring you that I am, with the truest esteem, Madam, your most obedient, humble servant,

A. POPE

CANTO I

What dire offense from am'rous causes springs,
What mighty contests rise from trivial things,
I sing—This verse to CARYLL, Muse! is due;
This, ev'n Belinda may vouchsafe to view:
Slight is the subject, but not so the praise,   5
If she inspire, and he approve my lays.
  Say what strange motive, Goddess! could compel
A well-bred lord t' assault a gentle belle?
O say what stranger cause, yet unexplored,
Could make a gentle belle reject a lord?   10
In tasks so bold, can little men engage,
And in soft bosoms dwells such mighty rage?

Sol through white curtains shot a tim'rous ray,
And oped those eyes that must eclipse the day;
Now lap dogs give themselves the rousing shake,   15
And sleepless lovers, just at twelve, awake:
Thrice rung the bell, the slipper knocked the ground,
And the pressed watch returned a silver sound.[3]
Belinda still her downy pillow pressed,
Her guardian Sylph prolonged the balmy rest.   20
'Twas he had summoned to her silent bed
The morning dream that hovered o'er her head.
A youth more glittering than a Birth-night beau,[4]
(That ev'n in slumber caused her cheek to glow)
Seemed to her ear his winning lips to lay,   25
And thus in whispers said, or seemed to say.
    "Fairest of mortals, thou distinguished care
Of thousand bright inhabitants of air!
If e'er one vision touched thy infant thought,
Of all the nurse and all the priest have taught,   30
Of airy elves by moonlight shadows seen,
The silver token, and the circled green,[5]
Or virgins visited by angel pow'rs,
With golden crowns and wreaths of heav'nly flow'rs,
Hear and believe! thy own importance know,   35
Nor bound thy narrow views to things below.
Some secret truths from learnèd pride concealed,
To maids alone and children are revealed:
What though no credit doubting wits may give?
The fair and innocent shall still believe.   40
Know then, unnumbered spirits round thee fly,
The light militia of the lower sky;
These, though unseen, are ever on the wing,
Hang o'er the box, and hover round the Ring.[6]
Think what an equipage thou hast in air,   45
And view with scorn two pages and a chair.[7]
As now your own, our beings were of old,
And once inclosed in woman's beauteous mold;
Thence, by a soft transition, we repair

[3] *sound* chimes to give the time
[4] *birth-night beau* gentleman dressed for a royal Birthday Ball. Costumes of both men and women were described in the newspapers.
[5] *token, green* a coin or a circle in the grass left by fairies
[6] *box, ring* at social affairs—a box at the theater or the riding circle in London's Hyde Park
[7] *chair* sedan chair, carried by servants

From earthly vehicles to these of air. 50
Think not, when woman's transient breath is fled,
That all her vanities at once are dead:
Succeeding vanities she still regards,
And though she plays no more, o'erlooks the cards.
Her joy in gilded chariots,[8] when alive, 55
And love of ombre,[9] after death survive.
For when the fair in all their pride expire,
To their first elements their souls retire:
The sprites of fiery termagants [10] in flame
Mount up, and take a Salamander's name. 60
Soft yielding minds to water glide away,
And sip, with nymphs, their elemental tea.[11]
The graver prude sinks downward to a Gnome,
In search of mischief still on earth to roam.
The light coquettes in Sylphs aloft repair, 65
And sport and flutter in the fields of air.
    "Know farther yet; whoever fair and chaste
Rejects mankind, is by some Sylph embraced:
For spirits, freed from mortal laws, with ease
Assume what sexes and what shapes they please. 70
What guards the purity of melting maids,
In courtly balls, and midnight masquerades,
Safe from the treach'rous friend, the daring spark,[12]
The glance by day, the whisper in the dark;
When kind occasion prompts their warm desires, 75
When music softens, and when dancing fires?
'Tis but their Sylph, the wise celestials know,
Though Honor is the word with men below.
    "Some nymphs there are, too conscious of their face,
For life predestined to the Gnomes' embrace. 80
These swell their prospects and exalt their pride,
When offers are disdained, and love denied.
Then gay ideas [13] crowd the vacant brain;
While peers, and dukes, and all their sweeping train,
And garters, stars, and coronets [14] appear, 85
And in soft sounds, "Your Grace" salutes their ear.
'Tis these that early taint the female soul,

---

[8] *gilded chariots* decorated carriages
[9] *ombre* a card game. See note for Canto III, line 27.
[10] *termagants* excitable, scolding women
[11] *tea* at that time pronounced *tā*, to rhyme with *away*
[12] *spark* a lively, showy man   [13] *ideas* images
[14] *garters, stars, coronets* badges of knighthood and royalty

Instruct the eyes of young coquettes to roll,
Teach infant cheeks a bidden blush to know,
And little hearts to flutter at a beau.   90
    "Oft when the world imagine women stray,
The Sylphs through mystic mazes guide their way,
Through all the giddy circle they pursue,
And old impertinence expel by new.
What tender maid but must a victim fall   95
To one man's treat, but for another's ball?
When Florio speaks, what virgin could withstand,
If gentle Damon [15] did not squeeze her hand?
With varying vanities, from ev'ry part,
They shift the moving toyshop of their heart;   100
Where wigs with wigs, with sword-knots [16] sword-knots strive,
Beaux banish beaux, and coaches coaches drive.
This erring mortals Levity may call,
Oh blind to truth! the Sylphs contrive it all.
    "Of these am I, who thy protection claim,   105
A watchful sprite, and Ariel is my name.
Late, as I ranged the crystal wilds of air,
In the clear mirror of thy ruling star
I saw, alas! some dread event impend,
Ere to the main this morning sun descend,   110
But heav'n reveals not what, or how, or where:
Warned by the Sylph, oh pious maid, beware!
This to disclose is all thy guardian can:
Beware of all, but most beware of man!"
    He said; when Shock,[17] who thought she slept too long,   115
Leaped up, and waked his mistress with his tongue.
'Twas then, Belinda, if report say true,
Thy eyes first opened on a billet-doux; [18]
Wounds, charms, and ardors were no sooner read,
But all the vision vanished from thy head.   120
    And now, unveiled, the toilet [19] stands displayed,
Each silver vase in mystic order laid.
First, robed in white, the nymph intent adores,
With head uncovered, the cosmetic [20] powers.
A heav'nly image in the glass appears,   125
To that she bends, to that her eye she rears;

---

[15] *Florio, Damon* type-names common to pastoral poetry
[16] *sword-knots* ribbons or tassels tied to the hilt of a sword
[17] *Shock* Belinda's lap dog
[18] *billet-doux* a love letter (literally, "sweet note")   [19] *toilet* dressing table
[20] *cosmetic* implies *cosmos* (the universal order) as well as decoration

Th' inferior priestess, at her altar's side,
Trembling, begins the sacred rites of pride.
Unnumbered treasures ope at once, and here
The various off'rings of the world appear;   130
From each she nicely culls with curious toil,
And decks the goddess with the glitt'ring spoil.
This casket India's glowing gems unlocks,
And all Arabia breathes from yonder box.
The tortoise here and elephant unite,   135
Transformed to combs, the speckled and the white.
Here files of pins extend their shining rows,
Puffs, powders, patches,21 Bibles, billet-doux.
Now awful Beauty puts on all its arms;
The fair each moment rises in her charms,   140
Repairs her smiles, awakens ev'ry grace,
And calls forth all the wonders of her face;
Sees by degrees a purer blush arise,
And keener lightnings quicken in her eyes.
The busy Sylphs surround their darling care;   145
These set the head, and those divide the hair,
Some fold the sleeve, while others plait the gown;
And Betty's praised for labors not her own.

CANTO II

Not with more glories, in th' ethereal plain,
The sun first rises o'er the purpled main,
Than, issuing forth, the rival of his beams
Launched on the bosom of the silver Thames.1
Fair nymphs, and well-dressed youths around her shone,   5
But every eye was fixed on her alone.
On her white breast a sparkling cross she wore,
Which Jews might kiss, and infidels adore.
Her lively looks a sprightly mind disclose,
Quick as her eyes, and as unfixed as those: 10
Favors to none, to all she smiles extends;
Oft she rejects, but never once offends.
Bright as the sun, her eyes the gazers strike,
And, like the sun, they shine on all alike.
Yet graceful ease, and sweetness void of pride,   15

---

21 *patches* small bits of black silk or court plaster worn on the face as adornment

---

1 *Thames* going by boat from London up the river Thames twelve miles to the palace of Hampton Court

Might hide her faults, if belles had faults to hide:
If to her share some female errors fall,
Look on her face, and you'll forget 'em all.
    This nymph, to the destruction of mankind,
Nourished two locks, which graceful hung behind   20
In equal curls, and well conspired to deck
With shining ringlets the smooth iv'ry neck.
Love in these labyrinths his slaves detains,
And mighty hearts are held in slender chains.
With hairy springes [2] we the birds betray,   25
Slight lines of hair surprise the finny prey,
Fair tresses man's imperial race ensnare,
And beauty draws us with a single hair.
    Th' adventurous Baron the bright locks admired;
He saw, he wished, and to the prize aspired.   30
Resolved to win, he meditates the way,
By force to ravish, or by fraud betray;
For when success a lover's toils attends,
Few ask, if fraud or force attained his ends.
    For this, ere Phoebus [3] rose, he had implored   35
Propitious Heaven, and ev'ry power adored,
But chiefly Love—to Love an altar built,
Of twelve vast French romances, neatly gilt.
There lay three garters, half a pair of gloves;
And all the trophies of his former loves;   40
With tender billet-doux he lights the pyre,
And breathes three am'rous sighs to raise the fire.
Then prostrate falls, and begs with ardent eyes
Soon to obtain, and long possess the prize:
The pow'rs gave ear, and granted half his prayer,   45
The rest, the winds dispersed in empty air.
    But now secure the painted vessel glides,
The sunbeams trembling on the floating tides,
While melting music steals upon the sky,
And softened sounds along the waters die.   50
Smooth flow the waves, the zephyrs gently play,
Belinda smiled, and all the world was gay.
All but the Sylph—with careful thoughts oppressed,
Th' impending woe sat heavy on his breast.
He summons straight his denizens [4] of air;   55
The lucid squadrons round the sails repair: [5]

---

[2] *springes* *(sprinjes)* traps made with a noose fastened to a spring
[3] *Phoebus* the sun   [4] *denizens* inhabitants: the Sylphs   [5] *repair* go

Soft o'er the shrouds aërial whispers breathe,
That seemed but zephyrs to the train beneath.
Some to the sun their insect-wings unfold,
Waft on the breeze, or sink in clouds of gold;   60
Transparent forms, too fine for mortal sight,
Their fluid bodies half dissolved in light.
Loose to the wind their airy garments flew,
Thin glitt'ring textures of the filmy dew,
Dipped in the richest tincture of the skies,   65
Where light disports in ever-mingling dyes,
While ev'ry beam new transient colors flings,
Colors that change whene'er they wave their wings.
Amid the circle, on the gilded mast,
Superior by the head, was Ariel placed;   70
His purple pinions opening to the sun,
He raised his azure wand, and thus begun.
  "Ye Sylphs and Sylphids, to your chief give ear,
Fays, Fairies, Genii, Elves, and Daemons, hear!
Ye know the spheres and various tasks assigned   75
By laws eternal to th' aërial kind.
Some in the fields of purest ether [6] play,
And bask and whiten in the blaze of day.
Some guide the course of wand'ring orbs on high,
Or roll the planets through the boundless sky.   80
Some less refined, beneath the moon's pale light,
Pursue the stars that shoot athwart the night,
Or suck the mists in grosser air below,
Or dip their pinions in the painted bow,[7]
Or brew fierce tempests on the wintry main,[8]   85
Or o'er the glebe [9] distill the kindly rain.
Others on earth o'er human race preside,
Watch all their ways, and all their actions guide:
Of these the chief the care of nations own,
And guard with arms divine the British throne.   90
  "Our humbler province is to tend the fair,
Not a less pleasing, though less glorious care;
To save the powder from too rude a gale,
Nor let th' imprisoned essences [10] exhale;
To draw fresh colors from the vernal flow'rs;   95
To steal from rainbows ere they drop in show'rs
A brighter wash; [11] to curl their waving hairs,

---

[6] *ether* the upper regions of space   [7] *painted bow* rainbow   [8] *main* sea
[9] *glebe* land   [10] *essences* perfumes or oils
[11] *wash* liquid for hair and skin

Assist their blushes, and inspire their airs;
Nay oft, in dreams, invention we bestow,
To change a flounce, or add a furbelow.[12]   100
    "This day, black omens threat the brightest Fair
That e'er deserved a watchful spirit's care;
Some dire disaster, or by force, or slight;
But what, or where, the Fates have wrapped in night.
Whether the nymph shall break Diana's law,[13]   105
Or some frail china jar receive a flaw;
Or stain her honor, or her new brocade;
Forget her prayers, or miss a masquerade;
Or lose her heart, or necklace, at a ball;
Or whether Heav'n has doomed that Shock must fall.   110
Haste, then, ye spirits! to your charge repair:
The fluttering fan be Zephyretta's care;
The drops [14] to thee, Brillante, we consign;
And, Momentilla, let the watch be thine;
Do thou, Crispissa, tend her fav'rite lock;   115
Ariel himself shall be the guard of Shock.
    "To fifty chosen Sylphs, of special note,
We trust th' important charge, the petticoat:
Oft have we known that sev'nfold fence to fail,
Though stiff with hoops, and armed with ribs of whale;   120
Form a strong line about the silver bound,
And guard the wide circumference around.
    "Whatever spirit, careless of his charge,
His post neglects, or leaves the fair at large,
Shall feel sharp vengeance soon o'ertake his sins,   125
Be stopped in vials, or transfixed with pins;
Or plunged in lakes of bitter washes lie,
Or wedged whole ages in a bodkin's eye: [15]
Gums and pomatums [16] shall his flight restrain,
While clogged he beats his silken wings in vain;   130
Or alum styptics [17] with contracting power
Shrink his thin essence like a rivelled [18] flower:
Or, as Ixion [19] fixed, the wretch shall feel
The giddy motion of the whirling mill,

---

[12] *furbelow* trimming   [13] *Diana's law* chastity
[14] *drops* pendant earrings   [15] *bodkin's eye* the eye of a large needle
[16] *Gums and pomatums* perfumed oils used especially to keep the hair in place
[17] *alum styptics* astringents   [18] *rivelled* wrinkled, shrivelled
[19] *Ixion* fastened to a turning wheel in Hades as punishment for loving Hera, queen of the gods

In fumes of burning chocolate shall glow,   135
And tremble at the sea that froths below!"
    He spoke; the spirits from the sails descend;
Some, orb in orb, around the nymph extend,
Some thrid [20] the mazy ringlets of her hair,
Some hang upon the pendants of her ear;   140
With beating hearts the dire event they wait,
Anxious, and trembling for the birth of Fate.

CANTO III

Close by those meads, for ever crowned with flow'rs,
Where Thames with pride surveys his rising tow'rs,
There stands a structure [1] of majestic frame,
Which from the neighb'ring Hampton takes its name.
Here Britain's statesmen oft the fall foredoom   5
Of foreign tyrants, and of nymphs at home;
Here thou, great Anna! [2] whom three realms [3] obey,
Dost sometimes counsel take—and sometimes tea.
    Hither the heroes and the nymphs resort,
To taste awhile the pleasures of a court;   10
In various talk th' instructive hours they passed,
Who gave the ball, or paid the visit last;
One speaks the glory of the British Queen,
And one describes a charming Indian screen;
A third interprets motions, looks, and eyes;   15
At ev'ry word a reputation dies.
Snuff, or the fan, supply each pause of chat,
With singing, laughing, ogling,[4] and all that.
    Meanwhile, declining from the noon of day,
The sun obliquely shoots his burning ray;   20
The hungry judges soon the sentence sign,
And wretches hang that jurymen may dine;
The merchant from th' Exchange [5] returns in peace,
And the long labors of the toilet cease—
Belinda now, whom thirst of fame invites,   25
Burns to encounter two adventrous knights,
At ombre [6] singly to decide their doom;

[20] *thrid* thread

---

[1] *structure* Hampton Court Palace   [2] *Anna* Queen Anne (1702–1714)
[3] *three realms* England, Wales, Scotland—united 1707
[4] *ogling* flirting by look or glance   [5] *Exchange* Stock Exchange
[6] *ombre* a three-handed card game of Spanish origin, especially fashionable
(*continued p. 304*)

And swells her breast with conquests yet to come.
Straight the three bands prepare in arms to join,
Each band the number of the sacred nine.   30
Soon as she spreads her hand, th' aërial guard
Descend, and sit on each important card:
First Ariel perched upon a Matadore,[7]
Then each, according to the rank they bore;
For Sylphs, yet mindful of their ancient race,   35
Are, as when women, wondrous fond of place.
    Behold, four Kings in majesty revered,
With hoary whiskers and a forky beard;
And four fair Queens whose hands sustain a flow'r,
Th' expressive emblem of their softer pow'r;   40
Four Knaves [8] in garbs succinct, a trusty band,
Caps on their heads, and halberds in their hand;
And particolored troops, a shining train,
Draw forth to combat on the velvet plain.[9]
    The skilful nymph reviews her force with care: 45
"Let Spades be trumps!" she said, and trumps they were.
    Now move to war her sable Matadores,
In show like leaders of the swarthy Moors.
Spadillio first, unconquerable lord!
Led off two captive trumps, and swept the board.   50
As many more Manillio forced to yield,

---

in the seventeenth and eighteenth centuries. It uses a 40-card deck (omitting the 10's, 9's, and 8's), a complex system of values and rules, and characteristic Spanish "war" terms for plays and trumps. One person—the high bidder or Ombre (from the Spanish *hombre,* man)—opposes the other two players, attempting to take more tricks than either of them. The players are dealt nine cards each; they agree upon the person who is to be Ombre (each has his turn to declare himself the challenger); and Ombre then names trumps. Ombre (and the others in turn) may discard and then draw from the stock of the remaining thirteen cards to build his hand. The play continues with each player laying out a card in turn, each trick of three cards going to the person with the highest trump or other ranking card. The highest cards, the Matadores, are always as follows: (1) Spadille—the ace of spades; (2) Manille —the low card of the trump suit (a black deuce or a red seven); (3) Basto— the ace of clubs. When they are not trumps, the red kings outrank the red aces. (See also the discussion of ombre in *The Rape of the Lock and Other Poems,* ed. Tillotson, App. C.)
[7] *Matadore* highest-ranking card   [8] *Knaves* jacks
[9] In the game which follows, Belinda wins the bid, names spades as trumps. She takes the first four tricks with (1) the ace of spades, (2) the deuce of spades, (3) the ace of clubs, and (4) the king of spades. The Baron wins the next four tricks with (5) the queen of spades, (6) the king of diamonds, (7) the queen of diamonds, and (8) the jack of diamonds. Belinda takes the last trick with the king of hearts.

And marched a victor from the verdant field.[10]
Him Basto followed, but his fate more hard
Gained but one trump and one plebeian card.[11]
With his broad saber next, a chief in years,   55
The hoary Majesty of Spades appears;
Puts forth one manly leg, to sight revealed;
The rest, his many-colored robe concealed.
The rebel Knave, who dares his prince engage,
Proves the just victim of his royal rage.   60
Ev'n mighty Pam,[12] that kings and queens o'erthrew
And mowed down armies in the fights of Loo,
Sad chance of war! now destitute of aid,
Falls undistinguished by the victor Spade!

    Thus far both armies to Belinda yield;   65
Now to the Baron fate inclines the field.
His warlike Amazon her host invades,
Th' imperial consort of the Crown of Spades.
The Club's black tyrant first her victim died,
Spite of his haughty mien, and barbarous pride: 70
What boots the regal circle on his head,
His giant limbs in state unwieldy spread;
That long behind he trails his pompous robe,
And, of all monarchs, only grasps the globe?

    The Baron now his Diamonds pours apace;   75
Th' embroidered King who shows but half his face,
And his refulgent Queen, with pow'rs combined
Of broken troops an easy conquest find.
Clubs, Diamonds, Hearts, in wild disorder seen,
With throngs promiscuous strow the level green.   80
Thus when dispersed a routed army runs,
Of Asia's troops, and Afric's sable sons,
With like confusion different nations fly,
Of various habit, and of various dye,
The pierced battalions disunited fall,   85
In heaps on heaps; one fate o'erwhelms them all.

    The Knave of Diamonds tries his wily arts,
And wins (oh shameful chance!) the Queen of Hearts.
At this, the blood the virgin's cheek forsook,
A livid paleness spreads o'er all her look;   90
She sees, and trembles at th' approaching ill,

[10] *verdant field* the green velvet of the table
[11] *plebeian card* a common or lower card
[12] *Pam* jack of clubs, a wild card in the game of loo

Just in the jaws of ruin, and codille.[13]
And now (as oft in some distempered State)
On one nice trick depends the gen'ral fate.
An Ace of Hearts steps forth: the King unseen   95
Lurked in her hand, and mourned his captive Queen.
He springs to vengeance with an eager pace,
And falls like thunder on the prostrate Ace.
The nymph exulting fills with shouts the sky;
The walls, the woods, and long canals reply.   100
    Oh thoughtless mortals! ever blind to fate,
Too soon dejected, and too soon elate!
Sudden these honors shall be snatched away,
And cursed for ever this victorious day.
    For lo! the board with cups and spoons is crowned, 105
The berries [14] crackle, and the mill turns round.
On shining altars of Japan [15] they raise
The silver lamp; the fiery spirits blaze.
From silver spouts the grateful liquors glide,
While China's earth [16] receives the smoking tide.   110
At once they gratify their scent and taste,
And frequent cups prolong the rich repast.
Straight hover round the Fair her airy band;
Some, as she sipped, the fuming liquor fanned,
Some o'er her lap their careful plumes displayed,   115
Trembling, and conscious of the rich brocade.
Coffee (which makes the politician wise,
And see through all things with his half-shut eyes)
Sent up in vapors to the Baron's brain
New stratagems, the radiant lock to gain.   120
Ah cease, rash youth! desist ere 'tis too late,
Fear the just gods, and think of Scylla's [17] fate!
Changed to a bird, and sent to flit in air,
She dearly pays for Nisus' injured hair!
    But when to mischief mortals bend their will,   125
How soon they find fit instruments of ill!
Just then, Clarissa drew with tempting grace
A two-edged weapon [18] from her shining case;

[13] *codille* defeat of the challenger (Ombre)
[14] *berries* coffee beans, freshly roasted and ground
[15] *altars of Japan* japanned (lacquered) tables   [16] *China's earth* dishes
[17] *Scylla* daughter of Nisus, whose life-giving lock of purple hair she gave to
his enemy Minos. She was changed to a bird, Nisus to a hawk.
[18] *two-edged weapon* scissors

So ladies in romance assist their knight,
Present the spear, and arm him for the fight.   130
He takes the gift with rev'rence, and extends
The little engine [19] on his fingers' ends;
This just behind Belinda's neck he spread,
As o'er the fragrant steams she bends her head:
Swift to the lock a thousand sprites repair,   135
A thousand wings, by turns, blow back the hair;
And thrice they twitched the diamond in her ear;
Thrice she looked back, and thrice the foe drew near.
Just in that instant, anxious Ariel sought
The close recesses of the virgin's thought;   140
As on the nosegay in her breast reclined,
He watched th' ideas rising in her mind,
Sudden he viewed, in spite of all her art,
An earthly lover lurking at her heart.
Amazed, confused, he found his pow'r expired,   145
Resigned to fate, and with a sigh retired.
    The peer now spreads the glittering forfex wide,
T' inclose the lock; now joins it, to divide.
Ev'n then, before the fatal engine closed,
A wretched Sylph too fondly interposed;   150
Fate urged the shears, and cut the Sylph in twain
(But airy substance soon unites again).
The meeting points the sacred hair dissever
From the fair head, for ever, and for ever!
    Then flashed the living lightning from her eyes,   155
And screams of horror rend th' affrighted skies.
Not louder shrieks to pitying Heav'n are cast,
When husbands or when lap dogs breathe their last;
Or when rich China vessels fallen from high,
In glitt'ring dust and painted fragments lie!   160
    "Let wreaths of triumph now my temples twine,"
(The victor cried) "the glorious prize is mine!
While fish in streams, or birds delight in air,
Or in a coach and six the British fair,
As long as *Atalantis* [20] shall be read,   165
Or the small pillow grace a lady's bed,
While visits shall be paid on solemn days,

[19] *engine* tool, instrument
[20] *Atalantis* a popular book of Court scandal (Mrs. Manley's *Atalantis: Secret Memoirs and Manners of several Persons of Quality, of Both Sexes*, London, 1709)

When numerous wax-lights [21] in bright order blaze,
While nymphs take treats, or assignations give,
So long my honor, name, and praise shall live!　　　170
　　What time would spare, from steel receives its date,
And monuments, like men, submit to fate!
Steel could the labor of the gods destroy,
And strike to dust th' imperial tow'rs of Troy;
Steel could the works of mortal pride confound,　　　175
And hew triumphal arches to the ground.
What wonder then, fair nymph! thy hairs should feel
The conquering force of unresisted steel?"

CANTO IV

But anxious cares the pensive nymph oppressed,
And secret passions labored in her breast.
Not youthful kings in battle seized alive,
Not scornful virgins who their charms survive,
Not ardent lovers robbed of all their bliss,　　　5
Not ancient ladies when refused a kiss,
Not tyrants fierce that unrepenting die,
Not Cynthia [1] when her manteau's [2] pinned awry,
E'er felt such rage, resentment, and despair,
As thou, sad virgin! for thy ravished hair.　　　10
　　For, that sad moment, when the Sylphs withdrew,
And Ariel weeping from Belinda flew,
Umbriel, a dusky, melancholy sprite,
As ever sullied the fair face of light,
Down to the central earth, his proper scene,　　　15
Repaired to search the gloomy cave of Spleen.[3]
　　Swift on his sooty pinions flits the Gnome,
And in a vapor reached the dismal dome.
No cheerful breeze this sullen region knows,
The dreaded East is all the wind that blows.　　　20
Here, in a grotto, sheltered close from air,
And screened in shades from day's detested glare,
She sighs for ever on her pensive bed,
Pain at her side, and Megrim [4] at her head.
　　Two handmaids wait the throne: alike in place,　　　25
But diff'ring far in figure and in face.

---

[21] *wax-lights* candles

[1] *Cynthia* the moon, goddess of chastity　　　[2] *manteau* robe
[3] *cave of Spleen* low spirits, melancholy, the "vapors"
[4] *Megrim* migraine headache

Here stood Ill-Nature like an ancient maid,
Her wrinkled form in black and white arrayed;
With store of prayers, for mornings, nights, and noons,
Her hand is filled; her bosom with lampoons.[5]   30
    There Affectation, with a sickly mien,
Shows in her cheek the roses of eighteen,
Practiced to lisp, and hang the head aside,
Faints into airs, and languishes with pride;
On the rich quilt sinks with becoming woe,   35
Wrapped in a gown, for sickness, and for show.
The fair ones feel such maladies as these,
When each new nightdress gives a new disease.
    A constant vapor o'er the palace flies;
Strange phantoms rising as the mists arise;   40
Dreadful, as hermit's dreams in haunted shades,
Or bright, as visions of expiring maids.
Now glaring fiends, and snakes on rolling spires,
Pale spectres, gaping tombs, and purple fires:
Now lakes of liquid gold, Elysian [6] scenes,   45
And crystal domes, and angels in machines.[7]
    Unnumbered throngs on every side are seen
Of bodies changed to various forms by Spleen.
Here living teapots stand, one arm held out,
One bent; the handle this, and that the spout: 50
A pipkin [8] there like Homer's tripod[9] walks;
Here sighs a jar, and there a goose pie talks;[10]
Men prove with child, as powerful fancy works,
And maids turned bottles, call aloud for corks.
    Safe passed the Gnome through this fantastic band,   55
A branch of healing spleenwort [11] in his hand.
Then thus addressed the pow'r: "Hail, wayward Queen!
Who rule the sex to fifty from fifteen:
Parent of vapors and of female wit,
Who give th' hysteric [12] or poetic fit,   60
On various tempers act by various ways,

---

[5] *lampoons* abusive personal satires   [6] *Elysian* as in Elysium or Paradise
[7] *angels in machines* Some stage spectacles had complicated machinery for
transformations, disappearances, and even flying performers.
[8] *pipkin* earthen pot
[9] *Homer's tripod* In the *Iliad* (XVIII) Homer tells of Vulcan's twenty tri-
pods, "placed on living wheels of massy gold," that rolled from place to
place, obedient to the wishes of the gods.
[10] *goose pie talks* According to Pope, "a Lady of distinction imagin'd herself
in this condition."
[11] *spleenwort* fern   [12] *hysteric* hysterical

Make some take physic, others scribble plays;
Who cause the proud their visits to delay,
And send the godly in a pet,[13] to pray.
A nymph there is, that all thy pow'r disdains,   65
And thousands more in equal mirth maintains.
But oh! if e'er thy Gnome could spoil a grace,
Or raise a pimple on a beauteous face,
Like citron waters [14] matrons' cheeks inflame,
Or change complexions at a losing game;   70
If e'er with airy horns I planted heads,[15]
Or rumpled petticoats, or tumbled beds,
Or caused suspicion when no soul was rude,
Or discomposed the headdress of a prude,
Or e'er to costive [16] lap dog gave disease,   75
Which not the tears of brightest eyes could ease:
Hear me, and touch Belinda with chagrin;
That single act gives half the world the spleen."
    The Goddess with a discontented air
Seems to reject him, though she grants his prayer.   80
A wondrous bag with both her hands she binds,
Like that where once Ulysses held the winds; [17]
There she collects the force of female lungs,
Sighs, sobs, and passions, and the war of tongues.
A vial next she fills with fainting fears,   85
Soft sorrows, melting griefs, and flowing tears.
The Gnome rejoicing bears her gifts away,
Spreads his black wings, and slowly mounts to day.
    Sunk in Thalestris' arms the nymph he found,
Her eyes dejected and her hair unbound.   90
Full o'er their heads the swelling bag he rent,
And all the Furies [18] issued at the vent.
Belinda burns with more than mortal ire,
And fierce Thalestris fans the rising fire.
"O wretched maid!" she spread her hands, and cried   95
(While Hampton's echoes, "Wretched maid!" replied),
"Was it for this you took such constant care
The bodkin,[19] comb, and essence to prepare?
For this your locks in paper durance bound,

[13] *pet* irritation, ill-humor
[14] *citron waters* brandy drink flavored with citron or lemon peel
[15] *heads* A cuckold was said to have horns on his brow.
[16] *costive* constipated   [17] *winds* See *Odyssey*, X.
[18] *Furies* in Greek mythology, avenging spirits
[19] *bodkin* hairpin

For this with tort'ring irons wreathed around? [20]   100
For this with fillets [21] strained your tender head,
And bravely bore the double loads of lead?
Gods! shall the ravisher display your hair,
While the fops envy, and the ladies stare!
Honor forbid! at whose unrivaled shrine   105
Ease, pleasure, virtue, all, our sex resign.
Methinks already I your tears survey,
Already hear the horrid things they say,
Already see you a degraded toast,[22]
And all your honor in a whisper lost!   110
How shall I, then, your helpless fame defend?
'Twill then be infamy to seem your friend!
And shall this prize, th' inestimable prize,
Exposed through crystal to the gazing eyes,
And heightened by the diamond's circling rays,[23]   115
On that rapacious hand for ever blaze?
Sooner shall grass in Hyde Park Circus grow,
And wits take lodgings in the sound of Bow; [24]
Sooner let earth, air, sea, to chaos fall,
Men, monkeys, lap dogs, parrots, perish all!"   120
   She said; then raging to Sir Plume repairs,
And bids her beau demand the precious hairs:
(Sir Plume, of amber snuffbox justly vain,
And the nice conduct [25] of a clouded [26] cane)
With earnest eyes, and round unthinking face,   125
He first the snuffbox opened, then the case,
And thus broke out—"My Lord, why, what the devil?
Z—ds! damn the lock! 'fore Gad, you must be civil!
Plague on't! 'tis past a jest—nay prithee, pox!
Give her the hair"—he spoke, and rapped his box.   130
   "It grieves me much" (replied the peer again)
"Who speaks so well should ever speak in vain.
But by this lock, this sacred lock I swear
(Which never more shall join its parted hair,
Which never more its honors shall renew,   135
Clipped from the lovely head where late it grew),
That while my nostrils draw the vital air,

---

[20] *locks . . . around* hair confined in curl papers with strips of lead
[21] *fillets* bands for binding the hair   [22] *toast* person honored with a drink
[23] *prize . . . rays* the lock set into a ring
[24] *sound of Bow* bells of St. Mary le Bow, a church in the unfashionable or commercial part of town.
[25] *nice conduct* exact carrying   [26] *clouded* mottled, with dark veins

This hand, which won it, shall for ever wear."
He spoke, and speaking, in proud triumph spread
The long-contended honors of her head.   140
   But Umbriel, hateful Gnome! forbears not so;
He breaks the vial whence the sorrows flow.
Then see! the nymph in beauteous grief appears,
Her eyes half-languishing, half-drowned in tears;
On her heaved bosom hung her drooping head,   145
Which, with a sigh, she raised; and thus she said:
   "For ever curs'd be this detested day,
Which snatched my best, my fav'rite curl away!
Happy! ah ten times happy had I been,
If Hampton Court these eyes had never seen!   150
Yet am not I the first mistaken maid,
By love of courts to num'rous ills betrayed.
Oh had I rather unadmired remained
In some lone isle, or distant northern land;
Where the gilt chariot never marks the way,   155
Where none learn ombre, none e'er taste bohea! [27]
There kept my charms concealed from mortal eye,
Like roses that in deserts bloom and die.
What moved my mind with youthful lords to roam?
Oh had I stayed, and said my prayers at home!   160
'Twas this, the morning omens seemed to tell:
Thrice from my trembling hand the patchbox fell;
The tottering china shook without a wind,
Nay, Poll sat mute, and Shock was most unkind!
A Sylph too warned me of the threats of fate,   165
In mystic visions, now believed too late!
See the poor remnants of these slighted hairs!
My hands shall rend what ev'n thy rapine spares:
These, in two sable ringlets taught to break,[28]
Once gave new beauties to the snowy neck.   170
The sister-lock now sits uncouth, alone,
And in its fellow's fate foresees its own;
Uncurled it hangs, the fatal shears demands;
And tempts, once more, thy sacrilegious hands.
Oh hadst thou, cruel! been content to seize   175
Hairs less in sight, or any hairs but these!"

CANTO V

She said: the pitying audience melt in tears.
But Fate and Jove had stopped the Baron's ears.

[27] *bohea* black tea   [28] *break* divide

In vain Thalestris with reproach assails,
For who can move when fair Belinda fails?
Not half so fixed the Trojan could remain, 5
While Anna begged and Dido raged in vain.[1]
Then grave Clarissa graceful waved her fan;
Silence ensued, and thus the nymph began.

"Say, why are beauties praised and honored most,
The wise man's passion, and the vain man's toast? 10
Why decked with all that land and sea afford,
Why angels called, and angel-like adored?
Why round our coaches crowd the white-gloved beaux,
Why bows the side-box from its inmost rows?
How vain are all these glories, all our pains, 15
Unless good sense preserve what beauty gains:
That men may say, when we the front-box [2] grace,
'Behold the first in virtue, as in face!'
Oh! if to dance all night, and dress all day,
Charmed the smallpox, or chased old age away; 20
Who would not scorn what housewife's cares produce,
Or who would learn one earthly thing of use?
To patch, nay ogle, might become a saint,
Nor could it sure be such a sin to paint.
But since, alas! frail beauty must decay, 25
Curled or uncurled, since locks will turn to grey;
Since painted, or not painted, all shall fade,
And she who scorns a man, must die a maid;
What then remains, but well our pow'r to use,
And keep good humor still whate'er we lose? 30
And trust me, dear! good humor can prevail,
When airs, and flights, and screams, and scolding fail.
Beauties in vain their pretty eyes may roll;
Charms strike the sight, but merit wins the soul."

So spoke the dame, but no applause ensued; 35
Belinda frowned, Thalestris called her prude.
"To arms, to arms!" the fierce virago [3] cries,
And swift as lightning to the combat flies.
All side in parties, and begin th' attack;
Fans clap, silks rustle, and tough whalebones crack; 40
Heroes' and heroines' shouts confus'dly rise,
And bass, and treble voices strike the skies.

[1] *Trojan . . . vain* The Trojan Aeneas was begged by Dido and her sister Anna to stay in Carthage.
[2] *side-box, front-box* positions of theater boxes
[3] *virago* an Amazon, or woman warrior

No common weapons in their hands are found,
Like gods they fight, nor dread a mortal wound.
    So when bold Homer makes the gods engage,   45
And heav'nly breasts with human passions rage;
'Gainst Pallas, Mars; Latona, Hermes [4] arms;
And all Olympus rings with loud alarms.
Jove's thunder roars, Heav'n trembles all around;
Blue Neptune storms, the bellowing deeps resound;   50
Earth shakes her nodding tow'rs, the ground gives way;
And the pale ghosts start at the flash of day!
    Triumphant Umbriel on a sconce's [5] height
Clapped his glad wings, and sat to view the fight:
Propped on their bodkin spears, the sprites survey   55
The growing combat, or assist the fray.
    While through the press enraged Thalestris flies,
And scatters death around from both her eyes,
A beau and witling [6] perished in the throng,
One died in metaphor, and one in song.   60
"O cruel nymph! a living death I bear,"
Cried Dapperwit,[7] and sunk beside his chair.
A mournful glance Sir Fopling [8] upwards cast,
"Those eyes are made so killing"—was his last.
Thus on Maeander's [9] flow'ry margin lies   65
Th' expiring swan, and as he sings he dies.
    When bold Sir Plume had drawn Clarissa down,
Chloe stepped in, and killed him with a frown;
She smiled to see the doughty hero slain,
But, at her smile, the beau revived again.   70
    Now Jove suspends his golden scales in air,
Weighs the men's wits against the lady's hair;
The doubtful beam long nods from side to side;
At length the wits mount up, the hairs subside.
    See fierce Belinda on the Baron flies,   75
With more than usual lightning in her eyes;
Nor feared the chief th' unequal fight to try,
Who sought no more than on his foe to die.

---

[4] *Pallas . . . Hermes* When the gods joined the battle in the Trojan War
(*Iliad*, XX), Pallas Athena and Hermes fought for the Greeks, Mars and
Latona for the Trojans.
[5] *sconce* a hanging candlestick   [6] *witling* a self-styled wit
[7] *Dapperwit* a foppish character in Wycherley's *Love in a Wood*
[8] *Sir Fopling* a character in Etherege's *The Man of Mode; or, Sir Fopling
Flutter* (see Dryden's epilogue, p. 272)
[9] *Maeander* a winding river in Phrygia

But this bold lord, with manly strength endued,
She with one finger and a thumb subdued: 80
Just where the breath of life his nostrils drew,
A charge of snuff the wily virgin threw;
The Gnomes direct, to every atom just,
The pungent grains of titillating dust.
Sudden, with starting tears each eye o'erflows,   85
And the high dome re-echoes to his nose.
    "Now meet thy fate," incensed Belinda cried,
And drew a deadly bodkin from her side.
(The same, his ancient personage to deck,
Her great-great-grandsire wore about his neck   90
In three seal rings; which after, melted down,
Formed a vast buckle for his widow's gown:
Her infant grandame's whistle next it grew,
The bells she jingled, and the whistle blew;
Then in a bodkin graced her mother's hairs,   95
Which long she wore, and now Belinda wears.)
    "Boast not my fall" (he cried) "insulting foe!
Thou by some other shalt be laid as low.
Nor think, to die dejects my lofty mind;
All that I dread is leaving you behind!   100
Rather than so, ah let me still survive,
And burn in Cupid's flames—but burn alive."
    "Restore the lock!" she cries; and all around
"Restore the lock!" the vaulted roofs rebound.
Not fierce Othello in so loud a strain   105
Roared for the handkerchief that caused his pain.[10]
But see how oft ambitious aims are crossed,
And chiefs contend till all the prize is lost!
The lock, obtained with guilt, and kept with pain,
In ev'ry place is sought, but sought in vain: 110
With such a prize no mortal must be blest,
So Heav'n decrees! with Heav'n who can contest?
    Some thought it mounted to the lunar sphere,
Since all things lost on earth, are treasured there.
There heroes' wits are kept in pond'rous vases,   115
And beaux' in snuffboxes and tweezer-cases.
There broken vows, and deathbed alms are found,
And lovers' hearts with ends of riband bound;
The courtier's promises, and sick man's prayers,
The smiles of harlots, and the tears of heirs,   120

[10] *Othello . . . pain* See *Othello*, IV.1

Cages for gnats, and chains to yoke a flea,
Dried butterflies, and tomes of casuistry.[11]
   But trust the Muse—she saw it upward rise,
Though marked by none but quick poetic eyes:
(So Rome's great founder to the heav'ns withdrew,   125
To Proculus alone confessed in view.) [12]
A sudden star, it shot through liquid air,
And drew behind a radiant trail of hair.
Not Berenice's lock [13] first rose so bright,
The heav'ns bespangling with disheveled light.   130
The Sylphs behold it kindling as it flies,
And pleased pursue its progress through the skies.
   This the beau monde [14] shall from the Mall [15] survey,
And hail with music its propitious ray.
This, the blest lover shall for Venus take,   135
And send up vows from Rosamonda's lake.[16]
This Partridge soon shall view in cloudless skies,
When next he looks through Galileo's eyes;
And hence th' egregious wizard shall foredoom
The fate of Louis, and the fall of Rome.[17]   140
   Then cease, bright nymph! to mourn thy ravished hair
Which adds new glory to the shining sphere!
Not all the tresses that fair head can boast
Shall draw such envy as the lock you lost.
For, after all the murders of your eye,   145
When, after millions slain, your self shall die;
When those fair suns shall set, as set they must,
And all those tresses shall be laid in dust;
This lock, the Muse shall consecrate to fame,
And 'midst the stars inscribe Belinda's name.   150

[11] *tomes of casuistry* books of arguments on delicate problems of right and wrong
[12] *Rome . . . view* Proculus saw Rome's founder, Romulus, taken to heaven.
[13] *Berenice's lock* Berenice, wife of Ptolemy III (d. 221 B.C.), dedicated her hair to Venus for his safe return from an expedition. It disappeared from the temple, and was said to have been carried to the heavens and made a constellation.
[14] *beau monde* fashionable society   [15] *Mall* promenade in St. James's Park
[16] *Rosamonda's lake* in St. James's Park
[17] *Partridge . . . Rome* John Partridge (1644–1715), almanac maker and amateur astrologer who regularly prophesied the defeat of Louis XIV and the fall of the Pope.

KNOW THEN THYSELF

Know then thyself, presume not God to scan;
The proper study of mankind is man.
Placed on this isthmus of a middle state,
A being darkly wise, and rudely great:
With too much knowledge for the skeptic side,   5
With too much weakness for the Stoic's pride,
He hangs between; in doubt to act, or rest;
In doubt to deem himself a god, or beast;
In doubt his mind or body to prefer;
Born but to die, and reas'ning but to err;   10
Alike in ignorance, his reason such,
Whether he thinks too little, or too much:
Chaos of thought and passion, all confused;
Still by himself abused, or disabused;
Created half to rise, and half to fall;   15
Great lord of all things, yet a prey to all;
Sole judge of truth, in endless error hurled:
The glory, jest, and riddle of the world!

An Essay on Man [1] (II, 1)

EPIGRAM

ENGRAVED ON THE COLLAR OF A DOG WHICH I GAVE
TO HIS ROYAL HIGHNESS

I am his Highness' dog at Kew;
Pray tell me, sir, whose dog are you?

CRITICISM

Lytton Strachey here attempts to define and evaluate Pope (and his period) through the poet's characteristic style: the use of the heroic couplet. In the same kind of approach, one might study Milton's blank verse or compare Shakespeare's and Donne's use of the sonnet form. Strachey does not consider individual poems; his is more the horizontal approach—with some con-

[1] *An Essay on Man* is composed of four epistles on the nature and state of man with respect to (I) the Universe; (II) Himself as an Individual; (III) Society; and (IV) Happiness. Pope intended it as both a "system of Ethics" and "a general Map of Man."

sideration of the history of the couplet and Pope's development as well as his general style. Neither does he treat Pope fully as a satirist and a wit. Pope's social criticism may also be studied in the specific statements and the ingenious structure of *The Rape of the Lock*; but to characterize him through the simplest element of his style is another valid and individual approach.

Pope and the Heroic Couplet [1]

LYTTON STRACHEY

Let us examine for a moment the technical instrument which Pope used—I mean the heroic couplet.

When he was a young man, the poet Walsh gave Pope a piece of advice. 'We have had great poets,' he said, 'but never one great poet that was correct. I recommend you to make your leading aim —correctness.' Pope took the advice, and became the most correct of poets. This was his chief title to glory in the eighteenth century; it was equally the stick that he was most frequently and rapturously beaten with, in the nineteenth. Macaulay, in his essay on Byron, devotes several pages of his best forensic style to an exposure and denunciation of the absurd futility of the 'correctness' of the school of Pope. There is in reality, he declared, only one kind of correctness in literature—that which 'has its foundation in truth and in the principles of human nature.' But Pope's so-called correctness was something very different. It consisted simply in a strict obedience to a perfectly arbitrary set of prosodic rules. His couplet was a purely artificial structure—the product of mere convention; and, so far from there being any possible poetic merit in the kind of correctness which it involved, this 'correctness' was in fact only 'another name for dullness and absurdity.' A short time ago, the distinguished poet, M. Paul Valéry, demolished Macaulay's argument —no doubt quite unconsciously—in an essay full of brilliant subtlety and charming wit. He showed conclusively the essentially poetic value of purely arbitrary conventions. But, for our purposes, so drastic a conclusion is unnecessary. For Macaulay was mistaken, not only in his theory, but in his facts. The truth

[1] A portion of Lytton Strachey's essay, "Pope" (the Leslie Stephen Lecture for 1925), first published in *Characters and Commentaries* by Lytton Strachey. (Copyright, 1933, by Harcourt, Brace & World, Inc.; renewed, 1961, by James Strachey. Reprinted by permission of Harcourt, Brace & World, Inc.)

is that the English classical couplet—unlike the French—had nothing conventional about it. On the contrary, it was the inevitable, the logical, the natural outcome of the development of English verse.

The fundamental element in the structure of poetry is rhythmical repetition. In England, the favourite unit of this repetition very early became the ten-syllabled iambic line. Now it is clear that the treatment of this line may be developed in two entirely different directions. The first of these developments is blank verse. Milton's definition of blank verse is well known, and it cannot be bettered: it consists, he says, 'in apt numbers, fit quantity of syllables, and the sense variously drawn out from one verse into another.' Its essence, in other words, is the combination formed by rhythmical variety playing over an underlying norm; and it is easy to trace the evolution of this wonderful measure from the primitive rigidity of Surrey to the incredible virtuosity of Shakespeare's later plays, where blank verse reaches its furthest point of development—where rhythmical variety is found in unparalleled profusion, while the underlying regularity is just, still, miraculously preserved. After Shakespeare, the combination broke down; the element of variety became so excessive that the underlying norm disappeared, with the result that the blank verse of the latest Elizabethans is virtually indistinguishable from prose.

But suppose the ten-syllabled iambic were treated in precisely the contrary manner. Suppose, instead of developing the element of variety to its maximum, the whole rhythmical emphasis were put upon the element of regularity. What would be the result? This was the problem that presented itself to the poets of the seventeenth century, when it appeared to them that the possibilities of blank verse were played out. (In reality they were not played out, as Milton proved; but Milton was an isolated and unique phenomenon.) Clearly, the most effective method of emphasising regularity is the use of rhyme; and the most regular form of rhyme is the couplet. Already, in the splendid couplets of Marlowe and in the violent couplets of Donne, we can find a foretaste of what the future had in store for the measure. Shakespeare, indeed, as if to show that there were no limits either to his comprehension or to his capacity, threw off a few lines which might have been written by Pope, and stuck them into the middle of *Othello*.[2] But it was not until the collapse of blank verse, about 1630, that the essential characteristics which lay concealed in the couplet began to be exploited. It was Waller who first fully apprehended the implications of regularity; and it is to this fact that his immense reputation during the succeeding hundred years was due. Waller disengaged the heroic couplet from the beautiful vagueness of Elizabethanism. He perceived what logically followed from a rhyme. He saw that regularity implied balance, that balance implied antithesis; he saw that balance also implied simplicity, that simplicity implied clarity and that clarity implied exactitude. The result was a poetical instrument contrary in every particular to blank verse—a form which, instead of being varied, unsymmetrical, fluid, complex, profound and indefinite, was regular, balanced, antithetical, simple, clear, and exact. But, though Waller was its creator, the heroic couplet remained, with him, in an embryonic state. Its evolution was slow; even Dryden did not quite bring it to perfection. That great genius, with all his strength and all his brilliance, lacked one quality without which no mastery of the couplet could be complete—the elegance of perfect finish. This was possessed by Pope. The most correct of poets—Pope was indeed that; it is his true title to glory. But the phrase does not mean that he obeyed more slavishly than anybody else a set of arbitrary rules. No, it means something entirely different: it means that the system of versification of which the principle is regularity reached in Pope's hands the final plenitude of its nature—its ultimate significance—its supreme consummation.

That Pope's verse is artificial there can be no doubt. But then there is only one kind of verse that is not artificial, and that is, bad verse. Yet it is true that there is a sense in which Pope's couplet is more artificial than, let us say, the later blank verse of Shakespeare—it has less resemblance to nature. It is regular and neat; but nature is 'divers et ondoyant'; and so is blank verse. Nature and blank verse are complicated; and Pope's couplet is simplicity itself. But what a profound art underlies

---

[2] 'She that in wisdom never was so frail
To change the cod's head for the salmon's tail;
She that could think, and ne'er disclose her mind;
See suitors following, and not look behind;
She was a wight, if ever such wight were,
To suckle fools and chronicle small beer.'

that simplicity! Pope's great achievement in English literature was the triumph of simplification. In one of his earliest works, the *Pastorals,* there is simplicity and nothing else; Pope had understood that if he could once attain to a perfect simplicity, all the rest would follow in good time—

> O deign to visit our forsaken seats,
> The mossy fountains, and the green retreats!
> Where'er you walk, cool gales shall fan the glade;
> Trees, where you sit, shall crowd into a shade;
> Where'er you tread, the blushing flow'rs shall rise,
> And all things flourish where you turn your eyes.

The lines flow on with the most transparent limpidity—

> But see, the shepherds shun the noon-day heat,
> The lowing herds to murm'ring brooks retreat,
> To closer shades the panting flocks remove;
> Ye Gods! and is there no relief for love?

Everything is obvious. The diction is a mass of *clichés;* the epithets are the most commonplace possible; the herds low, the brooks murmur, the flocks pant and remove, the retreats are green, and the flowers blush. The rhythm is that of a rocking-horse; and the sentiment is mere sugar. But what a relief! What a relief to have escaped for once from *le mot propre,* from subtle elaboration of diction and metre, from complicated states of mind, and all the profound obscurities of Shakespeare and Mr. T. S. Eliot! How delightful to have no trouble at all—to understand so very, very easily every single thing that is said!

This is Pope at his most youthful. As he matured, his verse matured with him. Eventually, his couplets, while retaining to the full their early ease, polish, and lucidity, became charged with an extraordinary weight. He was able to be massive, as no other wielder of the measure has ever been—

> Lo! thy dread empire, Chaos! is restored;
> Light dies before thy uncreating word;
> Thy hand, great Anarch! lets the curtain fall,
> And universal Darkness buries All.

Here the slow solemnity of the effect is produced by a most learned accumulation of accents and quantities; in some of the lines all the syllables save two are either long or stressed. At other times, he uses a precisely opposite method; in line after line he maintains, almost completely, the regular alternation of accented and unaccented syllables; and so conveys a wonderful impression of solidity and force—

> Proceed, great days! till learning fly the shore,
> Till Birch shall blush with noble blood no more,
> Till Thames see Eton's sons for ever play,
> Till Westminster's whole year be holiday,
> Till Isis' Elders reel, their pupils' sport,
> And Alma Mater lies dissolved in Port!

Perhaps the most characteristic of all the elements in the couplet is antithesis. Ordinary regularity demands that the sense should end with every line—that was a prime necessity; but a more scrupulous symmetry would require something more—a division of the line itself into two halves, whose meanings should correspond. And yet a further refinement was possible: each half might be again divided, and the corresponding divisions in the two halves might be so arranged as to balance each other. The force of neatness could no further go; and thus the most completely evolved type of the heroic line is one composed of four main words arranged in pairs, so as to form a double antithesis.

> Willing to wound, and yet afraid to strike

is an example of such a line, and Pope's poems are full of them. With astonishing ingenuity he builds up these exquisite structures, in which the parts are so cunningly placed that they seem to interlock spontaneously, and, while they are all formed on a similar model, are yet so subtly adjusted that they produce a fresh pleasure as each one appears. But that is not all. Pope was preeminently a satirist. He was naturally drawn to the contemplation of human beings, their conduct in society, their characters, their motives, their destinies; and the feelings which these contemplations habitually aroused in him were those of scorn and hatred. Civilisation illumined by animosity—such was his theme; such was the passionate and complicated material from which he wove his patterns of balanced precision and polished clarity. Antithesis penetrates below the structure; it permeates the whole conception of his work. Fundamental opposites clash, and are reconciled. The profundities of persons, the futilities of existence, the rage and spite of genius—these things are mixed together, and presented to our eyes in the shape of a Chinese box. The essence of all art is the accomplishment of the impossible. This cannot be done, we say; and it *is* done. What has happened? A magician has waved his wand. It is impossible that Pope should convey to us his withering sense of the wretchedness and emptiness of the fate of old women in society, in five lines, each containing four words, arranged in pairs, so as to form a double antithesis. But the magician waves his wand, and there it is—

> See how the world its veterans rewards!
> A youth of frolics, an old age of cards;
> Fair to no purpose, artful to no end,
> Young without lovers, old without a friend,
> A fop their passion, and their prize a sot;
> Alive ridiculous, and dead forgot!

And now, perhaps, we have discovered what may truly be said to have been Pope's 'poetic criticism of life.' His poetic criticism of life was, simply and solely, the heroic couplet.

WILLIAM BLAKE

[1757-1827]

WILLIAM BLAKE, son of a London hosier and haberdasher, became both an artist and a poet. Educated at home, in drawing school, and as an apprentice engraver, by 1778 he was working for himself on commissions from booksellers. The next five years held important events—his art exhibit at the Royal Academy (1780), his marriage to Catherine Boucher (1782), and the publication of his first book of poems, *Poetical Sketches* (1783). Blake, assisted by his wife, then developed the art of "illuminated printting," publishing his *Songs of Innocence* (1789) and *Songs of Experience* (1794), for which he made prints from copper plates engraved with text and illustrations and then hand colored the designs. From childhood Blake had been a visionary and mystic (he had seen God looking through the window, a tree full of angels, and the prophet Ezekiel). His poetry, also mystical, developed in two styles—the cryptic simplicity of the *Songs,* whose vision was always inside and behind things, sometimes with a double view; and the more sweeping, almost apocalyptic style of his prophetic books, such as *The Book of Thel* (1789) and *The First Book of Urizen* (1794). Influenced by the liberal ideas of Thomas Paine, he also wrote poems on the French and American revolutions, *Europe, A Prophecy* (1794) and *America, A Prophecy* (1794). In his later years, Blake continued to work on texts and illustrations of *Milton* (1804–*c.*1808) and *Jerusalem* (1804–*c.*1820), and at his death was a recognized artist in London. Blake recorded his visions of God and the Devil, man and the world, in both his poetic and his engraved lines, which fused to make the strong whirling motion of his art.

Introductory Readings

EDITION: *Complete Writings of William Blake,* ed. Geoffrey Keynes
(1957). LETTERS: *The Letters of William Blake,* ed. Geoffrey Keynes
(1956). BIOGRAPHY: Mona Wilson, *The Life of William Blake* (rev. ed.,
1928). CRITICISM: Max Plowman, *An Introduction to the Study of Blake*
(1927); Helen C. White, *The Mysticism of William Blake* (1927); Mark
Schorer, *William Blake: The Politics of Vision* (1946); Northrop Frye,
Fearful Symmetry (1947); H. M. Margoliouth, *William Blake* (1951);
Margaret Rudd, *Divided Image* [on Blake and Yeats] (1953).

SONGS OF INNOCENCE AND EXPERIENCE

"Shewing the Two Contrary States of the Human Soul"

SONGS OF INNOCENCE

INTRODUCTION

Piping down the valleys wild,
Piping songs of pleasant glee,
On a cloud I saw a child,
And he laughing said to me:

"Pipe a song about a Lamb!"   5
So I piped with merry chear.
"Piper, pipe that song again;"
So I piped: he wept to hear.

"Drop thy pipe, thy happy pipe;
Sing thy songs of happy chear:"   10
So I sung the same again,
While he wept with joy to hear.

"Piper, sit thee down and write
In a book, that all may read."
So he vanish'd from my sight,   15
And I pluck'd a hollow reed,

And I made a rural pen,
And I stain'd the water clear,
And I wrote my happy songs
Every child may joy to hear.   20

THE LAMB

Little Lamb, who made thee?
 Dost thou know who made thee?
Gave thee life, & bid thee feed
By the stream & o'er the mead;
Gave thee clothing of delight,   5
Softest clothing, wooly, bright;
Gave thee such a tender voice,
Making all the vales rejoice?
 Little Lamb, who made thee?
 Dost thou know who made thee?   10

 Little Lamb, I'll tell thee,
 Little Lamb, I'll tell thee:
He is called by thy name,
For he calls himself a Lamb.
He is meek, & he is mild;   15
He became a little child.
I a child, & thou a lamb,
We are called by his name.
 Little Lamb, God bless thee!
 Little Lamb, God bless thee!   20

THE ECCHOING GREEN

The Sun does arise,
And make happy the skies;
The merry bells ring
To welcome the Spring;
The skylark and thrush,   5
The birds of the bush,
Sing louder around
To the bells' chearful sound,
While our sports shall be seen
On the Ecchoing Green.   10

Old John, with white hair,
Does laugh away care,
Sitting under the oak,
Among the old folk.
They laugh at our play,   15
And soon they all say:

"Such, such were the joys
When we all, girls & boys,
In our youth time were seen
On the Ecchoing Green."   20

Till the little ones, weary,
No more can be merry;
The sun does descend,
And our sports have an end.
Round the laps of their mothers   25
Many sisters and brothers,
Like birds in their nest,
Are ready for rest,
And sport no more seen
On the darkening Green.   30

THE CHIMNEY SWEEPER

When my mother died I was very young,
And my father sold me while yet my tongue
Could scarcely cry " 'weep! 'weep! 'weep! 'weep!"
So your chimneys I sweep, & in soot I sleep.

There's little Tom Dacre, who cried when his head,   5
That curl'd like a lamb's back, was shav'd: so I said
"Hush, Tom! never mind it, for when your head's bare
You know that the soot cannot spoil your white hair."

And so he was quiet, & that very night,
As Tom was a-sleeping, he had such a sight!   10
That thousands of sweepers, Dick, Joe, Ned, & Jack,
Were all of them lock'd up in coffins of black.

And by came an Angel who had a bright key,
And he open'd the coffins & set them all free;
Then down a green plain leaping, laughing, they run,   15
And wash in a river, and shine in the Sun.

Then naked & white, all their bags left behind,
They rise upon clouds and sport in the wind;
And the Angel told Tom, if he'd be a good boy,
He'd have God for his father, & never want joy.   20

And so Tom awoke; and we rose in the dark,
And got with our bags & our brushes to work.
Tho' the morning was cold, Tom was happy & warm;
So if all do their duty they need not fear harm.

HOLY THURSDAY

'Twas on a Holy Thursday,[1] their innocent faces clean,
The children [2] walking two & two, in red & blue & green,
Grey-headed beadles [3] walk'd before, with wands as white as snow,
Till into the high dome of Paul's they like Thames' waters flow.

O what a multitude they seem'd, these flowers of London town!   5
Seated in companies they sit with radiance all their own.
The hum of multitudes was there, but multitudes of lambs,
Thousands of little boys & girls raising their innocent hands.

Now like a mighty wind they raise to heaven the voice of song,
Or like harmonious thunderings the seats of Heaven among.   10
Beneath them sit the aged men, wise guardians of the poor;
Then cherish pity, lest you drive an angel from your door.

LAUGHING SONG

When the green woods laugh with the voice of joy,
And the dimpling stream runs laughing by;
When the air does laugh with our merry wit,
And the green hill laughs with the noise of it;

When the meadows laugh with lively green,   5
And the grasshopper laughs in the merry scene,
When Mary and Susan and Emily
With their sweet round mouths sing "Ha, Ha, He!"

When the painted birds laugh in the shade,
Where our table with cherries and nuts is spread,   10
Come live & be merry, and join with me,
To sing the sweet chorus of "Ha, Ha, He!"

THE LITTLE BLACK BOY

My mother bore me in the southern wild,
And I am black, but O! my soul is white;
White as an angel is the English child,
But I am black, as if bereav'd of light.

[1] *Holy Thursday* in the Anglican Church, Ascension Day
[2] *children* charity children who gave concerts in St. Paul's Cathedral in London
[3] *beadles* mace-bearers who walked ahead of processions

My mother taught me underneath a tree, 5
And sitting down before the heat of day,
She took me on her lap and kissed me,
And pointing to the east, began to say:

"Look on the rising sun: there God does live,
And gives his light, and gives his heat away; 10
And flowers and trees and beasts and men receive
Comfort in morning, joy in the noonday.

"And we are put on earth a little space,
That we may learn to bear the beams of love;
And these black bodies and this sunburnt face 15
Is but a cloud, and like a shady grove.

"For when our souls have learn'd that heat to bear,
The cloud will vanish; we shall hear his voice,
Saying: 'Come out from the grove, my love & care,
And round my golden tent like lambs rejoice.' " 20

Thus did my mother say, and kissed me;
And thus I say to little English boy:
When I from black and he from white cloud free,
And round the tent of God like lambs we joy,

I'll shade him from the heat, till he can bear 25
To lean in joy upon our father's knee;
And then I'll stand and stroke his silver hair,
And be like him, and he will then love me.

SONGS OF EXPERIENCE

THE LITTLE GIRL LOST

In futurity
I prophetic see
That the earth from sleep
(Grave the sentence deep)

Shall arise and seek 5
For her maker meek;
And the desart wild
Become a garden mild.

In the southern clime,
Where the summer's prime   10
Never fades away,
Lovely Lyca lay.

Seven summers old
Lovely Lyca told;
She had wander'd long   15
Hearing wild birds' song.

"Sweet sleep, come to me
Underneath this tree.
Do father, mother weep,
Where can Lyca sleep?   20

"Lost in desart wild
Is your little child.
How can Lyca sleep
If her mother weep?

"If her heart does ake   25
Then let Lyca wake;
If my mother sleep,
Lyca shall not weep.

"Frowning, frowning night,
O'er this desart bright   30
Let thy moon arise
While I close my eyes."

Sleeping Lyca lay
While the beasts of prey,
Come from caverns deep,   35
View'd the maid asleep.

The kingly lion stood
And the virgin view'd,
Then he gamboll'd round
O'er the hallow'd ground.   40

Leopards, tygers, play
Round her as she lay,
While the lion old
Bow'd his mane of gold

And her bosom lick,   45
And upon her neck

From his eyes of flame
Ruby tears there came;

While the lioness
Loos'd her slender dress,   50
And naked they convey'd
To caves the sleeping maid.

THE LITTLE GIRL FOUND

All the night in woe
Lyca's parents go
Over vallies deep,
While the desarts weep.

Tired and woe-begone,   5
Hoarse with making moan,
Arm in arm seven days
They trac'd the desart ways.

Seven nights they sleep
Among shadows deep,   10
And dream they see their child
Starv'd in desart wild.

Pale, thro' pathless ways
The fancied image strays
Famish'd, weeping, weak,   15
With hollow piteous shriek.

Rising from unrest,
The trembling woman prest
With feet of weary woe:
She could no further go.   20

In his arms he bore
Her, arm'd with sorrow sore;
Till before their way
A couching lion lay.

Turning back was vain: 25
Soon his heavy mane
Bore them to the ground.
Then he stalk'd around,

Smelling to his prey;
But their fears allay   30

When he licks their hands,
And silent by them stands.

They look upon his eyes
Fill'd with deep surprise,
And wondering behold 35
A spirit arm'd in gold.

On his head a crown,
On his shoulders down
Flow'd his golden hair.
Gone was all their care. 40

"Follow me," he said;
"Weep not for the maid;
In my palace deep
Lyca lies asleep."

Then they followed 45
Where the vision led,
And saw their sleeping child
Among tygers wild.

To this day they dwell
In a lonely dell; 50
Nor fear the wolvish howl
Nor the lions' growl.

THE SICK ROSE [1]

O rose, thou art sick!
The invisible worm
That flies in the night,
In the howling storm,

Has found out thy bed 5
Of crimson joy,
And his dark secret love
Does thy life destroy.

THE FLY

Little Fly,
Thy summer's play

---

[1] Critical comment on this poem appears on p. 346.

My thoughtless hand
Has brush'd away.

Am not I   5
A fly like thee?
Or art not thou
A man like me?

For I dance,
And drink, & sing,   10
Till some blind hand
Shall brush my wing.

If thought is life
And strength & breath,
And the want   15
Of thought is death;

Then am I
A happy fly,
If I live
Or if I die.   20

THE TYGER [1]

Tyger! Tyger! burning bright
In the forests of the night,
What immortal hand or eye
Could frame thy fearful symmetry?

In what distant deeps or skies   5
Burnt the fire of thine eyes?
On what wings dare he aspire?
What the hand dare seize the fire?

And what shoulder, & what art,
Could twist the sinews of thy heart?   10
And when thy heart began to beat,
What dread hand? & what dread feet? [2]

---

[1] Critical comment on this poem appears on p. 347.
[2] *What . . . feet?* In Blake's original draft of "The Tyger," line 12 was connected to a five-line stanza which was later omitted. This line and the one which followed read:

> What dread hand & what dread feet
> Could fetch it from the furnace deep . . .

What the hammer? what the chain?
In what furnace was thy brain?
What the anvil? what dread grasp   15
Dare its deadly terrors clasp?

When the stars threw down their spears,
And water'd heaven with their tears,
Did he smile his work to see?
Did he who made the Lamb make thee?   20

Tyger! Tyger! burning bright
In the forests of the night,
What immortal hand or eye,
Dare frame thy fearful symmetry?

AH! SUN-FLOWER [1]

Ah, Sun-flower! weary of time,
Who countest the steps of the Sun,
Seeking after that sweet golden clime
Where the traveller's journey is done:

Where the Youth pined away with desire,   5
And the pale Virgin shrouded in snow,
Arise from their graves, and aspire
Where my Sun-flower wishes to go.

THE GARDEN OF LOVE

I went to the Garden of Love,
And saw what I never had seen:
A Chapel was built in the midst,
Where I used to play on the green.

And the gates of this Chapel were shut,   5
And "Thou shalt not" writ over the door;
So I turn'd to the Garden of Love
That so many sweet flowers bore;

And I saw it was filled with graves,
And tomb-stones where flowers should be;   10
And Priests in black gowns were walking their rounds,
And binding with briars my joys & desires.

[1] Critical comment on this poem appears on p. 347.

LONDON

I wander thro' each charter'd [1] street,
Near where the charter'd Thames does flow,
And mark in every face I meet
Marks of weakness, marks of woe.

In every cry of every Man,   5
In every Infant's cry of fear,
In every voice, in every ban,[2]
The mind-forg'd manacles I hear.

How the Chimney-sweeper's cry
Every black'ning Church appalls; [3]   10
And the hapless Soldier's sigh
Runs in blood down Palace walls.

But most thro' midnight streets I hear
How the youthful Harlot's curse
Blasts the new born Infant's tear,   15
And blights with plagues the Marriage hearse.

THE HUMAN ABSTRACT

Pity would be no more
If we did not make somebody Poor;
And Mercy no more could be
If all were as happy as we.

And mutual fear brings peace,   5
Till the selfish loves increase:
Then Cruelty knits a snare,
And spreads his baits with care.

He sits down with holy fears,
And waters the ground with tears;   10
Then Humility takes its root
Underneath his foot.

Soon spreads the dismal shade
Of Mystery over his head;

[1] *charter'd* marked out, bound for use. Compare *manacles*, l. 8. Another
version has "dirty."
[2] *ban* curse   [3] *appalls* literally, "to make pale"; to dismay

And the Catterpiller and Fly   15
Feed on the Mystery.

And it bears the fruit of Deceit,
Ruddy and sweet to eat;
And the Raven his nest has made   20
In its thickest shade.

The Gods of the earth and sea
Sought thro' Nature to find this Tree;
But their search was all in vain:
There grows one in the Human Brain.

A POISON TREE

I was angry with my friend:
I told my wrath, my wrath did end.
I was angry with my foe:
I told it not, my wrath did grow.

And I water'd it in fears,   5
Night & morning with my tears;
And I sunned it with smiles,
And with soft deceitful wiles.

And it grew both day and night,
Till it bore an apple bright;   10
And my foe beheld it shine,
And he knew that it was mine,

And into my garden stole
When the night had veil'd the pole:
In the morning glad I see   15
My foe outstretch'd beneath the tree.

OTHER POEMS

INFANT SORROW

My mother groan'd, my father wept;
Into the dangerous world I leapt,
Helpless, naked, piping loud,
Like a fiend hid in a cloud.

Struggling in my father's hands   5
Striving against my swaddling bands,

Bound & weary, I thought best
To sulk upon my mother's breast.

When I saw that rage was vain,
And to sulk would nothing gain,   10
Turning many a trick & wile,
I began to soothe & smile.

And I sooth'd day after day
Till upon the ground I stray;
And I smil'd night after night,   15
Seeking only for delight.

And I saw before me shine
Clusters of the wand'ring vine,
And many a lovely flower & tree
Stretch'd their blossoms out to me.   20

My father then with holy look,
In his hands a holy book,
Pronounc'd curses on my head
And bound me in a mirtle ¹ shade.

Why should I be bound to thee,   25
O my lovely mirtle tree?
Love, free love, cannot be bound
To any tree that grows on ground.

O, how sick & weary I
Underneath my mirtle lie,   30
Like to dung upon the ground
Underneath my mirtle bound.

Oft my mirtle sigh'd in vain
To behold my heavy chain;
Oft my father saw us sigh,   35
And laugh'd at our simplicity.

So I smote him & his gore
Stain'd the roots my mirtle bore.
But the time of youth is fled,
And grey hairs are on my head.   40

---

¹ *mirtle* The myrtle tree was sacred to Venus, goddess of love.

TO NOBODADDY [1]

Why art thou silent & invisible,
Father of Jealousy?
Why dost thou hide thy self in clouds
From every searching Eye?

Why darkness & obscurity   5
In all thy words & laws,
That none dare eat the fruit but from
The wily serpent's jaws?
Or is it because Secresy gains females' loud applause?

IF YOU TRAP THE MOMENT

If you trap the moment before it's ripe,
The tears of repentance you'll certainly wipe:
But if once you let the ripe moment go
You can never wipe off the tears of woe.

ETERNITY

He who bends to himself a joy
Does the winged life destroy;
But he who kisses the joy as it flies
Lives in eternity's sun rise.

THE MENTAL TRAVELLER [1]

I travel'd thro' a Land of Men,
A Land of Men & Women too,
And heard & saw such dreadful things
As cold Earth wanderers never knew.

For there the Babe is born in joy   5
That was begotten in dire woe;
Just as we Reap in joy the fruit
Which we in bitter tears did sow.

---

[1] *Nobodaddy* "Nobody's Daddy," as opposed to "Father of All." "Nobodaddy" was Blake's nickname for Urizen, the Father of Jealousy.

---

[1] Critical comment on this poem appears on p. 350.

And if the Babe is born a Boy
He's given to a Woman Old,   10
Who nails him down upon a rock,
Catches his shrieks in cups of gold.

She binds iron thorns around his head,
She pierces both his hands & feet,
She cuts his heart out at his side   15
To make it feel both cold & heat.

Her fingers number every Nerve,
Just as a Miser counts his gold;
She lives upon his shrieks & cries,
And she grows young as he grows old.   20

Till he becomes a bleeding youth,
And she becomes a Virgin bright;
Then he rends up his Manacles
And binds her down for his delight.

He plants himself in all her Nerves,   25
Just as a Husbandman his mould;
And she becomes his dwelling place
And Garden fruitful seventy fold.

An aged Shadow, soon he fades,
Wand'ring round an Earthly Cot,   30
Full filled all with gems & gold
Which he by industry had got.

And these are the gems of the Human Soul,
The rubies & pearls of a lovesick eye,
The countless gold of the akeing heart,   35
The martyr's groan & the lover's sigh.

They are his meat, they are his drink;
He feeds the Beggar & the Poor
And the wayfaring Traveller:
For ever open is his door.   40

His grief is their eternal joy;
They make the roofs & walls to ring;
Till from the fire on the hearth
A little Female Babe does spring.

And she is all of solid fire   45
And gems & gold, that none his hand

Dares stretch to touch her Baby form,
Or wrap her in his swaddling-band.

But She comes to the Man she loves,
If young or old, or rich or poor;   50
They soon drive out the aged Host,
A Beggar at another's door.

He wanders weeping far away,
Until some other take him in;
Oft blind & age-bent, sore distrest,   55
Untill he can a Maiden win.

And to allay his freezing Age
The Poor Man takes her in his arms;
The Cottage fades before his sight,
The Garden & its lovely Charms.   60

The Guests are scatter'd thro' the land,
For the Eye altering alters all;
The Senses roll themselves in fear,
And the flat Earth becomes a Ball;

The stars, sun, Moon, all shrink away,   65
A desart vast without a bound,
And nothing left to eat or drink,
And a dark desart all around.

The honey of her Infant lips,
The bread & wine of her sweet smile,   70
The wild game of her roving Eye,
Does him to Infancy beguile;

For as he eats & drinks he grows
Younger & younger every day;
And on the desart wild they both   75
Wander in terror & dismay.

Like the wild Stag she flees away,
Her fear plants many a thicket wild;
While he pursues her night & day,
By various arts of Love beguil'd,   80

By various arts of Love & Hate,
Till the wide desart planted o'er
With Labyrinths of wayward Love,
Where roam the Lion, Wolf & Boar,

Till he becomes a wayward Babe,   85
And she a weeping Woman Old.
Then many a Lover wanders here;
The Sun & Stars are nearer roll'd.

The trees bring forth sweet Extacy
To all who in the desert roam;   90
Till many a City there is Built,
And many a pleasant Shepherd's home.

But when they find the frowning Babe,
Terror strikes thro' the region wide:
They cry "The Babe! the Babe is Born!"   95
And flee away on Every side.

For who dare touch the frowning form,
His arm is wither'd to its root;
Lions, Boars, Wolves, all howling flee,
And every Tree does shed its fruit.   100

And none can touch that frowning form,
Except it be a Woman Old;
She nails him down upon the Rock,
And all is done as I have told.

THE CRYSTAL CABINET

The Maiden caught me in the Wild,
Where I was dancing merrily;
She put me into her Cabinet
And Lock'd me up with a golden Key.

This Cabinet is form'd of Gold   5
And Pearl & Crystal shining bright,
And within it opens into a World
And a little lovely Moony Night.

Another England there I saw,
Another London with its Tower,   10
Another Thames & other Hills,
And another pleasant Surrey Bower,

Another Maiden like herself,
Translucent, lovely, shining clear,
Threefold each in the other clos'd—   15
O, what a pleasant trembling fear!

O, what a smile! a threefold Smile
Fill'd me, that like a flame I burn'd;
I bent to Kiss the lovely Maid,
And found a Threefold Kiss return'd.   20

I strove to seize the inmost Form
With ardor fierce & hands of flame,
But burst the Crystal Cabinet,
And like a Weeping Babe became—

A weeping Babe upon the wild,   25
And Weeping Woman pale reclin'd,
And in the outward air again
I fill'd with woes the passing Wind.

AUGURIES[1] OF INNOCENCE

To see a World in a Grain of Sand
And a Heaven in a Wild Flower,
Hold Infinity in the palm of your hand
And Eternity in an hour.

A Robin Red breast in a Cage   5
Puts all Heaven in a Rage.
A dove house fill'd with doves & Pigeons
Shudders Hell thro' all its regions.
A dog starv'd at his Master's Gate
Predicts the ruin of the State.   10
A Horse misus'd upon the Road
Calls to Heaven for Human blood.
Each outcry of the hunted Hare
A fibre from the Brain does tear.
A Skylark wounded in the wing,   15
A Cherubim does cease to sing.
The Game Cock clip'd & arm'd for fight
Does the Rising Sun affright.
Every Wolf's & Lion's howl
Raises from Hell a Human Soul.   20
The wild deer, wand'ring here & there,
Keeps the Human Soul from Care.
The Lamb misus'd breeds Public strife
And yet forgives the Butcher's Knife.
The Bat that flits at close of Eve   25

[1] *auguries* prophecies, divinations, signs

Has left the Brain that won't Believe.
The Owl that calls upon the Night
Speaks the Unbeliever's fright.
He who shall hurt the little Wren
Shall never be belov'd by Men.   30
He who the Ox to wrath has mov'd
Shall never be by Woman lov'd.
The wanton Boy that kills the Fly
Shall feel the Spider's enmity.
He who torments the Chafer's sprite   35
Weaves a Bower in endless Night.
The Catterpiller on the Leaf
Repeats to thee thy Mother's grief.
Kill not the Moth nor Butterfly,
For the Last Judgment draweth nigh.   40
He who shall train the Horse to War
Shall never pass the Polar Bar.
The Beggar's Dog & Widow's Cat,
Feed them & thou wilt grow fat.
The Gnat that sings his Summer's song   45
Poison gets from Slander's tongue.
The poison of the Snake & Newt
Is the sweat of Envy's Foot.
The Poison of the Honey Bee
Is the Artist's Jealousy.   50
The Prince's Robes & Beggar's Rags
Are Toadstools on the Miser's Bags.
A truth that's told with bad intent
Beats all the Lies you can invent.
It is right it should be so;   55
Man was made for Joy & Woe;
And when this we rightly know
Thro' the World we safely go,
Joy & Woe are woven fine,
A Clothing for the Soul divine;   60
Under every grief & pine
Runs a joy with silken twine.
The Babe is more than swadling Bands;
Throughout all these Human Lands
Tools were made, & Born were hands,   65
Every Farmer Understands.
Every Tear from Every Eye
Becomes a Babe in Eternity;
This is caught by Females bright

And return'd to its own delight. 70
The Bleat, the Bark, Bellow & Roar
Are Waves that Beat on Heaven's Shore.
The Babe that weeps the Rod beneath
Writes Revenge in realms of death.
The Beggar's Rags, fluttering in Air, 75
Does to Rags the Heavens tear.
The Soldier, arm'd with Sword & Gun,
Palsied strikes the Summer's Sun.
The poor Man's Farthing is worth more
Than all the Gold on Afric's Shore. 80
One Mite wrung from the Labrer's hands
Shall buy & sell the Miser's Lands:
Or, if protected from on high,
Does that whole Nation sell & buy.
He who mocks the Infant's Faith 85
Shall be mock'd in Age & Death.
He who shall teach the Child to Doubt
The rotting Grave shall ne'er get out.
He who respects the Infant's faith
Triumphs over Hell & Death. 90
The Child's Toys & the Old Man's Reasons
Are the Fruits of the Two seasons.
The Questioner, who sits so sly,
Shall never know how to Reply.
He who replies to words of Doubt 95
Doth put the Light of Knowledge out.
The Strongest Poison ever known
Came from Caesar's Laurel Crown.
Nought can deform the Human Race
Like to the Armour's iron brace. 100
When Gold & Gems adorn the Plow
To peaceful Arts shall Envy Bow.
A Riddle or the Cricket's Cry
Is to Doubt a fit Reply.
The Emmet's Inch & Eagle's Mile 105
Make Lame Philosophy to smile.
He who Doubts from what he sees
Will ne'er Believe, do what you Please.
If the Sun & Moon should doubt,
They'd immediately Go out. 110
To be in a Passion you Good may do,
But no Good if a Passion is in you.
The Whore & Gambler, by the State

Licenc'd, build that Nation's Fate.
The Harlot's cry from Street to Street   115
Shall weave Old England's winding Sheet.
The Winner's Shout, the Loser's Curse,
Dance before dead England's Hearse.
Every Night & every Morn
Some to Misery are Born.   120
Every Morn & every Night
Some are Born to sweet delight.
Some are Born to sweet delight,
Some are Born to Endless Night.
We are led to Believe a Lie   125
When we see not Thro' the Eye
Which was Born in a Night to perish in a Night
When the Soul Slept in Beams of Light.
God Appears & God is Light
To those poor Souls who dwell in Night,   130
But does a Human Form Display
To those who Dwell in Realms of day.

THEL'S MOTTO

Does the Eagle know what is in the pit?
Or wilt thou go ask the Mole?
Can Wisdom be put in a silver rod?
Or Love in a golden bowl?

CRITICISM

Three selections on Blake poems illustrate in different ways the critical focus on symbolism (see the discussion in Chapter 1, pp. 9–10). All three writers attempt to show what Blake's images and figures stand for and what they represent, and so come to an understanding of the poems and a statement of their themes. One might ask if this approach is more likely to suit Blake's poems than those of Pope or Dryden; or if a study of Blake's kind of "simplicity" would give the same conclusions as those in Strachey's study of Pope's couplets (pp. 318–323).

Note some particular characteristics in the following essays: C. M. Bowra emphasizes the self-containment and individuality of "The Sick Rose" and "Ah! Sun-Flower" as poems separate from the author. In his interpretation of "The Tyger," Roy P.

Basler uses the approach of psychological criticism (see the discussion in Chapter 4, pp. 164–165), suggesting a symbolism of the "self" that does not, of course, cancel other interpretations. (Additional explications of "The Tyger" may be checked by consulting the bibliographical lists in the Preface.) In the third critical comment, Northrop Frye turns to archetypal patterns as the groundwork for his interpretation of "The Mental Traveller." The selections used here for illustration do not consider Blake's life or his other work; and though they focus on the individual poems, they are not concerned with the structure or the specific language or the pattern of imagery. Each critic makes only a general summary of the central symbolism of the poem as he sees it.

Blake's "The Sick Rose" and "Ah! Sun-Flower" [1]

C. M. BOWRA

Two examples must suffice to illustrate Blake's art of song, and each is equally wonderful. The first is "The Sick Rose." This poem illustrates in an astonishing way Blake's gift for distilling a complex imaginative idea into a few marvellously telling words. If we ask what the poem means, we can answer that it means what it says, and that this is perfectly clear. It conjures up the vision of a rose attacked in a stormy night by a destructive worm, and so Blake depicts it in his accompanying illustration. But, as in all symbolical poems, we can read other meanings into it and make its images carry a weight of secondary associations. We may say that it refers to the destruction of love by selfishness, of innocence by experience, of spiritual life by spiritual death. All these meanings it can bear, and it is legitimate to make it do so. But the actual poem presents something which is common and fundamental to all these themes, something which Blake has distilled so finely from many particular cases that it has their common, quintessential character. And this Blake sees with so piercing and so concentrated a vision that the poem has its own independent life and needs nothing to supplement it. If we wish to know more about Blake's views on the issues at which the

[1] Extracted from C. M. Bowra, *The Romantic Imagination* (Harvard University Press, 1949).

poem hints, we may find them in his prose works and prophetic books. But here he is a poet, and his thoughts are purified and transfigured in song.

My second example is "Ah! Sun-flower!" This poem raises questions similar to those raised by "The Sick Rose." Again a complex thought is distilled into two verses, and again what matters is the imaginative presentation which transports us in intense, excited delight. Here Blake's theme is not quite so single as in "The Sick Rose." He has transposed into this song his central ideas and feelings about all young men and young women who are robbed of their full humanity because they are starved of love. Because of this, the youth pines away with desire and the pale virgin is shrouded in snow. It is the pathos of their earthbound state that the song catches and makes significant through Blake's deep compassion. The central spring of the poem is the image of the sun-flower. The flower which turns its head to follow the sun's course and is yet rooted in the earth is Blake's symbol for all men and women whose lives are dominated and spoiled by a longing which they can never hope to satisfy, and who are held down to the earth despite their desire for release into some brighter, freer sphere. In this poem Blake expresses an idea which means a great deal to him, but he does not explain or elaborate it. He assumes that his poem will do its work by itself, and his reward is that "Ah! Sun-flower" belongs to that very rare and small class of poems in which inspiration carries words to a final enchantment.

Blake's "The Tyger" [1]

ROY P. BASLER

Consider the image presented in the first stanza [of "The Tyger"], and the question asked. What is the simplest communication made by the image? Terror in the beholder, power to harm in the image. Beyond this there is communication of something not wholly of this world. Tigers do not burn, though the color of the tiger may suggest fire; jungle forests may be so dark as to suggest night, but could not be with strict rational logic called

[1] A portion of the chapter "Psychological Interpretation of Literature," in Roy P. Basler, *Sex, Symbolism, and Psychology in Literature* (Rutgers University Press, 1948).

"forests of the night." What we have in the image is of the mind surely, but not of the rational conscious mind wholly. It is something of a dream image, conveying terror before a symbol of power to harm, and, like all dream images, made of the stuff known to the conscious mind but given in a fusion of non-sequiturs (fire-tiger-forest-night) which have nevertheless linking associations and analogies: tigers roam the forests, and darkness and fire (light) are archetypal opposites in any language or experience. The communication of fear before power to harm lies in what the poet and reader see as a mental image.

Continuing with the question asked in the first stanza, we find a query which supposes that the image has been created, "framed" by a hand, instructed by an eye, even as a painter paints a picture, and that the creator is perhaps immortal (not of this world) and the image awe-inspiring in symmetry (perfection). But the query is not a statement, please note. As a question it asks rather than answers "Whence came this image?" We shall keep this in mind to apply to the other questions asked in following stanzas, for the poet is not necessarily positing anything beyond the images.

The questions which continue in the rest of the poem reiterate and elaborate the question of the first stanza, the elaboration suggesting the possibility of an other-worldly or non-natural creator. Not until the next-to-last stanza, however, is there any specific, undebatable reference to deity. There, in an allusion to the unsuccessful revolt of the angels which provides *Paradise Lost* with its antecedent action, the question is put: Did God smile at the victorious conclusion of the war in heaven and then create something more terrible than Satan's pride? The allusion to the lamb provides an obvious contrast with the tiger, but also introduces a possible clue to allegory, since the lamb is the traditional symbol of peace and Christlike spirit. Biblical reference to the lion and the lamb as symbols of extremes in nature comes to mind at once, and the reader may leap to an interpretation of the tiger as the Antichrist, except that such an interpretation would be anticlimactic when the poet employs "dare" to replace "could" in repeating the first stanza as the poem's conclusion. There would be little daring involved for a supreme God who has smiled at the victorious conclusion of one struggle if he created nothing more terrible than the satanic power he had already vanquished. Surely the tiger does not represent Satan, but something more terrible, whether or not created by God. But perhaps the question is not meant by the poet to imply an affirmative answer, and we may do well to reconsider.

Upon reflection, the tiger may not represent the supernatural at all, but something within the soul of man. Blake's poetry testifies abundantly to the fact that he was most appalled by the infinite extremes of the human psyche, love-hate, trust-fear. Psychologically this symbolism has little that can be objected to. It provides a satisfactory symbolic climax in the poem's conclusion to match the dramatic climax of the rhetorical questions reached in the reference to deity in the next-to-last stanza, and, what is more significant, provides a powerful meaning which turns on the new word "dare" which replaces the "could" used in the first stanza. The question at last is: Would an immortal deity dare create on earth something more fearful than the power he had thrown out of heaven? The question is left to the reader for answer.

This seems to me the most satisfactory reading of the poem. The traditional interpretation that the tiger symbolizes the "Wrath of God" does not make sense to me now and did not when I first read the poem years ago, although I had then no alternative. It fails to make sense, not because the tiger is inapropos as a symbol of divine wrath, but because the dramatic framework includes deity as a possible creator of the tiger, not as the tiger itself. The poet's inclusive question is: What creator can be conceived capable of perpetrating man's scope for fear and hate?

The psychological implications of the poem are satisfying whether one answers the poet's question with God as creator, or with life-force as creator. From a Freudian point of view, the psyche encompasses the extremes symbolized in tiger and lamb no less than does the mythology which Blake created in his poetry. The orthodox Christian mythology does not encompass both extremes in deity, but does in man. The relegation of Satan to a secondary power, permitted to pursue evil by an absolute God who is thus responsible for the continuation of what He could at any moment terminate, is an anomaly which theology has rationalized but has never made wholly acceptable to human intelligence.

Hence Blake's question in this poem, like his questions in other poems, was meant in the eighteenth century to challenge orthodox theology and at the same time the too simply rational deism which was in intellectual favor at the time. Both deism and orthodox Christianity failed Blake, apparently, because they divorced the dual aspects of the soul on a supernatural plane, and deism failed even further by its impossible attempt to dismiss the darker aspect from this world by insisting that since a reasonable deity created it, "Whatever is, is right." Blake understood in his fashion, no less than Freud, the duality ruling the realm of the psyche.

Blake's "The Mental Traveller" [1]

NORTHROP FRYE

In Blake's poem *The Mental Traveller* we have a vision of the cycle of human life, from birth to death to rebirth. The two characters of the poem are a male and a female figure, moving in opposite directions, one growing old as the other grows young, and vice versa. The cyclical relation between them runs through four cardinal points: a son-mother phase, a husband-wife phase, a father-daughter phase, and a fourth phase of what Blake calls spectre and emanation, terms corresponding roughly to Shelley's alastor and epipsyche. None of these phases is quite true: the mother is only a nurse, the wife merely "bound down" for the male's delight, the daughter a changeling, and the emanation does not "emanate," but remains elusive. The male figure represents humanity, and therefore includes women—the "female will" in Blake becomes associated with women only when women dramatize or mimic the above relation in human life, as they do in the Courtly Love convention. The female figure represents the natural environment which man partially but never wholly subdues. The controlling symbolism of the poem, as the four phases suggest, is lunar.

To the extent that the encyclopaedic form concerns itself with the cycle of human life, an ambivalent female archetype appears in it, sometimes benevolent, sometimes sinister, but usually pre-

[1] Extracted from Northrop Frye, *Anatomy of Criticism* (Princeton University Press, 1957).

siding over and confirming the cyclical movement. One pole of her is represented by an Isis figure, a Penelope or Solveig who is the fixed point on which the action ends. The goddess who frequently begins and ends the cyclical action is closely related. This figure is Athene in the *Odyssey* and Venus in the *Aeneid;* in Elizabethan literature, for political reasons, usually some variant of Diana, like the Faerie Queen in Spenser. The *alma Venus* who suffuses Lucretius' great vision of life balanced in the order of nature is another version. Beatrice in Dante presides over not a cycle but a sacramental spiral leading up to deity, as does, in a far less concrete way, the *Ewig-Weibliche* of *Faust.* At the opposite pole is a figure—Calypso or Circe in Homer, Dido in Virgil, Cleopatra in Shakespeare, Duessa in Spenser, sometimes a "terrible mother" but often sympathetically treated—who represents the opposite direction from the heroic quest. Eve in Milton, who spirals man downward into the Fall, is the contrasting figure to Beatrice.

In the ironic age there are naturally a good many visions of a cycle of experience, often presided over by a female figure with lunar and femme fatale affiliations. Yeats's *Vision,* which Yeats was quite right in associating with *The Mental Traveller,* is based on this symbolism, and more recently Mr. Robert Graves' *The White Goddess* has expounded it with even greater learning and ingenuity. In Eliot's *Waste Land* the figure in the background is less "the lady of situations" than the androgynous Teiresias, and although there is a fire sermon and a thunder sermon, both with apocalyptic overtones, the natural cycle of water, the Thames flowing into the sea and returning through death by water in the spring rains, is the containing form of the poem. In Joyce's *Ulysses* a female figure at once maternal, marital, and meretricious, a Penelope who embraces all her suitors, merges in her sleep with the drowsy spinning earth, constantly affirming but never forming, and taking the whole book with her.

WILLIAM WORDSWORTH

[1770-1850]

WORDSWORTH was born at Cockermouth, in the Lake Country of England, his father an attorney and his family of the
landed gentry. He received his early education at the little town
of Hawkshead. In his Cambridge years and in travel on the Continent until 1793, Wordsworth was actively in sympathy with the
revolutionary movements in France. After his return to England,
he settled into a life of writing and travel, and, eventually, into
quieter conservatism. In 1798, he and his friend Coleridge (who
contributed four poems) anonymously published *Lyrical Ballads,*
a book that was to be a literary landmark. It was a primary influence in establishing a new style of writing and what was later
called the "Romantic Movement." The poems of *Lyrical Ballads* set the pattern for Wordsworth's later work—the simple,
direct, emotional treatment of nature and common life. In 1800
an enlarged edition of *Lyrical Ballads* was published, with Wordsworth's "Preface" stating his poetic creed and with his name on
the title page. After 1799, he lived in the Lake Country with his
sister Dorothy and his family (in 1802 he was married to Mary
Hutchinson, and they had four children). Wordsworth published continuously, his reputation grew, and in 1843 he became
Poet Laureate, succeeding Robert Southey. He worked on his
poetic autobiography, *The Prelude,* for many years before its
publication at the end of his career. He is buried at Grasmere;
his monument is in Westminster Abbey. All his life Wordsworth
used the subjects of landscape and sky, of simple people, and the
mysterious forces of life. Perhaps more than any other poet he
saw into, and with, the eye of nature.

Introductory Readings

EDITION: *The Poetical Works of William Wordsworth,* ed. Ernest de Selincourt and Helen Darbishire, 5 vols. (1940–1949). BIOGRAPHY: George McLean Harper, *William Wordsworth: His Life, Works, and Influence,* 2 vols. (rev. ed., 1929); *see also,* Wordsworth's autobiography, *The Prelude* (1850). CRITICISM: C. L. Patton, *The Rediscovery of Wordsworth* (1935); *Wordsworth and Coleridge: Studies in Honor of George McLean Harper,* ed. E. L. Griggs (1939); Newton P. Stallknecht, *Strange Seas of Thought* (1945); Helen Darbishire, *The Poet Wordsworth* (1950); *Wordsworth: Centenary Studies,* ed. Gilbert T. Dunklin (1951); Lascelles Abercrombie, *The Art of Wordsworth* (1952); F. W. Bateson, *Wordsworth: A Re-Interpretation* (1954).

THE TABLES TURNED

Up! up! my Friend, and quit your books;
Or surely you' ll grow double:
Up! up! my Friend, and clear your looks;
Why all this toil and trouble?

The sun, above the mountain's head,   5
A freshening lustre mellow
Through all the long green fields has spread,
His first sweet evening yellow.

Books! 't is a dull and endless strife:
Come, hear the woodland linnet,   10
How sweet his music! on my life,
There's more of wisdom in it.

And hark! how blithe the throstle [1] sings!
He, too, is no mean preacher:
Come forth into the light of things,   15
Let Nature be your teacher.

She has a world of ready wealth,
Our minds and hearts to bless—
Spontaneous wisdom breathed by health,
Truth breathed by cheerfulness.   20

One impulse from a vernal wood
May teach you more of man,
Of moral evil and of good,
Than all the sages can.

[1] *throstle* Scottish for thrush

Sweet is the lore which Nature brings;   25
Our meddling intellect
Mis-shapes the beauteous forms of things:—
We murder to dissect.

Enough of Science and of Art;
Close up those barren leaves;   30
Come forth, and bring with you a heart
That watches and receives.

LINES [1]

COMPOSED A FEW MILES ABOVE TINTERN ABBEY,[2] ON REVISITING THE BANKS OF THE WYE DURING A TOUR.
JULY 13, 1798

Five years have past; five summers, with the length
Of five long winters! and again I hear
These waters, rolling from their mountain-springs
With a soft inland murmur.—Once again
Do I behold these steep and lofty cliffs,   5
That on a wild secluded scene impress
Thoughts of more deep seclusion; and connect
The landscape with the quiet of the sky.
The day is come when I again repose
Here, under this dark sycamore, and view   10
These plots of cottage-ground, these orchard-tufts,
Which at this season, with their unripe fruits,
Are clad in one green hue, and lose themselves
'Mid groves and copses.[3] Once again I see
These hedge-rows, hardly hedge-rows, little lines   15
Of sportive wood run wild: these pastoral farms,
Green to the very door; and wreaths of smoke
Sent up, in silence, from among the trees!
With some uncertain notice, as might seem
Of vagrant dwellers in the houseless woods,   20

[1] Critical comment on this poem appears on p. 387.
[2] *Tintern Abbey* a ruined monastery situated in the valley of the Wye River in Monmouthshire, on the border of Wales. Wordsworth had taken a walking tour of the Wye country in 1793. He returned there with his sister Dorothy in 1798. "I have not ventured to call this Poem an Ode; but it was written with a hope that in the transitions and the impassioned music of the versification, would be found the principal requisites, of that species of composition."—Wordsworth, 1800.
[3] *copses* thickets

Or of some Hermit's cave, where by his fire
The Hermit sits alone.
                              These beauteous forms,
Through a long absence, have not been to me
As is a landscape to a blind man's eye:
But oft, in lonely rooms, and 'mid the din   25
Of towns and cities, I have owed to them
In hours of weariness, sensations sweet,
Felt in the blood, and felt along the heart;
And passing even into my purer mind,
With tranquil restoration:—feelings too   30
Of unremembered pleasure: such, perhaps,
As have no slight or trivial influence
On that best portion of a good man's life,
His little, nameless, unremembered, acts
Of kindness and of love. Nor less, I trust,   35
To them I may have owed another gift,
Of aspect more sublime; that blessed mood
In which the burthen of the mystery,
In which the heavy and the weary weight
Of all this unintelligible world,   40
Is lightened:—that serene and blessed mood,
In which the affections gently lead us on,—
Until, the breath of this corporeal frame
And even the motion of our human blood
Almost suspended, we are laid asleep   45
In body, and become a living soul:
While with an eye made quiet by the power
Of harmony, and the deep power of joy,
We see into the life of things.
                                    If this
Be but a vain belief, yet, oh! how oft—   50
In darkness and amid the many shapes
Of joyless daylight; when the fretful stir
Unprofitable, and the fever of the world,
Have hung upon the beatings of my heart—
How oft, in spirit, have I turned to thee,   55
O sylvan Wye! thou wanderer thro' the woods,
How often has my spirit turned to thee!

    And now, with gleams of half-extinguished thought,
With many recognitions dim and faint,
And somewhat of a sad perplexity,   60
The picture of the mind revives again:

While here I stand, not only with the sense
Of present pleasure, but with pleasing thoughts
That in this moment there is life and food
For future years. And so I dare to hope,   65
Though changed, no doubt, from what I was when first
I came among these hills; when like a roe
I bounded o'er the mountains, by the sides
Of the deep rivers, and the lonely streams,
Wherever nature led: more like a man   70
Flying from something that he dreads than one
Who sought the thing he loved. For nature then
(The coarser pleasures of my boyish days,
And their glad animal movements all gone by)
To me was all in all.—I cannot paint   75
What then I was. The sounding cataract
Haunted me like a passion: the tall rock,
The mountain, and the deep and gloomy wood,
Their colours and their forms, were then to me
An appetite; a feeling and a love,   80
That had no need of a remoter charm,
By thought supplied, nor any interest
Unborrowed from the eye.—That time is past,
And all its aching joys are now no more,
And all its dizzy raptures. Not for this   85
Faint I, nor mourn nor murmur; other gifts
Have followed; for such loss, I would believe,
Abundant recompense. For I have learned
To look on nature, not as in the hour
Of thoughtless youth; but hearing oftentimes   90
The still, sad music of humanity,
Nor harsh nor grating, though of ample power
To chasten and subdue. And I have felt
A presence that disturbs me with the joy
Of elevated thoughts; a sense sublime   95
Of something far more deeply interfused,
Whose dwelling is the light of setting suns,
And the round ocean and the living air,
And the blue sky, and in the mind of man:
A motion and a spirit, that impels   100
All thinking things, all objects of all thought,
And rolls through all things. Therefore am I still
A lover of the meadows and the woods,
And mountains; and of all that we behold
From this green earth; of all the mighty world   105

Of eye, and ear,—both what they half create,
And what perceive; well pleased to recognise
In nature and the language of the sense
The anchor of my purest thoughts, the nurse,
The guide, the guardian of my heart, and soul   110
Of all my moral being.
                            Nor perchance,
If I were not thus taught, should I the more
Suffer my genial spirits to decay:
For thou art with me here upon the banks
Of this fair river; thou my dearest Friend,[4]   115
My dear, dear Friend; and in thy voice I catch
The language of my former heart, and read
My former pleasures in the shooting lights
Of thy wild eyes. Oh! yet a little while
May I behold in thee what I was once,   120
My dear, dear Sister! and this prayer I make,
Knowing that nature never did betray
The heart that loved her; 'tis her privilege,
Through all the years of this our life, to lead
From joy to joy: for she can so inform   125
The mind that is within us, so impress
With quietness and beauty, and so feed
With lofty thoughts, that neither evil tongues,
Rash judgments, nor the sneers of selfish men,
Nor greetings where no kindness is, nor all   130
The dreary intercourse of daily life,
Shall e'er prevail against us, or disturb
Our cheerful faith, that all which we behold
Is full of blessings. Therefore let the moon
Shine on thee in thy solitary walk;   135
And let the misty mountain-winds be free
To blow against thee: and, in after years,
When these wild ecstasies shall be matured
Into a sober pleasure; when thy mind
Shall be a mansion for all lovely forms,   140
Thy memory be as a dwelling-place
For all sweet sounds and harmonies; oh! then,
If solitude, or fear, or pain, or grief,
Should be thy portion, with what healing thoughts
Of tender joy wilt thou remember me,   145
And these my exhortations! Nor, perchance—
If I should be where I no more can hear

[4] *Friend* Dorothy Wordsworth

Thy voice, nor catch from thy wild eyes these gleams
Of past existence—wilt thou then forget
That on the banks of this delightful stream   150
We stood together; and that I, so long
A worshipper of Nature, hither came
Unwearied in that service; rather say
With warmer love—oh! with far deeper zeal
Of holier love. Nor wilt thou then forget,   155
That after many wanderings, many years
Of absence, these steep woods and lofty cliffs,
And this green pastoral landscape, were to me
More dear, both for themselves and for thy sake!

SHE DWELT AMONG THE UNTRODDEN WAYS

She dwelt among the untrodden ways
   Beside the springs of Dove,[1]
A Maid whom there were none to praise
   And very few to love:

A violet by a mossy stone   5
   Half hidden from the eye!
—Fair as a star, when only one
   Is shining in the sky.

She lived unknown, and few could know
   When Lucy ceased to be;   10
But she is in her grave, and, oh,
   The difference to me!

A SLUMBER DID MY SPIRIT SEAL

A slumber did my spirit seal;
   I had no human fears:
She seemed a thing that could not feel
   The touch of earthly years.

No motion has she now, no force;   5
   She neither hears nor sees;
Rolled round in earth's diurnal [1] course,
   With rocks, and stones, and trees.

[1] *Dove* a stream in central England   [1] *diurnal* daily

MICHAEL

A PASTORAL POEM

If from the public way you turn your steps
Up the tumultuous brook of Green-head Ghyll,[1]
You will suppose that with an upright path
Your feet must struggle; in such bold ascent
The pastoral mountains front you, face to face.   5
But, courage! for around that boisterous brook
The mountains have all opened out themselves,
And made a hidden valley of their own.
No habitation can be seen; but they
Who journey thither find themselves alone   10
With a few sheep, with rocks and stones, and kites
That overhead are sailing in the sky.
It is in truth an utter solitude;
Nor should I have made mention of this Dell
But for one object which you might pass by,   15
Might see and notice not. Beside the brook
Appears a straggling heap of unhewn stones!
And to that simple object appertains
A story—unenriched with strange events,
Yet not unfit, I deem, for the fireside,   20
Or for the summer shade. It was the first
Of those domestic tales that spake to me
Of shepherds, dwellers in the valleys, men
Whom I already loved;—not verily
For their own sakes, but for the fields and hills   25
Where was their occupation and abode.
And hence this Tale, while I was yet a Boy
Careless of books, yet having felt the power
Of Nature, by the gentle agency
Of natural objects, led me on to feel   30
For passions that were not my own, and think
(At random and imperfectly indeed)
On man, the heart of man, and human life.
Therefore, although it be a history
Homely and rude, I will relate the same   35
For the delight of a few natural hearts;

[1] *Green-head Ghyll* a ravine or narrow valley near Grasmere in the Lake Country where Wordsworth lived

And, with yet fonder feeling, for the sake
Of youthful Poets, who among these hills
Will be my second self when I am gone.

Upon the forest-side in Grasmere Vale   40
There dwelt a Shepherd, Michael was his name;
An old man, stout of heart, and strong of limb.
His bodily frame had been from youth to age
Of an unusual strength: his mind was keen,
Intense, and frugal, apt for all affairs,   45
And in his shepherd's calling he was prompt
And watchful more than ordinary men.
Hence had he learned the meaning of all winds,
Of blasts of every tone; and oftentimes,
When others heeded not, He heard the South   50
Make subterraneous music, like the noise
Of bagpipers on distant Highland hills.
The Shepherd, at such warning, of his flock
Bethought him, and he to himself would say,
"The winds are now devising work for me!"   55
And, truly, at all times, the storm, that drives
The traveller to a shelter, summoned him
Up to the mountains: he had been alone
Amid the heart of many thousand mists,
That came to him, and left him, on the heights. 60
So lived he till his eightieth year was past.
And grossly that man errs, who should suppose
That the green valleys, and the streams and rocks,
Were things indifferent to the Shepherd's thoughts.
Fields, where with cheerful spirits he had breathed   65
The common air; hills, which with vigorous step
He had so often climbed; which had impressed
So many incidents upon his mind
Of hardship, skill or courage, joy or fear;
Which, like a book, preserved the memory   70
Of the dumb animals, whom he had saved,
Had fed or sheltered, linking to such acts
The certainty of honourable gain;
Those fields, those hills—what could they less? had laid
Strong hold on his affections, were to him   75
A pleasurable feeling of blind love,
The pleasure which there is in life itself.

His days had not been passed in singleness.
His Helpmate was a comely matron, old—

Though younger than himself full twenty years.   80
She was a woman of a stirring life,
Whose heart was in her house: two wheels she had
Of antique form; this large, for spinning wool;
That small, for flax; and if one wheel had rest
It was because the other was at work.   85
The Pair had but one inmate in their house,
An only Child, who had been born to them
When Michael, telling o'er his years, began
To deem that he was old,—in shepherd's phrase,
With one foot in the grave. This only Son,   90
With two brave sheep-dogs tried in many a storm,
The one of an inestimable worth,
Made all their household. I may truly say,
That they were as a proverb in the vale
For endless industry. When day was gone,   95
And from their occupations out of doors
The Son and Father were come home, even then,
Their labour did not cease; unless when all
Turned to the cleanly supper-board, and there,
Each with a mess of pottage and skimmed milk,   100
Sat round the basket piled with oaten cakes,
And their plain home-made cheese. Yet when the meal
Was ended, Luke (for so the Son was named)
And his old Father both betook themselves
To such convenient work as might employ   105
Their hands by the fire-side; perhaps to card
Wool for the Housewife's spindle, or repair
Some injury done to sickle, flail, or scythe,
Or other implement of house or field.

    Down from the ceiling, by the chimney's edge,   110
That in our ancient uncouth country style
With huge and black projection overbrowed
Large space beneath, as duly as the light
Of day grew dim the Housewife hung a lamp;
An aged utensil, which had performed   115
Service beyond all others of its kind.
Early at evening did it burn—and late,
Surviving comrade of uncounted hours,
Which, going by from year to year, had found,
And left, the couple neither gay perhaps   120
Nor cheerful, yet with objects and with hopes,
Living a life of eager industry.

And now, when Luke had reached his eighteenth year,
There by the light of this old lamp they sate,
Father and Son, while far into the night   125
The Housewife plied her own peculiar work,
Making the cottage through the silent hours
Murmur as with the sound of summer flies.
This light was famous in its neighbourhood,
And was a public symbol of the life   130
That thrifty Pair had lived. For, as it chanced,
Their cottage on a plot of rising ground
Stood single, with large prospect, north and south,
High into Easedale, up to Dunmail-Raise,[2]
And westward to the village near the lake;   135
And from this constant light, so regular,
And so far seen, the House itself, by all
Who dwelt within the limits of the vale,
Both old and young, was named THE EVENING STAR.

        Thus living on through such a length of years,   140
The Shepherd, if he loved himself, must needs
Have loved his Helpmate; but to Michael's heart
This son of his old age was yet more dear—
Less from instinctive tenderness, the same
Fond spirit that blindly works in the blood of all—   145
Than that a child, more than all other gifts
That earth can offer to declining man,
Brings hope with it, and forward-looking thoughts,
And stirrings of inquietude, when they
By tendency of nature needs must fail.   150
Exceeding was the love he bare to him,
His heart and his heart's joy! For often-times
Old Michael, while he was a babe in arms,
Had done him female service, not alone
For pastime and delight, as is the use   155
Of fathers, but with patient mind enforced
To acts of tenderness; and he had rocked
His cradle, as with a woman's gentle hand.

        And, in a later time, ere yet the Boy
Had put on boy's attire, did Michael love,   160
Albeit of a stern unbending mind,

---

[2] *Easedale, Dunmail-Raise* mountain places in the Lake Country near Grasmere

To have the Young-one in his sight, when he
Wrought in the field, or on his shepherd's stool
Sate with a fettered sheep before him stretched
Under the large old oak, that near his door   165
Stood single, and, from matchless depth of shade,
Chosen for the Shearer's covert from the sun,
Thence in our rustic dialect was called
The CLIPPING TREE, a name which yet it bears.
There, while they two were sitting in the shade,   170
With others round them, earnest all and blithe,
Would Michael exercise his heart with looks
Of fond correction and reproof bestowed
Upon the Child, if he disturbed the sheep
By catching at their legs, or with his shouts   175
Scared them, while they lay still beneath the shears.

And when by Heaven's good grace the boy grew up
A healthy Lad, and carried in his cheek
Two steady roses that were five years old;
Then Michael from a winter coppice cut   180
With his own hand a sapling, which he hooped
With iron, making it throughout in all
Due requisites a perfect shepherd's staff,
And gave it to the Boy; wherewith equipt
He as a watchman oftentimes was placed   185
At gate or gap, to stem or turn the flock;
And, to his office prematurely called,
There stood the urchin, as you will divine,
Something between a hindrance and a help;
And for this cause not always, I believe,   190
Receiving from his Father hire of praise;
Though nought was left undone which staff, or voice,
Or looks, or threatening gestures, could perform.

But soon as Luke, full ten years old, could stand
Against the mountain blasts; and to the heights,   195
Not fearing toil, nor length of weary ways,
He with his Father daily went, and they
Were as companions, why should I relate
That objects which the Shepherd loved before
Were dearer now? that from the Boy there came   200
Feelings and emanations—things which were
Light to the sun and music to the wind;
And that the old Man's heart seemed born again?

Thus in his Father's sight the Boy grew up:
And now, when he had reached his eighteenth year,   205
He was his comfort and his daily hope.

While in this sort the simple household lived
From day to day, to Michael's ear there came
Distressful tidings. Long before the time
Of which I speak, the Shepherd had been bound   210
In surety for his brother's son, a man
Of an industrious life, and ample means;
But unforeseen misfortunes suddenly
Had prest upon him; and old Michael now
Was summoned to discharge the forfeiture,   215
A grievous penalty, but little less
Than half his substance. This unlooked-for claim,
At the first hearing, for a moment took
More hope out of his life than he supposed
That any old man ever could have lost.   220
As soon as he had armed himself with strength
To look his trouble in the face, it seemed
The Shepherd's sole resource to sell at once
A portion of his patrimonial fields.
Such was his first resolve; he thought again,   225
And his heart failed him. "Isabel," said he,
Two evenings after he had heard the news,
"I have been toiling more than seventy years,
And in the open sunshine of God's love
Have we all lived; yet if these fields of ours   230
Should pass into a stranger's hand, I think
That I could not lie quiet in my grave.
Our lot is a hard lot; the sun himself
Has scarcely been more diligent than I;
And I have lived to be a fool at last   235
To my own family. An evil man
That was, and made an evil choice, if he
Were false to us; and if he were not false,
There are ten thousand to whom loss like this
Had been no sorrow. I forgive him;—but   240
'Twere better to be dumb than to talk thus.

"When I began, my purpose was to speak
Of remedies and of a cheerful hope.
Our Luke shall leave us, Isabel; the land
Shall not go from us, and it shall be free;   245
He shall possess it, free as is the wind

That passes over it. We have, thou know'st,
Another kinsman—he will be our friend
In this distress. He is a prosperous man,
Thriving in trade—and Luke to him shall go,   250
And with his kinsman's help and his own thrift
He quickly will repair this loss, and then
He may return to us. If here he stay,
What can be done? Where every one is poor,
What can be gained?"

                              At this the old Man paused,   255
And Isabel sat silent, for her mind
Was busy, looking back into past times.
There 's Richard Bateman, thought she to herself,
He was a parish-boy—at the church-door
They made a gathering for him, shillings, pence,   260
And halfpennies, wherewith the neighbours bought
A basket, which they filled with pedlar's wares;
And, with this basket on his arm, the lad
Went up to London, found a master there,
Who, out of many, chose the trusty boy   265
To go and overlook his merchandise
Beyond the seas; where he grew wondrous rich,
And left estates and monies to the poor,
And, at his birth-place, built a chapel floored
With marble, which he sent from foreign lands.   270
These thoughts, and many others of like sort,
Passed quickly through the mind of Isabel,
And her face brightened. The old Man was glad,
And thus resumed:— "Well, Isabel! this scheme
These two days has been meat and drink to me.   275
Far more than we have lost is left us yet.
—We have enough—I wish indeed that I
Were younger;—but this hope is a good hope.
Make ready Luke's best garments, of the best
Buy for him more, and let us send him forth   280
To-morrow, or the next day, or to-night;
—If he *could* go, the Boy should go tonight."

    Here Michael ceased, and to the fields went forth
With a light heart. The Housewife for five days
Was restless morn and night, and all day long   285
Wrought on with her best fingers to prepare
Things needful for the journey of her son.
But Isabel was glad when Sunday came

To stop her in her work: for, when she lay
By Michael's side, she through the last two nights   290
Heard him, how he was troubled in his sleep:
And when they rose at morning she could see
That all his hopes were gone. That day at noon
She said to Luke, while they two by themselves
Were sitting at the door, "Thou must not go: 295
We have no other Child but thee to lose,
None to remember—do not go away,
For if thou leave thy Father he will die."
The Youth made answer with a jocund voice;
And Isabel, when she had told her fears,   300
Recovered heart. That evening her best fare
Did she bring forth, and all together sat
Like happy people round a Christmas fire.

With daylight Isabel resumed her work;
And all the ensuing week the house appeared   305
As cheerful as a grove in Spring: at length
The expected letter from their kinsman came,
With kind assurances that he would do
His utmost for the welfare of the Boy;
To which, requests were added, that forthwith   310
He might be sent to him. Ten times or more
The letter was read over; Isabel
Went forth to show it to the neighbours round;
Nor was there at that time on English land
A prouder heart than Luke's. When Isabel   315
Had to her house returned, the old Man said,
"He shall depart to-morrow." To this word
The Housewife answered, talking much of things
Which, if at such short notice he should go,
Would surely be forgotten. But at length   320
She gave consent, and Michael was at ease.

Near the tumultuous brook of Green-head Ghyll,
In that deep valley, Michael had designed
To build a Sheep-fold; [3] and, before he heard
The tidings of his melancholy loss,   325

[3] *Sheepfold* "It may be proper to inform some readers that a sheepfold in
these mountains is an unroofed building of stone walls, with different divisions. It is generally placed by the side of a brook, for the convenience of
washing the sheep; but it is also useful as a shelter for them, and as a place
to drive them into, to enable the shepherds conveniently to single out one or
more for any particular purpose."—Wordsworth

For this same purpose he had gathered up
A heap of stones, which by the streamlet's edge
Lay thrown together, ready for the work.
With Luke that evening thitherward he walked:
And soon as they had reached the place he stopped,   330
And thus the old Man spake to him:—"My Son,
To-morrow thou wilt leave me: with full heart
I look upon thee, for thou art the same
That wert a promise to me ere thy birth,
And all thy life hast been my daily joy.   335
I will relate to thee some little part
Of our two histories; 'twill do thee good
When thou art from me, even if I should touch
On things thou canst not know of.——After thou
First cam'st into the world—as oft befalls   340
To new-born infants—thou didst sleep away
Two days, and blessings from thy Father's tongue
Then fell upon thee. Day by day passed on,
And still I loved thee with increasing love.
Never to living ear came sweeter sounds   345
Than when I heard thee by our own fire-side
First uttering, without words, a natural tune;
While thou, a feeding babe, didst in thy joy
Sing at thy Mother's breast. Month followed month,
And in the open fields my life was passed   350
And on the mountains; else I think that thou
Hadst been brought up upon thy Father's knees.
But we were playmates, Luke: among these hills,
As well thou knowest, in us the old and young
Have played together, nor with me didst thou   355
Lack any pleasure which a boy can know."
Luke had a manly heart; but at these words
He sobbed aloud. The old Man grasped his hand,
And said, "Nay, do not take it so—I see
That these are things of which I need not speak.   360
—Even to the utmost I have been to thee
A kind and a good Father: and herein
I but repay a gift which I myself
Received at others' hands; for, though now old
Beyond the common life of man, I still   365
Remember them who loved me in my youth.
Both of them sleep together: here they lived,
As all their Forefathers had done; and when
At length their time was come, they were not loth

To give their bodies to the family mould.   370
I wished that thou should'st live the life they lived,
But 'tis a long time to look back, my Son,
And see so little gain from the threescore years.
These fields were burthened when they came to me;
Till I was forty years of age, not more   375
Than half of my inheritance was mine.
I toiled and toiled; God blessed me in my work,
And till these three weeks past the land was free.
—It looks as if it never could endure
Another Master. Heaven forgive me, Luke,   380
If I judge ill for thee, but it seems good
That thou should'st go."
                            At this the old Man paused;
Then, pointing to the stones near which they stood,
Thus, after a short silence, he resumed:
"This was a work for us; and now, my Son,   385
It is a work for me. But, lay one stone—
Here, lay it for me, Luke, with thine own hands.
Nay, Boy, be of good hope;—we both may live
To see a better day. At eighty-four
I still am strong and hale;—do thou thy part;   390
I will do mine.—I will begin again
With many tasks that were resigned to thee:
Up to the heights, and in among the storms,
Will I without thee go again, and do
All works which I was wont to do alone,   395
Before I knew thy face.—Heaven bless thee, Boy!
Thy heart these two weeks has been beating fast
With many hopes; it should be so—yes—yes—
I knew that thou could'st never have a wish
To leave me, Luke: thou hast been bound to me   400
Only by links of love: when thou art gone,
What will be left to us!—But I forget
My purposes. Lay now the corner-stone,
As I requested; and hereafter, Luke,
When thou art gone away, should evil men   405
Be thy companions, think of me, my Son,
And of this moment; hither turn thy thoughts,
And God will strengthen thee: amid all fear
And all temptation, Luke, I pray that thou
May'st bear in mind the life thy Fathers lived,   410
Who, being innocent, did for that cause
Bestir them in good deeds. Now, fare thee well—

When thou return'st, thou in this place wilt see
A work which is not here: a covenant
'Twill be between us; but, whatever fate 415
Befall thee, I shall love thee to the last,
And bear thy memory with me to the grave."

The Shepherd ended here; and Luke stooped down,
And, as his Father had requested, laid
The first stone of the Sheep-fold. At the sight 420
The old Man's grief broke from him; to his heart
He pressed his Son, he kissed him and wept;
And to the house together they returned.
—Hushed was that House in peace, or seeming peace,
Ere the night fell:—with morrow's dawn the Boy 425
Began his journey, and when he had reached
The public way, he put on a bold face;
And all the neighbours, as he passed their doors,
Came forth with wishes and with farewell prayers,
That followed him till he was out of sight. 430

A good report did from their Kinsman come,
Of Luke and his well-doing: and the Boy
Wrote loving letters, full of wondrous news,
Which, as the Housewife phrased it, were throughout
"The prettiest letters that were ever seen." 435
Both parents read them with rejoicing hearts.
So, many months passed on: and once again
The Shepherd went about his daily work
With confident and cheerful thoughts; and now
Sometimes when he could find a leisure hour 440
He to that valley took his way, and there
Wrought at the Sheep-fold. Meantime Luke began
To slacken in his duty; and, at length,
He in the dissolute city gave himself
To evil courses: ignominy and shame 445
Fell on him, so that he was driven at last
To seek a hiding-place beyond the seas.

There is a comfort in the strength of love;
'Twill make a thing endurable, which else
Would overset the brain, or break the heart: 450
I have conversed with more than one who well
Remember the old Man, and what he was
Years after he had heard this heavy news.
His bodily frame had been from youth to age

Of an unusual strength. Among the rocks   455
He went, and still looked up to sun and cloud,
And listened to the wind; and, as before,
Performed all kinds of labour for his sheep,
And for the land, his small inheritance.
And to that hollow dell from time to time   460
Did he repair, to build the Fold of which
His flock had need. 'Tis not forgotten yet
The pity which was then in every heart
For the old Man—and 'tis believed by all
That many and many a day he thither went,   465
And never lifted up a single stone.

There, by the Sheep-fold, sometimes was he seen
Sitting alone, or with his faithful Dog,
Then old, beside him, lying at his feet.
The length of full seven years, from time to time,   470
He at the building of this Sheep-fold wrought,
And left the work unfinished when he died.
Three years, or little more, did Isabel
Survive her Husband: at her death the estate
Was sold, and went into a stranger's hand.   475
The Cottage which was named the EVENING STAR
Is gone—the ploughshare has been through the ground
On which it stood; great changes have been wrought
In all the neighbourhood:—yet the oak is left
That grew beside their door; and the remains   480
Of the unfinished Sheep-fold may be seen [4]
Beside the boisterous brook of Green-head Ghyll.

MY HEART LEAPS UP

My heart leaps up when I behold
      A rainbow in the sky:
So was it when my life began;
So is it now I am a man;
So be it when I shall grow old,   5
      Or let me die!
The Child is father of the Man;
And I could wish my days to be
Bound each to each by natural piety.

[4] *Sheep-fold may be seen* In her *Journal* (October 11, 1800) Dorothy Wordsworth describes how she and William found the sheepfold, "falling away."
It was "built nearly in the form of a heart unequally divided."

RESOLUTION AND INDEPENDENCE

I

There was a roaring in the wind all night;
The rain came heavily and fell in floods;
But now the sun is rising calm and bright;
The birds are singing in the distant woods;
Over his own sweet voice the Stock-dove broods;   5
The Jay makes answer as the Magpie chatters;
And all the air is filled with pleasant noise of waters.

II

All things that love the sun are out of doors;
The sky rejoices in the morning's birth;
The grass is bright with rain-drops;—on the moors   10
The hare is running races in her mirth;
And with her feet she from the plashy earth
Raises a mist; that, glittering in the sun,
Runs with her all the way, wherever she doth run.

III

I was a Traveller then upon the moor;   15
I saw the hare that raced about with joy;
I heard the woods and distant waters roar;
Or heard them not, as happy as a boy:
The pleasant season did my heart employ:
My old remembrances went from me wholly;   20
And all the ways of men, so vain and melancholy.

IV

But, as it sometimes chanceth, from the might
Of joy in minds that can no further go,
As high as we have mounted in delight
In our dejection do we sink as low;   25
To me that morning did it happen so;
And fears and fancies thick upon me came;
Dim sadness—and blind thoughts, I knew not, nor could name.

V

I heard the sky-lark warbling in the sky;
And I bethought me of the playful hare:
Even such a happy Child of earth am I;   30

Even as these blissful creatures do I fare;
Far from the world I walk, and from all care;
But there may come another day to me—
Solitude, pain of heart, distress, and poverty.   35

VI

My whole life I have lived in pleasant thought,
As if life's business were a summer mood;
As if all needful things would come unsought
To genial faith, still rich in genial good;
But how can He expect that others should   40
Build for him, sow for him, and at his call
Love him, who for himself will take no heed at all?

VII

I thought of Chatterton,[1] the marvellous Boy,
The sleepless Soul that perished in his pride;
Of Him [2] who walked in glory and in joy   45
Following his plough, along the mountain-side:
By our own spirits are we deified:
We Poets in our youth begin in gladness;
But thereof come in the end despondency and madness.

VIII

Now, whether it were by peculiar grace,   50
A leading from above, a something given,
Yet it befell, that, in this lonely place,
When I with these untoward thoughts had striven,
Beside a pool bare to the eye of heaven
I saw a Man [3] before me unawares: 55
The oldest man he seemed that ever wore grey hairs.

IX

As a huge stone is sometimes seen to lie
Couched on the bald top of an eminence;
Wonder to all who do the same espy,

---

[1] *Chatterton* Thomas Chatterton (1752–1770), brilliant young poet who committed suicide before he was recognized
[2] *Him* Robert Burns (1759–1796)
[3] *Man* The leech gatherer is described in Dorothy Wordsworth's *Journal* (October 3, 1800) as "an old man almost double. He had on a coat, thrown over his shoulders, above his waistcoat and coat. Under this he carried a bundle, and had an apron on and a night-cap. His face was interesting. He had dark eyes and a long nose. . . . His trade was to gather leeches, but now leeches are scarce, and he had not strength for it. He lived by begging . . ."

By what means it could thither come, and whence;   60
So that it seems a thing endued with sense:
Like a sea-beast crawled forth, that on a shelf
Of rock or sand reposeth, there to sun itself;

X

Such seemed this Man, not all alive nor dead,
Nor all asleep—in his extreme old age: 65
His body was bent double, feet and head
Coming together in life's pilgrimage;
As if some dire constraint of pain, or rage
Of sickness felt by him in times long past,
A more than human weight upon his frame had cast.   70

XI

Himself he propped, limbs, body, and pale face,
Upon a long grey staff of shaven wood:
And, still as I drew near with gentle pace,
Upon the margin of that moorish flood
Motionless as a cloud the old Man stood,   75
That heareth not the loud winds when they call
And moveth all together, if it move at all.

XII

At length, himself unsettling, he the pond
Stirred with his staff, and fixedly did look
Upon the muddy water, which he conned,   80
As if he had been reading in a book:
And now a stranger's privilege I took;
And, drawing to his side, to him did say,
"This morning gives us promise of a glorious day."

XIII

A gentle answer did the old Man make,   85
In courteous speech which forth he slowly drew:
And him with further words I thus bespake,
"What occupation do you there pursue?
This is a lonesome place for one like you."
Ere he replied, a flash of mild surprise   90
Broke from the sable orbs of his yet-vivid eyes,

XIV

His words came feebly, from a feeble chest,
But each in solemn order followed each,

With something of a lofty utterance drest—
Choice word and measured phrase, above the reach   95
Of ordinary men; a stately speech;
Such as grave Livers do in Scotland use,
Religious men, who give to God and man their dues.

XV

He told, that to these waters he had come
To gather leeches,[4] being old and poor: 100
Employment hazardous and wearisome!
And he had many hardships to endure:
From pond to pond he roamed, from moor to moor;
Housing, with God's good help, by choice or chance,
And in this way he gained an honest maintenance.   105

XVI

The old Man still stood talking by my side;
But now his voice to me was like a stream
Scarce heard; nor word from word could I divide;
And the whole body of the Man did seem
Like one whom I had met with in a dream;   110
Or like a man from some far region sent,
To give me human strength, by apt admonishment.

XVII

My former thoughts returned: the fear that kills;
And hope that is unwilling to be fed;
Cold, pain, and labour, and all fleshly ills;   115
And mighty Poets in their misery dead.
—Perplexed, and longing to be comforted,
My question eagerly did I renew,
"How is it that you live, and what is it you do?"

XVIII

He with a smile did then his words repeat;   120
And said, that, gathering leeches, far and wide
He travelled; stirring thus above his feet
The waters of the pools where they abide.
"Once I could meet with them on every side;
But they have dwindled long by slow decay;   125
Yet still I persevere, and find them where I may."

---

[4] *leeches* bloodsucking worms, still used by physicians in Wordsworth's time
to bleed the sick

XIX

While he was talking thus, the lonely place,
The old Man's shape, and speech—all troubled me:
In my mind's eye I seemed to see him pace
About the weary moors continually,   130
Wandering about alone and silently.
While I these thoughts within myself pursued,
He, having made a pause, the same discourse renewed.

XX

And soon with this he other matter blended,
Cheerfully uttered, with demeanour kind,   135
But stately in the main; and when he ended,
I could have laughed myself to scorn to find
In that decrepit Man so firm a mind.
"God," said I, "be my help and stay secure;
I'll think of the Leech-gatherer on the lonely moor!" 140

COMPOSED UPON WESTMINSTER BRIDGE,[1]

SEPTEMBER 3, 1802

Earth has not anything to show more fair:
Dull would he be of soul who could pass by
A sight so touching in its majesty:
This City now doth, like a garment, wear
The beauty of the morning; silent, bare,   5
Ships, towers, domes, theatres, and temples lie
Open unto the fields, and to the sky;
All bright and glittering in the smokeless air.
Never did sun more beautifully steep
In his first splendour, valley, rock, or hill;   10
Ne'er saw I, never felt, a calm so deep!
The river glideth at his own sweet will:
Dear God! the very houses seem asleep;
And all that mighty heart is lying still!

---

[1] "Written on the roof of a coach, on my way to France."—Wordsworth
  "We mounted the Dover Coach at Charing Cross. It was a beautiful morning. The city, St. Paul's, with the river and a multitude of little Boats made a most beautiful sight as we crossed Westminster Bridge. The houses were not overhung by their cloud of smoke, and they were spread out endlessly, yet the sun shone so brightly, with such a fierce light, that there was something like the purity of one of nature's own grand spectacles."—Dorothy Wordsworth

IT IS A BEAUTEOUS EVENING, CALM AND FREE

It is a beauteous evening, calm and free,
The holy time is quiet as a Nun
Breathless with adoration; the broad sun
Is sinking down in its tranquillity;
The gentleness of heaven broods o'er the Sea: 5
Listen! the mighty Being is awake,
And doth with his eternal motion make
A sound like thunder—everlastingly.
Dear Child! [1] dear Girl! that walkest with me here,
If thou appear untouched by solemn thought,   10
Thy nature is not therefore less divine:
Thou liest in Abraham's bosom [2] all the year;
And worshipp'st at the Temple's inner shrine,
God being with thee when we know it not.

LONDON, 1802 [1]

Milton! thou shouldst be living at this hour:
England hath need of thee: she is a fen
Of stagnant waters: altar, sword, and pen,
Fireside, the heroic wealth of hall and bower,
Have forfeited their ancient English dower   5
Of inward happiness. We are selfish men;
Oh! raise us up, return to us again;
And give us manners, virtue, freedom, power.
Thy soul was like a Star, and dwelt apart;
Thou hadst a voice whose sound was like the sea: 10
Pure as the naked heavens, majestic, free,
So didst thou travel on life's common way,
In cheerful godliness; and yet thy heart
The lowliest duties on herself did lay.

[1] *Child* Caroline, daughter of Wordsworth and Annette Vallon
[2] *Abraham's bosom* God's care

[1] One of a group of five sonnets about England written on Wordsworth's return from a visit to France. He writes, "I could not but be struck . . . with the vanity and parade of our own country, especially in great towns and cities, as contrasted with the quiet, and I may say the desolation, that the revolution had produced in France."

I WANDERED LONELY AS A CLOUD

I wandered lonely as a cloud
That floats on high o'er vales and hills,
When all at once I saw a crowd,
A host, of golden daffodils;
Beside the lake,[1] beneath the trees, 5
Fluttering and dancing in the breeze.

Continuous as the stars that shine
And twinkle on the milky way,
They stretched in never-ending line
Along the margin of a bay: 10
Ten thousand saw I at a glance,
Tossing their heads in sprightly dance.

The waves beside them danced; but they
Out-did the sparkling waves in glee:
A poet could not but be gay, 15
In such a jocund company:
I gazed—and gazed—but little thought
What wealth the show to me had brought:

For oft, when on my couch I lie
In vacant or in pensive mood, 20
They flash upon that inward eye
Which is the bliss of solitude;
And then my heart with pleasure fills,
And dances with the daffodils.

ODE:

INTIMATIONS OF IMMORTALITY FROM RECOLLECTIONS
OF EARLY CHILDHOOD

Wordsworth has written:
This was composed during my residence at Town-end, Grasmere. Two years at least passed between the writing of the four first stanzas and the remaining part. To the attentive and competent reader the whole sufficiently explains itself; but there may be no harm in adverting here to particular feelings or *experiences* of my own mind on which the structure of the poem partly

[1] *lake* Wordsworth identifies the place as Ullswater, the time March.

rests. Nothing was more difficult for me in childhood than to admit the notion of death as a state applicable to my own being.
I have said elsewhere—

> A simple child,
> That lightly draws its breath,
> And feels its life in every limb,
> What should it know of death!—

But it was not so much from feelings of animal vivacity that *my*
difficulty came as from a sense of the indomitableness of the
Spirit within me. I used to brood over the stories of Enoch and
Elijah, and almost to persuade myself that, whatever might become of others, I should be translated, in something of the same
way, to heaven. With a feeling congenial to this, I was often
unable to think of external things as having external existence,
and I communed with all that I saw as something not apart
from, but inherent in, my own immaterial nature. Many times
while going to school have I grasped at a wall or tree to recall
myself from this abyss of idealism to the reality. At that time I
was afraid of such processes. In later periods of life I have de-
plored, as we have all reason to do, a subjugation of an opposite
character, and have rejoiced over the remembrances, as is expressed in the lines—

> Obstinate questionings
> Of sense and outward things,
> Fallings from us, vanishings; etc.

To that dream-like vividness and splendor which invest objects
of sight in childhood, every one, I believe, if he would look back,
could bear testimony, and I need not dwell upon it here: but
having in the poem regarded it as presumptive evidence of a
prior state of existence, I think it right to protest against a conclusion, which has given pain to some good and pious persons,
that I meant to inculcate such a belief. It is far too shadowy
a notion to be recommended to faith, as more than an element
in our instincts of immortality. But let us bear in mind that,
though the idea is not advanced in revelation, there is nothing
there to contradict it, and the fall of Man presents an analogy in
its favor. Accordingly, a pre-existent state has entered into the
popular creeds of many nations; and, among all persons acquainted with classic literature, is known as an ingredient in
Platonic philosophy. Archimedes said that he could move the
world if he had a point whereon to rest his machine. Who has not
felt the same aspirations as regards the world of his own mind?

Having to wield some of its elements when I was impelled to write this poem on the 'Immortality of the Soul,' I took hold of the notion of pre-existence as having sufficient foundation in humanity for authorizing me to make for my purpose the best use of it I could as a poet.

> The Child is Father of the Man;
> And I could wish my days to be
> Bound each to each by natural piety.

I

There was a time when meadow, grove, and stream,
The earth, and every common sight,
    To me did seem
    Apparelled in celestial light,
The glory and the freshness of a dream.   5
It is not now as it hath been of yore;—
    Turn wheresoe'er I may,
    By night or day,
The things which I have seen I now can see no more.

II

    The Rainbow comes and goes,   10
    And lovely is the Rose,
    The Moon doth with delight
Look round her when the heavens are bare;
    Waters on a starry night
    Are beautiful and fair;   15
    The sunshine is a glorious birth;
    But yet I know, where'er I go,
That there hath past away a glory from the earth.

III

Now, while the birds thus sing a joyous song,
    And while the young lambs bound   20
    As to the tabor's [1] sound,
To me alone there came a thought of grief:
A timely utterance gave that thought relief,
    And I again am strong:
The cataracts blow their trumpets from the steep;   25
No more shall grief of mine the season wrong;
I hear the Echoes through the mountains throng,
The Winds come to me from the fields of sleep,
    And all the earth is gay;
    Land and sea   30

[1] *tabor* drum

Give themselves up to jollity,
　　And with the heart of May
　　Doth every Beast keep holiday;—
　　　Thou Child of Joy,
Shout round me, let me hear thy shouts, thou happy Shepherd-
　　　　boy!　　　　　　35

IV

Ye blessèd Creatures, I have heard the call
　　Ye to each other make; I see
The heavens laugh with you in your jubilee;
　　My heart is at your festival,
　　　My head hath its coronal,[2]　　　　40
The fulness of your bliss, I feel—I feel it all.
　　Oh evil day! if I were sullen
　　While Earth herself is adorning,
　　　This sweet May-morning,
　　And the Children are culling　　　　45
　　　On every side,
　　In a thousand valleys far and wide,
　　Fresh flowers; while the sun shines warm,
And the Babe leaps up on his Mother's arm:—
　　I hear, I hear, with joy I hear!　　　　50
　　—But there's a Tree, of many, one,
A single Field which I have looked upon,
Both of them speak of something that is gone:
　　　The Pansy at my feet
　　　Doth the same tale repeat:　　　　55
Whither is fled the visionary gleam?
Where is it now, the glory and the dream?

V

Our birth is but a sleep and a forgetting:
The Soul that rises with us, our life's Star,
　　　Hath had elsewhere its setting,　　　　60
　　　And cometh from afar:
　　Not in entire forgetfulness,
　　And not in utter nakedness,
But trailing clouds of glory do we come
　　From God, who is our home:　　　　65
Heaven lies about us in our infancy!
Shades of the prison-house begin to close
　　　Upon the growing Boy,
　　　　But He

[2] *coronal* crown

Beholds the light, and whence it flows, 70
He sees it in his joy;
The Youth, who daily farther from the east
Must travel, still is Nature's Priest,
And by the vision splendid
Is on his way attended; 75
At length the Man perceives it die away,
And fade into the light of common day.

VI

Earth fills her lap with pleasures of her own;
Yearnings she hath in her own natural kind,
And, even with something of a Mother's mind, 80
And no unworthy aim,
The homely Nurse doth all she can
To make her Foster-child, her Inmate Man,
Forget the glories he hath known,
And that imperial palace whence he came. 85

VII

Behold the Child among his new-born blisses,
A six years' Darling of a pigmy size!
See, where 'mid work of his own hand he lies,
Fretted by sallies of his mother's kisses,
With light upon him from his father's eyes! 90
See, at his feet, some little plan or chart,
Some fragment from his dream of human life,
Shaped by himself with newly-learned art:
A wedding or a festival,
A mourning or a funeral; 95
And this hath now his heart,
And unto this he frames his song:
Then will he fit his tongue
To dialogues of business, love, or strife;
But it will not be long 100
Ere this be thrown aside,
And with new joy and pride
The little Actor cons ³ another part;
Filling from time to time his "humorous stage" ⁴
With all the Persons, down to palsied Age, 105
That Life brings with her in her equipage;

³ *cons* studies
⁴ *"humorous stage"* plays (like those of Ben Jonson) in which characters represent the different humors or temperaments of man

As if his whole vocation
Were endless imitation.

VIII

Thou, whose exterior semblance doth belie
    Thy Soul's immensity;   110
Thou best Philosopher, who yet dost keep
Thy heritage, thou Eye among the blind,
That, deaf and silent, read'st the eternal deep,
Haunted for ever by the eternal mind,—
    Mighty Prophet! Seer blest!   115
    On whom those truths do rest,
Which we are toiling all our lives to find,
In darkness lost, the darkness of the grave;
Thou, over whom thy Immortality
Broods like the Day, a Master o'er a Slave,   120
A Presence which is not to be put by;
Thou little Child, yet glorious in the might
Of heaven-born freedom on thy being's height,
Why with such earnest pains dost thou provoke
The years to bring the inevitable yoke,   125
Thus blindly with thy blessedness at strife?
Full soon thy Soul shall have her earthly freight,
And custom lie upon thee with a weight,
Heavy as frost, and deep almost as life!

IX

    O joy! that in our embers   130
    Is something that doth live,
    That nature yet remembers
    What was so fugitive!
The thought of our past years in me doth breed
Perpetual benediction: not indeed   135
For that which is most worthy to be blest;
Delight and liberty, the simple creed
Of Childhood, whether busy or at rest,
With new-fledged hope still fluttering in his breast:—
    Not for these I raise   140
    The song of thanks and praise;
  But for those obstinate questionings
    Of sense and outward things,
    Fallings from us, vanishings;
  Blank misgivings of a Creature   145
Moving about in worlds not realised,

High instincts before which our mortal Nature
Did tremble like a guilty Thing surprised:
    But for those first affections,
      Those shadowy recollections,   150
   Which, be they what they may,
Are yet the fountain light of all our day,
Are yet a master light of all our seeing;
   Uphold us, cherish, and have power to make
Our noisy years seem moments in the being   155
Of the eternal Silence: truths that wake,
    To perish never;
Which neither listlessness, nor mad endeavour,
    Nor Man nor Boy,
Nor all that is at enmity with joy,   160
Can utterly abolish or destroy!
    Hence in a season of calm weather
    Though inland far we be,
Our Souls have sight of that immortal sea
    Which brought us hither,   165
   Can in a moment travel thither,
And see the Children sport upon the shore,
And hear the mighty waters rolling evermore.

X

Then sing, ye Birds, sing, sing a joyous song!
    And let the young Lambs bound   170
    As to the tabor's sound!
We in thought will join your throng,
    Ye that pipe and ye that play,
    Ye that through your hearts to-day
    Feel the gladness of the May!   175
What though the radiance which was once so bright
Be now for ever taken from my sight,
    Though nothing can bring back the hour
Of splendour in the grass, of glory in the flower;
    We will grieve not, rather find   180
    Strength in what remains behind;
    In the primal sympathy
    Which having been must ever be;
    In the soothing thoughts that spring
    Out of human suffering;   185
    In the faith that looks through death,
In years that bring the philosophic mind.

XI

And O, ye Fountains, Meadows, Hills, and Groves,
Forebode not any severing of our loves!
Yet in my heart of hearts I feel your might;   190
I only have relinquished one delight
To live beneath your more habitual sway.
I love the Brooks which down their channels fret,
Even more than when I tripped lightly as they;
The innocent brightness of a new-born Day   195
　　　Is lovely yet;
The Clouds that gather round the setting sun
Do take a sober colouring from an eye
That hath kept watch o'er man's mortality;
Another race hath been, and other palms are won.   200
Thanks to the human heart by which we live,
Thanks to its tenderness, its joys, and fears,
To me the meanest flower that blows can give
Thoughts that do often lie too deep for tears.

THE SOLITARY REAPER [1]

Behold her, single in the field,
Yon solitary Highland Lass!
Reaping and singing by herself;
Stop here, or gently pass!
Alone she cuts and binds the grain,   5
And sings a melancholy strain;
O listen! for the Vale profound
Is overflowing with the sound.

No Nightingale did ever chaunt
More welcome notes to weary bands   10
Of travellers in some shady haunt,
Among Arabian sands:
A voice so thrilling ne'er was heard
In spring-time from the Cuckoo-bird,
Breaking the silence of the seas   15
Among the farthest Hebrides.

Will no one tell me what she sings? [2]—
Perhaps the plaintive numbers [3] flow

[1] One of fifteen poems, "Memorials of a Tour in Scotland, 1803—"
[2] *what she sings* Wordsworth acknowledged a debt to Thomas Wilkinson's *Tour in Scotland*, circulated in manuscript before its publication in 1824. Wilkinson said that the girl was singing "in Erse," or Scottish Gaelic.
[3] *numbers* lines of poetry

For old, unhappy, far-off things,
And battles long ago: 20
Or is it some more humble lay,[4]
Familiar matter of to-day?
Some natural sorrow, loss, or pain,
That has been, and may be again?

Whate'er the theme, the Maiden sang   25
As if her song could have no ending;
I saw her singing at her work,
And o'er the sickle bending:—
I listened, motionless and still;
And, as I mounted up the hill,   30
The music in my heart I bore,
Long after it was heard no more.

THE WORLD IS TOO MUCH WITH US

The world is too much with us; late and soon,
Getting and spending, we lay waste our powers:
Little we see in Nature that is ours;
We have given our hearts away, a sordid boon!
This Sea that bares her bosom to the moon;   5
The winds that will be howling at all hours,
And are up-gathered now like sleeping flowers;
For this, for everything, we are out of tune;
It moves us not.—Great God! I'd rather be
A Pagan suckled in a creed outworn;   10
So might I, standing on this pleasant lea,
Have glimpses that would make me less forlorn;
Have sight of Proteus [1] rising from the sea;
Or hear old Triton [2] blow his wreathèd horn.

PERSONAL TALK

I

I am not One who much or oft delight
To season my fireside with personal talk.—

[4] lay song

---

[1] Proteus a sea-god who tended the seals of Poseidon and rose from the sea
at noon to sleep among them. If caught, he would prophesy the future, but
he characteristically changed into different shapes when seized.
[2] Triton son of Poseidon, shaped like a man with a dolphin's tail. He used
a trumpet made of a twisted sea shell to govern the waves.

Of friends, who live within an easy walk,
Or neighbours, daily, weekly, in my sight:
And, for my chance-acquaintance, ladies bright,   5
Sons, mothers, maidens withering on the stalk,
These all wear out of me, like Forms, with chalk
Painted on rich men's floors, for one feast-night.
Better than such discourse doth silence long,
Long, barren silence, square with my desire;   10
To sit without emotion, hope, or aim,
In the loved presence of my cottage-fire,
And listen to the flapping of the flame,
Or kettle whispering its faint undersong.

III

Wings have we,—and as far as we can go
We may find pleasure: wilderness and wood,
Blank ocean and mere sky, support that mood
Which with the lofty sanctifies the low.
Dreams, books, are each a world; and books, we know,   5
Are a substantial world, both pure and good:
Round these, with tendrils strong as flesh and blood,
Our pastime and our happiness will grow.
There find I personal themes, a plenteous store,
Matter wherein right voluble I am,   10
To which I listen with a ready ear;
Two shall be named, pre-eminently dear,—
The gentle Lady married to the Moor; [1]
And heavenly Una with her milk-white Lamb. [2]

SCORN NOT THE SONNET

Scorn not the Sonnet; Critic, you have frowned,
Mindless of its just honors; with this key
Shakespeare unlocked his heart; the melody
Of this small lute gave ease to Petrarch's [1] wound;
A thousand times this pipe did Tasso [2] sound;   5
With it Camöens [3] soothed an exile's grief;
The Sonnet glittered a gay myrtle leaf

[1] *Lady . . . Moor* Shakespeare's *Othello* (Desdemona and Othello)
[2] *Una . . . Lamb* Spenser's *Faerie Queene*

[1] *Petrarch* Italian poet (1304–1374) who wrote many sonnets addressed to Laura
[2] *Tasso* Italian poet (1544–1595)
[3] *Camöens* Portuguese poet (1524–1580) banished from court *c.*1547–1570

Amid the cypress with which Dante crowned
His visionary brow: a glow-worm lamp,
It cheered mild Spenser, called from Faery-land   10
To struggle through dark ways; and, when a damp
Fell round the path of Milton, in his hand
The Thing became a trumpet; whence he blew
Soul-animating strains—alas, too few!

CRITICISM

The following discussion of "Tintern Abbey"—poem and place—has more of the historical, biographical approach than the preceding critical selections have shown, but the account of the poem as it relates to place and time is only an entry into an understanding of its central theme. The essay also considers the metaphors, the symbols, and the structure of the poem. The reader will find that other critics have said more about "Tintern Abbey's" religious and philosophical content and about its relation to all of Wordsworth's work and his beliefs.

The Case of The Missing Abbey:
Wordsworth's "Lines" [1]
BERNICE SLOTE

Wordsworth wrote twelve sets of "Lines," some "left upon a Seat in a Yew-tree," or "suggested by a Portrait," or written "as a School Exercise," "in Early Spring," and "while sailing in a Boat at Evening." One of these sets of "Lines" is identified as "composed a few miles above Tintern Abbey, on revisiting the Banks of the Wye during a Tour." This title, perhaps to offset the ambiguity of "Lines," has almost universally been shortened to "Tintern Abbey," and is often indexed that way. Among the few exceptions are Abbie Findlay Potts in *Wordsworth's Prelude,* who uses "Lines . . . along the Wye"; and, interestingly enough, Wordsworth himself, who in the note to "Guilt and Sorrow" recalls beginning "the verses—'Five years have passed.'" Hardly anybody else calls "Tintern Abbey" anything else, and for most readers, at least in the periphery of the mind, looms the familiar picture of the ruins of the old Cistercian monastery, hill-

[1] Reprinted from *The Western Humanities Review,* XI (Winter, 1957).

shadowed along the Wye.

The image of the Abbey, supported by the textbook photographs, is often so strong that it is with a start that one realizes a poetic mystery. For, in fact, Tintern Abbey is nowhere in the poem called "Tintern Abbey," either by name, image, or the most remote reference.[2] Furthermore, as visitors to the Wye will discover, it is unlikely that the Abbey can be seen with any real effect from the spot where the title says Wordsworth composed the poem. At least, in the summer of 1954, all my efforts to sit under some sycamore and view the ruins from *a few miles above* the Abbey were unsuccessful. A further difficulty, of course, is that the poem was not actually composed under that sycamore at all, but a number of miles in the other direction from Tintern, with the ruins at Wordsworth's back. This is clearly a case of a missing Abbey.

The first facts we need to examine in the mystery are those of the contradictory accounts of the poem's composition. The poem says one thing; Wordsworth another. There are, then, two poetic origins—one dramatic and the other actual. The dramatic, or assumed circumstance, is given in the title. The "Lines" were supposedly "composed a few miles above Tintern Abbey" while Wordsworth was revisiting the banks of the Wye during a tour, July 13, 1798. (The previous visit, we know, had been in 1793.) The speaker of the poem is reposing under a "dark sycamore," hearing the waters of the Wye murmuring in the silence and viewing the river's "steep and lofty cliffs" and the farther green, somewhat inhabited, terrain. He begins his moments of reflection with a memory, "Five years have passed."

However, in the Fenwick note to the "Lines," Wordsworth gives the more factual account: "I began it upon leaving Tintern, after crossing the Wye, and concluded it just as I was entering Bristol in the evening, after a ramble of four or five days, with my Sister. Not a line of it was altered, and not any part of it written down till I reached Bristol."[3] William and

---

[2] I have found only one other comment on this fact. Royal Gettmann, in "A Literary Tour of England—Without Slides," *Phi Kappa Phi Journal*, XXXV (Oct. 1955), 18, says: "His not mentioning the abbey seemed to me one of the most remarkable things about the poem."

[3] The Duke of Argyle account, quoted in *Wordsworth's Poetical Works*, ed. E. de Selincourt (Oxford, 1944), II, 517, is that it took four days to compose the poem.

his sister Dorothy had been on a walking tour of the Wye country,[4] leaving Bristol on July 10, 1798, and going to Goodrich Castle, some twenty-seven miles up the Wye. They passed through Tintern on the way up and on the way back, stopped at Chepstow, and on the next day went back to Tintern. On July 13 they crossed the river there and returned to Bristol, William composing his "Lines" on the way. On that day, only the *dramatic speaker* of the poem could have been resting under the trees two or more miles up the river from the ruins.

It may be pertinent to our mystery to note that Wordsworth, in spite of his penchant for realistic, matter-of-fact titles, was quite aware of the poet's need to re-create imaginatively, using situations and images for the sake of the poem, rather than for history, and letting the unliteral be true. This he did in many other poems. In the note to "Lines written while sailing in a Boat at Evening," he points out that "This title is scarcely correct. It was during a solitary walk on the banks of the Cam that I was first struck with this appearance, and applied it to my own feelings in the manner here expressed, changing the scene to the Thames, near Windsor." "Guilt and Sorrow" concerns incidents on Salisbury Plain, but Wordsworth again notes, "of the features described as belonging to it, one or two are taken from other desolate parts of England." A more direct statement of Wordsworth's dramatic intentions is in the note to "An Evening Walk": "the plan of it has not been confined to a particular walk or an individual place,—a proof (of which I was unconscious at the time) of my unwillingness to submit the poetic spirit to the chains of fact and real circumstance. The country is idealized rather than described in any one of its local aspects."

One might say, then, that Wordsworth's factually realistic tone is often deceptive, one which may be assumed for a deliberate dramatic purpose. For example, it may be more effective for the speaker in a reflective, mystical poem to be seated in near solitude on the banks of the Wye than to be jogging through the dust of the Bristol road. And the very air of contemplative leisure dramatically suitable for the "Lines," is quite at variance with the actual circumstances, for having been "composed" on July 13, the poem was fairly hurled into the press, where Cottle

[4] A complete chronology of this tour is in John Bard McNulty, "Wordsworth's Tour of the Wye," *Modern Language Notes*, LX (May, 1945), 291–295.

the printer had *Lyrical Ballads* under way on July 18.[5] The truth of the poem may indeed lie somewhere outside both the physical scene and the position of the poet in that experience, or even the specific language or metaphors employed. It is a totality of fact unchained to move freely in the world of the poem, a fusion of both heard and unheard melodies.

In the dynamics of metaphor, such a fusion may sometimes operate like a montage, in which one image glows in a ghostly shadow through a scene, as the light of a blown candle is held for a moment on the retina. Sometimes this montage operates in the origin of a poem, sometimes in its actual structure. An experience or an image which is the conception of the living poem may be lost from the final lines: it has been transformed into another shape, or it has been diffused into the poem. For example, in Wordsworth's "Michael," the narrator sees the ruins of a sheepfold as "a straggling heap of unhewn stones." The actual sheepfold, Dorothy Wordsworth reports, was "built nearly in the form of a heart unequally divided." [6] Such an obvious, factual symbol seems too good to lose, yet nowhere in "Michael" does Wordsworth describe the ruined sheepfold as heart-shaped. But the heart symbol, though missing, is not dead. It has become the poem: the composite truth of the experience in "Michael," the ruin of an old man's dream, is truly a heart broken, unequally divided. This is a simple case of an origin discarded, but such a montage of images may function even more deeply in a poem. Here, I think, we may find the best clue to the missing Abbey. For in spite of all the apparent contradictions, the internal, poetic logic of Wordsworth's "Lines" does seem to reveal the mingled grey and green, the stone and grass, of Tintern Abbey. In order to see it clearly, we should look first at the Abbey, as it is in time.

Two things are blended in a ruin: time past evidenced in the still decay of the present, and nature moving with green ease through the works of man. Tintern Abbey today is an almost perfect dramatization of such a mingling of man and nature, with a religious meaning out of time. The floor of the Abbey is grass,

---

[5] D. W. to—? (18 July 1798), *Early Letters of William and Dorothy Wordsworth*, ed. E. de Selincourt (Oxford, 1935), p. 198.
[6] *Journals of Dorothy Wordsworth*, ed. E. de Selincourt (New York, 1941), I, 66.

the roof is the sky, and the great arched windows of the stand-ing grey stone walls are storied not with lives of saints but with the changing colors on the hills along the Wye. I once saw the altar window thick with green; the sod was soft, as in a meadow; but the solitude had currents of other presences, shadows of the monks who once were there. In a religious sense, the chapel walls are symbols, outlines only, that now define the sacrament of woods, stones, familiar fields.

The Tintern Abbey that William and Dorothy Wordsworth saw in 1798 must have been quite like the ruin of today. William Gilpin's travel book of 1782, *Observations on the River Wye,*[7] gives an account of "the noble ruin of Tintern-abbey":

It occupies a gentle eminence in the middle of a circular valley, beauti-fully screened on all sides by woody hills; through which the river winds its course; . . . the splendid ruin, contrasted with the objects of nature; and the elegant line formed by the summits of the hills, which include the whole; make all together a very inchanting piece of scenery.

On a near view, it is seen that

Nature has now made it her own. Time has worn off all traces of the rule: it has blunted the sharp edges of the chissel; and broken the regu-larity of opposing parts . . . Ivy, in masses uncommonly large, has taken possession of many parts of the wall; and gives a happy contrast to the grey-coloured stone, of which the building is composed.

Mosses cover the stone, as well, and give a rich finishing to the ruin. On the inside, "The roof is gone: but the walls, and pillars, and abutments, which supported it, are intire. . . . the whole area is reduced to one level; cleared of rubbish; and covered with neat turf, closely shorn. . . ." Tintern Abbey, concluded Gilpin, was an "awful piece of ruin," a "grand, and venerable remains." He objected somewhat to the neatness inside the ruined Abbey, but rejoiced that the outside was still in its "wild, and native rudeness." Wordsworth describes a similar scene "At Furness Abbey,"

> Man left this Structure to become Time's Prey,
> A soothing spirit follows in the way
> That Nature takes, her counter-work pursuing.
> See how her Ivy clasps the sacred Ruin . . .

[7] *Observations on the River Wye, and Several Parts of South Wales, &c. Rela-tive Chiefly to Picturesque Beauty; Made in the Summer of the Year 1770* (London, 1782), pp. 31–35.

And no doubt the travelers of 1798, touring the Wye for the conventional eighteenth-century purpose of viewing ruins and the picturesque, recognized in Tintern Abbey the same counterpoint of leaf and stone.

If the Abbey image appears to the reader of the "Lines," as it must have hung in Wordsworth's mind as he composed the poem (he had visited it several times in the days preceding), it may come by several routes. The poem, in one sense, draws on familiar scenes outside the frame of the lines: any "tour of the Wye" in 1798 carries with it some reference to the pleasure in landscape and in ruins like Goodrich Castle, Chepstow Castle, and Tintern Abbey. The title implies the conventional ruins and a prospect sweetly wild and pastoral. In another sense, it may well be that the Abbey is recognized in the poem through its ultimate transformation. Nature had made Tintern Abbey her own, life submerging decay with an aspect both gentle and awesome, and with the air of holiness that Wordsworth had sensed at other abbies (*Prelude* II, 107; "Old Abbies"). The most obvious quality in the physical grass-paved, leaf-windowed Abbey ruin is just that quality of mingling, of the interfusion of man and nature, and of the past in the present (time not cancelled, but contained). Wordsworth's poem is a hymn of mystical recognition and praise for the union, the totality, of the universe. This sense of total being is in the poem, not by a symbol, but by a complete structural development in which all separate things are fused. Without considering the complicated matter of Wordsworth's religious view of the world, we can note here the rather particular evidences of the "oneness" in the poem.

Interfusion as a structural principle in the "Lines" is first suggested by a blending of time. After five years, *again* the speaker hears the waters and views the wild, secluded scene. The present scene is actually the recall of the past. "Again" is used twice more to impress the double view, and the *memory* of such beauty is then described. When the speaker emerges from the thought of the past, the present contains "recognitions," and "The picture of the mind revives again." The phrase, "The sense/Of present pleasure," is one of the two points in the whole poem where the present is recognized for itself. The other is the speaker's reference to his sister, "For thou art with me." The thoughts immediately turn to the future, "That in this moment there is

life and food/For future years"; and after the further recall of
the speaker's changing attitudes toward nature, he addresses his
sister with a wish for the future influence of nature on her.
Even at the close he considers the continuity of all things, speaking of the moment on the river, in "this green pastoral landscape,"
as a thing not to be forgotten. Thus, in the present of the poem,
past and future time mingle. Even as the scenes of five years before became landscapes of sensation, so the mind will contain for
the future all "lovely forms" and harmonies of the present scene.
Even the two companions there on the river change time. The
speaker sees in his sister his former self, and imagines for her the
memoried future.

The scene along the Wye which is described in this montage
of past and present has further physical evidences of interfusion.
The landscape is connected with the quiet of the sky. The orchards are distinguished only in that they are *not* distinguished,
but "with their unripe fruits/Are clad in one green hue, and lose
themselves/'Mid groves and copses." Thus man's planting mingles with the natural scene. The hedge-rows, too, are hardly like
man's work, but "little lines/Of sportive wood run wild." The
green of the landscape extends to the very door of the "pastoral
farms." Smoke rises from the trees, as if from no house at all,
perhaps from the paradoxically "vagrant dwellers" in the woods,
or from some hermit's cave. The smoke, of course, is from the
charcoal furnaces in Tintern, but the silent mystery of the
wreaths is used dramatically as a part of the natural scene. Gilpin
described the smoke as "spreading its thin veil" over the hills, a
veil which "beautifully breaks their lines, and unites them with
the sky" (p. 12). In this landscape, the effect is to cancel lines,
obliterate distinctions, mingle man with nature and the pathless
woods.

The central passage of the "Lines" in which Wordsworth describes his relationship to nature is developed on the key phrase:
"something far more deeply interfused." Here, at the climax of
his hymn as a worshipper of nature, Wordsworth repeats his sense
of oneness, of the total fusion of all things, as his highest realization. His first love was purely an appetite, a singleness, nature
for itself with no "need of a remoter charm." But the next understanding is that man and the physical world are entwined,
that one must hear in all of it the "still, sad music of humanity."

With man a part of nature and their mutual harmony heard, there is still a further mystical realization of "something far more deeply interfused"—that is, mingled more completely throughout all things than any oneness man and the physical world can achieve. This motion, this spirit, "rolls through all things." It is the ultimate, pervasive life. The central theme is that "The unity of all hath been revealed" (*Prelude* II, 221). Through harmonious quiet and the language of the senses we thus "see into the life of things." Nature becomes more than the physical world, and more than man or his acts, but a totality whose life is interfusion.

The chief effect of the "Lines" is a sense of complete, harmonious blending and interaction: past, present, and future; the landscape with its muted, flowing lines; man's work and a natural wildness; all senses, memories, and revelations. And the *being* of the poem is exactly what the being of the physical Tintern Abbey suggests. As a poetic locale may be unliteral, as a real situation may be exchanged for an even more real creation, so the imagined body of the world may find its bone and blood through many a strange sea-change. Those who call the lines composed along the Wye "Tintern Abbey" may be impelled by more than a need to shorten the title. The Abbey is missing, it is true, but only because the image, the symbol, has in its turn been interfused with the dramatic situation of the poem. Man and his work, blended with the natural world to the exclusion of the formal shape of religion, but realizing a sacramental awareness of the mysterious power of complete nature—this is, in effect, what the image of the Abbey suggests. In a kind of poetic logic, the poem *is* Tintern Abbey.

SAMUEL TAYLOR COLERIDGE

[1772-1834]

COLERIDGE, the son of an Anglican clergyman, was born in Ottery St. Mary, Devonshire; he attended Christ's Hospital School in London and Jesus College, Cambridge. His life was restless, even from the beginning. He was briefly in the Light Dragoons, contemplated entering the Unitarian ministry, was associated with Robert Southey in Utopian schemes (Pantisocracy) for which a group proposed and then abandoned emigration to America. He began publishing poetry, edited a paper for a time, met William and Dorothy Wordsworth, and in 1798 with Wordsworth published the anonymous volume *Lyrical Ballads.* Coleridge's contribution of four poems included *The Rime of the Ancient Mariner,* but it did not appear under his name until 1817. In the next years he was ill, quarreled with the Wordsworths, separated from his family (he had married for convenience, later fell in love with Mrs. Wordsworth's sister). He lectured, published a periodical *(The Friend),* wrote some plays *(Remorse, Zapolya)* and more poems—"Christabel" (1816) and *Sibylline Leaves* (1817), which included "The Rime of the Ancient Mariner" with the marginal notes added. *Biographia Literaria,* his essays on literary history, was also published in 1817. Coleridge is known now as a man of diverse talents. As a poet, he is known best for his haunting poems of the supernatural. He was known to his friends for the brilliant shimmer of his talk and learning. And many read him now as a religious philosopher and wise critic.

Introductory Readings

EDITION: *The Complete Poetical Works,* ed. Ernest Hartley Coleridge (1912); *Biographia Literaria,* ed. J. Shawcross (1907). BIOGRAPHY: E. K.

Chambers, *Samuel Taylor Coleridge* (1938). CRITICISM: John Livingston Lowes, *The Road to Xanadu: A Study in the Ways of the Imagination* (rev. ed., 1930); Thomas M. Raysor, ed., "Introduction" to *Coleridge's Shakespearean Criticism* (1930); H. M. Margoliouth, *Wordsworth and Coleridge* (1953).

THE RIME OF THE ANCIENT MARINER [1]

IN SEVEN PARTS

ARGUMENT

How a Ship having passed the Line was driven by storms to the cold Country towards the South Pole; and how from thence she made her course to the tropical Latitude of the Great Pacific Ocean; and of the strange things that befell: and in what manner the Ancyent Marinere came back to his own Country.

PART 1

An ancient Mariner meeteth three gallants bidden to a wedding-feast, and detaineth one.

It is an ancient Mariner,
And he stoppeth one of three.
"By thy long grey beard and glittering eye,
Now wherefore stopp'st thou me?

"The Bridegroom's doors are opened wide,   5
And I am next of kin;
The guests are met, the feast is set:
May'st hear the merry din."

He holds him with his skinny hand,
"There was a ship," quoth he.   10
"Hold off! unhand me, grey-beard loon!"
Eftsoons [2] his hand dropt he.

He holds him with his glittering eye—
The Wedding-Guest stood still,
And listens like a three years' child: 15
The Mariner hath his will.

The Wedding-Guest is spellbound by the eye of the old seafaring man and constrained to hear his tale.

The Wedding-Guest sat on a stone:
He cannot choose but hear;
And thus spake on that ancient man,
The bright-eyed Mariner.   20

[1] Critical comment on this poem appears on p. 416.
[2] *Eftsoons* soon afterwards

"The ship was cheered, the harbor cleared,
Merrily did we drop
Below the kirk,[3] below the hill,
Below the light-house top.

*The Mariner tells how
the ship sailed south-
ward with a good wind
and fair weather, till it
reached the Line.*

The sun came up upon the left, 25
Out of the sea came he!
And he shone bright, and on the right
Went down into the sea.

Higher and higher every day,
Till over the mast at noon—" 30
The Wedding-Guest here beat his breast,
For he heard the loud bassoon.

*The Wedding-Guest
heareth the bridal
music; but the Mariner
continueth his tale.*

The bride hath paced into the hall,
Red as a rose is she;
Nodding their heads before her goes 35
The merry minstrelsy.

The Wedding-Guest he beat his breast,
Yet he cannot choose but hear;
And thus spake on that ancient man,
The bright-eyed Mariner. 40

*The ship driven by a
storm toward the
south pole.*

"And now the storm-blast came, and he
Was tyrannous and strong:
He struck with his o'ertaking wings,
And chased us south along.

With sloping masts and dipping prow, 45
As who pursued with yell and blow
Still treads the shadow of his foe,
And forward bends his head,
The ship drove fast, loud roared the blast,
And southward aye we fled. 50

And now there came both mist and snow,
And it grew wondrous cold:
And ice, mast-high, came floating by,
As green as emerald.

*The land of ice, and
of fearful sounds
where no living thing
was to be seen.*

And through the drifts the snowy clifts 55
Did send a dismal sheen:
Nor shapes of men nor beast we ken— [4]
The ice was all between.

[3] *kirk* church   [4] *ken* discern

The ice was here, the ice was there,
The ice was all around: 60
It cracked and growled, and roared and
   howled,
Like noises in a swound! [5]

Till a great sea-bird,
called the Albatross,
came through the
snow-fog, and was re-
ceived with great joy
and hospitality.

At length did cross an Albatross,
Thorough the fog it came;
As if it had been a Christian soul,   65
We hailed it in God's name.

It ate the food it ne'er had eat,
And round and round it flew.
The ice did split with a thunder-fit;
The helmsman steered us through!   70

And lo! the Albatross
proveth a bird of good
omen, and followeth
the ship as it returned
northward through fog
and floating ice.

And a good south wind sprung up behind;
The Albatross did follow,
And every day, for food or play,
Came to the mariner's hollo!

In mist or cloud, on mast or shroud,[6]   75
It perched for vespers [7] nine;
Whiles all the night, through fog-smoke
   white,
Glimmered the white moon-shine."

The ancient Mariner
inhospitably killeth the
pious bird of good
omen.

"God save thee, ancient Mariner!
From the fiends, that plague thee thus!—   80
Why look'st thou so?"—"With my cross-bow
I shot the Albatross!"

PART 2

"The Sun now rose upon the right:
Out of the sea came he,
Still hid in mist, and on the left   85
Went down into the sea.

And the good south wind still blew behind,
But no sweet bird did follow,
Nor any day for food or play
Came to the mariner's hollo!   90

His shipmates cry out
against the ancient

And I had done a hellish thing,
And it would work 'em woe:

[5] *swound* swoon
[7] *vespers* evening

[6] *shroud* ropes on the side of a ship

*Mariner, for killing
the bird of good luck.*

For all averred, I had killed the bird
That made the breeze to blow.
Ah, wretch! said they, the bird to slay,   95
That made the breeze to blow!

*But when the fog
cleared off they justify
the same, and thus
make themselves ac-
complices in the crime.*

Nor dim nor red, like God's own head,
The glorious Sun uprist:
Then all averred, I had killed the bird
That brought the fog and mist.   100
'Twas right, said they, such birds to slay,
That bring the fog and mist.

*The fair breeze con-
tinues; the ship enters
the Pacific Ocean, and
sails northward, even
till it reaches the Line.*

The fair breeze blew, the white foam flew,
The furrow followed free;
We were the first that ever burst   105
Into that silent sea.

*The ship hath been
suddenly becalmed.*

Down dropt the breeze, the sails dropt
     down,
'Twas sad as sad could be;
And we did speak only to break
The silence of the sea!   110

All in a hot and copper sky,
The bloody Sun, at noon,
Right up above the mast did stand,
No bigger than the Moon.

Day after day, day after day,   115
We stuck, nor breath nor motion;
As idle as a painted ship
Upon a painted ocean.

*And the Albatross
begins to be avenged.*

Water, water, every where,
And all the boards did shrink;   120
Water, water, every where,
Nor any drop to drink.

The very deep did rot: O Christ!
That ever this should be!
Yea, slimy things did crawl with legs   125
Upon the slimy sea.

*A Spirit had followed
them; one of the in-
visible inhabitants of*

About, about, in reel and rout
The death-fires [8] danced at night;

[8] *death-fires* corpse-candles, here phosphorescent appearances on ship and
water

this planet, neither departed souls nor angels; concerning whom the learned Jew, Josephus, and the Platonic Constantinopolitan, Michael Psellus, may be consulted. They are very numerous, and there is no climate or element without one or more.

The shipmates, in their sore distress, would fain throw the whole guilt on the ancient Mariner: in sign whereof they hang the dead sea-bird round his neck.

The water, like a witch's oils,
Burnt green, and blue and white.   130

And some in dreams assured were
Of the Spirit that plagued us so;
Nine fathom deep he had followed us
From the land of mist and snow.

And every tongue, through utter drought,
Was withered at the root;   136
We could not speak, no more than if
We had been choked with soot.

Ah! well-a-day! what evil looks
Had I from old and young!   140
Instead of the cross, the Albatross
About my neck was hung."

PART 3

"There passed a weary time. Each throat
Was parched, and glazed each eye.
A weary time! a weary time!   145
How glazed each weary eye,
When looking westward, I beheld
A something in the sky.

The ancient Mariner beholdeth a sign in the element afar off.

At first it seemed a little speck,
And then it seemed a mist;   150
It moved and moved, and took at last
A certain shape, I wist.[9]

A speck, a mist, a shape, I wist!
And still it neared and neared:
As if it dodged a water-sprite,   155
It plunged and tacked and veered.

At its nearer approach, it seemeth him to be a ship; and at a dear ransom he freeth his speech from the bonds of thirst.

With throats unslaked, with black lips
    baked,
We could nor laugh nor wail;
Through utter drought all dumb we stood!
I bit my arm, I sucked the blood,   160
And cried, A sail! a sail!

[9] *wist* knew

With throats unslaked, with black lips
  baked,
Agape they heard me call:

A flash of joy;

Gramercy! [10] they for joy did grin,
And all at once their breath drew in,   165
As they were drinking all.

And horror follows.
For can it be a ship
that comes onward
without wind or tide?

See! see! (I cried) she tacks no more!
Hither to work us weal; [11]
Without a breeze, without a tide,
She steadies with upright keel!   170

The western wave was all aflame.
The day was well nigh done!
Almost upon the western wave
Rested the broad bright Sun;
When that strange shape drove suddenly
Betwixt us and the Sun.   176

It seemeth him but the
skeleton of a ship.

And straight the Sun was flecked with bars,
(Heaven's Mother send us grace!)
As if through a dungeon-grate he peered
With broad and burning face.   180

Alas! (thought I, and my heart beat loud)
How fast she nears and nears!
Are those her sails that glance in the Sun,
Like restless gossameres?

And its ribs are seen
as bars on the face of
the setting Sun.
The Spectre-Woman
and her Deathmate,
and no other on board
the skeleton-ship.
Like vessel, like crew!

Are those her ribs through which the Sun
Did peer, as through a grate?   186
And is that Woman all her crew?
Is that a Death? and are there two?
Is Death that woman's mate?

Her lips were red, her looks were free, 190
Her locks were yellow as gold:
Her skin was as white as leprosy,
The Night-mare Life-in-Death was she,
Who thicks man's blood with cold.

Death and Life-in-
Death have diced for
the ship's crew, and
she (the latter) win-

The naked hulk alongside came,   195
And the twain were casting dice;
'The game is done! I've won! I've won!'
Quoth she, and whistles thrice.

[10] *Gramercy* Mercy on us   [11] *weal* good

neth the ancient Mariner.
No twilight within the courts of the Sun.

The Sun's rim dips; the stars rush out:
At one stride comes the dark;　　200
With far-heard whisper, o'er the sea,
Off shot the spectre-bark.

At the rising of the Moon,

We listened and looked sideways up!
Fear at my heart, as at a cup,
My life-blood seemed to sip!　　205
The stars were dim, and thick the night,
The steersman's face by his lamp gleamed
　　white;
From the sails the dew did drip—
Till clomb [12] above the eastern bar
The horned Moon, with one bright star
Within the nether tip.　　211

One after another,

One after one, by the star-dogged Moon,
Too quick for groan or sigh,
Each turned his face with a ghastly pang,
And cursed me with his eye.　　215

His shipmates drop down dead.

Four times fifty living men,
(And I heard nor sigh nor groan)
With heavy thump, a lifeless lump,
They dropped down one by one.

But Life-in-Death begins her work on the ancient Mariner.

The souls did from their bodies fly,—　　220
They fled to bliss or woe!
And every soul, it passed me by
Like the whizz of my cross-bow!"

PART 4

The Wedding-Guest feareth that a Spirit is talking to him.

"I fear thee, ancient Mariner!
I fear thy skinny hand!　　225
And thou art long, and lank, and brown,
As is the ribbed sea-sand.

But the ancient Mariner assureth him of his bodily life, and proceedeth to relate his horrible penance.

I fear thee and thy glittering eye,
And thy skinny hand, so brown."—
"Fear not, fear not, thou Wedding-Guest!
This body dropt not down.　　231

Alone, alone, all, all alone,
Alone on a wide, wide sea!

[12] *clomb* climbed

And never a saint took pity on
My soul in agony.   235

He despiseth the
creatures of the calm.

The many men, so beautiful!
And they all dead did lie:
And a thousand thousand slimy things
Lived on; and so did I.

And envieth that they
should live, and so
many lie dead.

I looked upon the rotting sea,   240
And drew my eyes away;
I looked upon the rotting deck,
And there the dead men lay.

I looked to heaven, and tried to pray;
But or ever a prayer had gusht,   245
A wicked whisper came, and made
My heart as dry as dust.

I closed my lids, and kept them close,
And the balls like pulses beat;
For the sky and the sea, and the sea and the
    sky   250
Lay like a load on my weary eye,
And the dead were at my feet.

But the curse liveth
for him in the eye of
the dead men.

The cold sweat melted from their limbs,
Nor rot nor reek did they:
The look with which they looked on me   255
Had never passed away.

In his loneliness and
fixedness he yearneth
towards the journeying
Moon, and the stars
that still sojourn, yet
still move onward; and
every where the blue
sky belongs to them,
and is their appointed
rest, and their native
country and their own
natural homes, which
they enter unan-
nounced, as lords that
are certainly expected
and yet there is a
silent joy at their
arrival.

An orphan's curse would drag to hell
A spirit from on high;
But oh! more horrible than that
Is a curse in a dead man's eye!   260
Seven days, seven nights, I saw that curse,
And yet I could not die.

The moving Moon went up the sky,
And nowhere did abide:
Softly she was going up,   265
And a star or two beside—

Her beams bemocked the sultry main,
Like April hoar-frost spread;
But where the ship's huge shadow lay,
The charmèd water burnt alway   270
A still and awful red.

By the light of the
Moon he beholdeth
God's creatures of the
great calm.

Beyond the shadow of the ship,
I watched the water-snakes:
They moved in tracks of shining white,
And when they reared, the elfish [13] light 275
Fell off in hoary flakes.

Within the shadow of the ship
I watched their rich attire:
Blue, glossy green, and velvet black,
They coiled and swam; and every track 280
Was a flash of golden fire.

Their beauty and
their happiness.

O happy living things! no tongue
Their beauty might declare:
A spring of love gushed from my heart,

He blesseth them in
his heart.

And I blessed them unaware: 285
Sure my kind saint took pity on me,
And I blessed them unaware.

The spell begins to
break.

The selfsame moment I could pray;
And from my neck so free
The Albatross fell off, and sank 290
Like lead into the sea."

PART 5

"Oh sleep! it is a gentle thing,
Beloved from pole to pole!
To Mary Queen the praise be given!
She sent the gentle sleep from Heaven, 295
That slid into my soul.

By grace of the holy
Mother, the ancient
Mariner is refreshed
with rain.

The silly [14] buckets on the deck,
That had so long remained,
I dreamt that they were filled with dew;
And when I awoke, it rained. 300

My lips were wet, my throat was cold,
My garments all were dank;
Sure I had drunken in my dreams,
And still my body drank.

I moved, and could not feel my limbs: 305
I was so light—almost
I thought that I had died in sleep,
And was a blessed ghost.

[13] *elfish* spectral   [14] *silly* poor

He heareth sounds and seeth strange sights and commotions in the sky and the elements.

And soon I heard a roaring wind:
It did not come anear;   310
But with its sound it shook the sails,
That were so thin and sere.

The upper air burst into life!
And a hundred fire-flags sheen,[15]
To and fro they were hurried about!   315
And to and fro, and in and out,
The wan stars danced between.

And the coming wind did roar more loud,
And the sails did sigh like sedge;
And the rain poured down from one black
      cloud;   320
The Moon was at its edge.

The thick black cloud was cleft, and still
The Moon was at its side:
Like waters shot from some high crag,
The lightning fell with never a jag,   325
A river steep and wide.

The bodies of the ship's crew are inspired and the ship moves on;

The loud wind never reached the ship,
Yet now the ship moved on!
Beneath the lightning and the Moon
The dead men gave a groan.   330

They groaned, they stirred, they all uprose,
Nor spake, nor moved their eyes;
It had been strange, even in a dream,
To have seen those dead men rise.

The helmsman steered, the ship moved on;
Yet never a breeze up blew;   336
The mariners all 'gan work the ropes,
Where they were wont to do;
They raised their limbs like lifeless tools—
We were a ghastly crew.   340

The body of my brother's son
Stood by me, knee to knee:
The body and I pulled at one rope,
But he said nought to me."

[15] *sheen* gleamed

But not by the souls of the men, nor by demons of earth or middle air, but by a blessed troop of angelic spirits, sent down by the invocation of the guardian saint.

"I fear thee, ancient Mariner!"   345
"Be calm, thou Wedding-Guest!
'Twas not those souls that fled in pain,
Which to their corses [16] came again,
But a troop of spirits blest:

For when it dawned—they dropped their
    arms,   350
And clustered round the mast;
Sweet sounds rose slowly through their
    mouths,
And from their bodies passed.

Around, around, flew each sweet sound,
Then darted to the Sun;   355
Slowly the sounds came back again,
Now mixed, now one by one.

Sometimes a-dropping from the sky
I heard the sky-lark sing;
Sometimes all little birds that are,   360
How they seemed to fill the sea and air
With their sweet jargoning! [17]

And now 'twas like all instruments,
Now like a lonely flute;
And now it is an angel's song,   365
That makes the heavens be mute.

It ceased; yet still the sails made on
A pleasant noise till noon,
A noise like of a hidden brook
In the leafy month of June,   370
That to the sleeping woods all night
Singeth a quiet tune.

Till noon we quietly sailed on,
Yet never a breeze did breathe:
Slowly and smoothly went the ship,   375
Moved onward from beneath.

The lonesome Spirit from the south pole carries on the ship as far as the Line, in obedience to the an-

Under the keel nine fathom deep,
From the land of mist and snow,
The Spirit slid: and it was he
That made the ship to go.   380

[16] *corses* corpses   [17] *jargoning* twittering

gelic troop, but still requireth vengeance.

The sails at noon left off their tune,
And the ship stood still also.

The Sun, right up above the mast,
Had fixed her to the ocean:
But in a minute she 'gan stir,   385
With a short uneasy motion—
Backwards and forwards half her length
With a short uneasy motion.

Then like a pawing horse let go,
She made a sudden bound: 390
It flung the blood into my head,
And I fell down in a swound.

The Polar Spirit's fellow demons, the invisible inhabitants of the element, take part in his wrong; and two of them relate, one to the other, that penance long and heavy for the ancient Mariner hath been accorded to the Polar Spirit, who returneth southward.

How long in that same fit I lay,
I have not to declare;
But ere my living life returned,   395
I heard, and in my soul discerned,
Two voices in the air.

'Is it he?' quoth one, 'Is this the man?
By him who died on cross,
With his cruel bow he laid full low   400
The harmless Albatross.

The Spirit who bideth by himself
In the land of mist and snow,
He loved the bird that loved the man
Who shot him with his bow.'   405

The other was a softer voice,
As soft as honey-dew:
Quoth he, 'The man hath penance done,
And penance more will do.' "

PART 6

FIRST VOICE

" 'But tell me, tell me! speak again,   410
Thy soft response renewing—
What makes that ship drive on so fast?
What is the ocean doing?'

SECOND VOICE

'Still as a slave before his lord,
The ocean hath no blast;   415

His great bright eye most silently
Up to the Moon is cast—

If he may know which way to go;
For she guides him smooth or grim.
See, brother, see! how graciously   420
She looketh down on him.'

FIRST VOICE

The Mariner hath
been cast into a
trance; for the angelic
power causeth the ves-
sel to drive northward
faster than human life
could endure.

'But why drives on that ship so fast,
Without or wave or wind?'

SECOND VOICE

'The air is cut away before,
And closes from behind.   425

Fly, brother, fly! more high, more high!
Or we shall be belated:
For slow and slow that ship will go,
When the Mariner's trance is abated.'

The supernatural mo-
tion is retarded; the
Mariner awakes, and
his penance begins
anew.

I woke, and we were sailing on   430
As in a gentle weather:
'Twas night, calm night, the moon was
            high;
The dead men stood together.

All stood together on the deck,
For a charnel-dungeon fitter: 435
All fixed on me their stony eyes,
That in the Moon did glitter.

The pang, the curse, with which they died,
Had never passed away:
I could not draw my eyes from theirs,   440
Nor turn them up to pray.

The curse is finally
expiated.

And now this spell was snapt: once more
I viewed the ocean green,
And looked far forth, yet little saw
Of what had else been seen—   445

Like one, that on a lonesome road
Doth walk in fear and dread,
And having once turned round, walks on,
And turns no more his head;

Because he knows, a frightful fiend   450
Doth close behind him tread.

But soon there breathed a wind on me,
Nor sound nor motion made:
Its path was not upon the sea,
In ripple or in shade.   455

It raised my hair, it fanned my cheek
Like a meadow-gale of spring—
It mingled strangely with my fears,
Yet it felt like a welcoming.

Swiftly, swiftly flew the ship,   460
Yet she sailed softly too:
Sweetly, sweetly blew the breeze—
On me alone it blew.

And the ancient Mariner beholdeth his native country.

Oh! dream of joy! is this indeed
The light-house top I see?   465
Is this the hill? is this the kirk?
Is this mine own countree?

We drifted o'er the harbor-bar,
And I with sobs did pray—
O let me be awake, my God!   470
Or let me sleep alway.

The harbor-bay was clear as glass,
So smoothly it was strewn!
And on the bay the moonlight lay,
And the shadow of the Moon.   475

The rock shone bright, the kirk no less,
That stands above the rock:
The moonlight steeped in silentness
The steady weathercock.

And the bay was white with silent light   480
Till, rising from the same,

The angelic spirits leave the dead bodies,

Full many shapes, that shadows were,
In crimson colors came.

A little distance from the prow
Those crimson shadows were: 485
I turned my eyes upon the deck—
Oh, Christ! what saw I there!

Each corse lay flat, lifeless and flat,
And, by the holy rood! [18]

*And appear in their
own forms of light.*

A man all light, a seraph-man,[19]   490
On every corse there stood.

This seraph-band, each waved his hand:
It was a heavenly sight!
They stood as signals to the land,
Each one a lovely light;   495

This seraph-band, each waved his hand,
No voice did they impart—
No voice; but oh! the silence sank
Like music on my heart.

But soon I heard the dash of oars,   500
I heard the Pilot's cheer;
My heard was turned perforce away,
And I saw a boat appear.

The Pilot and the Pilot's boy,
I heard them coming fast: 505
Dear Lord in Heaven! it was a joy
The dead men could not blast.

I saw a third—I heard his voice:
It is the Hermit good!
He singeth loud his godly hymns   510
That he makes in the wood.
He'll shrieve [20] my soul, he'll wash away
The Albatross's blood."

PART 7

*The Hermit of the
wood,*

"This Hermit good lives in that wood
Which slopes down to the sea.   515
How loudly his sweet voice he rears!
He loves to talk with marineres
That come from a far countree.

He kneels at morn, and noon, and eve—
He hath a cushion plump: 520
It is the moss that wholly hides
The rotted old oak-stump.

[18] *rood* cross   [19] *seraph* angel
[20] *shrieve* shrive: hear confession and forgive

The skiff-boat neared: I heard them talk,
'Why, this is strange, I trow!
Where are those lights so many and fair,
That signal made but now?'   526

Approacheth the ship
with wonder.

'Strange, by my faith!' the Hermit said—
'And they answered not our cheer!
The planks looked warped! and see those
    sails,
How thin they are and sere!   530
I never saw aught like to them,
Unless perchance it were

Brown skeletons of leaves that lag
My forest-brook along;
When the ivy-tod [21] is heavy with snow,   535
And the owlet whoops to the wolf below,
That eats the she-wolf's young.'

'Dear Lord! it hath a fiendish look—
(The Pilot made reply)
I am a-feared'—'Push on, push on!'   540
Said the Hermit cheerily.

The boat came closer to the ship,
But I nor spake nor stirred;
The boat came close beneath the ship,
And straight a sound was heard.   545

The ship suddenly
sinketh.

Under the water it rumbled on,
Still louder and more dread:
It reached the ship, it split the bay;
The ship went down like lead.

The ancient Mariner
is saved in the Pilot's
boat.

Stunned by that loud and dreadful sound,
Which sky and ocean smote,   551
Like one that hath been seven days drowned
My body lay afloat;
But swift as dreams, myself I found
Within the Pilot's boat.   555

Upon the whirl, where sank the ship,
The boat spun round and round;
And all was still, save that the hill
Was telling of the sound.

[21] *tod* bush

I moved my lips—the Pilot shrieked   560
And fell down in a fit;
The holy Hermit raised his eyes,
And prayed where he did sit.

I took the oars: the Pilot's boy,
Who now doth crazy go,   565
Laughed loud and long, and all the while
His eyes went to and fro.
'Ha! ha!' quoth he, 'full plain I see,
The Devil knows how to row.'

And now, all in my own countree,   570
I stood on the firm land!
The Hermit stepped forth from the boat,
And scarcely he could stand.

The ancient Mariner
earnestly entreateth
the Hermit to shrieve
him; and the penance
of life falls on him.

'O shrieve me, shrieve me, holy man!'
The Hermit crossed his brow.   575
'Say quick,' quoth he, 'I bid thee say—
What manner of man art thou?'

Forthwith this frame of mine was wrenched
With a woful agony,
Which forced me to begin my tale;   580
And then it left me free.

And ever and anon
throughout his future
life an agony con-
straineth him to travel
from land to land;

Since then, at an uncertain hour,
That agony returns:
And till my ghastly tale is told,
This heart within me burns.   585

I pass, like night, from land to land;
I have strange power of speech;
That moment that his face I see,
I know the man that must hear me:
To him my tale I teach.   590

What loud uproar bursts from that door!
The wedding-guests are there:
But in the garden-bower the bride
And bride-maids singing are:
And hark the little vesper bell,   595
Which biddeth me to prayer!

O Wedding-Guest! this soul hath been
Alone on a wide, wide sea:

So lonely 'twas, that God himself
Scarce seemèd there to be.   600

Oh sweeter than the marriage-feast,
'Tis sweeter far to me,
To walk together to the kirk
With a goodly company!—

To walk together to the kirk,   605
And all together pray,
While each to his great Father bends,
Old men, and babes, and loving friends,
And youths and maidens gay!

And to teach, by his
own example, love and   Farewell, farewell! but this I tell   610
reverence to all things   To thee, thou Wedding-Guest!
that God made and   He prayeth well, who loveth well
loveth.   Both man and bird and beast.

He prayeth best, who loveth best
All things both great and small;   615
For the dear God who loveth us,
He made and loveth all."

The Mariner, whose eye is bright,
Whose beard with age is hoar,
Is gone: and now the Wedding-Guest   620
Turned from the bridegroom's door.

He went like one that hath been stunned,
And is of sense forlorn: [22]
A sadder and a wiser man,
He rose the morrow morn.   625

KUBLA KHAN: [1]

OR, A VISION IN A DREAM. A FRAGMENT

Coleridge has written:
In the summer of the year 1797 [1798], the Author, then in ill
health, had retired to a lonely farmhouse between Porlock and
Linton, on the Exmoor confines of Somerset and Devonshire. In
consequence of a slight indisposition, an anodyne had been pre-

---

[22] *forlorn* forsaken

[1] Critical comment on this poem appears on p. 422.

scribed, from the effects of which he fell asleep in his chair at the moment he was reading the following sentence, or words of the same substance, in *Purchas's Pilgrimage:*—"Here the Khan Kubla commanded a palace to be built, and a stately garden thereunto: and thus ten miles of fertile ground were inclosed with a wall." The Author continued for about three hours in a profound sleep, at least of the external senses, during which time he has the most vivid confidence that he could not have composed less than from two to three hundred lines; if that indeed can be called composition in which all the images rose up before him as *things,* with a parallel production of the correspondent expressions, without any sensation or consciousness of effort. On awaking he appeared to himself to have a distinct recollection of the whole, and taking his pen, ink, and paper, instantly and eagerly wrote down the lines that are here preserved. At this moment he was unfortunately called out by a person on business from Porlock, and detained by him above an hour, and on his return to his room, found, to his no small surprise and mortification, that though he still retained some vague and dim recollection of the general purport of his vision, yet, with the exception of some eight or ten scattered lines and images, all the rest had passed away like the images on the surface of a stream into which a stone had been cast, but, alas! without the after restoration of the latter.

> In Xanadu [2] did Kubla Khan [3]
> A stately pleasure-dome decree:
> Where Alph,[4] the sacred river, ran
> Through caverns measureless to man
>   Down to a sunless sea.   5
> So twice five miles of fertile ground
> With walls and towers were girdled round:
> And there were gardens bright with sinuous rills,
> Where blossomed many an incense-bearing tree;
> And here were forests ancient as the hills,   10
> Enfolding sunny spots of greenery.

[2] *Xanadu* region in China
[3] *Kubla Khan* Mongol emperor (1259–1294), founder of the Mongol dynasty in China
[4] *Alph* The following passage may refer to the legends of the river Alpheus in southern Greece. The god of the river pursued his love, the nymph Arethusa, until she was changed into a fountain by Diana. The river Alpheus was said to pass under the sea from Greece to Sicily until it joined the stream of Arethusa.

But oh! that deep romantic chasm which slanted
Down the green hill athwart a cedarn [5] cover!
A savage place! as holy and enchanted
As e'er beneath a waning moon was haunted   15
By woman wailing for her demon-lover!
And from this chasm, with ceaseless turmoil seething,
As if this earth in fast thick pants were breathing,
A mighty fountain momently was forced:
Amid whose swift half-intermitted burst   20
Huge fragments vaulted like rebounding hail,
Or chaffy grain beneath the thresher's flail:
And 'mid these dancing rocks at once and ever
It flung up momently the sacred river.
Five miles meandering with a mazy motion   25
Through wood and dale the sacred river ran,
Then reached the caverns measureless to man,
And sank in tumult to a lifeless ocean:
And 'mid this tumult Kubla heard from far
Ancestral voices prophesying war!   30
    The shadow of the dome of pleasure
    Floated midway on the waves;
    Where was heard the mingled measure
    From the fountain and the caves.
It was a miracle of rare device,   35
A sunny pleasure-dome with caves of ice!

    A damsel with a dulcimer [6]
    In a vision once I saw:
    It was an Abyssinian maid,
    And on her dulcimer she played,   40
    Singing of Mount Abora.[7]
    Could I revive within me
    Her symphony and song,
    To such a deep delight 'twould win me,
That with music loud and long,   45
I would build that dome in air,
That sunny dome! those caves of ice!
And all who heard should see them there,
And all should cry, Beware! Beware!
His flashing eyes, his floating hair!   50

[5] *cedarn* cedar
[6] *dulcimer* stringed instrument played with small hammers, a harp
[7] *Mount Abora* not identified. (Etymologically it suggests a place oracular,
prophetic, or mystical.)

Weave a circle round him thrice,
And close your eyes with holy dread,
For he on honey-dew hath fed,
And drunk the milk of Paradise.

CRITICISM

The following essays are included here to show two distinct and important approaches in criticism. E. M. W. Tillyard discusses *The Rime of the Ancient Mariner* as a poem with several layers of meaning, or significance. This recognition of the complexity of a major poem is useful not only for the reading of Coleridge's poem, but also to indicate what might be done for other poems. A reader-critic might consider what simultaneous "meanings" emerge in poems like Pope's *The Rape of the Lock,* Keats's "Ode on a Grecian Urn," or Browning's "The Bishop Orders His Tomb." A poem does not mean one thing alone. The essay on "Kubla Khan" first concentrates on the poem, but by extension says much that helps to define Romanticism, as the term is used to describe the work of the poets from Wordsworth to Keats. Structure, theme, and unity in "Kubla Khan" are clarified by seeing it as a representative Romantic poem.

The Rime of the Ancient Mariner 1798 [1]

E. M. W. TILLYARD

. . . first let me explain that I shall not try to criticise the poem [the *Ancient Mariner*] in the sense of conveying something of the total effect. It is a rich and complicated poem, and to put in words the total effect issuing from this complication would be at once surpassingly difficult and unnecessary for the humbler objects I have in view. All I seek to do is to enumerate some of the layers of significance that go to make up the whole.

First, it is an exciting story, imitated from the old ballads, drawing much of its material from old books of travel, enlivened by touches of realistic natural description, yet partly appealing to that part of our natures that delights in superstitions and in the supernatural. Secondly, in spite of the supernatural happen-

[1] Reprinted from E. M. W. Tillyard, *Five Poems* (London: Chatto & Windus, 1948) by permission of The Macmillan Company.

ings, of which no rational explanation is given, the main events of the story happen logically in a sequence of cause and effect. In such a sequence the moral motive naturally enters, and the question arises of what this amounts to. Late in his life Coleridge censured the presence of a motivating morality. In reply to an objection of Mrs Barbauld that the poem lacked a moral he answered that it had too much:

It ought to have had no more moral than the Arabian Nights' tale of the merchant's sitting down to eat dates by the side of a well, and throwing the shells aside, and lo! a genie starts up, and says he *must* kill the aforesaid merchant, *because* one of the date shells had, it seems, put out the eye of the genie's son. [*Table Talk,* May 31, 1830]

Probably Coleridge was stung to perversity by Mrs Barbauld's being so stupid, and did not mean what he said. In truth, the moral story, the punishment of a crime, is the core of the poem; each part ends with a reference to the crime, the killing of the albatross: remove the moral, and the poem collapses. Granted the moral, we must beware of narrowing it to the familiar modern doctrine of kindness to animals. If the albatross had been a crow or vulture or other bird of ill omen, there would have been no crime in shooting it; yet by humanitarian standards the act would have been just as bad. The reasons for not shooting the albatross were superstitious or at least primitive. By standards of superstition animals are good or bad. It is unlucky to kill the good; the bad (the toad, for instance) can be persecuted to any extent. The albatross was a good bird, and they "hailed it in God's name." It was also their guest, and in a primitive world treachery to a guest was a terrible crime. Coleridge's gloss sums the matter up: "The ancient Mariner inhospitably killeth the pious bird of good omen." Whether the act itself apart from its consequences can be motivated is a matter of opinion. Should we simply accept it as a piece of plot-mechanism, like Lear's resolution to divide his kingdom, or should we detect a reason? Certainly there is a very simple reason to hand. The act could be interpreted as the essential act of devilment, the act of pride, of the unbridled assertion of the self. It was what Satan did when he rebelled and what Defoe made Crusoe do when he thrice rejected God's offer of a virtuous middle way of life. Whatever the answer, we are suitably impressed by the enormity of the mariner's crime and readily accept the straits into which he falls.

The way he gets out of these straits is also motivated but with a richness that makes it difficult not to encroach here on other layers of the poem's meaning. One reason for his escape is the sheer fulfilment of a frightful penance: he issues out of his prison like a prisoner who has served his time, whether repentant or not. And this punitive motive corresponds well enough to the purely superstitious crime of killing a bird of good omen. But there is the further reason of his blessing the water-snakes. And this was an act of repentance, a moral reversal of his grossly self-regarding act of killing the albatross, a forgetfulness of self in recognising the beauty of something quite independent. The crime, however, is not expiated at once. One of the two voices in the air says there is more penance to do. It is the one defect in the poem's structure that this further penance hardly exists and that the final expiation in line 442 ("And now this spell was snapt . . .") comes in very casually. Having learnt to expect motivation, we are disappointed when it is lacking. Even if we assume that the penance is now really complete, we still miss a further act of repentance to correspond to the blessing of the water-snakes. Thenceforward everything is credible in its context. The crime has been such that we accept the mariner's final doom of having periodically to relive his old experience through recounting his tale.

I have spoken of the simple narrative interest and of the moral motivation together because the second helps the first along: a logical is more emphatic than a mere casual sequence. As Lowes says in his *Road to Xanadu* [p. 299]: "The sequence which follows the Mariner's initial act accomplishes two ends: it unifies and it 'credibilizes' the poem." But Lowes notices something more about the morality: its truth to the ordinary experience of life. He writes [p. 298]:

> The train of cause and consequence is more than a consolidating factor of the poem. It happens to be life, as every human being knows it. You do a foolish or an evil deed, and its results come home to you. And they are apt to fall on others too. You repent, and a load is lifted from your soul. But you have not thereby escaped your deed. You attain forgiveness, but cause and effect work on unmoved, and life to the end may be the continued reaping of the repented deed's results.

Though this is not how we think of the poem when we read it, we do ratify Lowes's words on reflection. And they are important, for they convey a part of the meaning that is too often forgotten. And it is precisely the blend of this sheer truth to human experience with the narrative power, the fantastic happenings and the brilliant pictures that makes the *Ancient Mariner* so rich and so surprising.

But the *Ancient Mariner* is more than a fascinating story with a moral. It may be that H. I'A. Fausset is right in seeing it as an allegory of Coleridge's own life: his strange mind, his terrors, his loquacity. The Mariner, repeating his tale, may well be Coleridge, "seeking relief throughout his life in endless monologues." But even if Fausset is right, he is indicating a very minor layer of the poem's meaning. What matters is not that Coleridge should be speaking for himself but that he should be speaking for many others. Miss Bodkin in her *Archetypal Patterns in Poetry* chooses the *Ancient Mariner* as one of the poems "the ground of whose appeal is most evidently the impression of the inner life," but she rightly does not confine the inner life to Coleridge's. And if, as I think we should, we take the Mariner's voyage as a mental one, it should figure the adventures not of Coleridge alone but of all mental voyagers.

Once we postulate an allegory we are beset with dangers, above all with the temptation to grow excited, to see too much, to mistake a simple picturesque detail for a complicated moral truth. I will try to keep to the more obvious and plausible significances.

The general drift of the poem in its mental action can readily be recognised by two passages from other poets: Webster,

> My soul like to a ship in a black storm
> Is driven I know not whither;

and Shelley,

> The breath whose might I have invoked in song
> Descends on me; my spirit's bark is driven
> Far from the shore, far from the trembling throng
> Whose sails were never to the tempest given;
> The massy earth and sphered skies are riven.
> I am borne darkly, fearfully, afar!

The sea-voyage, then, indicates spiritual *adventure,* as the ordinary journey or pilgrimage indicates the course of normal life. And it is not everyone who goes out of his way to seek adventure. There is a passage in Coleridge's prose [*Biographia Literaria,* xii.] that both says this and has its bearing on the *Ancient Mariner.*

The first range of hills, that encircles the scanty vale of human life, is the horizon for the majority of its inhabitants. On *its* ridges the common sun is born and departs. From *them* the stars rise, and touching *them* they vanish. By the many, even this range, the natural limit and bulwark of the vale, is but imperfectly known. Its higher ascents are too often hidden by mists and clouds from uncultivated swamps, which few have courage or curiosity to penetrate. To the multitude below these vapours appear, now as the dark haunts of terrific agents, on which none may intrude with impunity; and now all aglow, with colours not their own, they are gazed at as the splendid palaces of happiness and power. But in all ages there have been a few, who measuring and sounding the rivers of the vale at the feet of their furthest inaccessible falls have learned, that the sources must be far higher and far inward; a few, who even in the level streams have detected elements, which neither the vale itself nor the surrounding mountains contained or could supply. . . . It is the essential mark of the true philosopher to rest satisfied with no imperfect light, as long as the impossibility of attaining a fuller knowledge has not been demonstrated.

The Ancient Mariner and his ship represent the small but persisting class of mental adventurers who are not content with the appearances surrounding them but who attempt to get behind. (It may be added that though the class is small it stands for a universal impulse which is dormant in most minds and not absent from them.) Further, and here I recognise the danger of seeing too much, it is possible that the different degrees of nearness to normality represented in the poem do correspond to the apprehension of such degrees in actual life. The harbour-town, occurring in a narrative, is less real than the wedding-guest and the wedding but more so than the realms visited in the voyage; and these degrees of reality can hardly be without their effect.

Granted that the Mariner and his voyage signify the mental adventure of an unusually inquiring spirit, the outline of that adventure becomes tolerably clear, while it would be senseless to seek more than an outline. From the social point of view these spiritual adventurers are criminals: they disturb the existing order and they imply a criticism of the accepted round of life: they are self-appointed outcasts. The shooting of the albatross in the present context was an anti-social act: something that by everyday rules would not be done. And the avenging spirit takes the Mariner into a region and a situation the utter loneliness of which is both the logical consequence and the avengement of his revolt against society. This same region is one more version of that aridity that besets all isolated mental voyagers at one stage of their voyage. Other versions are Donne's conceit of himself in *A Nocturnal upon St Lucy's Day* as the quintessence of the primeval nothingness out of which God created the world; the emptiness experienced by the poet in Shelley's *Alastor*, who, when he awakes from his dreams, sees the "garish hills" and "vacant woods," while his "wan eyes"

> Gaze on the empty scene as vacantly
> As ocean's moon looks on the moon in heaven;

and the landscape in Browning's *Childe Roland*. The Mariner escapes from his isolation by the enlargement of his sympathies in the manner least expected and he is allowed to return to common life. And he does so as a changed man. He has repented of his isolation; his greatest satisfaction is to worship in company with his fellows of all ages. But he is still the marked man, the outcast, the Wandering Jew, the victim of his own thoughts. Further, although he has been judged by society, he has the reward of the courage that propels the mental adventurer: that of arresting and disturbing and teaching those who have had no such experiences. And this ambivalent criterion enriches the poem incalculably.

But there may be yet one more important layer of meaning; something so simple and fundamental that it extends beyond the rarer sphere of self-imposed mental adventure to the common inevitable workings of the human mind. Miss Bodkin sees in the *Ancient Mariner* a rendering of the pattern of rebirth [*Archetypal Patterns in Poetry*, Chap. II.], which is at once the theme of tragedy and a very law of human life: the process of renovation through destruction. This theme is certainly present. It was only through the destruction of his old state of mind that the Mariner was able to achieve the new, enlarged state of mind that could include the water-snakes in its sympathies. But the *Ancient Mariner* is unlike the most satisfying works that render the theme, for instance the *Oresteia* or *Lycidas*, in that the renovation

brought about is less powerful than the thing from whose destruction it has sprung. There is nothing to correspond to the
thrust of energy that ends *Lycidas* with

> To-morrow to fresh woods, and pastures new.

The Ancient Mariner has been born again into a ghostly existence, not rejuvenated. And the haunting terror of the destructive experience remains the dominant theme of the poem:

> O Wedding-Guest! this soul hath been
> Alone on a wide wide sea.

The Romantic Unity of "Kubla Khan" [1]

RICHARD HARTER FOGLE

In his valuable book on *Keats' Craftsmanship,* M. R. Ridley
has cited *Kubla Khan* along with the "magic casements" passage
of Keats's "Nightingale" ode as the very essence of "the distilled
sorceries of Romanticism," and his statement is more or less
typical. This concept of "romantic magic" has its sanction and
is by no means to be discarded as pointless. In practice, however, it has had the unfortunate effect of discouraging critical
analysis; and it likewise plays into the hands of those of our
contemporaries who incline to look upon Romantic poetry as
a kind of moonlit mist, which dissolves at the touch of reality
and reason.

The fascinating but uncritical study of Lowes, with its emphasis upon the irrational and the unconscious, and its untiring
quest for sources, has had an equally unfortunate and discouraging influence. Only recently, with the work of Elisabeth
Schneider and others who have pointed the way, has it become
possible to think of *Kubla Khan* as other than a kind of magnificent freak and to treat it as an intelligible poem which lies
open to critical examination. And the influence of Lowes still
imposes upon the student the tyranny of source study. He has
opened so wide a field for speculation that scholars are still
inclined rather to revise or enlarge his conclusions than to
proceed to the task of the critic.

The study of possible sources for Coleridge's imagery is valu-

[1] Reprinted from *College English,* 13 (October, 1951)

able. Whatever we can get, in fact, in the way of information on the genesis and the circumstances of a poem is useful. Such information, however, can be dangerous if we exaggerate its function and substitute it for the poem itself. It is background, not foreground. To discover, for instance, a parallel between a passage in Plato and a poem of Coleridge is valuable when it adds to the poem's potential meaning; but the discovery is misused if Plato is permitted to determine what Coleridge is talking about. The proper place to study Coleridge's poetry is ultimately *The Poetical Works of Samuel Taylor Coleridge.*

By implication the foregoing incautious remarks bind this essay to a twofold effort: first, to give such an account of *Kubla Khan*'s "distilled sorceries" and "romantic magic" as will reconcile them with the rational and discursive processes of criticism; and, second, to account for them within the bounds of the poem. As to the first, no one need fear that our "romantic magic" will be dispelled, such a Pyrrhic victory as that lying quite beyond either the powers or the wishes of the present writer. As to the second, I hope for a generously loose construction as to what the bounds of the poem include.

A number of contentions must precede the specific examination of *Kubla Khan*. First, the immediate literary effect intended and obtained in it by Coleridge is pleasure—a pleasure which derives from that very "Romantic sorcery" of which we have spoken. This pleasure, as Pope says of Nature, is "the source, and end, and test" of poetic art. It is not necessary, of course, to claim that Coleridge has found the only means of attaining it. Second, this pleasure is in no way incompatible with even the profoundest meaning; is in fact inseparable from meaning. The basic criterion for poetry is in the broadest sense human interest: a poem should deal with a human situation of universal interest treated with sympathy, judgment, and insight. This human significance is not to be regarded as a monopoly of the classical or neoclassical humanist but belongs to the Romantic poet as well. Third, *Kubla Khan* embodies the Coleridgean doctrine of "the reconciliation of opposites." On this point be it added that the authority of the poem is at least equal to prose definitions of these doctrines; it is the living word, as opposed to the skeleton of abstract definition. Neither, however, is fully intelligible without the other. Finally, *Kubla Khan* is in the most essential sense a completed work, in that it symbolizes and comprehends the basic Romantic dilemma, a crucial problem of art.

To avoid misunderstanding, let us preface interpretation of the poem with a self-evident but necessary distinction. *Kubla Khan* is "fanciful" rather than "realistic"; the simplest, most basic pleasure it provides stems rather from its distance from actuality than from any verisimilitude or skilful imitation of matter of fact. It belongs in the category of what Dryden called "the fairy way of poetry," and consideration of its meaning must be controlled by our understanding of this limitation. With this conceded, however, we can still demonstrate the immensely important fact of its basic humanity and significance. The setting of *Kubla Khan* is pleasurable and well removed from any contact with the sharp edges of the actual; yet within its enchanted garden we shall find problems of the weightiest import. Thus the central situation of the poem is the spacious pleasure-garden of Kubla:

> So twice five miles of fertile ground
> With walls and towers were girdled round. . . .

And the poem itself is embodied in this garden, various, extensive, yet inclosed from the world without. But our estimate of the situation is incomplete if it ignores the implications of the towered walls. A reality against which we must fortify ourselves is hardly a reality which we can ignore. We must then extend our definition to include this implication and consider the core of the poem to reside in an opposition or stress between the garden, artificial and finite, and the indefinite, inchoate, and possibly turbulent outside world.

Since, however, what lies beyond the walls is only implied, not imaged, we must pass to whatever relationships exist inside them.

> In Xanadu did Kubla Khan
> A stately pleasure-dome decree. . . .

This pleasure-dome is the focal point of the physical setting and is correspondingly important. Within the bounds of the encircled garden, the pleasure-dome and the river are the opposites to be reconciled. The pleasure-dome is associated with Man, as Kubla is an emblem of Man; it figures his desire for pleasure and safety;

it stands for strictly human and finite values. The image of the dome suggests agreeable sensations of roundedness and smoothness; the creation of Man, its quasi-geometrical shape is simpler than the forms of Nature which surround it, yet blends with them. This dome, however, also evokes the religious—it is in some sort a temple, if only to the mere mortal Kubla Khan. And thus there is also a blending or interfusion with its opposite, the sacred river Alph.

The pleasure-dome is the chosen refuge of Kubla the mighty, the emperor whose every whim is law, who would have temptations toward *hubris*. It is the center of his retreat in his haughty withdrawal from a world unworthy of him. It is above and beyond Nature, a "miracle of rare device" in which Man transcends and circumvents mere natural processes. It stands amid an enormous garden in which a considerable segment of wild nature is isolated and imprisoned for the delight of the human Kubla.

> And there were gardens bright with sinuous rills,
> Where blossomed many an incense-bearing tree;
> And here were forests ancient as the hills,
> Enfolding sunny spots of greenery.

This description hints, however, that Nature here is an uneasy prisoner, or perhaps a prisoner who is bounded only during her own pleasure. The "forests ancient" suggest an existence unknown to man and uncoerced by human power, whose sway over it is temporary and precarious. It is a force and being unlike Man, busy about its own purposes and, like the serpent, inscrutable in the labyrinthine wanderings of the "sinuous rills" of the gardens.

Here one may affirm that this setting illustrates a typical Romantic conception of "the reconciliation of opposites" by means of a concrete, visual scene. By a process of shading and gradation in light and dark, in garden and forest, oppositions become blended, interfused, and unified; and this visual unification extends to the feelings and ideas which the scene evokes. This is the Romantic "picturesque," more fully to be seen in the landscape of Wordsworth's "Lines . . . above Tintern Abbey," with its complex blending of sky and valley, of Man and Nature, objectified in blending and gradation of color and form. In *Kubla Khan* the effect permits us simultaneously and with no sense of paradox or jar to receive the gardens as the elaborate plaything of a great potentate, the emblem of his pride, exclusiveness, and power, and also as an ironic commentary upon the impossibility of any real ownership of Nature.

These oppositions, however, are only a subtheme or prelude. The river is the true exemplar of nonhuman forces, subhuman and superhuman alike. Even the "deep romantic chasm" of its rising is incompatible with the order of Kubla's pleasure-grounds. It "slants athwart"; it cuts across the pattern. The simile of the "woman wailing for her demon-lover" invests it with the supernatural, the *Arabian Nights* wonder and fear of the jinni, beings unfriendly to man and yet obscurely connected with him.

Of the river itself most noticeable is the brevity of its surface course in relation to the hidden potentialities of its subterranean flowing:

> Five miles meandering with a mazy motion
> Through wood and dale the sacred river ran,
> Then reached the caverns measureless to man
> And sank in tumult to a lifeless ocean. . . .

Treated as a whole and in its relationship with the dome and the pleasure-grounds, the river is the primordial and the irrational, whatever lies beyond the control of the rational and conscious mind. The power of the source, vividly imaged in the dancing rocks—

> And from this chasm, with ceaseless turmoil seething
> As if this earth in fast thick pants were breathing,
> A mighty fountain momently was forced
> Amid whose swift half-intermitted burst
> Huge fragments vaulted like rebounding hail,
> Or chaffy grain beneath the thresher's flail:
> And 'mid these dancing rocks at once and ever
> It flung up momently the sacred river . . .

is a power beyond mortal man, even beyond Kubla Khan. This source is creation and birth, a force and urge at once frenetic and turbulent and also rhythmical and regular. At the mouth is death, icy and lifeless, where Alph in tumult returns to the underground. As with the source, powers unknown and uncontrollable are at work, descending at last to quiescence. Here are potentialities not of death absolutely but relative to what can be imagined and experienced.

Thus the opposition between river and dome. But here we must shift our emphasis, as previously with the pleasure-grounds themselves, more fully to Alph. The river is human life, past, present, and future, birth, life, and death. For five miles it runs upon the surface, consents, "meandering with a mazy motion," to harmonize with the order of Kubla's estate, to yield to his power. It is like Bede's famous bird which flies in a moment through the warm hall, swiftly proceeding from unknown birth to unknown death. And Kubla in his pleasure-dome is Man, living in his special cosmos of palace and garden, but hearing

> . . . the mingled measure
> From the fountain and the caves. . . .

Impulses unaccountable, creative and deadly alike, comprehending more of life than the reason can grasp. It is amid the tumult that Kubla hears the ominous prophecy of war, and this from the dying, the caves of ice. The poem as narrative can go no further than this, for the destruction is implied of Kubla's elaborate and artificial escape. The complex order and equilibrium of his existence are overset by the mere hint. This statement implies, of course, that the pattern must not within the poem be broken and that Kubla is never to emerge from his walled pleasure-grounds.

Yet in an important sense the pattern *is* broken in that Coleridge continues the lyric but abandons the story. Suddenly the imagery shifts to the "damsel with a dulcimer." This damsel, the Abyssinian maid, is most simply comparable to the muse invoked by the classical poet. She has, as has been suggested, a relation to Milton's heavenly muse Urania, as the stimulating speculations about the source of "Mount Abora" indicate. It is valuable to compare her also, as does Miss Schneider, to Platonic inspiration, the *furor poeticus* of the bard. Appropriately, however, to Coleridge's Romanticism and to the special context of *Kubla Khan,* she is wild and remote, with the glamour and terror of a far-off, mysterious land, marvelous, inaccessible, yet rich with the significant associations of literature. So Keats in a lyric much akin to *Kubla Khan:*

> I saw parched Abyssinia rouse and sing
> To the silver cymbals' ring!
> I saw the whelming vintage hotly pierce
> Old Tartary the fierce!—

The damsel is as well the ideal singer, the archetypal poet. The transmission of her song, if transmission there could be, would be like the conception of imitation in Longinus, where the divine fire passes from poet to poet, and Plato emulates Homer in the beneficent rivalry of genius. But Coleridge is modest, with the clear sense that the song can never be equaled:

> Could I revive within me
> Her symphony and song,
> To such a deep delight 'twould win me
> That with music loud and long
> I would build that dome in air. . . .

The phrase "deep delight" carries us into the problem of pleasure, more especially into the problem of the pleasure which the particular poem *Kubla Khan* should provide. This delight is for Coleridge as well as Wordsworth the prerequisite of poetic creation, the imaginative joy and effluence described in "Dejection: An Ode." But here it is also an effect peculiar to the poem itself: a kind of magic, an apparently naïve delight in the presentation of wonders, and in gorgeous images evoked in imagination in the sort of pleasure suggested by the classic ancient accounts of Plato, Aristotle, and Longinus.

This pleasure is also partly from variety and fulness—wonders which satisfy, as for a child at a carnival. These qualities are embodied not only in the imagery but in fulness and variety of melodic movement in the verse, which would bear more thorough discussion than can be given here. The word "symphony" in line 43 is not lightly or carelessly used. The delight is rounded and completed by the dark tinge of the "deep romantic chasm," the turbulent power of the river, the doom of the ancestral voices, and lastly by the mingling of dread and enchantment in the closing lines, where the holiness of the inspired poet is in a sense unholy too, an affair as it were of the infernal gods as much as the clear deity of Apollo.

The interpretation in earlier pages has attempted to demonstrate an essential profundity and universality in the theme of *Kubla Khan*. It remains to assert that pleasure is in no way incompatible with significance. In some contemporary poetry and criticism there seems implicit the notion that it is somehow dishonest and shameful to please, an attitude which has tellingly been termed "the new Puritanism." One feels inclined to renew the old question, "Dost thou think, because thou art virtuous, there shall be no more cakes and ale?" But in *Kubla Khan,* as probably in all good Romantic poetry, the pleasure which draws us within the poem is also inseparable from its full meaning. Imaginative delight in the wonders of the pleasure-ground is indispensable to the sense of their opposite. Fully to appreciate the theme's potentialities, we must be beguiled into believing momentarily in the permanency of the impermanent, the possibility of the impossible. The fullest meaning, a synthesis of antitheses, calls for feeling and imagination at full stretch, reconciled with intellectual scope and understanding. And pleasure, one may claim, is the basis and beginning of the process.

Our final contention re-emphasizes the depth and significance of *Kubla Khan.* It is in the truest sense a completed work, in that it symbolizes and comprehends the crucial Romantic dilemma. In a more obvious sense it is clearly unfinished: as a narrative it barely commences, and it shifts abruptly with the Abyssinian maid from objective to subjective. Considered as lyric, however, it is self-contained and whole. The Romantic poet as idealist and monist strives to include within his cosmos both actual and ideal, as in Coleridge, Wordsworth, Shelley, even Byron, and to some extent Keats. His attempt, however, coexists with his consciousness that he seeks the unattainable; the ideal can never be fully actualized. Thus in good Romantic poetry there is a continuous tension, compacted of the sense of the immense potentialities of his theme set off against the knowledge that they can only partially be realized. This tension and conflict can be reconciled and rendered valuable partly by the poet's own belief in the value of the attempt itself. The poet excels himself as it were by force; he is stimulated to creation rather than falling into despair. Above all, he benefits by understanding and accepting his dilemma even while trying to rise above it nonetheless.

And this is eminently the case with *Kubla Khan.* Coleridge provides a scene and experience too fine for common nature's daily food. With exquisite judgment he forbears the attempt to explain what can only be hinted and dramatizes instead what is lost in the very act of relinquishing it. But amid the master-artist's skilful manipulation of interest and suspense, his suggestions of "more than meets the eye," is the human interest, the complexity and spacious grasp, without which the rest would be nothing, could not separately exist. Properly understood, Romantic poetry is never a cheat, although it often labors under the disadvantage of being extremely agreeable.

JOHN KEATS

[1795-1821]

KEATS grew up in towns around London, attending school at
Enfield. His father, a livery stable manager, died in 1804, his
mother in 1810. The next year Keats was apprenticed to a surgeon
in Edmonton, but he was already deep in his own study of poetry.
Four years later, at twenty years of age, he became a medical
student at Guy's and St. Thomas's Hospitals in London, receiving his apothecary's certificate in 1816. By this time Keats was
determined to give full time to the writing of poetry; his first
book, *Poems,* was published in 1817. He had rapidly gained a
circle of close friends who believed in his genius—Leigh Hunt,
Robert Haydon, William Hazlitt, and many others. He also knew
Wordsworth, Coleridge, and Shelley. By the end of 1818, Keats
had had a number of disappointments. Both his 1817 volume and
Endymion (1818) had been the objects of scurrilous attacks from
Edinburgh magazines (partly for political and journalistic reasons). His brother George and his wife moved to America; and
his youngest brother, Thomas, died of tuberculosis. Yet in 1819
Keats wrote most of his greatest poetry ("The Eve of St. Agnes,"
"La Belle Dame sans Merci," the odes). He was then secretly engaged to Fanny Brawne, but his own illness was plainly upon
him by early 1820, and marriage became impossible. After the
publication of his final volume, *Lamia, Isabella, The Eve of St.
Agnes and Other Poems,* his friends sent him to Italy, accompanied by Joseph Severn, hoping that he might be cured. But in
1821, a few months past his twenty-fifth birthday, Keats died of
tuberculosis in Rome and was buried there in the Protestant
Cemetery. His letters, some of the greatest we have from any
writer, give a brilliant and moving picture of his searching mind,

his high aims and hard work, his engaging humanity. And his poetry is the rich and permanent fulfillment of what in his brief life may have seemed transient and incomplete.

Introductory Readings

EDITION: *The Poetical Works,* ed. H. W. Garrod (1939). LETTERS: *The Letters of John Keats,* 1814–1821, ed. Hyder E. Rollins, 2 vols. (1958). BIOGRAPHY: Sidney Colvin, *John Keats* (1917, 1925); Amy Lowell, *John Keats,* 2 vols. (1925); Dorothy Hewlett, *A Life of John Keats* (rev. ed., 1950). CRITICISM: Clarence D. Thorpe, *The Mind of John Keats* (1926); Walter J. Bate, *The Stylistic Development of Keats* (1945); Earl Wasserman, *The Finer Tone: Keats' Major Poems* (1953); John Middleton Murry, *Keats* (rev. ed., 1955); E. C. Pettet, *On the Poetry of Keats* (1957); Bernice Slote, *Keats and the Dramatic Principle* (1958); Bernard Blackstone, *The Consecrated Urn* (1959). See also, *The Keats Circle,* ed. Hyder E. Rollins, 2 vols. (1948).

ON FIRST LOOKING INTO CHAPMAN'S HOMER [1]

Much have I travell'd in the realms of gold,
  And many goodly states and kingdoms seen;
  Round many western islands have I been
Which bards in fealty [2] to Apollo [3] hold.
Oft of one wide expanse had I been told   5
  That deep-brow'd Homer ruled as his demesne; [4]
  Yet did I never breathe its pure serene
Till I heard Chapman [5] speak out loud and bold:
Then felt I like some watcher of the skies
  When a new planet swims into his ken; [6]   10
Or like stout Cortez [7] when with eagle eyes
  He star'd at the Pacific—and all his men
Look'd at each other with a wild surmise—
  Silent, upon a peak in Darien.[8]

[1] Critical comment on this poem appears on p. 461.
[2] *fealty* token or oath of faithfulness
[3] *Apollo* god of the sun, music, poetry   [4] *demesne* possession
[5] *Chapman* George Chapman (1559–1634) translated the *Iliad* and the *Odyssey* and other Homeric poems.
[6] *ken* sight
[7] *Cortez* See pp. 464–467 for a discussion of Keats's use of Cortez here.
[8] *Darien* a mountainous region of central Panama

ON THE GRASSHOPPER AND CRICKET

The poetry of earth is never dead:
  When all the birds are faint with the hot sun,
  And hide in cooling trees, a voice will run
From hedge to hedge about the new-mown mead;
That is the Grasshopper's—he takes the lead   5
  In summer luxury, [1]—he has never done
  With his delights; for when tired out with fun
He rests at ease beneath some pleasant weed.
The poetry of earth is ceasing never:
  On a lone winter evening, when the frost   10
    Has wrought a silence, from the stove there shrills
The Cricket's song, in warmth increasing ever,
  And seems to one in drowsiness half lost,
    The Grasshopper's among some grassy hills.

ON SEEING THE ELGIN MARBLES [1]

My spirit is too weak—mortality
  Weighs heavily on me like unwilling sleep,
  And each imagin'd pinnacle and steep
Of godlike hardship tells me I must die
Like a sick Eagle looking at the sky.   5
  Yet 'tis a gentle luxury to weep
  That I have not the cloudy winds to keep,
Fresh for the opening of the morning's eye.
Such dim-conceived glories of the brain
  Bring round the heart an indescribable feud;   10
So do these wonders a most dizzy pain,
  That mingles Grecian grandeur with the rude
Wasting of old Time—with a billowy main—
  A sun—a shadow of a magnitude.

ON THE SEA

It keeps eternal whisperings around
  Desolate shores, and with its mighty swell
  Gluts twice ten thousand Caverns, till the spell

[1] *luxury* intense enjoyment

[1] *Elgin Marbles* sculptured marble friezes and figures from the Parthenon in Athens, brought to England by Lord Elgin and placed in the British Museum in 1816

Of Hecate leaves them their old shadowy sound.
Often 'tis in such gentle temper found,   5
    That scarcely will the very smallest shell
    Be mov'd for days from where it sometime fell,
When last the winds of Heaven were unbound.
Oh ye! who have your eye-balls vex'd and tir'd,
    Feast them upon the wideness of the Sea;   10
        Oh ye! whose ears are dinn'd with uproar rude,
    Or fed too much with cloying melody—
        Sit ye near some old Cavern's Mouth and brood,
Until ye start, as if the sea-nymphs quir'd!

TO MRS. REYNOLDS'S CAT

Cat! who has pass'd thy grand climacteric,
    How many mice and rats hast in thy days
    Destroy'd?—How many tit bits stolen? Gaze
With those bright languid segments green, and prick
Those velvet ears—but pr'ythee do not stick   5
    Thy latent talons in me—and upraise
    Thy gentle mew—and tell me all thy frays
Of fish and mice, and rats and tender chick.
Nay, look not down, nor lick thy dainty wrists—
    For all the wheezy asthma,—and for all   10
    Thy tail's tip is nick'd off—and though the fists
    Of many a maid have given thee many a maul,
Still is that fur as soft as when the lists
    In youth thou enter'dst on glass-bottled wall.

ON SITTING DOWN TO READ *KING LEAR*
ONCE AGAIN

O golden-tongued Romance, with serene lute!
    Fair plumed Syren, Queen of far-away!
    Leave melodizing on this wintry day,
Shut up thine olden pages, and be mute:
Adieu! for, once again, the fierce dispute,   5
    Betwixt damnation and impassion'd clay
    Must I burn through; once more humbly assay [1]
The bitter-sweet of this Shakespearian fruit:

[1] *assay* test. A special meaning is "to try by tasting" (Oxford English Dictionary).

Chief Poet! and ye clouds of Albion,
   Begetters of our deep eternal theme! 10
When through the old oak Forest I am gone,
   Let me not wander in a barren dream,
But, when I am consumed in the fire,
Give me new Phœnix wings to fly at my desire.

WHEN I HAVE FEARS

When I have fears that I may cease to be
   Before my pen has glean'd my teeming brain,
Before high-pilèd books, in charact'ry, [1]
   Hold like rich garners [2] the full-ripen'd grain;
When I behold, upon the night's starr'd face, 5
   Huge cloudy symbols of a high romance,
And think that I may never live to trace
   Their shadows, with the magic hand of chance;
And when I feel, fair creature of an hour,
   That I shall never look upon thee more, 10
Never have relish in the faery power
   Of unreflecting love!—then on the shore
Of the wide world I stand alone, and think
Till love and fame to nothingness do sink.

LINES ON THE MERMAID TAVERN

   Souls of Poets dead and gone,
   What Elysium [1] have ye known,
   Happy field or mossy cavern,
   Choicer than the Mermaid Tavern? [2]
   Have ye tippled drink more fine 5
   Than mine host's Canary wine? [3]
   Or are fruits of Paradise
   Sweeter than those dainty pies
   Of venison? O generous food!
   Drest as though bold Robin Hood 10
   Would, with his maid Marian,
   Sup and bowse [4] from horn and can.

[1] *charact'ry* writing, language   [2] *garners* granaries

[1] *Elysium* Paradise
[2] *Mermaid Tavern* a celebrated London tavern frequented by the Elizabethan dramatists
[3] *Canary wine* made in the Canary Islands, similar to madeira
[4] *bowse* drink

I have heard that on a day
Mine host's sign-board flew away,
Nobody knew whither, till   15
An astrologer's old quill
To a sheepskin gave the story,
Said he saw you in your glory,
Underneath a new old sign
Sipping beverage divine,   20
And pledging with contented smack
The Mermaid in the Zodiac.

    Souls of Poets dead and gone,
What Elysium have ye known,
Happy field or mossy cavern,   25
Choicer than the Mermaid Tavern?

WHAT THE THRUSH SAID [1]

LINES FROM A LETTER TO JOHN HAMILTON REYNOLDS

O thou whose face hath felt the Winter's wind,
  Whose eye has seen the snow-clouds hung in mist,
  And the black elm tops 'mong the freezing stars,
To thee the spring will be a harvest-time.
O thou, whose only book has been the light   5
  Of supreme darkness which thou feddest on
Night after night when Phœbus was away,
  To thee the Spring shall be a triple morn.
O fret not after knowledge—I have none,
  And yet my song comes native with the warmth.   10
O fret not after knowledge—I have none,
  And yet the Evening listens. He who saddens
At thought of idleness cannot be idle,
And he's awake who thinks himself asleep.

A SONG ABOUT MYSELF

LINES FROM A LETTER TO FANNY KEATS

IV

There was a naughty Boy,
  And a naughty Boy was he,

[1] The thrush is speaking. Written in a letter to John Hamilton Reynolds
(Febraury 19, 1818), this poem is preceded by the sentence, "I have not read

He ran away to Scotland
  The people for to see—
    Then he found   5
    That the ground
    Was as hard,
    That a yard
    Was as long,
    That a song   10
    Was as merry,
    That a cherry
    Was as red—
    That lead
    Was as weighty,   15
    That fourscore
    Was as eighty,
    That a door
    Was as wooden
    As in England—   20
  So he stood in his shoes
  And he wonder'd,
    He wonder'd,
  He stood in his
    Shoes and he wonder'd.   25

WHERE'S THE POET?

Where's the Poet? show him! show him,
Muses nine! that I may know him!
'Tis the man who with a man
  Is an equal, be he King,
Or poorest of the beggar-clan,   5
  Or any other wondrous thing
A man may be 'twixt ape and Plato;
  'Tis the man who with a bird,
Wren or Eagle, finds his way to
  All its instincts; he hath heard   10
The Lion's roaring, and can tell
  What his horny throat expresseth,
And to him the Tiger's yell
  Comes articulate and presseth
  On his ear like mother-tongue.   15

---

any Book—the Morning said I was right—I had no idea but of the Morning, and the Thrush said I was right, seeming to say. . . ."

THE EVE OF ST. AGNES

I

St. Agnes' Eve [1]—Ah, bitter chill it was!
The owl, for all his feathers, was a-cold;
The hare limp'd trembling through the frozen grass,
And silent was the flock in woolly fold:
Numb were the Beadsman's [2] fingers, while he told   5
His rosary, and while his frosted breath,
Like pious incense from a censer old,
Seem'd taking flight for heaven, without a death,
Past the sweet Virgin's picture, while his prayer he saith.

II

His prayer he saith, this patient, holy man;   10
Then takes his lamp, and riseth from his knees,
And back returneth, meagre, barefoot, wan,
Along the chapel aisle by slow degrees:
The sculptur'd dead, on each side, seem to freeze,
Emprison'd in black, purgatorial rails: 15
Knights, ladies, praying in dumb orat'ries,[3]
He passeth by; and his weak spirit fails
To think how they may ache in icy hoods and mails.

III

Northward he turneth through a little door,
And scarce three steps, ere Music's golden tongue   20
Flatter'd to tears this aged man and poor;
But no—already had his deathbell rung:
The joys of all his life were said and sung:
His was harsh penance on St. Agnes' Eve:
Another way he went, and soon among   25
Rough ashes sat he for his soul's reprieve,
And all night kept awake, for sinners' sake to grieve.

IV

That ancient Beadsman heard the prelude soft;
And so it chanc'd, for many a door was wide,
From hurry to and fro. Soon, up aloft,   30
The silver, snarling trumpets 'gan to chide:

[1] *St. Agnes' Eve* January 20   [2] *Beadsman* one hired to pray for others
[3] *orat'ries* small chapels

The level chambers, ready with their pride,
Were glowing to receive a thousand guests:
The carved angels, ever eager-eyed,
Star'd, where upon their heads the cornice rests, 35
With hair blown back, and wings put cross-wise on their breasts.

V

At length burst in the argent [4] revelry,
With plume, tiara, and all rich array,
Numerous as shadows haunting fairily
The brain, new stuff'd, in youth, with triumphs gay 40
Of old romance. These let us wish away,
And turn, sole-thoughted, to one Lady there,
Whose heart had brooded, all that wintry day,
On love, and wing'd St. Agnes' saintly care,
As she had heard old dames full many times declare. 45

VI

They told her how, upon St. Agnes' Eve,
Young virgins might have visions of delight,
And soft adorings from their loves receive
Upon the honey'd middle of the night,
If ceremonies due they did aright; 50
As, supperless to bed they must retire,
And couch supine their beauties, lilly white;
Nor look behind, nor sideways, but require
Of Heaven with upward eyes for all that they desire.

VII

Full of this whim was thoughtful Madeline: 55
The music, yearning like a God in pain,
She scarcely heard: her maiden eyes divine,
Fix'd on the floor, saw many a sweeping train
Pass by—she heeded not at all: in vain
Came many a tiptoe, amorous cavalier, 60
And back retir'd; not cool'd by high disdain,
But she saw not: her heart was otherwhere:
She sigh'd for Agnes' dreams, the sweetest of the year.

VIII

She danc'd along with vague, regardless eyes,
Anxious her lips, her breathing quick and short: 65
The hallow'd hour was near at hand: she sighs

[4] *argent* silver

Amid the timbrels,[5] and the throng'd resort
Of whisperers in anger, or in sport;
'Mid looks of love, defiance, hate, and scorn,
Hoodwink'd with faery fancy; all amort,[6]   70
Save to St. Agnes and her lambs unshorn,
And all the bliss to be before to-morrow morn.

IX

So, purposing each moment to retire,
She linger'd still. Meantime, across the moors,
Had come young Porphyro, with heart on fire   75
For Madeline. Beside the portal doors,
Buttress'd from moonlight, stands he, and implores
All saints to give him sight of Madeline,
But for one moment in the tedious hours,
That he might gaze and worship all unseen;   80
Perchance speak, kneel, touch, kiss—in sooth such things have
    been.

X

He ventures in: let no buzz'd whisper tell:
All eyes be muffled, or a hundred swords
Will storm his heart, Love's fev'rous citadel:
For him, those chambers held barbarian hordes,   85
Hyena foemen, and hot-blooded lords,
Whose very dogs would execrations howl
Against his lineage: not one breast affords
Him any mercy, in that mansion foul,
Save one old beldame,[7] weak in body and in soul.   90

XI

Ah, happy chance! the aged creature came,
Shuffling along with ivory-headed wand,
To where he stood, hid from the torch's flame,
Behind a broad hall-pillar, far beyond
The sound of merriment and chorus bland: 95
He startled her; but soon she knew his face,
And grasp'd his fingers in her palsied hand,
Saying, "Mercy, Porphyro! hie thee from this place:
They are all here to-night, the whole blood-thirsty race!

[5] *timbrels* tambourines
[6] *all amort* alamort (*à la mort*) as if dead, dispirited
[7] *beldame* old woman

XII

"Get hence! get hence! there's dwarfish Hildebrand; 100
He had a fever late, and in the fit
He cursed thee and thine, both house and land:
Then there's that old Lord Maurice, not a whit
More tame for his gray hairs—Alas me! flit!
Flit like a ghost away."—"Ah, Gossip 8 dear, 105
We're safe enough; here in this arm-chair sit,
And tell me how"—"Good Saints; not here, not here;
Follow me, child, or else these stones will be thy bier."

XIII

He follow'd through a lowly archèd way,
Brushing the cobwebs with his lofty plume, 110
And as she mutter'd "Well-a—well-a-day!"
He found him in a little moonlight room,
Pale, lattic'd, chill, and silent as a tomb.
"Now tell me where is Madeline," said he,
"O tell me, Angela, by the holy loom 115
Which none but secret sisterhood may see,
When they St. Agnes' wool are weaving piously."

XIV

"St. Agnes! Ah! it is St. Agnes' Eve—
Yet men will murder upon holy days:
Thou must hold water in a witch's sieve,9 120
And be liege-lord of all the Elves and Fays,10
To venture so: it fills me with amaze
To see thee, Porphyro!—St. Agnes' Eve!
God's help! my lady fair the conjuror plays
This very night: good angels her deceive! 125
But let me laugh awhile, I've mickle 11 time to grieve."

XV

Feebly she laugheth in the languid moon,
While Porphyro upon her face doth look,
Like puzzled urchin on an agèd crone
Who keepeth clos'd a wond'rous riddle-book, 130
As spectacled she sits in chimney nook.

8 *Gossip* in the Elizabethan sense of "familiar acquaintance"
9 *witch's sieve* a sieve that will hold water, a sign of witchcraft
10 *Fays* fairies   11 *mickle* much

But soon his eyes grew brilliant, when she told
His lady's purpose; and he scarce could brook
Tears, at the thought of those enchantments cold,
And Madeline asleep in lap of legends old.   135

XVI

Sudden a thought came like a full-blown rose,
Flushing his brow, and in his pained heart
Made purple riot: then doth he propose
A stratagem, that makes the beldame start:
"A cruel man and impious thou art: 140
Sweet lady, let her pray, and sleep, and dream
Alone with her good angels, far apart
From wicked men like thee. Go, go!—I deem
Thou canst not surely be the same that thou didst seem."

XVII

"I will not harm her, by all saints I swear,"   145
Quoth Porphyro: "O may I ne'er find grace
When my weak voice shall whisper its last prayer,
If one of her soft ringlets I displace,
Or look with ruffian passion in her face:
Good Angela, believe me by these tears;   150
Or I will, even in a moment's space,
Awake, with horrid shout, my foemen's ears,
And beard them, though they be more fang'd than wolves and
      bears."

XVIII

"Ah! why wilt thou affright a feeble soul?
A poor, weak, palsy-stricken, churchyard thing,   155
Whose passing-bell [12] may ere the midnight toll;
Whose prayers for thee, each morn and evening,
Were never miss'd."—Thus plaining,[13] doth she bring
A gentler speech from burning Porphyro;
So woful, and of such deep sorrowing,   160
That Angela gives promise she will do
Whatever he shall wish, betide her weal [14] or woe.

XIX

Which was, to lead him, in close secrecy,
Even to Madeline's chamber, and there hide

[12] *passing-bell* death bell   [13] *plaining* complaining   [14] *weal* good

Him in a closet, of such privacy   165
That he might see her beauty unespied,
And win perhaps that night a peerless bride,
While legion'd faeries pac'd the coverlet,
And pale enchantment held her sleepy-eyed.
Never on such a night have lovers met,   170
Since Merlin [15] paid his Demon all the monstrous debt.

XX

"It shall be as thou wishest," said the Dame
"All cates [16] and dainties shall be stored there
Quickly on this feast-night: by the tambour frame [17]
Her own lute thou wilt see: no time to spare,   175
For I am slow and feeble, and scarce dare
On such a catering trust my dizzy head.
Wait here, my child, with patience; kneel in prayer
The while: Ah! thou must needs the lady wed,
Or may I never leave my grave among the dead."   180

XXI

So saying, she hobbled off with busy fear.
The lover's endless minutes slowly pass'd;
The dame return'd, and whisper'd in his ear
To follow her; with aged eyes aghast
From fright of dim espial. Safe at last,   185
Through many a dusky gallery, they gain
The maiden's chamber, silken, hush'd, and chaste;
Where Porphyro took covert, pleas'd amain.
His poor guide hurried back with agues [18] in her brain.

XXII

Her falt'ring hand upon the balustrade,   190
Old Angela was feeling for the stair,
When Madeline, St. Agnes' charmed maid,
Rose, like a mission'd spirit, unaware:
With silver taper's light, and pious care,
She turn'd, and down the aged gossip led   195
To a safe level matting. Now prepare,
Young Porphyro, for gazing on that bed;
She comes, she comes again, like ring-dove fray'd [19] and fled.

---

[15] *Merlin* in Arthurian legends, an evil magician   [16] *cates* delicacies
[17] *tambour frame* circular frame to hold material for embroidery
[18] *agues* spells of fever and chills   [19] *fray'd* frightened

XXIII

Out went the taper as she hurried in;
Its little smoke, in pallid moonshine, died: 200
She clos'd the door, she panted, all akin
To spirits of the air, and visions wide:
No uttered syllable, or, woe betide!
But to her heart, her heart was voluble,
Paining with eloquence her balmy side;   205
As though a tongueless nightingale should swell
Her throat in vain, and die, heart-stifled, in her dell.

XXIV

A casement high and triple-arch'd there was,
All garlanded with carven imag'ries
Of fruits, and flowers, and bunches of knot-grass,   210
And diamonded with panes of quaint device,
Innumerable of stains and splendid dyes,
As are the tiger-moth's deep-damask'd wings;
And in the midst, 'mong thousand heraldries,
And twilight saints, and dim emblazonings,   215
A shielded scutcheon [20] blush'd with blood of queens and kings.

XXV

Full on this casement shone the wintry moon,
And threw warm gules [21] on Madeline's fair breast,
As down she knelt for heaven's grace and boon;
Rose-bloom fell on her hands, together prest,   220
And on her silver cross soft amethyst,
And on her hair a glory, like a saint:
She seem'd a splendid angel, newly drest,
Save wings, for heaven:—Porphyro grew faint:
She knelt, so pure a thing, so free from mortal taint.   225

XXVI

Anon his heart revives: her vespers done,
Of all its wreathed pearls her hair she frees;
Unclasps her warmed jewels one by one;
Loosens her fragrant boddice; by degrees
Her rich attire creeps rustling to her knees: 230
Half-hidden, like a mermaid in sea-weed,
Pensive awhile she dreams awake, and sees,

[20] *scutcheon* escutcheon, a shield for a coat of arms
[21] *gules* the color red in heraldry, represented by parallel vertical lines

In fancy, fair St. Agnes in her bed,
But dares not look behind, or all the charm is fled.

XXVII

Soon, trembling in her soft and chilly nest,   235
In sort of wakeful swoon, perplex'd she lay,
Until the poppied warmth of sleep oppress'd
Her soothed limbs, and soul fatigued away;
Flown, like a thought, until the morrow-day;
Blissfully haven'd both from joy and pain;   240
Clasp'd like a missal [22] where swart Paynims [23] pray;
Blinded alike from sunshine and from rain,
As though a rose should shut, and be a bud again.

XXVIII

Stol'n to this paradise, and so entranced,
Porphyro gazed upon her empty dress,   245
And listen'd to her breathing, if it chanced
To wake into a slumberous tenderness;
Which when he heard, that minute did he bless,
And breath'd himself: then from the closet crept,
Noiseless as fear in a wide wilderness,   250
And over the hush'd carpet, silent, stept,
And 'tween the curtains peep'd, where, lo!—how fast she slept.

XXIX

Then by the bed-side, where the faded moon
Made a dim, silver twilight, soft he set
A table, and, half anguish'd, threw thereon   255
A cloth of woven crimson, gold, and jet:—
O for some drowsy Morphean amulet! [24]
The boisterous, midnight, festive clarion,
The kettle-drum, and far-heard clarinet,
Affray his ears, though but in dying tone:—   260
The hall door shuts again, and all the noise is gone.

XXX

And still she slept an azure-lidded sleep,
In blanched linen, smooth, and lavender'd,
While he from forth the closet brought a heap
Of candied apple, quince, and plum, and gourd;   265

---

[22] *missal* prayer book   [23] *Paynims* pagans
[24] *Morphean amulet* a charm of the god of dreams

With jellies soother [25] than the creamy curd,
And lucent syrops, tinct with cinnamon;
Manna and dates, in argosy transferr'd
From Fez; and spiced dainties, every one,
From silken Samarcand to cedar'd Lebanon.[26]   270

XXXI

These delicates he heap'd with glowing hand
On golden dishes and in baskets bright
Of wreathed silver: sumptuous they stand
In the retired quiet of the night,
Filling the chilly room with perfume light.—   275
"And now, my love, my seraph [27] fair, awake!
Thou art my heaven, and I thine eremite: [28]
Open thine eyes, for meek St. Agnes' sake,
Or I shall drowse beside thee, so my soul doth ache."

XXXII

Thus whispering, his warm, unnerved arm   280
Sank in her pillow. Shaded was her dream
By the dusk curtains:—'twas a midnight charm
Impossible to melt as iced stream:
The lustrous salvers [29] in the moonlight gleam;   285
Broad golden fringe upon the carpet lies:
It seem'd he never, never could redeem
From such a stedfast spell his lady's eyes;
So mus'd awhile, entoil'd in woofed [30] phantasies.

XXXIII

Awakening up, he took her hollow lute,—
Tumultuous,—and, in chords that tenderest be,   290
He play'd an ancient ditty, long since mute,
In Provence [31] call'd, "La belle dame sans mercy:" [32]
Close to her ear touching the melody;—
Wherewith disturb'd, she utter'd a soft moan:
He ceased—she panted quick—and suddenly   295
Her blue affrayed [33] eyes wide open shone:
Upon his knees he sank, pale as smooth-sculptured stone.

[25] *soother* smoother
[26] *Fez, Samarcand, Lebanon* the exotic world of Asia and the Mediterranean
[27] *seraph* angel   [28] *eremite* worshiping hermit   [29] *salvers* trays for food
[30] *woofed* woven
[31] *Provence* region of the troubadours in France
[32] *"La . . . mercy"* "the beautiful lady without mercy"
[33] *affrayed* frightened

XXXIV

Her eyes were open, but she still beheld,
Now wide awake, the vision of her sleep:
There was a painful change, that nigh expell'd   300
The blisses of her dream so pure and deep
At which fair Madeline began to weep,
And moan forth witless words with many a sigh;
While still her gaze on Porphyro would keep;
Who knelt, with joined hands and piteous eye,   305
Fearing to move or speak, she look'd so dreamingly.

XXXV

"Ah, Porphyro!" said she, "but even now
Thy voice was at sweet tremble in mine ear,
Made tuneable with every sweetest vow;
And those sad eyes were spiritual and clear: 310
How chang'd thou art! how pallid, chill, and drear!
Give me that voice again, my Porphyro,
Those looks immortal, those complainings dear!
Oh leave me not in this eternal woe,
For if thou diest, my Love, I know not where to go." 315

XXXVI

Beyond a mortal man impassion'd far
At these voluptuous accents, he arose,
Ethereal, flush'd, and like a throbbing star
Seen mid the sapphire heaven's deep repose;
Into her dream he melted, as the rose   320
Blendeth its odour with the violet,—
Solution sweet: meantime the frost-wind blows
Like Love's alarum pattering the sharp sleet
Against the window-panes; St. Agnes' moon hath set.

XXXVII

'Tis dark: quick pattereth the flaw [34]-blown sleet: 325
"This is no dream, my bride, my Madeline!"
'Tis dark: the iced gusts still rave and beat:
"No dream, alas! alas! and woe is mine!
Porphyro will leave me here to fade and pine.—
Cruel! what traitor could thee hither bring?   330
I curse not, for my heart is lost in thine,

[34] *flaw* gust

Though thou forsakest a deceived thing;—
A dove forlorn and lost with sick unpruned wing."

XXXVIII

"My Madeline! sweet dreamer! lovely bride!
Say, may I be for aye thy vassal blest?   335
Thy beauty's shield, heart-shap'd and vermeil [35] dyed?
Ah, silver shrine, here will I take my rest
After so many hours of toil and quest,
A famish'd pilgrim,—sav'd by miracle.
Though I have found, I will not rob thy nest   340
Saving of thy sweet self; if thou think'st well
To trust, fair Madeline, to no rude infidel.

XXXIX

"Hark! 'tis an elfin-storm from faery land,
Of haggard seeming, but a boon indeed:
Arise—arise! the morning is at hand;—   345
The bloated wassaillers [36] will never heed:—
Let us away, my love, with happy speed;
There are no ears to hear, or eyes to see,—
Drown'd all in Rhenish [37] and the sleepy mead: [38]
Awake! arise! my love, and fearless be,   350
For o'er the southern moors I have a home for thee."

XL

She hurried at his words, beset with fears,
For there were sleeping dragons all around,
At glaring watch, perhaps, with ready spears—
Down the wide stairs a darkling way they found.—   355
In all the house was heard no human sound.
A chain-droop'd lamp was flickering by each door;
The arras, [39] rich with horseman, hawk, and hound,
Flutter'd in the besieging wind's uproar;
And the long carpets rose along the gusty floor.   360

XLI

They glide, like phantoms, into the wide hall;
Like phantoms, to the iron porch, they glide;
Where lay the Porter, in uneasy sprawl,
With a huge empty flaggon by his side:

[35] *vermeil* vermilion   [36] *wassaillers* revelers   [37] *Rhenish* Rhine wine
[38] *mead* a drink with a sherry-like taste, made of fermented honey
[39] *arras* wall tapestry

The wakeful bloodhound rose, and shook his hide,　　365
But his sagacious eye an inmate owns:
By one, and one, the bolts full easy slide:—
The chains lie silent on the footworn stones;—
The key turns, and the door upon its hinges groans.

XLII

And they are gone: aye, ages long ago　　　　370
These lovers fled away into the storm.
That night the Baron dreamt of many a woe,
And all his warrior-guests, with shade and form
Of witch, and demon, and large coffin-worm,
Were long be-nightmar'd. Angela the old　　　375
Died palsy-twitch'd, with meagre face deform;
The Beadsman, after thousand aves told,
For aye unsought for slept among his ashes cold.

WHY DID I LAUGH

Why did I laugh to-night? No voice will tell:
　　No God, no Demon of severe response,
Deigns to reply from Heaven or from Hell.
　　Then to my human heart I turn at once.
Heart! Thou and I are here sad and alone;　　　5
　　Say, wherefore did I laugh? O mortal pain!
O Darkness! Darkness! ever must I moan,
　　To question Heaven and Hell and Heart in vain.
Why did I laugh? I know this Being's lease,
　　My fancy to its utmost blisses spreads;　　　10
Yet would I on this very midnight cease,
　　And the world's gaudy ensigns see in shreds;
Verse, Fame, and Beauty are intense indeed,
But Death intenser—Death is Life's high meed.

BRIGHT STAR

Bright star, would I were stedfast as thou art—
　　Not in lone splendour hung aloft the night
And watching, with eternal lids apart,
　　Like nature's patient, sleepless Eremite,[1]
The moving waters at their priestlike task　　　5
　　Of pure ablution [2] round earth's human shores,

---

[1] *Eremite* holy hermit　　　　　[2] *ablution* religious ritual of cleansing

Or gazing on the new soft fallen mask
  Of snow upon the mountains and the moors—
No—yet still stedfast, still unchangeable,
  Pillow'd upon my fair love's ripening breast,   10
To feel for ever its soft fall and swell,
  Awake for ever in a sweet unrest,
Still, still to hear her tender-taken breath,
And so live ever—or else swoon to death.

A DREAM,

AFTER READING DANTE'S EPISODE OF PAOLO AND FRANCESCA [1]

As Hermes once took to his feathers light,
  When lulled Argus, [2] baffled, swoon'd and slept,
So on a Delphic reed, [3] my idle spright [4]
  So play'd, so charm'd, so conquer'd, so bereft
The dragon-world of all its hundred eyes;   5
  And seeing it asleep, so fled away—
Not to pure Ida [5] with its snow-cold skies,
  Nor unto Tempe [6] where Jove griev'd a day;
But to that second circle of sad hell,
  Where 'mid the gust, the whirlwind, and the flaw   10
Of rain and hail-stones, lovers need not tell
  Their sorrows,—pale were the sweet lips I saw,
Pale were the lips I kiss'd, and fair the form
I floated with, about that melancholy storm.

LA BELLE DAME SANS MERCI [1]

A BALLAD

O what can ail thee, knight-at-arms,
  Alone and palely loitering?
The sedge has wither'd from the lake,
  And no birds sing.

[1] In Dante's *Divina Commedia* (Inferno, V)
[2] *Hermes, Argus* Argus had a hundred eyes, but Hermes lulled him to sleep with music and cut off his head. Hermes had winged cap and sandals.
[3] *Delphic reed* a pipe, or music of the gods.   [4] *spright* spirit
[5] *Ida* mountain in Greece, connected with the worship of Zeus
[6] *Tempe* valley in Greece often visited by the gods

[1] This is the first version of the poem, generally preferred to the later revised and published form.

O what can ail thee, knight-at-arms!   5
    So haggard and so woe-begone?
The squirrel's granary is full,
    And the harvest's done.

I see a lilly on thy brow,
    With anguish moist and fever dew,   10
And on thy cheeks a fading rose
    Fast withereth too.

I met a lady in the meads,
    Full beautiful—a faery's child,
Her hair was long, her foot was light,   15
    And her eyes were wild.

I made a garland for her head,
    And bracelets too, and fragrant zone; [2]
She look'd at me as she did love,
    And made sweet moan.   20

I set her on my pacing steed,
    And nothing else saw all day long,
For sidelong would she bend, and sing
    A faery's song.

She found me roots of relish [3] sweet,   25
    And honey wild, and manna [4] dew,
And sure in language strange she said—
    "I love thee true."

She took me to her elfin grot, [5]
    And there she wept, and sigh'd full sore,   30
And there I shut her wild wild eyes
    With kisses four.

And there she lulled me asleep,
    And there I dream'd—Ah! woe betide!
The latest dream I ever dream'd   35
    On the cold hill's side.

I saw pale kings and princes too,
    Pale warriors, death-pale were they all;

[2] *zone* belt   [3] *relish* taste or flavor
[4] *manna* probably referring to sustenance miraculously supplied to the Israelites in the Wilderness, though some trees and plants produce a liquid
called manna
[5] *grot* grotto

> They cried—"La Belle Dame sans Merci
>   Hath thee in thrall!" [6]   40
>
> I saw their starved lips in the gloam,
>   With horrid warning gaped wide,
> And I awoke and found me here,
>   On the cold hill's side.
>
> And this is why I sojourn here,   45
>   Alone and palely loitering,
> Though the sedge is wither'd from the lake,
>   And no birds sing.

ODE TO PSYCHE [1]

> O goddess! hear these tuneless numbers, wrung
>   By sweet enforcement and remembrance dear,
> And pardon that thy secrets should be sung
>   Even into thine own soft-conched ear:
> Surely I dreamt to-day, or did I see   5
>   The winged Psyche with awaken'd eyes?
> I wander'd in a forest thoughtlessly,
>   And, on the sudden, fainting with surprise,
> Saw two fair creatures, couched side by side
>   In deepest grass, beneath the whisp'ring roof   10
>   Of leaves and trembled blossoms, where there ran
>   A brooklet, scarce espied:
> 'Mid hush'd, cool-rooted flowers, fragrant-eyed,
>   Blue, silver-white, and budded Tyrian,[2]
> They lay calm-breathing on the bedded grass;   15
>   Their arms embraced, and their pinions too;
>   Their lips touch'd not, but had not bade adieu,
> As if disjoined by soft-handed slumber,
> And ready still past kisses to outnumber
>   At tender eye-dawn of aurorean love: 20
>   The winged boy I knew;
>   But who wast thou, O happy, happy dove?
>   His Psyche true!

[6] *thrall* enslavement, bondage

---

[1] *Psyche* In the legend of Cupid and Psyche, the lovers are represented as meeting nightly. Although Psyche has been forbidden to see Cupid, she does look at him while he is asleep. A drop of hot oil from her lamp falls on his shoulder and wakens him. Cupid leaves in anger, and they are reunited only when Psyche is made immortal. Psyche is taken as the personification of the human soul, is often represented as a moth or butterfly.

[2] *Tyrian* purple

O latest born and loveliest vision far
    Of all Olympus' faded hierarchy!   25
Fairer than Phœbe's [3] sapphire-region'd star,
    Or Vesper,[4] amorous glow-worm of the sky;
Fairer than these, though temple thou hast none,
        Nor altar heap'd with flowers;
Nor virgin-choir to make delicious moan   30
        Upon the midnight hours;
No voice, no lute, no pipe, no incense sweet
    From chain-swung censer teeming;
No shrine, no grove, no oracle, no heat
        Of pale-mouth'd prophet dreaming.   35

O brightest! though too late for antique vows,
    Too, too late for the fond believing lyre,
When holy were the haunted forest boughs,
    Holy the air, the water, and the fire;
Yet even in these days so far retir'd   40
    From happy pieties, thy lucent fans,
    Fluttering among the faint Olympians,
I see, and sing, by my own eyes inspir'd.
So let me be thy choir, and make a moan
        Upon the midnight hours;   45
Thy voice, thy lute, thy pipe, thy incense sweet
    From swinged censer teeming;
Thy shrine, thy grove, thy oracle, thy heat
        Of pale-mouth'd prophet dreaming.

Yes, I will be thy priest, and build a fane [5]   50
    In some untrodden region of my mind,
Where branched thoughts, new grown with pleasant pain,
    Instead of pines shall murmur in the wind:
Far, far around shall those dark-cluster'd trees
    Fledge the wild-ridged mountains steep by steep;   55
And there by zephyrs, streams, and birds, and bees,
    The moss-lain Dryads [6] shall be lull'd to sleep;
And in the midst of this wide quietness
A rosy sanctuary will I dress
With the wreath'd trellis of a working brain,   60
    With buds, and bells, and stars without a name,
With all the gardener Fancy e'er could feign,
    Who breeding flowers, will never breed the same:

[3] *Phoebe* Diana (the moon)   [4] *Vesper* the evening star (sometimes Venus)
[5] *fane* temple   [6] *Dryads* wood-nymphs

And there shall be for thee all soft delight
    That shadowy thought can win,   65
A bright torch, and a casement ope at night,
    To let the warm Love in!

ODE TO A NIGHTINGALE

I

My heart aches, and a drowsy numbness pains
    My sense, as though of hemlock [1] I had drunk,
Or emptied some dull opiate to the drains
    One minute past, and Lethe [2]-wards had sunk:
'Tis not through envy of thy happy lot,   5
    But being too happy in thine happiness,—
        That thou, light-winged Dryad [3] of the trees,
          In some melodious plot
    Of beechen green, and shadows numberless,
        Singest of summer in full-throated ease.   10

II

O, for a draught of vintage! that hath been
    Cool'd a long age in the deep-delved earth,
Tasting of Flora [4] and the country green,
    Dance, and Provençal song,[5] and sunburnt mirth!
O for a beaker full of the warm South,   15
    Full of the true, the blushful Hippocrene,[6]
        With beaded bubbles winking at the brim,
          And purple-stained mouth;
    That I might drink, and leave the world unseen,
        And with thee fade away into the forest dim: 20

III

Fade far away, dissolve, and quite forget
    What thou among the leaves hast never known,
The weariness, the fever, and the fret
    Here, where men sit and hear each other groan;

[1] *hemlock* a poisonous plant, used as a powerful sedative
[2] *Lethe* river of forgetfulness in Hades   [3] *Dryad* wood-nymph
[4] *Flora* goddess of flowers. Her festival came at the end of April and the
beginning of May.
[5] *Provençal song* Provence, in France; a medieval center of poetry and music
[6] *Hippocrene* the fountain of the Muses on Mount Helicon, the inspiration
of song and poetry

Where palsy shakes a few, sad, last gray hairs,   25
  Where youth grows pale, and spectre-thin, and dies;
    Where but to think is to be full of sorrow
      And leaden-eyed despairs,
  Where Beauty cannot keep her lustrous eyes,
    Or new Love pine at them beyond to-morrow.   30

IV

Away! away! for I will fly to thee,
  Not charioted by Bacchus and his pards,[7]
But on the viewless [8] wings of Poesy,
  Though the dull brain perplexes and retards:
Already with thee! tender is the night,   35
  And haply the Queen-Moon is on her throne,
    Cluster'd around by all her starry Fays; [9]
      But here there is no light,
  Save what from heaven is with the breezes blown
    Through verdurous glooms and winding mossy ways.   40

V

I cannot see what flowers are at my feet,
  Nor what soft incense hangs upon the boughs,
But, in embalmed [10] darkness, guess each sweet
  Wherewith the seasonable month endows
The grass, the thicket, and the fruit-tree wild;   45
  White hawthorn, and the pastoral eglantine; [11]
    Fast fading violets cover'd up in leaves;
      And mid-May's eldest child,
  The coming musk-rose, full of dewy wine,
    The murmurous haunt of flies on summer eves.   50

VI

Darkling [12] I listen; and, for many a time
  I have been half in love with easeful Death,
Call'd him soft names in many a mused rhyme,
  To take into the air my quiet breath;
Now more than ever seems it rich to die,   55
  To cease upon the midnight with no pain,

---

[7] *Bacchus and his pards* the god of fertility and wine, often attended by leopards. A Titian painting known to Keats represents Bacchus in a chariot drawn by leopards.
[8] *viewless* invisible   [9] *Fays* fairies
[10] *embalmed* made fragrant with spices and perfumes
[11] *eglantine* sweet-briar or honeysuckle   [12] *darkling* in darkness

While thou art pouring forth thy soul abroad
    In such an ecstasy!
Still wouldst thou sing, and I have ears in vain—
    To thy high requiem become a sod.   60

VII

Thou wast not born for death, immortal Bird!
    No hungry generations tread thee down;
The voice I hear this passing night was heard
    In ancient days by emperor and clown:
Perhaps the self-same song that found a path   65
    Through the sad heart of Ruth,[13] when, sick for home,
        She stood in tears amid the alien corn;
            The same that oft-times hath
    Charm'd magic casements, opening on the foam
    Of perilous seas, in faery lands forlorn.   70

VIII

Forlorn! the very word is like a bell
    To toll me back from thee to my sole self!
Adieu! the fancy cannot cheat so well
    As she is fam'd to do, deceiving elf.
Adieu! adieu! thy plaintive anthem fades   75
    Past the near meadows, over the still stream,
        Up the hill-side; and now 'tis buried deep
            In the next valley-glades:
    Was it a vision, or a waking dream?
    Fled is that music:—Do I wake or sleep?   80

ODE ON A GRECIAN URN [1]

I

Thou still unravish'd bride of quietness,
    Thou foster-child of silence and slow time,
Sylvan historian, who canst thus express
    A flowery tale more sweetly than our rhyme:
What leaf-fring'd legend haunts about thy shape   5
    Of deities or mortals, or of both,

---

[13] *Ruth* in the Biblical story, the woman who stayed in her husband's country even after his death

---

[1] *Grecian Urn* believed to be an imaginary urn, a composite of several Keats might have seen

In Tempe [2] or the dales of Arcady? [3]
What men or gods are these? What maidens loth?
    What mad pursuit? What struggle to escape?
        What pipes and timbrels? [4] What wild ecstasy?   10

II

Heard melodies are sweet, but those unheard
    Are sweeter; therefore, ye soft pipes, play on;
Not to the sensual ear, but, more endear'd,
    Pipe to the spirit ditties of no tone:
Fair youth, beneath the trees, thou canst not leave   15
    Thy song, nor ever can those trees be bare;
        Bold Lover, never, never canst thou kiss,
Though winning near the goal—yet, do not grieve;
    She cannot fade, though thou hast not thy bliss,
        For ever wilt thou love, and she be fair!   20

III

Ah, happy, happy boughs! that cannot shed
    Your leaves, nor ever bid the Spring adieu;
And, happy melodist, unwearied,
    For ever piping songs for ever new;
More happy love! more happy, happy love!   25
    For ever warm and still to be enjoy'd,
        For ever panting, and for ever young;
All breathing human passion far above,
    That leaves a heart high-sorrowful and cloy'd,
        A burning forehead, and a parching tongue.   30

IV

Who are these coming to the sacrifice?
    To what green altar, O mysterious priest,
Lead'st thou that heifer lowing at the skies,
    And all her silken flanks with garlands drest?
What little town by river or sea shore,   35
    Or mountain-built with peaceful citadel,
        Is emptied of this folk, this pious morn?
And, little town, thy streets for evermore

[2] *Tempe* a beautiful valley in Greece, supposed to be a favorite haunt of
Apollo
[3] *Arcady* Arcadia, a part of Greece surrounded by mountains, idealized in
myths
[4] *timbrels* tambourines

Will silent be; and not a soul to tell
Why thou art desolate, can e'er return.   40

V

O Attic [5] shape! Fair attitude! with brede [6]
Of marble men and maidens overwrought,
With forest branches and the trodden weed;
    Thou, silent form, dost tease us out of thought
As doth eternity: Cold Pastoral!   45
    When old age shall this generation waste,
        Thou shalt remain, in midst of other woe
Than ours, a friend to man, to whom thou say'st,
    "Beauty is truth, truth beauty,"—that is all
        Ye know on earth, and all ye need to know.   50

ODE ON MELANCHOLY [1]

I

No, no, go not to Lethe,[2] neither twist
Wolf's-bane,[3] tight-rooted, for its poisonous wine;
Nor suffer thy pale forehead to be kiss'd
By nightshade,[4] ruby grape of Proserpine; [5]
Make not your rosary of yew-berries,   5
    Nor let the beetle, nor the death-moth be
        Your mournful Psyche,[6] nor the downy owl

---

[5] *Attic* Greek   [6] *brede* interwoven design on the urn

[1] Keats once placed the following stanza first in the poem:

Though you should build a bark of dead men's bones,
    And rear a phantom gibbet for a mast,
Stitch creeds together for a sail, with groans
    To fill it out, blood-stained and aghast;
Although your rudder be a dragon's tail
    Long sever'd, yet still hard with agony,
        Your cordage large uprootings from the skull
Of bald Medusa, certes you would fail
    To find the Melancholy—whether she
        Dreameth in any isle of Lethe dull . . .

[2] *Lethe* river of forgetfulness in Hades
[3] *Wolf's-bane* poisonous plant
[4] *nightshade* plant with poisonous berries, sometimes called belladonna
[5] *Proserpine* queen of the underworld and death
[6] *Psyche* the soul, represented as a moth or butterfly. Cupid was Psyche's secret lover; only when she was made immortal could she be united with him.

A partner in your sorrow's mysteries;
  For shade to shade will come too drowsily,
    And drown the wakeful anguish of the soul.   10

II

But when the melancholy fit shall fall
  Sudden from heaven like a weeping cloud,
That fosters the droop-headed flowers all,
  And hides the green hill in an April shroud;
Then glut thy sorrow on a morning rose,   15
  Or on the rainbow of the salt sand-wave,
    Or on the wealth of globed peonies;
Or if thy mistress some rich anger shows,
  Emprison her soft hand, and let her rave,
    And feed deep, deep upon her peerless eyes.   20

III

She dwells with Beauty—Beauty that must die;
  And Joy, whose hand is ever at his lips
Bidding adieu; and aching Pleasure nigh,
  Turning to poison while the bee-mouth sips:
Ay, in the very temple of Delight   25
  Veil'd Melancholy has her sovran shrine,
    Though seen of none save him whose strenuous tongue
Can burst Joy's grape against his palate fine;
  His soul shall taste the sadness of her might,
    And be among her cloudy trophies hung.   30

TO AUTUMN

I

Season of mists and mellow fruitfulness,
  Close bosom-friend of the maturing sun;
Conspiring with him how to load and bless
  With fruit the vines that round the thatch-eves run;
To bend with apples the moss'd cottage-trees,   5
  And fill all fruit with ripeness to the core;
    To swell the gourd, and plump the hazel shells
With a sweet kernel; to set budding more,
  And still more, later flowers for the bees,
    Until they think warm days will never cease,   10
    For Summer has o'er-brimm'd their clammy cells.

II

Who hath not seen thee oft amid thy store?
   Sometimes whoever seeks abroad may find
Thee sitting careless on a granary floor,
   Thy hair soft-lifted by the winnowing wind;   15
Or on a half-reap'd furrow sound asleep,
   Drows'd with the fume of poppies, while thy hook
      Spares the next swath and all its twined flowers:
And sometimes like a gleaner thou dost keep
   Steady thy laden head across a brook;   20
   Or by a cyder-press, with patient look,
      Thou watchest the last oozings hours by hours.

III

Where are the songs of Spring? Ay, where are they?
   Think not of them, thou hast thy music too,—
While barred clouds bloom the soft-dying day,   25
   And touch the stubble-plains with rosy hue;
Then in a wailful choir the small gnats mourn
   Among the rivers sallows,[1] borne aloft
      Or sinking as the light wind lives or dies;
And full-grown lambs loud bleat from hilly bourn;[2]   30
   Hedge-crickets sing; and now with treble soft
   The red-breast whistles from a garden-croft; [3]
      And gathering swallows twitter in the skies.

CRITICISM

     The sonnet "On First Looking into Chapman's Homer" is
viewed here in its origins, its sources, and its personal significance to Keats. Accounts of the composition of a particular poem
are usually interesting, but not always important to its understanding. In this poem, however, the theme is directly related to
the reading of books. The essay does not attempt to analyze
language, music, and structure in the sonnet. The focus is on the
poem's history.

[1] *sallows* low-growing willows   [2] *bourn* region
[3] *garden-croft* tilled ground near a house

Of Chapman's Homer and Other Books [1]

BERNICE SLOTE

To Keats, books were life. What a poet made and how a man lived were all part of the same adventure to worlds unconfined and beautiful. One vivid example of how books and men behave together is the story of his sonnet "On First Looking into Chapman's Homer." It began on the October night in London in 1816 when he joined his friend Charles Cowden Clarke for some reading, even as the two had enjoyed many books together in the years since Keats was a student in the Enfield school of Clarke's father—books like Spenser's *Faerie Queene*, which had led Keats to a career as a poet.[2] Clarke now had been lent a "beautiful copy of the folio edition" of George Chapman's Elizabethan translation of Homer's *Iliad* and *Odyssey*. Keats and Clarke had read Homer in Pope's translation, but not in Chapman's. It was a book both famous and rare.

From 1611 to 1616, various editions and combinations of Chapman's translations of Homer had been printed. A good many of the copies now in rare-book collections are slightly different in details, but one "Chapman's Homer" in the Henry E. Huntington Library (San Marino, California) will serve as a model of the kind of book Keats used that night in Clarke's rooms. It is a folio of heavy paper, clear type, wide margins. The title pages and section headings are richly decorated with sharp, detailed engravings (both pictures and formal designs of geometric figures, scrolls, motifs). The title page reads: "The Whole Works of Homer; Prince of Poetts. In his Iliads, and Odysses. Translated according to the Greeke, by Geo: Chapman. London: printed for Nathaniell Butter." The introductory pages include a picture of Chapman (two moles on the left of his nose, a beard, and bald head fringed with curly hair); a dedication to Prince Henry; a knightly picture of the Prince holding a spear, with helmet and plumes at the side; and other dedications, compli-

---

[1] Reprinted (revised) from *College English*, 23 (January, 1962).
[2] For Clarke's account of Keats, books, and the evening with Chapman's Homer, see Charles and Mary Cowden Clarke, *Recollections of Writers* (New York: Charles Scribner's Sons, 1878), pp. 120–157; and *The Keats Circle*, ed. Hyder Edward Rollins (Harvard University Press, 1948), II, 146–150, 169.

ments, and prefaces to the reader in which Chapman extols
Homer's universal greatness. But what Homer was, says Chapman, "his workes shew most truly; to which (if you please) go
on and examine him." Certainly Keats and Clarke did go on,
and no doubt read one of the dedicatory sonnets which Chapman
had placed at the end of the "Iliads," for the poem to Robert
Cecyl, Earle of Salisburye, anticipates the general pattern of
imagery Keats would use in his sonnet, whose metaphors contain the earth (ll. 1–7), the skies (ll. 9–10), and the ocean (ll.
11–14). Chapman writes,

> So, none like Homer hath the World enspher'd;
> Earth, Seas, & heaven, fixt in his verse, and moving. . . .

"We read through the night," said Clarke, sampling the passages they knew best: from the *Iliad,* the conversation of the
Senators and Helen on the wall of Troy and Antenor's description of Ulysses as orator (Book III), the description of the shield
and helmet of Diomed (Book V), and Neptune's passage to the
Achive (Achaean) ships (Book XIII); from the *Odyssey,* the ship-
wreck of Ulysses (Book V). Clarke, writing years later, remembered the Keats of that night: "How distinctly is that earnest
stare, and protrusion of the upper lip now present with me, as
we came upon some piece of rough-hewn doric elevation in the
fine old poet. He sometimes shouted." They read late, but the
next morning a messenger brought Clarke Keats's new poem of
personal discovery, "On First Looking into Chapman's Homer."
    What was so vividly alive and exciting about this reading of
Homer? Chapman's lines *are* virile and bold, and the stories
themselves exciting; but in addition, *the poetry was read aloud.*
This was nothing unusual for the two friends. Clarke said that
he *had read to Keats* the "Epithalamion" of Spenser, and Keats
had responded physically—"his features and exclamations were
ecstatic." Keats read aloud, too: in *Cymbeline,* his eyes filled with
tears and his voice faltered at some of Imogen's lines. During
the night of Chapman's Homer, Clarke must have read many of
the passages, which he knew better than Keats. Clarke was a big
man and he had a big voice that would have filled the room.
Something of his presence can be guessed by the description of
Boythorn in Dickens's *Bleak House,* a character that in later
years his wife and his friends laughingly thought must have

been taken directly from Clarke.[3] Boythorn is an impetuous, loud, hearty, sturdy man with great lungs—"Talking, laughing, or snoring, they make the beams of the house shake." Boythorn (and no doubt Clarke) had a great laugh and a booming voice, and uttered every word with "roundness and fullness." Even by such an indirection we can picture the scene—Keats, slight and compact, listening to the big Clarke pounding away at heroes and seas and shipwrecks. No wonder Keats heard "Chapman speak out loud and bold." The poetry to Keats was not an intellectual maneuver; he was deeply and physically involved, with delighted stares when some passage struck him with a fresh surprise. And remember, *he sometimes shouted.*

Many who have read neither Pope nor Chapman may wonder what there was to shout about in Chapman's version of Homer. Pope's translation was, of course, in the standard ten-syllable line of the heroic couplet, most two-line units making a finished or closed segment. Chapman wrote in couplets, too, but the *Iliad* is put into longer lines of fourteen syllables and the couplets are not always closed. Therefore the breath is longer, more irregular, more racy. The *Odyssey* is in ten-syllable lines, but again the couplets are generally free and open. In addition, Chapman's language is usually more colorful, more imaginatively exciting. For example, Chapman's description of Ulysses as orator throws us into a storm:

> But when out of his ample breast he gave his great voice passe
> And words that flew about our eares like drifts of winter's snow,
> None thenceforth might contend with him . . . (III, 242–244)

Pope's version puts us neatly into the schoolroom:

> But when he speaks, what elocution flows!
> Soft as the fleeces of descending snows
> The copious accents fall, with easy art;
> Melting they fall, and sink into the heart!

Keats liked Chapman's vivid phrases: Neptune's "immortall moving feet" (XIII, 19), and (of Ulysses shipwrecked) "The sea had soakt his heart through" (V, 612), which was limply handled by Pope as, "And lost in lassitude lay all the man." Chapman's Homer was a poet whose world was brilliantly alive. And now

[3] Richard D. Altick, *The Cowden Clarkes* (London: Oxford University Press, 1948), pp. 79–80.

Keats knew for himself.

Part of Keats's excitement about Homer was tied up with a happy fusion of two other general imaginative experiences, those of classical mythology and the literature of travel and exploration. In school, Clarke said, Keats had "devoured rather than read" all the school library, "which consisted principally of abridgments of all the voyages and travels of any note" as well as a number of histories. The books that attracted him most, however, were those on mythology: Tooke's *Pantheon,* Lemprière's *Classical Dictionary,* Spence's *Polymetis,* and, of course, Ovid. Books of history and mythology helped in the generation of Keats's poem, for its metaphor was principally the union of these two streams: it portrayed, in terms of geographical discovery, the world of Apollo.[4]

All the high adventure and desperate undertaking of the early voyagers, explorers, and discoverers must have appealed to Keats. One of the books we know he studied is William Robertson's *History of America,* and in it we can trace the geographical-historical framework of the sonnet.[5] Robertson tells mainly of certain "realms of gold," the treasure lands of the Portuguese and Spanish explorers, who sought and eventually found Mexico and Peru, passing literally the "western islands" on the way. One map in Robertson's *History* shows most prominently the range of islands from Cuba and the Caribbean westward through the Gulf of Mexico to Darien, in Central America, and the lands north of it. The question of why Cortez, instead of Balboa, seems to be discovering the Pacific from a peak in Darien has not been answered to everyone's satisfaction. Some critics have argued that Keats simply made a mistake. Others have sensibly pointed out that the metaphor of discovery does not need to mean "the first by anyone" (for Keats had read Homer before, and others had known Chapman's translation).[6] But we also recognize the in-

---

[4] Only these primary sources are considered here. They do not, of course, exclude the addition of other sources that have been suggested for the images of the sonnet. See especially B. Ifor Evans on John Bonnycastle's *An Introduction to Astronomy* (*Essays and Studies of the English Association,* 1931), and the general discussion in Claude Lee Finney, *The Evolution of Keats's Poetry* (Harvard University Press, 1936), I, 120–128.

[5] I have used the fourth edition of William Robertson, *The History of America* (London, 1783), 3 vols. Page references are in the text.

[6] See Charles C. Walcutt, "Keats' 'On First Looking into Chapman's Homer,'" *Explicator,* V (June, 1947), 56; and the more complete discussion in C. V. Wicker, "Cortez—Not Balboa," *College English,* 17 (April, 1956), 383–387.

escapable parallel between the scene in the last lines of the poem and that in Robertson's account of Balboa's discovery of the Pacific. Like others, Balboa was looking for the golden land of Peru. Robertson tells how with tremendous difficulty he crossed the marshes and mountains of Darien, searching for a rumored ocean that might be their way. Finally, near one summit,

> Balboa commanded his men to halt, and advanced alone to the summit, that he might be the first who should enjoy a spectacle which he had so long desired. As soon as he beheld the South Sea stretching in endless prospect below him, he fell on his knees, and lifting up his hands to Heaven, returned thanks to God, who had conducted him to a discovery so beneficial to his country, and so honourable to himself. His followers, observing his transports of joy, rushed forward to join in his wonder, exultation and gratitude [I, 250–251].

Another view is that Cortez was taken (consciously or unconsciously) as a blend of all the conquistadors, even as the heroes of legend and myth take on the feats of lesser figures.[7] It is most likely that Keats was thinking of the total story of Robertson's New World, in which Cortez was clearly the principal actor, and he simply used the most dramatic single scene he remembered to embody the act and the emotion of discovery.

However, several other passages in Robertson, not usually noted, have some bearing on both the factual problem and the symbolic direction of Keats's poem. For one thing, Cortez had the *type* of experience Keats describes. Descending from the mountains of Chalco, Cortez and his party saw before them the "prospect" of Montezuma's Mexico, fields "stretching farther than the eye could reach," a lake "resembling the sea in extent," and the capital city rising upon an island:

> the scene so far exceeded their imagination, that some believed the fanciful descriptions of romance were realized, and that its enchanted palaces and gilded domes were presented to their sight; others could hardly persuade themselves that this wonderful spectacle was any thing more than a dream. As they advanced, their doubts were removed, but their amazement increased [II, 276].

Furthermore, *according to Robertson,* Cortez did see the Pacific, and from Darien. Going on in the *History* to the close of the extensive account of Cortez's conquest of Mexico, we read that his

---

[7] See Joseph Warren Beach, "Keats's Realms of Gold," PMLA (March, 1934), 246–257. This article is the most complete account of Keats's use of Robertson as material for the sonnet on Chapman's Homer.

last schemes were to find some strait to afford easy passage between the Gulf of Mexico and the Pacific, and in 1530 he
searched, though unsuccessfully, through the isthmus of Darien.
Eventually he crossed to the Pacific side of the isthmus and made
his further voyages from ports on the other side of Darien. From
there he discovered another land of gold of which he had often
heard—the peninsula of California—and surveyed the gulf of
the Vermilion Sea between it and New Spain (II, 393–394). Moreover, Pizarro in 1529, financed by Cortez, had also marched
across Darien to Panama and from there made the conquest of
Peru, that really golden land of the fabled Incas (III, 16–19).
Just how the scenes were shifted we do not know, but in one
moment, one man, Keats did focus all of the long and difficult
search that saw in wonder that its dream had been made possible.
The great expanse of the sea-world was the immediate cause of
wonder. But it was not only the ocean but the lands beyond—
California, Sonora, Peru—that made the discovery supreme. Now
they could be reached. Chapman was, after all, the *way* to the
world of Homer. As the Pacific could (and did) bring explorers to
the lands of gold, so Chapman's lines could make the world of
Greek story real, actual, and alive for Keats. He could at last
breathe its very air.

But we must turn from the stream of history to the stream of
myth, and other books. Keats had suggested that the world of the
imagination had its own geography to explore. With this figure
he combined the myth of Apollo, god of poetry and therefore
the ruler of its lands. But he had also learned from the textbooks
of mythology he had studied that no god is one thing alone.
Apollo is also associated with the sun, light, growth, and life.
The realms of gold are in harmony with him. Spence in *Polymetis* [8] describes Apollo's shining face, the brightness beaming
from his eyes, the crown of twelve rays on his head. His chariot
of gold has a rose-colored harness studded with precious stones.
In Tooke's *Pantheon* [9] he is pictured with a halo of light, and
it is said that he "shines in Garments embroidered with Gold."
Apollo the Sun "by his Light makes all Things manifest." In his
own "Ode to Apollo" a year before (1815) Keats had already
combined Apollo's gold with the poet Homer. In the god's

[8] Joseph Spence, *Polymetis* (London, 1747), p. 185.
[9] Andrew Tooke, *The Pantheon* (London, 1774), pp. 29–30, 87.

"western halls of gold" bards strike their lyres, "Whose chords are solid rays, and twinkle radiant fires." One bard is Homer who "with his nervous arms/ Strikes the twanging harp of war." Another characteristic of Apollo, according to Tooke, is the "Perspicuity and Sharpness of his Eyes" that "do most fitly represent the Foresight of Prophecy." Even if the "eagle eyes" in the sonnet were suggested by Titian's picture of Cortez, as many think, the effect of the two comparisons in the sestet of the poem is to put the "watcher of the skies" and the explorer gazing seaward from the mountain peak into harmony with the visionary quality of Apollo's view. The hawk, after all, was favored by Apollo because he "has Eyes as bright as the sun." Neither Cortez nor the watcher of the skies *is* Apollo, but the discoverer in the world of poetry would have sight suitable to Apollo's realm. Finally, Apollo is the god of harmony, growth, and life. The images of Keats's poem do trace the great cosmic circle of earth and ocean and the planets of the sky, and the vision that might contain it, even as Keats had described the epic itself in his "Epistle to Charles Cowden Clarke" (September, 1816) as king of all, "Round, vast, and spanning all like Saturn's ring." The sonnet on Chapman's Homer unites both history and myth, both human understanding and godlike vision.

Among the books Keats owned at the time of his death (less than five years after he wrote the sonnet) was listed "Marmontel's Incas" [10]—Jean Francois Marmontel's *Les Incas,* a history-romance of the Incas of Peru, which first appeared in Paris in 1777, with a later English translation published in Dublin, 1797. There is no indication whether Keats had the French or English version, or when it came into his possession. But whether he read it early or late (as cause or continuation of an idea), this book, too, joins in the fused worlds of the sonnet—Apollo's realms of gold. The Incas, Robertson said in his *History,* were called "children of the Sun" and were sent by their parent, "who beheld with pity the miseries of the human race, to instruct and to reclaim them" (III, 22). The central theme of Marmontel is that the Incas were indeed the children of the sun, and much of the book is devoted to accounts of the temples and rituals of sun-worship. Their sun-god—Apollo, in other lands—pours forth "in one great stream of light, the principles of warmth, of

[10] *The Keats Circle,* I, 259.

life, and of fertility." [11] The sonnet, "On First Looking into Chapman's Homer," is a motif for the finding of such illumination: it is not so much about reading as about the stirring of life. Certainly Keats's personal quest under Apollo ended before it should, but as his poem records, he knew well how the creative imagination—in reading as well as in writing—could make life outreach space and time.

[11] *The Incas* (Dublin, 1797), I, 4.

ALFRED, LORD TENNYSON

[1809-1892]

TENNYSON came from an English clergyman's family in Somersby, Lincolnshire; attended Trinity College, Cambridge; and by 1832 had published two volumes of poetry. When Arthur Hallam, his friend in Cambridge and fiancé of his sister Emily, died in Vienna in 1832, Tennyson began work on his elegy, *In Memoriam,* though it was not published until 1850. (Before that time came the 1842 *Poems,* including "Morte d'Arthur" and "Locksley Hall," and in 1847, *The Princess.*) The year of 1850 had two other important events—Tennyson married Emily Sellwood, and he was made Poet Laureate to succeed Wordsworth. The Tennyson poems continued to use two principal sources— the Arthurian stories and Greek myth. *Idylls of the King* appeared in 1859, *The Holy Grail* in 1869; some of his last poems —*Demeter* (1889) and *The Death of Oenone* (1892)—were on the classical themes. Tennyson's fame was unquestioned, even with Queen Victoria, and in 1883 he was given a title. Tennyson also wrote seven plays, although *Becket* was his only real success. He died near Haslemere, England, and was buried in Westminster Abbey. Tennyson had the perfect touch for the melodious line, became the master of a silken melancholy. His poetry is often nostalgic for other worlds; it also reveals (*In Memoriam,* "Locksley Hall") some of the doubts that haunted even the sure Victorians.

Introductory Readings

EDITION: *The Works of Tennyson,* ed. Hallam Lord Tennyson (1920). BIOGRAPHY: Charles Tennyson, *Alfred Tennyson* (1949). CRITICISM: A. C. Bradley, *A Commentary on Tennyson's In Memoriam* (1920); Harold Nicolson, *Tennyson* (1923); Paull F. Baum, *Tennyson: Sixty Years After* (1948); Frank Lawrence Lucas, *Tennyson* (1957).

THE LADY OF SHALOTT [1]

PART I

On either side the river lie
Long fields of barley and of rye,
That clothe the wold [2] and meet the sky;
And thro' the field the road runs by
    To many-tower'd Camelot; [3]   5
And up and down the people go,
Gazing where the lilies blow
Round an island there below,
    The island of Shalott.

Willows whiten, aspens quiver,   10
Little breezes dusk and shiver
Thro' the wave that runs for ever
By the island in the river
    Flowing down to Camelot.
Four gray walls, and four gray towers,   15
Overlook a space of flowers,
And the silent isle imbowers
    The Lady of Shalott.

By the margin, willow-veil'd,
Slide the heavy barges trail'd   20
By slow horses; and unhail'd
The shallop [4] flitteth silken-sail'd
    Skimming down to Camelot:
But who hath seen her wave her hand?
Or at the casement seen her stand?   25
Or is she known in all the land,
    The Lady of Shalott?

Only reapers, reaping early
In among the bearded barley,
Hear a song that echoes cheerly   30

[1] Story taken from an Italian novelette, *Donna di Scalotta*. "Shalott" and "Astolat" are the same words, but Tennyson said he had not heard of Elaine, the Lily Maid of Astolat, when he wrote this poem.
[2] *wold* plain
[3] *Camelot* the city of King Arthur's court and Round Table. In the Italian story, it is on the sea.
[4] *shallop* small open boat

From the river winding clearly,
    Down to tower'd Camelot:
And by the moon the reaper weary,
Piling sheaves in uplands airy,
Listening, whispers " 'Tis the fairy   35
    Lady of Shalott."

PART II

There she weaves by night and day
A magic web with colors gay.
She has heard a whisper say,
A curse is on her if she stay   40
    To look down to Camelot.
She knows not what the curse may be,
And so she weaveth steadily,
And little other care hath she,
    The Lady of Shalott.   45

And moving thro' a mirror clear
That hangs before her all the year,
Shadows of the world appear.
There she sees the highway near
    Winding down to Camelot: 50
There the river eddy whirls,
And there the surly village-churls,
And the red cloaks of market girls,
    Pass onward from Shalott.

Sometimes a troop of damsels glad,   55
An abbot on an ambling pad,[5]
Sometimes a curly shepherd-lad,
Or long-hair'd page in crimson clad,
    Goes by to tower'd Camelot;
And sometimes thro' the mirror blue   60
The knights come riding two and two:
She hath no loyal knight and true,
    The Lady of Shalott.

But in her web she still delights
To weave the mirror's magic sights,   65
For often thro' the silent nights
A funeral, with plumes and lights
    And music, went to Camelot:

[5] *pad* a slow-paced horse

Or when the moon was overhead,
Came two young lovers lately wed: 70
"I am half sick of shadows," said
    The Lady of Shalott.

PART III

A bow-shot from her bower-eaves,
He rode between the barley-sheaves.
The sun came dazzling thro' the leaves,   75
And flamed upon the brazen greaves [6]
    Of bold Sir Lancelot.
A red-cross knight for ever kneel'd
To a lady in his shield,
That sparkled on the yellow field,   80
    Beside remote Shalott.

The gemmy bridle glitter'd free,
Like to some branch of stars we see
Hung in the golden Galaxy.
The bridle bells rang merrily   85
    As he rode down to Camelot:
And from his blazon'd baldric [7] slung
A mighty silver bugle hung,
And as he rode his armor rung,
    Beside remote Shalott.   90

All in the blue unclouded weather
Thick-jewell'd shone the saddle-leather,
The helmet and the helmet-feather
Burn'd like one burning flame together,
    As he rode down to Camelot;   95
As often thro' the purple night,
Below the starry clusters bright,
Some bearded meteor, trailing light,
    Moves over still Shalott.

His broad clear brow in sunlight glow'd;   100
On burnish'd hooves his war-horse trode;
From underneath his helmet flow'd
His coal-black curls as on he rode,
    As he rode down to Camelot.
From the bank and from the river   105
He flash'd into the crystal mirror,

---

[6] *brazen greaves* brass leg armor   [7] *baldric* shoulder strap

"Tirra lirra," by the river
    Sang Sir Lancelot.

She left the web, she left the loom,
She made three paces thro' the room,   110
She saw the water-lily bloom,
She saw the helmet and the plume,
    She look'd down to Camelot.
Out flew the web and floated wide;
The mirror crack'd from side to side;   115
"The curse is come upon me," cried
    The Lady of Shalott.

PART IV

In the stormy east-wind straining,
The pale yellow woods were waning,
The broad stream in his banks complaining,   120
Heavily the low sky raining
    Over tower'd Camelot;
Down she came and found a boat
Beneath a willow left afloat,
And round about the prow she wrote   125
    The Lady of Shalott.

And down the river's dim expanse
Like some bold seër in a trance,
Seeing all his own mischance—
With a glassy countenance   130
    Did she look to Camelot.
And at the closing of the day
She loosed the chain, and down she lay;
The broad stream bore her far away,
    The Lady of Shalott.   135

Lying, robed in snowy white
That loosely flew to left and right—
The leaves upon her falling light—
Thro' the noises of the night
    She floated down to Camelot: 140
And as the boat-head wound along
The willowy hills and fields among,
They heard her singing her last song,
    The Lady of Shalott.

Heard a carol, mournful, holy,   145
Chanted loudly, chanted lowly,

Till her blood was frozen slowly,
And her eyes were darken'd wholly,
　　Turn'd to tower'd Camelot.
For ere she reach'd upon the tide　　150
The first house by the water-side,
Singing in her song she died,
　　The Lady of Shalott.

Under tower and balcony,
By garden-wall and gallery,　　155
A gleaming shape she floated by,
Dead-pale between the houses high,
　　Silent into Camelot.
Out upon the wharfs they came,
Knight and burgher, lord and dame,　　160
And round the prow they read her name,
　　The Lady of Shalott.

Who is this? and what is here?
And in the lighted palace near
Died the sound of royal cheer;　　165
And they cross'd themselves for fear,
　　All the knights at Camelot:
But Lancelot mused a little space;
He said, "She has a lovely face;
God in his mercy lend her grace,　　170
　　The Lady of Shalott."

THE LOTOS-EATERS

"Courage!" he [1] said, and pointed toward the land,
"This mounting wave will roll us shoreward soon."
In the afternoon they came unto a land
In which it seemèd always afternoon.
All round the coast the languid air did swoon,　　5
Breathing like one that hath a weary dream.
Full-faced above the valley stood the moon;
And, like a downward smoke, the slender stream
Along the cliff to fall and pause and fall did seem.

A land of streams! some, like a downward smoke,　　10
Slow-dropping veils of thinnest lawn, did go;
And some thro' wavering lights and shadows broke,

[1] *he* Odysseus

Rolling a slumbrous sheet of foam below.
They saw the gleaming river seaward flow
From the inner land; far off, three mountain-tops,   15
Three silent pinnacles of aged snow,
Stood sunset-flush'd; and, dew'd with showery drops,
Up-clomb the shadowy pine above the woven copse.

The charmed sunset linger'd low adown
In the red West: thro' mountain clefts the dale   20
Was seen far inland, and the yellow down
Border'd with palm, and many a winding vale
And meadow, set with slender galingale; [2]
A land where all things always seem'd the same!
And round about the keel with faces pale,   25
Dark faces pale against that rosy flame,
The mild-eyed melancholy Lotos-eaters [3] came.

Branches they bore of that enchanted stem,
Laden with flower and fruit, whereof they gave
To each, but whoso did receive of them   30
And taste, to him the gushing of the wave
Far far away did seem to mourn and rave
On alien shores; and if his fellow spake,
His voice was thin, as voices from the grave;
And deep-asleep he seem'd, yet all awake,   35
And music in his ears his beating heart did make.

They sat them down upon the yellow sand,
Between the sun and moon upon the shore;
And sweet it was to dream of Fatherland,
Of child, and wife, and slave; but evermore   40
Most weary seem'd the sea, weary the oar,
Weary the wandering fields of barren foam.
Then some one said, "We will return no more";
And all at once they sang, "Our island home
Is far beyond the wave; we will no longer roam."   45

CHORIC SONG

I

There is sweet music here that softer falls
Than petals from blown roses on the grass,

[2] *galingale* sedge (papyrus)
[3] *Lotos-eaters* a fabled people who lived on the fruit of the lotus shrub, becoming dreamy and indolent

Or night-dews on still waters between walls
Of shadowy granite, in a gleaming pass;
Music that gentlier on the spirit lies,   5
Than tired eyelids upon tired eyes;
Music that brings sweet sleep down from the blissful skies.
Here are cool mosses deep,
And thro' the moss the ivies creep,
And in the stream the long-leaved flowers weep,   10
And from the craggy ledge the poppy hangs in sleep.

II

Why are we weigh'd upon with heaviness,
And utterly consumed with sharp distress,
While all things else have rest from weariness?
All things have rest: why should we toil alone,   15
We only toil, who are the first of things,
And make perpetual moan,
Still from one sorrow to another thrown;
Nor ever fold our wings,
And cease from wanderings,   20
Nor steep our brows in slumber's holy balm;
Nor harken what the inner spirit sings,
"There is no joy but calm!"
Why should we only toil, the roof and crown of things?

III

Lo! in the middle of the wood,   25
The folded leaf is woo'd from out the bud
With winds upon the branch, and there
Grows green and broad, and takes no care,
Sun-steep'd at noon, and in the moon
Nightly dew-fed; and turning yellow   30
Falls, and floats adown the air.
Lo! sweeten'd with the summer light,
The full-juiced apple, waxing over-mellow,
Drops in a silent autumn night.
All its allotted length of days   35
The flower ripens in its place,
Ripens and fades, and falls, and hath no toil,
Fast-rooted in the fruitful soil.

IV

Hateful is the dark-blue sky,
Vaulted o'er the dark-blue sea.   40

Death is the end of life; ah, why
Should life all labor be?
Let us alone. Time driveth onward fast,
And in a little while our lips are dumb.
Let us alone. What is it that will last?   45
All things are taken from us, and become
Portions and parcels of the dreadful Past.
Let us alone. What pleasure can we have
To war with evil? Is there any peace
In ever climbing up the climbing wave?   50
All things have rest, and ripen toward the grave
In silence—ripen, fall, and cease:
Give us long rest or death, dark death, or dreamful ease.

V

How sweet it were, hearing the downward stream,
With half-shut eyes ever to seem   55
Falling asleep in a half-dream!
To dream and dream, like yonder amber light,
Which will not leave the myrrh-bush [4] on the height;
To hear each other's whisper'd speech;
Eating the Lotos day by day,   60
To watch the crisping ripples on the beach,
And tender curving lines of creamy spray;
To lend our hearts and spirits wholly
To the influence of mild-minded melancholy;
To muse and brood and live again in memory,   65
With those old faces of our infancy
Heap'd over with a mound of grass,
Two handfuls of white dust, shut in an urn of brass!

VI

Dear is the memory of our wedded lives,
And dear the last embraces of our wives   70
And their warm tears: but all hath suffer'd change:
For surely now our household hearths are cold:
Our sons inherit us: our looks are strange:
And we should come like ghosts to trouble joy.
Or else the island princes over-bold   75
Have eat our substance, and the minstrel sings
Before them of the ten years' war in Troy,
And our great deeds, as half-forgotten things.
Is there confusion in the little isle?

[4] *myrrh-bush* grown in Africa and Arabia, source of perfumes

Let what is broken so remain.   80
The Gods are hard to reconcile:
'T is hard to settle order once again.
There *is* confusion worse than death,
Trouble on trouble, pain on pain,
Long labor unto aged breath,   85
Sore task to hearts worn out by many wars
And eyes grown dim with gazing on the pilot-stars.

VII

But, propt on beds of amaranth and moly,[5]
How sweet—while warm airs lull us, blowing lowly—
With half-dropt eyelid still,   90
Beneath a heaven dark and holy,
To watch the long bright river drawing slowly
His waters from the purple hill—
To hear the dewy echoes calling
From cave to cave thro' the thick-twined vine—   95
To watch the emerald-color'd water falling
Thro' many a wov'n acanthus-wreath [6] divine!
Only to hear and see the far-off sparkling brine,
Only to hear were sweet, stretch'd out beneath the pine.

VIII

The Lotos blooms below the barren peak: 100
The Lotos blows by every winding creek:
All day the wind breathes low with mellower tone:
Thro' every hollow cave and alley lone
Round and round the spicy downs the yellow Lotos-dust is blown.
We have had enough of action, and of motion we,   105
Roll'd to starboard, roll'd to larboard, when the surge was seeth-
    ing free,
Where the wallowing monster spouted his foam-fountains in the
    sea.
Let us swear an oath, and keep it with an equal mind,
In the hollow Lotos-land to live and lie reclined
On the hills like Gods together, careless of mankind.   110
For they lie beside their nectar, and the bolts are hurl'd
Far below them in the valleys, and the clouds are lightly curl'd
Round their golden houses, girdled with the gleaming world;
Where they smile in secret, looking over wasted lands,

[5] *amaranth and moly* legendary immortal flowers and herbs
[6] *acanthus-wreath* leaves of a prickly plant whose shape is used as ornamenta-
tion on classical columns (Corinthian and Byzantine)

Blight and famine, plague and earthquake, roaring deeps and
    fiery sands, 115
Clanging fights, and flaming towns, and sinking ships, and pray-
    ing hands.
But they smile, they find a music centred in a doleful song
Steaming up, a lamentation and an ancient tale of wrong,
Like a tale of little meaning tho' the words are strong;
Chanted from an ill-used race of men that cleave the soil, 120
Sow the seed, and reap the harvest with enduring toil,
Storing yearly little dues of wheat, and wine and oil;
Till they perish and they suffer—some, 'tis whisper'd—down in
    hell
Suffer endless anguish, others in Elysian valleys dwell,
Resting weary limbs at last on beds of asphodel.[7] 125
Surely, surely, slumber is more sweet than toil, the shore
Than labor in the deep mid-ocean, wind and wave and oar;
Oh, rest ye, brother mariners, we will not wander more.

ULYSSES

It little profits that an idle king,
By this still hearth, among these barren crags,
Match'd with an aged wife,[1] I mete and dole
Unequal laws unto a savage race,
That hoard, and sleep, and feed, and know not me. 5
I cannot rest from travel: I will drink
Life to the lees: all times I have enjoy'd
Greatly, have suffer'd greatly, both with those
That loved me, and alone; on shore, and when
Thro' scudding drifts the rainy Hyades [2] 10
Vext the dim sea: I am become a name;
For always roaming with a hungry heart
Much have I seen and known; cities of men
And manners, climates, councils, governments,
Myself not least, but honor'd of them all; 15
And drunk delight of battle with my peers,
Far on the ringing plains of windy Troy.
I am a part of all that I have met;
Yet all experience is an arch wherethro'
Gleams that untravell'd world whose margin fades 20

---

[7] *asphodel* daffodils: immortal flowers of Elysium

[1] *wife* Penelope
[2] *Hyades* stars in the constellation of Taurus that determine rainy weather

For ever and for ever when I move.
How dull it is to pause, to make an end,
To rust unburnish'd, not to shine in use!
As tho' to breathe were life! Life piled on life
Were all too little, and of one to me   25
Little remains: but every hour is saved
From that eternal silence, something more,
A bringer of new things; and vile it were
For some three suns to store and hoard myself,
And this gray spirit yearning in desire   30
To follow knowledge like a sinking star,
Beyond the utmost bound of human thought.
　　This is my son, mine own Telemachus,
To whom I leave the sceptre and the isle—
Well-loved of me, discerning to fulfil   35
This labor, by slow prudence to make mild
A rugged people, and thro' soft degrees
Subdue them to the useful and the good.
Most blameless is he, centred in the sphere
Of common duties, decent not to fail   40
In offices of tenderness, and pay
Meet adoration to my household gods,
When I am gone. He works his work, I mine.
　　There lies the port; the vessel puffs her sail:
There gloom the dark broad seas. My mariners,   45
Souls that have toil'd, and wrought, and thought with me—
That ever with a frolic welcome took
The thunder and the sunshine, and opposed
Free hearts, free foreheads—you and I are old;
Old age hath yet his honor and his toil;   50
Death closes all: but something ere the end,
Some work of noble note, may yet be done,
Not unbecoming men that strove with Gods.
The lights begin to twinkle from the rocks:
The long day wanes: the slow moon climbs: the deep   55
Moans round with many voices. Come, my friends,
'Tis not too late to seek a newer world.
Push off, and sitting well in order smite
The sounding furrows; for my purpose holds
To sail beyond the sunset, and the baths   60
Of all the western stars, until I die.
It may be that the gulfs will wash us down:
It may be we shall touch the Happy Isles,[3]

[3] *Happy Isles* islands of Paradise for the dead

And see the great Achilles,[4] whom we knew.
Tho' much is taken, much abides; and tho'   65
We are not now that strength which in old days
Moved earth and heaven, that which we are, we are;
One equal temper of heroic hearts,
Made weak by time and fate, but strong in will
To strive, to seek, to find, and not to yield.   70

TITHONUS [1]

THE woods decay, the woods decay and fall,
The vapors weep their burthen to the ground,
Man comes and tills the field and lies beneath,
And after many a summer dies the swan.
Me only cruel immortality   5
Consumes: I wither slowly in thine arms,
Here at the quiet limit of the world,
A white-hair'd shadow roaming like a dream
The ever-silent spaces of the East,
Far-folded mists, and gleaming halls of morn.   10
    Alas! for this gray shadow, once a man—
So glorious in his beauty and thy choice,
Who madest him thy chosen, that he seem'd
To his great heart none other than a God!
I ask'd thee, "Give me immortality."   15
Then didst thou grant mine asking with a smile,
Like wealthy men who care not how they give.
But thy strong Hours indignant work'd their wills,
And beat me down and marr'd and wasted me,
And tho' they could not end me, left me maim'd   20
To dwell in presence of immortal youth,
Immortal age beside immortal youth,
And all I was, in ashes. Can thy love,
Thy beauty, make amends, tho' even now,
Close over us, the silver star,[2] thy guide,   25
Shines in those tremulous eyes that fill with tears
To hear me? Let me go; take back thy gift:
Why should a man desire in any way

---

[4] *Achilles* Greek hero who fought with Ulysses in the Trojan war

[1] *Tithonus* a mortal loved by Aurora. She obtained from Zeus the gift of
immortality for him, but forgot to ask that he have eternal youth. Tithonus
was finally changed into a grasshopper.
[2] *silver star* morning-star

To vary from the kindly race of men,
Or pass beyond the goal of ordinance   30
Where all should pause, as is most meet for all?

A soft air fans the cloud apart; there comes
A glimpse of that dark world where I was born.
Once more the old mysterious glimmer steals
From thy pure brows, and from thy shoulders pure,   35
And bosom beating with a heart renew'd.
Thy cheek begins to redden thro' the gloom,
Thy sweet eyes brighten slowly close to mine.
Ere yet they blind the stars, and the wild team
Which love thee, yearning for thy yoke, arise,   40
And shake the darkness from their loosen'd manes,
And beat the twilight into flakes of fire.

Lo! ever thus thou growest beautiful
In silence, then before thine answer given
Departest, and thy tears are on my cheek.   45

Why wilt thou ever scare me with thy tears,
And make me tremble lest a saying learnt,
In days far-off, on that dark earth, be true?
"The Gods themselves cannot recall their gifts."

Ay me! ay me! with what another heart   50
In days far-off, and with what other eyes
I used to watch—if I be he that watch'd—
The lucid outline forming round thee; saw
The dim curls kindle into sunny rings;
Changed with thy mystic change, and felt my blood   55
Glow with the glow that slowly crimson'd all
Thy presence and thy portals, while I lay,
Mouth, forehead, eyelids, growing dewy-warm
With kisses balmier than half-opening buds
Of April, and could hear the lips that kiss'd   60
Whispering I knew not what of wild and sweet,
Like that strange song I heard Apollo sing,
While Ilion [3] like a mist rose into towers.

Yet hold me not for ever in thine East:
How can my nature longer mix with thine?   65
Coldly thy rosy shadows bathe me, cold
Are all thy lights, and cold my wrinkled feet
Upon thy glimmering thresholds, when the steam
Floats up from those fields about the homes
Of happy men that have the power to die,   70

[3] *Ilion* Troy, built by Apollo and Neptune for the father of Tithonus

And grassy barrows of the happier dead.
Release me, and restore me to the ground;
Thou seest all things, thou wilt see my grave:
Thou wilt renew thy beauty morn by morn;
I earth in earth forget these empty courts,   75
And thee returning on thy silver wheels.

LOCKSLEY HALL [1]

Comrades, leave me here a little, while as yet 't is early morn;
Leave me here, and when you want me, sound upon the bugle-
   horn.

'T is the place, and all around it, as of old, the curlews call,
Dreary gleams [2] about the moorland flying over Locksley Hall;

Locksley Hall, that in the distance overlooks the sandy tracts,   5
And the hollow ocean-ridges roaring into cataracts.

Many a night from yonder ivied casement, ere I went to rest,
Did I look on great Orion sloping slowly to the West.

Many a night I saw the Pleiads, rising thro' the mellow shade,
Glitter like a swarm of fireflies tangled in a silver braid.   10

Here about the beach I wander'd, nourishing a youth sublime
With the fairy tales of science, and the long result of Time;

When the centuries behind me like a fruitful land reposed;
When I clung to all the present for the promise that it closed:

When I dipt into the future far as human eye could see;   15
Saw the Vision of the world and all the wonder that would be.—

In the Spring a fuller crimson comes upon the robin's breast;
In the Spring the wanton lapwing gets himself another crest;

In the Spring a livelier iris changes on the burnish'd dove;
In the Spring a young man's fancy lightly turns to thoughts of
   love.   20

Then her cheek was pale and thinner than should be for one so
   young,
And her eyes on all my motions with a mute observance hung.

And I said, "My cousin Amy, speak, and speak the truth to me,
Trust me, cousin, all the current of my being sets to thee."

---

[1] The poem is about an imaginary place and hero.
[2] *gleams* of light, not the curlews, according to Tennyson

On her pallid cheek and forehead came a color and a light,   25
As I have seen the rosy red flushing in the northern night.

And she turn'd—her bosom shaken with a sudden storm of sighs—
All the spirit deeply dawning in the dark of hazel eyes—

Saying, "I have hid my feelings, fearing they should do me
  wrong";
Saying, "Dost thou love me, cousin?" weeping, "I have loved thee
  long."   30

Love took up the glass of Time, and turn'd it in his glowing
  hands;
Every moment, lightly shaken, ran itself in golden sands.

Love took up the harp of Life, and smote on all the chords with
  might;
Smote the chord of Self, that, trembling, pass'd in music out of
  sight.

Many a morning on the moorland did we hear the copses ring,
And her whisper throng'd my pulses with the fulness of the
  Spring.   36

Many an evening by the waters did we watch the stately ships,
And our spirits rush'd together at the touching of the lips.

O my cousin, shallow-hearted! O my Amy, mine no more!
O the dreary, dreary moorland! O the barren, barren shore!   40

Falser than all fancy fathoms, falser than all songs have sung,
Puppet to a father's threat, and servile to a shrewish tongue!

Is it well to wish thee happy?—having known me—to decline
On a range of lower feelings and a narrower heart than mine!

Yet it shall be: thou shalt lower to his level day by day,   45
What is fine within thee growing coarse to sympathize with clay.

As the husband is, the wife is: thou art mated with a clown,
And the grossness of his nature will have weight to drag thee
  down.

He will hold thee, when his passion shall have spent its novel
  force,
Something better than his dog, a little dearer than his horse.   50

What is this? his eyes are heavy; think not they are glazed with
  wine.
Go to him: it is thy duty: kiss him: take his hand in thine.

It may be my lord is weary, that his brain is overwrought:
Soothe him with thy finer fancies, touch him with thy lighter
    thought.

He will answer to the purpose, easy things to understand—   55
Better thou wert dead before me, tho' I slew thee with my hand!

Better thou and I were lying, hidden from the heart's disgrace,
Roll'd in one another's arms, and silent in a last embrace.

Cursed be the social wants that sin against the strength of youth!
Cursed be the social lies that warp us from the living truth!   60

Cursed be the sickly forms that err from honest Nature's rule!
Cursed be the gold that gilds the straiten'd forehead of the fool!

Well—'t is well that I should bluster!—Hadst thou less unworthy
    proved—
Would to God—for I had loved thee more than ever wife was
    loved.

Am I mad, that I should cherish that which bears but bitter
    fruit?   65
I will pluck it from my bosom, tho' my heart be at the root.

Never, tho' my mortal summers to such length of years should
    come
As the many-winter'd crow that leads the clanging rookery home.

Where is comfort? in division of the records of the mind?
Can I part her from herself, and love her, as I knew her, kind?   70

I remember one that perish'd: sweetly did she speak and move:
Such a one do I remember, whom to look at was to love.

Can I think of her as dead, and love her for the love she bore?
No—she never loved me truly: love is love for evermore.

Comfort? comfort scorn'd of devils! this is truth the poet sings,   75
That a sorrow's crown of sorrow is remembering happier things.

Drug thy memories, lest thou learn it, lest thy heart be put to
    proof,
In the dead unhappy night, and when the rain is on the roof.

Like a dog, he hunts in dreams, and thou art staring at the wall,
Where the dying night-lamp flickers, and the shadows rise and
    fall.   80

Then a hand shall pass before thee, pointing to his drunken sleep,
To thy widow'd marriage-pillows, to the tears that thou wilt weep.

Thou shalt hear the "Never, never," whisper'd by the phantom
     years,
And a song from out the distance in the ringing of thine ears;

And an eye shall vex thee, looking ancient kindness on thy pain.
Turn thee, turn thee on thy pillow: get thee to thy rest again.   86

Nay, but Nature brings thee solace; for a tender voice will cry.
'T is a purer life than thine, a lip to drain thy trouble dry.

Baby lips will laugh me down: my latest rival brings thee rest.
Baby fingers, waxen touches, press me from the mother's breast.

O, the child too clothes the father with a dearness not his due.   91
Half is thine and half is his: it will be worthy of the two.

O, I see thee old and formal, fitted to thy petty part,
With a little hoard of maxims preaching down a daughter's heart.

"They were dangerous guides the feelings—she herself was not
     exempt—   95
Truly, she herself had suffer'd"—Perish in thy self-contempt!

Overlive it—lower yet—be happy! wherefore should I care?
I myself must mix with action, lest I wither by despair.

What is that which I should turn to, lighting upon days like
     these?
Every door is barr'd with gold, and opens but to golden keys.   100

Every gate is throng'd with suitors, all the markets overflow.
I have but an angry fancy: what is that which I should do?

I had been content to perish, falling on the foeman's ground,
When the ranks are roll'd in vapor, and the winds are laid with
     sound.

But the jingling of the guinea helps the hurt that Honor feels,   105
And the nations do but murmur, snarling at each other's heels.

Can I but relive in sadness? I will turn that earlier page.
Hide me from my deep emotion, O thou wondrous Mother-Age!

Make me feel the wild pulsation that I felt before the strife,
When I heard my days before me, and the tumult of my life;   110

Yearning for the large excitement that the coming years would
    yield,
Eager-hearted as a boy when first he leaves his father's field,

And at night along the dusky highway near and nearer drawn,
Sees in heaven the light of London flaring like a dreary dawn;

And his spirit leaps within him to be gone before him then,   115
Underneath the light he looks at, in among the throngs of men:

Men, my brothers, men the workers, ever reaping something new:
That which they have done but earnest of the things that they
    shall do:

For I dipt into the future, far as human eye could see,
Saw the Vision of the world, and all the wonder that would be;

Saw the heavens fill with commerce, argosies of magic sails,   121
Pilots of the purple twilight, dropping down with costly bales;

Heard the heavens fill with shouting, and there rain'd a ghastly
    dew
From the nations' airy navies grappling in the central blue;

Far along the world-wide whisper of the south-wind rushing
    warm,   125
With the standards of the peoples plunging thro' the thunder-
    storm;

Till the war-drum throbb'd no longer, and the battle-flags were
    furl'd
In the Parliament of man, the Federation of the world.

There the common sense of most shall hold a fretful realm in
    awe,
And the kindly earth shall slumber, lapt in universal law.   130

So I triumph'd ere my passion sweeping thro' me left me dry,
Left me with the palsied heart, and left me with the jaundiced
    eye;

Eye, to which all order festers, all things here are out of joint:
Science moves, but slowly, slowly, creeping on from point to
    point:

Slowly comes a hungry people, as a lion, creeping nigher,   135
Glares at one that nods and winks behind a slowly-dying fire.

Yet I doubt not thro' the ages one increasing purpose runs,
And the thoughts of men are widen'd with the process of the suns.

What is that to him that reaps not harvest of his youthful joys,
Tho' the deep heart of existence beat for ever like a boy's?   140

Knowledge comes, but wisdom lingers, and I linger on the shore,
And the individual withers, and the world is more and more.

Knowledge comes, but wisdom lingers, and he bears a laden breast,
Full of sad experience, moving toward the stillness of his rest.

Hark, my merry comrades call me, sounding on the bugle-horn,   145
They to whom my foolish passion were a target for their scorn:

Shall it not be scorn to me to harp on such a moulder'd string?
I am shamed thro' all my nature to have loved so slight a thing.

Weakness to be wroth with weakness! woman's pleasure, woman's pain—
Nature made them blinder motions bounded in a shallower brain: 150

Woman is the lesser man, and all thy passions, match'd with mine,
Are as moonlight unto sunlight, and as water unto wine—

Here at last, where nature sickens, nothing. Ah, for some retreat
Deep in yonder shining Orient, where my life began to beat;

Where in wild Mahratta-battle [3] fell my father evil-starr'd;—   155
I was left a trampled orphan, and a selfish uncle's ward.

Or to burst all links of habit—there to wander far away,
On from island unto island at the gateways of the day.

Larger constellations burning, mellow moons and happy skies,
Breadths of tropic shade and palms in cluster, knots of Paradise.

Never comes the trader, never floats an European flag,   161
Slides the bird o'er lustrous woodland, swings the trailer from the crag;

Droops the heavy-blossom'd bower, hangs the heavy-fruited tree—
Summer isles of Eden lying in dark-purple spheres of sea.

There methinks would be enjoyment more than in this march of mind,   165
In the steamship, in the railway, in the thoughts that shake mankind.

[3] *Mahratta-battle* in India

There the passions cramp'd no longer shall have scope and
   breathing space;
I will take some savage woman, she shall rear my dusky race.

Iron-jointed, supple-sinew'd, they shall dive, and they shall run,
Catch the wild goat by the hair, and hurl their lances in the
   sun;   170

Whistle back the parrot's call and leap the rainbows of the brooks,
Not with blinded eyesight poring over miserable books—

Fool, again the dream, the fancy! but I *know* my words are wild,
But I count the gray barbarian lower than the Christian child.

I, to herd with narrow foreheads, vacant of our glorious gains, 175
Like a beast with lower pleasures, like a beast with lower pains!

Mated with a squalid savage—what to me were sun or clime?
I the heir of all the ages, in the foremost files of time—

I that rather held it better men should perish one by one,
Than that earth should stand at gaze like Joshua's moon in
   Ajalon! [4]   180

Not in vain the distance beacons. Forward, forward let us range,
Let the great world spin for ever down the ringing grooves of
   change.

Thro' the shadow of the globe we sweep into the younger day:
Better fifty years of Europe than a cycle of Cathay.[5]

Mother-Age (for mine I knew not) help me as when life begun:
Rift the hills, and roll the waters, flash the lightnings, weigh the
   Sun.   186

O, I see the crescent promise of my spirit hath not set.
Ancient founts of inspiration well thro' all my fancy yet.

Howsoever these things be, a long farewell to Locksley Hall!
Now for me the woods may wither, now for me the roof-tree
   fall.   190

Comes a vapor from the margin, blackening over heath and holt,
Cramming all the blast before it, in its breast a thunderbolt.

Let it fall on Locksley Hall, with rain or hail, or fire or snow;
For the mighty wind arises, roaring seaward, and I go.

[4] *Joshua's moon in Ajalon* During a battle in Palestine, Joshua commanded
the moon to stand still in the valley of Ajalon, and the sun on Gibeon.
[5] *Cathay* China, or the East

BREAK, BREAK, BREAK

Break, break, break,
  On thy cold gray stones, O Sea!
And I would that my tongue could utter
  The thoughts that arise in me.

O well for the fisherman's boy,   5
  That he shouts with his sister at play!
O well for the sailor lad,
  That he sings in his boat on the bay!

And the stately ships go on
  To their haven under the hill;   10
But O for the touch of a vanish'd hand,
  And the sound of a voice that is still!

Break, break, break,
  At the foot of thy crags, O Sea!
But the tender grace of a day that is dead   15
  Will never come back to me.

THE EAGLE

FRAGMENT

He clasps the crag with crooked hands;
Close to the sun in lonely lands,
Ring'd with the azure world, he stands.

The wrinkled sea beneath him crawls;
He watches from his mountain walls,   5
And like a thunderbolt he falls.

SONGS AND LYRICS FROM
THE PRINCESS

TEARS, IDLE TEARS

Tears, idle tears, I know not what they mean,
Tears from the depth of some divine despair
Rise in the heart, and gather to the eyes,
In looking on the happy Autumn-fields,
And thinking of the days that are no more.   5

Fresh as the first beam glittering on a sail,
That brings our friends up from the underworld,
Sad as the last which reddens over one
That sinks with all we love below the verge;
So sad, so fresh, the days that are no more.   10

Ah, sad and strange as in dark summer dawns
The earliest pipe of half-awaken'd birds
To dying ears, when unto dying eyes
The casement slowly grows a glimmering square;
So sad, so strange, the days that are no more.   15

Dear as remember'd kisses after death,
And sweet as those by hopeless fancy feign'd
On lips that are for others; deep as love,
Deep as first love, and wild with all regret;
O Death in Life, the days that are no more.   20

NOW SLEEPS THE CRIMSON PETAL

Now sleeps the crimson petal, now the white;
Nor waves the cypress in the palace walk;
Nor winks the gold fin in the porphyry [1] font:
The fire-fly wakens: waken thou with me.

Now droops the milk-white peacock like a ghost,   5
And like a ghost she glimmers on to me.

Now lies the Earth all Danaë [2] to the stars,
And all thy heart lies open unto me.

Now slides the silent meteor on, and leaves
A shining furrow, as thy thoughts in me.   10

Now folds the lily all her sweetness up,
And slips into the bosom of the lake:
So fold thyself, my dearest, thou, and slip
Into my bosom and be lost in me.

COME DOWN, O MAID

"Come down, O maid, from yonder mountain height:
What pleasure lives in height (the shepherd sang),

[1] *porphyry* dark-red or purple rock flecked with crystals
[2] *Danaë* visited by Jupiter in the form of a shower of gold. She became the
mother of Perseus.

In height and cold, the splendor of the hills?
But cease to move so near the heavens, and cease
To glide a sunbeam by the blasted pine,   5
To sit a star upon the sparkling spire;
And come, for Love is of the valley, come,
For Love is of the valley, come thou down
And find him; by the happy threshold, he,
Or hand in hand with Plenty in the maize,   10
Or red with spirted [1] purple of the vats,
Or foxlike in the vine; nor cares to walk
With Death and Morning on the Silver Horns,[2]
Nor wilt thou snare him in the white ravine,
Nor find him dropt upon the firths of ice,[3]   15
That huddling slant in furrow-cloven falls
To roll the torrent out of dusky doors:
But follow; let the torrent dance thee down
To find him in the valley; let the wild
Lean-headed eagles yelp alone, and leave   20
The monstrous ledges there to slope, and spill
Their thousand wreaths of dangling water-smoke,
That like a broken purpose waste in air:
So waste not thou; but come; for all the vales
Await thee; azure pillars of the hearth   25
Arise to thee; the children call, and I
Thy shepherd pipe, and sweet is every sound,
Sweeter thy voice, but every sound is sweet;
Myriads of rivulets hurrying thro' the lawn,
The moan of doves in immemorial elms,   30
And murmuring of innumerable bees."

IN MEMORIAM [1]

1

I held it truth, with him who sings
    To one clear harp in divers tones,
    That men may rise on stepping-stones
Of their dead selves to higher things.

[1] *spirted* spurted   [2] *Silver Horns* Silberhorn, a mountain peak
[3] *firths of ice* arms of the sea containing glaciers

[1] A series of 133 lyrics (including a prologue and epilogue) written as a tribute to the memory of Tennyson's friend, the brilliant and promising Arthur Henry Hallam, who died in 1833 at the age of twenty-two.

But who shall so forecast the years 5
   And find in loss a gain to match?
    Or reach a hand thro' time to catch
The far-off interest of tears?

Let Love clasp Grief lest both be drown'd,
   Let darkness keep her raven gloss: 10
    Ah, sweeter to be drunk with loss,
To dance with Death, to beat the ground,

Than that the victor Hours should scorn
   The long result of love, and boast,
    "Behold the man that loved and lost, 15
But all he was is overworn."

7

Dark house, by which once more I stand
   Here in the long unlovely street,[2]
    Doors, where my heart was used to beat
So quickly, waiting for a hand,

A hand that can be clasp'd no more— 5
   Behold me, for I cannot sleep,
    And like a guilty thing I creep
At earliest morning to the door.

He is not here; but far away
   The noise of life begins again, 10
    And ghastly thro' the drizzling rain
On the bald street breaks the blank day.

54

Oh yet we trust that somehow good
   Will be the final goal of ill,
    To pangs of nature, sins of will,
Defects of doubt, and taints of blood;

That nothing walks with aimless feet; 5
   That not one life shall be destroy'd,
    Or cast as rubbish to the void,
When God hath made the pile complete;

That not a worm is cloven in vain;
   That not a moth with vain desire 10
    Is shrivell'd in a fruitless fire,
Or but subserves another's gain.

[2] *street* Hallam lived at 67 Wimpole Street, London

Behold, we know not anything;
   I can but trust that good shall fall
   At last—far off—at last, to all,   15
And every winter change to spring.

So runs my dream: but what am I?
   An infant crying in the night:
   An infant crying for the light:
And with no language but a cry.   20

55

The wish, that of the living whole
   No life may fail beyond the grave,
   Derives it not from what we have
The likest God within the soul?

Are God and Nature then at strife,   5
   That Nature lends such evil dreams?
   So careful of the type she seems,
So careless of the single life;

That I, considering everywhere
   Her secret meaning in her deeds,   10
   And finding that of fifty [3] seeds
She often brings but one to bear,

I falter where I firmly trod,
   And falling with my weight of cares
   Upon the great world's altar-stairs   15
That slope thro' darkness up to God,

I stretch lame hands of faith, and grope,
   And gather dust and chaff, and call
   To what I feel is Lord of all,
And faintly trust the larger hope.   20

56

"So careful of the type?" but no.
   From scarped cliff and quarried stone
   She cries, "A thousand types are gone:
I care for nothing, all shall go.

"Thou makest thine appeal to me: 5
   I bring to life, I bring to death:
   The spirit does but mean the breath:
I know no more." And he, shall he,

---

[3] *fifty* Tennyson noted that "fifty" should be "myriad."

Man, her last work, who seem'd so fair,
   Such splendid purpose in his eyes,   10
   Who roll'd the psalm to wintry skies,
Who built him fanes of fruitless prayer,

Who trusted God was love indeed
   And love Creation's final law—
   Tho' Nature, red in tooth and claw   15
With ravine, shriek'd against his creed—

Who loved, who suffer'd countless ills,
   Who battled for the True, the Just,
   Be blown about the desert dust,
Or seal'd within the iron hills?   20

No more? A monster then, a dream,
   A discord. Dragons of the prime,
   That tare each other in their slime,
Were mellow music match'd with him.

O life as futile, then, as frail!   25
   O for thy voice to soothe and bless!
   What hope of answer, or redress?
Behind the veil, behind the veil.

106

Ring out, wild bells, to the wild sky,
   The flying cloud, the frosty light:
   The year is dying in the night;
Ring out, wild bells, and let him die.

Ring out the old, ring in the new,   5
   Ring, happy bells, across the snow:
   The year is going, let him go;
Ring out the false, ring in the true.

Ring out the grief that saps the mind,
   For those that here we see no more;   10
   Ring out the feud of rich and poor,
Ring in redress to all mankind.

Ring out a slowly dying cause,
   And ancient forms of party strife;
   Ring in the nobler modes of life,   15
With sweeter manners, purer laws.

Ring out the want, the care, the sin,
   The faithless coldness of the times;

Ring out, ring out my mournful rhymes,
But ring the fuller minstrel in.   20

Ring out false pride in place and blood,
    The civic slander and the spite;
    Ring in the love of truth and right,
Ring in the common love of good.

Ring out old shapes of foul disease;   25
    Ring out the narrowing lust of gold;
    Ring out the thousand wars of old,
Ring in the thousand years of peace.

Ring in the valiant man and free,
    The larger heart, the kindlier hand;   30
    Ring out the darkness of the land,
Ring in the Christ that is to be.

119

Doors, where my heart was used to beat
    So quickly, not as one that weeps
    I come once more; the city sleeps;
I smell the meadow in the street;

I hear a chirp of birds; I see   5
    Betwixt the black fronts long-withdrawn
    A light-blue lane of early dawn,
And think of early days and thee,

And bless thee, for thy lips are bland,
    And bright the friendship of thine eye;   10
    And in my thoughts with scarce a sigh
I take the pressure of thine hand.

130

Thy voice is on the rolling air;
    I hear thee where the waters run;
    Thou standest in the rising sun,
And in the setting thou art fair.

What art thou then? I cannot guess;   5
    But tho' I seem in star and flower
    To feel thee some diffusive power,
I do not therefore love thee less.

My love involves the love before;
    My love is vaster passion now;   10

Tho' mix'd with God and Nature thou,
I seem to love thee more and more.

Far off thou art, but ever nigh;
   I have thee still, and I rejoice;
   I prosper, circled with thy voice;   15
I shall not lose thee tho' I die.

131

O living will [4] that shalt endure
   When all that seems shall suffer shock,
   Rise in the spiritual rock,
Flow thro' our deeds and make them pure,

That we may lift from out of dust   5
   A voice as unto him that hears,
   A cry above the conquer'd years
To one that with us works, and trust,

With faith that comes of self-control,
   The truths that never can be proved   10
   Until we close with all we loved,
And all we flow from, soul in soul.

FLOWER IN THE CRANNIED WALL

Flower in the crannied wall,
I pluck you out of the crannies,
I hold you here, root and all, in my hand,
Little flower—but *if* I could understand
What you are, root and all, and all in all,   5
I should know what God and man is.

CROSSING THE BAR

Sunset and evening star,
   And one clear call for me!
And may there be no moaning of the bar,
   When I put out to sea,

But such a tide as moving seems asleep,   5
   Too full for sound and foam,
When that which drew from out the boundless deep
   Turns again home.

[4] *living will* free-will, according to Tennyson

Twilight and evening bell,
    And after that the dark!   10
And may there be no sadness of farewell,
    When I embark;

For tho' from out our bourne of Time and Place
    The flood may bear me far,
I hope to see my Pilot face to face   15
    When I have crost the bar.

CRITICISM

As a contrast to the detailed and factual accounts of poems
in some preceding essays, the following illustrates the general
appreciation, or evaluation, of a poet that is another kind of
criticism. Like the brief sketch of Shakespeare's characteristics
in the sonnets (p. 199), this piece attempts to give an over-all
(even personal) view of Tennyson rather than specific instances.
It is, in effect, a summary of a poet, not of his work.

Tennyson [1]

GEORGE SAINTSBURY

It is not improper . . . to endeavour to state—leaving out the
graces that can never be stated, and are more important than all
the others—the points in which this new excellence of Tennyson
differed from the excellences of his forerunners. One of them,
not the least important, but the least truly original, because something distantly resembling it had been seen before in Keats and
Shelley, is the combined application of pictorial and musical
handling. Not, of course, that all poets had not endeavoured to
depict their subjects vividly and to arrange the picture in a
melodious frame of sound, not that the best of them had not
also endeavoured to convey, if it were possible, the colours into
the sense, the sense into the music. But partly as a result of
the natural development and acquired practice of the language,
partly for the very reason that the arts both of painting and
music had themselves made independent progress, most of all,
perhaps, because Tennyson was the first poet in English of the

---

[1] Extracted from George Saintsbury, *A History of Nineteenth Century Literature* (Macmillan, 1896).

very greatest genius who dared not to attempt work on the great scale, but put into short pieces (admitting, of course, of infinite formal variety) what most of his forerunners would have spun into long poems—the result here is, as a rule, far in advance of those forerunners in this respect. . . . About [his poetry] there clung and rang a peculiar dreamy slow music which was heard for the first time, and which has never been reproduced. . . .

But there is something more to be noted still. The poet had caught and was utilising the spirit of his time in two ways, one of them almost entirely new. That he constantly sang the subjective view of nature may be set down to the fact that he came after Wordsworth, though the fact that he sang it without the Wordsworthian dryness and dulness must be set down to his own credit. But in that sense of the history of former times which is perhaps the chief glory of the nineteenth century in matters of thought he had been anticipated by no one. He might not have attained it without Scott and Byron, but his expression of it was hardly conditioned in the very slightest degree by the expression either of Byron or of Scott. They were not in strictness men of the nineteenth century; he was, and he represented the very best features of his time in attending, from its point of view mainly, to the features of better times. . . .

A very little more may, perhaps, still be said about this great poet,—great in the character and variety of his accomplishment, in the volume of it, and, above all, in the extraordinarily sustained quality of his genius and the length of time during which it dominated and pervaded the literature of his country. The influences of Pope and Dryden were weak in force and merely external in effect, the influence of Byron was short-lived, that of Wordsworth was partial and limited, in comparison with the influence of Tennyson. Of this, as of a mere historical fact, there can be no dispute among those who care to inform themselves of the facts and to consider them coolly. Of his intrinsic merit, as opposed to his influential importance, it is not of course possible to speak so peremptorily. Among the great volume of more or less unfavourable criticism which such a career was sure to call forth, two notes perhaps were the most dominant, the most constant, and (even fervent admirers may admit) the least unjust. He was accused of a somewhat excessive prettiness, a sort of dandyism and coquetry in form, and of a certain want of

profundity in matter. The last charge is the more unprofitable
in discussion, for it turns mainly on vast and vague questions of
previous definition. "What is thought?" "What is profundity?"
a by no means jesting demurrer may object, and he will not soon
be cleared out of the way. And it will perhaps seem to some
that what is called Tennyson's lack of profundity consists only in
a disinclination on his part to indulge in what the Germans call
the *Schwätzerei,* the endless, aimless talkee-talkee about "thoughtful" things in which the nineteenth century has indulged beyond
the record of any since what used to be called the Dark Ages. On
the real "great questions" Tennyson was not loth to speak, and
spoke gravely enough; even to the ephemeralities, as we have said,
he paid rather too much than too little attention. But he did not
go into the ins and outs of them as some of his contemporaries
did, and as other contemporaries thought fitting. He usually
neglected the negligible; and perhaps it would not hurt him with
posterity if he had neglected it a little more, though it hurt him a
little with contemporaries that he neglected it as much as he did.

The charge of prettiness is to be less completely ruled out;
though it shows even greater mistake in those who do more than
touch very lightly on it. In the earliest forms of the earlier
poems not seldom, and occasionally in even the latest forms of
the later, the exquisiteness of the poet's touch in music and in
painting, in fancy and in form, did sometimes pass into something like finicalness, into what is called in another language
mignardise. But this was only the necessary, and, after he was out
of his apprenticeship, the minimised effect of his great poetical
quality—that very quality of exquisiteness in form, in fancy, in
painting, and in music which has just been stated. We have, it
must be admitted, had greater poets than Tennyson. Shakespeare,
Spenser, Milton, Shelley, undoubtedly deserve this preference to
him; Wordsworth and Keats may deserve it. But we have had
none so uniformly, and over such a large mass of work, exquisite.
In the lighter fantastic veins he may sometimes be a little unsure
in touch and taste; in satire and argument a little heavy, a
little empty, a little rhetorical; in domestic and ethical subjects
a little tame. But his handlings of these things form a very
small part of his work. And in the rest none of all these faults
appears, and their absence is due to the fact that nothing inter-
feres with the exquisite perfection of the form. Some faults have

been found with Tennyson's rhymes, though this is generally hypercriticism; and in his later years he was a little too apt to accumulate tribrachs in his blank verse, a result of a mistaken sense of the true fact that he was better at slow rhythms than at quick, and of an attempt to cheat nature. But in all other respects his versification is by far the most perfect of any English poet, and results in a harmony positively incomparable. So also his colour and outline in conveying the visual image are based on a study of natural fact and a practice in transferring it to words which are equally beyond comparison. Take any one of a myriad of lines of Tennyson, and the mere arrangement of vowels and consonants will be a delight to the ear; let any one of a thousand of his descriptions body itself before the eye, and the picture will be like the things seen in a dream, but firmer and clearer.

EDITORS' NOTE: To compare with Saintsbury in the nineteenth century, here is W. H. Auden in a twentieth-century summary of Tennyson:

He had a large, loose-limbed body, a swarthy complexion, a high, narrow forehead, and huge bricklayer's hands; in youth he looked like a gypsy; in age like a dirty old monk; he had the finest ear, perhaps, of any English poet; he was also undoubtedly the stupidest; there was little about melancholia that he didn't know; there was little else that he did. [Introduction to *A Selection from the Poems of Alfred Lord Tennyson*, ed. W. H. Auden (Doubleday, 1947), p. x]

ROBERT BROWNING

[1812-1889]

ROBERT BROWNING was a Londoner, of a cultured family (his father, a bank clerk, was a learned man). He was educated in private schools and the University of London. *Paracelsus* (1835) began his series of poems on Renaissance and medieval Italy; *Sordello* (1840) gave him a reputation for obscurity. Browning's trademark soon became the dramatic poem, and with his shorter lyrics and dramatic monologues he created a whole gallery of voices. In 1846, books of the previous five years (*Pippa Passes, Dramatic Lyrics, Dramatic Romances and Lyrics*) were collected into one volume. That year, too, he married Elizabeth Barrett, a poet then better known than he. Until Elizabeth's death in 1861, the Brownings spent their years in Italy, where their son was born and where Browning's interest in art brought new themes into his poems. Some of his later books are *Men and Women* (1855), *Dramatis Personae* (1864), and *The Ring and the Book* (1868–1869). He spent his last years actively writing in England and Italy. He was popular, though he was studied by the fashionable Browning societies as the "difficult" modern poet of his day. In his life Browning had prosperity and fame. And surviving far beyond his time are his brilliantly spoken, truly observed sketches of human character.

Introductory Readings

EDITION: *The Complete Poetical Works of Robert Browning,* ed. Augustine Birrell, 2 vols. (1919). BIOGRAPHY: W. H. Griffin and H. C. Minchin, *The Life of Robert Browning* (rev. ed., 1938); Betty Miller, *Robert Browning: A Portrait* (1952). CRITICISM: W. C. DeVane, *A Browning Handbook* (rev. ed., 1955); Henry Charles Duffin, *Amphibian: A Reconsideration of Browning* (1956); Roma A. King, Jr., *The Bow & the Lyre* (1957); John Norman Bryson, *Browning* (1959).

MY LAST DUCHESS' [1]

FERRARA [2]

That's my last Duchess painted on the wall,
Looking as if she were alive. I call
That piece a wonder, now: Frà Pandolf's [3] hands
Worked busily a day, and there she stands.
Will't please you sit and look at her? I said   5
"Frà Pandolf" by design, for never read
Strangers like you that pictured countenance,
The depth and passion of its earnest glance,
But to myself they turned (since none puts by
The curtain I have drawn for you, but I)   10
And seemed as they would ask me, if they durst,
How such a glance came there; so, not the first
Are you to turn and ask thus. Sir, 'twas not
Her husband's presence only, called that spot
Of joy into the Duchess' cheek: perhaps   15
Frà Pandolf chanced to say, "Her mantle laps
Over my lady's wrist too much," or "Paint
Must never hope to reproduce the faint
Half-flush that dies along her throat:" such stuff
Was courtesy, she thought, and cause enough   20
For calling up that spot of joy. She had
A heart—how shall I say?—too soon made glad,
Too easily impressed; she liked whate'er
She looked on, and her looks went everywhere.
Sir, 'twas all one! My favor at her breast,   25
The dropping of the daylight in the West,
The bough of cherries some officious fool
Broke in the orchard for her, the white mule
She rode with round the terrace—all and each
Would draw from her alike the approving speech,   30
Or blush, at least. She thanked men,—good! but thanked
Somehow—I know not how—as if she ranked
My gift of a nine-hundred-years-old name
With anybody's gift. Who'd stoop to blame
This sort of trifling? Even had you skill   35
In speech—(which I have not)—to make your will

---

[1] Critical comment on this poem appears on p. 530.
[2] *Ferrara* an Italian city-state that flourished during the Renaissance
[3] *Frà Pandolf* an imaginary artist

Quite clear to such an one, and say, "Just this
Or that in you disgusts me; here you miss,
Or there exceed the mark"—and if she let
Herself be lessoned so, nor plainly set   40
Her wits to yours, forsooth, and made excuse,
—E'en then would be some stooping; and I choose
Never to stoop. Oh sir, she smiled, no doubt,
Whene'er I passed her; but who passed without
Much the same smile? This grew; I gave commands;   45
Then all smiles stopped together. There she stands
As if alive. Will't please you rise? We'll meet
The company below, then. I repeat,
The Count your master's known munificence
Is ample warrant that no just pretence   50
Of mine for dowry will be disallowed;
Though his fair daughter's self, as I avowed
At starting, is my object. Nay, we'll go
Together down, sir. Notice Neptune,[4] though,
Taming a sea-horse, thought a rarity,   55
Which Claus [5] of Innsbruck cast in bronze for me!

SOLILOQUY OF THE SPANISH CLOISTER

I

Gr-r-r—there go, my heart's abhorrence!
    Water your damned flower-pots, do!
If hate killed men, Brother Lawrence,
    God's blood, would not mine kill you!
What? your myrtle-bush wants trimming?   5
    Oh, that rose has prior claims—
Needs its leaden vase filled brimming?
    Hell dry you up with its flames!

II

At the meal we sit together:
    Salve tibi! [1] I must hear   10
Wise talk of the kind of weather,
    Sort of season, time of year:
*Not a plenteous cork-crop: scarcely
    Dare we hope oak-galls, I doubt:*

---

[4] *Neptune* a statue of the sea god   [5] *Claus* another imaginary artist

[1] *Salve tibi!* hail to you

What's the Latin name for "parsley"?   15
 What's the Greek name for Swine's Snout?

III

Whew! We'll have our platter burnished,
  Laid with care on our own shelf!
With a fire-new spoon we're furnished,
  And a goblet for ourself,   20
Rinsed like something sacrificial
  Ere 'tis fit to touch our chaps—
Marked with L. for our initial!
  (He-he! There his lily snaps!)

IV

Saint, forsooth! While brown Dolores   25
  Squats outside the Convent bank
With Sanchicha, telling stories,
  Steeping tresses in the tank,
Blue-black, lustrous, thick like horsehairs,
  —Can't I see his dead eye glow,   30
Bright as 'twere a Barbary corsair's? [2]
  (That is, if he'd let it show!)

V

When he finishes refection,[3]
  Knife and fork he never lays
Cross-wise, to my recollection,   35
  As do I, in Jesu's praise.
I the Trinity illustrate,
  Drinking watered orange-pulp—
In three sips the Arian [4] frustrate;
  While he drains his at one gulp.   40

VI

Oh, those melons? If he's able
  We're to have a feast! so nice!
One goes to the Abbot's table,
  All of us get each a slice.
How go on your flowers? None double?   45
  Not one fruit-sort can you spy?

[2] *Barbary corsair* pirate from northwest coast of Africa
[3] *refection* repast, light meal
[4] *Arian* Arius was a fourth-century heretic who denied the doctrine of the trinity, or Christ's equality with God.

Strange!—And I, too, at such trouble,
   Keep them close-nipped on the sly!

VII

There's a great text in Galatians,[5]
   Once you trip on it, entails   50
Twenty-nine distinct damnations,
   One sure, if another fails:
If I trip him just a-dying,
   Sure of heaven as sure can be,
Spin him round and send him flying   55
   Off to hell, a Manichee? [6]

VIII

Or, my scrofulous French novel
   On gray paper with blunt type!
Simply glance at it, you grovel
   Hand and foot in Belial's [7] gripe: 60
If I double down its pages
   At the woeful sixteenth print,
When he gathers his greengages,
   Ope a sieve and slip it in't?

IX

Or, there's Satan!—one might venture   65
   Pledge one's soul to him, yet leave
Such a flaw in the indenture
   As he'd miss till, past retrieve,
Blasted lay that rose-acacia
   We're so proud of! *Hy, Zy, Hine.*[8]   70
'St, there's Vespers! *Plena gratiâ*
   Ave, Virgo! [9] Gr-r-r—you swine!

[5] *Galatians* where there are many passages difficult to interpret
[6] *Manichee* a believer in the Manichaean heresy, a concept of two kingdoms, one good, the other evil, both equal in strength: so long as man is in the flesh, he is in the power of the Kingdom of Darkness
[7] *Belial* the Devil
[8] *Hy, Zy, Hine* perhaps the vesper bells, or maybe a curse
[9] *Plena . . . Virgo* Full of grace, Hail Virgin (for "Hail Mary, full of Grace," opening of a vespers prayer)

HOME-THOUGHTS, FROM ABROAD

I

Oh, to be in England
Now that April's there,
And whoever wakes in England
Sees, some morning, unaware,
That the lowest boughs and the brushwood sheaf   5
Round the elm-tree bole are in tiny leaf,
While the chaffinch sings on the orchard bough
In England—now!

II

And after April, when May follows,
And the whitethroat builds, and all the swallows!   10
Hark, where my blossomed pear-tree in the hedge
Leans to the field and scatters on the clover
Blossoms and dewdrops—at the bent spray's edge—
That's the wise thrush; he sings each song twice over,
Lest you should think he never could recapture   15
The first fine careless rapture!
And though the fields look rough with hoary dew,
All will be gay when noontide wakes anew
The buttercups, the little children's dower
—Far brighter than this gaudy melon-flower!   20

THE BISHOP ORDERS HIS TOMB
AT SAINT PRAXED'S CHURCH

ROME, 15—

Vanity, saith the preacher, vanity!
Draw round my bed: is Anselm keeping back?
Nephews [1]—sons mine . . . ah God, I know not! Well—
She, men would have to be your mother once,
Old Gandolf envied me, so fair she was!   5
What's done is done, and she is dead beside,
Dead long ago, and I am Bishop since,
And as she died so must we die ourselves,
And thence ye may perceive the world's a dream.
Life, how and what is it? As here I lie   10

[1] *Nephews* his illegitimate sons

In this state-chamber, dying by degrees,
Hours and long hours in the dead night, I ask
"Do I live, am I dead?" Peace, peace seems all.
Saint Praxed's ever was the church for peace;
And so, about this tomb of mine. I fought   15
With tooth and nail to save my niche, ye know:
—Old Gandolf cozened [2] me, despite my care;
Shrewd was that snatch from out the corner South
He graced his carrion with, God curse the same!
Yet still my niche is not so cramped but thence   20
One sees the pulpit o' the epistle-side,[3]
And somewhat of the choir, those silent seats,
And up into the aery dome where live
The angels, and a sunbeam's sure to lurk:
And I shall fill my slab of basalt there,   25
And 'neath my tabernacle take my rest,
With those nine columns [4] round me, two and two,
The odd one at my feet where Anselm stands:
Peach-blossom marble all, the rare, the ripe
As fresh-poured red wine of a mighty pulse.[5]   30
—Old Gandolf with his paltry onion-stone,[6]
Put me where I may look at him! True peach,
Rosy and flawless: how I earned the prize!
Draw close: that conflagration of my church
—What then? So much was saved if aught were missed!   35
My sons, ye would not be my death? Go dig
The white-grape vineyard where the oil-press stood,
Drop water gently till the surface sink,
And if ye find . . . Ah God, I know not, I! . . .
Bedded in store of rotten fig-leaves soft,   40
And corded up in a tight olive-frail,[7]
Some lump, ah God, of *lapis lazuli*,[8]
Big as a Jew's head cut off at the nape,
Blue as a vein o'er the Madonna's breast . . .
Sons, all have I bequeathed you, villas, all,   45
That brave Frascati [9] villa with its bath,
So, let the blue lump poise between my knees,
Like God the Father's globe on both his hands

---

[2] *cozened* cheated   [3] *epistle-side* as one faces the altar, the right side
[4] *tabernacle . . . columns* a canopy, supported by columns, over the tomb
[5] *pulse* strength   [6] *onion-stone* poor grade of marble likely to split
[7] *olive-frail* basket for holding olives
[8] *lapis lazuli* a semiprecious, blue stone
[9] *Frascati* a town in the Alban hills, near Rome

Ye worship in the Jesu Church so gay,
For Gandolf shall not choose but see and burst!   50
Swift as a weaver's shuttle fleet our years:
Man goeth to the grave, and where is he?
Did I say basalt for my slab, sons? Black—
'Twas ever antique-black I meant! How else
Shall ye contrast my frieze to come beneath?   55
The bas-relief in bronze ye promised me,
Those Pans [10] and Nymphs ye wot [11] of, and perchance
Some tripod, thyrsus,[12] with a vase or so,
The Saviour at his sermon on the mount,
Saint Praxed in a glory,[13] and one Pan   60
Ready to twitch the Nymph's last garment off,
And Moses with the tables . . . but I know
Ye mark me not! What do they whisper thee,
Child of my bowels, Anselm? Ah, ye hope
To revel down my villas while I gasp   65
Bricked o'er with beggar's mouldy travertine [14]
Which Gandolf from his tomb-top chuckles at!
Nay, boys, ye love me—all of jasper, then!
'Tis jasper ye stand pledged to, lest I grieve.
My bath must needs be left behind, alas!   70
One block, pure green as a pistachio-nut,
There's plenty jasper somewhere in the world—
And have I not Saint Praxed's ear to pray
Horses for ye, and brown Greek manuscripts,
And mistresses with great smooth marbly limbs?   75
—That's if ye carve my epitaph aright,
Choice Latin, picked phrase, Tully's [15] every word,
No gaudy ware like Gandolf's second line—
Tully, my masters? Ulpian [16] serves his need!
And then how I shall lie through centuries,   80
And hear the blessed mutter of the mass,
And see God made and eaten all day long,
And feel the steady candle-flame, and taste
Good strong thick stupefying incense-smoke!
For as I lie here, hours of the dead night,   85

[10] *Pans* fun-loving gods of flocks and pastures, part goat, part man
[11] *wot* know
[12] *tripod, thyrsus* three-legged stool of priest of the Delphic Oracle; a staff
used in the rites of Bacchus
[13] *in a glory* with a halo   [14] *travertine* a form of limestone
[15] *Tully's* classical style of Latin, as written by Marcus Tullius Cicero
[16] *Ulpian* Domitius Ulpianus, whose Latin style was regarded as inferior

Dying in state and by such slow degrees,
I fold my arms as if they clasped a crook,[17]
And stretch my feet forth straight as stone can point,
And let the bedclothes, for a mortcloth,[18] drop
Into great laps and folds of sculptor's-work: 90
And as yon tapers dwindle, and strange thoughts
Grow, with a certain humming in my ears,
About the life before I lived this life,
And this life too, popes, cardinals and priests,
Saint Praxed at his sermon on the mount,   95
Your tall pale mother with her talking eyes,
And new-found agate urns as fresh as day,
And marble's language, Latin pure, discreet,
—Aha, ELUCESCEBAT [19] quoth our friend?
No Tully, said I, Ulpian at the best!   100
Evil and brief hath been my pilgrimage.
All *lapis*, all, sons! Else I give the Pope
My villas! Will ye ever eat my heart?
Ever your eyes were as a lizard's quick,
They glitter like your mother's for my soul,   105
Or ye would heighten my impoverished frieze,
Piece out its starved design, and fill my vase
With grapes, and add a vizor [20] and a Term,[21]
And to the tripod ye would tie a lynx
That in his struggle throws the thyrsus down,   110
To comfort me on my entablature
Whereon I am to lie till I must ask
"Do I live, am I dead?" There, leave me, there!
For ye have stabbed me with ingratitude
To death—ye wish it—God, ye wish it! Stone—   115
Gritstone, a-crumble! Clammy squares which sweat
As if the corpse they keep were oozing through—
And no more *lapis* to delight the world!
Well go! I bless ye. Fewer tapers there,
But in a row: and, going, turn your backs   120
—Ay, like departing altar-ministrants,
And leave me in my church, the church for peace,
That I may watch at leisure if he leers—
Old Gandolf, at me, from his onion-stone,
As still he envied me, so fair she was!   125

---

[17] *crook* shepherd's crook, the bishop's symbol   [18] *mortcloth* funeral pall
[19] *Elucescebat* "he was famous"; the classical form would be elucebat
[20] *vizor* mask   [21] *Term* a bust of the Roman god Terminus

MEETING AT NIGHT

I

The gray sea and the long black land;
And the yellow half-moon large and low;
And the startled little waves that leap
In fiery ringlets from their sleep,
As I gain the cove with pushing prow,   5
And quench its speed i' the slushy sand.

II

Then a mile of warm sea-scented beach;
Three fields to cross till a farm appears;
A tap at the pane, the quick sharp scratch
And blue spurt of a lighted match,   10
And a voice less loud, thro' its joys and fears,
Than the two hearts beating each to each!

PARTING AT MORNING

Round the cape of a sudden came the sea,
And the sun looked over the mountain's rim:
And straight was a path of gold for him,
And the need of a world of men for me.

ANDREA DEL SARTO [1]

CALLED "THE FAULTLESS PAINTER"

But do not let us quarrel any more,
No, my Lucrezia; bear with me for once:
Sit down and all shall happen as you wish.
You turn your face, but does it bring your heart?
I'll work then for your friend's friend, never fear,   5
Treat his own subject after his own way,
Fix his own time, accept too his own price,
And shut the money into this small hand
When next it takes mine. Will it? tenderly?
Oh, I'll content him,—but to-morrow, Love!   10
I often am much wearier than you think,

[1] *Andrea del Sarto* (1486–1531), Italian painter. son of a tailor

This evening more than usual, and it seems
As if—forgive now—should you let me sit
Here by the window with your hand in mine
And look a half-hour forth on Fiesole,[2]   15
Both of one mind, as married people use,
Quietly, quietly the evening through,
I might get up to-morrow to my work
Cheerful and fresh as ever. Let us try.
To-morrow, how you shall be glad for this!   20
Your soft hand is a woman of itself,
And mine the man's bared breast she curls inside.
Don't count the time lost, neither; you must serve [3]
For each of the five pictures we require:
It saves a model. So! keep looking so—   25
My serpentining beauty, rounds on rounds!
—How could you ever prick those perfect ears,
Even to put the pearl there! oh, so sweet—
My face, my moon, my everybody's moon,
Which everybody looks on and calls his,   30
And, I suppose, is looked on by in turn,
While she looks—no one's: very dear, no less.
You smile? why, there's my picture ready made,
There's what we painters call our harmony!
A common grayness silvers everything,—   35
All in a twilight, you and I alike
—You, at the point of your first pride in me
(That's gone you know),—but I, at every point;
My youth, my hope, my art, being all toned down
To yonder sober pleasant Fiesole.   40
There's the bell clinking from the chapel-top;
That length of convent-wall across the way
Holds the trees safer, huddled more inside;
The last monk leaves the garden; days decrease,
And autumn grows, autumn in everything.   45
Eh? the whole seems to fall into a shape
As if I saw alike my work and self
And all that I was born to be and do,
A twilight-piece. Love, we are in God's hand.
How strange now, looks the life he makes us lead;   50
So free we seem, so fettered fast we are!
I feel he laid the fetter: let it lie!
This chamber for example—turn your head—

---

[2] *Fiesole* suburb of Florence   [3] *serve* as a model

All that's behind us! You don't understand
Nor care to understand about my art, 55
But you can hear at least when people speak:
And that cartoon,[4] the second from the door
—It is the thing, Love! so such things should be—
Behold Madonna!—I am bold to say.
I can do with my pencil what I know, 60
What I see, what at bottom of my heart
I wish for, if I ever wish so deep—
Do easily, too—when I say, perfectly,
I do not boast, perhaps: yourself are judge,
Who listened to the Legate's [5] talk last week, 65
And just as much they used to say in France.
At any rate 'tis easy, all of it!
No sketches first, no studies, that's long past:
I do what many dream of, all their lives,
—Dream? strive to do, and agonize to do, 70
And fail in doing. I could count twenty such
On twice your fingers, and not leave this town,
Who strive—you don't know how the others strive
To paint a little thing like that you smeared
Carelessly passing with your robes afloat,— 75
Yet do much less, so much less, Someone says,
(I know his name, no matter)—so much less!
Well, less is more, Lucrezia: I am judged.
There burns a truer light of God in them,
In their vexed beating stuffed and stopped-up brain, 80
Heart, or whate'er else, than goes on to prompt
This low-pulsed forthright craftsman's hand of mine.
Their works drop groundward, but themselves, I know,
Reach many a time a heaven that's shut to me,
Enter and take their place there sure enough, 85
Though they come back and cannot tell the world.
My works are nearer heaven, but I sit here.
The sudden blood of these men! at a word—
Praise them, it boils, or blame them, it boils too.
I, painting from myself and to myself, 90
Know what I do, am unmoved by men's blame
Or their praise either. Somebody remarks
Morello's [6] outline there is wrongly traced,
His hue mistaken; what of that? or else,

[4] *cartoon* preliminary drawing for a painting
[5] *Legate* the Pope's representative
[6] *Morello* a mountain north of Florence

Rightly traced and well ordered; what of that?   95
Speak as they please, what does the mountain care?
Ah, but a man's reach should exceed his grasp,
Or what's a heaven for? All is silver-gray
Placid and perfect with my art: the worse!
I know both what I want and what might gain,   100
And yet how profitless to know, to sigh
"Had I been two, another and myself,
Our head would have o'erlooked the world!" No doubt.
Yonder's a work now, of that famous youth
The Urbinate [7] who died five years ago.   105
('Tis copied, George Vasari [8] sent it me.)
Well, I can fancy how he did it all,
Pouring his soul, with kings and popes to see,
Reaching, that heaven might so replenish him,
Above and through his art—for it gives way;   110
That arm is wrongly put—and there again—
A fault to pardon in the drawing's lines,
Its body, so to speak: its soul is right,
He means right—that, a child may understand.
Still, what an arm! and I could alter it: 115
But all the play, the insight and the stretch—
Out of me, out of me! And wherefore out?
Had you enjoined them on me, given me soul,
We might have risen to Rafael, I and you!
Nay, Love, you did give all I asked, I think—   120
More than I merit, yes, by many times.
But had you—oh, with the same perfect brow,
And perfect eyes, and more than perfect mouth,
And the low voice my soul hears, as a bird
The fowler's pipe, and follows to the snare—   125
Had you, with these the same, but brought a mind!
Some women do so. Had the mouth there urged
"God and the glory! never care for gain.
The present by the future, what is that?
Live for fame, side by side with Agnolo! [9]   130
Rafael is waiting: up to God, all three!"
I might have done it for you. So it seems:
Perhaps not. All is as God over-rules.
Beside, incentives come from the soul's self;
The rest avail not. Why do I need you?   135

[7] *The Urbinate* the great artist Raphael (1483–1520), born in Urbino
[8] *George [Giorgio] Vasari* author of the classic *Lives of the Painters*
[9] *Agnolo* Michelangelo (1475–1564)

What wife had Rafael, or has Agnolo?
In this world, who can do a thing, will not;
And who would do it, cannot, I perceive:
Yet the will's somewhat—somewhat, too, the power—
And thus we half-men struggle. At the end,   140
God, I conclude, compensates, punishes.
'Tis safer for me, if the award be strict,
That I am something underrated here,
Poor this long while, despised, to speak the truth.
I dared not, do you know, leave home all day,   145
For fear of chancing on the Paris lords.
The best is when they pass and look aside;
But they speak sometimes; I must bear it all.
Well may they speak! That Francis,[10] that first time,
And that long festal year at Fontainebleau!   150
I surely then could sometimes leave the ground,
Put on the glory, Rafael's daily wear,
In that humane great monarch's golden look,—
One finger in his beard or twisted curl
Over his mouth's good mark that made the smile,   155
One arm about my shoulder, round my neck,
The jingle of his gold chain in my ear,
I painting proudly with his breath on me,
All his court round him, seeing with his eyes,
Such frank French eyes, and such a fire of souls   160
Profuse, my hand kept plying by those hearts,—
And, best of all, this, this, this face beyond,
This in the background, waiting on my work,
To crown the issue with a last reward!
A good time, was it not, my kingly days?   165
And had you not grown restless . . . but I know—
'Tis done and past; 'twas right, my instinct said;
Too live the life grew, golden and not gray,
And I'm the weak-eyed bat no sun should tempt
Out of the grange whose four walls make his world.   170
How could it end in any other way?
You called me, and I came home to your heart.
The triumph was—to reach and stay there; since
I reached it ere the triumph, what is lost?
Let my hands frame your face in your hair's gold,   175
You beautiful Lucrezia that are mine!

[10] *Francis* King Francis I of France (1494–1547) brought Andrea to Fontainebleau as a court painter, but Andrea, at Lucrezia's request, returned to Italy
after a year.

"Rafael did this, Andrea painted that;
The Roman's [11] is the better when you pray,
But still the other's Virgin was his wife—"
Men will excuse me. I am glad to judge   180
Both pictures in your presence; clearer grows
My better fortune, I resolve to think.
For, do you know, Lucrezia, as God lives,
Said one day Agnolo, his very self,
To Rafael . . . I have known it all these years . . .   185
(When the young man was flaming out his thoughts
Upon a palace-wall for Rome to see,
Too lifted up in heart because of it)
"Friend, there's a certain sorry little scrub
Goes up and down our Florence, none cares how,   190
Who, were he set to plan and execute
As you are, pricked on by your popes and kings,
Would bring the sweat into that brow of yours!"
To Rafael's!—And indeed the arm is wrong.
I hardly dare . . . yet, only you to see,   195
Give the chalk here—quick, thus the line should go!
Ay, but the soul! he's Rafael! rub it out!
Still, all I care for, if he spoke the truth,
(What he? why, who but Michel Agnolo?
Do you forget already words like those?)   200
If really there was such a chance, so lost,—
Is, whether you're—not grateful—but more pleased.
Well, let me think so. And you smile indeed!
This hour has been an hour! Another smile?
If you would sit thus by me every night   205
I should work better, do you comprehend?
I mean that I should earn more, give you more.
See, it is settled dusk now; there's a star;
Morello's gone, the watch-lights show the wall,
The cue-owls [12] speak the name we call them by.   210
Come from the window, love,—come in, at last,
Inside the melancholy little house
We built to be so gay with. God is just.
King Francis [13] may forgive me: oft at nights
When I look up from painting, eyes tired out,   215
The walls become illumined, brick from brick
Distinct, instead of mortar, fierce bright gold,

[11] *Roman's* Raphael's   [12] *cue-owls* a species of small owl
[13] *King Francis may forgive me* It was thought that Andrea used funds from
King Francis, meant for pictures, to build a house for Lucrezia.

That gold of his I did cement them with!
Let us but love each other. Must you go?
That Cousin [14] here again? he waits outside?   220
Must see you—you, and not with me? Those loans?
More gaming debts to pay? you smiled for that?
Well, let smiles buy me! have you more to spend?
While hand and eye and something of a heart
Are left me, work's my ware, and what's it worth?   225
I'll pay my fancy. Only let me sit
The gray remainder of the evening out,
Idle, you call it, and muse perfectly
How I could paint, were I but back in France,
One picture, just one more—the Virgin's face,   230
Not yours this time! I want you at my side
To hear them—that is, Michel Agnolo—
Judge all I do and tell you of its worth.
Will you? To-morrow, satisfy your friend.
I take the subjects for his corridor,   235
Finish the portrait out of hand—there, there,
And throw him in another thing or two
If he demurs; the whole should prove enough
To pay for this same Cousin's freak. Beside,
What's better and what's all I care about,   240
Get you the thirteen scudi [15] for the ruff!
Love, does that please you? Ah, but what does he,
The Cousin! what does he to please you more?

I am grown peaceful as old age to-night.
I regret little, I would change still less.   245
Since there my past life lies, why alter it?
The very wrong to Francis!—it is true
I took his coin, was tempted and complied,
And built this house and sinned, and all is said.
My father and my mother died of want.   250
Well, had I riches of my own? you see
How one gets rich! Let each one bear his lot.
They were born poor, lived poor, and poor they died:
And I have labored somewhat in my time
And not been paid profusely. Some good son   255
Paint my two hundred pictures—let him try!
No doubt, there's something strikes a balance. Yes,
You loved me quite enough, it seems to-night.

[14] *Cousin* Lucrezia's lover   [15] *scudi* coins, worth about $1 each

This must suffice me here. What would one have?
In heaven, perhaps, new chances, one more chance—   260
Four great walls in the New Jerusalem,
Meted [16] on each side by the angel's reed,[17]
For Leonard,[18] Rafael, Agnolo and me
To cover—the three first without a wife,
While I have mine! So—still they overcome   265
Because there's still Lucrezia,—as I choose.

Again the Cousin's whistle! Go, my Love.

A GRAMMARIAN'S FUNERAL

SHORTLY AFTER THE REVIVAL OF LEARNING IN EUROPE

LET us begin and carry up this corpse,
  Singing together.
Leave we the common crofts,[1] the vulgar thorpes [2]
  Each in its tether
Sleeping safe on the bosom of the plain,   5
  Cared-for till cock-crow:
Look out if yonder be not day again
  Rimming the rock-row!
That's the appropriate country; [3] there, man's thought,
  Rarer, intenser,   10
Self-gathered for an outbreak, is it ought,
  Chafes in the censer.
Leave we the unlettered plain its herd and crop;
  Seek we sepulture
On a tall mountain, cited to the top,   15
  Crowded with culture!
All the peaks soar, but one the rest excels;
  Clouds overcome it;
No! yonder sparkle is the citadel's
  Circling its summit.   20
Thither our path lies; wind we up the heights:
  Wait ye the warning?
Our low life was the level's and the night's;
  He's for the morning.

---

[16] *Meted* measured   [17] *reed* measuring rod
[18] *Leonard* Leonardo da Vinci (1452–1519). Leonardo da Vinci, Raphael, and
Michelangelo were the three great painters of the Renaissance.

---

[1] *crofts* small fields   [2] *thorpes* villages
[3] *appropriate country* best place for burying a grammarian

Step to a tune, square chests, erect each head,   25
 'Ware [4] the beholders!
This is our master, famous, calm, and dead,
 Borne on our shoulders.

Sleep, crop and herd! sleep, darkling thorpe and croft,
 Safe from the weather!   30
He, whom we convoy to his grave aloft,
 Singing together,
He was a man born with thy face and throat,
 Lyric Apollo! [5]
Long he lived nameless: how should spring take note   35
 Winter would follow?
Till lo, the little touch, and youth was gone!
 Cramped and diminished,
Moaned he, "New measures, other feet anon!
 My dance is finished?"   40
No, that's the world's way: (keep the mountain-side,
 Make for the city!)
He knew the signal, and stepped on with pride
 Over men's pity;
Left play for work, and grappled with the world   45
 Bent on escaping:
"What's in the scroll," [6] quoth he, "thou keepest furled?
 Show me their shaping,
Theirs who most studied man, the bard and sage,—
 Give!"—So, he gowned him,[7]   50
Straight got by heart that book to its last page:
 Learned, we found him.
Yea, but we found him bald too, eyes like lead,
 Accents uncertain:
"Time to taste life," another would have said,   55
 "Up with the curtain!"
This man said rather, "Actual life comes next?
 Patience a moment!
Grant I have mastered learning's crabbed text,
 Still there's the comment.   60
Let me know all! Prate not of most or least,
 Painful or easy!
Even to the crumbs I'd fain eat up the feast,
 Ay, nor feel queasy."

[4] *'Ware* beware [5] *Lyric Apollo* the sun god who was also god of art
[6] *scroll* manuscript [7] *he gowned him* put on the academic gown

Oh, such a life as he resolved to live,   65
    When he had learned it,
When he had gathered all books had to give!
    Sooner, he spurned it.
Image the whole, then execute the parts—
    Fancy the fabric   70
Quite, ere you build, ere steel strike fire from quartz,
    Ere mortar dab brick!

(Here's the town-gate reached: there's the market-place
    Gaping before us.)
Yea, this in him was the peculiar grace   75
    (Hearten our chorus!)
That before living he'd learn how to live—
    No end to learning:
Earn the means first—God surely will contrive
    Use for our earning.   80
Others mistrust and say, "But time escapes:
    Live now or never!"
He said, "What's time? Leave Now for dogs and apes!
    Man has Forever."
Back to his book then: deeper drooped his head: 85
    Calculus [8] racked him:
Leaden before, his eyes grew dross of lead:
    Tussis [9] attacked him.
"Now, master, take a little rest!"—not he!
    (Caution redoubled,   90
Step two abreast, the way winds narrowly!)
    Not a whit troubled
Back to his studies, fresher than at first,
    Fierce as a dragon
He (soul-hydroptic[10] with a sacred thirst)   95
    Sucked at the flagon.
Oh, if we draw a circle premature,
    Heedless of far gain,
Greedy for quick returns of profit, sure
    Bad is our bargain!   100
Was it not great? did not he throw on God,
    (He loves the burthen)—
God's task to make the heavenly period
    Perfect the earthen?

[8] *Calculus* a disease caused by the formation in the body of a solid concretion, or stone
[9] *Tussis* a cough   [10] *soul-hydroptic* soul-thirsty

Did not he magnify the mind, show clear   105
    Just what it all meant?
He would not discount life, as fools do here,
    Paid by instalment.
He ventured neck or nothing—heaven's success
    Found, or earth's failure: 110
"Wilt thou trust death or not?" He answered "Yes:
    Hence with life's pale lure!"
That low man seeks a little thing to do,
    Sees it and does it:
This high man, with a great thing to pursue,   115
    Dies ere he knows it.
That low man goes on adding one to one,
    His hundred's soon hit:
This high man, aiming at a million,
    Misses an unit.   120
That, has the world here—should he need the next,
    Let the world mind him!
This, throws himself on God, and unperplexed
    Seeking shall find him.
So, with the throttling hands of death at strife,   125
    Ground he at grammar;
Still, thro' the rattle,[11] parts of speech were rife:
    While he could stammer
He settled *Hoti's* business—let it be!—
    Properly based *Oun*—   130
Gave us the doctrine of the enclitic *De*,[12]
    Dead from the waist down.
Well, here's the platform, here's the proper place:
    Hail to your purlieus,
All ye highfliers of the feathered race,   135
    Swallows and curlews!
Here's the top-peak; the multitude below
    Live, for they can, there:
This man decided not to Live but Know—
    Bury this man there?   140
Here—here's his place, where meteors shoot, clouds form,
    Lightnings are loosened,
Stars come and go! Let joy break with the storm,
    Peace let the dew send!

[11] *rattle* death-rattle
[12] *Hoti, Oun, De* Greek particles of only modest significance on which the grammarian did the definitive scholarship. The *enclitic* word is that which loses its own accent in becoming attached to another word.

Lofty designs must close in like effects: 145
    Loftily lying,
Leave him—still loftier than the world suspects,
    Living and dying.

"TRANSCENDENTALISM: A POEM
IN TWELVE BOOKS" [1]

Stop playing, poet! May a brother speak?
'Tis you speak, that's your error. Song's our art:
Whereas you please to speak these naked thoughts
Instead of draping them in sights and sounds.
—True thoughts, good thoughts, thoughts fit to treasure up!   5
But why such long prolusion [2] and display,
Such turning and adjustment of the harp,
And taking it upon your breast, at length,
Only to speak dry words across its strings?
Stark-naked thought is in request enough: 10
Speak prose and hollo it till Europe hears!
The six-foot Swiss tube, braced about with bark,
Which helps the hunter's voice from Alp to Alp—
Exchange our harp for that,—who hinders you?

    But here's your fault; grown men want thought, you think;   15
Thought's what they mean by verse, and seek in verse.
Boys seek for images and melody,
Men must have reason—so, you aim at men.
Quite otherwise! Objects throng our youth, 'tis true;
We see and hear and do not wonder much: 20
If you could tell us what they mean, indeed!
As German Boehme [3] never cared for plants
Until it happed, a-walking in the fields,
He noticed all at once that plants could speak,
Nay, turned with loosened tongue to talk with him.   25
That day the daisy had an eye indeed—
Colloquized with the cowslip on such themes!
We find them extant yet in Jacob's prose.
But by the time youth slips a stage or two
While reading prose in that tough book he wrote   30

---

[1] *"Transcendentalism"* an imaginary poem filled with abstractions, here
criticized by another poet who favors concrete language
[2] *prolusion* an introductory exercise
[3] *German Boehme* Jakob Boehme (1575–1624), a mystic who saw the world as
a manifestation of God

(Collating and emendating the same
And settling on the sense most to our mind),
We shut the clasps and find life's summer past.
Then, who helps more, pray, to repair our loss—
Another Boehme with a tougher book   35
And subtler meanings of what roses say,—
Or some stout Magic like him of Halberstadt,[4]
John, who made things Boehme wrote thoughts about?
He with a "look you!" vents a brace of rhymes,
And in there breaks the sudden rose herself,   40
Over us, under, round us every side,
Nay, in and out the tables and the chairs
And musty volumes, Boehme's book and all,—
Buries us with a glory, young once more,
Pouring heaven into this shut house of life.   45

      So come, the harp back to your heart again!
You are a poem, though your poem's naught.
The best of all you showed before, believe,
Was your own boy-face o'er the finer chords
Bent, following the cherub at the top   50
That points to God with his paired half-moon wings.

ABT VOGLER [1]

(AFTER HE HAS BEEN EXTEMPORIZING UPON THE MUSICAL INSTRUMENT OF HIS INVENTION.)

I

Would that the structure brave, the manifold music I build,
    Bidding my organ obey, calling its keys to their work,
Claiming each slave of the sound, at a touch, as when Solomon
      willed [2]
    Armies of angels that soar, legions of demons that lurk,
Man, brute, reptile, fly,—alien of end and of aim,   5

---

[4] *Mage like him of Halberstadt* a magician like the one of Halberstadt, Johannes Teutonicus, whose "vegetable stone" controlled the growth of plants

[1] *Abt Vogler* George Vogler (1749–1814) was a noted German musician, famed for his extemporizing as he played, and inventor of the Orchestrion, an organ of wide range and compact size.
[2] *Solomon willed* According to legend, Solomon controlled "armies of angels" and "legions of demons" through a seal which bore the "ineffable Name" of God.

Adverse, each from the other heaven-high, hell-deep re-
    moved,—
Should rush into sight at once as he named the ineffable Name,
    And pile him a palace straight, to pleasure the princess he
    loved!

II

Would it might tarry like his, the beautiful building of mine,
    This which my keys in a crowd pressed and importuned to
    raise!   10
Ah, one and all, how they helped, would dispart now and now
    combine,
    Zealous to hasten the work, heighten their master his praise!
And one would bury his brow with a blind plunge down to hell,
    Burrow awhile and build, broad on the roots of things,
Then up again swim into sight, having based me my palace
    well,   15
    Founded it, fearless of flame, flat on the nether springs.

III

And another would mount and march, like the excellent minion
    he was,
    Ay, another and yet another, one crowd but with many a
    crest,
Raising my rampired walls of gold as transparent as glass,
    Eager to do and die, yield each his place to the rest: 20
For higher still and higher (as a runner tips with fire,
    When a great illumination surprises a festal night—
Outlining round and round Rome's dome [3] from space to spire)
    Up, the pinnacled glory reached, and the pride of my soul
    was in sight.

IV

In sight? Not half! for it seemed, it was certain, to match man's
    birth,   25
    Nature in turn conceived, obeying an impulse as I;
And the emulous heaven yearned down, made effort to reach the
    earth,
    As the earth had done her best, in my passion, to scale the
    sky:
Novel splendors burst forth, grew familiar and dwelt with mine,
    Not a point nor peak but found and fixed its wandering
    star;   30

[3] *Rome's dome* St. Peter's of Rome, whose dome is illuminated on important
occasions

Meteor-moons, balls of blaze: and they did not pale nor pine,
    For earth had attained to heaven, there was no more near
        nor far.

V

Nay more; for there wanted not who walked in the glare and
    glow,
    Presences plain in the place; or, fresh from the Protoplast,[4]
Furnished for ages to come, when a kindlier wind should blow, 35
    Lured now to begin and live, in a house to their liking at
        last;
Or else the wonderful Dead who have passed through the body
    and gone,
    But were back once more to breathe in an old world worth
    their new:
What never had been, was now; what was, as it shall be anon;
    And what is,—shall I say, matched both? for I was made per-
    fect too.   40

VI

All through my keys that gave their sounds to a wish of my soul,
    All through my soul that praised as its wish flowed visibly
    forth,
All through music and me! For think, had I painted the whole,
    Why, there it had stood, to see, nor the process so wonder-
    worth:
Had I written the same, made verse—still, effect proceeds from
    cause,   45
    Ye know why the forms are fair, ye hear how the tale is told;
It is all triumphant art, but art in obedience to laws,
    Painter and poet are proud in the artist-list enrolled:—

VII

But here is the finger of God, a flash of the will that can,
    Existent behind all laws, that made them and, lo, they are! 50
And I know not if, save in this, such gift be allowed to man,
    That out of three sounds he frame, not a fourth sound, but
    a star.
Consider it well: each tone of our scale in itself is naught;
    It is everywhere in the world—loud, soft, and all is said:
Give it to me to use! I mix it with two in my thought: 55
    And, there! Ye have heard and seen: consider and bow the
    head!

[4] *fresh from the Protoplast* newly created

VIII

Well, it is gone at last, the palace of music I reared;
    Gone! and the good tears start, the praises that come too
        slow;
For one is assured at first, one scarce can say that he feared,
    That he even gave it a thought, the gone thing was to go. 60
Never to be again! But many more of the kind
    As good, nay, better perchance: is this your comfort to me?
To me, who must be saved because I cling with my mind
    To the same, same self, same love, same God: ay, what was,
        shall be.

IX

Therefore to whom turn I but to thee, the ineffable Name? 65
    Builder and maker, thou, of houses not made with hands!
What, have fear of change from thee who art ever the same?
    Doubt that thy power can fill the heart that thy power ex-
        pands?
There shall never be one lost good! What was, shall live as be-
        fore;
    The evil is null, is naught, is silence implying sound; 70
What was good shall be good, with, for evil, so much good more;
    On the earth the broken arcs; in the heaven, a perfect round.

X

All we have willed or hoped or dreamed of good shall exist;
    Not its semblance, but itself; no beauty, nor good, nor power
Whose voice has gone forth, but each survives for the melodist 75
    When eternity affirms the conception of an hour.
The high that proved too high, the heroic for earth too hard,
    The passion that left the ground to lose itself in the sky,
Are music sent up to God by the lover and the bard;
    Enough that he heard it once: we shall hear it by-and-by. 80

XI

And what is our failure here but a triumph's evidence
    For the fulness of the days? Have we withered or agonized?
Why else was the pause prolonged but that singing might issue
        thence?
    Why rushed the discords in but that harmony should be
        prized?
Sorrow is hard to bear, and doubt is slow to clear, 85
    Each sufferer says his say, his scheme of the weal and woe:

But God has a few of us whom he whispers in the ear;
  The rest may reason and welcome: 'tis we musicians know.

XII

Well, it is earth with me; silence resumes her reign:
  I will be patient and proud, and soberly acquiesce.   90
Give me the keys. I feel for the common chord again,
  Sliding by semitones, till I sink to the minor,—yes,
And I blunt it into a ninth, and I stand on alien ground,
  Surveying awhile the heights I rolled from into the deep;
Which, hark, I have dared and done, for my resting-place is
    found,   95
  The C Major of this life: so, now I will try to sleep.[5]

PROSPICE [1]

Fear death?—to feel the fog in my throat,
  The mist in my face,
When the snows begin, and the blasts denote
  I am nearing the place,
The power of the night, the press of the storm,   5
  The post of the foe;
Where he stands, the Arch Fear in a visible form,
  Yet the strong man must go:
For the journey is done and the summit attained,
  And the barriers fall,   10
Though a battle's to fight ere the guerdon be gained,
  The reward of it all.
I was ever a fighter, so—one fight more,
  The best and the last!
I would hate that death bandaged my eyes, and forbore,   15
  And bade me creep past.
No! let me taste the whole of it, fare like my peers
  The heroes of old,
Bear the brunt, in a minute pay glad life's arrears
  Of pain, darkness and cold.   20
For sudden the worst turns the best to the brave,
  The black minute's at end,

---

[5] (ll. 91–96) *common chord* the fundamental tone, from which the musician descends to a minor key which is "alien ground," and which gives way to a "resting-place," or *C Major,* representing the level of everyday life

---

[1] *prospice* look forward

And the elements' rage, the fiend-voices that rave,
  Shall dwindle, shall blend,
Shall change, shall become first a peace out of pain,   25
  Then a light, then thy breast,
O thou soul of my soul! [2] I shall clasp thee again,
  And with God be the rest!

HOUSE

I

Shall I sonnet-sing you about myself?
  Do I live in a house you would like to see?
Is it scant of gear, has it store of pelf?
  "Unlock my heart with a sonnet-key?" [1]

II

Invite the world, as my betters have done?   5
  "Take notice: this building remains on view,
Its suites of reception every one,
  Its private apartment and bedroom too;

III

"For a ticket, apply to the Publisher."
  No: thanking the public, I must decline.   10
A peep through my window, if folk prefer;
  But, please you, no foot over threshold of mine!

IV

I have mixed with a crowd and heard free talk
  In a foreign land where an earthquake chanced:
And a house stood gaping, naught to balk   15
  Man's eye wherever he gazed or glanced.

V

The whole of the frontage shaven sheer,
  The inside gaped: exposed to day,
Right and wrong and common and queer,
  Bare, as the palm of your hand, it lay.   20

---

[2] *soul of my soul* the poet's dead wife

[1] *"Unlock . . . sonnet-key?"* Browning's poem is an answer to Wordsworth's "Scorn Not the Sonnet" (p. 386), in which Wordsworth argues that Shakespeare "unlocked his heart" in his sonnet sequence.

VI

The owner? Oh, he had been crushed, no doubt!
"Odd tables and chairs for a man of wealth!
What a parcel of musty old books about!
He smoked,—no wonder he lost his health!

VII

"I doubt if he bathed before he dressed.   25
A brazier?—the pagan, he burned perfumes!
You see it is proved, what the neighbors guessed:
His wife and himself had separate rooms."

VIII

Friends, the goodman of the house at least
Kept house to himself till an earthquake came: 30
'Tis the fall of its frontage permits you feast
On the inside arrangement you praise or blame.

IX

Outside should suffice for evidence:
And whoso desires to penetrate
Deeper, must dive by the spirit-sense—   35
No optics like yours, at any rate!

X

"Hoity toity! A street to explore,
Your house the exception! *'With this same key
Shakespeare unlocked his heart,'* once more!"
Did Shakespeare? If so, the less Shakespeare he!   40

CRITICISM

Detective-critics who search for the real-life counterparts for
the characters and events of literature are sometimes rewarded
by illuminating comparisons: they can see the writer in action as
he changes life to the life of art. Here is one note on a possible
Duke for Browning's "My Last Duchess." But the reader should
also consult the article by Louis S. Friedland, "Ferrara and *My
Last Duchess*" (*Studies in Philology*, XXXIII [1936]), in which
the writer suggests plausibly that the model was Alfonzo II.
Neither of these articles tries to analyze the poem itself. For one
example of the approach which studies the situation and the

Duke as Browning presents them, see Leonard Nathanson, "Browning's 'My Last Duchess,'" *The Explicator*, XIX (June, 1961), 68.

"My Last Duchess" [1]

JOHN D. REA

In reading "My Last Duchess" I had, until recently, supposed that Browning had no one duke in mind, but was merely representing in the character of the duke many of the qualities of Italy in the sixteenth century. The duke embodies the love for art, the passion of the collector, with the moral unscrupulousness that Browning was soon to portray again in another sixteenth-century dignitary in "The Bishop Orders His Tomb at St. Praxed's Church." Of late, however, I have come to believe that Browning had in mind one special duke, Vespasiano Gonzaga, and one interesting incident of his career, taken probably either from his life by Ireneo Affó, published at Parma in 1780, or the earlier life by Alessandro Lisca, Verona, 1592—just such out-of-the-way volumes as Browning and his father delighted in.

Vespasiano Gonzaga, Duke of Sabbioneta (a town founded by him, about fifty miles from Ferrara), belonged to one of the most eminent families of northern Italy, tracing its origin back to the Emperor Lothaire, who ruled in the ninth century. ("My gift of a nine-hundred-years-old name"). The family during the Renaissance was famous for its patronage of art. Duke Vespasiano built his city to indulge his tastes more magnificently. For its adornment he summoned famous painters and sculptors from everywhere; his own splendid palace still contains portraits of members of his family and mural decorations representing scenes from mythology, all to be reached by the broad staircase down which the duke and the count's representative go at the end of Browning's poem.

The duke was married three times, the first time to a gay young Sicilian girl, daughter of Don Antonio di Cardona, named Diana; she is the Duchess of Browning's poem. Diana is described as unusually lively and pretty; her coquettishness aroused her stern husband's suspicions. Affó, quoting Lisca, remarks that the duke

---

[1] Reprinted from *Studies in Philology*, XXIX (January, 1932).

may have feared disgrace to his family by her conduct "since he was always quoting the old saying of Caesar, that the wife of a great man must be free not merely from wrongdoing, but from any suspicion of wrongdoing." At the time when the duke discovered confirmation of his suspicions his wife suddenly and mysteriously disappeared. Affó hesitates to conjecture what was the fate of the lady; he remarks that he does not feel able to say how she met her death, but that the belief was that she was "removed by violence from the world." The duke himself, in a letter, commented laconically that it had pleased God to call his wife to him; "she died suddenly of apoplexy without being able to speak a word." "I gave commands," Browning puts it; "then all smiles stopped together." In view of Affó's non-commital attitude it is easy to see why Browning gives no more definite statement and why, when questioned about his meaning, he seemed reluctant to give a very positive answer as to whether the duke had his duchess murdered.

Lisca, quoted by Affó, gives an account of the duke's appearance and some of his characteristics that helps to make the identity of Browning's duke somewhat more certain. He is described as tall, pale, with blue eyes and long neck: very dignified. "Strange to say, but true, he never let fall a word he might be sorry for, even in anger, never had a lowly thought." (Nihil umquam humile cogitavit.)

> Who'd stoop to blame
> This sort of trifling.
>
>   . . .
>
> E'en then would be some stooping and I choose
> Never to stoop.

It often happens that an author who finds material in a work that he can use, as Browning apparently did in Affó's life of Vespasiano Gonzaga, picks up other hints that he can make use of elsewhere. In reading Affó's life I was therefore especially pleased to find on page 4 the name of a churchman, Gandolfo. To any reader of Browning this would bring to mind Gandolf, the rival of the Bishop, in "The Bishop Orders His Tomb at St. Praxed's Church." Two pages later came further confirmation that I was following Browning's trail, in the sentence "Vna tamen in dies elucescebat tua virtus major." Elucescebat! "Not Cicero; Ulpian at the best," said the Bishop contemptuously, sneering at the word in Gandolf's epitaph; "Dog-Latin" Browning called it in a letter to Rossetti. I read on, looking for other connections with the Bishop, dying, with his sons around him, and making his legacies, but conditioning them on the building of a splendid tomb, from materials he had long been collecting and hoarding, and in the church he had helped to build and adorn.

> As here I lie
> In this state-chamber, dying by degrees.

At the end of Affó's *Life* is an account of the duke's making of his will, in his beloved palace, dying in state among his household and dictating his bequests: "Jacens in lecto in quadam camera superiore palatii praefati" says the will. "First let my daughter be bound and obligated to erect in that church a tomb of marble, in which my body will be placed, on the construction and adornment of which she will be bound and obligated to spend fifteen hundred scudi, besides the stones necessary to adorn the aforesaid tomb, which I have had brought from Rome." On the tomb is to be placed, the will goes on, a statue of the duke. The daughter is further bound to spend twenty-five hundred scudi in beautifying the church where the tomb is to be placed.

There is one further link in our chain of evidence. "My Last Duchess" appeared in *Bells and Pomegranates No. 3;* its companion piece, "St. Praxed's Church," appeared in *Bells and Pomegranates No. 7.* In this same number appeared "The Flight of the Duchess," which looks suspiciously like a re-working of the story of the stern duke and the gay young duchess, with a different outcome. Still more noteworthy is the fact that "The Tomb at St. Praxed's" had earlier appeared in *Hood's Magazine,* March, 1845, and part of "The Flight of the Duchess" (the first nine sections) in the same magazine the next month. Apparently Browning had developed the Bishop from his earlier portrait of the duke, and then had tried the story of the duchess again, at greater length and with a different ending. It is tempting to find echoes of the same material in two later poems, "The Statue and the Bust" and "Bishop Blougram's Apology"; but in the last named the bishop has become strangely merged with or reincarnated in Cardinal Wiseman.

GERARD MANLEY HOPKINS

[1844-1889]

HOPKINS, the Jesuit priest-poet, was born in Stratford, Essex, England, to an Anglican family of both business and literary interests. In school, Hopkins won some poetry prizes. His first ambition was to be a painter. While he was at Oxford (1863–1867) he became a Roman Catholic (1866) and studied under John Henry Newman, who had also been a convert. Hopkins was ordained a priest in 1877. He served in several parishes (Oxford, Liverpool, Glasgow, Chesterfield) until 1881, then taught classics at Stonyhurst College. In 1884 he went to Dublin, where he had the Chair of Classics at University College and a Fellowship at the Royal University of Ireland. He died in Dublin of typhoid fever. Though Hopkins wrote poetry continuously, only a few poems were published during his lifetime, and not until 1918, when his friend Robert Bridges edited his work, did the world know much of him. But his individual poetics, the sensuous excitement of his language, and his deep religious passion have given Hopkins a distinctive place in English poetry.

Introductory Readings

EDITION: *Poems*, ed. W. H. Gardner, preface and notes by Robert Bridges (3rd ed., 1948). BIOGRAPHY: W. H. Gardner, *Gerard Manley Hopkins, 1844–1889* (rev. ed., 1948–1949). CRITICISM: *Immortal Diamond: Studies in Gerard Manley Hopkins*, ed. Norman Weyand and Raymond V. Schoder (1949); Geoffrey Grigson, *Gerard Manley Hopkins* (1955).

HEAVEN-HAVEN

A NUN TAKES THE VEIL

I have desired to go
Where springs not fail,

533

To fields where flies no sharp and sided hail
And a few lilies blow.

And I have asked to be   5
Where no storms come,
Where the green swell is in the havens dumb,
And out of the swing of the sea.

THE WRECK OF THE DEUTSCHLAND

TO THE HAPPY MEMORY OF FIVE FRANCISCAN NUNS
EXILES BY THE FALK LAWS [1] DROWNED BETWEEN
MIDNIGHT AND MORNING OF DEC. 7TH, 1875

Gerard Manley Hopkins wrote to R. W. Dixon, Oct. 5, 1878:
". . . when in the winter of '75 the *Deutschland* was wrecked in
the mouth of the Thames and five Franciscan nuns, exiles from
Germany by the Falck Laws, aboard of her were drowned I was
affected by the account and happening to say so to my rector he
said that he wished some one would write a poem on the subject.
On this hint I set to work and, though my hand was out at first,
produced one. I had long had haunting my ear the echo of a new
rhythm which now I realized on paper . . . I do not say the idea
is altogether new . . . but no one has professedly used it and
made it the principle throughout, that I know of . . . However,
I had to mark the stresses . . . and a great many more oddnesses
could not but dismay an editor's eye, so that when I offered it to
our magazine *The Month* . . . they dared not print it."

Synopsis

W. H. GARDNER

Part the First (stanzas 1–10):
  Meditation on God's infinite power and masterhood, on the
direct mystical "stress" or intuitive knowledge by which man,
the dependent finite creature, apprehends the majesty and terror,
the beauty and love of his Maker. Not only through beauty and
joy do we know Him. Since the Incarnation and Passion, the
human heart has become sensitized to the deeper mystery of suffering and loss—the paradox of God's mastery and mercy. Adoration to Him! May he subjugate and save His rebellious creature,
man.

[1] *Falk Laws* Prussian anti-Catholic measures passed under Bismarck, 1873–1875.
Some were promoted by Adalbert Falk, minister of cults.

Part the Second.

(Stanzas 11-17): Sudden, unexpected disaster overtook the *Deutschland,* with her emigrants and exiles bound for America. A hurricane of wind and snow drove her on to a sandbank. For a whole night without succour, the passengers and crew of the crippled and settling ship were buffeted by the elements: many were drowned.

(Stanzas 17-31): Amid the tumult and horror, the voice of a nun is heard calling on Christ to "come quickly." (She was one of five Franciscan exiles: surely Five, the number of Christ's wounds, is the symbol of Sacrifice and the heavenly Reward.) But what did she mean? Her cry came from the heart of all suffering humanity. Man seeks deliverance not from danger (which is stimulating) but from the remorseless daily round of toil and disappointment. That deliverance comes only from Christ, who succeeded by failure; His Passion holds the promise of heaven in an otherwise "unshapeable" existence (st. 29). This nun read the symbol aright: the pain and tragedy of life elucidate, and are themselves elucidated by, the Redemption. In the nun the meaning of Christ is reborn (a second Virgin Birth!). Touched by the finger of God (as the poet had been) she had created faith and hope in those around her.

(Stanzas 32-5): Return to the theme of Part the First: the poet adores the majesty and inscrutable wisdom of God. The dead nun, prophetess of the Faith indomitable and resurgent, is asked to intercede for the conversion of "rare-dear Britain."

PART THE FIRST

1

Thou mastering me
God! giver of breath and bread;
World's strand, sway of the sea;
Lord of living and dead;
Thou hast bound bones and veins in me, fastened me flesh,   5
And after it almost unmade, what with dread,
Thy doing: and dost thou touch me afresh?
Over again I feel thy finger and find thee.

2

I did say yes
O at lightning and lashed rod;   10
Thou heardst me truer than tongue confess
Thy terror, O Christ, O God;

Thou knowest the walls, altar and hour and night:
The swoon of a heart that the sweep and the hurl of thee
trod
Hard down with a horror of height: 15
And the midriff astrain with leaning of, laced with fire of stress.

3

The frown of his face
Before me, the hurtle of hell
Behind, where, where was a, where was a place?
I whirled out wings that spell   20
And fled with a fling of the heart to the heart of the Host.
And heart, but you were dovewinged, I can tell,
Carrier-witted,[2] I am bold to boast,
To flash from the flame to the flame then, tower from the grace
to the grace.

4

I am soft sift   25
In an hourglass – at the wall
Fast, but mined with a motion, a drift,
And it crowds and it combs to the fall;
I steady as a water in a well, to a poise, to a pane,
But roped with, always, all the way down from the tall   30
Fells or flanks of the voel,[3] a vein
Of the gospel proffer, a pressure, a principle, Christ's gift.

5

I kiss my hand
To the stars, lovely-asunder
Starlight, wafting him out of it; and   35
Glow, glory in thunder;
Kiss my hand to the dappled-with-damson [4] west:
Since, tho' he is under the world's splendour and wonder,
His mystery must be instressed, stressed;
For I greet him the days I meet him, and bless when I under-
stand.   40

6

Not out of his bliss
Springs the stress felt
Nor first from heaven (and few know this)

---

[2] *carrier-witted* disposed to move like a carrier (bird)
[3] *voel* mountain in Wales   [4] *damson* plum-color

Swings the stroke dealt –
Stroke and a stress that stars and storms deliver,   45
That guilt is hushed by, hearts are flushed by and melt –
But it rides time like riding a river
(And here the faithful waver, the faithless fable and miss).

7

It dates from day
Of his going in Galilee;   50
Warm-laid grave of a womb-life grey;
Manger, maiden's knee;
The dense and the driven Passion, and frightful sweat;
Thence the discharge of it, there its swelling to be,
Though felt before, though in high flood yet –   55
What none would have known of it, only the heart, being hard at
bay,

8

Is out with it! Oh,
We lash with the best or worst
Word last! How a lush-kept plush-capped sloe [5]
Will, mouthed to flesh-burst,   60
Gush! – flush the man, the being with it, sour or sweet,
Brim, in a flash, full! – Hither then, last or first,
To hero of Calvary, Christ,'s feet –
Never ask if meaning it, wanting it, warned of it – men go.

9

Be adored among men,   65
God, three-numberèd form;
Wring thy rebel, dogged in den,
Man's malice, with wrecking and storm.
Beyond saying sweet, past telling of tongue,
Thou art lightning and love, I found it, a winter and
warm;   70
Father and fondler of heart thou hast wrung:
Hast thy dark descending and most art merciful then.

10

With an anvil-ding
And with fire in him forge thy will
Or rather, rather then, stealing as Spring   75
Through him, melt him but master him still:

[5] *sloe* dark purple, sour fruit of the blackthorn

Whether at once, as once at a crash Paul,
Or as Austin,[6] a lingering-out swéet skíll,
   Make mercy in all of us, out of us all
Mastery, but be adored, but be adored King.   80

PART THE SECOND

11

   'Some find me a sword; some
   The flange and the rail; flame,
Fang, or flood' goes Death on drum,
   And storms bugle his fame.
But wé dream we are rooted in earth – Dust!   85
Flesh falls within sight of us, we, though our flower the same,
   Wave with the meadow, forget that there must
The sour scythe cringe,[7] and the blear [8] share come.

12

   On Saturday sailed from Bremen,
   American-outward-bound,   90
Take settler and seamen, tell men with women,
   Two hundred souls in the round –
O Father, not under thy feathers nor ever as guessing
The goal was a shoal, of a fourth the doom to be drowned;
   Yet did the dark side of the bay of thy blessing   95
Not vault them, the millions of rounds of thy mercy not reeve [9]
   even them in?

13

   Into the snows she sweeps,
   Hurling the haven behind,
The Deutschland, on Sunday; and so the sky keeps,
   For the infinite air is unkind,   100
And the sea flint-flake, black-backed in the regular blow,
Sitting Eastnortheast, in cursed quarter, the wind;
   Wiry and white-fiery and whirlwind-swivellèd snow
Spins to the widow-making unchilding unfathering deeps.

14

   She drove in the dark to leeward,   105
   She struck – not a reef or a rock

---

[6] *Austin* Augustine   [7] *cringe* bend   [8] *blear* dull   [9] *reeve* gather

But the combs of a smother of sand: night drew her
   Dead to the Kentish Knock;[10]
And she beat the bank down with her bows and the ride of
      her keel:
The breakers rolled on her beam with ruinous shock;   110
   And canvas and compass, the whorl [11] and the wheel
Idle for ever to waft her or wind her with, these she endured.

15

Hope had grown grey hairs,
   Hope had mourning on,
Trenched with tears, carved with cares,   115
   Hope was twelve hours gone;
And frightful a nightfall folded rueful a day
   Nor rescue, only rocket and lightship, shone,
And lives at last were washing away:
To the shrouds they took, – they shook in the hurling and horri-
      ble airs.   120

16

One stirred from the rigging to save
   The wild woman-kind below,
With a rope's end round the man, handy and brave –
   He was pitched to his death at a blow,
For all his dreadnought breast and braids of thew: 125
   They could tell him for hours, dandled the to and fro
Through the cobbled foam-fleece, what could he do
With the burl [12] of the fountains of air, buck and the flood of the
      wave?

17

They fought with God's cold –
   And they could not and fell to the deck   130
(Crushed them) or water (and drowned them) or rolled
   With the sea-romp over the wreck.
Night roared, with the heart-break hearing a heart-broke
      rabble,
   The woman's wailing, the crying of child without check –
Till a lioness arose breasting the babble,   135
A prophetess towered in the tumult, a virginal tongue told.

---

[10] *Kentish Knock* sandbank near the mouth of the Thames
[11] *whorl* screw-propeller   [12] *burl* roundness

18

Ah, touched in your bower of bone
Are you! turned for an exquisite smart,
Have you! make words break from me here all alone,
Do you! – mother of being in me, heart.   140
O unteachably after [13] evil, but uttering truth,
Why tears! is it? tears; such a melting, a madrigal [14] start!
Never-eldering revel and river of youth,
What can it be, this glee? the good you have there of your own?

19

Sister, a sister calling   145
A master, her master and mine! –
And the inboard seas run swirling and hawling;
The rash smart sloggering [15] brine
Blinds her; but she that weather sees one thing, one;
Has one fetch [16] in her: she rears herself to divine   150
Ears, and the call of the tall nun
To the men in the tops and the tackle rode over the storm's
brawling.

20

She was first of a five and came
Of a coifèd sisterhood.
(O Deutschland, double a desperate name!   155
O world wide of its good!
But Gertrude,[17] lily, and Luther, are two of a town,
Christ's lily and beast of the waste wood:
From life's dawn it is drawn down,
Abel is Cain's brother and breasts they have sucked the same.)   160

21

Loathed for a love men knew in them,
Banned by the land of their birth,
Rhine refused them. Thames would ruin them;
Surf, snow, river and earth
Gnashed: but thou art above, thou Orion [18] of light;   165
Thy unchancelling [19] poising palms were weighing the
worth,

---

[13] *after* go after   [14] *madrigal* song   [15] *sloggering* dealing heavy blows
[16] *fetch* shift
[17] *Gertrude* thirteenth-century German saint who lived near Luther's birth-place
[18] *Orion* constellation (the hunter)   [19] *unchancelling* unlatticed

Thou martyr-master: in thy sight
Storm flakes were scroll-leaved flowers, lily showers – sweet heaven
was astrew in them.

22

Five! the finding [20] and sake
And cipher of suffering Christ.   170
Mark, the mark is of man's make
And the word of it Sacrificed.
But he scores it in scarlet himself on his own bespoken,
Before-time-taken, dearest prizèd and priced –
Stigma, signal, cinquefoil [21] token   175
For lettering of the lamb's fleece, ruddying of the rose-flake.

23

Joy fall to thee, father Francis,   6
Drawn to the Life that died;
With the gnarls of the nails in thee, niche of the lance,
his
Lovescape [22] crucified   180
And seal of his seraph-arrival! and these thy daughters
And five-livèd and leavèd favour and pride,
Are sisterly sealed in wild waters,
To bathe in his fall-gold mercies, to breathe in his all-fire glances.

24

Away in the loveable west,   185
On a pastoral forehead of Wales,
I was under a roof here, I was at rest,
And they the prey of the gales;
She to the black-about air, to the breaker, the thickly
Falling flakes, to the throng that catches and quails   190
Was calling 'O Christ, Christ, come quickly':
The cross to her she calls Christ to her, christens her wild-worst
Best.

25

The majesty! what did she mean?
Breathe, arch and original Breath.
Is it love in her of the being as her lover had been?   195
Breathe, body of lovely Death.

[20] *finding* device
[21] *cinquefoil* design of five leaves, often in a circle or arch
[22] *Lovescape* pattern of Christ's wounds

They were else-minded then, altogether, the men
Woke thee with a *we are perishing* in the weather of Gen-
　　　nesareth.[23]
Or is it that she cried for the crown then,
The keener to come at the comfort for feeling the combating
　　　keen?　　　　　　　　　　　　　　　　　　　　200

26

For how to the heart's cheering
The down-dugged ground-hugged grey
Hovers off, the jay-blue heavens appearing
Of pied and peeled May!
Blue-beating and hoary-glow height; or night, still higher,　205
With belled fire and the moth-soft Milky Way,
What by your measure is the heaven of desire,
The treasure never eyesight got, nor was ever guessed what for
　　　the hearing?

27

No, but it was not these.
The jading [24] and jar of the cart,　　　　　　　　210
Time's tasking, it is fathers that asking for ease
Of the sodden-with-its-sorrowing heart,
Not danger, electrical horror; then further it finds
The appealing of the Passion is tenderer in prayer apart:
Other, I gather, in measure her mind's　　　　　　215
Burden, in wind's burly [25] and beat of endragonèd seas.

28

But how shall I . . . make me room there:
Reach me a . . . Fancy, come faster –
Strike you the sight of it? Look at it loom there,
Thing that she . . . there then! the Master,　　　220
Ipse, the only one, Christ, King, Head:
He was to cure the extremity where he had cast her;
Do, deal, lord it with living and dead;
Let him ride, her pride, in his triumph, despatch and have done
　　　with his doom there.

29

Ah! there was a heart right　　　　　　　　225
There was single eye!

[23] *Gennesareth* The Sea of Galilee is located on the plain of Gennesareth.
[24] *jading* tiring　　　　　　　　　[25] *burly* bluster

Read the unshapeable shock night
And knew the who and the why;
Wording it how but by him that present and past,
Heaven and earth are word of, worded by? –   230
The Simon Peter of a soul! to the blast
Tarpeian 26-fast, but a blown beacon of light.

30

Jesu, heart's light,   6
Jesu, maid's son,
What was the feast followed the night   235
Thou hadst glory of this nun? –
Feast 27 of the one woman without stain.
For so conceivèd, so to conceive thee is done;
But here was heart-throe, birth of a brain,
Word, that heard and kept thee and uttered thee outright.   240

31

Well, she has thee for the pain, for the
Patience; but pity of the rest of them!
Heart, go and bleed at a bitterer vein for the
Comfortless unconfessed of them –
No not uncomforted: lovely-felicitous Providence   245
Finger of a tender of, O of a feathery delicacy, the breast of the
Maiden could obey so, be a bell to, ring of it, and
Startle the poor sheep back! is the shipwrack then a harvest, does
tempest carry the grain for thee?

32

I admire thee, master of the tides,
Of the Yore-flood,28 of the year's fall;   250
The recurb and the recovery of the gulf's sides,
The girth of it and the wharf of it and the wall;
Stanching, quenching ocean of a motionable 29 mind;
Ground of being, and granite of it: past all
Grasp God, throned behind   255
Death with a sovereignty that heeds but hides, bodes but abides;

33

With a mercy that outrides
The all of water, an ark

26 *Tarpeian* denoting a rock-face on the Capitoline hill in Rome
27 *Feast* of the Immaculate Conception, December 8
28 *Yore-flood* the flood of old   29 *motionable* restless

For the listener; for the lingerer with a love glides
  Lower than death [30] and the dark;   260
A vein for the visiting of the past-prayer, pent in prison,
  The-last-breath penitent spirits – the uttermost mark
    Our passion-plungèd giant risen,
The Christ of the Father compassionate, fetched in the storm of
    his strides.

34

Now burn, new born to the world,   265
  Doubled-naturèd name,
The heaven-flung, heart-fleshed, maiden-furled
  Miracle-in-Mary-of-flame,
Mid-numbered He in three of the thunder-throne!
Not a dooms-day dazzle in his coming nor dark as he came;
  Kind, but royally reclaiming his own;   271
A released shower, let flash to the shire, not a lightning of fire
    hard-hurled.

35

Dame, at our door
  Drowned, and among our shoals,
Remember us in the roads, the heaven-haven of the
    Reward: 275
  Our King back, oh, upon English souls!
Let him easter in us, be a dayspring to the dimness of us, be
    a crimson-cresseted [31] east,
More brightening her, rare-dear Britain, as his reign rolls,
Pride, rose, prince, hero of us, high-priest,
Our hearts' charity's hearth's fire, our thoughts' chivalry's throng's
    Lord.   280

GOD'S GRANDEUR

The world is charged with the grandeur of God.
  It will flame out, like shining from shook foil; [1]
  It gathers to a greatness, like the ooze of oil
Crushed. Why do men then now not reck [2] his rod?
Generations have trod, have trod, have trod;   5
  And all is seared with trade; bleared, smeared with toil;

---

[30] *lower than death* Purgatory   [31] *cresseted* torched

---

[1] *shook foil* leaf or tinsel that glares or glints   [2] *reck* take heed of

And wears man's smudge and shares man's smell: the soil
Is bare now, nor can foot feel, being shod.

And for all this, nature is never spent;
  There lives the dearest freshness deep down things;   10
And though the last lights off the black West went
  Oh, morning, at the brown brink eastward, springs –
Because the Holy Ghost over the bent
  World broods with warm breast and with ah! bright wings.

THE STARLIGHT NIGHT

Look at the stars! look, look up at the skies!
  O look at all the fire-folk sitting in the air!
  The bright boroughs, the circle-citadels there!
Down in dim woods the diamond delves! [1] the elves'-eyes!
The grey lawns cold where gold, where quickgold lies!   5
  Wind-beat whitebeam! airy abeles [2] set on a flare!
  Flake-doves sent floating forth at a farmyard scare! –
Ah well! it is all a purchase, all is a prize.

Buy then! bid then! – What? [3] – Prayer, patience, alms, vows.
Look, look: a May-mess, like on orchard boughs!   10
  Look! March-bloom, like on mealed-with-yellow sallows! [4]
These are indeed the barn; withindoors house
The shocks.[5] This piece-bright paling [6] shuts the spouse
  Christ home, Christ and his mother and all his hallows.[7]

SPRING

Nothing is so beautiful as spring –
  When weeds, in wheels, shoot long and lovely and lush;
  Thrush's eggs look little low heavens, and thrush
Through the echoing timber does so rinse and wring [1]
The ear, it strikes like lightnings to hear him sing;   5
  The glassy [2] peartree leaves and blooms, they brush
  The descending blue; that blue is all in a rush
With richness; the racing lambs too have fair their fling.

---

[1] *delves* pits   [2] *abeles* white poplars   [3] *What?* What price?
[4] *sallows* low willows   [5] *shocks* of grain   [6] *paling* fencing
[7] *hallows* saints

---

[1] *rinse and wring* sound like water cleansing and swirling
[2] *glassy* shining

What is all this juice and all this joy?
A strain of the earth's sweet being in the beginning   10
In Eden garden. – Have, get, before it cloy,
  Before it cloud, Christ, lord, and sour with sinning,
Innocent mind and Mayday in girl and boy,
  Most, O maid's child, thy choice and worthy the winning.

THE WINDHOVER: [1]

TO CHRIST OUR LORD

I caught this morning morning's minion,[2] king-
  dom of daylight's dauphin,[3] dapple-dawn-drawn Falcon, in his
    riding
Of the rolling level underneath him steady air, and striding
High there, how he rung upon the rein of a wimpling [4] wing
In his ecstasy! then off, off forth on swing,   5
  As a skate's heel sweeps smooth on a bow-bend: the hurl and
    gliding
Rebuffed the big wind. My heart in hiding
Stirred for a bird, – the achieve of, the mastery of the thing!

Brute beauty and valour and act, oh, air, pride, plume, here
  Buckle! [5] AND the fire that breaks from thee then, a billion   10
Times told lovelier, more dangerous, O my chevalier! [6]
  No wonder of it: shéer plód [7] makes plough down sillion [8]
Shine, and blue-bleak embers, ah my dear,
  Fall, gall themselves, and gash gold-vermilion.

PIED [1] BEAUTY

Glory be to God for dappled things –
  For skies of couple-colour as a brinded cow;
    For rose-moles all in stipple upon trout that swim;
Fresh-firecoal chestnut-falls; finches' wings;
  Landscape plotted and pieced – fold, fallow,[2] and plough;   5
    And áll trádes, their gear and tackle and trim.[3]

---

[1] *Windhover* a falcon that hovers in the air with its head to the wind. Critical comment on this poem appears on p. 551.
[2] *minion* favorite   [3] *dauphin* king's heir
[4] *wimpling* twisting and turning   [5] *Buckle* collapse   [6] *chevalier* knight
[7] *plod* trudging   [8] *sillion* furrow

---

[1] *Pied* mingled, varied colors. Also *dappled, couple-colour, brinded* (ll. 1–2)
[2] *fallow* uncultivated land   [3] *gear, tackle, trim* equipment of the trades

All things counter,[4] original, spare, strange;
   Whatever is fickle, freckled (who knows how?)
     With swift, slow; sweet, sour; adazzle, dim;
He fathers-forth whose beauty is past change: 10
             Praise him.

THE CANDLE INDOORS

Some candle clear burns somewhere I come by.
I muse at how its being puts blissful back
With yellowy moisture mild night's blear-all black,
Or to-fro tender trambeams truckle [1] at the eye.
By that window what task what fingers ply,   5
I plod wondering, a-wanting, just for lack
Of answer the eagerer a-wanting Jessy or Jack
There   God to aggrándise, God to glorify. –

Come you indoors, come home; your fading fire
Mend first and vital candle in close heart's vault: 10
You there are master, do your own desire;
What hinders? Are you beam-blind, yet to a fault
In a neighbour deft-handed? are you that liar
And, cast by conscience out, spendsavour salt? [2]

FELIX RANDAL

Felix Randal the farrier,[1] O he is dead then? my duty all ended,
Who have watched his mould of man, big-boned and hardy-
   handsome
Pining, pining, till time when reason rambled in it and some
Fatal four disorders, fleshed there,[2] all contended?

Sickness broke him. Impatient he cursed at first, but mended   5
Being anointed and all; [3] though a heavenlier heart began some
Months earlier, since I had our sweet reprieve and ransom

---

[4] *counter* contrary

---

[1] *trambeams truckle* silken threads of light move in submission to the eye's
movements, or move toward the eye
[2] *beam-blind . . . salt* probably references to the (Biblical) beam that one
may disregard in his own eye while watching for motes in others, and to
salt that has lost its savor

---

[1] *farrier* blacksmith   [2] *fleshed there* brought into his body
[3] *anointed and all* given Extreme Unction

Tendered to him. Ah well, God rest him all road ever[4] he
    offended!

This seeing the sick endears them to us, us too it endears.
My tongue had taught thee comfort, touch had quenched thy
    tears,   10
Thy tears that touched my heart, child, Felix, poor Felix Randal;

How far from then forethought of, all thy more boisterous years,
When thou at the random[5] grim forge, powerful amidst peers,
Didst fettle[6] for the great grey drayhorse his bright and battering
    sandal!

SPRING AND FALL:

TO A YOUNG CHILD

Márgarét, are you gríeving
Over Goldengrove unleaving?
Leáves, líke the things of man, you
With your fresh thoughts care for, can you?
Áh! ás the heart grows older   5
It will come to such sights colder
By and by, nor spare a sigh
Though worlds of wanwood leafmeal[1] lie;
And yet you wíll weep and know why.
Now no matter, child, the name: 10
Sórrow's springs áre the same.
Nor mouth had, no nor mind, expressed
What heart heard of, ghost guessed:
It ís the blight man was born for,
It is Margaret you mourn for.   15

AS KINGFISHERS CATCH FIRE

As kingfishers catch fire, dragonflies dráw fláme;
As tumbled over rim in roundy wells
Stones ring; like each tucked[1] string tells, each hung bell's

---

[4] *all road ever* all ways in which   [5] *random* masonry of irregular stones
[6] *fettle* make ready

---

[1] *wanwood leafmeal* referring to dull woods and crushed leaves in a late fall
landscape

---

[1] *tucked* plucked

Bow swung finds tongue to fling out broad its name;
Each mortal thing does one thing and the same:　　　　5
Deals out that being indoors each one dwells;
Selves ² – goes itself; *myself* it speaks and spells;
Crying *Whát I dó is me: for that I came.*

Í say móre: the just man justices;
Kéeps gráce: thát keeps all his goings graces;　　　　10
Acts in God's eye what in God's eye he is –
Chríst – for Christ plays in ten thousand places,
Lovely in limbs, and lovely in eyes not his
To the Father through the features of men's faces.

NO WORST, THERE IS NONE

No worst, there is none. Pitched past pitch of grief,
More pangs will, schooled at forepangs, wilder wring.
Comforter, where, where is your comforting?
Mary, mother of us, where is your relief?
My cries heave, herds-long; ¹ huddle in a main, a chief　5
Woe, world-sorrow; on an age-old anvil wince and sing –
Then lull, then leave off. Fury had shrieked 'No ling-
ering! Let me be fell: ² force ³ I must be brief.'

　O the mind, mind has mountains; cliffs of fall
Frightful, sheer, no-man-fathomed. Hold them cheap　10
May who ne'er hung there. Nor does long our small
Durance deal with that steep or deep. Here! creep,
Wretch, under a comfort serves in a whirlwind: ⁴ all
Life death does end and each day dies with sleep.

I WAKE AND FEEL THE FELL OF DARK

I wake and feel the fell ¹ of dark, not day.
What hours, O what black hoürs we have spent
This night! what sights you, heart, saw; ways you went!
And more must, in yet longer light's delay.
　　　With witness I speak this. But where I say　5
Hours I mean years, mean life. And my lament

---

² *selves* makes the self

---

¹ *herds-long* not separate but in accumulation　　　² *fell* cruel
³ *force* perforce　　　⁴ *under . . . whirlwind* under whatever comfort available

---

¹ *fell* cruelty

Is cries countless, cries like dead letters sent
To dearest him that lives alas! away.

I am gall,[2] I am heartburn. God's most deep decree
Bitter would have me taste: my taste was me;　　10
Bones built in me, flesh filled, blood brimmed the curse.
Selfyeast of spirit a dull dough sours. I see
The lost are like this, and their scourge to be
As I am mine, their sweating selves; but worse.

THAT NATURE IS A HERACLITEAN [1] FIRE
AND OF THE
COMFORT OF THE RESURRECTION

Cloud-puffball, torn tufts, tossed pillows I flaunt forth, then
　　chevy [2] on an air-
built thoroughfare: heaven-roysterers, in gay-gangs I they throng;
　　they glitter in marches.
Down roughcast, down dazzling whitewash, I wherever an elm
　　arches,
Shivelights [3] and shadowtackle [4] in long I lashes lace, lance, and
　　pair.
Delightfully the bright wind boisterous I ropes, wrestles, beats
　　earth bare　　5
Of yestertempest's creases; I in pool and rut peel parches
Squandering ooze to squeezed I dough, crust, dust; stanches,[5]
　　starches [6]
Squadroned masks [7] and manmarks I treadmire toil there
Footfretted [8] in it. Million-fuelèd, I nature's bonfire burns on.
But quench her bonniest, dearest I to her, her clearest-selvèd
　　spark　　10
Man, how fast his firedint, I his mark on mind, is gone!
Both are in an unfathomable, all is in an enormous dark
Drowned. O pity and indig I nation! Manshape, that shone
Sheer off, disseveral,[9] a star, I death blots black out; nor mark
　　　　　Is any of him at all so stark　　15

[2] *gall* bitter substance

---

[1] *Heraclitean* of Heraclitus (*c.*535–*c.*457), who believed all things are in flux,
governed by the principle of fire and changing through all the elements of
fire, water, earth, air.
[2] *chevy* scamper　　　　　　　　　　[3] *shivelights* splinters of light
[4] *shadowtackle* ropes of shadow　　　[5] *stanches* stops
[6] *starches* stiffens　　　　　　　　[7] *squadroned masks* fixed expressions
[8] *footfretted* foot-marked　　　　　[9] *disseveral* separate

WALT WHITMAN

[1891-1892]

WALT WHITMAN was born of a Quaker family on Long Island, New York. In his early years he taught school; started and abandoned a newspaper; was a printer, editor, and journalist in New York, Brooklyn, and New Orleans; built and sold houses. But his poetry was his main work, and he collected it in the one book that would change and grow with him. In 1855 he published the first edition of *Leaves of Grass* at his own expense; eight later editions, from 1856 to 1891–1892 were constantly expanded and rearranged. In *Leaves of Grass* Whitman startled the reading world with his new style of poetry. In strong-voiced, free rhythms he dramatically presented his belief in the possibilities of America and the worth of the individual person. During the Civil War, Whitman worked as a journalist and wounddresser, later as a government clerk in Washington. *Democratic Vistas,* a major essay on the American scene, was published in 1871. In his last years Whitman was a semi-invalid, living in Camden, New Jersey. But by then (with the 1881 edition of *Leaves of Grass*) he was famous. Whitman is now considered by many to be the great American poet, not so much as a social optimist but as a philosophic poet who chanted the mystic spiral of creative life and the unity of all things.

Introductory Readings

EDITION: *The Complete Writings of Walt Whitman,* ed. Richard M. Bucke et al, 10 vols. (1902); *The Complete Poetry and Selected Prose,* ed. James E. Miller, Jr. (1959). BIOGRAPHY: Gay Wilson Allen, *The Solitary Singer: A Critical Biography of Walt Whitman* (1955). CRITICISM: Gay Wilson Allen, *Walt Whitman Handbook* (1946); Richard Chase, *Walt Whitman Reconsidered* (1955); James E. Miller, Jr., *A Critical*

Guide to Leaves of Grass (1957); see also, *Leaves of Grass: The First (1855) Edition,* ed. with introduction by Malcolm Cowley (1959).

ONE'S-SELF I SING

One's-self I sing, a simple separate person,
Yet utter the word Democratic, the word En-Masse.[1]

Of physiology from top to toe I sing,
Not physiognomy alone nor brain alone is worthy for the Muse,
    I say the form complete is worthier far,
The Female equally with the Male I sing.   5

Of Life immense in passion, pulse, and power,
Cheerful, for freest action form'd under the laws divine,
The Modern Man I sing.

SONG OF MYSELF

SECTION 44

It is time to explain myself [1]—let us stand up.

What is known I strip away,
I launch all men and women forward with me into the Unknown.

The clock indicates the moment—but what does eternity indicate?

We have thus far exhausted trillions of winters and summers,   5
There are trillions ahead, and trillions ahead of them.

Births have brought us richness and variety,
And other births will bring us richness and variety.

I do not call one greater and one smaller,
That which fills its period and place is equal to any.   10

Were mankind murderous or jealous upon you, my brother, my
    sister?
I am sorry for you, they are not murderous or jealous upon me,
All has been gentle with me, I keep no account with lamentation,
(What have I to do with lamentation?)

[1] *En-Masse* all together, as a whole

[1] *explain myself* At this point in his long, mystical poem, the poet begins an "explanation" of his intuitive knowledge that he transcends time and space. In Section 44 he asserts his immortality by identifying himself with all time, but not at the expense of diminishing the *now.*

I am an acme of things accomplish'd, and I an encloser of things
 to be.   15

My feet strike an apex of the apices [2] of the stairs,
On every step bunches of ages, and larger bunches between the
 steps,
All below duly travel'd, and still I mount and mount.

Rise after rise bow the phantoms behind me,   19
Afar down I see the huge first Nothing, I know I was even there,
I waited unseen and always, and slept through the lethargic mist,
And took my time, and took no hurt from the fetid carbon.

Long I was hugg'd close—long and long.

Immense have been the preparations for me,
Faithful and friendly the arms that have help'd me.   25

Cycles ferried my cradle, rowing and rowing like cheerful boat-
 men,
For room to me stars kept aside in their own rings,
They sent influences to look after what was to hold me.

Before I was born out of my mother generations guided me,
My embryo has never been torpid, nothing could overlay it. 30

For it the nebula cohered to an orb,
The long slow strata piled to rest it on,
Vast vegetables gave it sustenance,
Monstrous sauroids [3] transported it in their mouths and deposited
 it with care.

All forces have been steadily employ'd to complete and delight
 me,   35
Now on this spot I stand with my robust soul!

CROSSING BROOKLYN FERRY

1

Flood-tide below me! I see you face to face!
Clouds of the west—sun there half an hour high—I see you also
 face to face.

[2] *apex of the apices* peak or tip—of the several ages of the past and more to
come
[3] *Monstrous sauroids* large, lizard-like animals

Crowds of men and women attired in the usual costumes, how
    curious you are to me!
On the ferry-boats the hundreds and hundreds that cross, return-
    ing home, are more curious to me than you suppose,   4
And you that shall cross from shore to shore years hence are more
    to me, and more in my meditations, than you might suppose.

2

The impalpable sustenance of me from all things at all hours of
    the day,   6
The simple, compact, well-join'd scheme, myself disintegrated,
    every one disintegrated yet part of the scheme,
The similitudes [1] of the past and those of the future,
The glories strung like beads on my smallest sights and hearings,
    on the walk in the street and the passage over the river,   9
The current rushing so swiftly and swimming with me far away,
The others that are to follow me, the ties between me and them,
The certainty of others, the life, love, sight, hearing of others.

Others will enter the gates of the ferry and cross from shore to
    shore,
Others will watch the run of the flood-tide,
Others will see the shipping of Manhattan north and west, and
    the heights of Brooklyn to the south and east,   15
Others will see the islands large and small;
Fifty years hence, others will see them as they cross, the sun half
    an hour high,
A hundred years hence, or ever so many hundred years hence,
    others will see them,
Will enjoy the sunset, the pouring-in of the flood-tide, the falling-
    back to the sea of the ebb-tide.

3

It avails not, time nor place—distance avails not,   20
I am with you, you men and women of a generation, or ever so
    many generations hence,
Just as you feel when you look on the river and sky, so I felt,
Just as any of you is one of a living crowd, I was one of a crowd,
Just as you are refresh'd by the gladness of the river and the
    bright flow, I was refresh'd,
Just as you stand and lean on the rail, yet hurry with the swift
    current, I stood yet was hurried,   25
Just as you look on the numberless masts of ships and the thick-
    stemm'd pipes of steamboats, I look'd.

[1] *similitudes* likenesses, similarities

I too many and many a time cross'd the river of old,
Watched the Twelfth-month sea-gulls, saw them high in the air
    floating with motionless wings, oscillating their bodies,
Saw how the glistening yellow lit up parts of their bodies and left
    the rest in strong shadow,
Saw the slow-wheeling circles and the gradual edging toward the
    south,   30
Saw the reflection of the summer sky in the water,
Had my eyes dazzled by the shimmering track of beams,
Look'd at the fine centrifugal spokes of light round the shape of
    my head in the sunlit water,
Look'd on the haze on the hills southward and south-westward,
Look'd on the vapor as it flew in fleeces tinged with violet,   35
Look'd toward the lower bay to notice the vessels arriving,
Saw their approach, saw aboard those that were near me,
Saw the white sails of schooners and sloops, saw the ships at
    anchor,
The sailors at work in the rigging or out astride the spars,
The round masts, the swinging motion of the hulls, the slender
    serpentine pennants,   40
The large and small steamers in motion, the pilots in their pilot-
    houses,
The white wake left by the passage, the quick tremulous whirl of
    the wheels,
The flags of all nations, the falling of them at sunset,
The scallop-edged waves in the twilight, the ladled cups, the
    frolicsome crests and glistening,
The stretch afar growing dimmer and dimmer, the gray walls of
    the granite storehouses by the docks,   45
On the river the shadowy group, the big steam-tug closely flank'd
    on each side by the barges, the hay-boat, the belated lighter,
On the neighboring shore the fires from the foundry chimneys
    burning high and glaringly into the night,
Casting their flicker of black contrasted with wild red and yellow
    light over the tops of houses, and down into the clefts of
    streets.

4

These and all else were to me the same as they are to you,
I loved well those cities, loved well the stately and rapid river,   50
The men and women I saw were all near to me,
Others the same—others who look back on me because I look'd
    forward to them,
(The time will come, though I stop here to-day and to-night.)

5

What is it then between us?　　　　　54
What is the count of the scores or hundreds of years between us?

Whatever it is, it avails not—distance avails not, and place avails
　　not,　　　　　56
I too lived, Brooklyn of ample hills was mine,
I too walk'd the streets of Manhattan island, and bathed in the
　　waters around it,
I too felt the curious abrupt questionings stir within me.
In the day among crowds of people sometimes they came upon
　　me,　　　　　60
In my walks home late at night or as I lay in my bed they came
　　upon me,
I too had been struck from the float [2] forever held in solution,
I too had receiv'd identity by my body,
That I was I knew was of my body, and what I should be I knew
　　I should be of my body.

6

It is not upon you alone the dark patches fall,　　　　　65
The dark threw its patches down upon me also,
The best I had done seem'd to me blank and suspicious,
My great thoughts as I supposed them, were they not in reality
　　meagre?
Nor is it you alone who know what it is to be evil,
I am he who knew what it was to be evil,　　　　　70
I too knitted the old knot of contrariety,[3]
Blabb'd,[4] blush'd, resented, lied, stole, grudg'd,
Had guile, anger, lust, hot wishes I dared not speak,
Was wayward, vain, greedy, shallow, sly, cowardly, malignant,
The wolf, the snake, the hog, not wanting in me,　　　　　75
The cheating look, the frivolous word, the adulterous wish, not
　　wanting,
Refusals, hates, postponements, meanness, laziness, none of these
　　wanting,
Was one with the rest, the days and haps [5] of the rest,
Was call'd by my nighest name by clear loud voices of young men
　　as they saw me approaching or passing,
Felt their arms on my neck as I stood, or the negligent leaning of
　　their flesh against me as I sat,　　　　　80

[2] *float* dissolved substance distributed throughout liquid
[3] *knot of contrariety* wayward or evil behavior　　　[4] *Blabb'd* talked wildly
[5] *haps* events or accidents

Saw many I loved in the street or ferry-boat or public assembly,
    yet never told them a word,
Lived the same life with the rest, the same old laughing, gnawing,
    sleeping,
Play'd the part that still looks back on the actor or actress,
The same old role, the role that is what we make it, as great as we
    like,
Or as small as we like, or both great and small.   85

7

Closer yet I approach you,
What thought you have of me now, I had as much of you—I laid
    in my stores in advance,
I consider'd long and seriously of you before you were born.

Who was to know what should come home to me?
Who knows but I am enjoying this?   90
Who knows, for all the distance, but I am as good as looking at
    you now, for all you cannot see me?

8

Ah, what can ever be more stately and admirable to me than mast-
    hemm'd Manhattan?
River and sunset and scallop-edg'd waves of flood-tide?
The sea-gulls oscillating their bodies, the hay-boat in the twilight,
    and the belated lighter?
What gods can exceed these that clasp me by the hand, and with
    voices I love call me promptly and loudly by my nighest
    name as I approach?   95
What is more subtle than this which ties me to the woman or man
    that looks in my face?
Which fuses me into you now, and pours my meaning into you?

We understand then do we not?
What I promis'd without mentioning it, have you not accepted?
What the study could not teach—what the preaching could not
    accomplish is accomplish'd, is it not?   100

9

Flow on, river! flow with the flood-tide, and ebb with the ebb-tide!
Frolic on, crested and scallop-edg'd waves!
Gorgeous clouds of the sunset! drench with your splendor me, or
    the men and women generations after me!
Cross from shore to shore, countless crowds of passengers!

Stand up, tall masts of Mannahatta! stand up, beautiful hills of
　　Brooklyn!   105
Throb, baffled and curious brain! throw out questions and an-
　　swers!
Suspend here and everywhere, eternal float of solution!
Gaze, loving and thirsting eyes, in the house or street or public
　　assembly!
Sound out, voices of young men! loudly and musically call me by
　　my nighest name!
Live, old life! play the part that looks back on the actor or ac-
　　tress!   110
Play the old role, the role that is great or small according as one
　　makes it!
Consider, you who peruse me, whether I may not in unknown
　　ways be looking upon you;
Be firm, rail over the river, to support those who lean idly, yet
　　haste with the hasting current;
Fly on, sea-birds! fly sideways, or wheel in large circles high in
　　the air;
Receive the summer sky, you water, and faithfully hold it till all
　　downcast eyes have time to take it from you!   115
Diverge, fine spokes of light, from the shape of my head, or any
　　one's head, in the sunlit water!
Come on, ships from the lower bay! pass up or down, white-sail'd
　　schooners, sloops, lighters!
Flaunt away, flags of all nations! be duly lower'd at sunset!
Burn high your fires, foundry chimneys! cast black shadows at
　　nightfall! cast red and yellow light over the tops of the houses!
Appearances, now or henceforth, indicate what you are,   120
You necessary film, continue to envelop the soul,
About my body for me, and your body for you, be hung our
　　divinest aromas,
Thrive, cities—bring your freight, bring your shows, ample and
　　sufficient rivers,
Expand, being than which none else is perhaps more spiritual,
Keep your places, objects than which none else is more lasting. 125

You have waited, you always wait, you dumb, beautiful ministers,[6]
We receive you with free sense at last, and are insatiate hence-
　　forward,
Not you any more shall be able to foil us, or withhold yourselves
　　from us,

[6] *ministers* the contents of the world, objects which make vivid sense impressions

We use you, and do not cast you aside—we plant you perma-
nently within us,
We fathom you not—we love you—there is perfection in you also,
You furnish your parts toward eternity,   131
Great or small, you furnish your parts toward the soul.

OUT OF THE CRADLE ENDLESSLY ROCKING

Out of the cradle endlessly rocking,
Out of the mocking-bird's throat, the musical shuttle,
Out of the Ninth-month midnight,
Over the sterile sands and the fields beyond, where the child leav-
ing his bed wander'd alone, bareheaded, barefoot,
Down from the shower'd halo,   5
Up from the mystic play of shadows twining and twisting as if
they were alive,
Out from the patches of briers and blackberries,
From the memories of the bird that chanted to me,
From your memories sad brother, from the fitful risings and fall-
ings I heard,
From under that yellow half-moon late-risen and swollen as if
with tears,   10
From those beginning notes of yearning and love there in the
mist,
From the thousand responses of my heart never to cease,
From the myriad thence-arous'd words,
From the word stronger and more delicious than any,
From such as now they start the scene revisiting,   15
As a flock, twittering, rising, or overhead passing,
Borne hither, ere all eludes me, hurriedly,
A man, yet by these tears a little boy again,
Throwing myself on the sand, confronting the waves,
I, chanter of pains and joys, uniter of here and hereafter,   20
Taking all hints to use them, but swiftly leaping beyond them,
A reminiscence sing.

Once Paumanok,[1]
When the lilac-scent was in the air and Fifth-month grass was
growing,
Up this seashore in some briers,   25
Two feather'd guests from Alabama, two together,
And their nest, and four light-green eggs spotted with brown,
And every day the he-bird to and fro near at hand,

[1] *Paumanok* Indian name for Manhattan

And every day the she-bird crouch'd on her nest, silent, with
    bright eyes,
And every day I, a curious boy, never too close, never disturbing
    them,   30
Cautiously peering, absorbing, translating.

Shine! shine! shine!
Pour down your warmth, great sun!
While we bask, we two together.

Two together!   35
Winds blow south, or winds blow north,
Day come white, or night come black,
Home, or rivers and mountains from home,
Singing all time, minding no time,
While we two keep together.   40

Till of a sudden,
May-be kill'd, unknown to her mate,
One forenoon the she-bird crouch'd not on the nest,
Nor return'd that afternoon, nor the next,
Nor ever appear'd again.   45

And thenceforward all summer in the sound of the sea,
And at night under the full of the moon in calmer weather,
Over the hoarse surging of the sea,
Or flitting from brier to brier by day,
I saw, I heard at intervals the remaining one, the he-bird,   50
The solitary guest from Alabama.

Blow! blow! blow!
Blow up sea-winds along Paumanok's shore;
I wait and I wait till you blow my mate to me.

Yes, when the stars glisten'd,   55
All night long on the prong of a moss-scallop'd stake,
Down almost amid the slapping waves,
Sat the lone singer wonderful causing tears.

He call'd on his mate,
He pour'd forth the meanings which I of all men know.   60

Yes my brother I know,
The rest might not, but I have treasur'd every note,
For more than once dimly down to the beach gliding,
Silent, avoiding the moonbeams, blending myself with the
    shadows,

Recalling now the obscure shapes, the echoes, the sounds and
    sights after their sorts,   65
The white arms out in the breakers tirelessly tossing,
I, with bare feet, a child, the wind wafting my hair,
Listen'd long and long.

Listen'd to keep, to sing, now translating the notes,
Following you my brother.   70

Soothe! soothe! soothe!
Close on its wave soothes the wave behind,
And again another behind embracing and lapping, every one
    close,
But my love soothes not me, not me.

Low hangs the moon, it rose late,   75
It is lagging [2]*—O I think it is heavy with love, with love.*

O madly the sea pushes upon the land,
With love, with love.

O night! do I not see my love fluttering out among the breakers?
What is that little black thing I see there in the white?   80

Loud! loud! loud!
Loud I call to you, my love!
High and clear I shoot my voice over the waves,
Surely you must know who is here, is here,
You must know who I am, my love.   85

Low-hanging moon!
What is that dusky spot in your brown yellow?
O it is the shape, the shape of my mate!
O moon do not keep her from me any longer.

Land! land! O land!   90
Whichever way I turn, O I think you could give me my mate back
    again if you only would,
For I am almost sure I see her dimly whichever way I look.

O rising stars!
Perhaps the one I want so much will rise, will rise with some of
    you.

O throat! O trembling throat!   95
Sound clearer through the atmosphere!
Pierce the woods, the earth,
Somewhere listening to catch you must be the one I want.

[2] *lagging* falling behind

Shake out carols!
Solitary here, the night's carols!   100
Carols of lonesome love! death's carols!
Carols under that lagging, yellow, waning moon!
O under that moon where she droops almost down into the sea!
O reckless despairing carols.

But soft! sink low!   105
Soft! let me just murmur,
And do you wait a moment you husky-nois'd sea,
For somewhere I believe I heard my mate responding to me,
So faint, I must be still, be still to listen,
But not altogether still, for then she might not come immediately
*   to me.*   110

Hither my love!
Here I am! here!

With this just-sustain'd note I announce myself to you,
This gentle call is for you my love, for you.

Do not be decoy'd elsewhere,   115
That is the whistle of the wind, it is not my voice,
That is the fluttering, the fluttering of the spray,
Those are the shadows of leaves.

O darkness! O in vain!
O I am very sick and sorrowful.   120

O brown halo in the sky near the moon, drooping upon the sea!
O troubled reflection in the sea!
O throat! O throbbing heart!
And I singing uselessly, uselessly all the night.

O past! O happy life! O songs of joy!   125
In the air, in the woods, over fields,
Loved! loved! loved! loved! loved!
But my mate no more, no more with me!
We two together no more.

The aria sinking,   130
All else continuing, the stars shining,
The winds blowing, the notes of the bird continuous echoing,
With angry moans the fierce old mother incessantly moaning,
On the sands of Paumanok's shore gray and rustling,
The yellow half-moon enlarged, sagging down, drooping, the face
     of the sea almost touching,   135

The boy ecstatic, with his bare feet the waves, with his hair the
    atmosphere dallying,
The love in the heart long pent, now loose, now at last tumultu-
    ously bursting,
The aria's meaning, the ears, the soul, swiftly depositing,
The strange tears down the cheeks coursing,
The colloquy there, the trio, each uttering,   140
The undertone, the savage old mother incessantly crying,
To the boy's soul's questions sullenly timing, some drown'd secret
    hissing,
To the outsetting bard.

Demon or bird! (said the boy's soul,)
Is it indeed toward your mate you sing? or is it really to me?   145
For I, that was a child, my tongue's use sleeping, now I have heard
    you,
Now in a moment I know what I am for, I awake,
And already a thousand singers, a thousand songs, clearer, louder
    and more sorrowful than yours,
A thousand warbling echoes have started to life within me, never
    to die.

O you singer solitary, singing by yourself, projecting me,   150
O solitary me listening, never more shall I cease perpetuating
    you,
Never more shall I escape, never more the reverberations,
Never more the cries of unsatisfied love be absent from me,
Never again leave me to be the peaceful child I was before what
    there in the night,
By the sea under the yellow and sagging moon,   155
The messenger there arous'd, the fire, the sweet hell within,
The unknown want, the destiny of me.

O give me the clew! (it lurks in the night here somewhere,)
O if I am to have so much, let me have more!

A word then, (for I will conquer it,)   160
The word final, superior to all,
Subtle, sent up—what is it?—I listen;
Are you whispering it, and have been all the time, you sea waves?
Is that it from your liquid rims and wet sands?

Whereto answering, the sea,   165
Delaying not, hurrying not,
Whisper'd me through the night, and very plainly before day-
    break,

Lisp'd to me the low and delicious word death,
And again death, death, death, death,
Hissing melodious, neither like the bird nor like my arous'd
  child's heart,   170
But edging near as privately for me rustling at my feet,
Creeping thence steadily up to my ears and laving me softly all
  over
Death, death, death, death, death.

Which I do not forget,
But fuse the song of my dusky demon and brother,   175
That he sang to me in the moonlight on Paumanok's gray beach,
With the thousand responsive songs at random,
My own songs awaked from that hour,
And with them the key, the word up from the waves,
The word of the sweetest song and all songs,   180
That strong and delicious word which, creeping to my feet,
(Or like some old crone rocking the cradle, swathed in sweet gar-
  ments, bending aside,)
The sea whisper'd me.

WHEN I HEARD THE LEARN'D ASTRONOMER

When I heard the learn'd astronomer,
When the proofs, the figures, were ranged in columns before me,
When I was shown the charts and diagrams, to add, divide, and
  measure them,
When I sitting heard the astronomer where he lectured with
  much applause in the lecture-room,
How soon unaccountable I became tired and sick,   5
Till rising and gliding out I wander'd off by myself,
In the mystical moist night air, and from time to time,
Look'd up in perfect silence at the stars.

WHEN LILACS LAST IN THE DOORYARD BLOOM'D

1

When lilacs [1] last in the dooryard bloom'd,
And the great star early droop'd in the western sky in the night,
I mourn'd, and yet shall mourn with ever-returning spring.

[1] *lilacs* Lincoln was assassinated in April, 1865, when lilacs were in bloom.
The lilacs become symbolic of the poet's love for Lincoln, the star identifies
with Lincoln, and the hermit-thrush represents the spiritual reconciliation
to Lincoln's death.

Ever-returning spring, trinity sure to me you bring,
Lilac blooming perennial and drooping star in the west,   5
And thought of him I love.

2

O powerful western fallen star!
O shades of night—O moody, tearful night!
O great star disappear'd—O the black murk that hides the star!
O cruel hands that hold me powerless—O helpless soul of me!   10
O harsh surrounding cloud that will not free my soul.

3

In the dooryard fronting an old farm-house near the white-wash'd
   palings,
Stands the lilac-bush tall-growing with heart-shaped leaves of rich
   green,
With many a pointed blossom rising delicate, with the perfume
   strong I love,
With every leaf a miracle—and from this bush in the dooryard,   15
With delicate-color'd blossoms and heart-shaped leaves of rich
   green,
A sprig with its flower I break.

4

In the swamp in secluded recesses,
A shy and hidden bird is warbling a song.

Solitary the thrush,   20
The hermit withdrawn to himself, avoiding the settlements,
Sings by himself a song.

Song of the bleeding throat,
Death's outlet song of life, (for well dear brother I know,
If thou was not granted to sing thou would'st surely die.)   25

5

Over the breast of the spring, the land, amid cities,
Amid lanes and through old woods, where lately the violets peep'd
   from the ground, spotting the gray debris,
Amid the grass in the fields each side of the lanes, passing the end-
   less grass,
Passing the yellow-spear'd wheat, every grain from its shroud in
   the dark-brown fields uprisen,
Passing the apple-tree blows of white and pink in the orchards,   30

Carrying a corpse to where it shall rest in the grave,
Night and day journeys a coffin.

6

Coffin that passes through lanes and streets,
Through day and night with the great cloud darkening the land,
With the pomp of the inloop'd flags with the cities draped in
　　black,　　　　　　　　　　　　　　　　　　　　　　　35
With the show of the States themselves as of crape-veil'd women
　　standing,
With processions long and winding and the flambeaus of the
　　night,
With the countless torches lit, with the silent sea of faces and the
　　unbared heads,
With the waiting depot, the arriving coffin, and the sombre faces,
With dirges through the night, with the thousand voices rising
　　strong and solemn,　　　　　　　　　　　　　　　　40
With all the mournful voices of the dirges pour'd around the
　　coffin,
The dim-lit churches and the shuddering organs—where amid
　　these you journey,
With the tolling tolling bells' perpetual clang,
Here, coffin that slowly passes,
I give you my sprig of lilac.　　　　　　　　　　　　　　45

7

(Nor for you, for one alone,
Blossoms and branches green to coffins all I bring,
For fresh as the morning, thus would I chant a song for you O
　　sane and sacred death.

All over bouquets of roses,
O death, I cover you over with roses and early lilies,　　　　50
But mostly and now the lilac that blooms the first,
Copious I break, I break the sprigs from the bushes,
With loaded arms I come, pouring for you,
For you and the coffins all of you O death.)

8

O western orb sailing the heaven,　　　　　　　　　　　55
Now I know what you must have meant as a month since I
　　walk'd,
As I walk'd in silence the transparent shadowy night,

As I saw you had something to tell as you bent to me night after
    night,
As you droop'd from the sky low down as if to my side, (while the
    other stars all look'd on,)
As we wander'd together the solemn night, (for something I know
    not what kept me from sleep,)   60
As the night advanced, and I saw on the rim of the west how full
    you were of woe,
As I stood on the rising ground in the breeze in the cool trans-
    parent night,
As I watch'd where you pass'd and was lost in the netherward
    black of the night,
As my soul in its trouble dissatisfied sank, as where you sad orb,
Concluded, dropt in the night, and was gone.   65

9

Sing on there in the swamp,
O singer bashful and tender, I hear your notes, I hear your call,
I hear, I come presently, I understand you,
But a moment I linger, for the lustrous star has detain'd me,
The star my departing comrade holds and detains me.   70

10

O how shall I warble myself for the dead one there I loved?
And how shall I deck my song for the large sweet soul that has
    gone?
And what shall my perfume be for the grave of him I love?

Sea-winds blown from east and west,
Blown from the Eastern sea and blown from the Western sea, till
    there on the prairies meeting,   75
These and with these and the breath of my chant,
I'll perfume the grave of him I love.

11

O what shall I hang on the chamber walls?
And what shall the pictures be that I hang on the walls,
To adorn the burial-house of him I love?   80

Pictures of growing spring and farms and homes,
With the Fourth-month eve at sundown, and the gray smoke
    lucid and bright,
With floods of the yellow gold of the gorgeous, indolent, sinking
    sun, burning, expanding the air,

With the fresh sweet herbage under foot, and the pale green
leaves of the trees prolific,
In the distance the flowing glaze, the breast of the river, with a
wind-dapple here and there,   85
With ranging hills on the banks, with many a line against the
sky, and shadows,
And the city at hand with dwellings so dense, and stacks of chimneys,
And all the scenes of life and the workshops, and the workmen
homeward returning.

12

Lo, body and soul—this land,
My own Manhattan with spires, and the sparkling and hurrying
tides, and the ships,   90
The varied and ample land, the South and the North in the light,
Ohio's shores and flashing Missouri,
And ever the far-spreading prairies cover'd with grass and corn.

Lo, the most excellent sun so calm and haughty,
The violet and purple morn with just-felt breezes,
The gentle soft-born measureless light,   95
The miracle spreading bathing all, the fulfill'd noon,
The coming eve delicious, the welcome night and the stars,
Over my cities shining all, enveloping man and land.

13

Sing on, sing on you gray-brown bird,
Sing from the swamps, the recesses, pour your chant from the
bushes,   100
Limitless out of the dusk, out of the cedars and pines.

Sing on dearest brother, warble your reedy song,
Loud human song, with voice of uttermost woe,

O liquid and free and tender!
O wild and loose to my soul—O wondrous singer,   105
You only I hear—yet the star holds me, (but will soon depart,)
Yet the lilac with mastering odor holds me.

14

Now while I sat in the day and look'd forth,
In the close of the day with its light and the fields of spring, and
the farmers preparing their crops,

In the large unconscious scenery of my land with its lakes and
 forests,   110
In the heavenly aerial beauty, (after the perturb'd winds and the
 storms,)
Under the arching heavens of the afternoon swift passing, and the
 voices of children and women,
The many-moving sea-tides, and I saw the ships how they sail'd,
And the summer approaching with richness, and the fields all
 busy with labor,
And the infinite separate houses, how they all went on, each with
 its meals and minutia of daily usages,   115
And the streets how their throbbings throbb'd, and the cities pent
 —lo, then and there,
Falling upon them all and among them all, enveloping me with
 the rest,
Appear'd the cloud, appear'd the long black trail,
And I knew death, its thought, and the sacred knowledge of
 death.
Then with the knowledge of death as walking one side of me, 120
And the thought of death close-walking the other side of me,
And I in the middle as with companions, and as holding the
 hands of companions,
I fled forth to the hiding receiving night that talks not,
Down to the shores of the water, the path by the swamp in the
 dimness,
To the solemn shadowy cedars and ghostly pines so still. 125

And the singer so shy to the rest receiv'd me,
The gray-brown bird I know receiv'd us comrades three,
And he sang the carol of death, and a verse for him I love.

From deep secluded recesses,
From the fragrant cedars and the ghostly pines so still, 130
Came the carol of the bird.

And the charm of the carol rapt me,
As I held as if by their hands my comrades in the night,
And the voice of my spirit tallied the song of the bird.

Come lovely and soothing death,   135
Undulate round the world, serenely arriving, arriving,
In the day, in the night, to all, to each,
Sooner or later delicate death.

Prais'd be the fathomless universe,
For life and joy, and for objects and knowledge curious, 140

And for love, sweet love—but praise! praise! praise!
For the sure-enwinding arms of cool-enfolding death.

Dark mother always gliding near with soft feet,
Have none chanted for thee a chant of fullest welcome?
Then I chant it for thee, I glorify thee above all,   145
I bring thee a song that when thou must indeed come, come un-
falteringly.

Approach strong deliveress,
When it is so, when thou hast taken them I joyously sing the
dead,
Lost in the loving floating ocean of thee,
Laved in the flood of thy bliss O death.   150

From me to thee glad serenades,
Dances for thee I propose saluting thee, adornments and feastings
for thee,
And the sights of the open landscape and the high-spread sky are
fitting,
And life and the fields, and the huge and thoughtful night.

The night in silence under many a star,   155
The ocean shore and the husky whispering wave whose voice I
know,
And the soul turning to thee O vast and well-veil'd death,
And the body gratefully nestling close to thee.

Over the tree-tops I float thee a song,
Over the rising and sinking waves, over the myriad fields and the
prairies wide,   160
Over the dense-pack'd cities all and the teeming wharves and
ways,
I float this carol with joy, with joy to thee O death.

15

To the tally of my soul,
Loud and strong kept up the gray-brown bird,
With pure deliberate notes spreading filling the night.   165

Loud in the pines and cedars dim,
Clear in the freshness moist and the swamp-perfume,
And I with my comrades there in the night.

While my sight that was bound in my eyes unclosed,
As to long panoramas of visions.   170

And I saw askant [2] the armies,
I saw as in noiseless dreams hundreds of battle-flags,
Borne through the smoke of the battles and pierc'd with missiles
    I saw them,
And carried hither and yon through the smoke, and torn and
    bloody,
And at last but a few shreds left on the staffs, (and all in si-
    lence,)   175
And the staffs all splinter'd and broken.

I saw battle-corpses, myriads of them,
And the white skeletons of young men, I saw them,
I saw the debris and debris of all the slain soldiers of the war,
But I saw they were not as was thought,   180
They themselves were fully at rest, they suffer'd not,
The living remain'd and suffered, the mother suffered,
And the wife and the child and the musing comrade suffer'd,
And the armies that remain'd suffer'd.

16

Passing the visions, passing the night,   185
Passing, unloosing the hold of my comrade's hands,
Passing the song of the hermit bird and the tallying song of my
    soul,
Victorious song, death's outlet song, yet varying ever-altering
    song,
As low and wailing, yet clear the notes, rising and falling, flood-
    ing the night,
Sadly sinking and fainting, as warning and warning, and yet
    again bursting with joy,   190
Covering the earth and filling the spread of the heaven,
As that powerful psalm in the night I heard from recesses,
Passing, I leave thee lilac with heart-shaped leaves,
I leave thee there in the door-yard, blooming, returning with
    spring.

I cease from my song for thee,   195
From my gaze on thee in the west, fronting the west, communing
    with thee,
O comrade lustrous with silver face in the night.

Yet each to keep and all, retrievements out of the night,
The song, the wondrous chant of the gray-brown bird,
And the tallying chant, the echo arous'd in my soul,   200

---

[2] *askant* with mistrust

With the lustrous and drooping star with the countenance full of
    woe,
With the holders holding my hand nearing the call of the bird,
Comrades mine and I in the midst, and their memory ever to
    keep, for the dead I loved so well,
For the sweetest, wisest soul of all my days and lands—and this
    for his dear sake,
Lilac and star and bird twined with the chant of my soul,   205
There in the fragrant pines and the cedars dusk and dim.

SPARKLES FROM THE WHEEL

Where the city's ceaseless crowd moves on the livelong day,
Withdrawn I join a group of children watching, I pause aside
    with them.

By the curb toward the edge of the flagging,
A knife-grinder works at his wheel sharpening a great knife,
Bending over he carefully holds it to the stone, by foot and
    knee,   5
With measur'd tread he turns rapidly, as he presses with light but
    firm hand,
Forth issue then in copious golden jets,
Sparkles from the wheel.

The scene and all its belongings, how they seize and affect me,
The sad sharp-chinn'd old man with worn clothes and broad
    shoulder-band of leather,   10
Myself effusing [1] and fluid, a phantom curiously floating, now
    here absorb'd and arrested,
The group, (an unminded point set in a vast surrounding,)
The attentive, quiet children, the loud, proud, restive base of the
    streets,
The low hoarse purr of the whirling stone, the light-press'd blade,
Diffusing, dropping, sideways-darting, in tiny showers of gold,   15
Sparkles from the wheel.

PASSAGE TO INDIA

1

Singing my days,
Singing the great achievements of the present,
Singing the strong light works of engineers,

[1] *effusing* pouring out

Our modern wonders,[1] (the antique ponderous Seven outvied,)
In the Old World the east the Suez canal,   5
The New by its mighty railroad spann'd,
The seas inlaid with eloquent gentle wires;
Yet first to sound, and ever sound, the cry with thee O soul,
The Past! the Past! the Past!

The Past—the dark unfathom'd retrospect!   10
The teeming gulf—the sleepers and the shadows!
The past—the infinite greatness of the past!
For what is the present after all but a growth out of the past?
(As a projectile form'd, impell'd, passing a certain line, still
     keeps on,
So the present, utterly form'd, impell'd by the past.)   15

2

Passage O soul to India!
Eclaircise [2] the myths Asiatic, the primitive fables.

Not you alone proud truths of the world,
Nor you alone ye facts of modern science,
But myths and fables of eld, Asia's, Africa's fables,   20
The far-darting beams of the spirit, the unloos'd dreams,
The deep diving bibles and legends,
The daring plots of the poets, the elder religions;
O you temples fairer than lilies pour'd over by the rising sun!
O you fables spurning the known, eluding the hold of the known,
     mounting to heaven!   25
You lofty and dazzling towers, pinnacled, red as roses, burnish'd
     with gold!
Towers of fables immortal fashion'd from mortal dreams!
You too I welcome and fully the same as the rest!
You to with joy I sing.

Passage to India!   30
Lo, soul, seest thou not God's purpose from the first?
The earth to be spann'd, connected by network,
The races, neighbors, to marry and be given in marriage,
The oceans to be cross'd, the distant brought near,
The lands to be welded together.   35
A worship new I sing,

[1] *Our modern wonders* Specific reference is to three engineering feats finished
shortly after the middle of the nineteenth century: the Suez canal, the trans-
continental railroad, and the transatlantic cable.
[2] *Eclaircise* clear up, explain

You captains, voyagers, explorers, yours,
You engineers, you architects, machinists, yours,
You, not for trade or transportation only,
But in God's name, and for thy sake O soul. 40

3

Passage to India!
Lo soul for thee of tableaus twain,
I see in one the Suez canal initiated, open'd,
I see the procession of steamships, the Empress Eugenie's leading the van,
I mark from on deck the strange landscape, the pure sky, the level sand in the distance, 45
I pass swiftly the picturesque groups, the workmen gather'd,
The gigantic dredging machines.

In one again, different, (yet thine, all thine, O soul, the same,)
I see over my own continent the Pacific railroad surmounting every barrier,
I see continual trains of cars winding along the Platte carrying freight and passengers, 50
I hear the locomotives rushing and roaring, and the shrill steam-whistle,
I hear the echoes reverberate through the grandest scenery in the world,
I cross the Laramie plains, I note the rocks in grotesque shapes, the buttes,
I see the plentiful larkspur and wild onions, the barren, colorless, sage-deserts,
I see in glimpses afar or towering immediately above me the great mountains, I see the Wind river and the Wahsatch mountains, 55
I see the Monument mountain and the Eagle's Nest, I pass the Promontory, I ascend the Nevadas,
I scan the noble Elk mountain and wind around its base,
I see the Humboldt range, I thread the valley and cross the river,
I see the clear waters of lake Tahoe, I see forests of majestic pines,
Or crossing the great desert, the alkaline plains, I behold enchanting mirages of waters and meadows, 60
Marking through these and after all, in duplicate slender lines,
Bridging the three or four thousand miles of land travel,
Tying the Eastern to the Western sea,
The road between Europe and Asia.

(Ah Genoese thy dream! thy dream!   65
Centuries after thou art laid in thy grave,
The shore thou foundest verifies thy dream.)

4

Passage to India!
Struggles of many a captain, tales of many a sailor dead,
Over my mood stealing and spreading they come,   70
Like clouds and cloudlets in the unreach'd sky.

Along all history, down the slopes,
As a rivulet running, sinking now, and now again to the surface
    rising,
A ceaseless thought, a varied train—lo, soul, to thee, thy sight,
    they rise,
The plans, the voyages again, the expeditions,   75
Again Vasco de Gama [3] sails forth,
Again the knowledge gain'd, the mariner's compass,
Lands found and nations born, thou born America,
For purpose vast, man's long probation fill'd,
Thou rondure of the world at last accomplish'd.   80

5

O vast Rondure, swimming in space,
Cover'd all over with visible power and beauty,
Alternate light and day and the teeming spiritual darkness,
Unspeakable high processions of sun and moon and countless
    stars above,
Below, the manifold grass and waters, animals, mountains,
    trees,   85
With inscrutable purpose, some hidden prophetic intention,
Now first it seems my thought begins to span thee.

Down from the gardens of Asia descending radiating,
Adam and Eve appear, then their myriad progeny after them,
Wandering, yearning, curious, with restless explorations,   90
With questionings, baffled, formless, feverish, with never-happy
    hearts,
With that sad incessant refrain, *Wherefore unsatisfied soul?* and
    Whither O mocking life?

Ah who shall soothe these feverish children?
Who justify these restless explorations?

[3] *Vasco de [da] Gama* Portuguese navigator who discovered a sea route to
India

Who speak the secret of impassive earth?   95
Who bind it to us? what is this separate Nature so unnatural?
What is this earth to our affections? (unloving earth, without a
    throb to answer ours,
Cold earth, the place of graves.)

Yet soul be sure the first intent remains, and shall be carried out,
Perhaps even now the time has arrived.   100

After the seas are all cross'd, (as they seem already cross'd,)
After the great captains and engineers have accomplish'd their
    work,
After the noble inventors, after the scientists, the chemist, the
    geologist, ethnologist,
Finally shall come the poet worthy that name,
The true son of God shall come singing his songs.   105

Then not your deeds only O voyagers, O scientists and inventors,
    shall be justified,
All these hearts as of fretted children shall be sooth'd,
All affection shall be fully responded to, the secret shall be told,
All these separations and gaps shall be taken up and hook'd and
    link'd together,
The whole earth, this cold, impassive, voiceless earth, shall be
    completely justified,   110
Trinitas divine shall be gloriously accomplish'd and compacted
    by the true son of God, the poet,
(He shall indeed pass the straits and conquer the mountains,
He shall double the cape of Good Hope to some purpose,)
Nature and Man shall be disjoin'd and diffused no more,
The true son of God shall absolutely fuse them.   115

6

Year at whose wide-flung door I sing!
Year of the purpose accomplish'd!
Year of the marriage of continents, climates and oceans!
(No mere doge of Venice now wedding the Adriatic,)
I see O year in you the vast terraqueous globe given and giving
    all,   120
Europe to Asia, Africa join'd, and they to the New World,
The lands, geographies, dancing before you, holding a festival
    garland,
As brides and bridegrooms hand in hand.

Passage to India!
Cooling airs from Caucasus far, soothing cradle of man,   125
The river Euphrates flowing, the past lit up again.

Lo soul, the retrospect brought forward,
The old, most populous, wealthiest of earth's lands,
The streams of the Indus and the Ganges and their many afflu-
    ents,
(I my shores of America walking to-day behold, resuming all,) 130
The tale of Alexander on his warlike marches suddenly dying,
On one side China and on the other side Persia and Arabia,
To the south the great seas and the bay of Bengal,
The flowing literatures, tremendous epics, religions, castes,
Old occult Brahma interminably far back, the tender and junior
    Buddha,   135
Central and southern empires and all their belongings, possessors,
The wars of Tamerlane, the reign of Aurungzebe,
The traders, rulers, explorers, Moslems, Venetians, Byzantium,
    the Arabs, Portuguese,
The first travelers famous yet, Marco Polo, Batouta the Moor,
Doubts to be solv'd, the map incognita, blanks to be fill'd, 140
The foot of man unstay'd, the hands never at rest,
Thyself O soul that will not brook a challenge.
The mediæval navigators rise before me,
The world of 1492, with its awaken'd enterprise,
Something swelling in humanity now like the sap of the earth in
    spring,   145
The sunset splendor of chivalry declining.

And who art thou sad shade?
Gigantic, visionary, thyself a visionary,
With majestic limbs and pious beaming eyes,
Spreading around with every look of thine a golden world, 150
Enhuing it with gorgeous hues.

As the chief histrion,[4]
Down to the footlights walks in some great scena,
Dominating the rest I see the Admiral himself,
(History's type of courage, action, faith,)   155
Behold him sail from Palos leading his little fleet,
His voyage behold, his return, his great fame,
His misfortunes, calumniators, behold him a prisoner, chain'd,
Behold his dejection, poverty, death.

(Curious in time I stand, noting the efforts of heroes,   160
Is the deferment long? bitter the slander, poverty, death?
Lies the seed unreck'd for centuries in the ground? lo, to God's
    due occasion,
Uprising in the night, it sprouts, blooms,
And fills the earth with use and beauty.)

[4] *histrion* actor

7

Passage indeed O soul to primal thought,   165
Not lands and seas alone, thy own clear freshness,
The young maturity of brood and bloom,
To realms of budding bibles.

O soul, repressless, I with thee and thou with me,
Thy circumnavigation of the world begin,   170
Of man, the voyage of his mind's return,
To reason's early paradise,
Back, back to wisdom's birth, to innocent intuitions,
Again with fair creation.

8

O we can wait no longer,   175
We too take ship O soul,
Joyous we too launch out on trackless seas,
Fearless for unknown shores on waves of ecstasy to sail,
Amid the wafting winds, (thou pressing me to thee, I thee to me,
    O soul,)
Caroling free, singing our song of God,   180
Chanting our chant of pleasant exploration.
With laugh and many a kiss,
(Let others deprecate, let others weep for sin, remorse, humilia-
    tion,)
O soul, thou pleasest me, I thee.

Ah more than any priest O soul we too believe in God,   185
But with the mystery of God we dare not dally.

O soul thou pleasest me, I thee,
Sailing these seas or on the hills, or waking in the night,
Thoughts, silent thoughts, of Time and Space and Death, like
    waters flowing,
Bear me indeed as through the regions infinite,   190
Whose air I breathe, whose ripples hear, lave me all over,
Bathe me O God in thee, mounting to thee,
I and my soul to range in range of thee.

O Thou transcendent,
Nameless, the fibre and the breath,   195
Light of the light, shedding forth universes, thou centre of them,
Thou mightier centre of the true, the good, the loving,
Thou moral, spiritual fountain—affection's source—thou reser-
    voir,

(O pensive soul of me—O thirst unsatisfied—waitest not there?
Waitest not haply for us somewhere there the Comrade per-
fect?)   200
Thou pulse—thou motive of the stars, suns, systems,
That, circling, move in order, safe, harmonious,
Athwart the shapeless vastnesses of space,
How should I think, how breathe a single breath, how speak, if
out of myself,
I could not launch, to those, superior universes?   205

Swiftly I shrivel at the thought of God,
At Nature and its wonders, Time and Space and Death,
But that I, turning, call to thee O soul, thou actual Me,
And lo, thou gently masterest the orbs,
Thou matest Time, smilest content at Death,   210
And fillest, swellest full the vastnesses of Space.

Greater than stars or suns,
Bounding O soul thou journeyest forth;
What love than thine and ours could wider amplify?
What aspirations, wishes, outvie thine and ours O soul?   215
What dreams of the ideal? what plans of purity, perfection,
strength,
What cheerful willingness for others' sake to give up all?
For others' sake to suffer all?

Reckoning ahead O soul, when thou, the time achiev'd,
The seas all cross'd, weather'd the capes, the voyage done, 220
Surrounded, copest, frontest God, yieldest, the aim attain'd,
As fill'd with friendship, love complete, the Elder Brother found,
The Younger melts in fondness in his arms.

9

Passage to more than India!
Are thy wings plumed indeed for such far flights?   225
O soul, voyagest thou indeed on voyages like those?
Disportest thou on waters such as those?
Soundest below the Sanscrit and the Vedas?
Then have thy bent [5] unleash'd.

Passage to you, your shores, ye aged fierce enigmas!   230
Passage to you, to mastership of you, ye strangling problems!
You, strew'd with the wrecks of skeletons, that, living, never
reach'd you.

[5] *bent* concentrated energy

Passage to more than India!
O secret of the earth and sky!
Of you O waters of the sea! O winding creeks and rivers!   235
Of you O woods and fields! of you strong mountains of my land!
Of you O prairies! of you gray rocks!
O morning red! O clouds! O rain and snows!
O day and night, passage to you!

O sun and moon and all you stars! Sirius and Jupiter!   240
Passage to you!

Passage, immediate passage! the blood burns in my veins!
Away O soul! hoist instantly the anchor!
Cut the hawsers—haul out—shake out every sail!
Have we not stood here like trees in the ground long enough?   245
Have we not grovel'd here long enough, eating and drinking like
    mere brutes?
Have we not darken'd and dazed ourselves with books long
    enough?

Sail forth—steer for the deep waters only,
Reckless O soul, exploring, I with thee, and thou with me,
For we are bound where mariner has not yet dared to go,   250
And we will risk the ship, ourselves and all.

O my brave soul!
O farther farther sail!
O daring joy, but safe! are they not all the seas of God?
O farther, farther, farther sail!   255

TO A LOCOMOTIVE IN WINTER

Thee for my recitative,
Thee in the driving storm even as now, the snow, the winter-day
    declining,
Thee in thy panoply, thy measur'd dual throbbing and thy beat
    convulsive,
Thy black cylindric body, golden brass and silvery steel,
Thy ponderous side-bars, parallel and connecting rods, gyrating,
    shuttling at thy sides,   5
Thy metrical, now swelling pant and roar, now tapering in the
    distance,
Thy great protruding head-light fix'd in front,
Thy long, pale, floating vapor-pennants, tinged with delicate pur-
    ple,

The dense and murky clouds out-belching from thy smoke-stack,
Thy knitted frame, thy springs and valves, the tremulous twinkle
  of thy wheels,   10
Thy train of cars behind, obedient, merrily following,
Through gale or calm, now swift, now slack, yet steadily career-
  ing;
Type of the modern—emblem of motion and power—pulse of
  the continent,
For once come serve the Muse and merge in verse, even as here I
  see thee,
With storm and buffeting gusts of wind and falling snow,   15
By day thy warning ringing bell to sound its notes,
By night thy silent signal lamps to swing.

Fierce-throated beauty!
Roll through my chant with all thy lawless music, thy swinging
  lamps at night,
Thy madly-whistled laughter, echoing, rumbling like an earth-
  quake, rousing all,   20
Law of thyself complete, thine own track firmly holding,
(No sweetness debonair of tearful harp or glib piano thine,)
Thy trills of shrieks by rocks and hills return'd,
Launch'd o'er the prairies wide, across the lakes,
To the free skies unpent and glad and strong.   25

CRITICISM

   Criticism frequently goes beyond the single poem, yet stays
within a single author, tracing out some stylistic or thematic
pattern in a series of poems. The following essay concentrates
on one single element—mysticism—that connects four of Whitman's major poems written over a period of several years. By
focusing on a single recurring theme, the essay remains largely
silent on the significant elements that distinguish these four
poems. The reader will find other essays, or he may write one
himself, demonstrating the individuality of these poems by
analysis of structure, imagery, or meaning.

The Mysticism of Whitman [1]

JAMES E. MILLER, JR.

Many discussions of mysticism have been stopped before they begin, simply because no agreement could be reached on a definition of such a vague and disputable term. Without becoming tied up in semantic knots distinguishing among religious, psychological, or philosophical concepts, I propose that we define mysticism, along with William James in *The Varieties of Religious Experience*, as a state of consciousness characterized by the *noetic* (states of transcendent, non-intellectual insight, revelation) and the *ineffable* (the "knowledge" cannot be imparted; to be known it must be experienced). This minimum definition should be an acceptable area of truce for the skeptical, who view the mystical experience as a purely psychological phenomenon, and the orthodox, who are committed to an official definition.

With this definition we should be able to make a brief exploration of Whitman's poetry, discovering where signs of mysticism appear. For the sake of clarity and emphasis, we shall pass over many minor instances of mystical moments (such as those in "Prayer of Columbus"), and even the major example of "Song of Myself" (which has been repeatedly analyzed for its mysticism), and concentrate on four key poems, each a masterpiece of its kind, which in their chronological arrangement admirably demonstrate Whitman's development over his most productive and creative period of fifteen years, from about 1855 to 1870.

"Crossing Brooklyn Ferry" (1856) is a "public" philosophical poem dramatizing and celebrating the part played by the "dumb, beautiful ministers" (all the diverse inventory of the universe) in bestowing spiritual insight into the unity of all mankind. "Out of the Cradle Endlessly Rocking" (1860) is a "private" love poem which describes the symbolic love experience that granted spiritual insight into the meaning of death—and the origin of the poetic impulse. "When Lilacs Last in the Dooryard Bloom'd" (1865) is an elegy which dramatizes the grief at a national loss

[1] Reprinted (revised) from *The Emerson Society Quarterly* (First Quarter, 1961).

that, through its profundity, results in "knowledge of death" and spiritual insight into eternity. "Passage to India" (1871) is a religious chant on the achievement of man in circling the globe, and concludes in an ecstatic apprehension of divine presence that culminates in spiritual insight into the nature of man's fate. All these poems turn in their crucial passages on some kind of intuitive insight that is both profoundly revealing and ultimately ineffable. All of them are, by whatever definition, deeply mystical in nature.

Of all four poems, "Crossing Brooklyn Ferry" seems the most deeply involved in the materials and content of the world. Indeed, it is the physical body of the world, the world as perceived through all the senses, that leads to the poem's spiritual assertion. The dramatic structure of the poem is essentially mystical—the successive stages constitute a progression toward ultimate mystical penetration of the barriers to union, as indicated by the carefully spaced and timed outcries—"It avails not, time nor place —distance avails not" (Sec. 3), "Whatever it is, it avails not— distance avails not and place avails not" (Sec. 5), "Closer yet I approach you" (Sec. 7), and finally: "We understand then do we not? / What I promis'd without mentioning it, have you not accepted?" (Sec. 8). All these assertions confirm two movements in the poem, one on the surface, the other subterranean, the latter more vital than but only hinted at by, the former. Just what is understood or accepted is what the "study could not teach—what the preaching could not accomplish"—it is intuitive awareness of unity that fuses Whitman into the reader, that resolves all things into one. It is a *mystical* knowledge, not intellectual but spiritual in origin.

In "Crossing Brooklyn Ferry" Whitman focused on an unexceptional event, the common experience of multitudes in making their daily rounds, to dramatize a kind of mysticism of the masses; in "Out of the Cradle Endlessly Rocking," the central event is secluded and private, a part of the poet's distant past. We might speculate that Whitman (following the process of what T. S. Eliot called the objective correlative) transfigured his personal emotions (a disappointed love affair?) into art by inventing (or fusing out of many events) a set of symbols that correlate with (but do not necessarily—even symbolically—re-create) original experience. The poet's emotional distance is achieved not only by placing the event in his boyhood (he is singing a reminiscence), but also by becoming an observer of the tragic love of the mockingbirds. But the narrative of the poem is not related for its own sake: the meaning of the poem lies in the mystical knowledge bestowed by the experience enabling (or compelling) the boy to become a poet. As elsewhere in Whitman, this knowledge is never fully revealed, only hinted at. In the latter part of the poem, after "tallying" the he-bird's carol of unsatisfied love, the boy passionately invokes the night for a "clew"; and in answer to his spirit's anguished cry, the sea sounds repeatedly the single word "death," pouring its mystic meaning into the boy's ecstatic soul ("Creeping thence steadily up to my ears and laving me softly all over / Death, death, death, death, death"). Out of this mystical experience, out of insight into the mystic link of love and death, comes the boy's assurance of his role and theme as a poet.

Of Whitman's four major poems, "When Lilacs Last in the Dooryard Bloom'd," and "Out of the Cradle" seem more closely related than the others. Both involve the nature of love and the grief of death, and both conclude with mystic affirmation. But in the elegy the love is less personal, more exalted, as symbolized by the dooryard lilacs of the title. The western star suggests Lincoln, and the black cloud obscuring it represents his assassination. And it is the bird, the hermit-thrush, with its secluded and ecstatic eulogy of death as the "dark mother" and "deliveress," that finally brings about a reconciliation of the grief. The poet's visit with the hermit-thrush in the swamp cedars (and his soul's "tally" of the bird's song) is a symbolic dramatization of the mystical experience. While he listens, the "pure deliberate notes" of the bird pour into him (much as did the sea's voice in "Out of the Cradle"), and in his ecstatic, trance-like state, he sees beyond human ken: "While my sight that was bound in my eyes unclosed, / As to long panoramas of visions." The "visions" begin with the grim confusion and chaos of the battle-field, with its "debris of all the slain soldiers," but end with intuitive realization that it is the dead who are at rest, the living who suffer. The bird's spiritually "tallied" song together with the poet's vision represent an ultimate mystical affirmation much like that inspired by the bird's song and the sea's voice in "Out of the Cradle": in both poems, the dramatic speaker (or the poet) un-

dergoes an experience that appears the very essence of the mystical.

Of all Whitman's poems, "Passage to India" seems the most
ecstatic, perhaps in part because of the recurring fervent and
intimate address to the soul ("Passage O soul to India!"). Although it seems closer in structure to "Crossing Brooklyn Ferry,"
it differs markedly in its attitude toward the material world.
Whereas "Crossing Brooklyn Ferry" celebrated the physical contents of the world as the "ministers" that furnished their part
to the soul, "Passage to India" calls for a spiritual achievement
to match the engineering feats of the Suez Canal, the trans-
Atlantic cable, and the trans-continental railroad in rounding
the globe. In the first poem Whitman's love affair is with the
world's body, in the second with the world's soul. But both
affairs are Platonic—or mystical. In "Crossing Brooklyn Ferry,"
the poet achieves a spiritual fusion with the reader and all mankind; in "Passage to India" he merges with his own soul—and
with God. The spiritual India for which the poet seeks passage
is remote in both space and time; only by transcending both, as
he does metaphorically in the early sections of the poem with
their eager encompassment of the "vast Rondure, swimming in
space" and "all history," running its course "down the slopes" of
time—only by embracing them as One in his expanding vision is
he granted (in the latter part of the poem) his mystic merge beyond their barriers. As he soars in his mystic vision into the
"regions infinite," where he hears the "ripples" and is "laved
. . . all over" (much as the boy-poet by the seaside in "Out of
the Cradle"), he cries out in spiritual ecstasy: "Bathe me O God
in thee, mounting to thee,/ I and my soul to range in range of
thee." This seems to be the moment of mystic Union, for there
follows the frantic search for language to express the ineffable—
"Thou transcendent,/ Nameless, the fibre and the breath," "Light
of the light, shedding forth universes," "Thou moral, spiritual
fountain," "thou reservoir." More than Whitman's other poems,
"Passage to India" represents imaginative achievement of the
mystic goal, Union with the One—or, as Whitman puts it in
one striking metaphor—"the Elder Brother found,/ The Younger
melts in fondness in his arms."

Whatever the origin of the mysticism in Whitman, whether in
some specific experience or in his imagination, it seems clear that

his most dynamic literary connections run more deeply than merely to Emersonian Transcendentalism or even to Wordsworthian romanticism. He goes back in a vital way to a prophetic poet like Blake, whom he did not know, or looks forward to a prophetic philosopher like Nietzsche, whom he could not have read. And although Whitman has been called many poets—poet of democracy, poet of sex, poet of science—it might be that he will have had the last word in his frequent assertion that his "religious" themes dominated *Leaves of Grass*. Certainly in his great and memorable poems, the mystical current is strong, and other themes seem to be carried along by its sheer power and vitality.

Whitman's mysticism bears strong resemblances to both Christian and Oriental mysticism; but as his other themes mingle and intermix with his mysticism—his strong materialism, his assertion of self, his restless vagabondage, his celebrated sexuality—he seems to defy any kind of traditional classification. In the last analysis, Whitman's temperament seems eminently unsuited to the selflessness of the Christian mystic and to the passivity of the Oriental. He is far too much bound up in his own consciousness and self-hood and far too fully committed to wandering the open road. It is possible that Whitman, out of multiple obscure sources and out of his own soul, created a unique mysticism designed for America, a "democratic" mysticism available to every man on equal terms, embracing both the body and the soul, science and myth, life and death, the active and passive, material and spiritual. But whatever the ultimate nature of his mysticism, it must be granted a central role in the meaning of his greatest poetry in *Leaves of Grass*.

EMILY DICKINSON

[1830-1886]

EMILY DICKINSON lived all her life in Amherst, Massachusetts. Her father was a lawyer, a Congressman, and the treasurer of Amherst College (where Emily attended the Academy). Her additional schooling at Mount Holyoke Female Seminary, and brief trips to Washington, Cambridge, and Boston, were her only physical views outside; but in her life inside she was in touch with both the center of things and even farther worlds. She wrote more than 1700 poems for herself and her friends; only seven were published (anonymously) in her lifetime. Their significance and Emily's position as a major American poet are only now being defined, for the poems that were found after her death had a strange history of piecemeal publication from 1890 to the definitive edition of 1955. In them little is revealed directly about her personal life, though many persons have conjectured much. Friends with literary interests were Helen Hunt Jackson and Thomas Wentworth Higginson. She is thought to have had a deep but private attachment for the Reverend Charles Wadsworth of Philadelphia, and in later years for Otis P. Lord, associate justice of the Supreme Court of Massachusetts and her father's friend. The poems are best read for themselves—sharp, witty, compact lines that contain some absolutes of experience. In her poems, Emily Dickinson tells "all the truth" but tells it "slant."

Introductory Readings

EDITION: *The Complete Poems of Emily Dickinson,* ed. Thomas H. Johnson (1960). LETTERS: *The Letters of Emily Dickinson,* ed. Thomas H. Johnson, 3 vols. (1958). BIOGRAPHY AND CRITICISM: George F. Whicher, *This Was a Poet: A Critical Biography of Emily Dickinson* (1938, 1952); Henry W. Wells, *Introduction to Emily Dickinson* (1947); Richard

Chase, *Emily Dickinson* (1951); Thomas H. Johnson, *Emily Dickinson: An Interpretive Biography* (1955); Charles R. Anderson, *Emily Dickinson's Poetry: Stairway of Surprise* (1960).

67

Success is counted sweetest
By those who ne'er succeed.
To comprehend [1] a nectar
Requires sorest need.

Not one of all the purple Host   5
Who took the Flag today
Can tell the definition
So clear of Victory

As he defeated—dying—
On whose forbidden ear   10
The distant strains of triumph
Burst agonized and clear!

99

New feet within my garden go—
New fingers stir the sod—
A Troubadour upon the Elm
Betrays the solitude.

New children play upon the green—   5
New Weary sleep below—
And still the pensive Spring returns—
And still the punctual snow!

108

Surgeons must be very careful
When they take the knife!
Underneath their fine incisions
Stirs the Culprit—*Life!*

126

To fight aloud, is very brave—
But *gallanter,* I know

[1] *comprehend* really understand (not just taste)

Who charge within the bosom
The Cavalry of Wo—

Who win, and nations do not see—   5
Who fall—and none observe—
Whose dying eyes, no Country
Regards with patriot love—

We trust, in plumed procession
For such, the Angels go—   10
Rank after Rank, with even feet—
And Uniforms of Snow.

181

I lost a World—the other day!
Has Anybody found?
You'll know it by the Row of Stars
Around it's forehead bound.

A Rich man—might not notice it—   5
Yet—to my frugal Eye,
Of more Esteem than Ducats—[1]
Oh find it—Sir—for me!

182

If I should'nt be alive
When the Robins come,
Give the one in Red Cravat,
A Memorial crumb.

If I could'nt thank you,   5
Being fast asleep,
You will know I'm trying
With my Granite lip!

185

"Faith" is a fine invention
When Gentlemen can *see*—
But *Microscopes* are prudent
In an Emergency.

[1] *Ducats* gold coins

191

The Skies cant keep their secret!
They tell it to the Hills—
The Hills just tell the Orchards—
And they—the Daffodils!

A Bird—by chance—that goes that way—   5
Soft overhears the whole—
If I should bribe the little Bird—
Who knows but *she* would tell?

I think I wont—however—
It's finer—not to know—   10
If Summer were *an Axiom*—
What sorcery had *Snow?*

So keep your secret—Father!
I would not—if I could,
Know what the Sapphire Fellows, do,   15
In your new-fashioned world!

214

I taste a liquor never brewed—
From Tankards scooped in Pearl—
Not all the Frankfort Berries [1]
Yield such an Alcohol!

Inebriate of Air—am I—   5
And Debauchee of Dew—
Reeling—thro endless summer days—
From inns of Molten Blue—

When "Landlords" turn the drunken Bee
Out of the Foxglove's door—   10
When Butterflies—renounce their "drams"—
I shall but drink the more!

Till Seraphs swing their snowy Hats—
And Saints—to windows run—
To see the little Tippler   15
From Manzanilla come! [2]

[1] *Frankfort Berries* another version: *Vats upon the Rhine*
[2] *From Manzanilla come!* Manzanilla, Cuba, exporter of rum. Another version: *Leaning against the—Sun—*

215

What is—"Paradise"—
Who live there—
Are they "Farmers"—
Do they "hoe"—
Do they know that this is "Amherst"—   5
And that I—am coming—too—

Do they wear "new shoes"—in "Eden"—
Is it always pleasant—there—
Wont they scold us—when we're hungry—
Or tell God—how cross we are—   10

You are sure there's such a person
As "a Father"—in the sky—
So if I get lost—there—ever—
Or do what the Nurse calls "die"—
I shant walk the "Jasper" [1]—barefoot—   15
Ransomed folks—wont laugh at me—
Maybe—"Eden" a'nt so lonesome
As New England used to be!

254

"Hope" is the thing with feathers—
That perches in the soul—
And sings the tune without the words—
And never stops—at all—

And sweetest—in the Gale—is heard—   5
And sore must be the storm—
That could abash the little Bird
That kept so many warm—

I've heard it in the chillest land—
And on the strangest Sea—   10
Yet, never, in Extremity,
It asked a crumb—of Me.

258

There's a certain Slant of light,
Winter Afternoons—

---

[1] *"Jasper"* variety of quartz; in the Bible probably a dark **green or** opalescent stone adorning Paradise

That oppresses, like the Heft
Of Cathedral Tunes—

Heavenly Hurt, it gives us— 5
We can find no scar,
But internal difference,
Where the Meanings, are—

None may teach it—Any—
'Tis the Seal Despair— 10
An imperial affliction
Sent us of the Air—

When it comes, the Landscape listens—
Shadows—hold their breath—
When it goes, 'tis like the Distance 15
On the look of Death—

276

Many a phrase has the English language—
I have heard but one—
Low as the laughter of the Cricket,
Loud, as the Thunder's Tongue—

Murmuring, like old Caspian Choirs,[1] 5
When the Tide's a' lull—
Saying itself in new inflection—
Like a Whippowil—

Breaking in bright Orthography
On my simple sleep— 10
Thundering it's Prospective—
Till I stir, and weep—

Not for the Sorrow, done me—
But the push of Joy—
Say it again, Saxon! 15
Hush—Only to me!

280

I felt a Funeral, in my Brain,
And Mourners to and fro

[1] *Caspian Choirs* choirs of Greek orthodox churches

Kept treading—treading—till it seemed
That Sense was breaking through—

And when they all were seated,   5
A Service, like a Drum—
Kept beating—beating—till I thought
My Mind was going numb—

And then I heard them lift a Box
And creak across my Soul   10
With those same Boots of Lead, again,
Then Space—began to toll,

As all the Heavens were a Bell,
And Being, but an Ear,
And I, and Silence, some strange Race   15
Wrecked, solitary, here—

And then a Plank in Reason, broke,
And I dropped down, and down—
And hit a World, at every plunge,
And Finished knowing—then—   20

288

I'm Nobody! Who are you?
Are you—Nobody—too?
Then there's a pair of us!
Dont tell! they'd banish us—you know!

How dreary—to be—Somebody!   5
How public—like a Frog—
To tell your name—the livelong June—
To an admiring Bog!

303

The Soul selects her own Society—
Then—shuts the Door—
To her divine Majority—
Present no more—

Unmoved—she notes the Chariots—pausing—   5
At her low Gate—
Unmoved—an Emperor be kneeling
Upon her Mat—

I've known her—from an ample nation—
Choose One—   10
Then—close the Valves of her attention—
Like Stone—

311

It sifts from Leaden Sieves—
It powders all the Wood.
It fills with Alabaster Wool
The Wrinkles of the Road—

It makes an Even Face   5
Of Mountain, and of Plain—
Unbroken Forehead from the East
Unto the East again—

It reaches to the Fence—
It wraps it Rail by Rail   10
Till it is lost in Fleeces—
It deals Celestial Vail

To Stump, and Stack—and Stem—
A Summer's empty Room—
Acres of Joints, where Harvests were,   15
Recordless, but for them—

It Ruffles Wrists of Posts
As Ankles of a Queen—
Then stills it's Artisans—like Ghosts—
Denying they have been—   20

324

Some keep the Sabbath going to Church—
I keep it, staying at Home—
With a Bobolink for a Chorister—
And an Orchard, for a Dome—

Some keep the Sabbath in Surplice—   5
I just wear my Wings—
And instead of tolling the Bell, for Church,
Our little Sexton—sings.

God preaches, a noted Clergyman—
And the sermon is never long,   10

So instead of getting to Heaven, at last—
I'm going, all along.

328

A Bird came down the Walk—
He did not know I saw—
He bit an Angleworm in halves
And ate the fellow, raw,

And then he drank a Dew   5
From a convenient Grass—
And then hopped sidewise to the Wall
To let a Beetle pass—

He glanced with rapid eyes
That hurried all around—   10
They looked like frightened Beads, I thought—
He stirred his Velvet Head

Like one in danger, Cautious,
I offered him a Crumb
And he unrolled his feathers   15
And rowed him softer home—

Than Oars divide the Ocean,
Too silver for a seam—
Or Butterflies, off Banks of Noon
Leap, plashless as they swim.   20

335

'Tis not that Dying hurts us so—
'Tis Living—hurts us more—
But Dying—is a different way—
A Kind behind the Door—

The Southern Custom—of the Bird—   5
That ere the Frosts are due—
Accepts a better Latitude—
We—are the Birds—that stay.

The Shiverers round Farmer's doors—
For whose reluctant Crumb—   10
We stipulate—till pitying Snows
Persuade our Feathers Home

371

A precious—mouldering pleasure—'tis—
To meet an Antique Book—
In just the Dress his Century wore—
A privilege—I think—

His venerable Hand to take—   5
And warming in our own—
A passage back—or two—to make—
To Times when he—was young—

His quaint opinions—to inspect—
His thought to ascertain   10
On Them[e]s concern our mutual mind—
The Literature of Man—

What interested Scholars—most—
What Competitions ran—
When Plato—was a Certainty—   15
And Sophocles—a Man—

When Sappho—was a living Girl—
And Beatrice wore
The Gown that Dante—deified—
Facts Centuries before   20

He traverses—familiar—
As One should come to Town—
And tell you all your Dreams—were true—
He lived—where Dreams were born—

His presence is Enchantment—   25
You beg him not to go—
Old Volumes shake their Vellum Heads
And tantalize—just so—

429

The Moon is distant from the Sea—
And yet, with Amber Hands—
She leads Him—docile as a Boy—
Along appointed Sands—

He never misses a Degree—   5
Obedient to Her Eye

He comes just so far—toward the Town—
Just so far—goes away—

Oh, Signor, Thine, the Amber Hand—
And mine—the distant Sea—   10
Obedient to the least command
Thine eye impose on me—

435

Much Madness is divinest Sense—
To a discerning Eye—
Much Sense—the starkest Madness—
'Tis the Majority
In this, as All, prevail—   5
Assent—and you are sane—
Demur—you're straightway dangerous—
And handled with a Chain—

441

This is my letter to the World
That never wrote to Me—
The simple News that Nature told—
With tender Majesty

Her Message is committed   5
To Hands I cannot see—
For love of Her—Sweet—countrymen—
Judge tenderly—of Me

445

'Twas just this time, last year, I died.
I know I heard the Corn,
When I was carried by the Farms—
It had the Tassels on—

I thought how yellow it would look—   5
When Richard went to mill—
And then, I wanted to get out,
But something held my will.

I thought just how Red—Apples wedged
The Stubble's joints between—   10

And Carts went stooping round the fields
To take the Pumpkins in—

I wondered which would miss me, least,
And when Thanksgiving, came,
If Father'd multiply the plates—   15
To make an even Sum—

And would it blur the Christmas glee
My Stocking hang too high
For any Santa Claus to reach
The Altitude of me—   20

But this sort, grieved myself,
And so, I thought the other way,
How just this time, some perfect year—
Themself, should come to me—

449

I died for Beauty—but was scarce
Adjusted in the Tomb
When One who died for Truth, was lain
In an adjoining Room—

He questioned softly "Why I failed"?   5
"For Beauty," I replied—
"And I—for Truth—Themself are One—
We Bretheren, are," He said—

And so, as Kinsmen, met a Night—
We talked between the Rooms—   10
Until the Moss had reached our lips—
And covered up—our names—

465

I heard a Fly buzz—when I died—
The Stillness in the Room
Was like the Stillness in the Air—
Between the Heaves of Storm—

The Eyes around—had wrung them dry—   5
And Breaths were gathering firm
For that last Onset—when the King
Be witnessed—in the Room—

I willed my Keepsakes—Signed away
What portion of me be   10
Assignable—and then it was
There interposed a Fly—

With Blue—uncertain stumbling Buzz—
Between the light—and me—
And then the Windows failed—and then   15
I could not see to see—

494

Going to Him! Happy letter!
Tell Him—
Tell Him the page I did'nt write—
Tell Him—I only said the Syntax—
And left the Verb and the pronoun out—   5
Tell Him just how the fingers hurried—
Then—how they waded—slow—slow—
And then you wished you had eyes in your pages—
So you could see what moved them so—

Tell Him—it was'nt a Practised Writer—   10
You guessed—from the way the sentence toiled—
You could hear the Boddice tug, behind you—
As if it held but the might of a child—
You almost pitied it—you—it worked so—
Tell Him—no—you may quibble there—   15
For it would split His Heart, to know it—
And then you and I, were silenter.

Tell Him—Night finished—before we finished—
And the Old Clock kept neighing "Day"!
And you—got sleepy—and begged to be ended—   20
What could it hinder so—to say?
Tell Him—just how she sealed you—Cautious!
But—if He ask where you are hid
Until tomorrow—Happy letter!
Gesture Coquette—and shake your Head!   25

511

If you were coming in the Fall,
I'd brush the Summer by

With half a smile, and half a spurn,
As Housewives do, a Fly.

If I could see you in a year,   5
I'd wind the months in balls—
And put them each in separate Drawers,
For fear the numbers fuse—

If only Centuries, delayed,
I'd count them on my Hand,   10
Subtracting, till my fingers dropped
Into Van Dieman's Land.[1]

If certain, when this life was out—
That your's and mine, should be—
I'd toss it yonder, like a Rind,   15
And take Eternity—

But, now, uncertain of the length
Of this, that is between,
It goads me, like the Goblin Bee—
That will not state—it's sting.   20

520

I started Early—Took my Dog—
And visited the Sea—
The Mermaids in the Basement
Came out to look at me—

And Frigates—in the Upper Floor   5
Extended Hempen Hands—
Presuming Me to be a Mouse—
Aground—upon the Sands—

But no Man moved Me—till the Tide
Went past my simple Shoe—   10
And past my Apron—and my Belt
And past my Boddice—too—

And made as He would eat me up—
As wholly as a Dew
Upon a Dandelion's Sleeve—   15
And then—I started—too—

---

[1] *Van Dieman's Land* Tasmania, island state of Australia

And He—He followed—close behind—
I felt His Silver Heel
Upon my Ancle—Then my Shoes
Would overflow with Pearl—   20

Until We met the Solid Town—
No One He seemed to know—
And bowing—with a Mighty look—
At me—The Sea withdrew—

556

The Brain, within it's Groove
Runs evenly—and true—
But let a Splinter swerve—
'Twere easier for You—

To put a Current back—   5
When Floods have slit the Hills—
And scooped a Turnpike for Themselves—
And trodden out the Mills—

585

I like to see it lap the Miles—
And lick the Valleys up—
And stop to feed itself at Tanks—
And then—prodigious step

Around a Pile of Mountains—   5
And supercilious peer
In Shanties—by the sides of Roads—
And then a Quarry pare

To fit it's sides
And crawl between   10
Complaining all the while
In horrid—hooting stanza—
Then chase itself down Hill—

And neigh like Boanerges— [1]
Then—prompter than a Star   15
Stop—docile and omnipotent
At it's own stable door—

---

[1] *Boanerges* "sons of thunder"; hence, any loud preacher or orator

620

It makes no difference abroad—
The Seasons—fit—the same—
The Mornings blossom into Noons—
And split their Pods of Flame—

Wild flowers—kindle in the Woods—   ·   5
The Brooks slam—all the Day—
No Black bird bates his Banjo —
For passing Calvary—

Auto da Fe [1]—and Judgment—
Are nothing to the Bee—   10
His separation from His Rose—
To Him—sums Misery—

622

To know just how He suffered—would be dear—
To know if any Human eyes were near
To whom He could entrust His wavering gaze—
Until it settled broad—on Paradise—

To know if He was patient—part content—   5
Was Dying as He thought—or different—
Was it a pleasant Day to die—
And did the Sunshine face His way—

What was His furthest mind—Of Home—or God—
Or what the Distant say—   10
At news that He ceased Human Nature
Such a Day—

And Wishes—Had He Any—
Just His Sigh—Accented—
Had been legible—to Me—   15
And was He Confident until
Ill fluttered out—in Everlasting Well—

And if He spoke What name was Best—
What last

[1] *Auto da Fe* publicly proclaimed judgment passed on victims of the Spanish Inquisition courts

What One broke off with   20
At the Drowsiest—

Was He afraid—or tranquil—
Might He know
How Conscious Consciousness—could grow—
Till Love that was—and Love too best to be—   25
Meet—and the Junction be Eternity

636

The Way I read a Letter's—this—
'Tis first—I lock the Door—
And push it with my fingers—next—
For transport it be sure—

And then I go the furthest off   5
To counteract a knock—
Then draw my little Letter forth
And slowly pick the lock—

Then—glancing narrow, at the Wall—
And narrow at the floor   10
For firm Conviction of a Mouse
Not exorcised before—

Peruse how infinite I am
To no one that You—know—
And sigh for lack of Heaven—but **not**   15
The Heaven God bestow—

640

I cannot live with You—
It would be Life—
And Life is over there—
Behind the Shelf

The Sexton keeps the Key to—   5
Putting up
Our Life—His Porcelain—
Like a Cup—

Discarded of the Housewife—
Quaint—or Broke—   10

A newer Sevres [1] pleases—
Old Ones crack—

I could not die—with You—
For One must wait
To shut the Other's Gaze down—   15
You—could not—

And I—Could I stand by
And see You—freeze—
Without my Right of Frost—
Death's privilege?   20

Nor could I rise—with You—
Because Your Face
Would put out Jesus'—
That New Grace

Glow plain—and foreign   25
On my homesick Eye—
Except that You than He
Shone closer by—

They'd judge Us—How—
For You—served Heaven—You know,   30
Or sought to—
I could not—

Because You saturated Sight—
And I had no more Eyes
For sordid excellence   35
As Paradise

And were You lost, I would be—
Though My Name
Rang loudest
On the Heavenly fame—   40

And were You—saved—
And I—condemned to be
Where You were not—
That self—were Hell to Me—

So We must meet apart—   45
You there—I—here—
With just the Door ajar

[1] *Sevres* French porcelain

That Oceans are—and Prayer—
And that White Sustenance—
Despair—   50

650

Pain—has an Element of Blank—
It cannot recollect
When it begun—or if there were
A time when it was not—

It has no Future—but itself—   5
It's Infinite contain
It's Past—enlightened to perceive
New Periods—of Pain

664

Of all the Souls that stand create—
I have elected—One—
When Sense from Spirit—files away—
And Subterfuge—is done—
When that which is—and that which was—   5
Apart—intrinsic—stand—
And this brief Tragedy of Flesh—
Is shifted—like a Sand—
When Figures show their royal Front—
And Mists—are carved away,   10
Behold the Atom—I preferred—
To all the lists of Clay!

670

One need not be a Chamber—to be Haunted—
One need not be a House—
The Brain has Corridors—surpassing
Material Place—

Far safer, of a Midnight Meeting   5
External Ghost
Than it's interior Confronting—
That Cooler Host.

Far safer, through an Abbey gallop,
The Stones a'chase—   10
Than Unarmed, one's a'self encounter—
In lonesome Place—

Ourself behind ourself, concealed—
Should startle most—
Assassin hid in our Apartment   15
Be Horror's least.

The Body—borrows a Revolver—
He bolts the Door—
O'erlooking a superior spectre—
Or More—   20

701

A Thought went up my mind today—
That I have had before—
But did not finish—some way back—
I could not fix the Year—

Nor where it went—nor why it came   5
The second time to me—
Nor definitely, what it was—
Have I the Art to say—

But somewhere—in my Soul—I know—
I've met the Thing before—   10
It just reminded me—'twas all—
And came my way no more—

712

Because I could not stop for Death—
He kindly stopped for me—
The Carriage held but just Ourselves—
And Immortality.

We slowly drove—He knew no haste   5
And I had put away
My labor and my leisure too,
For His Civility—

We passed the School, where Children strove
At Recess—in the Ring—   10

We passed the Fields of Gazing Grain—
We passed the Setting Sun—

Or rather—He passed Us—
The Dews drew quivering and chill—
For only Gossamer, my Gown—   15
My Tippet—only Tulle— [1]

We paused before a House that seemed
A Swelling of the Ground—
The Roof was scarcely visible—
The Cornice—in the Ground—   20

Since then—'tis Centuries—and yet
Feels shorter than the Day
I first surmised the Horses Heads
Were toward Eternity—

937

I felt a Cleaving in my Mind—
As if my Brain had split—
I tried to match it—Seam by Seam—
But could not make them fit.

The thought behind, I strove to join   5
Unto the thought before—
But Sequence ravelled out of Sound
Like Balls—upon a Floor.

986

A narrow Fellow in the Grass
Occasionally rides—
You may have met Him—did you not
His notice sudden is—
The Grass divides as with a Comb—   5
A spotted shaft is seen—
And then it closes at your feet
And opens further on—

He likes a Boggy Acre
A Floor too cool for Corn—   10
Yet when a Boy, and Barefoot—

[1] *My Tippet—only Tulle*—Her scarf, usually fur or wool, is only thin silk.

I more than once at Noon
Have passed, I thought, a Whip lash
Unbraiding in the Sun
When stooping to secure it   15
It wrinkled, and was gone—

Several of Nature's People
I know, and they know me—
I feel for them a transport
Of cordiality—   20

But never met this Fellow
Attended, or alone
Without a tighter breathing
And Zero at the Bone—

997

Crumbling is not an instant's Act
A fundamental pause
Delapidation's processes
Are organized Decays.

'Tis first a Cobweb on the Soul   5
A Cuticle of Dust
A Borer in the Axis
An Elemental Rust—

Ruin is formal—Devils work
Consecutive and slow—   10
Fail in an instant, no man did
Slipping—is Crashe's law.

1052

I never saw a Moor—
I never saw the Sea—
Yet know I how the Heather looks
And what a Billow be.

I never spoke with God   5
Nor visited in Heaven—
Yet certain am I of the spot
As if the Checks were given—

1075

The Sky is low—the Clouds are mean.
A Travelling Flake of Snow
Across a Barn or through a Rut
Debates if it will go—

A Narrow Wind complains all Day   5
How some one treated him
Nature, like Us is sometimes caught
Without her Diadem.

1100

The last Night that She lived
It was a Common Night
Except the Dying—this to Us
Made Nature different

We noticed smallest things—   5
Things overlooked before
By this great light upon our Minds
Italicized—as 'twere.

As We went out and in
Between Her final Room   10
And Rooms where Those to be alive
Tomorrow were, a Blame

That Others could exist
While She must finish quite
A Jealousy for Her arose   15
So nearly infinite—

We waited while She passed—
It was a narrow time—
Too jostled were Our Souls to speak
At length the notice came.   20

She mentioned, and forgot—
Then lightly as a Reed
Bent to the Water, struggled scarce—
Consented, and was dead—

And We—We placed the Hair—   25
And drew the Head erect—

And then an awful leisure was
Belief to regulate—

1126

Shall I take thee, the Poet said
To the propounded word?
Be stationed with the Candidates
Till I have finer tried—

The Poet searched Philology   5
And was about to ring
For the suspended Candidate
There came unsummoned in—

That portion of the Vision
The Word applied to fill   10
Not unto nomination
The Cherubim reveal—

1129

Tell all the Truth but tell it slant—
Success in Circuit lies
Too bright for our infirm Delight
The Truth's superb surprise
As Lightning to the Children eased   5
With explanation kind
The Truth must dazzle gradually
Or every man be blind—

1206

The Show is not the Show
But they that go—
Menagerie to me
My Neighbor be—
Fair Play—   5
Both went to see—

1298

The Mushroom is the Elf of Plants—
At Evening, it is not—

At Morning, in a Truffled Hut
It stop upon a Spot

As if it tarried always   5
And yet it's whole Career
Is shorter than a Snake's Delay
And fleeter than a Tare—

'Tis Vegetation's Juggler—
The Germ of Alibi—   10
Doth like a Bubble antedate
And like a Bubble, hie—

I feel as if the Grass was pleased
To have it intermit—
This surreptitious scion   15
Of Summer's circumspect.

Had Nature any supple Face
Or could she one contemn—
Had Nature an Apostate— [1]
That Mushroom—it is Him!   20

1409

Could mortal lip divine
The undeveloped Freight
Of a delivered syllable
'Twould crumble with the weight.

1452

Your thoughts dont have words every day
They come a single time
Like signal esoteric sips
Of the communion Wine
Which while you taste so native seems   5
So easy so to be
You cannot comprehend its price
Nor it's infrequency

1463

A Route of Evanescence
With a revolving Wheel—

[1] *Apostate* one who throws over his allegiance

A Resonance of Emerald—
A Rush of Cochineal— [1]
And every Blossom on the Bush   5
Adjusts it's tumbled Head—
The mail from Tunis, probably,
An easy Morning's Ride—

1540

As imperceptibly as Grief
The Summer lapsed away—
Too imperceptible at last
To seem like Perfidy—
A Quietness distilled   5
As Twilight long begun,
Or Nature spending with herself
Sequestered Afternoon—
The Dusk drew earlier in—
The Morning foreign shone—   10
A courteous, yet harrowing Grace,
As Guest, that would be gone—
And thus, without a Wing
Or service of a Keel [1]
Our Summer made her light escape   15
Into the Beautiful.

1547

Hope is a subtle Glutton—
He feeds upon the Fair—
And yet—inspected closely
What Abstinence is there—

His is the Halcyon Table—   5
That never seats but One—
And whatsoever is consumed
The same amount remain—

1732

My life closed twice before its close;
It yet remains to see

---

[1] *Keel* a ship

[1] *Cochineal* a red dye

If Immortality unveil
A third event to me,

So huge, so hopeless to conceive 5
As these that twice befel.
Parting is all we know of heaven,
And all we need of hell.

1755

To make a prairie it takes a clover and one bee,
One clover, and a bee,
And revery.
The revery alone will do,
If bees are few. 5

1760

Elysium is as far as to
The very nearest Room
If in that Room a Friend await
Felicity or Doom—

What fortitude the Soul contains, 5
That it can so endure
The accent of a coming Foot—
The opening of a Door—

CRITICISM

This essay illustrates criticism at its most paradoxical: its conclusion is that Emily Dickinson's poem is both brilliant and a
failure. In reality, much criticism is devoted to analysis that un-
covers both virtues and defects, successes and failures. (For a discussion of this kind of critical-analysis, see Chapter 3, pp. 137–
141). The book from which the following essay was taken (see
note) will yield the reader many other approaches to Emily
Dickinson's poetry—especially analysis of thematic patterns that
connect clusters of poems.

A Brilliant Failure: Emily Dickinson's "My Life Had Stood—A Loaded Gun" [1]

CHARLES R. ANDERSON

[Emily Dickinson once] found an instrument adequate to render her need for fulfillment through absolute commitment to love's service:

> My Life had stood—a Loaded Gun—
> In Corners—till a Day
> The Owner passed—identified—
> And carried Me away—
>
> And now We roam in Sovreign Woods—
> And now We hunt the Doe—
> And every time I speak for Him—
> The Mountains straight reply—
>
> And do I smile, such cordial light
> Upon the Valley glow—
> It is as a Vesuvian face
> Had let its pleasure through—
>
> And when at Night—Our good Day done—
> I guard My Master's Head—
> 'Tis better than the Eider-Duck's
> Deep Pillow—to have shared—
>
> To foe of His—I'm deadly foe—
> None stir the second time—
> On whom I lay a Yellow Eye—
> Or an emphatic Thumb—
>
> Though I than He—may longer live
> He longer must—than I—
> For I have but the power to kill,
> Without—the power to die—

The poem begins with a brilliant conceit. Fused from the ambiguous abstraction 'Life' and the explicit concretion 'Loaded Gun,' it expresses the charged potential of the human being who remains dormant until 'identified' into conscious vitality. 'At last,

[1] Extracted from Charles R. Anderson, *Emily Dickinson's Poetry: Stairway of Surprise* (copyright © 1960 by Charles R. Anderson. Reprinted by permission of Holt, Rinehart and Winston, Inc.) The text of "My Life Had Stood" (copyright 1929, © 1957, by Martha Dickinson Bianchi) is reprinted from *The Complete Poems of Emily Dickinson,* ed. Thomas H. Johnson, by permission of Little, Brown & Co.

to be identified!' another poem began. And when she heard of a friend's engagement to be married she wrote: 'The most noble congratulation it ever befell me to offer—is that you are yourself. Till it has loved—no man or woman can become itself—Of our first Creation we are unconscious.'

The paradox of finding oneself through losing oneself in love is rendered in her poem by one word: she achieves *identity* when the lover claims her as his own. The ecstasy of being swept up into the possession of another led her once to an extravagant succession of similes. She was borne along 'With swiftness, as of Chariots,' then lifted up into the ether by a balloon, while 'This World did drop away.' In the gun poem she puts far more in a single line, 'And carried Me away,' the double meaning encompassing both the portage of the gun and the transport of the beloved. The first stanza presents a tightly knit unit:

> My Life had stood—a Loaded Gun—
> In Corners—till a Day
> The Owner passed—identified—
> And carried Me away—

Its shock value inheres in the extreme disparity between the two things compared, incongruous in all ways except the startling points of likeness that can be ferreted out. The trap lies in the great precision needed to avoid confusing them, the vital but subjective 'Life' and the objective but inanimate 'Gun.' If she had chosen to use the strict method of metaphysical poetry, the succeeding stanzas would have been devoted to complicating and reconciling these disparities until they coalesce violently in the end.

Instead, after a brief setting introducing her over-image, she proceeds to develop it by the ballad narrative, to which her chosen metrical pattern was so well suited. In another sense, her poem is a domestication on American soil of the tradition of courtly love. The knight has turned pioneer, his quest a hunting expedition in the wilderness, his bower a cabin with feather-pillow and trusty rifle at his head, his lady the frontier wife who shares his hardships and adventures. In such a folk version of the troubadour lyric, the ballad stanza properly replaces the intricate Provençal forms. In the special climate of frontier America, another turn is given to the convention. Since the male provider is unavoidably committed to the strenuous life, here it is the woman who celebrates the softer arts, pledging eternal fidelity and the rapture of love's service. So the courtly roles are reversed: he is only the adored 'Master' while she is the joyous servant, which accounts for her assuming the active role in the love-game.

The hunting action of the second and third stanzas is given over to its devotional aspects. As steadfast companion, her words of love ring out in the gun's explosion, echoed by the mountains; her looks of love are the 'cordial light' of its fire, like the glow of Vesuvius in eruption. The quarry they hunt, 'the Doe,' is appropriate to the romantic theme. But to counterbalance the danger of sentimentalism she makes a pervasive use of hyperbole, suggesting the tall-tale mode of western humor. The protective action of the next two stanzas portrays the service of love. To guard his sleep is better than to share his bed. This may only mean that she places a higher value on giving him peace than on enjoying connubial bliss, though there is a curious suggestion that the love is never fulfilled in physical union. To give him security also calls forth an unquestioning loyalty destructive of his enemies, the jealous anger of the flashing muzzle's 'Yellow Eye' being a particularly happy extension of the image with which she began, the 'Loaded Gun.' Standing for the amorous potential of a newly vitalized life, this has been sustained through all the narrative center, successfully taking the risks inherent in this anatomical-mechanical fusion of part to part—'speak,' 'smile,' 'face,' and 'eye' applying to the gun as well as to love's servant. With 'thumb' it seems to break down in a shift of agency. Only the 'Owner' has a thumb to raise the hammer, and a finger to fire the gun, but here it fires itself. Her gun-life has so usurped the initiative as to reduce his function to hunting while she herself does the shooting. One of the hazards of the private poet is that the self tends to become the only reality. The lover here certainly plays a negative role.

The final stanza presents a more serious problem to be resolved. A metaphysical poet would have brought his series of shocks to rest in some unexpected figure evolved out of the initial conceit, but her gun only survives in the teasing antithesis of 'kill' and 'die.' A balladist would have rung down the curtain with an ending in surprise comedy or stark tragedy. Instead, she makes a third switch in technique and concludes with an aphorism that seems to have little structural relation to the rest of the poem:

> Though I than He—may longer live
> He longer must—than I—
> For I have but the power to kill,
> Without—the power to die—

If this poem was a deliberate attempt to weld a new form from all these disparate ones—folk ballad, troubadour lyric, tall tale, metaphysical and aphoristic verse—it was a bold experiment even though it did not quite come off. But though the conclusion is a disturbing departure in mode, it may be ventured that its thematic relevance is such as to make it a resolution of all that has gone before. Perhaps this is a poem about the limitations of mortal love and a yearning for the superior glories of the immortal kind. If this is so, then the last stanza is not a moralistic commentary on the narrative but the very meaning which the elaborated image finally creates.

The clues for such an interpretation are not planted thick enough, but there are some. The joys of merely sheltering the beloved are preferred to sharing the marriage bed. And this is the kind of love that finds its expression not in an earthly paradise but in roaming woods that are described here as 'Sovreign,' one of a cluster of words running through her poems to evoke the celestial estate. Earthly love, in spite of the ecstasy of passion and the bliss of service, she was forced to conclude is mortal. Such is the inanimate but loaded gun, once it has been touched into life by being identified by the owner. The physical existence of the gun, her mortal love, may outlast the earthly life of her master, the 'Owner,' but in immortality he will outlive it. So she too must have the 'power to die' into heavenly love in order to become immortal. Limited by her gun-body she has only the 'power to kill,' including paradoxically the soul of the beloved, by making him too enamored of the Eden of this life. In the plaintive 'I have but the power to kill' there may even be the backfire of a suicidal wish, to free him from the encumbrance of her mortal love. It may be reasonably objected that this meaning is too fragmentarily embodied in the poem; and the breakdown of the conclusion into prose brands it, when judged by the highest poetic standards, as a failure. But it is a brilliant one, repaying close study. Moreover, the theme here suggested, though conjectural, is in keeping with the whole trend of her love poetry and will help to illuminate it.

WILLIAM BUTLER YEATS

[1865-1939]

WILLIAM BUTLER YEATS, born near Dublin, was the son of an Irish artist. He was educated at home and in schools in England and Ireland. In his first poetry, Yeats worked in the spell of the Irish mythology (as in *The Wanderings of Oisin*). During his life he was an important figure in movements for the future of Ireland—its literary revival and its political independence. The literary revival meant the use of Irish themes, legends, and history. And it resulted in the establishment (by Lady Gregory and others) of the Abbey Theatre in Dublin. Yeats himself wrote a number of verse plays, like *The Land of Heart's Desire* (1894). Many early poems were written to the actress Maud Gonne, who was important to Yeats; but he married Georgie Hyde-Lees in 1917. At that time, he had also joined the movement for Irish independence; in 1922 he was elected senator of the Irish Free State. Yeats had been publishing many volumes of poetry, including *The Wind Among the Reeds* (1899), *In the Seven Woods* (1903), *The Wild Swans at Coole* (1917), and *Michael Robartes and the Dancer* (1920); and in 1923 he won the Nobel Prize for Literature. Yeats had developed a personal mysticism, his own mythology, and his own theories of history (*A Vision*, 1925, revised in 1937). His last books, like *The Tower* (1928), show the harder, more cryptic poetry that succeeded the early music and romance. This change in a forty-year career is described by Yeats himself in "The Circus Animals' Desertion" (p. 640). It is best read in his complete poems, where the variety, depth, and magic of the Yeats lines are clear.

Introductory Readings

EDITION: *The Collected Poems* (1949); *The Variorum Edition of the Poems of William Butler Yeats,* ed. Peter Allt and Russell K. Alspach

(1957). LETTERS: *The Letters of W. B. Yeats*, ed. Allan Wade (1954). BIOGRAPHY: *The Autobiography of William Butler Yeats* (1938); Joseph Hone, *William Butler Yeats* (1942, 1943); Richard Ellmann, *Yeats, the Man and the Masks* (1948). CRITICISM: *The Permanence of Yeats: Selected Criticism*, ed. James Hall and Martin Steinmann (1950); Richard Ellmann, *The Identity of Yeats* (1954); F. A. C. Wilson, *W. B. Yeats and Tradition* (1958); John Unterecker, *A Reader's Guide to William Butler Yeats* (1959).

THE LAKE ISLE OF INNISFREE

I will arise and go now, and go to Innisfree,
And a small cabin build there, of clay and wattles [1] made:
Nine bean-rows will I have there, a hive for the honeybee,
And live alone in the bee-loud glade.

And I shall have some peace there, for peace comes dropping
    slow,   5
Dropping from the veils of the morning to where the cricket sings;
There midnight's all a glimmer, and noon a purple glow,
And evening full of the linnet's wings.

I will arise and go now, for always night and day
I hear lake water lapping with low sounds by the shore;   10
While I stand on the roadway, or on the pavements grey,
I hear it in the deep heart's core.

WHEN YOU ARE OLD

When you are old and grey and full of sleep,
And nodding by the fire, take down this book,
And slowly read, and dream of the soft look
Your eyes had once, and of their shadows deep;

How many loved your moments of glad grace,   5
And loved your beauty with love false or true,
But one man loved the pilgrim soul in you,
And loved the sorrows of your changing face;

And bending down beside the glowing bars,
Murmur, a little sadly, how Love fled   10
And paced upon the mountains overhead
And hid his face amid a crowd of stars.

[1] *wattles* interwoven twigs and branches used for construction

THE SONG OF WANDERING AENGUS [1]

I went out to the hazel wood,
Because a fire was in my head,
And cut and peeled a hazel wand,
And hooked a berry to a thread;
And when white moths were on the wing,   5
And moth-like stars were flickering out,
I dropped the berry in a stream
And caught a little silver trout.

When I had laid it on the floor
I went to blow the fire aflame,   10
But something rustled on the floor,
And some one called me by my name:
It had become a glimmering girl
With apple blossom in her hair
Who called me by my name and ran   15
And faded through the brightening air.

Though I am old with wandering
Through hollow lands and hilly lands,
I will find out where she has gone,
And kiss her lips and take her hands;   20
And walk among long dappled grass,
And pluck till time and times are done
The silver apples of the moon,
The golden apples of the sun.

THE FIDDLER OF DOONEY

When I play on my fiddle in Dooney,
Folk dance like a wave of the sea;
My cousin is priest in Kilvarnet,
My brother in Mocharabuiee.

I passed my brother and cousin: 5
They read in their books of prayer;
I read in my book of songs
I bought at the Sligo fair.

When we come at the end of time
To Peter sitting in state,   10

[1] *Aengus* Angus, Celtic god of love

He will smile on the three old spirits,
But call me first through the gate;

For the good are always the merry,
Save by an evil chance,
And the merry love the fiddle,   15
And the merry love to dance:

And when the folk there spy me,
They will all come up to me,
With 'Here is the fiddler of Dooney!'
And dance like a wave of the sea.   20

ADAM'S CURSE

We sat together at one summer's end,
That beautiful mild woman, your close friend,
And you and I, and talked of poetry.
I said, 'A line will take us hours maybe;
Yet if it does not seem a moment's thought,   5
Our stitching and unstitching has been naught.

Better go down upon your marrow-bones
And scrub a kitchen pavement, or break stones
Like an old pauper, in all kinds of weather;
For to articulate sweet sounds together   10
Is to work harder than all these, and yet
Be thought an idler by the noisy set
Of bankers, schoolmasters, and clergymen
The martyrs call the world.'

                 And thereupon   15
That beautiful mild woman for whose sake
There's many a one shall find out all heartache
On finding that her voice is sweet and low
Replied, 'To be born woman is to know—
Although they do not talk of it at school—   20
That we must labour to be beautiful.'

I said, 'It's certain there is no fine thing
Since Adam's fall but needs much labouring.
There have been lovers who thought love should be
So much compounded of high courtesy   25
That they would sigh and quote with learned looks
Precedents out of beautiful old books;
Yet now it seems an idle trade enough.'

We sat grown quiet at the name of love;
We saw the last embers of daylight die,   30
And in the trembling blue-green of the sky
A moon, worn as if it had been a shell
Washed by time's waters as they rose and fell
About the stars and broke in days and years.

I had a thought for no one's but your ears: 35
That you were beautiful, and that I strove
To love you in the old high way of love;
That it had all seemed happy, and yet we'd grown
As weary-hearted as that hollow moon.

THE COMING OF WISDOM WITH TIME

Though leaves are many, the root is one;
Through all the lying days of my youth
I swayed my leaves and flowers in the sun;
Now I may wither into the truth.

TO A FRIEND WHOSE WORK HAS
COME TO NOTHING

Now all the truth is out,
Be secret and take defeat
From any brazen throat,
For how can you compete,
Being honour bred, with one   5
Who, were it proved he lies,
Were neither shamed in his own
Nor in his neighbours' eyes?
Bred to a harder thing
Than Triumph, turn away   10
And like a laughing string
Whereon mad fingers play
Amid a place of stone,
Be secret and exult,
Because of all things known   15
That is most difficult.

THE WILD SWANS AT COOLE

The trees are in their autumn beauty,
The woodland paths are dry,

Under the October twilight the water
Mirrors a still sky;
Upon the brimming water among the stones   5
Are nine-and-fifty swans.

The nineteenth autumn has come upon me
Since I first made my count;
I saw, before I had well finished,
All suddenly mount   10
And scatter wheeling in great broken rings
Upon their clamorous wings.

I have looked upon those brilliant creatures,
And now my heart is sore.
All's changed since I, hearing at twilight,   15
The first time on this shore,
The bell-beat of their wings above my head,
Trod with a lighter tread.

Unwearied still, lover by lover,
They paddle in the cold   20
Companionable streams, or climb the air;
Their hearts have not grown old;
Passion or conquest, wander where they will,
Attend upon them still.

But now they drift on the still water,   25
Mysterious, beautiful;
Among what rushes will they build,
By what lake's edge or pool
Delight men's eyes, when I awake some day
To find they have flown away?   30

IN MEMORY OF MAJOR ROBERT GREGORY [1]

1

Now that we're almost settled in our house [2]
I'll name the friends that cannot sup with us
Beside a fire of turf in th' ancient tower,
And having talked to some late hour
Climb up the narrow winding stair to bed: 5
Discoverers of forgotten truth

---

[1] *Major Robert Gregory* son of Yeats's friend, Lady Augusta Gregory. He was an aviator in World War I and was killed in action over Italy.
[2] *house* Yeats and his bride are settled in their home and are discussing friendships that might bring marital quarreling (l. 13).

Or mere companions of my youth,
All, all are in my thoughts to-night being dead.

2

Always we'd have the new friend meet the old
And we are hurt if either friend seem cold,   10
And there is salt to lengthen out the smart
In the affections of our heart,
And quarrels are blown up upon that head;
But not a friend that I would bring
This night can set us quarrelling,   15
For all that come into my mind are dead.

3

Lionel Johnson [3] comes the first to mind,
That loved his learning better than mankind,
Though courteous to the worst; much falling he
Brooded upon sanctity   20
Till all his Greek and Latin learning seemed
A long blast upon the horn that brought
A little nearer to his thought
A measureless consummation that he dreamed.

4

And that enquiring man John Synge [4] comes next,   25
That dying chose the living world for text
And never could have rested in the tomb
But that, long travelling, he had come
Towards nightfall upon certain set apart
In a most desolate stony place,   30
Towards nightfall upon a race
Passionate and simple like his heart.

5

And then I think of old George Pollexfen,[5]
In muscular youth well known to Mayo men
For horsemanship at meets or at racecourses,   35
That could have shown how pure-bred horses
And solid men, for all their passion, live
But as the outrageous stars incline

[3] *Lionel Johnson* writer friend of Yeats who died after he had been drinking
[4] *John Synge* the playwright who wrote about the simple Aran Islanders
[5] *George Pollexfen* Yeats's astrologer uncle who was an excellent horseman

By opposition, square and trine;
Having grown sluggish and contemplative.   40

6

They were my close companions many a year,
A portion of my mind and life, as it were,
And now their breathless faces seem to look
Out of some old picture-book;
I am accustomed to their lack of breath,   45
But not that my dear friend's dear son,
Our Sidney [6] and our perfect man,
Could share in that discourtesy of death.

7

For all things the delighted eye now sees
Were loved by him: the old storm-broken trees   50
That cast their shadows upon road and bridge;
The tower set on the stream's edge;
The ford where drinking cattle make a stir
Nightly, and startled by that sound
The water-hen must change her ground;   55
He might have been your heartiest welcomer.

8

When with the Galway foxhounds he would ride
From Castle Taylor to the Roxborough side
Or Esserkelly plain, few kept his pace;
At Mooneen he had leaped a place   60
So perilous that half the astonished meet
Had shut their eyes; and where was it
He rode a race without a bit?
And yet his mind outran the horses' feet.

9

We dreamed that a great painter had been born   65
To cold Clare rock and Galway rock [7] and thorn,
To that stern colour and that delicate line
That are our secret discipline
Wherein the gazing heart doubles her might.
Soldier, scholar, horseman, he,   70

[6] *Sidney* Sir Philip Sidney (1554–1586), who was considered the perfect knight
—the embodiment of all that was best in chivalry
[7] *Clare rock and Galway rock* Clare and Galway are counties of Ireland.

And yet he had the intensity
To have published all to be a world's delight.

10

What other could so well have counselled us
In all lovely intricacies of a house
As he that practised or that understood   75
All work in metal or in wood,
In moulded plaster or in carven stone?
Soldier, scholar, horseman, he,
And all he did done perfectly
As though he had but that one trade alone.   80

11

Some burn damp faggots, others may consume
The entire combustible world in one small room
As though dried straw, and if we turn about
The bare chimney is gone black out
Because the work had finished in that flare.   85
Soldier, scholar, horseman, he,
As 'twere all life's epitome.
What made us dream that he could comb grey hair?

12

I had thought, seeing how bitter is that wind
That shakes the shutter, to have brought to mind   90
All those that manhood tried, or childhood loved
Or boyish intellect approved,
With some appropriate commentary on each;
Until imagination brought
A fitter welcome; but a thought   95
Of that late death took all my heart for speech.

EASTER 1916 [1]

I have met them at close of day
Coming with vivid faces
From counter or desk among grey
Eighteenth-century houses.
I have passed with a nod of the head   5
Or polite meaningless words,

[1] *Easter 1916* At Easter, 1916, Connolly and Pearse (named in the last stanza)
led their Irish compatriots against British rule. The rebellion was quickly
stamped out, but became a celebrated instance of heroism.

Or have lingered awhile and said
Polite meaningless words,
And thought before I had done
Of a mocking tale or a gibe   10
To please a companion
Around the fire at the club,
Being certain that they and I
But lived where motley is worn:
All changed, changed utterly: 15
A terrible beauty is born.

That woman's [2] days were spent
In ignorant good-will,
Her nights in argument
Until her voice grew shrill.   20
What voice more sweet than hers
When, young and beautiful,
She rode to harriers?
This man [3] had kept a school
And rode our wingèd horse;   25
This other [4] his helper and friend
Was coming into his force;
He might have won fame in the end,
So sensitive his nature seemed,
So daring and sweet his thought.   30
This other man [5] I had dreamed
A drunken, vainglorious lout.
He had done most bitter wrong
To some who are near my heart,
Yet I number him in the song;   35
He, too, has resigned his part
In the casual comedy;
He, too, has been changed in his turn,
Transformed utterly:
A terrible beauty is born.   40

Hearts with one purpose alone
Through summer and winter seem
Enchanted to a stone
To trouble the living stream.

[2] *That woman's* a long-time friend of Yeats, Constance Gore-Booth, Countess
Markiewicz, who became interested in politics through Yeats's encouragement
[3] *This man* Pearse   [4] *This other* MacDonagh
[5] *This other man* MacBride, husband of Maud Gonne, the actress loved by
Yeats

The horse that comes from the road   45
The rider, the birds that range
From cloud to tumbling cloud,
Minute by minute they change;
A shadow of cloud on the stream
Changes minute by minute;   50
A horse-hoof slides on the brim,
And a horse plashes within it;
The long-legged moor-hens dive,
And hens to moor-cocks call;
Minute by minute they live: 55
The stone's in the midst of all.

Too long a sacrifice
Can make a stone of the heart.
O when may it suffice?
That is Heaven's part, our part   60
To murmur name upon name,
As a mother names her child
When sleep at last has come
On limbs that had run wild.
What is it but nightfall?   65
No, no, not night but death;
Was it needless death after all?
For England may keep faith
For all that is done and said.
We know their dream; enough   70
To know they dreamed and are dead;
And what if excesses of love
Bewildered them till they died?
I write it out in a verse—
MacDonagh and MacBride   75
And Connolly and Pearse
Now and in time to be,
Wherever green is worn,
Are changed, changed utterly:
A terrible beauty is born.   80

September 25, 1916

THE ROSE TREE

'O words are lightly spoken,'
Said Pearse to Connolly,[1]

---

[1] *Pearse, Connolly* leaders of the Irish insurrection against British rule, Easter, 1916; captured and executed. See Yeats's poem, "Easter 1916."

'Maybe a breath of politic words
Has withered our Rose Tree; [2]
Or maybe but a wind that blows   5
Across the bitter sea.'

'It needs to be but watered,'
James Connolly replied,
'To make the green come out again
And spread on every side,   10
And shake the blossom from the bud
To be the garden's pride.'

'But where can we draw water,'
Said Pearse to Connolly,
'When all the wells are parched away?   15
O plain as plain can be
There's nothing but our own red blood
Can make a right Rose Tree.'

THE SECOND COMING

Turning and turning in the widening gyre
The falcon cannot hear the falconer; [1]
Things fall apart; the centre cannot hold;
Mere anarchy is loosed upon the world,
The blood-dimmed tide is loosed, and everywhere   5
The ceremony of innocence is drowned;
The best lack all conviction, while the worst
Are full of passionate intensity.

Surely some revelation is at hand;
Surely the Second Coming is at hand.   10
The Second Coming! Hardly are those words out
When a vast image out of *Spiritus Mundi* [2]
Troubles my sight: somewhere in sands of the desert
A shape with lion body and the head of a man,
A gaze blank and pitiless as the sun,   15
Is moving its slow thighs, while all about it
Reel shadows of the indignant desert birds.
The darkness drops again; but now I know

[2] *Rose Tree* symbol of Ireland, withered under British rule, to be brought to life again only by rebellion

[1] *gyre . . . falconer* The falcon in its spiral flight soars beyond the falconer—as man has lost touch with stable values.
[2] *Spiritus Mundi* World Spirit

That twenty centuries [3] of stony sleep
Were vexed to nightmare by a rocking cradle,   20
And what rough beast, its hour come round at last,
Slouches towards Bethlehem to be born?

SAILING TO BYZANTIUM [1]

I

That is no country for old men. The young
In one another's arms, birds in the trees,
—Those dying generations—at their song,
The salmon-falls, the mackerel-crowded seas,
Fish, flesh, or fowl, commend all summer long   5
Whatever is begotten, born, and dies.
Caught in that sensual music all neglect
Monuments of unageing intellect.

II

An aged man is but a paltry thing,
A tattered coat upon a stick, unless   10
Soul clap its hands and sing, and louder sing
For every tatter in its mortal dress,
Nor is there singing school but studying
Monuments of its own magnificence;
And therefore I have sailed the seas and come   15
To the holy city of Byzantium.

III

O sages standing in God's holy fire
As in the gold mosaic of a wall,
Come from the holy fire, perne in a gyre,[2]
And be the singing-masters of my soul.   20
Consume my heart away; sick with desire
And fastened to a dying animal
It knows not what it is; and gather me
Into the artifice of eternity.

---

[3] *twenty centuries* the era of Christ, now to give way to some bestial anti-Christ

---

[1] *Byzantium* ancient Christian capital of the East, here symbolic of the world of the imagination and spirit. Critical comment on this poem appears on p. 642.
[2] *perne in a gyre* spiral like a hawk in flight

IV

Once out of nature I shall never take   25
My bodily form from any natural thing,
But such a form as Grecian goldsmiths make
Of hammered gold and gold enamelling
To keep a drowsy Emperor awake;
Or set upon a golden bough to sing   30
To lords and ladies of Byzantium
Of what is past, or passing, or to come.

LEDA AND THE SWAN [1]

A sudden blow: the great wings beating still
Above the staggering girl, her thighs caressed
By the dark webs, her nape caught in his bill,
He holds her helpless breast upon his breast.

How can those terrified vague fingers push   5
The feathered glory from her loosening thighs?
And how can body, laid in that white rush,
But feel the strange heart beating where it lies?

A shudder in the loins engenders there
The broken wall, the burning roof and tower   10
And Agamemnon [2] dead.
                              Being so caught up,
So mastered by the brute blood of the air,
Did she put on his knowledge with his power
Before the indifferent beak could let her drop?

AMONG SCHOOL CHILDREN

I

I walk through the long schoolroom questioning;
A kind old nun in a white hood replies;
The children learn to cipher and to sing,
To study reading-books and histories,
To cut and sew, be neat in everything   5
In the best modern way—the children's eyes

[1] *Leda, swan* Leda was loved by Zeus in the form of a swan; resulting from the union were Helen and Clytemnestra.
[2] *Agamemnon* When he returned from the Trojan wars, Agamemnon was killed by Clytemnestra and her lover.

In momentary wonder stare upon
A sixty-year-old smiling public man.

II

I dreamed of a Ledaean body,[1] bent
Above a sinking fire, a tale that she   10
Told of a harsh reproof, or trivial event
That changed some childish day to tragedy—
Told, and it seemed that our two natures blent
Into a sphere from youthful sympathy,
Or else, to alter Plato's parable,[2]   15
Into the yoke and white of the one shell.

III

And thinking of that fit of grief or rage
I look upon one child or t'other there
And wonder if she stood so at that age—
For even daughters of the swan can share   20
Something of every paddler's heritage—
And had that color upon cheek or hair,
And thereupon my heart is driven wild:
She stands before me as a living child.

IV

Her present image floats into the mind—   25
Did Quattrocento[3] finger fashion it
Hollow of cheek as though it drank the wind
And took a mess of shadows for its meat?
And I though never of Ledaean kind
Had pretty plumage once—enough of that,   30
Better to smile on all that smile, and show
There is a comfortable kind of old scarecrow.

V

What youthful mother, a shape upon her lap
Honey of generation[4] had betrayed,

---

[1] *Ledaean body* a body like that of Leda, loved by Zeus as a swan. Yeats remembers his youthful love, Maud Gonne.

[2] *Plato's parable* In the Symposium, Aristophanes indicates that humans were once sexually whole and self-contained, and only later split into male and female.

[3] *Quattrocento* 15th century, here referring to such painters as Raphael and Michelangelo

[4] *Honey of generation* refers to sweetness of procreation

And that must sleep, shriek, struggle to escape   35
As recollection or the drug decide,
Would think her son, did she but see that shape
With sixty or more winters on its head,
A compensation for the pang of his birth,
Or the uncertainty of his setting forth?   40

VI

Plato thought [5] nature but a spume that plays
Upon a ghostly paradigm of things;
Solider Aristotle played the taws
Upon the bottom of a king of kings; [6]
World-famous golden-thighed Pythagoras [7]   45
Fingered upon a fiddle-stick or strings
What a star sang and careless Muses heard:
Old clothes upon old sticks to scare a bird.

VII

Both nuns and mothers worship images,
But those the candles light are not as those   50
That animate a mother's reveries,
But keep a marble or a bronze repose.
And yet they too break hearts—O Presences [8]
That passion, piety or affection knows,
And that all heavenly glory symbolise—   55
O self-born mockers of man's enterprise;

VIII

Labor is blossoming or dancing where
The body is not bruised to pleasure soul,
Nor beauty born out of its own despair,
Nor blear-eyed wisdom out of midnight oil.   60
O chestnut-tree, great-rooted blossomer,
Are you the leaf, the blossom or the bole?
O body swayed to music, O brightening glance,
How can we know the dancer from the dance?

[5] *Plato thought* Plato looked upon the world as a reflection of the ideal.
[6] *Aristotle . . . taws . . . kings* (ll. 43–44) Aristotle believed in the solidity of reality, and used his leather strap on Alexander, his pupil.
[7] *Pythagoras* discoverer of the musical scale who believed in a celestial harmony
[8] *Presences* the ideals or the images of lovers, nuns, or mothers ("passion, piety or affection")

FOR ANNE GREGORY

'Never shall a young man,
Thrown into despair
By those great honey-coloured
Ramparts at your ear,
Love you for yourself alone   5
And not your yellow hair.'

'But I can get a hair-dye
And set such colour there,
Brown, or black, or carrot,
That young men in despair   10
May love me for myself alone
And not my yellow hair.'

'I heard an old religious man
But yesternight declare
That he had found a text to prove   15
That only God, my dear,
Could love you for yourself alone
And not your yellow hair.'

BYZANTIUM [1]

The unpurged images [2] of day recede;
The Emperor's drunken soldiery are abed;
Night resonance recedes, night-walkers' song
After great cathedral gong;
A starlit or a moonlit dome disdains   5
All that man is,
All mere complexities,
The fury and the mire of human veins.

Before me floats an image,[3] man or shade,
Shade more than man, more image than a shade;   10
For Hades' bobbin bound in mummy-cloth [4]

[1] *Byzantium* symbolic of the world of the imagination; see "Sailing to Byzantium"
[2] *unpurged images* unpurged because they are not purified by artistic conception
[3] *image* a perfect (non-living) soul
[4] *Hades' bobbin . . . mummy-cloth* The soul, as a bobbin, is imprisoned and deadened by the experiences of life, or a mummy-cloth.

May unwind the winding path;
A mouth that has no moisture and no breath
Breathless mouths [5] may summon;
I hail the superhuman;   15
I call it death-in-life and life-in-death.

Miracle, bird or golden handiwork,
More miracle than bird or handiwork,
Planted on the star-lit golden bough,
Can like the cocks of Hades [6] crow,   20
Or, by the moon embittered, scorn aloud
In glory of changeless metal
Common bird or petal
And all complexities of mire or blood.

At midnight on the Emperor's pavement flit   25
Flames that no faggot feeds, nor steel has lit,
Nor storm disturbs, flames begotten of flame,
Where blood-begotten spirits come
And all complexities of fury leave,
Dying into a dance,   30
An agony of trance,
An agony of flame that cannot singe a sleeve.

Astraddle on the dolphin's mire and blood,
Spirit after spirit! [7] The smithies break the flood,
The golden smithies of the Emperor!   35
Marbles of the dancing floor
Break bitter furies of complexity,
Those images that yet
Fresh images beget,
That dolphin-torn, that gong-tormented sea.[8]   40

[5] *Breathless mouths* the imaginative, who may summon to their imagination the purified (or unwound) soul
[6] *Miracle . . . cocks of Hades* (ll. 17–20) The image become work of art (a "bird or golden handiwork") transcends reality and may crow like the Hades' heralds of rebirth.
[7] *Astraddle on the dolphin's mire . . . spirit!* (ll. 33–34) The images of art derive from experience (the dolphin is a sexual symbol) and beget still other images (compare the "blood-begotten spirits" of l. 28).
[8] *sea* The sea is life, with all its torment of blood and flesh (dolphin) and awareness of time passing (gong-tormented); only the smithies of the Emperor, or the artists, can "break the flood" (l. 34) of life—transcend it.

CRAZY JANE TALKS WITH THE BISHOP

I met the Bishop on the road
And much said he and I.
'Those breasts are flat and fallen now,
Those veins must soon be dry;
Live in a heavenly mansion,   5
Not in some foul sty.'

'Fair and foul are near of kin,
And fair needs foul,' I cried.
'My friends are gone, but that's a truth
Nor grave nor bed denied,   10
Learned in bodily lowliness
And in the heart's pride.

'A woman can be proud and stiff
When on love intent;
But Love has pitched his mansion in   15
The place of excrement;
For nothing can be sole or whole
That has not been rent.'

AFTER LONG SILENCE

Speech after long silence; it is right,
All other lovers being estranged or dead,
Unfriendly lamplight hid under its shade,
The curtains drawn upon unfriendly night,
That we descant and yet again descant   5
Upon the supreme theme of Art and Song:
Bodily decrepitude is wisdom; young
We loved each other and were ignorant.

THE CIRCUS ANIMALS' DESERTION

I

I sought a theme and sought for it in vain,
I sought it daily for six weeks or so.
Maybe at last, being but a broken man,
I must be satisfied with my heart, although
Winter and summer till old age began   5

My circus animals were all on show,
Those stilted boys, that burnished chariot,
Lion and woman and the Lord knows what.[1]

II

What can I but enumerate old themes?
First that sea-rider Oisin [2] led by the nose   10
Through three enchanted islands, allegorical dreams,
Vain gaiety, vain battle, vain repose,
Themes of the embittered heart, or so it seems,
That might adorn old songs or courtly shows;
But what cared I that set him on to ride,   15
I, starved for the bosom of his faery bride?

And then a counter-truth filled out its play,
The Countess Cathleen [3] was the name I gave it;
She, pity-crazed, had given her soul away,
But masterful Heaven had intervened to save it.   20
I thought my dear must her own soul destroy,
So did fanaticism and hate enslave it,
And this brought forth a dream and soon enough
This dream itself had all my thought and love.

And when the Fool and Blind Man stole the bread   25
Cuchulain [4] fought the ungovernable sea;
Heart-mysteries there, and yet when all is said
It was the dream itself enchanted me:
Character isolated by a deed
To engross the present and dominate memory.   30
Players and painted stage took all my love,
And not those things that they were emblems of.

III

Those masterful images because complete
Grew in pure mind, but out of what began?

[1] *Those stilted boys . . . what* (ll. 7–8) Yeats here refers to his early themes, his young lovers and his ominous prophecies.
[2] *Oisin* One of Yeats's earlier works, *The Wanderings of Oisin*, was based on the old Irish legend of the famous warrior, Oisin, who was lured by a fairy woman into long wandering in the Celtic fairyland.
[3] *The Countess Cathleen* another early work by Yeats, for which Maud Gonne served as the model; but as Yeats says (ll. 23–24), the dream ultimately transcended the reality
[4] *Cuchulain* legendary Irish warrior, variously reported mortal and son of the sun god, fought the sea in defense of his land; the incident mentioned here is the climax of Yeats's play, *On Baile's Strand*.

A mound of refuse or the sweepings of a street,   35
Old kettles, old bottles, and a broken can,
Old iron, old bones, old rags, that raving slut
Who keeps the till. Now that my ladder's [5] gone,
I must lie down where all the ladders start,
In the foul rag-and-bone shop of the heart.   40

CRITICISM

Sometimes criticism of a particular literary work is written to illustrate a "critical system." The following essay has been used as a practical illustration of the critical theory of what has sometimes been called the neo-Aristotelian school of criticism, a type which emphasizes the comprehensive analysis of the elements in a poem which contribute to its unique effect, both in meaning and emotion. [See Elder Olson's "An Outline of Poetic Theory," *Critics and Criticism*, ed. R. S. Crane (1952), for more information on this critical approach.] In his essay on "Sailing to Byzantium," Olson tries to show *how* and *why* the poem makes the meanings it makes and has the effect it has. By close and detailed analysis of the poem, line by line, stanza by stanza, he invites us to a deeper understanding and fuller appreciation.

"Sailing to Byzantium" by William Butler Yeats [1]

ELDER OLSON

In *Sailing to Byzantium* an old man faces the problem of old age, of death, and of regeneration, and gives his decision. Old age, he tells us, excludes a man from the sensual joys of youth; the world appears to belong completely to the young, it is no place for the old; indeed, an old man is scarcely a man at all—he is an empty artifice, an effigy merely, of a man; he is a tattered coat upon a stick. This would be very bad, except that the young also are excluded from something; rapt in their sensuality, they are ignorant utterly of the world of the spirit. Hence if old age frees a man from sensual passion, he may rejoice in the liberation

---

[5] *ladder* The ladder of creativity or art; art begins in reality, however morbid, but ends in transcendence.

[1] A portion of Elder Olson's essay, "Sailing to Byzantium," first published in the *University of Kansas City Review*, VIII (Spring, 1942).

of the soul; he is admitted into the realm of the spirit; and his rejoicing will increase according as he realizes the magnificence of the soul. But the soul can best learn its own greatness from the great works of art; hence he turns to those great works, but in turning to them, he finds that these are by no means mere effigies, or monuments, but things which have souls also; these live in the noblest element of God's fire, free from all corruption; hence he prays for death, for release from his mortal body; and since the insouled monuments exhibit the possibility of the soul's existence in some other matter than flesh, he wishes reincarnation, not now in a mortal body, but in the immortal and changeless embodiment of art.

There are thus the following terms, one might say, from which the poem suspends: the condition of the young, who are spiritually passive although sensually active; the condition of the merely old, who are spiritually and physically impotent; the condition of the old, who, although physically impotent, are capable of spiritual activity; the condition of art considered as inanimate— i. e., the condition of things which are merely monuments; and finally the condition of art considered as animate—as of such things as artificial birds which have a human soul. The second term, impotent and unspiritual old age, is a privative, a repugnant state which causes the progression through the other various alternative terms, until its contrary is encountered. The first and third terms are clearly contraries of each other: taken together as animate nature they are further contrary to the fourth term, inanimate art. None of these terms represents a wholly desirable mode of existence; but the fifth term, which represents such a mode, amalgamates the positive elements and eliminates the negative elements of both nature and art, and effects thus a resolution of the whole, for now the soul is present, as it would not be in art, nor is it passive, as it would be in the young and sensual mortal body, nor is it lodged in a "dying animal," as it would be in the body of the aged man; the soul is now free to act in its own supremacy and in full cognizance of its own excellence, and its embodiment is now incorruptible and secure from all the ills of flesh.

About these several oppositions the poem forms. The whole turns on the old man's realization, now that he is in the presence of the images of Byzantium, that these images have souls; there are consequently two major divisions which divide the poem precisely in half, the first two stanzas presenting art as inanimate, the second two, as animate; and that this is the case can be seen from such signs as that in the first half of the poem the images are stated as passive objects—they are twice called "monuments," they are merely objects of contemplation, they may be neglected or studied, visited or not visited, whereas in stanzas III and IV they are treated as gods which can be prayed to for life or death, as beings capable of motion from sphere to sphere, as instructors of the soul, as sages possessed of wisdom; and the curious shift in the manner of consideration is signalized by the subtle phrasing of the first two lines of stanza III: "O sages standing in God's holy fire/ As in the gold mosaic of a wall." According to the first part, the images at Byzantium were images, and one should have expected at most some figurative apostrophe to them: "O images set in the gold mosaic of a wall, much as the sages stand in God's holy fire": but here the similitude is reversed, and lest there should be any error, the sages are besought to come from the holy fire and begin the tuition of the soul, the destruction of the flesh.

Within these two halves of the poem, further divisions may be found, coincident with the stanzaic divisions. Stanza I presents a rejection of passion, stanza II an acceptance of intellection; then, turning on the realization that art is insouled, stanza III presents a rejection of the corruptible embodiment, and stanza IV, an acceptance of the incorruptible. There is an alternation, thus, of negative and affirmative: out of passion into intellection, out of corruption into permanence, in clear balance, the proportion being I : II :: III : IV; and what orders these sections is their dialectical sequence. That is, passion must be condemned before the intellect can be esteemed; the intellect must operate before the images can be known to be insouled; the realization that the images are insouled precedes the realization that the body may be dispensed with; and the reincarnation of the soul in some changeless medium can be recognized as a possibility only through the prior recognition that the flesh is not the necessary matter of the soul. The parallel opposition of contraries constitutes a sharp demarcation; in stanza I a mortal bird of nature amid natural trees sings a brief song of sensual joy in praise of mortal things, of "whatever is begotten, born, and dies"; in stanza IV an immortal and artificial bird set in an artificial tree sings an eternal song of spiritual joy in praise of eternal things, of "what is past, or passing, or to come"; and similarly, in stanza II a living thing is found to be an inanimate artifice, "a tattered coat upon a stick," incapable of motion, speech, sense or knowledge whereas in stanza III what had appeared to be inanimate artifice is found to possess a soul, and hence to be capable of all these. A certain artificial symmetry in the argument serves to distinguish these parts even further; stanzas I and IV begin with the conclusions of their respective arguments, whereas II and III end with their proper conclusions, and I is dependent upon II for the substantiation of its premisses, as IV is dependent upon III.

This much indication of the principal organization of the work permits the explication, in terms of this, of the more elementary proportions. The first line of stanza I presents immediately, in its most simple statement, the condition which is the genesis of the whole structure: "That is no country for old men"; old men are shut out from something, and the remainder of the first six lines indicates precisely what it is from which they are excluded. The young are given over to sensual delight, in which old men can no longer participate. But a wall, if it shuts out, also shuts in; if the old are excluded from something, so are the young; lines 7 and 8, consequently, exhibit a second sense in which "That is no country for old men," for the young neglect all intellectual things. Further, the use of "that" implies a possible "this"; that is, there is a country for the old as for the young; and, again, the use of "that" implies that the separation from the country of the young is already complete. The occupation of the young is shrewdly stated: at first sight the human lovers "in one another's arms" have, like the birds at their song, apparently a romantic and sentimental aura; but the curious interpolation of "Those dying generations" in the description of the birds foreshadows the significance they are soon to have; and the phrases immediately following remove all sentimentality: "the salmon-falls, the mackerel-crowded seas" intend the ascent of salmon to the head-waters, the descent of mackerel to the deep seas in the spawning season, and the ironic intention is clear: all—the human lovers, the birds, the fish, do but spawn, but copulate, and this is their whole being; and if the parallel statement does not make this sufficiently evident, the summation of all in terms merely of animal genera—"fish, flesh, or fowl"—is unmistakable. The country of the young, then, is in its air, in its waters, and on its earth, from headwaters to ocean, wholly given over to sensuality; its inhabitants "commend all summer long" anything whatsoever, so long as it be mortal and animal—they commend "whatever is begotten, born, and dies"; and while they "commend" because they have great joy, that which they praise, they who praise, and their praise itself are ephemeral, for these mortals praise the things of mortality, and their commendation, like their joy, lasts but a summer, a mating season. The concluding lines of the stanza remove all ambiguity, and cancel all possibility of a return to such a country; even if the old man could, he would not return to a land where "caught in that sensual music, all neglect / Monuments of unageing intellect." The young are "caught," they are really passive and incapable of free action; and they neglect those things which are unageing.

Merely to end here, however, with a condemnation of youthful sensuality would be unsatisfactory; as the second stanza expounds, old age itself is no solution; the old man cannot justly say, like Sophocles when he was asked whether he regretted the loss of youth and love, "Peace; most gladly have I escaped the thing of which you speak; I feel as if I had escaped from a mad and furious master"; for merely to be old is merely to be in a state of privation, it is to be "a paltry thing / A tattered coat upon a stick," it is to be the merest scarecrow, the merest fiction and semblance of a man, an inanimate rag upon a dead stick. A man merely old, then, is worse off than youth; if the souls of the young are captive, the old have, in this sense at least, no souls at all. Something positive must be added; and if the soul can wax and grow strong as the body wanes, then every step in the dissolution of the body—"every tatter in its mortal dress"—is cause for a further augmentation of joy. But this can occur only if the soul can rejoice in its own power and magnificence; this rejoicing is possible only if the soul knows of its own magnificence, and this knowledge is possible only through the contemplation of monuments which recall that magnificence. The soul of the aged must be strong to seek that which youth neglects. Hence the old must seek Byzantium; that is the country of the old; it is reached by sailing the seas, by breaking utterly with the country of the young; all passion must be left behind, the soul must be free to study the emblems of unchanging things.

Here the soul should be filled with joy; it should, by merely "studying," commend changeless things with song, as youth commends the changing with song; it would seem that the problem has been resolved, and the poem hence must end; but the contemplation of the monuments teaches first of all that these are no mere monuments but living things, and that the soul cannot grow into likeness with these beings of immortal embodiment unless it cast off its mortal body utterly. Nor is joy possible until the body be dissolved; the heart is still sick with the impossible desires of the flesh, it is still ignorant of its circumstances, and no song is possible to the soul while even a remnant of passion remains. Hence the old man prays to the sages who really stand in God's holy fire and have merely the semblance of images in gold mosaic; let them descend, "perning in a gyre," that is, moving in the circular motion which alone is possible to eternal things, let them consume with holy fire the heart which is the last seat of passion and ignorance, let them instruct the soul, let them gather it into the artifice of eternity and make the old man like themselves; even Byzantium, so long as the flesh be present, is no country for old men.

What it is to be like these, the soul, as yet uninstructed, can only conjecture; at any rate, with the destruction of the flesh it will be free of its ills; and if, as in Plato's myth of Er, the soul after death is free to choose some new embodiment, it will never again elect the flesh which is so quickly corruptible and which enslaves it to passion; it will choose some such form of art as that of the artificial birds in Theophilus' garden [2] it will be of incorruptible and passionless gold; and it will dwell among leaves and boughs which are also of incorruptible and passionless metal. And now all sources of conflict are resolved in this last: the old has become the ageless; impotency has been exchanged for a higher power; the soul is free of passion and free for its joy, and

---

[2] In his note to the poem (*Collected Poems*, New York, 1933, p. 450) Yeats remarks: "I have read somewhere that in the Emperor's palace at Byzantium was a tree made of gold and silver, and artificial birds that sang." Undoubtedly the Emperor was Theophilus (829–842), and the birds conform to the descriptions of certain automata constructed for him by Leo Mathematicus and John Hylilas. Cf. *Hist. Byzan. Script. post Theoph.*, Anon. Cont. Theoph., 107; Constantini Manassis, *Brev. Hist.*, 107; and Michaeli Glycae, *Annales*, 292. See also Gibbon, *Decline and Fall*, Chapter LIII, and George Finlay, *History of the Byzantine Empire* (London, 1906), pp. 140, 148, where further references are given.

it sings as youth once sang, but now of "What is past, and passing, and to come"—of the divisions of Eternity—rather than of "Whatever is begotten, born, and dies"—of the divisions of mortal time. And it has here its country, its proper and permanent habitation.

ROBERT FROST

[1875-   ]

ROBERT FROST was born in San Francisco. His parents were both teachers, his father also a journalist. Frost moved east to school at Dartmouth and Harvard, married, and from 1900 to 1912 lived in New Hampshire working as a farmer, teacher, and unpublished poet. Although Frost is identified with American subjects and the New England voice, his first two books, *A Boy's Will* (1913) and *North of Boston* (1914), were published in England, where Ezra Pound was one of the first to praise him. Frost had moved to England in 1912, but after 1915 returned to America to live in New Hampshire and Vermont, where he has been writing, farming, teaching at universities, lecturing, giving poetry readings, and in general reaching the world with his cryptic, conversational poems out of nature. He has received four Pulitzer prizes: 1924, for *New Hampshire* (1923); 1931, for *Collected Poems* (1930); 1937, for *A Further Range* (1936); and 1943, for *A Witness Tree* (1942). Frost has published more than a dozen volumes of poetry, including two verse plays, *A Masque of Reason* and *A Masque of Mercy*. Although his poetry often sounds simple, it is more curved than direct, usually irreverent, and full of surprise. He has spent his whole life as a poet in what he calls "a lover's quarrel with the world."

Introductory Readings

EDITION: *Complete Poems* (1949). BIOGRAPHY AND CRITICISM: Gorham Munson, *Robert Frost: A Study in Sensibility and Good Sense* (1927); Lawrance Thompson, *Fire and Ice: The Art and Thought of Robert Frost* (1942); Sidney Cox, *A Swinger of Birches: A Portrait of Robert Frost* (1957); Elizabeth Shepley Sergeant, *Robert Frost: The Trial by Existence* (1960).

THE PASTURE

I'm going out to clean the pasture spring;
I'll only stop to rake the leaves away
(And wait to watch the water clear, I may):
I sha'n't be gone long.—You come too.

I'm going out to fetch the little calf   5
That's standing by the mother. It's so young
It totters when she licks it with her tongue.
I sha'n't be gone long.—You come too.

MOWING

There was never a sound beside the wood but one,
And that was my long scythe whispering to the ground.
What was it it whispered? I knew not well myself;
Perhaps it was something about the heat of the sun,
Something, perhaps, about the lack of sound—   5
And that was why it whispered and did not speak.
It was no dream of the gift of idle hours,
Or easy gold at the hand of fay or elf:
Anything more than the truth would have seemed too weak
To the earnest love that laid the swale in rows,   10
Not without feeble-pointed spikes of flowers
(Pale orchises [1]), and scared a bright green snake.
The fact is the sweetest dream that labor knows.
My long scythe whispered and left the hay to make.

MENDING WALL

Something there is that doesn't love a wall,
That sends the frozen-ground-swell under it,
And spills the upper boulders in the sun;
And makes gaps even two can pass abreast.
The work of hunters is another thing: 5
I have come after them and made repair
Where they have left not one stone on a stone,
But they would have the rabbit out of hiding,
To please the yelping dogs. The gaps I mean,
No one has seen them made or heard them made,   10

[1] *orchises* orchids

But at spring mending-time we find them there.
I let my neighbor know beyond the hill;
And on a day we meet to walk the line
And set the wall between us once again.
We keep the wall between us as we go.   15
To each the boulders that have fallen to each.
And some are loaves and some so nearly balls
We have to use a spell to make them balance:
'Stay where you are until our backs are turned!'
We wear our fingers rough with handling them.   20
Oh, just another kind of outdoor game,
One on a side. It comes to little more:
There where it is we do not need the wall:
He is all pine and I am apple orchard.
My apple trees will never get across   25
And eat the cones under his pines, I tell him.
He only says, 'Good fences make good neighbors.'
Spring is the mischief in me, and I wonder
If I could put a notion in his head:
'*Why* do they make good neighbors? Isn't it   30
Where there are cows? But here there are no cows.
Before I built a wall I'd ask to know
What I was walling in or walling out,
And to whom I was like to give offense.
Something there is that doesn't love a wall,   35
That wants it down.' I could say 'Elves' to him,
But it's not elves exactly, and I'd rather
He said it for himself. I see him there
Bringing a stone grasped firmly by the top
In each hand, like an old-stone savage armed.   40
He moves in darkness as it seems to me,
Not of woods only and the shade of trees.
He will not go behind his father's saying,
And he likes having thought of it so well
He says again, 'Good fences make good neighbors.'   45

AFTER APPLE-PICKING

My long two-pointed ladder's sticking through a tree
Toward heaven still,
And there's a barrel that I didn't fill
Beside it, and there may be two or three
Apples I didn't pick upon some bough.   5

But I am done with apple-picking now.
Essence of winter sleep is on the night,
The scent of apples: I am drowsing off.
I cannot rub the strangeness from my sight
I got from looking through a pane of glass   10
I skimmed this morning from the drinking trough
And held against the world of hoary grass.
It melted, and I let it fall and break.
But I was well
Upon my way to sleep before it fell,   15
And I could tell
What form my dreaming was about to take.
Magnified apples appear and disappear,
Stem end and blossom end,
And every fleck of russet showing clear.   20
My instep arch not only keeps the ache,
It keeps the pressure of a ladder-round.
I feel the ladder sway as the boughs bend.
And I keep hearing from the cellar bin
The rumbling sound   25
Of load on load of apples coming in.
For I have had too much
Of apple-picking: I am overtired
Of the great harvest I myself desired.
There were ten thousand thousand fruit to touch,   30
Cherish in hand, lift down, and not let fall.
For all
That struck the earth,
No matter if not bruised or spiked with stubble,
Went surely to the cider-apple heap   35
As of no worth.
One can see what will trouble
This sleep of mine, whatever sleep it is.
Were he not gone,
The woodchuck could say whether it's like his   40
Long sleep, as I describe its coming on,
Or just some human sleep.

THE ROAD NOT TAKEN

Two roads diverged in a yellow wood,
And sorry I could not travel both
And be one traveler, long I stood

And looked down one as far as I could
To where it bent in the undergrowth;   5

Then took the other, as just as fair,
And having perhaps the better claim,
Because it was grassy and wanted wear;
Though as for that the passing there
Had worn them really about the same,   10

And both that morning equally lay
In leaves no step had trodden black.
Oh, I kept the first for another day!
Yet knowing how way leads on to way,
I doubted if I should ever come back.   15

I shall be telling this with a sigh
Somewhere ages and ages hence:
Two roads diverged in a wood, and I—
I took the one less traveled by,
And that has made all the difference.   20

BIRCHES

When I see birches bend to left and right
Across the lines of straighter darker trees,
I like to think some boy's been swinging them.
But swinging doesn't bend them down to stay
As ice-storms do. Often you must have seen them   5
Loaded with ice a sunny winter morning
After a rain. They click upon themselves
As the breeze rises, and turn many-colored
As the stir cracks and crazes their enamel.
Soon the sun's warmth makes them shed crystal shells   10
Shattering and avalanching on the snow-crust—
Such heaps of broken glass do sweep away
You'd think the inner dome of heaven had fallen.
They are dragged to the withered bracken by the load,
And they seem not to break; though once they are bowed   15
So low for long, they never right themselves:
You may see their trunks arching in the woods
Years afterwards, trailing their leaves on the ground
Like girls on hands and knees that throw their hair
Before them over their heads to dry in the sun.   20
But I was going to say when Truth broke in
With all her matter-of-fact about the ice-storm

I should prefer to have some boy bend them
As he went out and in to fetch the cows—
Some boy too far from town to learn baseball,   25
Whose only play was what he found himself,
Summer or winter, and could play alone.
One by one he subdued his father's trees
By riding them down over and over again
Until he took the stiffness out of them,   30
And not one but hung limp, not one was left
For him to conquer. He learned all there was
To learn about not launching out too soon
And so not carrying the tree away
Clear to the ground. He always kept his poise   35
To the top branches, climbing carefully
With the same pains you use to fill a cup
Up to the brim, and even above the brim.
Then he flung outward, feet first, with a swish,
Kicking his way down through the air to the ground.   40
So was I once myself a swinger of birches.
And so I dream of going back to be.
It's when I'm weary of considerations,
And life is too much like a pathless wood
Where your face burns and tickles with the cobwebs   45
Broken across it, and one eye is weeping
From a twig's having lashed across it open.
I'd like to get away from earth awhile
And then come back to it and begin over.
May no fate willfully misunderstand me   50
And half grant what I wish and snatch me away
Not to return. Earth's the right place for love:
I don't know where it's likely to go better.
I'd like to go by climbing a birch tree,
And climb black branches up a snow-white trunk   55
Toward heaven, till the tree could bear no more,
But dipped its top and set me down again.
That would be good both going and coming back.
One could do worse than be a swinger of birches.

THE WITCH OF COÖS [1]

I stayed the night for shelter at a farm
Behind the mountain, with a mother and son,
Two old-believers. They did all the talking.

[1] *Coös* a county in northern New Hampshire

MOTHER. Folks think a witch who has familiar spirits
She could call up to pass a winter evening, 5
But won't, should be burned at the stake or something.
Summoning spirits isn't 'Button, button,
Who's got the button,' I would have them know.

SON. Mother can make a common table rear
And kick with two legs like an army mule. 10

MOTHER. And when I've done it, what good have I done?
Rather than tip a table for you, let me
Tell you what Ralle the Sioux Control once told me.
He said the dead had souls, but when I asked him
How could that be—I thought the dead were souls, 15
He broke my trance. Don't that make you suspicious
That there's something the dead are keeping back?
Yes, there's something the dead are keeping back.

SON. You wouldn't want to tell him what we have
Up attic, mother? 20

MOTHER. Bones—a skeleton.

SON. But the headboard of mother's bed is pushed
Against the attic door: the door is nailed.
It's harmless. Mother hears it in the night
Halting perplexed behind the barrier 25
Of door and headboard. Where it wants to get
Is back into the cellar where it came from.

MOTHER. We'll never let them, will we, son! We'll never!

SON. It left the cellar forty years ago
And carried itself like a pile of dishes 30
Up one flight from the cellar to the kitchen,
Another from the kitchen to the bedroom,
Another from the bedroom to the attic,
Right past both father and mother, and neither stopped it.
Father had gone upstairs; mother was downstairs. 35
I was a baby: I don't know where I was.

MOTHER. The only fault my husband found with me—
I went to sleep before I went to bed,
Especially in winter when the bed
Might just as well be ice and the clothes snow. 40
The night the bones came up the cellar-stairs
Toffile had gone to bed alone and left me,

But left an open door to cool the room off
So as to sort of turn me out of it.
I was just coming to myself enough   45
To wonder where the cold was coming from,
When I heard Toffile upstairs in the bedroom
And thought I heard him downstairs in the cellar.
The board we had laid down to walk dry-shod on
When there was water in the cellar in spring   50
Struck the hard cellar bottom. And then someone
Began the stairs, two footsteps for each step,
The way a man with one leg and a crutch,
Or a little child, comes up. It wasn't Toffile:
It wasn't anyone who could be there.   55
The bulkhead double-doors were double-locked
And swollen tight and buried under snow.
The cellar windows were banked up with sawdust
And swollen tight and buried under snow.
It was the bones. I knew them—and good reason.   60
My first impulse was to get to the knob
And hold the door. But the bones didn't try
The door; they halted helpless on the landing,
Waiting for things to happen in their favor.
The faintest restless rustling ran all through them.   65
I never could have done the thing I did
If the wish hadn't been too strong in me
To see how they were mounted for this walk.
I had a vision of them put together
Not like a man, but like a chandelier.   70
So suddenly I flung the door wide on him.
A moment he stood balancing with emotion,
And all but lost himself. (A tongue of fire
Flashed out and licked along his upper teeth.
Smoke rolled inside the sockets of his eyes.)   75
Then he came at me with one hand outstretched,
The way he did in life once; but this time
I struck the hand off brittle on the floor,
And fell back from him on the floor myself.
The finger-pieces slid in all directions.   80
(Where did I see one of those pieces lately?
Hand me my button-box—it must be there.)
I sat up on the floor and shouted, 'Toffile,
It's coming up to you.' It had its choice
Of the door to the cellar or the hall.   85
It took the hall door for the novelty,

And set off briskly for so slow a thing,
Still going every which way in the joints, though,
So that it looked like lightning or a scribble,
From the slap I had just now given its hand.   90
I listened till it almost climbed the stairs
From the hall to the only finished bedroom,
Before I got up to do anything;
Then ran and shouted, 'Shut the bedroom door,
Toffile, for my sake!' 'Company?' he said,   95
'Don't make me get up; I'm too warm in bed.'
So lying forward weakly on the handrail
I pushed myself upstairs, and in the light
(The kitchen had been dark) I had to own
I could see nothing. 'Toffile, I don't see it.   100
It's with us in the room though. It's the bones.'
'What bones?' 'The cellar bones—out of the grave.'
That made him throw his bare legs out of bed
And sit up by me and take hold of me.
I wanted to put out the light and see   105
If I could see it, or else mow the room,
With our arms at the level of our knees,
And bring the chalk-pile down. 'I'll tell you what—
It's looking for another door to try.
The uncommonly deep snow has made him think   110
Of his old song, *The Wild Colonial Boy,*
He always used to sing along the tote road.
He's after an open door to get outdoors.
Let's trap him with an open door up attic.'
Toffile agreed to that, and sure enough,   115
Almost the moment he was given an opening,
The steps began to climb the attic stairs.
I heard them. Toffile didn't seem to hear them.
'Quick!' I slammed to the door and held the knob.
'Toffile, get nails.' I made him nail the door shut   120
And push the headboard of the bed against it.
Then we asked was there anything
Up attic that we'd ever want again.
The attic was less to us than the cellar.
If the bones liked the attic, let them have it.   125
Let them stay in the attic. When they sometimes
Come down the stairs at night and stand perplexed
Behind the door and headboard of the bed,
Brushing their chalky skull with chalky fingers,
With sounds like the dry rattling of a shutter,   130

That's what I sit up in the dark to say—
To no one any more since Toffile died.
Let them stay in the attic since they went there.
I promised Toffile to be cruel to them
For helping them be cruel once to him.   135

SON. We think they had a grave down in the cellar.

MOTHER. We know they had a grave down in the cellar.

SON. We never could find out whose bones they were.

MOTHER. Yes, we could too, son. Tell the truth for once.
They were a man's his father killed for me.   140
I mean a man he killed instead of me.
The least I could do was to help dig their grave.
We were about it one night in the cellar.
Son knows the story: but 'twas not for him
To tell the truth, suppose the time had come.   145
Son looks surprised to see me end a lie
We'd kept all these years between ourselves
So as to have it ready for outsiders.
But tonight I don't care enough to lie—
I don't remember why I ever cared.   150
Toffile, if he were here, I don't believe
Could tell you why he ever cared himself. . . .

She hadn't found the finger-bone she wanted
Among the buttons poured out in her lap.
I verified the name next morning: Toffile.   155
The rural letter box said Toffile Lajway.

FIRE AND ICE

Some say the world will end in fire,
Some say in ice.
From what I've tasted of desire
I hold with those who favor fire.
But if it had to perish twice,   5
I think I know enough of hate
To say that for destruction ice
Is also great
And would suffice.

STOPPING BY WOODS ON A SNOWY EVENING

Whose woods these are I think I know.
His house is in the village though;
He will not see me stopping here
To watch his woods fill up with snow.

My little horse must think it queer 5
To stop without a farmhouse near
Between the woods and frozen lake
The darkest evening of the year.

He gives his harness bells a shake
To ask if there is some mistake. 10
The only other sound's the sweep
Of easy wind and downy flake.

The woods are lovely, dark and deep.
But I have promises to keep,
And miles to go before I sleep, 15
And miles to go before I sleep.

A HILLSIDE THAW

To think to know the country and not know
The hillside on the day the sun lets go
Ten million silver lizards out of snow!
As often as I've seen it done before
I can't pretend to tell the way it's done. 5
It looks as if some magic of the sun
Lifted the rug that bred them on the floor
And the light breaking on them made them run.
But if I thought to stop the wet stampede,
And caught one silver lizard by the tail, 10
And put my foot on one without avail,
And threw myself wet-elbowed and wet-kneed
In front of twenty others' wriggling speed,—
In the confusion of them all aglitter,
And birds that joined in the excited fun 15
By doubling and redoubling song and twitter,
I have no doubt I'd end by holding none.

It takes the moon for this. The sun's a wizard
By all I tell; but so's the moon a witch.

From the high west she makes a gentle cast   20
And suddenly, without a jerk or twitch,
She has her spell on every single lizard.
I fancied when I looked at six o'clock
The swarm still ran and scuttled just as fast.
The moon was waiting for her chill effect.   25
I looked at nine: the swarm was turned to rock
In every lifelike posture of the swarm,
Transfixed on mountain slopes almost erect.
Across each other and side by side they lay.
The spell that so could hold them as they were   30
Was wrought through trees without a breath of storm
To make a leaf, if there had been one, stir.
It was the moon's: she held them until day,
One lizard at the end of every ray.
The thought of my attempting such a stay!   35

SPRING POOLS

These pools that, though in forests, still reflect
The total sky almost without defect,
And like the flowers beside them, chill and shiver,
Will like the flowers beside them soon be gone,
And yet not out by any brook or river,   5
But up by roots to bring dark foliage on.

The trees that have it in their pent-up buds
To darken nature and be summer woods—
Let them think twice before they use their powers
To blot out and drink up and sweep away   10
These flowery waters and these watery flowers
From snow that melted only yesterday.

ACQUAINTED WITH THE NIGHT

I have been one acquainted with the night.
I have walked out in rain—and back in rain.
I have outwalked the furthest city light.

I have looked down the saddest city lane.
I have passed by the watchman on his beat   5
And dropped my eyes, unwilling to explain.

I have stood still and stopped the sound of feet
When far away an interrupted cry
Came over houses from another street,

But not to call me back or say good-by;   10
And further still at an unearthly height,
One luminary clock against the sky

Proclaimed the time was neither wrong nor right.
I have been one acquainted with the night.

WEST-RUNNING BROOK

'Fred, where is north?'

                              'North? North is there, my love.
The brook runs west.'

                              'West-running Brook then call it.'
(West-running Brook men call it to this day.)   5
'What does it think it's doing running west
When all the other country brooks flow east
To reach the ocean? It must be the brook
Can trust itself to go by contraries
The way I can with you—and you with me—   10
Because we're—we're—I don't know what we are.
What are we?'

                              'Young or new?'

                              'We must be something.
We've said we two. Let's change that to we three.   15
As you and I are married to each other,
We'll both be married to the brook. We'll build
Our bridge across it, and the bridge shall be
Our arm thrown over it asleep beside it.
Look, look, it's waving to us with a wave   20
To let us know it hears me.'

                              'Why, my dear,
That wave's been standing off this jut of shore—'
(The black stream, catching on a sunken rock,
Flung backward on itself in one white wave,   25
And the white water rode the black forever,
Not gaining but not losing, like a bird
White feathers from the struggle of whose breast
Flecked the dark stream and flecked the darker pool
Below the point, and were at last driven wrinkled   30
In a white scarf against the far shore alders.)
'That wave's been standing off this jut of shore

Ever since rivers, I was going to say,
Were made in heaven. It wasn't waved to us.'

'It wasn't, yet it was. If not to you   35
It was to me—in an annunciation.'

'Oh, if you take it off to lady-land,
As't were the country of the Amazons
We men must see you to the confines of
And leave you there, ourselves forbid to enter;—   40
It is your brook! I have no more to say.'

'Yes, you have, too. Go on. You thought of something.'
'Speaking of contraries, see how the brook
In that white wave runs counter to itself.
It is from that in water we were from   45
Long, long before we were from any creature.
Here we, in our impatience of the steps,
Get back to the beginning of beginnings,
The stream of everything that runs away.
Some say existence like a Pirouot   50
And Pirouette,[1] forever in one place,
Stands still and dances, but it runs away,
It seriously, sadly, runs away
To fill the abyss' void with emptiness.
It flows beside us in this water brook,   55
But it flows over us. It flows between us
To separate us for a panic moment.
It flows between us, over us, and *with* us.
And it is time, strength, tone, light, life, and love—
And even substance lapsing unsubstantial;   60
The universal cataract of death
That spends to nothingness—and unresisted,
Save by some strange resistance in itself,
Not just a swerving, but a throwing back,
As if regret were in it and were sacred.   65
It has this throwing backward on itself
So that the fall of most of it is always
Raising a little, sending up a little.
Our life runs down in sending up the clock.
The brook runs down in sending up our life.   70
The sun runs down in sending up the brook.
And there is something sending up the sun.

[1] *Pirouot . . . Pirouette* male and female characters in French comic pantomime; a pirouette is a whirling about on one foot or on the toes in ballet

It is this backward motion toward the source,
Against the stream, that most we see ourselves in,
The tribute of the current to the source.   75
It is from this in nature we are from.
It is most us.'

           'Today will be the day
You said so.'

            'No, today will be the day   80
You said the brook was called West-running Brook.'

'Today will be the day of what we both said.'

DEPARTMENTAL

An ant on the tablecloth
Ran into a dormant moth
Of many times his size.
He showed not the least surprise.
His business wasn't with such.   5
He gave it scarcely a touch,
And was off on his duty run.
Yet if he encountered one
Of the hive's enquiry squad
Whose work is to find out God   10
And the nature of time and space,
He would put him onto the case.
Ants are a curious race;
One crossing with hurried tread
The body of one of their dead   15
Isn't given a moment's arrest—
Seems not even impressed.
But he no doubt reports to any
With whom he crosses antennae,
And they no doubt report   20
To the higher up at court.
Then word goes forth in Formic: [1]
'Death's come to Jerry McCormic,
Our selfless forager Jerry.
Will the special Janizary [2]   25
Whose office it is to bury
The dead of the commissary

---

[1] *Formic* acid, occurring in some ants   [2] *Janizary* Turkish soldier

Go bring him home to his people.
Lay him in state on a sepal.[3]
Wrap him for shroud in a petal.   30
Embalm him with ichor [4] of nettle.
This is the word of your Queen.'
And presently on the scene
Appears a solemn mortician;
And taking formal position   35
With feelers calmly atwiddle,
Seizes the dead by the middle,
And heaving him high in air,
Carries him out of there.
No one stands round to stare.   40
It is nobody else's affair.

It couldn't be called ungentle.
But how thoroughly departmental.

DESERT PLACES

Snow falling and night falling fast, oh, fast
In a field I looked into going past,
And the ground almost covered smooth in snow,
But a few weeds and stubble showing last.

The woods around it have it—it is theirs.   5
All animals are smothered in their lairs.
I am too absent-spirited to count;
The loneliness includes me unawares.

And lonely as it is that loneliness
Will be more lonely ere it will be less—   10
A blanker whiteness of benighted snow
With no expression, nothing to express.

They cannot scare me with their empty spaces
Between stars—on stars where no human race is.
I have it in me so much nearer home   15
To scare myself with my own desert places.

MOON COMPASSES

I stole forth dimly in the dripping pause
Between two downpours to see what there was.

[3] *sepal* a leaf of the calyx   [4] *ichor* fluid in the veins of the gods

And a masked moon had spread down compass rays
To a cone mountain in the midnight haze,
As if the final estimate were hers,   5
And as it measured in her calipers,
The mountain stood exalted in its place.
So love will take between the hands a face. . . .

NEITHER OUT FAR NOR IN DEEP

The people along the sand
All turn and look one way.
They turn their back on the land.
They look at the sea all day.

As long as it takes to pass   5
A ship keeps raising its hull;
The wetter ground like glass
Reflects a standing gull.

The land may vary more;
But wherever the truth may be—   10
The water comes ashore,
And the people look at the sea.

They cannot look out far.
They cannot look in deep.
But when was that ever a bar   15
To any watch they keep?

THE SPAN OF LIFE

The old dog barks backward without getting up.
I can remember when he was a pup.

COME IN

As I came to the edge of the woods,
Thrush music—hark!
Now if it was dusk outside,
Inside it was dark.

Too dark in the woods for a bird   5
By sleight of wing
To better its perch for the night,
Though it still could sing.

The last of the light of the sun
That had died in the west   10
Still lived for one song more
In a thrush's breast.

Far in the pillared dark
Thrush music went—
Almost like a call to come in   15
To the dark and lament.

But no, I was out for stars:
I would not come in.
I meant not even if asked,
And I hadn't been.   20

DIRECTIVE

Back out of all this now too much for us,
Back in a time made simple by the loss
Of detail, burned, dissolved, and broken off
Like graveyard marble sculpture in the weather,
There is a house that is no more a house   5
Upon a farm that is no more a farm
And in a town that is no more a town.
The road there, if you'll let a guide direct you
Who only has at heart your getting lost,
May seem as if it should have been a quarry—   10
Great monolithic [1] knees the former town
Long since gave up pretense of keeping covered.
And there's a story in a book about it:
Besides the wear of iron wagon wheels
The ledges show lines ruled southeast northwest,   15
The chisel work of an enormous Glacier
That braced his feet against the Arctic Pole.
You must not mind a certain coolness from him
Still said to haunt this side of Panther Mountain.
Nor need you mind the serial ordeal   20
Of being watched from forty cellar holes
As if by eye pairs out of forty firkins. [2]
As for the woods' excitement over you
That sends light rustle rushes to their leaves,
Charge that to upstart inexperience.   25

[1] *monolithic* made in large slabs of stone
[2] *firkin* small wooden container for butter

Where were they all not twenty years ago?
They think too much of having shaded out
A few old pecker-fretted apple trees.[3]
Make yourself up a cheering song of how
Someone's road home from work this once was,   30
Who may be just ahead of you on foot
Or creaking with a buggy load of grain.
The height of the adventure is the height
Of country where two village cultures faded
Into each other. Both of them are lost.   35
And if you're lost enough to find yourself
By now, pull in your ladder road behind you
And put a sign up CLOSED to all but me.
Then make yourself at home. The only field
Now left's no bigger than a harness gall.   40
First there's the children's house of make believe,
Some shattered dishes underneath a pine,
The playthings in the playhouse of the children.
Weep for what little things could make them glad.
Then for the house that is no more a house,   45
But only a belilaced cellar hole,
Now slowly closing like a dent in dough.
This was no playhouse but a house in earnest.
Your destination and your destiny's
A brook that was the water of the house,   50
Cold as a spring as yet so near its source,
Too lofty and original to rage.
(We know the valley streams that when aroused
Will leave their tatters hung on barb and thorn.)
I have kept hidden in the instep arch   55
Of an old cedar at the waterside
A broken drinking goblet like the Grail [4]
Under a spell so the wrong ones can't find it,
So can't get saved, as Saint Mark says they mustn't.
(I stole the goblet from the children's playhouse.)   60
Here are your waters and your watering place.
Drink and be whole again beyond confusion.

[3] *pecker-fretted apple trees* apple trees fretted (decorated or damaged) by
woodpeckers
[4] *Grail* the goblet from which Christ drank at the Last Supper; according
to legend it could be seen only by the pure

CRITICISM

When a reader has read deeply into the entire poetry of a single poet, he soon discovers that poems begin to illuminate each other, that images which seemed simple become complex, while complex images turn simple. The following essay concentrates on a single image, the dark woods, in Frost's poetry. By the time the critic has traced it through all the poems, he has discovered a meaning for the dark woods that no analysis, however intense, of a single poem would yield. By focusing on specific appearances of recurring image, the critic finds his way to some persuasive generalizations about the psychological symbolism in Frost's poetry. There are, of course, many other ways of seeing the individual poems. An adventurous reader will discover many perspectives of his own.

From Woods to Stars: a Pattern of Imagery in Robert Frost's Poetry [1]

JOHN T. OGILVIE

Leaves are all my darker mood

Together with "Birches," "Mending Wall," "The Road Not Taken," "After Apple-Picking," and a dozen or so other familar descriptive pieces, "Stopping by Woods on a Snowy Evening" is one of Robert Frost's most admired poems. The beginning poetry student in particular is likely to take to it, for quite understandable reasons: its diction is unpretentious and subtly musical; it presents an engaging picture and hints at a "story" without too much taxing the imagination; it is short and seemingly unambiguous. And the teacher, from his side, likewise welcomes the opportunity to present a poem that can be enjoyed purely for its visual and verbal interest without having to be subjected to a rigorous search for "hidden meanings." But, as experienced readers of this poem know, "Stopping by Woods" has a disconcerting way of deepening in dimension as one looks at it, of

[1] Extracted from John T. Ogilvie's essay, "From Woods to Stars: A Pattern of Imagery in Robert Frost's Poetry," first published in the *South Atlantic Quarterly,* 58 (Winter, 1959).

darkening in tone, until it emerges as a full-blown critical and pedagogical problem. One comes to feel that there *is* more in the poem than is given to the senses alone. But how is one to treat a poem which has so simple and clear a descriptive surface, yet which somehow implies a complex emotional attitude? To what extent and in what ways is one's experience of the poem different from, or the same as, the poet's experience? Can one's "feeling" about the poem be either proved or disproved, when so few footholds for interpretation are offered by the poem itself? Is *any* interpretation bound to be the result of "reading in" meanings of one's own?

These questions are too delicate to be acted upon hastily. Certainly, to construe the poem, as some critics have, as expressing a "humanistic" or "agnostic" view of life, or as projecting an unconscious "death-wish," is to impose a pretty heavy burden upon so brief and unassuming a lyric. Although it would be a mistake wholly to reject these interpretations, nevertheless it is unlikely that any one of them can be established as a conclusive reading solely on the evidence of the single poem. "Stopping by Woods," I believe, represents one of those junctures where the critic must enlarge on his findings through searching comparisons with other of the author's productions. Taken in isolation, "Stopping by Woods" gives only a partial view (and for some readers possibly a misleading view) of what is actually an absorbing and central concern in Frost's poetry. The collaboration of a number of related poems is required to reveal this preoccupation in its entirety.

The visible sign of the poet's preoccupation—the word is not too strong—is the recurrent image, particularly in his earlier work, of dark woods and trees. Often, as in the lyric with which we have begun, the world of the woods (for such in effect it becomes), a world offering perfect quiet and solitude, exists side by side with the realization that there is also another world, a world of people and social obligations. Both worlds have claims on the poet. He stops by woods on this "darkest evening of the year" to watch them "fill up with snow," and lingers so long that his "little horse" shakes his harness bells "to ask if there is some mistake." The poet is put in mind of the "promises" he has to keep, of the miles he still must travel. We are not told, however, that the call of social responsibility proves stronger than the attraction of the woods, which are "lovely" as well as "dark and deep"; the poet and his horse have not moved on at the poem's end. The dichotomy of the poet's obligations both to the woods and to a world of "promises"—the latter filtering like a barely heard echo through the almost hypnotic state induced by the woods and falling snow—is what gives this poem its singular interest. If its "meanings" were more overt, it would be less interesting, less an authentically conveyed experience. The artfulness of "Stopping by Woods" consists in the way the two worlds are established and balanced. The poet is aware that the woods by which he is stopping belong to someone in the village; they are owned by the world of men. But at the same time they are *his*, the poet's woods, too, by virtue of what they mean to him in terms of emotion and private signification.

In Frost's first book, *A Boy's Will* (1913), we find a dark-woods imagery used repeatedly. It is not too much to say that the quiet drama of youthful love portrayed in the subjective lyrics of this volume takes place within the constant shadow of surrounding trees. That the trees are themselves part of this drama, and not simply descriptive background, is evident from such pieces as "Going for Water" and "A Dream Pang," in which the act of withdrawing into "forest" and "wood" becomes the very subject of the poem and is endowed with an undefined, almost ritualistic significance. In the first poem, husband and wife enter a wood together on a moonlit autumn evening to get water from a brook. In the second, the poet dreams that he has "withdrawn in forest," his song "swallowed up in leaves. . . ." He watches his wife, who comes to the edge of the forest in search of him, "behind low boughs the trees let down outside," but does not call to her, though it costs him a "sweet pang" not to do so. The overtones here may be too "romantic" for most readers, but the psychological pattern symbolized is of considerable interest in a total view of Frost's poetry.

The imagery of dark woods, woven so indelibly into the texture of these early poems, persists in succeeding collections. "The Road Not Taken," introductory to *Mountain Interval* (1916), can be read as a further commentary on the price of the poet's dedication. The two roads that "diverged in a yellow wood" represent a critical choice between two ways of life. The poet takes "the one less traveled by," the lonelier road which, we can presume, leads deeper into the wood. Knowing "how way leads on to way," he doubts that he "should ever come back." His choice has made "all the difference," yet it is a choice that he shall be recounting "with a sigh . . . ages and ages hence." He is thinking also of "the road not taken." The dark woods, though they hold a salutary privacy, impose a stern isolation, an isolation endured not without cost. In the poem "An Encounter," the poet pictures himself "half boring through, half climbing through a swamp of cedar," weary and overheated, and sorry he had ever left the road he knew. While resting, he looks skyward and sees above him "a barkless specter," a telegraph pole "dragging yellow strands of wire with something in it from men to men." This unexpected intrusion of the outer world of human society into the poet's inner world of trackless wood is occasion for ironic inquiry:

> "You here?" I said. "Where aren't you nowadays?
> And what's the news you carry—if you know?
> And tell me where you're off for—Montreal?
> Me? I'm not off for anywhere at all.
> Sometimes I wander out of beaten ways
> Half looking for the orchid Calypso."

The poet's quest, in contrast to the unswerving telegraph lines, appears to lack direction and purpose. The poet is alone, in communication only with himself.

In all of these poems, the imagery of woods, trees, and leaves is so intimately and persistently identified with certain psychological states as to assume a symbolic significance. The dark woods represent the privacy of the self, the sacred domain where poetry is made. Their area is the area of the poet's introspective life, his subjective experience. The pattern of feelings established by this recurrent imagery is fluctuating and ambivalent. The poet guards and cherishes the woods as his own, but there are times when he must close his windows against them and turn outward toward the larger world of social intercourse. There is lurking terror in his woods as well as keen pleasure, numbing loneliness as well as quiet satisfaction; one can as much lose himself there as find himself. This becomes more apparent as the poet grows older and his introspective life deepens. In "Leaves

Compared with Flowers" (*A Further Range*) he confesses that "leaves are all my darker mood," and finally he reaches a point when he cannot be enticed into the dark woods at all.

When viewed as part of this pattern, such a poem as "Stopping by Woods" is put into meaningful perspective. What appears to be "simple" is shown to be not *really* simple, what appears to be innocent not *really* innocent. "Sight and insight," Frost has said, "are the whole business of the poet." They are also the whole business of the poet's readers. What to sight is presented as a literal scene, to insight is revealed as the objectification of a psychological state. The nature of that state is complex. The poet is fascinated and lulled by the empty wastes of white and black. The repetition of "sleep" in the final two lines suggests that he may succumb to the influences that are at work. There is no reason to suppose that these influences are benignant. It is, after all, "the darkest evening of the year," and the poet is alone "between the woods and frozen lake." His one bond with the security and warmth of the "outer" world, the "little horse" who wants to be about his errand, is an unsure one. The ascription of "lovely" to this scene of desolate woods, effacing snow, and black night complicates rather than alleviates the mood when we consider how pervasive are the connotations of dangerous isolation and menacing death. The same imagistic elements work more overtly toward the same end in "The Onset" (also from *New Hampshire*, 1923) and "Desert Places" (*A Further Range*), one of Frost's starkest expressions of the isolated self.

THOMAS STEARNS ELIOT

[1888-   ]

T. S. ELIOT is an American-English poet. He was born in St. Louis, Missouri; attended Harvard, the Sorbonne, and Oxford; and by 1915 had settled in England where he worked as teacher, bank clerk, and editor. His first books—*Prufrock and Other Observations* (1917), *Poems* (1920), and especially *The Waste Land* (1922)—were in style and theme the perfect expressions of postwar disillusionment. They affected more than a generation of writers. Through the 20's and 30's other volumes appeared: *Journey of the Magi* (1927), *Marina* (1930), *Sweeney Agonistes* (1932), and in a change of pace, *Old Possum's Book of Practical Cats* (1939). After Eliot's strong turn to Anglicanism in the late 1920's, his poetry was no longer of the waste land, but of religious themes and convictions. Particularly important in these later poems are *Ash Wednesday* (1930) and *Four Quartets* (1939–1943). In 1935 Eliot began writing verse plays, *Murder in the Cathedral* (1935) and *The Cocktail Party* (1949) having considerable success on the stage. Eliot has also written notable literary criticism and essays, including *The Sacred Wood* (1920) and *Notes Toward the Definition of Culture* (1948). He has been a British subject and Anglican since 1927; is the director of the publishing firm of Faber and Faber. In 1948 he received the Nobel Prize for Literature. Through both his poetry and his criticism, T. S. Eliot has been one of the most important influences on the literature of our time.

Introductory Readings

EDITION: *The Complete Poems and Plays,* 1909–1950 (1952). CRITICISM: F. O. Matthiessen, *The Achievement of T. S. Eliot* (rev. ed. 1947); Helen Gardner, *The Art of T. S. Eliot* (1949); Grover Smith, Jr.,

T. S. Eliot's Poetry and Plays (1956); George Williamson, *A Reader's Guide to T. S. Eliot* (1953).

THE LOVE SONG OF J. ALFRED PRUFROCK

> *S'io credesse che mia risposta fosse*
> *A persona che mai tornasse al mondo,*
> *Questa fiamma staria senza piu scosse.*
> *Ma perciocche giammai di questo fondo*
> *Non torno vivo alcun, s'i'odo il vero,*
> *Senza tema d'infamia ti rispondo.*[1]

Let us go then, you and I,
When the evening is spread out against the sky
Like a patient etherised upon a table;
Let us go, through certain half-deserted streets,
The muttering retreats   5
Of restless nights in one-night cheap hotels
And sawdust restaurants with oyster-shells:
Streets that follow like a tedious argument
Of insidious intent
To lead you to an overwhelming question . . .   10
Oh, do not ask, "What is it?"
Let us go and make our visit.

In the room the women come and go
Talking of Michelangelo.

The yellow fog that rubs its back upon the window-
     panes,   15
The yellow smoke that rubs its muzzle on the window-
     panes
Licked its tongue into the corners of the evening,
Lingered upon the pools that stand in drains,
Let fall upon its back the soot that falls from chimneys,
Slipped by the terrace, made a sudden leap,   20
And seeing that it was a soft October night,
Curled once about the house, and fell asleep.

And indeed there will be time
For the yellow smoke that slides along the street,

[1] From Canto XXVII of Dante's *Inferno:* "If I thought my answer were to one who could return to the world, I would not reply, but as none ever did return alive from this depth, without fear of infamy I answer thee." The speaker is one of the lost souls who has been asked his name.

Rubbing its back upon the window-panes; 25
There will be time, there will be time
To prepare a face to meet the faces that you meet;
There will be time to murder and create,
And time for all the works and days [2] of hands
That lift and drop a question on your plate; 30
Time for you and time for me,
And time yet for a hundred indecisions,
And for a hundred visions and revisions,
Before the taking of a toast and tea.

    In the room the women come and go 35
Talking of Michelangelo.

    And indeed there will be time
To wonder, "Do I dare?" and, "Do I dare?"
Time to turn back and descend the stair,
With a bald spot in the middle of my hair— 40
[They will say: "How his hair is growing thin!"]
My morning coat, my collar mounting firmly to the chin,
My necktie rich and modest, but asserted by a simple
    pin—
[They will say: "But how his arms and legs are thin!"]
Do I dare 45
Disturb the universe?
In a minute there is time
For decisons and revisions which a minute will reverse.

    For I have known them all already, known them all:—
Have known the evenings, mornings, afternoons, 50
I have measured out my life with coffee spoons;
I know the voices dying with a dying fall
Beneath the music from a farther room.
    So how should I presume?

    And I have known the eyes already, known them all— 55
The eyes that fix you in a formulated phrase,
And when I am formulated, sprawling on a pin,
When I am pinned and wriggling on the wall,
Then how should I begin
To spit out all the butt-ends of my days and ways? 60
    And how should I presume?

---

[2] *works and days* The Greek poet Hesiod wrote *Works and Days,* about farming, in the eighth century B.C.

And I have known the arms already, known them all—
Arms that are braceleted and white and bare
[But in the lamplight, downed with light brown hair!]
Is it perfume from a dress   65
That makes me so digress?
Arms that lie along a table, or wrap about a shawl.
     And should I then presume?
     And how should I begin?

. . . . . .

Shall I say, I have gone at dusk through narrow streets   70
And watched the smoke that rises from the pipes
Of lonely men in shirt-sleeves, leaning out of win-
     dows? . . .

     I should have been a pair of ragged claws
Scuttling across the floors of silent seas.

. . . . . .

And the afternoon, the evening, sleeps so peacefully!   75
Smoothed by long fingers,
Asleep . . . tired . . . or it malingers,
Stretched on the floor, here beside you and me.
Should I, after tea and cakes and ices,
Have the strength to force the moment to its crisis?   80
But though I have wept and fasted, wept and prayed,
Though I have seen my head [grown slightly bald]
     brought in upon a platter,[3]
I am no prophet—and here's no great matter;
I have seen the moment of my greatness flicker,
And I have seen the eternal Footman hold my coat,
     and snicker,   85
And in short, I was afraid.

     And would it have been worth it, after all,
After the cups, the marmalade, the tea,
Among the porcelain, among some talk of you and me,
Would it have been worth while,   90
To have bitten off the matter with a smile,
To have squeezed the universe into a ball[4]

---

[3] *upon a platter* an allusion to John the Baptist, whose head was presented
on a platter to the queen on the order of King Herod
[4] *universe into a ball* Compare Andrew Marvell's "To His Coy Mistress":
"Let us roll all our strength, and all/ Our sweetness, up into one ball:/ And
tear our pleasures with rough strife,/ Thorough the iron gates of life."

To roll it toward some overwhelming question,
To say: "I am Lazarus, come from the dead,
Come back to tell you all, I shall tell you all"— 95
If one, settling a pillow by her head,
    Should say: "That is not what I meant at all.
    That is not it, at all."

And would it have been worth it, after all,
Would it have been worth while, 100
After the sunsets and the dooryards and the sprinkled
    streets,
After the novels, after the teacups, after the skirts that
    trail along the floor—
And this, and so much more?—
It is impossible to say just what I mean!
But as if a magic lantern threw the nerves in patterns
    on a screen: 105
Would it have been worth while
If one, settling a pillow or throwing off a shawl,
And turning toward the window, should say:
    "That is not it at all,
    That is not what I meant, at all." 110

        .   .   .   .   .

No! I am not Prince Hamlet, nor was meant to be;
Am an attendant lord, one that will do
To swell a progress, start a scene or two,
Advise the prince; no doubt, an easy tool,
Deferential, glad to be of use, 115
Politic, cautious, and meticulous;
Full of high sentence, but a bit obtuse;
At times, indeed, almost ridiculous—
Almost, at times, the Fool.

    I grow old . . . I grow old . . . 120
I shall wear the bottoms of my trousers rolled.

    Shall I put my hair behind? Do I dare to eat a peach?
I shall wear white flannel trousers, and walk upon the
    beach.
I have heard the mermaids singing, each to each.

    I do not think that they will sing to me. 125

    I have seen them riding seaward on the waves
Combing the white hair of the waves blown back
When the wind blows the water white and black.

We have lingered in the chambers of the sea
By sea-girls wreathed with seaweed red and brown   130
Till human voices wake us, and we drown.

PRELUDES

I

The winter evening settles down
With smell of steaks in passageways.
Six o'clock.
The burnt-out ends of smoky days.
And now a gusty shower wraps   5
The grimy scraps
Of withered leaves about your feet
And newspapers from vacant lots;
The showers beat
On broken blinds and chimney-pots,   10
And at the corner of the street
A lonely cab-horse steams and stamps.
And then the lighting of the lamps.

II

The morning comes to consciousness
Of faint stale smells of beer   15
From the sawdust-trampled street
With all its muddy feet that press
To early coffee-stands.
With the other masquerades
That time resumes,   20
One thinks of all the hands
That are raising dingy shades
In a thousand furnished rooms.

III

You tossed a blanket from the bed,
You lay upon your back, and waited;   25
You dozed, and watched the night revealing
The thousand sordid images
Of which your soul was constituted;
They flickered against the ceiling.
And when all the world came back   30
And the light crept up between the shutters

And you heard the sparrows in the gutters,
You had such a vision of the street
As the street hardly understands;
Sitting along the bed's edge, where   35
You curled the papers from your hair,
Or clasped the yellow soles of feet
In the palms of both soiled hands.

IV

His soul stretched tight across the skies
That fade behind a city block,   40
Or trampled by insistent feet
At four and five and six o'clock;
And short square fingers stuffing pipes,
And evening newspapers, and eyes
Assured of certain certainties,   45
The conscience of a blackened street
Impatient to assume the world.

I am moved by fancies that are curled
Around these images, and cling:
The notion of some infinitely gentle   50
Infinitely suffering thing.

Wipe your hand across your mouth, and laugh;
The worlds revolve like ancient women
Gathering fuel in vacant lots.

GERONTION [1]

*Thou hast nor youth nor age
But as it were an after dinner sleep
Dreaming of both.*[2]

Here I am, an old man in a dry month,
Being read to by a boy, waiting for rain.
I was neither at the hot gates
Nor fought in the warm rain
Nor knee deep in the salt marsh, heaving a cutlass,   5
Bitten by flies, fought.
My house is a decayed house,

---

[1] Critical comment on this poem appears on p. 688.
   Gerontion Greek, meaning "little old man"
[2] From Shakespeare's *Measure for Measure* (III, i). The Duke is remarking
on the unreality and futility of life

And the jew squats on the window sill, the owner,
Spawned in some estaminet [3] of Antwerp,
Blistered in Brussels, patched and peeled in London.   10
The goat coughs at night in the field overhead;
Rocks, moss, stonecrop, iron, merds.
The woman keeps the kitchen, makes tea,
Sneezes at evening, poking the peevish gutter.
                    I an old man   15
A dull head among windy spaces.

Signs are taken for wonders. "We would see a sign!"
The word within a word, unable to speak a word,[4]
Swaddled with darkness. In the juvescence [5] of the year
Came Christ the tiger   20

In depraved May, dogwood and chestnut, flowering
    judas,
To be eaten,[6] to be divided, to be drunk
Among whispers; by Mr. Silvero
With caressing hands, at Limoges
Who walked all night in the next room;   25

By Hakagawa, bowing among the Titians;
By Madame de Tornquist, in the dark room
Shifting the candles; Fräulein von Kulp [7]
Who turned in the hall, one hand on the door.
                    Vacant shuttles   30
Weave the wind. I have no ghosts,
An old man in a draughty house
Under a windy knob.

After such knowledge, what forgiveness? Think now
History has many cunning passages, contrived corridors   35
And issues, deceives with whispering ambitions,
Guides us by vanities. Think now
She gives when our attention is distracted
And what she gives, gives with such supple confusions
That the giving famishes the craving. Gives too late   40
What's not believed in, or if still believed,

[3] *estaminet* small cafe, tavern
[4] *unable to speak a word* Christ was God's word, but when born an infant was of course without speech.
[5] *juvescence* juvenescence, youth (here, spring)
[6] *To be eaten* reference to communion
[7] *Silvero, Hakagawa, de Tornquist, von Kulp* disparate examples of people to whom communion has become debased and meaningless

In memory only, reconsidered passion. Gives too soon
Into weak hands, what's thought can be dispensed with
Till the refusal propagates a fear. Think
Neither fear nor courage saves us. Unnatural vices 45
Are fathered by our heroism. Virtues
Are forced upon us by our impudent crimes.
These tears are shaken from the wrath-bearing tree.[8]

    The tiger [9] springs in the new year. Us he devours.
      Think at last
We have not reached conclusion, when I 50
Stiffen in a rented house. Think at last
I have not made this show purposelessly
And it is not by any concitation [10]
Of the backward devils.
I would meet you upon this honestly. 55
I that was near your heart was removed therefrom
To lose beauty in terror, terror in inquisition.
I have lost my passion: why should I need to keep it
Since what is kept must be adulterated?
I have lost my sight, smell, hearing, taste and touch: 60
How should I use them for your closer contact?

    These with a thousand small deliberations
Protract the profit of their chilled delirium,
Excite the membrane, when the sense has cooled,
With pungent sauces, multiply variety 65
In a wilderness of mirrors. What will the spider do,
Suspend its operations, will the weevil
Delay? De Bailhache, Fresca, Mrs. Cammel,[11] whirled
Beyond the circuit of the shuddering Bear [12]
In fractured atoms. Gull against the wind, in the windy
    straits 70
Of Belle Isle, or running on the Horn,
White feathers in the snow, the Gulf claims,
And an old man driven by the Trades
To a sleepy corner.

                 Tenants of the house, 75
Thoughts of a dry brain in a dry season.

[8] *tree* the tree of the knowledge of good and evil
[9] *tiger* the resurrected Christ in all his power (see line 20)
[10] *concitation* stirring up   [11] *De Bailhache . . . Cammel* random names
[12] *Bear* Ursa Major, the constellation

THE HOLLOW MEN

Mistah Kurtz—he dead.[1]

A penny for the Old Guy [2]

I

We are the hollow men
We are the stuffed men
Leaning together
Headpiece filled with straw. Alas!
Our dried voices, when   5
We whisper together
Are quiet and meaningless
As wind in dry grass
Or rats' feet over broken glass
In our dry cellar   10

Shape without form, shade without colour,
Paralysed force, gesture without motion;

Those who have crossed
With direct eyes, to death's other Kingdom [3]
Remember us—if at all—not as lost   15
Violent souls, but only
As the hollow men
The stuffed men.

II

Eyes I dare not meet in dreams
In death's dream kingdom [4]   20
These do not appear:
There, the eyes are

[1] A key line in Joseph Conrad's *Heart of Darkness:* Kurtz, the main character, abandons civilization for the African jungle, and as he lies dying, seems allowed a glimpse into the heart of things or the nature of man—and his only exclamation: "The horror! The horror!"
[2] A reference to Guy Fawkes Day in England, when straw effigies of Guy Fawkes are made. In the 1605 plot to blow up the House of Commons, Fawkes was caught and executed.
[3] *crossed . . . to death's other Kingdom* crossed over the river Acheron to Hell
[4] *death's dream kingdom* the present, unreal, meaningless "kingdom" of the hollow men, suspended impotently between the tortures of hell and the bliss of heaven

Sunlight on a broken column
There, is a tree swinging
And voices are   25
In the wind's singing
More distant and more solemn
Than a fading star.

   Let me be no nearer
In death's dream kingdom   30
Let me also wear
Such deliberate disguises
Rat's coat, crowskin, crossed staves
In a field
Behaving as the wind behaves   35
No nearer—

   Not that final meeting
In the twilight kingdom

III

This is the dead land
This is cactus land
Here the stone images   40
Are raised, here they receive
The supplication of a dead man's hand
Under the twinkle of a fading star.

   Is it like this   45
In death's other kingdom
Waking alone
At the hour when we are
Trembling with tenderness
Lips that would kiss   50
Form prayers to broken stone.

IV

The eyes are not here
There are no eyes here
In this valley of dying stars
In this hollow valley   55
This broken jaw of our lost kingdoms

   In this last of meeting places
We grope together

And avoid speech
Gathered on this beach of the tumid river [5]   60

  Sightless, unless
The eyes reappear
As the perpetual star
Multifoliate rose [6]
Of death's twilight kingdom   65
The hope only
Of empty men.

                        V

Here we go round the prickly pear
Prickly pear prickly pear
Here we go round the prickly pear   70
At five o'clock in the morning.

  Between the idea
And the reality
Between the motion
And the act   75
Falls the shadow
                  For Thine is the Kingdom

  Between the conception
And the creation
Between the emotion   80
And the response
Falls the Shadow
                  Life is very long

  Between the desire
And the spasm   85
Between the potency
And the existence
Between the essence
And the descent
Falls the Shadow.   90
                  For Thine is the Kingdom

  For Thine is
Life is
For Thine is the

[5] *tumid river* the Acheron
[6] *Multifoliate rose* In Dante, Paradise takes the form of a rose, the petals
formed from the souls of the blessed.

This is the way the world ends   95
This is the way the world ends
This is the way the world ends
Not with a bang but a whimper.

SWEENEY AMONG THE NIGHTINGALES

ὤμοι, πέπληγμαι καιρίαν πληγὴν ἔσω [1]

Apeneck Sweeney spreads his knees
Letting his arms hang down to laugh,
The zebra stripes along his jaw
Swelling to maculate [2] giraffe.

The circles of the stormy moon   5
Slide westward toward the River Plate,
Death and the Raven [3] drift above
And Sweeney guards the hornèd gate. [4]

Gloomy Orion and the Dog [5]
Are veiled; and hushed the shrunken seas;   10
The person in the Spanish cape
Tries to sit on Sweeney's knees

Slips and pulls the table cloth
Overturns a coffee-cup,
Reorganized upon the floor   15
She yawns and draws a stocking up;

The silent man in mocha brown
Sprawls at the window-sill and gapes;
The waiter brings in oranges
Bananas figs and hothouse grapes;   20

The silent vertebrate in brown
Contracts and concentrates, withdraws;
Rachel *née* Rabinovitch
Tears at the grapes with murderous paws;

She and the lady in the cape   25
Are suspect, thought to be in league;

[1] In *Agamemnon* by Aeschylus, the king is stabbed by his wife and cries out: "Alas, I have been struck a mortal blow."
[2] *maculate* spotted or striped
[3] *Death and the Raven* The raven, associated with death, is the constellation Corvus.
[4] *horned gate* the gate of Hades through which issue true dreams
[5] *Orion and the Dog* the hunter constellation near Canis, the dog constellation

Therefore the man with heavy eyes
Declines the gambit,[6] shows fatigue,

Leaves the room and reappears
Outside the window, leaning in,   30
Branches of wistaria
Circumscribe a golden grin;

The host with someone indistinct
Converses at the door apart,
The nightingales are singing near   35
The Convent of the Sacred Heart,

And sang within the bloody wood
When Agamemnon cried aloud,[7]
And let their liquid siftings fall
To stain the stiff dishonoured shroud.   40

JOURNEY OF THE MAGI

'A cold coming we had of it,
Just the worst time of the year
For a journey, and such a long journey:
The ways deep and the weather sharp,
The very dead of winter.'[1]   5
And the camels galled, sore-footed, refractory,
Lying down in the melting snow.
There were times we regretted
The summer palaces on slopes, the terraces,
And the silken girls bringing sherbet.[2]   10
Then the camel men cursing and grumbling
And running away, and wanting their liquor and
    women,
And the night-fires going out, and the lack of shelters,
And the cities hostile and the towns unfriendly
And the villages dirty and charging high prices: 15
A hard time we had of it.

---

[6] *gambit* a move or lead   [7] *Agamemnon cried aloud* as in the epigraph

---

[1] *'A cold . . . winter'* (ll. 1–5) a close paraphrase of a passage in Lancelot Andrewes' Christmas Day sermon, 1622 (*Works*, I, 257). Andrewes asks further if the Magi will worship the child in a manger: "Will they not step back at the sight, repent themselves of their journey, and wish themselves at home again?"
[2] *sherbet* a fruit drink

At the end we preferred to travel all night,
Sleeping in snatches,
With the voices singing in our ears, saying
That this was all folly.   20

   Then at dawn we came down to a temperate valley,
Wet, below the snow line, smelling of vegetation;
With a running stream and a water-mill beating the
    darkness,
And three trees [3] on the low sky,
And an old white horse galloped away in the meadow.   25
Then we came to a tavern with vine-leaves over the
    lintel,
Six hands at an open door dicing for pieces of silver,
And feet kicking the empty wine-skins.
But there was no information, and so we continued
And arrived at evening, not a moment too soon   30
Finding the place; it was (you may say) satisfactory.

   All this was a long time ago, I remember,
And I would do it again, but set down
This set down
This: were we led all that way for   35
Birth or Death? There was a Birth, certainly,
We had evidence and no doubt. I had seen birth and
    death,
But had thought they were different; this Birth was
Hard and bitter agony for us, like Death, our death.
We returned to our places, these Kingdoms,   40
But no longer at ease here, in the old dispensation,[4]
With an alien people clutching their gods.
I should be glad of another death.

CRITICISM

   The following criticism is not so much about a poem in history as about history in a poem—the cultural and intellectual
concepts of history that Eliot reveals in "Gerontion." Here is an
emphasis on *idea,* or thought, as it is involved in a poem, rather
than on the structure or the language, although much of the discussion of idea must be in terms of the metaphors and allusions

[3] *three trees* suggestive of the three crosses of Calvary
[4] *old dispensation* old order (pagan)

that the poet has used. Not all readers agree on what the function of the poet in society should be; but a consideration of what he is saying as prophet (or "unacknowledged legislator," as Shelley said) is another valid critical approach.

"Gerontion" and the Meaning of History [1]

HARVEY GROSS

The appeal to history is the sin against the Holy Ghost.
—CARDINAL MANNING

In the twenty-fifth chapter of *The Education,* Henry Adams describes with characteristic metaphoric violence his feelings about history. Trained to think that history had an ultimate meaning, that in the sequence of events there was some corresponding sequence of cause and effect, Adams discovers at the end of his researches that there is no understandable pattern; the best that Adams can tell us is that history is force: "and thus it happens that, after ten years' pursuit, he found himself lying in the Gallery of Machines at the Great Exposition of 1900, his historical neck broken by the sudden irruption of forces totally new."

What breaks Adams' historical neck renders Gerontion, the "I" or voice of Eliot's poem, blind and impotent. The central, dramatic concern in *Gerontion* is history as it actually seems, the devastating, indefinable, almost mystical force driving Europe toward cultural dissolution and moral despair; and history as it is philosophically or existentially understood, a shattering, crippling Idea of history. *Gerontion* gives literary expression to Karl Mannheim's contention that historicism is the only possible *Weltanschauung* in an age dominated by historical force and obsessed with the idea of history.

So overwhelming is this Idea it leaves the protagonist of Eliot's poem symbolically incapable of action. However, Gerontion has lost only sight and passion; he retains his honesty. Though he talks about history, he is no false prophet. His speculations on past and future are not urged "by any concitation / Of the back-

[1] A portion of Harvey Gross's essay, " 'Gerontion' and the Meaning of History," first published in PMLA, LXXIII (June, 1958).

ward devils" (ll. 53–54). "The backward devils" are those who pry into history for excitement or malign power. Eliot's allusion is to the legendary false prophets—soothsayers, seers, mantics— of Dante's fourth *bolgia* (*Inferno* xx) whose heads have been twisted to the rear and who are thus forced to walk backwards. Remembering their punishment, Gerontion pleads the rightness of his own motives for assuming the prophet's role. He does so neither for gain (like Madame Sosostris in *The Waste Land*), nor to dismay the credulous (like Madame de Tornquist in *Gerontion*). He tells us candidly "I would meet you upon this honestly."

What does Gerontion meet us upon? It is the historical situation as seen by a nearly disembodied consciousness. Gerontion is blind, with gifts of foresight; his public experience is universal in time and space; his private life is apparently epicene. He dramatizes the complex of ideas about history, and in one great passage comments explicitly on the questionable value of historical knowledge. These ideas, or more properly, speculations, are broadly philosophic; they touch on the senility of European culture, on the intolerable pressure of the past, and on the power and the baffling direction of the historical process. Eliot is then, in *Gerontion*, a "philosopher of history"; not because he gives a systematic account of historical process, but because he gives hints about the possible meaning and value of the past, and a view of history as a dynamic, generating force. The poet as philosopher of history is also a prophet. The prophetic voice speaks out of heightened historical consciousness, naming the things we have all felt and respond to—uncontrollable change; the fault in the structure of society; the transvaluation of all values.

The opening of *Gerontion* is an astonishing compression of what Western civilization means in memory ("In memory only, reconsidered passion") to the old man. Gerontion was neither "at the hot gates"—Thermopylae, the archetypal scene of Greek heroism—nor "in the salt marsh, heaving a cutlass" in what seem to be Elizabethan wars of exploration. He has total recall; he was witness to the birth of Christ and he is a spectator at the decline of the West. His personality merges with historical figures and with characters from the history of literature. He speaks with the words of Edward FitzGerald, the blind translator of

the *Rubáiyát,* or with the rhetoric of the Jacobean tragedians.
The pressure of this historical awareness paralyzes his capacity
to act. We recall how Nietzsche denounced his historicizing contemporaries for overstressing the importance of historical knowledge; he saw this burdensome sense of the past as a chief malady
of the modern world, leaving terrible scars on the individual
personality and on the culture of nations. Gerontion cannot act
because he cannot rid himself of his past; like Henry Adams he
is an injured victim of the historical sense.

Nor is Gerontion capable of religious belief; in a world dominated by history, matters for belief are historical reconstructions:

> History . . . Gives too late
> What's not believed in, or if still believed,
> In memory only, reconsidered passion.

Gerontion would see a sign, witness a rebirth of belief, but historical knowledge has destroyed the capacity for wonder and il-
lusion. He in effect *knows too much* about the past of religion,
about its anthropological sources and its relation to primitive
myth: "In the juvescence of the year / Came Christ the tiger."
Gerontion sees Christ as a culture hero who comes when the
flowering trees bloom, in the season of the slain gods. Christ the
tiger stalks us from the jungles of comparative religion. Eliot
tells us that religious energy needs fertile cultural soil, realized
in lush vegetation and sexual activity. The tiger is virile and
potent. In contrast, Gerontion is impotent, having "lost sight,
smell, hearing, taste, and touch."

Nietzsche observed that the historical sense destroys the religious sense; by knowing too much about a religion's past, we
recognize its absurdities and untruths. There can be no passionate belief until history has been forgotten: "Eine Religion,
zum Beispiel, die in historisches Wissen, unter dem Walten der
reinen Gerechtigkeit, umgesetzt werden soll, die durch und
durch wissenchaftlich erkannt werden soll, ist am Ende dieses
Weges zugleich vernichtet." The participants in the obscure
and sinister Communion, those who have eaten, divided, and
drunk Christ the tiger, are not communicants of a living, passionately believed and *felt* religion. Mr. Silvero, Madame de
Tornquist, Hakagawa, and Fräulein von Kulp make ironic gestures toward Western religious tradition, toward what they know

"In memory only," toward what history tells them. And Communion is not only the Christian ritual, it is also Eliot's symbol for participation in Western culture and membership in modern society. The names, suggesting the "international set," underline the nature of the modern European world with its disturbing juxtaposition of Spaniard and German, Gentile and Jew, Oriental and Westerner. Society is international, polyglot, and above all "historical."

The poem begins in revery with a stream of broken historical images and recollected meetings. However, with the line "After such knowledge, what forgiveness?" Eliot drops the dramatic mode and proposes, in a sustained conceptual passage, an attitude toward history. The tone is hortatory; the argument is closely reasoned:

> After such knowledge, what forgiveness? Think now
> History has many cunning passages, contrived corridors
> And issues, deceives with whispering ambitions,
> Guides us by vanities. Think now
> She gives when our attention is distracted
> And what she gives, gives with such supple confusions
> That the giving famishes the craving. Gives too late
> What's not believed in, or if still believed,
> In memory only, reconsidered passion. Gives too soon
> Into weak hands, what's thought can be dispensed with
> Till the refusal propagates a fear. Think
> Neither fear nor courage saves us. Unnatural vices
> Are fathered by our heroism. Virtues
> Are forced upon us by our impudent crimes.
> These tears are shaken from the wrath-bearing tree.

Gerontion's knowledge is a total awareness of the decline of European civilization, and an obsessive, debilitating belief in that decline. A mongrelized society and a polluted culture leave Gerontion little hope for physical regeneration; moral failure and religion known only in historical reconstruction point to no clear hope for spiritual salvation. He waits for a terrifying development, a new and destructive display of historical energy. Like Henry Adams he is prepared, and even eager, for violence: "The tiger springs in the new year. Us he devours."

But there is still time to consider the past. What does historical knowledge tell us about man's salvation? Very little, and this little dangerous:

> Think now
> History has many cunning passages, contrived corridors
> And issues, deceives with whispering ambitions,
> Guides us by vanities.

"Think now": Gerontion urges us to an effort of will. He moves from reverie to intellectual commitment to a position. The concept of history is a multiple one; and in the poem it has at least three meanings: Gerontion's own past; his allegorical past, which is the history of Western culture from Thermopylae to the nineteenth century and the immediate European present. Thus Madame de Tornquist and Mr. Silvero are part of Gerontion's personal history; "the hot gates" and "Christ the tiger" form moral and religious elements in Western culture; the Jew of Antwerp, Brussels, and London is a scapegoat for all whose lives are international and uprooted. To Gerontion history is memory of the race, the memory of heroic actions, the memory of his own symbolic past with its distressing lack of continuity.

Because history is so various, "has many cunning passages," it cannot be trusted to guide men in right action. Because the passages and issues—*issues* in the sense of exits but also in the sense of points of dispute or matters for decision—are already built and prepared, there is the implication that the course of history is determined. Man is doomed to haunt these corridors and be misled by the whispers and garbled voices. Yet history itself cannot be blamed: the past means what Gerontion and men in general (for Gerontion's is the voice of prophecy naming what men feel and respond to) wish it to mean at any convenient moment. For men will be urged by expediency or self-interest, or inflamed by the delusion that they are acting for the good of all. "History guides us by vanities."

Out of the bewildering experiences of the past, human pride selects the examples necessary to justify its wickedness, to excuse its irresponsibility, and to rationalize away its weakness and brutality. History "guides us by vanities" because it shows man what he wants to see, not what is right. Those who derive their moral values from historical examples see only the confused image of themselves. The fault is not believing that history is determined and therefore irrevocable, but acting as if it were. Deluded men excuse their actions by appealing to the past or to what they have convinced themselves is an inflexible historical process. To say, as Marx said, that violence is the midwife of history, and consequently the use of terror and purge is forced upon the revolutionary by the "justice" of "History," is to be guided by vanity and distracted with "supple confusions":

> Think now
> She gives when our attention is distracted
> And what she gives, gives with such supple confusions
> That the giving famishes the craving.

The past will affect us when we are least aware, and it is then we are tricked and misled. History is susceptible to the grossest misinterpretations; her confusions are supple because we can distort the past to suit our own ends. Eliot makes history feminine. Her attractions lead us on, at great peril, to bafflement and destruction. What history gives is so devious that we finally refuse her questionable generosity; her gifts do not satisfy, but create a more intense, more terrible longing:

> the giving famishes the craving. Gives too late
> What's not believed in, or if still believed,
> In memory only, reconsidered passion.

The questions of faith and passion are abstracted from the previous considerations of religion and sex. There is the insistence on passion as a necessary part of belief. We have the great examples of the Christian past "in memory only"; belief is intellectual effort, "reconsidered passion," and it is no longer rooted in the soil of our behavior and existence.

Gerontion's next imperative strengthens the notion that history is determined, impervious to individual action, whether for good or evil:

> Think
> Neither fear nor courage saves us. Unnatural vices
> Are fathered by our heroism. Virtues
> Are forced upon us by our impudent crimes.

The forces of history render the ethical will haphazard in action; we do the right things for the wrong reasons; our deliberate evil results in unexpected, unaccountable good. History has its own will which it makes known in an age of social violence and world war. Perhaps there has never been a time when individual man has felt himself so powerless before this will; he lives in an agony of events he abhors, and he faces values he can only regard with moral loathing. Gerontion is the protesting, apologetic voice of individual man in the grip of the historical process. He faces annihilation, yet would have his final say, "would meet you upon this honestly."

Gerontion's apology ends with an allusion to the Tree of Good and Evil: "These tears are shaken from the wrath-bearing tree." Shaken, that is, from the ancestral branches of moral knowledge. In an age when the politician's appeal to history is a daily sin against the Holy Ghost, Gerontion brings up the embarrassing questions of right and wrong and individual responsibility. Stemming from the Tree is the original loss of innocence, past all forgiveness: the moral theme of Gerontion's apology. This whole passage, then, can be considered a justification for loss of innocence—a justification which self-consciously refuses to accept the premise of its argument. The premise is that man is misled by history, and that, consequently, he may evade the moral responsibilities of action. But there is no forgiveness; even though men will protest that they have been tricked by history's cunning passages, confused by Clio's stumbling, garbled voice.

Earlier the polygot communicants (Mr. Silvero, Hakagawa, Fräulein von Kulp) eat the body of Christ; now, in ironic retribution, "The tiger springs in the new year. Us he devours." The eaters are eaten. They had made a gesture of piety to propitiate a god believed "in memory only." Now the tiger devours what remains of a culture it once ("in the juvescence of the year") initiated. A "new year" is the start of a new historical cycle: Gerontion waits for the inevitable completion of the old era and the onslaught of the new. Compare Eliot's image of a Second Coming with Yeats's:

> And what rough beast, its hour come round at last,
> Slouches toward Bethlehem to be born?

Yeats's beast is not Christ. And in his new appearance "Christ the tiger" is like Yeats's beast: the image of a new, destructive force.

The tiger and the rough beast are emblems of historical movement. They carry overtones of religious meaning, but they are not, in their contexts, religious symbols. The rough beast lumbers toward Bethlehem, but Yeats is no Christian philosopher of history. He is a philosophical naturalist who makes dramatic and not doctrinal use of Christian symbols. For Yeats historical movement exists in nature; it originates in primitive unreason and in the mythic stupidity of the blood.

Both Yeats and Eliot parallel Henry Adams' "dynamic" theory of history. Like the virgin and the dynamo, Christ the tiger and the rough beast symbolize the irrational power of history: its relentless movement ("slouches toward Bethlehem"), or its sudden violence ("The tiger springs . . . "). History, then, is energy, force, physical vitality. Gerontion asserts this when he speaks with the altered words of Beatrice, the lustful heroine of Middleton's *The Changeling:*

> I that was near your heart was removed therefrom
> To lose beauty in terror, terror in inquisition.

The irony is that the hot-blooded Beatrice dies in a swirl of Renaissance violence; while Gerontion, without "sight, smell, hearing, taste, and touch," decays in a rented house. His excitements must be stimulated by artificial means, in contrast to Beatrice and the other active women and men of an age when passionate action was possible. Although Beatrice is damned, she had the vitality of her sin; Gerontion in his debility can only

> Excite the membrane, when the sense has cooled,
> With pungent sauces, multiply variety
> In a wilderness of mirrors.

The poem ends with a burst of natural violence: it is total destruction. Gerontion suggests that a new age is imminent and that the turbulence at the end of the poem may proceed from a yet unknown, unnamed source of historical energy. Historical movement does not cease; civilization may decline in a chaotic present, but the process goes on:

> Think at last
> We have not reached conclusion, when I
> Stiffen in a rented house.

His decline does not mark the end of history. Even his own destruction in the whirlwind of historical force is a cause for remote hope. The death agonies of an old civilization may be the birth trauma of a new age.

Gerontion once more evokes the "international set" and the boarders who share his house:

> De Bailhache, Fresca, Mrs. Cammel, whirled
> Beyond the circuit of the shuddering Bear
> In fractured atoms.

Through some Einsteinian metamorphosis these people are changed from mass to energy, and their scattered substance is blown by the cold winds of space. The violence at the end comes as a purgation, a clean sweep of the world and the old man's mind. The desire for annihilation is stressed. Since his world has grown so corrupt, Gerontion eagerly looks toward irrational force to destroy what remains of a decayed culture. As Adams gave up "the sequence of men," saw that "the sequence of society could lead no further," and attached himself to the principle of force, so Gerontion awaits the final violence of history.

DYLAN THOMAS

[1914-1953]

DYLAN THOMAS was a Welsh bard, a singing, chanting poet. He was born in Swansea, Wales, where his father was a teacher. His first volumes of poetry—*18 Poems* (1934) and *Twenty-Five Poems* (1936)—caught attention, for the Thomas poems were fresh and violent, whirling with words and mysteries. Thomas continued to live and write in London and Wales. He married Caitlin Macnamara in 1936, had three children, and settled in a sea-hung house at Laugharne. He worked for the B.B.C., reading poetry; wrote for newspapers, films, and radio; was an anti-aircraft gunner in the war. With his prose autobiography, *A Portrait of the Artist as a Young Dog* (1940), *New Poems* (1943), and *Deaths and Entrances* (1946) Thomas reached maturity as a writer. In his last years he engaged in a series of lecture tours in America, which were to end tragically in his illness and death in New York at the age of 39. Thomas became a legend in his own lifetime, partly because of his personal magnetism, but also because he was the first—with his compelling voice—to make poetry readings and poetry records popular. More than anyone before him he released the voice of the poem, not only for himself but for others. In his own work (including his many prose pieces and the play for voices, *Under Milk Wood*) Thomas appealed because of the rich excitement of his language and the elemental themes he explored.

Introductory Readings

EDITION: *Collected Poems, 1934–1952* (1952). LETTERS: *Dylan Thomas: Letters to Vernon Watkins,* ed. Vernon Watkins (1957). BIOGRAPHY: John Malcolm Brinnin, *Dylan Thomas in America* (1955); Caitlin Thomas, *Leftover Life to Kill* (1957). CRITICISM: Henry Treece, *Dylan*

Thomas (1949); Derek Stanford, *Dylan Thomas, A Literary Study* (1954); Elder Olson, *The Poetry of Dylan Thomas* (1954).

THE FORCE THAT THROUGH THE GREEN FUSE DRIVES THE FLOWER

The force that through the green fuse drives the flower
Drives my green age; that blasts the roots of trees
Is my destroyer.
And I am dumb to tell the crooked rose
My youth is bent by the same wintry fever.   5

The force that drives the water through the rocks
Drives my red blood; that dries the mouthing streams
Turns mine to wax.
And I am dumb to mouth unto my veins
How at the mountain spring the same mouth sucks.   10

The hand that whirls the water in the pool
Stirs the quicksand; that ropes [1] the blowing wind
Hauls [2] my shroud sail.[3]
And I am dumb to tell the hanging man
How of my clay is made the hangman's lime.   15

The lips of time leech [4] to the fountain head;
Love drips and gathers, but the fallen blood
Shall calm her sores.
And I am dumb to tell a weather's wind
How time has ticked a heaven round the stars.   20

And I am dumb to tell the lover's tomb
How at my sheet goes the same crooked worm.

ESPECIALLY WHEN THE OCTOBER WIND

Especially when the October wind
With frosty fingers punishes my hair,
Caught by the crabbing sun [1] I walk on fire
And cast a shadow crab upon the land,
By the sea's side, hearing the noise of birds,   5

---

[1] *ropes* ties or catches.
[2] *Hauls* pulls or draws; also, with nautical connotations of trimming sails or changing course to sail nearer the wind
[3] *shroud sail* The life-force becomes death.
[4] *leech* cling, as the bloodsucking leech was once used for supposed healing

---

[1] *crabbing sun* crab-fishing sun; or, sun with rays like the claws of a crab

Hearing the raven cough in winter sticks,
My busy heart who shudders as she talks
Sheds the syllabic blood and drains her words.

Shut, too, in a tower of words, I mark
On the horizon walking like the trees   10
The wordy shapes of women, and the rows
Of the star-gestured children in the park.
Some let me make you of the vowelled beeches,
Some of the oaken voices, from the roots
Of many a thorny shire [2] tell you notes,   15
Some let me make you of the water's speeches.

Behind a pot of ferns the wagging clock
Tells me the hour's word, the neural meaning [3]
Flies on the shafted disk,[4] declaims the morning
And tells the windy weather in the cock.   20
Some let me make you of the meadow's signs;
The signal grass that tells me all I know
Breaks with the wormy winter through the eye.
Some let me tell you of the raven's sins.

Especially when the October wind   25
(Some let me make you of autumnal spells,
The spider-tongued,[5] and the loud hill of Wales)
With fists of turnips punishes the land,
Some let me make you of the heartless words.
The heart is drained that, spelling in the scurry   30
Of chemic blood,[6] warned of the coming fury.
By the sea's side hear the dark-vowelled birds.

AFTER THE FUNERAL

(IN MEMORY OF ANN JONES [1])

After the funeral, mule praises, brays,
Windshake of sailshaped ears, muffle-toed tap

[2] *shire* province or county
[3] *neural meaning* sensations or impressions from nerves, rather than the rational understanding of the mind
[4] *shafted disk* the clock face, with the hands becoming more like heraldic spears or arrows that would propel the meaning to another level
[5] *spider-tongued* both many (as a spider has many legs) and magical (as related to spells)
[6] *chemic blood* alchemical, involved in transmutations

---

[1] *Ann Jones* Thomas's elderly cousin

Tap happily of one peg in the thick
Grave's foot, blinds down the lids, the teeth in black,
The spittled eyes, the salt ponds in the sleeves,   5
Morning smack of the spade that wakes up sleep,
Shakes a desolate boy who slits his throat
In the dark of the coffin and sheds dry leaves,
That breaks one bone to light with a judgment clout,[2]
After the feast of tear-stuffed time and thistles   10
In a room with a stuffed fox and a stale fern,
I stand, for this memorial's sake, alone
In the snivelling hours with dead, humped Ann
Whose hooded, fountain heart once fell in puddles
Round the parched worlds of Wales and drowned each sun   15
(Though this for her is a monstrous image blindly
Magnified out of praise; her death was a still drop;
She would not have me sinking in the holy
Flood of her heart's fame; she would lie dumb and deep
And need no druid [3] of her broken body).   20
But I, Ann's bard on a raised hearth, call all
The seas to service that her wood-tongued virtue
Babble like a bellbuoy over the hymning heads,
Bow down the walls of the ferned and foxy woods
That her love sing and swing through a brown chapel,   25
Bless her bent spirit with four, crossing birds.[4]
Her flesh was meek as milk, but this skyward statue
With the wild breast and blessed and giant skull
Is carved from her in a room with a wet window
In a fiercely mourning house in a crooked year.   30
I know her scrubbed and sour humble hands
Lie with religion in their cramp, her threadbare
Whisper in a damp word, her wits drilled hollow,
Her fist of a face died clenched on a round pain;
And sculptured Ann is seventy years of stone.   35
These cloud-sopped, marble hands, this monumental
Argument of the hewn voice, gesture and psalm,
Storm me forever over her grave until
The stuffed lung of the fox twitch and cry Love
And the strutting fern lay seeds on the black sill.   40

[2] *clout* blow; also, a clod of earth
[3] *druid* an ancient Celtic priestly bard who would celebrate her
[4] *four, crossing birds* a religious symbol (the sign of the Cross) made out of
the rhythms of nature, as the seas also swing bell-like in their tides

TWENTY-FOUR YEARS

Twenty-four years remind the tears of my eyes.
(Bury the dead for fear that they walk to the grave in labour.)
In the groin of the natural doorway I crouched like a tailor
Sewing a shroud for a journey
By the light of the meat-eating sun.[1]   5
Dressed to die, the sensual strut begun,
With my red veins full of money,
In the final direction of the elementary town
I advance for as long as forever is.

A REFUSAL TO MOURN THE DEATH, BY FIRE,
OF A CHILD IN LONDON

Never until the mankind making
Bird beast and flower
Fathering and all humbling [1] darkness
Tells with silence the last light breaking
And the still hour   5
Is come of the sea tumbling in harness [2]

And I must enter again the round
Zion [3] of the water bead
And the synagogue of the ear of corn
Shall I let pray the shadow of a sound   10
Or sow my salt seed
In the least valley of sackcloth [4] to mourn

The majesty and burning of the child's death.
I shall not murder
The mankind of her going with a grave truth   15
Nor blaspheme down the stations of the breath [5]

[1] *meat-eating sun* the life-giving sun, symbol of time, seen also as the destroyer
of life

[1] *mankind . . . humbling* modifier of "darkness"
[2] *tumbling in harness* moving violently but in the tidal order that marks
the known universe
[3] *Zion* the holy place (and temple) of the Israelites, symbol of Old Testament
religious origins
[4] *sackcloth* Biblical symbol of mourning
[5] *stations of the breath* stations of the Cross, or signs of the Passion of Christ
transferred to the life (breath) of mortal man

With any further
Elegy of innocence and youth.

Deep with the first dead lies London's daughter,
Robed in the long friends,   20
The grains beyond age, the dark veins of her mother,
Secret by the unmourning water
Of the riding Thames.
After the first death, there is no other.

POEM IN OCTOBER

It was my thirtieth year to heaven
Woke to my hearing from harbour and neighbour wood
    And the mussel [1] pooled and the heron
        Priested shore
      The morning beckon   5
With water praying and call of seagull and rook
And the knock of sailing boats on the net webbed wall
      Myself to set foot [2]
        That second
In the still sleeping town and set forth.   10

My birthday began with the water-
Birds and the birds of the winged trees flying my name
    Above the farms and the white horses
        And I rose
      In rainy autumn   15
And walked abroad in a shower of all my days.
High tide and the heron dived when I took the road
      Over the border
        And the gates
Of the town closed as the town awoke.   20

A springful of larks in a rolling
Cloud and the roadside bushes brimming with whistling
    Blackbirds and the sun of October
        Summery
      On the hill's shoulder,   25
Here were fond [3] climates and sweet singers suddenly
Come in the morning where I wandered and listened

---

[1] *mussel* shellfish
[2] Lines 2–8 may be read "hearing . . . The morning beckon . . . Myself to
set foot."
[3] *fond* loving, tender

       To the rain wringing
         Wind blow cold
   In the wood faraway under me.   30

     Pale rain over the dwindling harbour
And over the sea wet church the size of a snail
     With its horns through mist and the castle
         Brown as owls
       But all the gardens   35
Of spring and summer were blooming in the tall tales
Beyond the border and under the lark full cloud.
       There could I marvel
         My birthday
   Away but the weather turned around.   40

     It turned away from the blithe country
And down the other air and the blue altered sky
     Streamed again a wonder of summer
         With apples
       Pears and red currants   45
And I saw in the turning so clearly a child's
Forgotten mornings when he walked with his mother
       Through the parables
         Of sun light
   And the legends of the green chapels [4]   50

     And the twice told fields of infancy
That his tears burned my cheeks and his heart moved in mine.
     These were the woods the river and sea
         Where a boy
       In the listening   55
Summertime of the dead [5] whispered the truth of his joy
To the trees and the stones and the fish in the tide.
       And the mystery
         Sang alive
   Still in the water and singingbirds.   60

     And there could I marvel my birthday
Away but the weather turned around. And the true
     Joy of the long dead child sang burning
         In the sun.
       It was my thirtieth   65
Year to heaven stood there then in the summer noon

[4] *green chapels* trees and woods
[5] *Summertime of the dead* past boyhood. See also l. 63.

Though the town below lay leaved with October blood.
        O may my heart's truth
              Still be sung
On this high hill in a year's turning.   70

THE HUNCHBACK IN THE PARK

The hunchback in the park [1]
A solitary mister
Propped between trees and water
From the opening of the garden lock
That lets the trees and water enter   5
Until the Sunday sombre bell at dark

Eating bread from a newspaper
Drinking water from the chained cup [2]
That the children filled with gravel
In the fountain basin where I sailed my ship   10
Slept at night in a dog kennel [3]
But nobody chained him up.

Like the park birds he came early
Like the water he sat down
And Mister they called Hey mister   15
The truant boys from the town
Running when he had heard them clearly
On out of sound

Past lake and rockery [4]
Laughing when he shook his paper   20
Hunchbacked in mockery
Through the loud zoo of the willow groves
Dodging the park keeper
With his stick that picked up leaves.

And the old dog sleeper   25
Alone between nurses and swans
While the boys among willows
Made the tigers jump out of their eyes
To roar on the rockery stones
And the groves were blue with sailors   30

[1] *park* Cwmdonkin Park, in Thomas's childhood home of Swansea, Wales
[2] *chained cup* literally, a drinking cup chained to a public fountain, still common in some countries
[3] *dog kennel* perhaps not literally, but at least in a poor, inhuman place
[4] *rockery* rock garden

Made all day until bell time [5]
A woman figure without fault
Straight as a young elm
Straight and tall from his crooked bones
That she might stand in the night   35
After the locks and chains

All night in the unmade park
After the railings and shrubberies
The birds the grass the trees the lake
And the wild boys innocent as strawberries   40
Had followed the hunchback
To his kennel in the dark.

DO NOT GO GENTLE INTO THAT GOOD NIGHT [1]

Do not go gentle into that good night,
Old age should burn and rave at close of day;
Rage, rage against the dying of the light.

Though wise men at their end know dark is right,
Because their words had forked no lightning they   5
Do not go gentle into that good night.

Good men, the last wave by, crying how bright
Their frail deeds might have danced in a green bay,
Rage, rage against the dying of the light.

Wild men who caught and sang the sun in flight,   10
And learn, too late, they grieved it on its way,
Do not go gentle into that good night.

Grave men, near death, who see with blinding sight
Blind eyes could blaze like meteors and be gay,
Rage, rage against the dying of the light.   15

And you, my father, there on the sad height,
Curse, bless, me now with your fierce tears, I pray.
Do not go gentle into that good night.
Rage, rage against the dying of the light.

---

[5] *bell time* closing time

[1] A villanelle, addressed to Thomas's dying father. Critical comment on this poem appears on p. 716.

IN MY CRAFT OR SULLEN ART

In my craft or sullen [1] art
Exercised in the still night
When only the moon rages
And the lovers lie abed
With all their griefs in their arms,   5
I labour by singing light
Not for ambition or bread
Or the strut and trade of charms
On the ivory stages [2]
 But for the common wages   10
Of their most secret heart.

Not for the proud man apart
From the raging moon I write
On these spindrift [3] pages
Nor for the towering dead [4]   15
With their nightingales and psalms
But for the lovers, their arms
Round the griefs of the ages,
Who pay no praise or wages
Nor heed my craft or art.   20

FERN HILL [1]

Now as I was young and easy under the apple boughs
About the lilting house and happy as the grass was green,
    The night above the dingle [2] starry,
        Time let me hail and climb
    Golden in the heydays [3] of his eyes,   5
And honoured among wagons I was prince of the apple towns
And once below a time [4] I lordly had the trees and leaves

[1] *sullen* stubborn, intractable; in context, however, more in its original sense
of lonely (from Latin, *solus,* alone)
[2] Although a number of specific interpretations of these lines have been offered, the only certainty is that they suggest the beautiful, the artificial, and
the pretended.
[3] *spindrift* ephemeral seaspray
[4] *towering dead* principally, the dead great poets

[1] Critical comment on this poem appears on p. 714.
[2] *dingle* a deep, wooded hollow
[3] *heydays* the most excited, exalted times
[4] *below a time* out of and before this time, almost to the point of unreality

Trail with daisies and barley
Down the rivers of the windfall light.[5]

And as I was green and carefree, famous among the barns   10
About the happy yard and singing as the farm was home,
In the sun that is young once only,
Time let me play and be
Golden in the mercy of his means,
And green and golden I was huntsman and herdsman, the calves
Sang to my horn, the foxes on the hills barked clear and cold,   16
And the sabbath rang slowly
In the pebbles of the holy streams.

All the sun long it was running, it was lovely, the hay
Fields high as the house, the tunes from the chimneys, it was air   20
And playing, lovely and watery
And fire green as grass.
And nightly under the simple stars
As I rode to sleep the owls were bearing the farm away,
All the moon long I heard, blessed among stables, the nightjars [6]
Flying with the ricks,[7] and the horses   26
Flashing into the dark.

And then to awake, and the farm, like a wanderer white
With the dew, come back, the cock on his shoulder: it was all
Shining, it was Adam and maiden,   30
The sky gathered again
And the sun grew round that very day.
So it must have been after the birth of the simple light
In the first, spinning place,[8] the spellbound horses walking warm
Out of the whinnying green stable   35
On to the fields of praise.

And honoured among foxes and pheasants by the gay house
Under the new made clouds and happy as the heart was long,
In the sun born over and over,
I ran my heedless ways,   40
My wishes raced through the house high hay [9]
And nothing I cared, at my sky blue trades, that time allows
In all his tuneful turning so few and such morning songs

[5] *windfall light* both the falling light of day and light gone (blown down by the wind of time)
[6] *nightjars* birds that sometimes have a whirring sound
[7] *ricks* haystacks
[8] *first, spinning place* movement of creation and the earth
[9] *house high hay* haystacks high as a house

Before the children green and golden
Follow him out of grace,   45

Nothing I cared, in the lamb white days, that time would take me
Up to the swallow thronged loft by the shadow of my hand,
In the moon that is always rising,
Nor that riding to sleep
I should hear him fly with the high fields   50
And wake to the farm forever fled from the childless land.
Oh as I was young and easy in the mercy of his means,
Time held me green and dying
Though I sang in my chains like the sea.

OVER SIR JOHN'S HILL

Over Sir John's hill,[1]
The hawk on fire hangs still;
In a hoisted cloud, at drop of dusk, he pulls to his claws
And gallows, up the rays of his eyes the small birds of the bay
And the shrill child's play   5
Wars
Of the sparrows and such who swansing,[2] dusk, in wrangling
    hedges.
And blithely they squawk
To fiery tyburn [3] over the wrestle of elms until
The flash the noosed hawk   10
Crashes, and slowly the fishing holy stalking heron
In the river Towy [4] below bows his tilted headstone.

Flash, and the plumes crack,
And a black cap of jack-
Daws [5] Sir John's just hill dons, and again the gulled [6] birds
    hare [7]   15
To the hawk on fire, the halter height, over Towy's fins,[8]
In a whack of wind.

[1] *Sir John's hill* a wooded hill and headland jutting into the water at Laugharne, Thomas's home in Wales
[2] *swansing* In legend, the swan sings a most beautiful song just before death.
[3] *tyburn* Tyburn was the place of public execution by hanging in Middlesex (near Marble Arch in modern London) until the late eighteenth century. With *gallows* (l. 4) and *noosed* (l. 10), the central figure of the poem is established.
[4] *Towy* (tou'ē) a river in Wales flowing southwest to Carmarthen Bay, near the place where Thomas lived
[5] *jackdaws* chattering, thieving birds   [6] *gulled* deceived, tricked
[7] *hare* harry, worry   [8] *fins* fish

There
Where the elegiac [9] fisherbird [10] stabs and paddles
In the pebbly dab [11]-filled   20
Shallow and sedge, and 'dilly dilly,' [12] calls the loft hawk,[13]
'Come and be killed,'
I open the leaves of the water at a passage
Of psalms and shadows among the pincered sandcrabs prancing

And read, in a shell,   25
Death clear as a buoy's bell:
All praise of the hawk on fire in hawk-eyed dusk be sung,
When his viperish fuse [14] hangs looped with flames under the
    brand
Wing,[15] and blest shall
Young   30
Green chickens of the bay and bushes cluck, 'dilly dilly,
Come let us die.'
We grieve as the blithe birds, never again, leave shingle [16] and
    elm,
The heron and I,
I young Aesop fabling to the near night by the dingle [17]   35
Of eels, saint heron hymning in the shell-hung distant

Crystal harbour vale
Where the sea cobbles [18] sail,
And wharves of water where the walls dance and the white cranes
    stilt.
It is the heron and I, under judging Sir John's elmed   40
Hill, tell-tale the knelled
Guilt
Of the led-astray birds whom God, for their breast of whistles,
Have mercy on,
God in his whirlwind silence save, who marks the sparrows
    hail,   45
For their souls' song.
Now the heron grieves in the weeded verge.[19] Through windows
Of dusk and water I see the tilting whispering

[9] *elegiac* mournful, commemorating the dead
[10] *fisherbird* the heron, both priest and killer   [11] *dab* small flat fish
[12] *dilly* sometimes a call to ducks   [13] *loft hawk* hawk high or aloft
[14] *fuse* the imagined rope of execution
[15] *brand/Wing* wing both marked with fire and ready to brand or burn others
[16] *shingle* beach, or small pebbles on a shore   [17] *dingle* hollow
[18] *cobbles* stones, pebbles   [19] *verge* margin of the river

Heron, mirrored, go,
As the snapt feathers snow,   50
Fishing in the tear of the Towy. Only a hoot owl
Hollows,[20] a grassblade blown in cupped hands, in the looted
     elms
And no green cocks or hens
Shout
Now on Sir John's hill. The heron, ankling the scaly   55
Lowlands of the waves,
Makes all the music; and I who hear the tune of the slow,
Wear-willow river, grave,
Before the lunge of the night, the notes on this time-shaken
Stone for the sake of the souls of the slain birds sailing.   60

POEM ON HIS BIRTHDAY

In the mustardseed sun,[1]
By full tilt river and switchback sea
    Where the cormorants [2] scud,
In his house on stilts high among beaks
    And palavers [3] of birds   5
This sandgrain day in the bent bay's grave
    He celebrates and spurns
His driftwood thirty-fifth wind turned age;
    Herons spire and spear.

Under and round him go   10
Flounders, gulls, on their cold, dying trails,
    Doing what they are told,
Curlews [4] aloud in the congered [5] waves
    Work at their ways to death,
And the rhymer in the long tongued room,   15
    Who tolls his birthday bell,
Toils towards the ambush of his wounds;
    Herons, steeple stemmed, bless.

---

[20] *Hollows* halloos, or calls (as to the hounds in hunting)

---

[1] *mustardseed sun* of yellow color, comparatively small (see "sandgrain day,"
l. 6), but also with Biblical connotations: "The kingdom of heaven is like
to a grain of *mustard seed*, . . . which is the least of all seeds." Matthew
xiii, 31
[2] *cormorants* voracious black sea birds   [3] *palavers* useless chattering
[4] *curlews* wading birds with long curved bills
[5] *congered* filled with congers, or eels that live in salt water

In the thistledown fall,
He sings towards anguish; finches fly   20
  In the claw tracks of hawks
On a seizing sky; small fishes glide
  Through wynds [6] and shells of drowned
Ship towns to pastures of otters. He
  In his slant, racking [7] house   25
And the hewn coils of his trade perceives
  Herons walk in their shroud,

  The livelong river's robe
Of minnows wreathing around their prayer;
  And far at sea he knows,   30
Who slaves to his crouched, eternal end
  Under a serpent cloud,
Dolphins [8] dive in their turnturtle [9] dust,
  The rippled seals streak down
To kill and their own tide daubing blood   35
  Slides good in the sleek mouth.

  In a cavernous, swung
Wave's silence, wept white angelus [10] knells.
  Thirty-five bells sing struck
On skull and scar where his loves lie wrecked,   40
  Steered by the falling stars.
And to-morrow weeps in a blind cage
  Terror will rage apart
Before chains break to a hammer flame
  And love unbolts the dark   45

  And freely he goes lost
In the unknown, famous light of great
  And fabulous, dear God.
Dark is a way and light is a place,
  Heaven that never was   50
Nor will be ever is always true,
  And, in that brambled void,
Plenty as blackberries in the woods
  The dead grow for His joy.

---

[6] *wynds* narrow cross-streets   [7] *racking* strained, dislocated
[8] *Dolphins* sea-mammals, smaller than whales, who leap and turn over in the waves
[9] *turnturtle* turned over, upset. In a less literal sense, dolphins are turnturtle in that they feed on fish but sometimes eat their own kind.
[10] *angelus* bell for daily devotions commemorating the incarnation, here implying the opposite sense

There he might wander bare   55
With the spirits of the horseshoe bay
    Or the stars' seashore dead,
Marrow of eagles, the roots of whales
    And wishbones of wild geese,
With blessed, unborn God and His Ghost,   60
    And every soul His priest,
Gulled and chanter [11] in young Heaven's fold
    Be at cloud quaking peace,

But dark is a long way.
He, on the earth of the night, alone   65
    With all the living, prays,
Who knows the rocketing wind will blow
    The bones out of the hills,
And the scythed boulders bleed, and the last
    Rage shattered waters kick   70
Masts and fishes to the still quick stars,
    Faithlessly unto Him

Who is the light of old
And air shaped Heaven where souls grow wild
    As horses in the foam: 75
Oh, let me midlife mourn by the shrined
    And druid herons' vows [12]
The voyage to ruin I must run,
    Dawn ships clouted [13] aground,
Yet, thou I cry with tumbledown tongue,   80
    Count my blessings aloud:

Four elements and five
Senses, and man a spirit in love
    Tangling through this spun slime
To his nimbus [14] bell cool kingdom come   85
    And the lost, moonshine domes,
And the sea that hides his secret selves
    Deep in its black, base bones,
Lulling of spheres in the seashell flesh,
    And this last blessing most,   90

[11] *Gulled and chanter* both one who is fooled and one who celebrates and asserts his belief. Compare the preceding stanza.
[12] *druid herons' vows* the herons as priests. The ancient Celtic druids were priests and bards, holy and magical.
[13] *clouted* struck by blows   [14] *nimbus* bright cloud or halo, sign of holiness

That the closer I move
To death, one man through his sundered hulks,[15]
   The louder the sun blooms
And the tusked, ramshackling sea [16] exults;
   And every wave of the way   95
And gale I tackle, the whole world then,
   With more triumphant faith
Than ever was since the world was said,
   Spins its morning of praise,

   I hear the bouncing hills   100
Grow larked and greener at berry brown
   Fall and the dew larks sing
Taller this thunderclap spring, and how
   More spanned with angels ride
The mansouled fiery islands! Oh,   105
   Holier then their eyes,
And my shining men no more alone
   As I sail out to die.

CRITICISM

These two essays on Dylan Thomas turn to the poet as artist. The account of the development of his "Do Not Go Gentle into That Good Night" reveals some of the effort through which Thomas found what he needed to say. A comparison of his early prose statement of the content with the finished version will be its own comment on the art of making a poem. [See the discussion of a poet's revisions in Chapter 4, pp. 159–162.] The second essay, on "Fern Hill," considers primarily the unifying elements, or motifs. But both critics also arrive at conclusions about the central themes of the poems, and they both suggest relationships with other poems (the great elegies) and poets (Wordsworth and Whitman). Thus an explication may begin with technique and end with meaning. Even in a single criticism, a poem may be seen to have several dimensions.

---

[15] *sundered hulks* broken ships
[16] *tusked, ramshackling sea* sea not only filled with tusked creatures, but itself toothed or equipped for destruction, and (ramshackling) wrecking and plundering

Motifs in Dylan Thomas' "Fern Hill" [1]

DEREK STANFORD

Thomas' chief other reminiscential piece,[2] *Fern Hill,* has claims to be considered his finest composition. Its status is that of major poetry.

If one sought to describe this poem within the compass of a single phrase, it might be called "an elegy in praise of lost youth." Lament and celebration sound throughout the work: the latter strongly at the beginning, the former gaining tone as the poem progresses.

But, as with all great threnodies in English—with Milton's *Lycidas,* Gray's *Elegy,* Shelley's *Adonais,* and Arnold's *Thyrsis*— the particularity of the cause of grief is lost in a sorrow which speaks for all men. Nostalgic recollection of a child's farm holi- day is the leaping-off point for the poem; but—once launched— so intense and poignant a memory overtakes the poet, that his words convey more than a merely topographical homesickness. The farm becomes Eden before the Fall, and time the angel with a flaming sword.

But no such intrusive personification operates within the poem. The farm is invested with a light as radiant as the un- forfeited Garden, and time exercises its function as irrevocably as God's excluding angel. So, though at the end we are faced with nothing worse than a farm-stead which cannot be re-visited, in actual poetic terms we have experienced the states of in- nocence and eternity, and been subjected to corruption, time, and change.

The poem is constructed from six nine-line stanzas, with only an infrequent rhyme. The absence of rhyme suffices to make the lyrically undulating lines more natural. The artifice and archi- tectonic of the poem consists not in the usual technical devices, but in the repetition, in later stanzas, of *motifs* established in the first. These *motifs* are not worked out with any mechanical regularity; and their place and precedence in the poem are not formally observed. The *motifs* I find to be mainly three: that of

[1] Extracted from Derek Stanford, *Dylan Thomas* (Citadel Press, 1954; Neville Spearman Limited, 1954).
[2] A discussion of "Poem in October" precedes this passage.—*Editors' note.*

the unwitting situation of childhood; that of the delight in this situation; that of time's operation, by which the situation becomes a fate.

The first of the three is associated with such phrases as "Now as I was young and easy," "And as I was green and carefree." The second *motif* is present in "honoured among wagons I was prince of the apple towns," "green and golden I was huntsman and herdsman," "honoured among foxes and pheasants by the gay house." The third *motif* is repeated, after its initial appearance—

> Time let me hail and climb
> Golden in the heydays of his eyes

in

> In the sun that is young once only,
> Time let me play and be
> Golden in the mercy of his means,

in

> And nothing I cared, at my sky blue trades, that time allows
> In all his tuneful turning so few and such morning songs

and

> Nothing I cared, in the lamb white days, that time would take me
> Up to the swallow thronged loft by the shadow of my hand,

All three motives come together in the last three lines of the poem:

> Oh as I was young and easy in the mercy of his means,
> Time held me green and dying
> Though I sang in my chains like the sea.

They form, as it were, a great resolving chord.

These are but three of the poem's many notes of development. In its six stanzas, we are escorted on a journey from innocence to experience. This direction also marks a journey from grace to corruption, from unity to dissolution. One of the most subtle features of this poem is the manner in which the growing presence of these latter qualities is expressed by a chilling of imagery. The first two stanzas are full of effects of sunlight; and then, in the third, nocturnal objects enter. We hear "the owls" "All the moon long" "bearing the farm away." So far, the images are not sinister; but the first touch of coolness has been conveyed.

In the sixth stanza, this chillness grows rapidly. Time takes the child

> Up to the swallow thronged loft by the shadow of [his] hand
> In the moon that is always rising,

The eeriness of the first line, with its suggestion of an evil presence or a mysterious double in the flickering movement of the shadows, and of the ghostly appearance of the swallows in the dim lights of the loft, distils a feeling of sin and death. And now "the sun born over and over" (which assured us in the fifth stanza) yields to "the moon which is always rising"—a symbol of the growing cold: that of a contracting imagination and heart. By the light of this moon the happy day-time vision of the farm vanished, and when the light returns it is to discover

> the farm forever fled from the childless land.

The Making of a Poem: Dylan Thomas' "Do Not Go Gentle into That Good Night" [1]

OLIVER EVANS

The poem under consideration is a villanelle belonging to that period of Thomas' activity which is generally thought to be his most successful, *i.e.*, the period of the early forties, to which also belong such poems as *Fern Hill*, the threnody which some critics have held to be his most important work; [2] *A Refusal to Mourn the Death of a Child, by Fire, in London* (which William Empson so admired); [3] *Poem in October;* and *In My Craft or Sullen Art.*

Thomas was especially fond of the stricter poetic forms (one recalls his experiments with poems in the shape of triangles and diamonds, reminiscent of George Herbert's *Wings*) and indeed in his facility with rhymes and metres was probably unsurpassed by any of his contemporaries with the possible exception of Auden. His formal virtuosity recalls that of Hopkins and Swin-

[1] Reprinted from *English Miscellany* (Rome, 1955).
[2] Derek Stanford, *Dylan Thomas*, London, Spearman & Calder, 1954, p. 105: "in my estimation, Thomas' finest poem." Again, p. 110: "Thomas' *Fern Hill* has claims to be his finest composition. Its status is that of major poetry."
[3] "How to Understand a Modern Poem," *Strand*, March, 1947.

burne, though of course where Swinburne is concerned that is the only point of comparison. It would be difficult to imagine a stricter metrical discipline than that imposed by the villanelle, which employs only two rhymes in constant proximity: the poet who can avoid creating an effect of monotony and artificiality under such stringent conditions is an accomplished poet indeed. The form challenges all of Thomas' resources as a versifier and as a poet; how successfully he met this challenge may be apparent to anyone who reads the final version of the poem as it appears in the Collected Edition of 1952.

The poem succeeds not only in the negative sense that it avoids monotony and artificiality, but also in the positive sense of making an important statement about life and death, and this is no small achievement in the villanelle: one would have to go back to the earliest French practitioners of that form to find so satisfactory an example. The poem is addressed to Thomas' father, who is on his deathbed, and it urges the old man not to accept death "wisely," that is calmly, even though he may be convinced that this is the proper way in which to meet it. Instead he wants his father to die struggling, to "rage against the dying of the light," to die *naturally* (since it is natural for men to resist death) rather than philosophically.

It is important that we realize this distinction between a natural and a philosophical attitude toward death, for otherwise it becomes difficult to reconcile the poem with Thomas' general pantheism manifest in such poems as *The Force that Through the Green Fuse Drives the Flower* and *And Death Shall Have No Dominion*.

Philosophically Thomas is very close to Wordsworth and his religion of nature, and perhaps closer still to Whitman (whom he very much admired) and his belief in a World Soul. But the comfort of philosophy, he says in this poem, is a cold comfort to a man faced with the immediate prospect of his own death: it is one thing to talk about, even to believe in, the unimportance of death in the abstract, and quite another thing for the indi-vidual to die as if the event were of small moment for him. It is asking too much of a man who is still alive. There is in fact no more natural a sign of life than the desire for its continuance, and the more passionate the desire the more alive the person: thus the poet, who does not wish to see his father die, is merely urging the old man to live as long as possible, to postpone the inevitable surrender of his identity. Thomas, too, is here speaking as a son rather than as a philosopher.

There is still another idea at work in the poem, more apparent in its earlier stages (as will be seen) than in the final version. This is the notion that only the man who has lived the ideal, the perfect life can be expected to accept death easily. Only he who has lived to the fullest extent of his capacities is ready to die and will do so without a struggle. The others are tortured by the thought of what they *might* have done (and might still do, if only it were not too late!). They "see with blinding sight" how blind they have been in the past and lament "how bright their frail deeds might have danced in a green bay." The poet is saying that most men, at the end, are conscious of a sense of wasted opportunity, and the belated desire to compensate for it is the reason why they want to go on living. Only the perfect man will die easily, and of course the perfect man does not exist. The perfect man is not the natural man.

Thomas is not thinking here of wasted opportunity in a practical sense—in the sense, for example, which Longfellow intends in *A Psalm of Life*, when he flatly, and in so many words, enjoins the reader to be "up and doing," and to "act, that each tomorrow / Find us further than today." The worksheets of Thomas' poem make it clear that he had something very different in mind. In one of the earliest versions we find the following prose jottings, a kind of blueprint for the body of the poem, as later they become the substance of Stanzas 3, 4, 5, and 6:

> Very near death they [4] see that life could have been
> wonderful, and they rage against the dying of the light.
> There could have been light all their days
> even at the darkest times, but they had worked
> against it, so they cannot die gently.
>
> They understand, now they are dying, that
> impossible love could have been their sun but
> that they helped to kill it, and so they rage
> aginst its dying.
>
> Now you, my father, have taught me this.

[4] One is reminded of the line by Dante Gabriel Rossetti: "They die not, never having lived" (Sonnet XXXV, *The House of Life*), and of a line by William Morris: "Because they, living not, can ne'er be dead," at the opening of *The Earthly Paradise;* cf. also the closing lines of Robert Browning's *In a Gondola.*

In a later version we find the lines, intended as the first two of Stanza 5:

> All men, dying, suffer the same dark sight:
> Impossible love that cannot stay.

And in a still later reworking:

> All men dying mark in their dark plight
> The sun of love was slain on the first day.

What Thomas is saying is that experience blunts man's original capacity for love: "The sun of love was slain on the first day." Man is born innocent and good, but from the very day of his birth the world serves to corrupt him and destroy in him the power of perfect (*i.e.*, "impossible") love. It is a theme immediately familiar to anyone who knows Wordsworth and Whitman, not to mention the whole latter-day school of American Transcendentalism (Emerson, Thoreau, etc.); and the wasted opportunities are the occasions when one acted according to the dictates of the world (*i.e.*, the world of rational experience) rather than those of one's own heart, thus stifling the sun of love. The morality of the poem is in fact the exact antithesis of that of Longfellow's.

But the poem is not easily apprehended on a moral level; that is, it is not quite clear where the ethical responsibility lies. On the surface Thomas appears to assign it to the individual, who cannot die easily because "his words had forked no lightning," because his deeds had been too frail "to dance in a green bay," and because his eyes had refused to "blaze like meteors and be gay." But this condition is inevitable and universal, existing from the very day of birth, so that there can be no ethical point if the poem is viewed as the indictment of an individual or even of mankind as a whole. It is not a matter which one may choose for himself, except perhaps relatively, and where there is no choice there is no morality. The "fault," assuming Thomas intended a moral meaning at all, which it is clear from a study of the manuscripts that he did,[5] is that of the "world"—the world of narrowing social institutions, of stultifying conventions, of cramping *mores*. To the extent that the individual revolts against

---

[5] In a very early version Stanza 3 takes a frankly religious turn:

> So near to God, they see that He shone bright
> Even in the bad days, and, lying brave,
> Rage, rage against the dying of the light.

these he may be said to have earned the right to die with a clear conscience, and I take it that this is the moral burden of the poem.

Thomas may have felt that this meaning was stated too baldly in the early versions, or he may have felt that it competed too strongly with the other theme of the poem (and in this connection it is interesting to speculate to what extent the two are, after all, compatible in a poem of this type), for he subordinated it in later versions to the urgent appeal expressed in the crucial recurring line, "Do not go gentle into that good night." Nevertheless, it is implicit in the second line of every stanza except the first and last (the structure of the poem is marvelously ordered), and these are the only lines in the poem which are likely to cause the reader any difficulty.

GLOSSARY

accent—a greater force, or stress, given to a syllable or word than to those around it. In describing the pattern of accents (or *beats,* or *stresses*) in poetry, the stressed syllable is marked "–" and the unstressed syllable "⌣." *Poet* (– ⌣); *until* (⌣ –). Not all accents have the same force, but in general their arrangement or pattern is the groundwork of the rhythm of poetry. See *meter, rhythm.*

alexandrine—a line of six metrical feet (generally, six accents). The last line of each stanza in Keats's "The Eve of St. Agnes" is an alexandrine. See *foot.*

allegory—a narrative of related characters and events that represent other things, usually abstractions (ideas or moral concepts). See "Lully, Lulley"; Chapter 1, pp. 10–11.

alliteration—the repetition of a consonant sound at the beginnings of words or accented syllables. "I wake and *f*eel the *f*ell of *d*ark, not *d*ay"— Hopkins.

ambiguity—double meaning. In its deliberate use in poetry and criticism, it refers to a word or image which has a complexity of meaning, involving several things at the same time.

anapestic—a rhythm of three-syllable feet, the accent on the third syllable (⌣⌣ –). See *meter.*

archetype—a universally used symbolic pattern of human experience (the cycle of death and rebirth, the triangle, the search, the enchantress or fatal woman). Sometimes used to mean the simple original form (situation or character) which is later developed and varied. See Chapter 4, pp. 167–168.

assonance—repetition or agreement of vowel sounds. "The pl*o*wman h*o*meward pl*o*ds his w*ea*ry w*ay*"—Gray. This line also illustrates *alliteration* in the use of *p*'s and *w*'s.

ballad—a narrative poem in simple short rhythms, usually written in four-line stanzas, often with repetitions and refrains. See Chapter 2, pp. 37–48. *Popular ballads* are those of anonymous folk origins, preserved by oral tradition and often sung ("Lord Randal"). *Literary ballads* are those composed with deliberate use of the ballad conventions: a forceful, often tragic story of love and war or the supernatural, told without comment or much detail, often in dramatic form with many repetitions and familiar phrases (Keats, "La Belle Dame sans Merci").

ballad stanza—usually a four-line stanza with alternating four-beat and three-beat lines and rhyming *abcb* ("Sir Patrick Spens"). In effect, it is a seven-beat couplet. Some ballad stanzas, however, have four-beat lines throughout. Some rhyme *abab*.

ballade—a French form of three stanzas of eight or ten lines and a concluding *envoi* of four or five lines. Only three rhymes are used throughout, and they must appear in the same order in each stanza.

beat—the recurrence of accented or stressed syllables. See *rhythm, accent.*

blank verse—unrhymed iambic pentameter. The lines are arranged continuously rather than in stanzas. See Milton, *Paradise Lost.*

caesura—a pause within a line of poetry, determined by punctuation, natural sense, or word arrangement.

> "So long lives this, / / and this gives life to thee"—SHAKESPEARE.

> "That's my last Duchess / / painted on the wall"—BROWNING.

closed couplet—two rhyming lines, the second coming to a full stop or period. See *couplet.*

> Slight is the subject, but not so the praise,
> If she inspire, and he approve my lays.
> —POPE

conceit—an elaborate, extended metaphor, most common in Elizabethan poetry (Donne, "The Ecstasy").

connotation—the emotions and ideas, as well as other imagery, suggested by a word or image.

consonance—repetition or agreement of consonant sounds. Note the *m*'s, *n*'s, *d*'s, and *b*'s in the following lines:

> The moan of doves in immemorial elms,
> And murmuring of innumerable bees.
> —TENNYSON

conventions—habitual devices in certain kinds of poetry, understood as necessary to the type (as in *pastoral* poetry, *elegies, odes*).

couplet—two successive rhyming lines.

> How vainly men themselves amaze
> To win the palm, the oak, or bays;
> —MARVELL

See also *heroic couplet, closed couplet.*

dactylic—rhythm of three-syllable feet, the accent on the first syllable (- ∪∪). See *foot, meter.*

denotation—the exact literal meaning of a word.

didactic—that which is primarily intended to instruct. See Chapter 2, pp. 82–83.

dimeter—a two-beat line (two feet). See *foot, meter.*

double rhyme—correspondence of sound in two final syllables (*sowing/ mowing*).

dramatic monologue—a speech or meditation by a person (not the poet) in which character and situation are revealed. See Browning, "Andrea del Sarto"; Tennyson, "Ulysses."

elegy—a lyrical poem in memory of the dead, either an individual (Milton, "Lycidas") or a group (Gray, "Elegy Written in a Country Churchyard").

empathy—the imaginative act of becoming one with another object and partaking in its feelings and identity. To be distinguished from *sympathy,* which is the sharing of like feelings.

end-stopped line—one in which a natural pause, from punctuation or sense, comes at the end of the line. "Earth has not anything to show more fair:"—Wordsworth. Compare *enjambement, run-on lines.*

English sonnet—see *Shakespearean sonnet.*

enjambement—the carrying-over of the natural phrasing from one line to the next. Opposed to the end-stopped line.

> Dull would he be of soul who could pass by
> A sight so touching in its majesty:
> —Wordsworth

epic—a long narrative poem of heroic subject, usually identified with the history and ideals of some people or nation (Homer, *Iliad;* Milton, *Paradise Lost*).

epigram—a short, witty poem of two or four lines on a single idea (Harington, "Treason").

epithalamion—a poem honoring a marriage.

feminine ending—lines ending (and sometimes rhyming) on unaccented syllables. See the last lines of the stanzas of Herrick's "Corinna's Going A-Maying" (*decaying / Maying*).

figures of speech—various kinds of unliteral language. See *simile, metaphor, synecdoche, metonymy, hyperbole, personification;* Chapter 1, pp. 7–10.

foot—the unit of measurement (or meter) in a line of poetry; usually a group of syllables containing one accented and one or more unaccented syllables. Two-syllable feet may have the accent on the second syllable (*iambic* ∪ –) or the first (*trochaic* – ∪). Three-syllable feet may have the accent on the first syllable (*dactyllic* – ∪ ∪) or the last syllable (*anapestic* ∪ ∪ –). Some variations are the *spondee* with two

accented syllables (– –) and the *pyrrhic* foot, with no accents (◡ ◡).
Coleridge wrote some lines called "Metrical Feet," beginning

> Trochee trips from long to short;
> From long to long in solemn sort
> Slow Spondee stalks; strong foot! yet ill able
> Ever to come up with Dactyl trisyllable
> Iambics march from short to long;—
> With a leap and a bound the swift Anapests throng. . . .

free verse—lines of irregular length and no exact metrical arrangement
or rhyme pattern, although rhyme and other musical devices may be
used at will and there will be an over-all rhythmic movement in the
poem. See Whitman, "Out of the Cradle Endlessly Rocking."

French forms—poems of exact and intricate patterns. See *ballade, villanelle, rondel, sestina* (also an Italian form).

genre—a literary form or type. The genre, or category, to which a
poem belongs may be determined primarily by form or arrangement
(sonnet), purpose (elegy), or origins (pastoral). See Chapter 2.

heptameter—a seven-beat line (seven feet). See *foot, meter.*

heroic couplet—two rhyming lines in iambic pentameter. See Pope,
The Rape of the Lock; couplet.

hexameter—a six-beat line (six feet). See *foot, meter.*

Horatian ode—ode after the manner of the Latin poet Horace (65–8
B.C.), in regular stanzas, often in a light or satirical tone. See Chapter
2, p. 68; *ode, irregular ode, Pindaric ode.*

hyperbole—a figure of speech: an exaggerated statement, impossible or
unbelievable if taken literally.

iambic—rhythm of two-syllable feet, the accent on the second syllable
(◡ –). See *foot, meter.*

imagery—language calling up sensory responses (sight, taste, hearing,
touch, taste), most apparent in descriptive poetry and necessary in
all figurative or metaphorical language, where abstractions are made
concrete and combinations of imagery are used to evoke new responses.

incremental repetition—in ballads, the repetition of lines or words in
successive stanzas, accompanied by slight changes that develop the
story. See the questions and answers in "Lord Randal."

invocation—often in the epic, an address to a god or a muse to ask
help for the poet. See the opening of *Paradise Lost.*

irony—in language, statements which mean the opposite of what is
literally said. In situations and events, an outcome which is the opposite of what is normally expected or hoped for.

irregular ode—a variation of the *Pindaric ode,* like those of Abraham
Cowley (1618–1667), using stanzas that change form (as in the Pindaric

strophe, antistrophe, and *epode*) but in no consistent order. Such stanzas vary from free verse in that they do have patterns of rhythm and rhyme that give them a recognizable form and shape. See Wordsworth, "Ode: Intimations of Immortality." See *ode, Pindaric ode, Horatian ode.*

Italian sonnet—see *Petrarchan sonnet.*

lyric—a musical poem. Originally, one intended to be sung. As developed, a subjective, emotional poem. See Chapter 2, pp. 55–76.

masculine ending—lines ending, and sometimes rhyming, on an accented syllable.

metaphor—a figure of speech in which the resemblance of two apparently unlike things is stated, directly or by implication. See Chapter 1, pp. 7–9.

metaphysical—in poetry, usually a description of the 17th-century poets (Donne, Vaughan, Herbert, Marvell) who used philosophical or scientific language and dramatic, startling metaphors. See Chapter 2, pp. 86–90.

meter—the formal arrangement of accented and unaccented syllables in a line or lines of poetry. See *foot,* and also *anapestic, dactylic, iambic, trochaic;* and *monometer, dimeter, trimeter, tetrameter, pentameter, hexameter.* See Chapter 1, pp. 12–14.

metonymy—a figure of speech in which one thing is called by the name of a closely related object.

mock epic—a poem in which trivial subjects are presented with epic grandeur and with the conventions and apparent tone of a serious epic (Pope, *The Rape of the Lock*).

monometer—a one-beat line (one foot). See *foot, meter.*

motif—a recurring detail (person, object, situation, image, symbol) that may determine the directions, the tone, and the import of a poem.

myth—a story incorporating divine meanings, the supernatural, or mysteries of experience, in terms of human events, giving form to gods or to god-like power (Keats, "Ode to Psyche"; Yeats, "Leda and the Swan"). In criticism, myth overlaps with archetype to describe those memorable, universal representations of man's experience or his explanation of what he believes but does not understand. In myth, it is the psychological, not the factual, truth that is important.

objective correlative—T. S. Eliot's term for the set of objects, situations, or events that are the formula of a particular emotion in the poet, and can through their incorporation in a poem evoke that emotion in the reader. It is the outside equivalent for the inside emotion.

occasional poetry—written on or about some particular event, or for a certain day or occasion (Milton, "On the Late Massacre in Piemont";

Dryden, "A Song for St. Cecilia's Day").

octave—the unit of the first eight lines in a *Petrarchan sonnet.*

ode—a serious, lyrical composition, usually honoring or meditating upon some subject. See Chapter 2, pp. 68–71; *irregular ode; Horatian ode.*

onomatopoeia—words (or language) whose sound resembles what is described (*crash, tinkle*).

ottava rima—an eight-line stanza, rhyming *abababcc.*

oxymoron—the combination of opposing words or elements ("pleasing woe"). A kind of paradox.

paradox—an apparent contradiction but an actual truth.

parody—an imitation of an author's general style or a particular work, often intended to be satirical.

pastoral—incorporating the conventions of idealized country life, especially of shepherds. See Chapter 2, pp. 91–96; *pastoral elegy.*

pastoral elegy—a lament for the dead which follows certain conventions of classical poetry: all persons become shepherds and nymphs, events are of rural life, elements of myth are introduced. See Chapter 2, pp. 71–72.

pathetic fallacy—a form of personification in which human feelings and reactions are given to inanimate objects ("the stones wept").

pause—a stop in the voice when reading poetry, thus marking phrases, punctuation, and inevitably though slightly, the ends of lines. Pauses and their timing—along with quantity, accent, and general sound and movement—help to form rhythm.

pentameter—a five-beat line (five feet). See *foot, meter.*

personification—representing a thing or an abstraction as a human form with human characteristics. See Chapter 1, p. 10.

Petrarchan sonnet—a poem with an octave (eight lines) rhyming *abbaabba* and a sestet (six lines) rhyming *cdecde* or in varying arrangements of two or three rhymes. The sense usually divides into parts corresponding to the form. After the manner of Petrarch (1304–1374); also called *Italian sonnet.* See Sidney's "With How Sad Steps, O Moon"; Chapter 2, p. 63; *sonnet.*

Pindaric ode—one patterned on the Greek choral ode as written by Pindar (522–443 B.C.). The true Pindaric ode has varying stanzas in three major parts: (1) the *strophe,* sung by the Greek chorus as it turns toward one side; (2) the *antistrophe,* or contrasting movement, sung as the chorus turns to the other side; (3) the *epode,* sung as the chorus stands still. See *ode; Horatian ode; irregular ode.*

prosody—the science or technique of versification.

pun—language that can be taken two or more ways because of words identical in sound but different in meaning. Related to *ambiguity,* but depending more on external resemblances than on involved meanings.

pyrrhic foot—a unit of two unaccented syllables (⌣ ⌣). See *foot, meter.*

quantity—the length of time used in pronouncing a syllable. The quantity of *moon* is longer than that of *sit.*

quatrain—a four-line stanza, rhyming in any pattern. Compare Wordsworth's "A Slumber Did My Spirit Seal" and Tennyson's *In Memoriam.*

refrain—lines or words repeated at the ends of stanzas, especially used in songs and ballads.

rhyme—similarity of sounds in words or the last syllable or syllables of words. Exact or perfect rhymes have the same final vowel and final consonants but different consonants preceding the vowel. *Set* and *met* are exact rhymes. The repetition of the same sounds (*set* and *set*) is not rhyme. Rhyme may occur at the ends of lines or irregularly within the lines.

rhythm—the continuous pattern of rising and falling sound in a line or passage. In poetry, rhythm is usually regular, determined by the arrangement of accented and unaccented syllables, and given musical variation by the arrangement of pauses, quantity, and sounds. See *foot, meter.*

rime royal—a seven-line stanza in iambic pentameter, rhyming *ababbcc.*

rondel (rondeau)—poems in variations of the exact French forms in which only a few rhymes are used and certain whole lines are repeated in a set form, often to get slightly different meanings in their recombinations.

run-on lines—those in which the phrasing carries over to the next line. See *enjambement.*

satire—depiction of a subject in terms to make it ridiculous or the object of laughter or scorn, often by using exaggeration, irony, or reversals of meaning and position.

scansion—the system of describing the formal metrical pattern of a poem. If one attempts to "scan" a poem (that is, mark out the pattern of accents or feet), it is important to remember that good poets always vary the predominant meter by slipping in occasional extra syllables, substituting a different type of foot, or mixing long and short lines. Otherwise the lines would be too monotonous. It is perhaps more important to determine the over-all rhythm of a poem than to become too involved with minute technical decisions on meter.

sestet—the unit of the last six lines in a Petrarchan sonnet.

sestina—a poem of six stanzas of six lines each, and a last stanza of three lines. Only two rhymes are used throughout, the same words making up the rhymes of each stanza, though always in a different order.

Shakespearean sonnet—a poem of three quatrains and a concluding couplet, in iambic pentameter, rhyming *abab cdcd efef gg.* Also called the *English sonnet.* See Shakespeare, "That Time of Year"; *Petrarchan sonnet; sonnet.*

simile—a comparison of two apparently unlike things, using the words "like" or "as." See Chapter 1, pp. 7–8.

slant rhyme—a correspondence in sound, though not as formally exact as true rhyme *(lane/loan; lake/lace).* See the poems of Emily Dickinson: *rhyme.*

sonnet—a poem of fourteen lines, in iambic pentameter, using one of several set rhyme schemes. See *Petrarchan sonnet* and *Shakespearean sonnet;* Chapter 2, pp. 62–67.

Spenserian stanza—a nine-line stanza, the first eight in iambic pentameter and the last in iambic hexameter (an alexandrine). Used by Spenser in *The Faerie Queene.* See Keats, "The Eve of St. Agnes."

spondee—a unit or foot of two accented syllables (– –). See *foot, meter.*

sprung rhythm—G. M. Hopkins' term for a metrical pattern of feet that have one accented syllable but no fixed number of unaccented syllables in each. See Chapter 1, p. 14.

stanza—a division of lines in the metrical pattern of the poem, corresponding in effect to a paragraph in prose. Stanza patterns are generally uniform within a poem, but some odes, in particular, have varying stanzas of elaborate structure.

strophe (strophic)—see *Pindaric ode* for the traditional meaning. In general use, the term may describe a sectional unit within a poem where the form is gained not from stanzas of set patterns but from passages of internal unity that rise and fall to a sense of completion. Long poems in free verse often show a strophic movement.

synecdoche—a figure of speech, in which a part of a thing is used to represent the whole. See Chapter 1, pp. 7–10.

tetrameter—a four-beat line (four feet). See *foot, meter.*

threnody—a dirge or *elegy.*

tone—the dominant attitude or manner (melancholy, apologetic, angry, playful, pensive).

tradition—in poetry as elsewhere, a long-established manner or form. Individual poems may differ from each other and yet harmonize with styles, subjects, and attitudes that have been established before them. See Chapter 2.

tribrach—a foot of three unaccented syllables (⌣ ⌣ ⌣). See *foot, meter.*

trimeter—a three-beat line (three feet). See *foot, meter.*

trochaic—rhythm of two-syllable feet, the accent on the first syllable
(– ᴗ). See *foot, meter.*

verse—generally, language in regular rhythm; poetry as opposed to
prose. Technically (in prosody), a line of poetry.

villanelle—a poem of five three-line stanzas and a final quatrain. Two
rhymes are used throughout, and some lines are repeated. See
Thomas, "Do Not Go Gentle into That Good Night."

INDEX